THE SUPER-ATHLETES

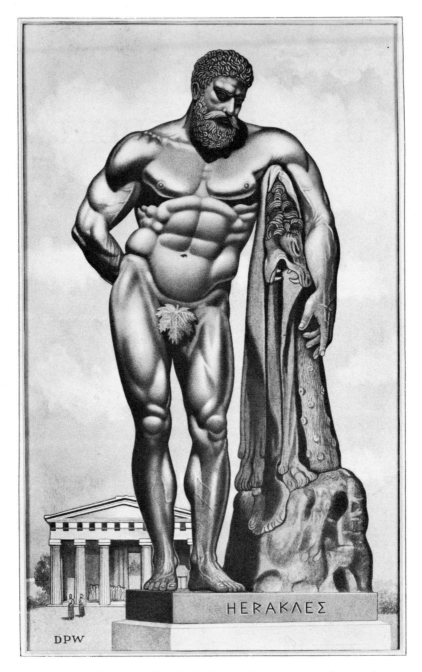

Herakles (Roman: Hercules), the mythological founder of the Olympic Games. After a watercolor painting by the author, 1957.

THE
SUPER-
ATHLETES

by

David P. Willoughby

South Brunswick and New York: A. S. Barnes and Company
London: Thomas Yoseloff Ltd

Library of Congress Catalog Card Number: 72-88302

A. S. Barnes and Co., Inc.
Cranbury, New Jersey 08512

Thomas Yoseloff Ltd
108 New Bond Street
London W1Y OQX, England

It is only to be expected that in a book of statistics of the scope of the present one, many errors will appear, even though every reasonable effort has been made to avoid them. The author will therefore be grateful for any corrections sent to him by readers, as well as for the report of any authenticated feats not already listed herein. All correspondence should be addressed:

David P. Willoughby,
c/o A. S. Barnes & Co., Inc.,
Cranbury,
New Jersey

ISBN: 0-498-06651-7

Printed in the United States of America

If arithmetic, mensuration, and weighing
be taken away from any art,
that which remains will not be much
. . . For measure and proportion
always pass into beauty and excellence.

PLATO (in Philebus)

Contents

Part 3. WOMEN ATHLETES AND GYMNASTS AND
THEIR RECORDS

List of Plates

List of Tables

List of Figures

Foreword

I am continually amazed when I hear of performances that have been made in the world of athletics, especially when these performances have been made with the aid of weight-training.

A good portion of the improvement in modern athletics is largely due to the fact that more people have incorporated weight-training and weight-lifting as a regular part of their training schedule.

I can testify that regular training is of benefit in the attainment of world class athletic performances, as I have attained five American Records all of which were due to my regular and specialized training with the weights.

I would like to extend my personal congratulations to all of the men of the "Iron Game," for they are a special group of athletes which are unique unto their own. A great feeling of brotherhood and comradeship exists whenever a few of the men of the Iron Game gather for sport or for fun.

To David Willoughby, I also extend congratulations for bringing together, within a single binding, many feats of strength and athletic prowess which heretofore have not been brought to light.

In *The Super-Athletes* he lists an almost incredible range of performances. In addition, he presents records on just about everything in the line of physical effort that has ever been in print. Without the aid of David Willoughby, world authority, historian and statistician of strongmen and feats of strength, many feats of physical endeavor would never have been brought to the attention of the public.

It all makes fascinating reading.

George M. Frenn
1967 National Champion and World
Record Holder for the 56-Pound
Weight Throw. 1967 National
Champion and National Record
Holder for 242-Pound Class
Power Lifting.

Introduction

While there are countless record-books and periodicals devoted to the publication of athletic performances in standardized sports, hardly ever does a book appear that describes and evaluates the *unstandardized* and *unofficial* feats of human strength and endurance that are constantly occurring and that have occurred since the dawn of history. In the present volume an attempt is made to bring together and comment on the merits of some of the more remarkable manifestations of physical power that have been made both by athletes and non-athletes since the days of the ancient Greeks.

Although the conventional record-books give, for example, the listed world records in track and field sports, the records themselves do not always express the various elements that enter into them. Accordingly, it is often difficult to assess the merits of a feat unless one takes into account certain factors that do not appear in the "record" itself. For instance, if one asks how fast a man can run, it is customary to quote the current world record in the 100-yard dash, and to convert the time over this distance into miles per hour. Thus, during recent years, the "fastest human" would be the U.S. sprinter Robert Hayes, whose 100 yards in 9.1 seconds would be reckoned as equalling 22.48 miles per hour. However, an analysis of Hayes's 100-yard record shows that during the *fastest stage* of his sprint he was moving at a rate of 100 yards in 7⅓ seconds, or no less than 27.9 miles per hour. A detailed account of how this figure was arrived at is given in Chapter 15.

In other track and field events, similar analyses can be made; and when they are made, the official records in these events come to have more meaning, and enable the various competitors to be judged more fairly as to their true potentialities. Especially is this true of such events as shot-putting, high jumping, and pole vaulting, in which, during recent years, new techniques and (in vaulting) new apparatus have made it necessary to make ample allowances for the presumed lesser records of earlier performers (see Part 2).

Then there are sports which are comparatively new to the American public, although they have been practiced in this country by enthusiasts for generations. One such sport is weightlifting. Unfortunately, about this activity the average American sports-writer knows practically nothing. As a result, he often makes absurd statements concerning the possibilities of muscular strength. Having once been a champion weightlifter myself, and having written about weightlifting and strong-men for over forty years, I find it a pleasure to present some historical and statistical data on these subjects in Part 1. That the sport of weightlifting is making great strides in popularity is shown by the fact that in the Olympic Games over a *hundred* contestants now regularly appear. Also, it has been said—possibly with some exaggeration—that in the Soviet Union alone there are about *two million* weightlifters.

To sum up, while conventional sports records may be found in any manual devoted to the subject, the figures for such records do not always tell the whole story, and the facts themselves are confined to standardized events. Such formally-presented records omit many interesting facts and speculations connected with human physical limits. How, for example, do men and women athletes actually compare? How high, straight up, can a man jump? From what height has a man jumped *downward* without injury? Is it possible for a strong-man to bite a nail in two? Has anyone ever performed a *double* back somersault off the ground without the aid of a springboard? Can a man really outrun a horse? The answers to these and hundreds of similar questions are usually difficult to find— *if* the average reader can find them at all. It is the author's purpose in the present volume to provide answers to a few, at least, of the innumerable questions connected with the strength and stamina of the human machine, and perhaps in the process to clear up some of the misconceptions and fallacies surrounding the subject.

It will be noted that in this review—so far as "sports" are concerned— emphasis is placed on such activities as require muscular and organic strength rather than skill and patience. For this reason the champions in such events as auto racing, motorcycling, yachting, hunting and fishing, billiards, chess, card-playing, etc. must be omitted from my account of super-athletes, since these pastimes—while possibly requiring endurance of a sort—can in most instances be engaged in by persons of ordinary (or even inferior) physique.

Additional exclusions from the present volume are the familiar player-by-player statistics on baseball, football, basketball, boxing, tennis, etc., which are steadily published in numerous popular books on these subjects and which limited space forbids repeating here. A few *original* contributions are presented herein concerning outstanding performers in baseball, boxing, and tennis; but these observations deal with *individual champions* rather than the statistical histories of the sports. Since in certain team sports, such as basketball, soccer, ice hockey, etc. the performance of the individual cannot be exactly measured (as it can be in track and field, swimming, etc.) but can only be surmised on the basis of games won, there are many unquestioned "super-athletes" who must be omitted from the present book.

In Part I of this volume I have drawn mainly on my own collection of statistics as gathered from various books and periodicals in English, French, and German. However, in this process I have had a considerable amount of assistance from a number of fellow-enthusiasts. Especially helpful have been: Edgar Müller, of Braunschweig, West Germany; Ottley R. Coulter, of Lemont Furnace, Pennsylvania; Ian "Mac" Batchelor, of Los Angeles, California; George Russell Weaver, of St. Petersburg, Florida; Siegmund Klein, of New York City; Leo Gaudreau, of West Peabody, Mass.; John Fuhrmann, of Portland, Oregon; Roberto Villar-Kelly Heydrich, of Havana, Cuba; the late Raymond Van Cleef, of San Jose, California; and the late Tromp van Diggelen, of Cape Town, South Africa. To these and all other contributors to the data on feats of strength published herein, I extend grateful thanks. I am indebted also to Peary Rader, the publisher of *Iron Man* magazine, for his kind permission to republish a number of illustrations which appeared previously in my series, *The Kings of Strength*, in *Iron Man*, as well as certain photographs from other accounts in *Iron Man* and *Lifting News*.

In Part II here—on track and field events, and swimming—I have drawn, for recent records, mainly on the periodical *Track and Field News* (Los Altos, Calif.); the comprehensive volume, *A World History of Track and Field Athletics*, 1864–1964, by R. L. Quercetani (Oxford Univ. Press); and *The Encyclopedia of Sports*, by the late Frank G. Menke (4th rev. ed., A. S. Barnes and Co., New Jersey). For miscellaneous and unofficial performances of merit in these fields, I have made use of extensive information personally collected during the last fifty years from newspapers, sports magazines, and other sources in various parts of the world.

It is, of course, impossible in any compilation of athletic records to keep strictly "up to date." The most that can be done is to *try* to keep abreast of happenings up until the time the manuscript is sent to the publisher. Most of the records quoted in Part 1 of this volume are correct, to the best of my knowledge and belief, up to January 1, 1969, and certain track and field records to as recently as September 14, 1969. If any listed performer feels that I have slighted him by not quoting his latest and best record, I can assure him that this is wholly unintentional, and is merely the consequence of limited facilities on my part for keeping abreast of records made throughout the world and not always widely publicized.

Several other differences, or innovations, also occur in the present volume. One of these is the inclusion of certain records made by *professional* athletes. Many a sports-writer appears to be averse to mentioning professionals in the same breath with amateurs, as though the professionals somehow enjoyed extra advantages. With the possible exception of certain old-time families of circus athletes, or gymnasts, in which training was commenced in childhood, and the performer's continued earning power depended on his or her professional superiority, it is doubtful whether any athletes in history trained longer or harder than do the amateurs of today. This is true particularly of performers in non-seasonal sports, who are obliged to work at their specialties steadily—in some events, *daily*—throughout the year. For if they do not, some close competitor will forge ahead of them, and so make them ineligible for major awards (e.g., participation in national and world competitions, including trips abroad).

So, in the present study, we are not concerned with extraneous differences between amateurs and professionals, but are interested primarily in recording the *best* (i.e., most efficient) performances in the various forms of athletics and gymnastics regardless of by whom performed, and in analyzing these outstanding records in an endeavor to learn what *bodily conformations* and what *techniques* are responsible for them. If a 300-pound "strong-man" is able to put the shot 50 feet or farther without any "form" whatever, little can be gained from a contemplation of his performance. But if a 180-pound athlete, by the skillful use of strength and speed, can achieve the same distance in this event, it should be of benefit to all future shot-putters to learn, if possible, just "how" he does it.

In short, the dominant thought herein with regards to athletes is not "how much did he get for it?" but rather, "of what is the human machine capable?"

As to what, or who, constitutes a "super-athlete," a fair definition would be: "Any person who holds a world (or even a national) record—or who has turned in the best performance—in any feat requiring an exceptional degree of muscular or vital power." Indeed, the term "record," as used in the present volume, is not restricted to the single best performance of its kind. It embraces also such "runner-up" performances as manifestly could be made only by "super-athletes" in their fields. And in point of merit—as shall be shown—many an old-time record surpasses a more recent or even a present-day one of its kind.

Finally, in reply to those who feel that modern man is degenerating physically and simply does not compare in strength or stamina with races or tribes who live under primitive or "natural" conditions, it should be reassuring to note that the records of modern athletics, sport, industry, and medical science combine to show that the civilized portion of the human race is bigger, stronger, and healthier in general today than ever before in history. And the prospects—barring some unforeseen catastrophe—are that this improvement will continue.

David P. Willoughby

Laguna Beach, California

THE SUPER-ATHLETES

Part 1.
FEATS OF STRENGTH

1.

Feats of Strength In Ancient Times

Since the earliest days of the human race, physical strength above the ordinary has been admired, envied, and striven for by the majority of men. Indeed, the more primitive a tribe, the more robust has been their conception of a hero and leader. And while every now and then the presence of extraordinary muscular power occurs naturally in some favored individual, as a result of heredity or a chance mutation, more often it is the result of long and arduous training toward that end. Whatever the cause, strong-men and their accomplishments have been a source of wonder and discussion among the rest of humanity since before the dawn of history.

While the term "ancient," in reference to sport, is commonly restricted to athletes and gladiators of Greek and Roman times, actually the procedure of training for strength was practiced at still-earlier centers of culture—those of Egypt, Crete, Phoenicia (now Syria and Lebanon), Babylonia, India, and China, for example. In most of these places the actual exploits of champion athletes and warriors became so magnified as the stories were handed down that today it is difficult or impossible to tell where fact ends and fable begins. In the following recounting of such ancient feats, suspected embellishments are omitted.

Since the recorded accomplishments of real strong-men are remarkable and numerous enough, we can also dispense here with references to such mythological or supernatural heroes as the Greek Herakles, the Hebrew Samson, the Babylonian Gilgamesh, the Egyptian Horus, and other figures of epic renown. If there were any "giants in the earth in those days," they are equally present today!

MILO. Perhaps the most famous actual strong-man of antiquity was the Greek athlete Milo, who was born in the province of Crotona (now called Calabria), in Italy, about 558 B.C. Although many different feats —some obviously exaggerated—have been attributed to him, perhaps his

best-known performance was that of carrying a four-year-old heifer on
his shoulders the full length of the stadium at Olympia, a distance of
over 600 feet. The difficulty in this exploit would have been more in
supporting the bulk of the animal on his *shoulders* than in carrying
its weight the aforementioned distance, since even a cow of small
breed, weighing perhaps 900 or 1000 lbs., presents a very bulky body,
requiring an extensive support. About thirty years ago, a strong-man
of Germantown, Tennessee, named Herbert Mann by daily practice
became able to carry a young bull, weighing 600 pounds, up to a
distance of 185 yards. But Mann did not support the animal on his
shoulders, but on his *back and hips*, which was a much less taxing
position. He discontinued the practice of thus carrying the young bull,
even for a short distance, after it had reached a weight of 840 pounds
and was becoming unruly in disposition.

To return to Milo, his prowess in the Olympic and other games of
his day proved that in man-to-man combat he was invincible. Besides
being the acknowledged strongest man of his time, he was the wrestling
champion in six Olympian, seven Pythian, nine Nemean, and ten
Isthmian games—a period of strenuous competition covering some 24
years. Finally, in Milo's seventh Olympic appearance, wrestling was
cancelled from the program because, as one observer put it, "neither
god nor man durst stand against him!" A massive bronze statue of
Milo was made by the Greek sculptor Damoas. There being some
discussion as to how it should be moved, Milo singlehandedly carried
the ponderous image and set it in position in the Altis at Olympia.

THEAGENES.   Another great Greek athlete was Theagenes, who was born
about 505 B.C. in Thasos, an island in the Aegean Sea off the coast of
Thrace. As he was primarily a prize-fighter, his record in this field
is given in Chapter 6. However, that he must have been extraordinarily
strong in lifting as well is indicated by the story that when only *nine
years of age* he carried off on his shoulders a life-sized bronze statue
of an Olympic athlete that had stood in the public square. Such a
statue, even if hollow, must have weighed at least 500 pounds!

POLYDAMAS.   This gigantic athlete was reputed by Pausanias to have
been in his day the largest man in all Greece. One estimate, made from
a statue of Polydamas (but which may have been larger than life-size),
puts his height at 6 feet 8 inches and his weight at 300 pounds.
Such physical dimensions are not uncommon among professional wrestlers
today; but it should be considered that in the time of Polydamas the
entire population of Greece was probably not over two million persons.
Like Hercules, Polydamas is reputed to have slain, with his bare hands
only, a full-grown lion (for comments on the possibility of such a feat,
see Chapter 18). Another of Polydamas's exploits, it is said, was to hold

back a chariot with one hand, even if a pair of horses was striving to pull the chariot forward (see Chapter 3). Officially, Polydamas was victor in the pancratium (a contest involving both boxing and wrestling) in the Olympic Games of 408 B.C. King Darius I of Persia, having heard of Polydamas and his tremendous strength, invited him to his court. There, he pitted against the Greek athlete three of his strongest guards, from a troop called the Immortals. The story is that Polydamas killed all three guardsmen, even though they had opposed him together. It will be noted that among these ancient peoples, in which a state of war was usually present or pending, all athletes, including the strong-men and wrestlers, had to be trained hand-to-hand *fighters* as well.

MAXIMINUS. Evidently one of the strongest of ancient strong-men was the Roman Emperor Gaius Julius Verus Maximinus, who was born in 186 and ruled from 235 to 238 A.D. Maximinus, who was originally a shepherd from Thrace, was in stature a true giant, standing about 8 feet 1 inch in height. If muscularly developed "in proportion" to this height—which it is said he was—Maximinus would have weighed close to 500 pounds.* This weight and muscularity would seem to be confirmed by the statement that Maximinus, in his youth, had defeated ordinary heavyweight wrestlers two and three at a time, as though they were children, and "without getting out of breath." Indeed, it is said he possessed tremendous endurance in running and other prolonged efforts, as well as prodigious momentary strength. Evidently he was endowed with muscles and physical power proportionate to his great height. The accompanying illustration (Plate 1) of a marble bust of Maximinus, which was made presumably by a contemporary sculptor, indicates however that the giant was afflicted with the glandular condition known as acromegaly (evidenced in the overdeveloped lower jaw and the large features); and it is known that some individuals having this disorder exhibit extraordinary physical strength during a certain stage of the condition (although later they become exceedingly weak). Another evidence of Maximinus's having had acromegaly was the reference to his hands being of enormous size. This circumstance was gradually exaggerated by hearsay until writers, later on, credited the giant with wearing his wife's bracelet as a thumb-ring! Unfortunately, Maximinus's great strength and physique were not accompanied by a kindly disposition. As a ruler he became so tyrannical and feared that one night three soldiers of the Praetorian Guard entered the tent where he and his son were sleeping and killed them. This was on June 17, 238 A.D.

---

* There are at least two sculptured busts of Maximinus in existence—one in the Louvre and one in the Capitoline Museum, Rome—and these portraits indicate that this giant was of a rather rangy build. A fair estimate would be that he weighed just over 400 pounds.

Among the few instances of actual weights being lifted by Greek and Roman strong-men are the following. During archeological excavations made at Olympia, a block of red sandstone weighing 315 pounds and dating from the 6th century B.C. was unearthed. On the stone was an inscription saying that an athlete named Bybon had, using one hand only, 'thrown' the stone over his head.* Another, still larger block, weighing 1058 pounds, and also from the 6th century B.C., was found at Santorin. On it was inscribed the statement, 'Eumastas, the son of Critobulus, lifted me from the ground.'

The merits of these two feats depend as much on the *positions* adopted for lifting (which are not stated) as on the poundages raised. In the first lift, by Bybon, the weight certainly was not *thrown*, as the inscription has been translated. Even if it had been slowly raised above the lifter's head with one hand, as in the present-day style called the "bent press," it would—in the form of a rock, rather than a barbell or a dumbbell— have surpassed any similar lift made by a modern strong-man. So, it leaves one wondering just *how* the 315-pound rock was raised. In the second-mentioned lift—that of raising a 1058-pound block just off the ground—the merit of the feat would depend not only on the style used in the lifting, but also on the *shape* of the stone. If of cubic shape—as the term "block" suggests—and if lifted with the hands alone, less difficulty would be presented than if the stone were of a rounded or egg-like shape. But it is exceedingly unlikely that this block was ever lifted off the ground with the hands alone, since the weight itself (1058 pounds) is nearly *twice* as great as that capable of being lifted by any one of the greatest modern strong-men (cf. Louis Cyr, Chapter 4). And if the block was raised by means of a belt or *harness* worn by the lifter, the merit of the performance would be so ordinary as not to be worth recording.

The lifting and carrying feats of several Roman strong-men have been recorded by various historians of their time. A professional athlete named Athanatus, at one of his exhibitions in the arena, was said by Pliny to have walked about while wearing a cuirass (breastplate and back-plate) of *lead* weighing 500 pounds, and with a pair of greaves (boots reaching to the knees) each weighing 250 pounds upon his legs. This performance by Athanatus, if actually accomplished with the aforementioned poundages, would have been a phenomenal example of carrying power and leg strength.

Julius Valens, a centurion of the guard of Augustus Caesar, could raise on his back and hips, by stooping under the weight, a wagon loaded with hogsheads of wine; how many, it is not stated. But since

---

* The dimensions of this 315-pound stone block have been given as: 68x38x33 cm. (=26¾x15x13 inches).

even the smallest-sized hogshead (a barrel containing 63 gallons) would weigh close to 500 pounds, perhaps Valens lifted a sufficient number of them in the wagon to result in a creditable feat. Again, Valens could carry a full-grown mule on his back (the weight not stated), or hold back a chariot, as Polydamas did, against the pull of the horses harnessed to it. These and other of his feats of strength were inscribed on his tombstone.

Fusius Salvius, of about the same period, could climb a flight of stairs, or a ladder, while carrying 100 pounds on his feet, 100 pounds in his hands, and 200 pounds on his shoulders. This poundage, however, has been greatly exceeded in the stair-climbing and ladder-climbing performances of various modern strong-men (Chapter 5).

Venetianello, another Roman, was said to be able to break the lower leg bone (tibia) of an ox by pulling upwards on it against his knee; to bend and twist bars of iron "as thick as a man's finger . . . as though they had been softened by fire"; and to carry (how far, it is not stated) a wooden beam 20 feet long and a foot "thick," occasionally shifting it from one shoulder to the other. (If by "thick" was meant *square,* such a beam, if of oak, would have weighed at least 800 lbs.). For comparison with the latter carrying feat, see that assertedly performed by Horace Barré, Chapter 5.

To sum up the feats performed by ancient strong-men, in most cases it is difficult to assess them at their true merits. Some were quite credible, while others were exaggerated to a preposterous degree (as, for example, the statement made by Pausanias that Milo could break a bowstring by tying it horizontally around his head above the eyebrows and then contracting his temporal muscles!).* Most of these feats, especially where weights were being lifted, suffer from their incomplete descriptions. Since the historians and travelers who recorded such stories were rarely if ever themselves trained athletes, their negligence in describing the feats fully and accurately is understandable. In any case, it is highly improbable that any of the Greek and Roman strong-men and wrestlers were capable of surpassing the best efforts of modern athletes in any direction. This may be inferred from the fact that the men of those days averaged only 5 feet 5 to 5 feet 6 inches in height, and the number of weightlifters and wrestlers among them was far less than the number competing today. Occasional muscular giants, like Polydamas and Maximinus (who was of Gothic descent), were probably exceedingly strong, even discounting the exaggerations attending their feats as recounted. But that their abilities were unique and unprecedented is unlikely in the extreme.

---

* In some translations (e.g., Depping, 1873, p. 17), this feat by Milo is described as having been accomplished by retaining his breath and breaking the cord "by the swelling and pressure of the veins." (1)

2.
Feats of Strength In Medieval and Early Modern Times

During the Middle Ages (c. 400–1400 A.D.) perhaps the physically most robust men, as a group, were the Vikings, who roved the northern seas during the ninth century. As these men took particular joy in battle, naturally their strength was acquired or used mainly in such activity. The most highly respected individuals were those who could wield the heaviest axes or swords, draw the strongest bows, throw the heaviest spears, or, in general, overcome the greatest number of the enemy. The galley-boats in which the Vikings did their roving were relatively small craft, and to keep one of these boats moving it was necessary that it be rowed *continuously*, 24 hours a day, using only two or three shifts of men. On such a schedule, it is understandable how these select warrior-oarsmen developed extraordinary strength, stamina, and physique.

Some descendants of the early Norse supermen may be living today in northern Norway. In 1925, a Captain Peterson gave an account to the press about these men, who have followed the trade of deep-sea fishing, generation after generation, for the past thousand years. According to Peterson, among these fishermen individuals seven feet tall are not uncommon, and their strength and endurance are phenomenal. They have no gasoline engines, and they think nothing of rowing their heavy boats thirty miles to sea to haul their nets, and then rowing back again with a boat-load of fish. Their diet consists almost entirely of dried fish and black (rye) bread, like that of the Finns who have produced so many champion athletes.

But the Vikings were not the only group to produce mighty fighting men during medieval times. All the way back to the sixth-century King Arthur of Britain, each of our ancestral nations today looks with pride to its particular champion or champions of strength and valor. In the accounts of these men, however, it is only natural to suspect, here and there, some fable interwoven with the facts.

Roland (or Orlando), a nephew of the famous Frankish Emperor Charlemagne (742–814), was the hero of many romantic tales and a man of prodigious strength. Legend says that he could deliver with his sword a blow so mighty that it would split an enemy warrior clear in two, right through his armor (cf. Scanderberg, p. 36). History books tell how, when Roland was dying in the valley of Roncevaux (N. Spain), and wished to break his good sword Durandal, he struck a rock with it which split under the blow and thus formed the pass between Spain and France known as the Gap of Roland (!). This was in the year 778 A.D.

William I, "the Conqueror," who was King of England from 1066 to 1087, could, it is said, vault into a saddle while clad in full armor. It is said also that he could pull a bow while on horseback that no other man could pull when standing.

Count Baldouin I, of Flanders (1058–1118 A.D.), was surnamed "Bras de Fer" ("arm of iron") because of his tremendous strength. Once, when attacked by a bear, while alone and without weapons, he was said to have strangled the beast with his bare hands! (See Chapter 18).

An examination of the armor worn by soldiers of the Middle Ages shows that an average-sized man of those times was decidedly smaller than an average-sized man of today. Possibly the medieval man averaged as little as 5 feet 6½ inches and 135 pounds. A suggestion has been made that many of the fighters may have been immature youths rather than full-grown men. Despite all this, there can be no doubt that most of the military *leaders* of those days were large individuals of powerful physique. For example, Edward III, who was king of England from 1327 to 1377, used a sword so big and heavy that two ordinary men were required to wield it. It is said that this enormous sword may still be seen in the Tower of London. Robert the Bruce, liberator and king of Scotland (1306–1329), slew with one blow of his battle-axe the iron-helmeted Bohun, giant of King Edward's invading army. Robert's axe, no less than Edward's sword, would take two ordinary men to handle. Bruce's greatest captain was the famous Sir James "Black" Douglas, who also wielded a "two-man" sword. He stood 6 feet 8 inches, weighed 280 pounds, and had exceedingly broad shoulders. Sir William Wallace, the Scottish hero (1272?–1305), also had a two-handed sword which only he was strong enough to use. The sword, some fragments of which may be seen in the castle in Edinburgh, was seven feet in length and weighed 40 pounds!* But about the men who used such swords all that is told, usually, is their prowess in battle, and rarely

---

* However, sometime about 1850, the "Cape Breton Giant," Angus MacAskill, on a visit to Edinburgh, wielded Wallace's sword, which at that time presumably was intact.

is any information given about their ability in other manifestations of strength.

Ericus, the second king of Denmark, was a man of tall stature and great physical power. Of him it is recorded that from a sitting position he could throw a stone or a spear to a greater distance than an ordinary man who stood; or that, also sitting, he could pull a rope against four strong men and draw them to him. (These accounts make one wonder what the king was capable of when standing!)

Marko Kralyevic, a 14th-century prince of Serbia, was a giant of a man and renowned for his strength. This he displayed mainly by his prowess in battle. During Serbia's war with Turkey at that time, Marko was said to have mown down a *thousand* Turkish soldiers with his six-foot, 50-pound sword. He could lift a full-grown ox on his back and shoulders, and (it is said) could muscle-out 112 pounds in each hand. He was killed in battle in 1394.

Scanderberg (*c.* 1404–1467), King of Albania, whose real name was Georges Castriota, was a ruler at the end of the Middle Ages who was famed for his great strength. He used a scimitar which was almost as renowned as the Durandal of Roland, or the Excalibur of King Arthur. Like Roland, Scanderberg was said to be able to cleave in two a soldier who was clad in armor from head to foot. His scimitar was so huge and heavy that none of his contemporaries could use it like himself. (It would be interesting to test, on a dummy, just how much force would be required to cleave an armor-covered figure in two, and whether the force would be beyond the power of a champion strong-man or swordsman of today.)

Of comparable strength to Scanderberg with a sword was "fearless De Courcey," Lord of Ulster, who lived in the 13th century. Historians state that one day in the presence of the king of England, De Courcey clove a steel helmet with one blow of his sword, and sank his weapon so deeply into the wooded block on which it stood that not a man at court except himself could pull the sword out again.

Louis de Boufflers, nicknamed "The Robust," who lived in 1534, could break a horseshoe with his bare hands. The same feat has been attributed to the great Renaissance artist Leonardo da Vinci (cf. John Grunn Marx, Chapter 4).

Antony Payne, a Cornish giant of the 16th century, stood 7 feet 4 inches tall and was "wide-chested, ample-limbed, and symmetrical in figure." He was quick and agile as well as strong, and excelled in games and sports of all kinds. Once—"because a taunting butcher doubted his strength for the feat"—Payne walked from Kilkhampton to Stowe (these towns are no longer on the map, but they were about 2½ miles apart) with the dressed carcass of a hog weighing 336 pounds on his shoulders. In "putting the stone," Payne, it is said, cast a rough block (weight not stated) a "full ten paces" beyond the point reached by ordinary putters.* This was at the "hurler's ground" at Stowe. Another exploit of Payne's was to carry on his back a donkey loaded with fuel logs, on account of the loitering of the boy leading the donkey.

A feat similar to the latter one by Payne is attributed by the French writer Froissart to a Spanish nobleman named Ernaulton, who was "tall and strong, and big-limbed, but not over-fleshy." Ernaulton, finding himself in the castle of Foix with several lords who complained of the severe cold and the feebleness of the fire in the hall where they were, and having noticed in the courtyard some donkeys loaded with wood, went down, put one of the animals on his back and lightly remounted the staircase of 24 steps, entered the hall, and dumped the donkey and the logs in the middle of the hearth.

During the reign of Louis XIV (1643–1715), there was a Major Barsaba who, it is said, was so strong that by squeezing the leg of a horse he broke the bones of it. One day, as a prank, Barsaba entered a smithy and asked the smith for a piece of tempered iron. The smith set about to satisfy him; but while the man's back was turned, Barsaba lifted the anvil from its place on a block and hid it under his cloak. The smith, who wished to hammer the iron, was astonished to find nothing on which to place it, and was amazed when the major calmly replaced the anvil on its block.

In the year 1716, in London, there was a 25-year-old giant named Thomas Fisher, "7 feet 5 inches high, and in every way proportionable." This giant was so strong that he could hold a 10-pound weight at arm's length for *12 minutes*, continuously.

George of Fransburg, Baron of Mindelheim, was said to be able to check a galloping horse simply by grabbing its bridle. He could carry a cannon (weight not stated) on his shoulders. "His joints seemed to be made of horn, and he wrested twisted ropes and horseshoes asunder by his bare hands."

Czar Peter I, of Russia, who succeeded to the throne at the age of ten, later became known as "Peter the Great" (see Plate 1). When he reached maturity he stood 6 feet 8½ inches in height, and was so strong that he could break silver coins with his fingers. He also had a tremendous constitution, which enabled him to work all day even though he had just finished a night-long drinking bout. He was a prodigious eater, too; in fact, just about everything in his makeup was on a colossal scale. But not his longevity, for he died at the age of 53.

---

* If we assume, conservatively, that the weight of the "rough block" was 14 pounds, and that the ordinary competitors put this weight 30 ft., if Payne put the weight "ten paces" (=25 ft.?) farther, he would have reached 55 ft. This would have been equivalent to about *51 ft.* with a 16-pound shot! (See Part 2).

Johann Karl von Eckenberg was a German professional strong-man who toured Europe in the early part of the 18th century, under the name of "Samson." He was perhaps one of the first exhibitors to do harness-lifting, chain-breaking, and similar spectacular feats. Although he was only of medium size, he performed heavy supporting feats using cannons, horses, and numbers of men, as in the so-called "Tomb of Hercules" (see Chapter 5). Some of von Eckenberg's exhibition numbers are shown in Plate 1, which is a reproduction of a contemporary engraving.

William Joyce (or Joy?) was a Kentish strong-man who lived toward the close of the 17th century. On November 15, 1699, he was called to Kensington Palace to demonstrate some of his feats before King William III. First, Joyce lifted from the ground a chunk of solid lead weighing 2254½ pounds (by what means, it is not said, but probably it was some kind of a harness lift). Secondly, after a thick rope had been fastened about his waist, a draft horse, fastened to the other end of the rope, was unable to pull him from where he "stood" (or reclined, with his feet against a brace?). Thirdly, tying the same rope between two heavy posts, by a blow of his fist he broke the rope. Finally, grasping one of the latter posts, by a single violent pull he broke it down. Joyce's tombstone bears the following epitaph:

> Herculean hero famed for strength,
> At last lies here, his breadth and length.
> See how the mighty man is done,
> In death the strong and weak are one;
> And the same judgment doth befall
> Goliath great as David small.

Maurice, Count of Saxony, the hero of Fontenoy, more generally known as Maurice Saxe, possessed great natural strength, especially in his arms and hands. On the occasion of a certain luncheon given by the Count for a party of huntsmen, no corkscrew could be found with which to open the wine bottles. "What does it matter?" asked Maurice; and taking a long nail, he twisted it into a corkscrew shape with his fingers, and with this improvised implement opened half a dozen bottles. He could also break with his hands the strongest horseshoes. At wrist-wrestling, in which Maurice was unbeatable, his most difficult victory, strange to say, came in a contest against a woman! This was Mlle. Gauthier, an actress, who was then performing at the Comedie Francaise. The Count said that of all the persons who had striven against him in this arm test, Mlle. Gauthier had held out the longest. She indeed had uncommon strength, for she could roll up with her fingers a heavy dish of pewter or silver plate.

The old-time English pugilist, Tom Johnson (68.5 in., 203 pounds), whose first public boxing match was in 1783, when he was 33, had remarkable strength and endurance. When he was 21 years of age he worked on the Thames wharves. His job was to carry sacks of wheat and corn from the wharves to the warehouses. It is recorded that when one of his co-workers was ill, and could not provide for his family, Johnson took over his absent colleague's job as well as his own, carrying twice the load. It is further said that Johnson, through years of work with heavy sacks, finally became able to take a sack of wheat in one hand and swing it around his head as if it were an Indian club! Hearing that the porters of Paris were accustomed to carry on their shoulders sacks of flour weighing 159 kilograms (about 350 pounds), and to climb stairs with them, Johnson duplicated the feat with *three* sacks, and on one occasion *four* sacks, the total weight of which was 1400 pounds.

William Ball, of Shropshire, England, who lived in the latter part of the eighteenth century, weighed 560 pounds at a height of only 5 feet 9½ inches. His arm measured 27 inches, calf 25 inches, and chest 70 inches. He worked in an iron foundry and possessed enormous strength. On one occasion, it is said, he carried in his hands a piece of iron, weighing about 1000 pounds, "from the ball furnace to the forge hammer."

In the town of Blyth, England, in 1798, there was a blacksmith named William Carr, who was locally famous for his impromptu feats of strength. Carr stood 6 feet 4 inches and weighed 336 pounds. On one occasion, it is related, he carried a 1120-pound anchor across his shoulders for a distance of half a mile!

Angus MacAskill (1825–1863), of Nova Scotia, was known as "the Cape Breton Giant." He stood 7 feet 9 inches and weighed 425 pounds. At one time, he was exhibited by the showman P. T. Barnum, along with the midget "Tom Thumb." While MacAskill may actually have been very strong, his alleged feats of strength have been so extravagantly exaggerated that it is impossible now to learn what he really could do. His most oft-cited feat was in shouldering a heavy anchor on a wharf in Halifax and walking a short distance with it. The weight of this anchor has been stated (by various misinformed writers) to have been between 1500 and 2700 lbs. However, in some correspondence with Dr. W. R. Bird, of the Historic Sites Advisory Council of the Province of Nova Scotia,* it develops that, "It is generally agreed the anchor weighed 600 pounds." Much heavier poundages than that have been shouldered and carried by men of considerably smaller size than MacAskill (See Chapter 5).

---

* Personal communication, June 10, 1966.

3.
Thomas Topham—an 18th-Century Prodigy of Strength

It will be seen, from the foregoing brief review, that many men of extraordinary physical power appeared at intervals during the long period from the time of the Vikings up to the 19th century. However, of them all, only one, so far as I am aware, would seem to warrant being classed as a *phenomenon* of strength. This was the famous Thomas Topham (pronounced Tuf'-um), of London, who lived from 1710 to 1749. Topham in his prime weighed only 14 stone (196 lbs.) at a height of 5 ft. 10 in. But there is some evidence that he may have possessed unique muscular leverage, because of his tendons being attached farther from the joints than is the case in ordinary men, no matter how muscular. Again, Topham's muscles themselves may have possessed a greater number of fibers for a given cross-sectional area than other men's. Finally, his voice was described as being so deep as "scarcely seemed human." Such a voice, as well as a greater-than-ordinary stimulation of the muscles, could have resulted from a hyperfunctioning of the adrenal glands.

The chief single source of information on Topham's physical strength is a chapter in Volume 1 (pp. 289–290) of the two-volume work, *A Course of Experimental Philosophy* (London, 1763), by Dr. John Theophilus Desaguliers (1683–1744), an English physicist, who personally witnessed many of Topham's feats and public performances. Most other sources, of which there are many, appear to have drawn on Desagulier's account, although here and there additional scraps of information appear.

Thomas Topham was born in London in 1710. His father was a carpenter, and he (Thomas) was brought up to follow the same occupation. However, as he gradually became aware that his physical strength was something far out of the ordinary, he did not follow the trade of carpenter after the age of 24. At that time he took over the managing of the Red Lion Inn, a tavern located at the corner of the City Road,

London. This location was chosen, it was said, so that Topham could keep conveniently informed of what went on in the nearby boxing and athletic club in the London parish known as Moorfields.

The first public exhibition given by Topham (who was then about 25) was to resist the pull of a horse. He accomplished this by bracing his feet against a low stone wall, which at the time divided the district of Moorfields (where Topham then lived) into Upper and Lower Moorfields. (An Inn called "The Strong Man," in East Smithfield, used a sign that showed Topham resisting the pull of a draft horse by bracing his feet against a *post*. This sign remained in place until at least 1802, possibly later). Later, he pulled against two horses, bracing his feet against two tree-stumps in the ground. However, on this occasion he took a disadvantageous position, in which the line of pull was too much forward and *upward*, rather than horizontal. As a result, he was jerked from his seat and had one of his knee-caps shattered against one of the stumps. The injury deprived him of most of the strength of that leg, and afterwards caused him to walk with a slight limp. It was the opinion of Dr. Desaguliers that if Topham had only braced himself properly, he could have resisted the pull not only of two, but of *four* horses "without the least inconvenience."

About a year later (that is, in 1736), Topham appeared in the town of Derby as a performer in public. In order for him to perform his exhibition he had to make application to an alderman named Cooper for permission. This magistrate was skeptical of the feats Topham claimed to do, since Topham's appearance, when dressed, was not unlike that of other men. However, when he disrobed down to his athletic attire, he was found by Cooper to be "extremely muscular," with armpits and hams "full of muscles and tendons."

Here are some feats Dr. Desaguliers saw Topham perform in the year 1741 (and described in the aforementioned *A Course in Experimental Philosophy*):

1. He broke seven or eight short and strong pieces of tobacco-pipe by the strength (flexion?) of his middle finger, having laid them, one at a time, across the backs of his first and third fingers.

2. Having placed under his garter the bowl of a strong tobacco pipe, his legs being bent, he broke the pipe into pieces merely by contracting the flexor tendons of his thigh, without altering the bending of his leg.

3. He broke another such pipe-bowl between his first and second fingers simply by pressing the fingers together sideways [!].

4. He took an iron kitchen-poker, about a yard long and three inches in circumference, and holding it in his right hand struck it

upon his bared left forearm with such force that the poker was bent nearly to a right angle.

5. He lifted a mill stone weighing 800 pounds (or 8 hundredweight?) with his hands only, standing in a frame above it and taking hold of a chain that was fastened to it.

As may be deduced from some of the above feats, Topham possessed phenomenal strength in his hands and fingers, and it was very easy for him to bend iron bars, roll up metal dishes, and perform similar feats. In the British Museum there was for a time a pewter dish, on the back of which was inscribed: "April 3, 1737. Thomas Topham, of London, carpenter, rolled up this dish (made of the hardest pewter) by the strength of his hands, in the presence of Dr. Jno. Theop. Desaguliers . . ." (and then are listed seven other witnesses).

Of Topham, it was said that, "the bodies he touched seemed to have lost the power of gravitation, and both weakness and feeling he seemed destitute of." The following is a copy of an original printed announcement of Topham's performance in the town of Derby:

By Desire of Several Gentlemen and Ladies, at the Play-House
in the Castle-Yard, on Tuesday next, being the 10th of February, 1736

Mr. Topham the Strong Man, from Islington, performs all his Feats of Strength, as he did before the Royal Society in that Way: particularly, to bend a large Iron Poker of three Inches Circumference over his naked Arm; he bends another Iron Poker of two Inches and a Quarter around his neck; he fairly breaks a Rope that will bear two Thousand Weight; and rolls up a Strong Pewter Dish by the Strength of his Fingers of Seven Pound Weight. He gripes [that is, compresses, D.P.W.] a strong Pewter Quart Pot in one Hand, by the Strength of his Fingers, at Arm's Length, in an Instant. He lays the back Part of his Head on one Chair, and his Heels on another, and suffers four corpulent men to stand on his Body and heaves them up and down. At the same time, with Pleasure, he heaves up a large Table of Six Foot long by the Strength of his Teeth, with half a hundred Weight hanging at the farthest end; and dances two corpulent Men, one in each Arm, and snaps his fingers all the time.

Pit, one Shilling; Gallery, Sixpence.
Beginning exactly at 6 o'clock.

The foregoing recital of an 18th-century "theatre" program, with its quaint use of capitalized words, is interesting in more ways than one. Where can one now get an orchestra seat for a shilling, and what evening performance takes place as early as 6 o'clock? But mainly, let us look further into the details of the above feats by Topham.

Concerning the bending of the iron bar around his neck, Topham was also able subsequently to *unbend* the bar, which was a more difficult feat, since the muscles which bring the elbows backward are not nearly so strong as those which bring them forward. This would indicate that Topham's ability in bending a bar forward around his neck was considerably greater than his exhibition feat with the poker. Possibly he could bend thus a bar even three inches in circumference—that is, nearly an inch in diameter!

In lifting the six-foot-long table with his teeth, Topham used a mouthpiece of leather fastened at one end of the table for his teeth to grip upon, and the two table-legs nearest him rested on top of his knees. He then raised or levered the far end of the table (to which the 56-pound weight was attached) to a level higher than his mouth. Incidentally, among many so-called "strong-men" there is a tendency to discredit or ridicule such feats as teeth-lifting, lifting or supporting with the hair, resisting the impact of blows to the body, etc., on the grounds that such feats are not legitimate manifestations of muscular power. This is certainly a debatable question. In Topham's case, it would appear to be simply an indication that he was strong all over—in his teeth and jaws no less than in his body, arms and legs.

In breaking the rope (of about two inches in circumference, or ⅝ of an inch in diameter), which was capable of supporting two thousand weight (2240 pounds), Topham used a harness that fit over his shoulders. However, on at least one occasion the rope was so long (or elastic) that it stretched without breaking, even when Topham had fully straightened his legs. He finally broke the rope, it is said, by raising his heels from the ground and using "other muscles that are weaker" (!). And it should be remembered that when Dr. Desaguliers saw Topham perform this rope-breaking feat, Topham, as a result of his shattered kneecap, had only one "good" leg. This was also the case when Topham did his famous harness lift with three casks weighing together 1836 pounds. This feat was performed on Bath Street, Coldbath Fields, London, on May 28, 1741, in honor of the naval victory attained by Admiral Vernon, when he captured the seaport of Carthagena, Spain, on April 1, 1741. The Admiral himself was present among the thousands of spectators who witnessed Topham's remarkable lift (see Plate 2). These public exhibitions, by the way, were Topham's undoing as an inn proprietor, at least at the Red Lion Inn, since evidently he could not give ample attention to both occupations at the same time. However, after having failed at the Red Lion, we read of his taking over the management of another inn, at Islington.

Occasionally in his stage exhibitions, Topham, despite his injured leg, would also display his ability as a wrestler. In one contemporary account it was said that, "To wind up his performance, he took on six wrestlers, one after the other, and brought each to the ground in an unconscious form, within five minutes" [total time]. From this it would appear that once Topham got hold of a man, that was the end of the wrestling match!

Even Topham's voice was in keeping with his gigantic muscular power. For a time he sang solos to the accompaniment of the organ in St. Werburgh's Church in Derby, but his voice was described as "more terrible than sweet . . . scarcely seemed human." His voice was an exceedingly deep bass.

Once an ostler at the Virgin Inn, where Topham had put up, said something that insulted the strong-man. Topham immediately took one of the kitchen-pokers from the mantlepiece and bent it around the ostler's neck like a handkerchief (see Plate 2). Later, he released the innkeeper from his embarrassing predicament by unbending the iron bar. As one reporter wrote: "Had Topham not abounded with good nature, the men might have been in fear for the safety of their persons, and the women for that of their pewter shelves. One blow from him [Topham] would forever have silenced those heroes of the boxing arena, Johnson and Mendoza."

But besides exhibition feats and everyday incidents like the one just related, Topham was given to pranks that he perpetrated just for the fun of them. Once, for instance, upon finding a night-watchman fast asleep in his sentry-box, near Chiswell Street, Topham took both, and carrying the load with the greatest of ease, at length dropped the watchman and his guardhouse over the wall of Tindall's cemetery. The poor watchman, still only half awake, probably wondered whether he was still in the land of the living! Another time, while sitting at the window of an inn, as a butcher went by under the window laboriously carrying a quarter of beef on his shoulder, Topham relieved him of it with such ease and dexterity that the butcher thought it must have been the Devil who thus flew away with his load (see Plate 2). On yet another occasion, "being persuaded by one of his acquaintances to accompany him aboard a West Indian boat in the river and being presented with a cocoanut, he astonished those around him by cracking it "close to his ear" with the same ease that an ordinary person would crack an eggshell. When the mate of the ship made some irrelevant remark, Topham replied by saying that he could just as easily crack the bowsprit (of the mate's boat) over his head."

On another day, when a footrace was being run on the Hackney Road, a fellow with a horse and cart kept attempting to keep close to the runners, much to the annoyance of the spectators. Topham, who was one of them, stepped into the road, seized the rear end of the cart, and in spite of all the driver's exertions in whipping his horse to go forward, he drew them both backwards, with ease and quickness; and while the spectators cheered, the driver, raging, would have used his whip upon Topham but for the fear of being pulled or crushed to pieces.

At one of Topham's stage exhibitions, he was said to have taken a Mr. Chambers, Vicar of All Saints Church, who weighed 27 stone (378 pounds) and "raised him with one hand." That is all that was said, and it leaves one in wonder as to how the one-hand lift was performed. If to arm's length overhead, in a standing position, it would have been an unprecedented feat of pressing strength, since Topham, according to Dr. Desaguliers, used no tricks or artifices in lifting, and made no attempt to have his strength appear greater than it actually was. And we can hardly imagine that the "bent press" style of one-arm overhead lifting, as perfected by Arthur Saxon and a few other professional strong-men some 160 years later, was even conceived of by the primitively strong Topham.

Again, Topham was said to have been able to take a "200 weight with his little finger and move it gently over his head." A 200 weight in English measure is 224 pounds; and here again, if Topham was actually able to lift such a poundage over his head in the manner presumably indicated, he would easily have been the strongest man of modern times. But just his feats with the iron bars, pewter plates, and the cocoanut leave little doubt that he must have possessed terrific strength in his arms and hands. And that all parts of his physique were proportionately strong is shown by his "harness lift," his breaking of the 2-inch-circumference rope, and his breaking of the pipe-bowls with his fingers and his leg-tendons. So we can only surmise, in the absence of any exact contemporary description, that he must have been phenomenally strong also in all kinds of pressing, curling, and other typical weightlifter's feats.

Likewise, before the injury to one of his knees, there is every reason to believe that his legs were as strong, proportionately, as his arms and upper-body. One account, in fact, tells about how, as a youth, he could leap over a fence, hurdle-style, while carrying a full-grown girl. Another tells of his jogging along for a half-mile while carrying on one shoulder a barrel of nails weighing three hundredweight (336 lbs.). As for general or all-around strength, what would take more than the pulling-up of carriages drawn by horses, as Topham had a habit of doing just for fun. On one occasion, when he must have felt especially energetic, he is said to have lifted bodily a heavy horse "over a turnpike gate"!

But Topham had a prolonged period of trouble at home with a wife who was unfaithful to him. Finally, unable to endure the condition longer, he beat his wife severely, then stabbed himself and died from the effects several days later. The date was August 10, 1749, and Topham was just 39 years of age. He was buried in the churchyard of St. Leonard's, in Shoreditch.

4.
An Introduction to Modern Weightlifting

While the average sports fan may not be aware of it, the literature on strong-men and weightlifting is very extensive. A considerable number of books have been published on the subject (see Bibliography), and at the present time numerous periodicals in England and the United States, France, Germany, Russia and other European countries give their readers the results of the latest weightlifting competitions and the most efficacious methods of training with weights. While in a less organized form the sport of weightlifting dates back to antiquity, for our purpose it can be considered to have gotten under way as a more or less *standardized* form of athletics about the middle of the 19th century, both in Europe and the United States.

The former leading authority on weightlifting in France, Prof. Edmond Desbonnet, claimed to have "founded" physical culture (including weight-training?) there in 1885; and in Germany a controlling organization for heavy athletics (weightlifting and wrestling), the *Deutschen Athletik Sports-Verbandes* (DASV), was founded in 1891. About this time also there was a beginning wave of enthusiasm for competitive weightlifting in Austria. But long before these dates there were traveling professional strong-men who used barbells and dumbbells to demonstrate their strength to the public. In the United States, no great interest was shown until about 1902, when Alan Calvert founded the Milo Bar-Bell Company in Philadelphia; he started the manufacture of practical, plate-loading barbells and dumbbells for use by amateurs, and began publishing the little magazine *Strength*, which demonstrated, in text and photographs, the benefits and pleasures to be derived from "progressive weight-lifting" (barbell and dumbbell exercises). From Calvert's time until the present day, interest in weightlifting has increased at an accelerating rate until, as mentioned elsewhere, there are today probably about 3500 regular contestants* in the United States

---

* Plus perhaps several hundred thousand non-competing *trainees* (one source says 2½ *million!*).

and perhaps in Russia as many as 1,000,000. With the intense and incessant competition provided by such numbers, it is not surprising that the world records in weightlifting are being bettered almost daily.

It is not my purpose here to present a *history* of weightlifting, which in itself would require a book.* Rather, my object is to provide readers with a list of the most outstanding *performances* in the sport, and to confine myself biographically to the following series of 20 well-known strong-men, both professional and amateur, who by their record performances and public exhibitions have perhaps done the most to create general interest in the subject. But before giving these accounts, it should be well to define some of the chief terms used in competitive weightlifting (including bodybuilding with weights), so that readers who are not familiar with the sport may know what the various lifts and exercises are called.

A. DEFINITIONS OF SOME OF THE TERMS USED IN WEIGHTLIFTING

1. PRESS. To "press" a weight (either a barbell or, if with one hand, a dumbbell) means to raise the weight from the chest or shoulders to arms' length overhead (either in a standing or a lying position) by strength of the arm and shoulder muscles, *without assisting in any way with the legs.*

a. *Military Press.* This means to press a weight in a standing position while keeping the body perfectly *erect* in an "at attention" (heels together) military position. *No bending backward* (or, if with one hand, *sideward*) *at the waist is permitted.*

b. *Olympic Press.* This is the style of pressing a barbell with both arms used in all official 3-lift Olympic weightlifting competitions. Back in the 1890s, when the Olympic or French style of pressing was first standardized, the amount of weight possible in this style was only 4 or 5 percent more than in a strictly performed Military Press. Since that time, the rules governing the Olympic Press have been relaxed or departed from more and more, so that today (in some contests, and depending on the whim of the referee) an unlimited amount of backbending—and sometimes even a start with a knee-jerk—is permitted (or overlooked). As a result, an Olympic "Press" today may in poundage be as much as 18 or 19 percent more than a true Military Press. Such a lift should be called a "push" or a "jerk," *not* a press, as will be seen from the following definitions.

---

* Readers who are interested in this aspect of weightlifting are referred to my series in *Iron Man* (Alliance, Nebraska), entitled *The Kings of Strength,* which was published steadily in that magazine from May 1956 to April 1963.

c. *Continental Press.* In Europe, in the early days of organized weight-lifting, two different "schools" of lifting prevailed. One, the French or classic school, performed all lifts in a "clean" style, where form was all-important and the weights, in being shouldered, were not permitted to come into contact with the body. This style was followed in France, Belgium, Luxembourg, Spain, Italy, and the Scandinavian countries. The second school, which embraced what was termed the "Continental" style of lifting, was followed in Germany, Austria, Russia, and some of the Balkan countries. It permitted, in pressing, an unlimited amount of back-bend; and the weights could be taken to the shoulders in any manner desired, so long, of course, as there was no outside assistance. To facilitate this, lifters (who were mostly big, heavy men with large waists) wore a belt with a large buckle, onto which the barbell handle was rested in all "two-movement" lifts to the shoulders. Since, in pressing, a backbend was permitted, the so-called "Continental press" should really be called—as it sometimes was—a two hands *push.* (A *press* is where the weight is steadily raised above the shoulders solely by exten-sion of the arms. Where this movement is combined with a back-bend —so that the arms are straightened only partially by *raising* the weight, and partially by sinking back *under* it—the lift becomes a *push.*) The present-day Olympic "press" is thus hardly distinguishable from the old-time Continental *push.*

d. *Bench Press.* This lift, as its name implies, is performed with the lifter lying supine on a bench. Usually, the lifter's feet rest on the floor, his knees being bent over one end of the bench. The bench, which is about 4 feet long, must, according to the rules, be not less than 10 inches nor more than 12 inches in width, and not less than 14 inches nor more than 18 inches in height. Official records in this style are performed always with a barbell (although, in exercising, additional results in strength and development may be obtained by using a pair of dumb-bells). The lift is started by supporting the barbell on straight arms— where it has either been handed to the lifter or taken by him off supports —lowering it to the chest, and after a pause of 2 seconds at the chest, pressed to arms' length. The bar may be grasped with the hands any desired distance apart, but during the pressing of the barbell no "bridging" (raising the buttocks from the bench) is permitted.

e. *Bent Press.* This lift has no connection with the Bench Press, even though the two names could be confused. The Bent Press is a style of one-arm lifting that allows of the greatest poundage being put overhead. For an illustration of the starting position in this lift, see Plate 11. Actually, the Bent Press is a combination of lifting and *supporting.* Whereas in the usual "press" lift the weight is steadily raised until the arm, or arms, are straight, in the Bent Press the body is bent forward and sideways away from the *stationary* weight. This bending away is continued until the lifting arm becomes straight (at the elbow) by reason of the *shoulder being lowered below the level of the supported elbow.* While some form of the Bent Press was used perhaps as early as a hundred years ago, this style of one-arm lifting was brought to a high stage of efficiency by Eugen Sandow in the early 1890s, and virtually to perfection by Arthur Saxon about ten years later (see Chapter 4).

2. JERK. To "jerk" a weight is to heave or toss it from the shoulders to arms' length overhead by bending and then restraightening the knees with a snap. It amounts to pressing (by arm strength) combined with jumping (by leg strength). Jerking may be done with either one or both arms, with either a barbell or a dumbbell, or a pair of barbells or dumbbells. A lifter who is proficient in the jerk will raise about 40 percent more weight overhead, two hands, than in a Military press. This greater poundage is made possible, not only by the legs giving the impetus in the jerk, but also to a subsequent "knee-dip" under the rising weight being made and the arms thereby straightened by the *lowering* of the body.

3. CLEAN. To "clean" a weight means to bring it from the ground to the shoulders, in a single continuous movement, clear, or "clean" of the body. In contrast, in the "Continental" style of shouldering, the barbell or dumbbells may be rested on the knees, waist (belt), or chest, prior to coming to rest at the shoulders. Certain writers, presumably unfamiliar with weightlifting, or just careless, have used the term "Continental clean." This is meaningless, since a lift to the shoulders has to be *either* "clean" or "Continental." It cannot simultaneously be *both*!

4. SNATCH. This style of lifting is similar to "cleaning" a weight to the shoulders, except that in the "snatch" the weight is brought all the way to arms' length overhead without a pause. The "snatch" consists of a quick, strong upward pull, followed by a knee-dip (either by squatting or by "splitting" the feet fore and aft). In the two-hand "snatch" with a barbell, approximately 80 percent as much weight can be handled as in the *two hands clean* (and jerk). These two lifts—the snatch and the clean and jerk—along with the two hands Olympic *press*, constitute the three standard events used in all present-day Olympic lifting competitions. In the *one-hand* snatch, about 62 or 63 percent as much weight can be handled as in the two hands *clean* to the shoulders.

5. SQUAT. This is a recognized "power lift" event as well as a bodily posture! The lift is accomplished by first supporting a barbell across the shoulders, then bending the knees as far as possible and arising. The feet are kept *flat* (on the heels) throughout. In the case of heavy record

attempts, the barbell may be placed on the lifter's shoulders by two or more assistants. The rule stipulates that the lifter shall then "bend the knees and lower the body until the top levels of the thighs are below parallel with the platform." But this is an elastic definition; and in many cases heavyweight performers have such thick thighs and calves that the knees cannot be bent to the stipulated extent. In such cases the lift should be called a "half-squat" (rather than accepted as a full squat), and rated in merit accordingly. A fairer—though less practicable—test of leg strength would be the Back Lift with platform (see below).

6. CURL. To "curl" a weight means to first take it to the "hang" position (at arms' length in front of the body) and then slowly raise it from the thighs to the shoulders in a *semi-circular* movement, flexing the forearms on the upperarms. During the "curling" movement, the elbows should be kept fairly close to the sides, but will necessarily move forward in order for the bar to come to a resting position near the shoulders. During this lift the body must be kept *erect*, with no bending backward at the waist, and the legs kept straight. Also, the barbell (or dumbbell) must be slowly "curled", not swung to the shoulders. In grasping the barbell, the *palms* of the hands should face forwards. If the *knuckles* face forward, less weight is possible, and the lift becomes known as a *Reverse* curl.

7. DEAD LIFT. This is perhaps the simplest of all styles of weightlifting, since it means merely to pick up a barbell from the ground to an erect position with either both hands or one hand. According to the late W. A. Pullum, British weightlifting instructor and record holder, the two hands dead lift constitutes "the fundamental test of a man's bodily strength." However, this definition would be valid only if the height of the barbell handle from the ground bore a constant ratio to the height of the lifter. On the contrary, the lifter, regardless of his stature, is required to lift on a barbell having plates or discs a maximum of 45 centimeters (17.72 inches) in diameter. The diameter of the barbell handle is usually 28 millimeters (1.10 inches). This means that the bottom of the bar is about 8.3 inches from the ground. Accordingly, to grasp the bar, a tall man has to bend forward to a greater extent than a short man, thereby putting greater leverage on his lower back muscles. But the rules, as they exist, make no provision for a barbell handle of *adjustable* height from the ground. As a result, one of the best performances on record in the two hands dead lift was made by a short man who had long arms, and therefore had to bend his back to a minimum extent.

8. SWING. In this form of lifting, which may be executed with either one hand or with both hands together, the weight (usually a dumbbell, although it may also be a kettlebell, or a ringweight) is swung from the

ground to arms' length overhead with the lifting arm, or arms, kept *straight*. The "poundage possibility" in this style (in the *one* hand swing) is a little less than in the one hand *snatch*.

9. MUSCLING-OUT. To "muscle-out" a weight means to hold it at arm's length straight out from the shoulder. The lift may be performed either with the palm up or the knuckles up; it requires more strength in the latter style. When performed with the hands held sideways, palms up, with a pair of dumbbells, kettlebells, or ringweights, the lift is known as the "crucifix." The most meritorious feats of "muscling-out" are those performed with the body *erect* and the arms rigidly *straight*. But as in most other lifts, certain performers, in order to make better "records," adopt easier positions. Thus in the "crucifix" various so-called records have been made in which the performers bent backwards at the waist until their chests were nearly horizontal, thereby transferring much of the lifting strain from the shoulders to the powerful front chest (pectoral) muscles. When a strict, upright carriage of the body is adopted, the "poundage possibility" in the Crucifix lift is 60 percent of that in a correct, two hands Military Press with barbell.

The lifts described above are those most often used or referred to in the sport of weightlifting today.* The Two Hands Olympic Press, Two Hands Snatch, and Two Hands Clean and Jerk are the three standard barbell lifts used today in all Olympic, World, National, and regional championship competitions; while the Bench Press, Squat, and Two Hands Dead Lift with barbell are the styles most often used in the so-called "Power Lift" contests. Participation in the Power Lifts—so far as establishing records is concerned—is largely confined to the United States and Canada, although there is also a certain amount of practice of them in the British Isles, where they are gradually becoming more popular. In Australia, too, increased interest is being shown.

In addition to the aforementioned lifts, there are at least *fifty other styles* of lifting weights that have, at one time or another, been used to such an extent that rules were drawn up for their performance. Certain once-popular lifts, such as the Back Lift, the Harness Lift, and the

---

* It should be added that in all the aforementioned lifts there are certain additional rules that must be followed wherever an official contest is being held, or an attempt at a record is being made. These rulings have to do mainly with the *positions* of the body and the barbell (or other weight) at the start and at the completion of the lift. For example, in all lifts it is required that the finishing position be held until the referee counts "One," "Two" (two seconds). Again, except in recumbent lifts, no part of the body other than the feet is allowed to come into contact with the floor, even where no assistance is gained thereby. However, while these rules must be adhered to in order to gain official recognition, their application does not always, or necessarily, indicate the true respective *potentialities* of the various contestants.

Hand-and-Thigh Lift were used at first by professional strong-men as a means of exhibiting their strength in a manner that permitted the handling of impressively heavy poundage. But these lifts are too cumbersome and time-consuming to make practicable their use in widespread competition in various bodyweight classes, such as those taking place today in Olympic and Power Lift contests. Finally, there are still other lifts, which have evolved from various barbell *exercises,* for which records are listed. These lifts—such as the Abdominal Raise (sit-up, with a barbell held behind the neck), the Lateral (straight-arm) Raise Lying, the Pull-over at Arms' Length, and the Pull-over and Press in Wrestler's Bridge position—are more or less self-explanatory and will be mentioned later on in connection with miscellaneous weightlifting records.

Now, it is opportune to list (in chronological order, more or less) the 20 strong-men previously mentioned as having, by their public exhibitions and record performances, perhaps done the most to arouse general interest in weightlifting and other feats of strength. Many more such men could be cited; but those listed below should suffice here to present a diversified cross-section of what has been called "The Iron Game." The large group of weightlifters who have identified themselves almost strictly with the three two-arm Olympic lifts are rated separately on their performances in these lifts in a later listing.

B. BRIEF BIOGRAPHIES OF TWENTY FAMOUS MODERN STRONG-MEN

(Note: The listings are in approximate chronological order, and do not necessarily indicate respective merit)*

1. "APOLLON." In the book, *Les Rois de la Force* ("The Kings of Strength"), published by Prof. Edmond Desbonnet in Paris in 1911, the professor gave brief biographies of hundreds of strong-men of numerous nationalities. However, of all these men there were only two that Desbonnet termed "super-athletes," and to them he devoted a separate chapter. The two "super-athletes" were Louis Cyr, of Canada, and Louis Uni, of France. Cyr was popularly known as "the Canadian Samson." This title originated in his early days as a professional strong-man, when, in order to liken himself to the Biblical Samson, he wore his hair down to his shoulders. Louis Uni went almost always under the professional name of "Apollon" (pronounced Ap'ah-lon'). Desbonnet regarded the sheer, muscular powers of Cyr and Apollon to be so far beyond the ordinary as to deserve special mention.

Apollon (b. Jan. 21, 1862, in Marsillargues, France) was a tall, heavily-

---

* Nor do the respective *lengths* of these brief accounts, which are based largely on how *interesting* each strong-man's career was.

built, dark-complexioned man, standing 6 feet 2.8 inches and weighing in solid, muscular condition about 260 pounds (see Plate 3). He was noted especially for his feats of grip and forearm strength (some of which are described below). But he was strong all over, with tremendous development of the legs as well as the arms and shoulders.

Perhaps the greatest feat performed by Apollon was an accidental, unrehearsed one that, unfortunately, was not measurable in pounds. It occurred during the course of one of his regular stage performances at the Folies-Bergere, in 1889. At one point in his act, Apollon took the part of an escaping prisoner, pursued by guards. Running from them, he came to a heavy, barred iron gate, which was locked. Throwing off his cloak, he presented a figure of herculean power. Grasping two of the iron bars, with a mighty effort he would force them apart and make good his escape. But before his performance on this particular evening, evidently some jokester had bribed the blacksmith who made the iron gate (and who had the job of restraightening the bent portions after each performance) to *temper* or harden the iron bars. When these steel-like bars were grasped by Apollon, he found himself unable to bend them. Meanwhile, his small wife, who was standing in the wings, and who thought Apollon was merely in one of his lazy moods, urged the giant to get to work. Forgetting all acting, and with grim determination, Apollon drew on the full measure of his colossal strength. Finally, bathed in perspiration, he was able actually to bend the tempered bars far enough to force his body through. Utterly exhausted, he staggered to the footlights and told the audience that he was unable to continue his act. But the spectators were satisfied that they had witnessed an altogether extraordinary exhibition of human physical power.

Another prodigious impromptu feat performed by Apollon was the following. It occurred during his engagement at the Varieties Theatre in Lille in 1892. One day Apollon heard that some rival strong-men—three Germans known as "The Rasso Trio"—were coming to see his act that afternoon and if possible to wrest from him his title of "Strongest Man." It was presumed that the particular member of the Trio who would attempt this was one Godfrey Nordmann. He was indeed a huge fellow and—as he appeared bundled up in his winter overcoat—looked even bigger than Apollon. Quite perturbed by this unexpected turn, Apollon asked his friend Batta to fix up one of his barbells so that it would weigh much more. This particular bell, empty, weighed 143 pounds. However, it had a handle so thick (over 2½ inches) that few lifters could raise it to the shoulders. Batta loaded the two hollow spheres with sand, which made the bell weigh 198 pounds, but Apollon declared that it was still too light. He then asked Batta to send for more sand, so as to fill the smaller spheres also. Then, as the time for the performance was approaching, he retired to his dressingroom. Paul Pons, the famous heavyweight wrestler, who was with Batta, suggested a prank. "Why bother with sand?" he asked. "Here are two solid iron spheres; slip them on and the big fellow will never know the difference." Batta, who loved a joke, complied with glee. The solid spheres were put on the bar in place of the sand-filled ones, and the barbell was found to now weigh 341 pounds.

The performance began at 2 P.M. Sitting in the first row, sure enough, were the three Rassos, waiting to see what Apollon could lift. After performing for their benefit several difficult feats with lighter weights, Apollon rolled out the big, thick-handled barbell. Batta and Pons, shaking with excitement, prepared to make a speedy exit. But they need not have worried! Evidently Apollon never even suspected that the weight might have been changed. Grasping the bar with both hands, he cleaned it in a flash, jerk-pressed it overhead, passed his right hand to the center of the bar, let go with his left hand, and to cap the performance stood on his left foot alone, raising his right leg out straight. Allowing the bell to drop, he caught it in the bend of his elbows, tossed it up, grasped it in midair and set it gently on the floor. It is difficult to conceive of a man so strong that he either ignored, or did not notice, the difference in weight between a barbell weighing in the neighborhood of 200 pounds and another weighing no less than 341! Yet that is the way Apollon reacted on the stage at the Varieties Theatre that afternoon in 1892.

The Rassos came forward to test the weight of the barbell that Apollon had handled as if a toy, but even the huge Nordmann was barely able to lift the bell off the floor. Batta and Pons, who had thought that for once Apollon would be stumped, were stupified by the manner in which he had played with the 341-pound weight (see Plate 3).

Even the latter poundage may not have represented Apollon's maximum lift overhead with both hands. At one time, while searching the junkyards of Paris for a weight with which he could safely challenge all rivals, he came across and purchased a pair of railway wheels, mounted on an axle, that weighed altogether 118 kilos or 260 pounds. This he used as a barbell in his contest with Batta in 1889. Later on, by the same procedure, he obtained a much heavier set of wheels, weighing 166½ kilos or 367 pounds. The story of these wheels is given in detail below.

In 1927, when Apollon was about 65, he appeared in the motion picture *Mare Nostrum*, which was directed by Rex Ingram. In it he took the part of a retired sea captain.

Various feats of weightlifting performed by Apollon are described under their specific headings later in this chapter. Apollon died on October 18, 1928, in Paris, from an abscess of the throat.

2. LOUIS CYR. (See Plate 4). This world-renowned French-Canadian strong-man was born in a small village, St. Cyprien de Napierville, near Montreal, on October 11, 1863. His father was only of average size, but his mother was a veritable female Hercules, standing 6 ft. 1½ ins. and weighing some 267 pounds! His mother's parents also were large and strong, the father standing 6 ft. 4 in. and weighing 260 pounds. Evidently Louis was to inherit breadth and girth rather than height, for when full-grown he stood only 5 ft. 8½ in. But he weighed anywhere from 270 to 315 pounds, even when he was in his prime of activity, and was a colossus of all-around strength—be it in lifting, working, or rough-and-tumble fighting!

Once, when Cyr was only 17, and weighing 225 lbs., he came upon a driver whose heavily-laden wagon was mired in a rain-soaked road. Knee-deep in the mud, young Louis got his back under the wagon and raised it up while the driver's horses pulled it out. Thus, perhaps, was born the idea for his "Back Lift," in which later on, as a professional strong-man, he would raise on a platform on his back as many as 20 men.

At 18, Cyr was matched in a strength-test against David Michaud, who at the time claimed to be the strongest man in Canada. The test chosen was that of lifting with the hands alone, just off the ground, the heaviest field stone. After several lifts with lighter stones, Cyr finally raised an unwieldy granite boulder weighing 480 lbs., which Michaud had failed to budge.

While still 18, and shortly after he had married, Cyr worked for several months as a lumberjack. His foreman, observing young Cyr's extraordinary strength, urged him to exhibit his abilities to the world at large—not to just a few admiring woodsmen. Responding to this advice, Cyr for the next several years trained diligently with various weightlifting paraphernalia that he had managed to gather together, to prepare himself for a career as a "strong-man."

While working for awhile as a patrolman in an outlying branch of the police department in Montreal, Cyr had an experience that catapulted him into the headlines. While going about his rounds, Cyr happened upon two (some accounts say three) burly thugs engaged in a fight with knives. Stepping between them (Cyr had the reputation of being absolutely fearless), the young officer, who was surprisingly agile (considering his size) as well as strong, quickly disarmed and subdued the fighters. Then—there being no conveyance at hand—he calmly carried the two inert lawbreakers, one under each arm (some accounts add to this a third man, whom Cyr held in front of him!) to the nearest police station! This spectacular arrest focused widespread attention upon its real-life hero.

In New York City, among the many there who happened to read about Cyr's exploit, was the sports-promoter Richard K. Fox, who was publisher of the popular weekly, *The Police Gazette*. Some time after the episode, Cyr came under Fox's patronage. Seeing some of the feats that Cyr could perform, Fox was so impressed that he backed Cyr as the "Strongest Man in the World," and offered $5000 to anyone who could duplicate even one of Cyr's many routine examples of strength.

Among the many top-notch strong-men to be defeated in contests with Cyr, while he was on tour periodically in the United States and Canada during the years 1885–1891, were "Cyclops" (Franz Bienkowski) "the coin-breaker"; Sebastian Miller; the aforementioned David Michaud (in several subsequent matches); Richard Pennell; the Montreal strong-man, Hector Decarie; and the great Swedish weightlifter, August Johnson. Eugen Sandow, who was at his best as a weightlifter during the years 1891–1894, was repeatedly challenged by Cyr during this period. Richard Fox, Cyr's sponsor, even had a diamond-studded championship belt made up, to be presented to the winner; but the hoped-for contest either never took place or was kept quiet if it did.

While as mentioned before, Cyr weighed at his best (*c.* 1892–1896) in the neighborhood of 300 pounds, he nevertheless carried a great deal of excess fat even though his body and limbs were solid to the touch. His true *muscular* bodyweight was probably about 235 to 240 pounds. As he stood only 5 feet 8½ inches, Cyr's build was thus close to maximum for his height; and it is in relation to his probable *muscular* bodyweight —not his actual weight—that his feats of strength should be judged.

The lift for which Cyr was most famous was his Back Lift (with platform). But his performances in this style of lifting are surrounded with confusion. Nearly all weightlifting historians quote his best lift in this event as having been 4300 pounds. This poundage he is supposed to have raised on May 27, 1895, at Austin & Stone's Museum in Boston. But on that occasion, nothing was weighed. The alleged 4300 pounds was the total of the 18 men on the platform (each of whom *stated* his own bodyweight), plus the weight of the platform. Assuming that the platform weighed 500 pounds—a liberal estimate—it would mean the *average* weight of the 18 men Cyr lifted was about 211 pounds. This, while possible, was not likely.* Several contemporary strong-men, who knew Cyr, seemed to concur in the belief that Cyr's best effort in the Back Lift was somewhere between 3900 and 4000 pounds. On the basis of his other lifts, it would appear that Cyr *should* have been capable of *more* than 4000 pounds, but somehow, despite all his practice in the

---

* On another occasion, Cyr lifted *16* men on his platform, the total weight of which was known to be 3626 pounds. On the same basis, 18 men and the platform would have weighed about 4000 pounds.

Back Lift, he never seemed to have acquired an efficient *technique* in that style—a technique comparable, for instance, to that possessed in 1907 by Warren L. Travis (see below).

While Cyr's hands were larger than average for his height, particularly in their width (each of his hands was about 7¾ inches long and 4¼ inches wide), they were appreciably smaller than those of various contemporary strong-men: "Apollon," John Marx, Charles Jefferson, and Sebastian Miller, for instance. Yet Cyr, by reason of his phenomenal forearm development (his forearms were *twice* the size of the wrists!), had a vise-like grip and was a past-master at handling heavy objects such as sacks and barrels, as well as barbells and dumbbells having very thick handles. One of his most remarkable demonstrations of strength—an entirely unrehearsed one—was as follows. One evening in 1892, when Cyr was exhibiting in London at the Royal Aquarium and was making a one-arm lift with a thick-handled dumbbell weighing 240 pounds, someone in the audience sounded (to Cyr, at least) as though he were expressing skepticism of the announced poundage of the bell. Lowering the dumbbell from his shoulder until it hung at his side like a briefcase, and still carrying it, Cyr walked over to the suspected miscreant and told him to either test the weight himself or shut up! Then, swinging the ponderous dumbbell back to his shoulder, Cyr completed his lift by heaving the weight overhead! Other weightlifters who witnessed this performance (among them the one-time British Amateur champion, Tom Pevier), in recounting the feat referred to Cyr's strength in tones of awe.

The various lifts made by Cyr in other styles are listed later in this chapter and in Chapter 5 under their respective classifications. Cyr's preeminence as a strong-man was shown by the fact that he never side-stepped a contest, and was never defeated during his long reign before the public (1881–1906). Unfortunately, Cyr was a champion eater and a heavy drinker as well as a strong-man, and these excesses contributed to his demise at the early age of 49, of Bright's disease. He passed away in Montreal on November 10, 1912.

3. HORACE BARRÉ (pronounced barr-ā'). (See Plate 5.) Nearly equal to Cyr in all-around strength, but lacking Cyr's showmanship and fighting spirit, was his one-time protegé, Horace Barré, who was born in Montreal on March 25, 1872. Barré in his physical prime, about 1896, stood 5 feet 9 inches and weighed about 275 pounds. However, like Cyr, he later on became obese and then weighed well over 300 pounds. In putting up a dumbbell with one arm, Barré succeeded with a weight of 275 pounds, thus surpassing Cyr's record of 273¼ pounds, which Cyr had made in London in 1892. Another fine feat of strength performed by Barré was to curl with one arm, while standing erect, a 100-pound dumb-

bell. In doing this, he kept his hand in a position midway between pronation and supination, as in carrying a suitcase. This left indicated that Barré was probably capable of a military two-arm curl with barbell of between 215 and 220 pounds. In a correct crucifix lift, holding out two dumbbells, it appears that he was capable of about 175 pounds (90 right hand, 85 left hand). With a pair of dumbbells he pressed 280 pounds, and in the two arm jerk (taking the barbell to the shoulders in two movements) he equalled Cyr's official record by doing 347 pounds. Actually, Barré could jerk 380 pounds if the weight were placed at his shoulders, which lift must have constituted a world record in 1896. In the Back Lift, Barré's record was 3890 pounds. But like Cyr, Barré evidently did not take care of his health after he had retired from competition, as he died at the age of 46, in 1918.

4. HENRY HOLTGREWE. (See Plate 5). Another powerfully-built weightlifter—a contemporary of Louis Cyr and Horace Barré—was Henry Holtgrewe, of Cincinnati. Holtgrewe was born in Hanover, Germany, in 1872. He was descended from several generations of large and powerful ancestors. Henry came to the United States at an early age, and settled in Cincinnati. There, he followed the career of a tavern-keeper and restaurateur. In his spare time he delighted in practicing and performing feats of strength; and in this field he became so proficient that he was known as "The Cincinnati Strong-man." At a height of 5 feet 9 inches, Holtgrewe weighed at his best about 280 pounds, thus being comparable in physique with Horace Barré and only slightly less heavy-built than Louis Cyr. In putting up a weight with one arm, he surpassed the records both of Cyr and Barré by doing 287 pounds. That even this poundage was not his limit was shown by the fact that he could perform the lift (which was made on a thick-handled, unbalanced barbell) almost any time he tried it. The style he employed was probably somewhere between a side press and a bent press, and was done largely by sheer strength.

Another stamina-requiring feat performed by Holtgrewe was to raise overhead three separate weights that totalled 380 pounds. First, he put up a heavy barbell with his right arm; next, using his left arm, he picked up a lighter weight (probably a kettlebell or a ringweight) which he hung onto the thumb of his right hand; finally, using again his left arm, he raised a third weight from the ground to arm's length overhead. This was an even more drawn-out lift than the "Two Hands Anyhow, with barbell and ringweight" performed some ten years later by Arthur Saxon (see below), even though the total poundage was considerably less. Holtgrewe, like Saxon, was partial to the use of bells having very thick handles. This alone stopped most smaller-handed competitors. It also accounted largely for the exceptional development of Holtgrewe's forearms, which measured a clean 15½ inches. It is said that in "wrist wrestling" (see Chapter 5) and similar feats of arm strength he was never defeated.

Like Cyr and Barré, Holtgrewe was very strong in the Back Lift. In 1904, at Redlands Field, Cincinnati, he is said to have lifted on his back with a platform the players of two opposing baseball teams, an estimated weight of 4103 pounds. However, as in Louis Cyr's claimed 4300-pound Back Lift, the estimated weight of Holtgrewe's lift appears excessive. The bodyweight of professional baseball players averages about 178 pounds. Accordingly, 18 players (two teams) would weigh 3204 pounds. This, with a 500-pound backlifting platform, would make 3704 pounds. Even if the ball players whom Holtgrewe lifted weighed over 180 pounds each, it is highly unlikely that they averaged 200 pounds —which they would have had to do unless Holtgrewe's platform weighed over 500 pounds. So, evidently this alleged record of Holtgrewe's in the Back Lift, as in the case of Louis Cyr, has suffered from having been "estimated" rather than accurately weighed. But for all this, that Holtgrewe was a remarkable strong-man is indicated by the fact that Warren L. Travis (see below), who later on made world records in deadweight lifting, always referred to Henry as "the great Holtgrewe." This close-to-the-top strong-man died on January 1, 1917, at the age of 54 years.

5. EUGEN SANDOW. (See Plates 6 and 7). Despite the superiority in sheer physical power of men like "Apollon," Cyr, Barré, Holtgrewe, and certain other exhibitors of the 'nineties, the greatest of them all—from the standpoints of artistry and showmanship—was the peerless Eugen Sandow. For it was Sandow, more than any performer who had preceded him, who raised feats of strength out of the grunt-and-groan category and made them spectacular and entertaining. He was enabled to do this largely by reason of his remarkable physique, in which was combined versatile strength with panther-like grace and agility. Because of his possession of these qualities in a high measure, Sandow could truly be called a "super-athlete." This separated him from most of his numerous rivals, some of whom were stronger than Sandow but the majority of whom could only be called "strong-men" and nothing more.

Eugen Sandow, whose real name was Frederick Mueller, was born in Königsberg, East Prussia, on April 2, 1867. Prior to becoming a "strong-man," he had been a circus acrobat; and there is evidence that he had visited the United States about 1887 in a gymnastic (Roman ring) act. This, accordingly, was *before* his supposed first appearance in the United States, in 1893.* In the latter year, he appeared first at the Casino, in

---

* Also, about 1890, Sandow had appeared in one of the first motion pictures made by Thomas A. Edison. This was in East Orange, New Jersey.

New York City. Later in 1893 he secured an engagement at the Trocadero Theater in Chicago, where meanwhile the World's Columbian Exposition was being held. At the Trocadero, Sandow came under the management of the later-to-become-famous impresario, Florenz Ziegfeld.

Actually, Sandow's first chance at fame had come in London, in 1889. At that time, strength acts were popular, and the reigning performers in this field in London were two Continental strong-men having the names, respectively, of Charles Sampson and "Cyclops" (Franz Bienkowski). As a team, they were currently performing at the Royal Aquarium, where they were offering prizes to anyone who could duplicate certain of their feats. Attracted by the magnitude of these prizes—and the possibility of capitalizing on a successful venture—Sandow, accompanied by his manager, Louis Attila, on the evening of October 29 "jumped the stage" at the Aquarium and defeated Cyclops in four separate feats of weight-lifting. Four evenings later (November 2, 1889), at the same venue, Sandow defeated Sampson, in a contest of bar-bending and chain and wire breaking. To furnish an idea of the impact on the public of the latter contest, here is a sample quotation from a contemporary London newspaper: "If the fate of the Empire had depended on the outcome, no greater interest could have been shown." (It was said that front-row tickets to this show sold for as much as $250 a seat!)

As a result of his victory over Sampson, Sandow was the recipient of many theatrical offers. From then on, his success appeared assured; and from 1890 to 1905 he enjoyed extended engagements in the British Isles, Continental Europe, the United States, South Africa, and Australia. At the Trocadero Theater in Chicago, his salary was reputed to be $3500 a week. After retiring from the stage, Sandow founded his Institute, or "school," of Physical Culture, in London. This he followed with numerous branch "schools" throughout the British Empire. Becoming a British subject, he became also "Instructor by Appointment to His Majesty George V."

Although the extraordinary amount of publicity surrounding Sandow during his professional career caused a great many people to believe that he was "The Strongest Man in the World," actually the only record in weightlifting ever established by Sandow was his put-up with one arm of 269 pounds, which he performed in London late in 1891. This lift was made in the "bent press" style, using the right arm. The weight (a barbell with spherical ends) was shouldered by first standing it on end and then tilting it over. As the barbell was not sufficiently long for this purpose, Sandow stood it on a 9-inch block before levering it to his shoulder. But this record was to be short-lived, for on January 19, 1892, at the Royal Aquarium, before a record-sized audience of some 5000 persons, the huge French-Canadian strong-man, Louis Cyr, put up a *dumbbell* weighing 273¼ pounds mainly by sheer strength.

As mentioned at the beginning of this account, Sandow was endowed
with marked *agility* as well as exceptional strength; and he appeared to
best advantage where the feats were of an acrobatic or gymnastic nature.
In fact, his physique was that of a "herculean gymnast" rather than a
typical strong-man (he stood 5 feet 7.7 inches, and at his best weighed
186 pounds, his development from the hips up being disproportionate
for that of his legs, fine as the latter were). One of Sandow's spectacular
feats was to perform a standing back somersault while holding in each
hand a 35-pound dumbbell.* Sometimes he varied this by doing it blindfolded on a handkerchief, or over the back of a chair. Another feat was
to hold, hanging in front of him, a 125-pound barbell, and then to jump
over it (between his hands) forward and backward. In chinning, according to Al Treloar (who was for a time Sandow's assistant), Sandow
could do a one-arm chin with a single one of any of his ten fingers,
including the thumbs! Treloar told me that he saw Sandow do these
chins on a loop of rope which was suspended back-stage. When chinning
with one of his thumbs, Sandow contrived to assist it with the palm
of his hand, but it was a terrific feat nevertheless.

Other lifts and feats performed by Sandow are listed later in this
chapter and in Chapter 5 under their respective headings. Sandow died
in London on October 14, 1925, assertedly from a cerebral hemorrhage.

6. JOHN MARX. (See Plate 8). This famous strong-man, whose real name
was Grünn, was known as "The Luxembourg Hercules." He was in
his prime during the 'nineties—a period in which competition among
professional strong-men was so intense as to cause many to resort to
faked performances. It is to Marx's credit that he did not have to
stoop to such deception. His strength was so genuine, and his showmanship so polished and professional, that he had little difficulty in
keeping his name steadily before the public in the leading theaters and
music-halls of England and the Continent.

Marx was born in Mondort, Luxembourg, on August 27, 1868. His
father was a blacksmith, as was his grandfather. For a time, as a
young man, John followed the same calling; but with an urge to see
the world strong within him, he emigrated to the United States. There,
in St. Louis, he obtained employment in a brewery, his specific job
being the loading of heavy, beer-filled barrels onto delivery wagons.
One day he was observed by a travelling professional strong-man named
Aloysius Marx, who hired him on the spot. The two men worked up
a "strong-act" and went to England, where they appeared in various
music-halls under the name, "The Brothers Marx."

---

* The dumbbells were *announced* as weighing 56 pounds each. This poundage
Sandow could probably have done as a *limit* feat.

PLATE 1

(Left) A statue of Milo, by Dumont, in the Louvre. The sculptor has shown the famous Greek strong-man in his old age, attempting to pull apart the stump, which had been partially split by woodcutters. The story is that the wedge fell out, causing the wood to spring back and imprison Milo's hands, and that in that position he was devoured by wild beasts. This highly unlikely happening has been recounted by countless authors as though it were historical fact! (1)

(Right) A marble bust in the Louvre of the Roman Emperor Gaius Julius Verus Maximinus, who was a giant 8 ft., 1 in. in height and was said to be "proportionately strong." He ruled from 235 to 238 A.D. (2)

This drawing by Clyde James Newman shows Milo carrying a bullock rather than the generally-stated four-year-old heifer. (3)

Some feats of Karl von Eckenberg (c. 1715), which provided a basis for those performed by other strong-men centuries later. (5)

Peter I ("The Great"), Czar of Russia from 1682 to 1725, was a man of extraordinary stature and strength. (4)

63

PLATE 2

A copy of an old wood engraving, showing Thomas Topham making his famous "Harness Lift" of 1836 lbs., in London, May 28, 1741. Since one of his legs was of very little use due to an injury, he was forced to perform the lift mostly with the strength of one leg and his arms. This made the feat even more outstanding. (6)

Topham supporting a falling building. (7)

Here we see Topham calming down two insolent customers. (8)

Topham punishing an insulting innkeeper. (9)

Here we see Topham returning a quarter of beef. Incidents shown in drawings are described in text. (10)

PLATE 3

A favorite pose of Apollon, taken when he was about 30 years of age and at the zenith of his career (1892). (11)

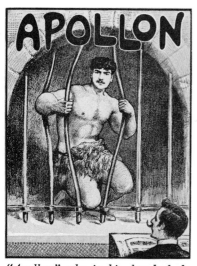

"Apollon," who in his day had the largest muscular arms on record, as he appeared in the "Escaping Prisoner" sequence of his act at the Folies-Bergere in Paris, 1889, from a contemporary drawing. (12)

An artist's illustration of the historical meeting of Apollon and the Rassos. Here, Apollon jerked and then shifted into one hand a thick-handled barbell weighing 341 lbs. (13)

PLATE 4

Louis Cyr, "The Canadian Samson," c. 1893. (14)

A wood-engraving that was published in The Police Gazette *in the 1890s, showing the manner in which Louis Cyr performed his famous "back-lift." (15)*

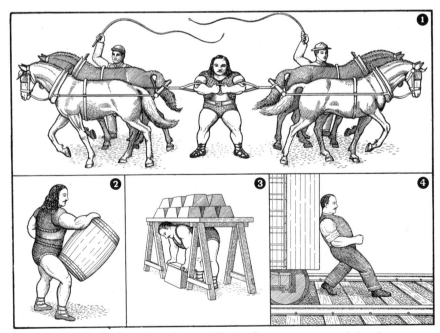

Some of the herculean feats of Louis Cyr, as interpreted by the author.

1) resisting the pull of two 1000-lb. horses on each arm 2) shouldering with one hand a barrel of sand and water weighing 445 lbs. 3) lifting on his back a platform loaded with pig-iron, weighing 3536 lbs. 4) pushing a loaded freight car up a slight grade. (This was actually done using both legs together, as in a Back Lift.) (16)

66

PLATE 5

Horace Barre, above, at the age of 18, was already a very husky strong man and making Canadian records (17). In the photo below we see him in 1896 when he was at his best (18). At the right he is dressed in the fashion of the day, ready to go out on the town. (19)

Henry Holtgrewe, "The Cincinnati Strong-man." (20)

PLATE 6

Eugen Sandow displaying his mighty muscles to swooning feminine admirers backstage. (From a contemporary illustration in The Police Gazette, New York.) (23)

(Left) Eugen Sandow at the age of 26 (1893), in one of the "club studies" taken of him by the well-known portrait photographer, Napoleon Sarony, in New York City. (21)

Prof. Louis Attila, who trained Sandow for the career of strong-man. He was instrumental also in bringing various other athletes into professional prominence. (22)

Sandow in 1891, in his stage costume of pink shirt, black leotard, and Roman sandals. It was about this time, in London, that he made his one-arm press record of 269 lbs. (24)

PLATE 7

Some stage feats performed by Eugen Sandow.

(1) The "human bridge," supporting a horse and rider. Later on, Sandow used two horses (large ponies), one on each end of the plank. Still later, he used three ponies, the center pony being a small one which was trained to "see-saw" the plank by shifting its weight from one side of the center to the other. (2) The "bent press," with a hollow-ended barbell holding two small persons. (3) The "Roman Column," in which Sandow, holding a barbell or a man, would bring his body from a hanging to an upright position. (4) Supporting a "horse" (actually a pony, weighing perhaps 350 lbs.) on one arm, a good part of the weight resting on his neck and shoulders. After the pony was hoisted into place (with a block and tackle), Sandow would walk with it across the stage. Needless to say, all these feats were extremely spectacular, and "took" exceedingly well with the audience. (25)

PLATE 8

(Above) Two poses of George Hackenschmidt taken about 1905, at the age of 27. (26, 27) (Right) "Hack" at the age of 20 (1898), when he was making weightlifting records. (28)

John Grünn Marx, "The Luxembourg Hercules," who was champion at breaking horseshoes. (29)

After awhile, the two men separated, and John put on his own act, under the name "John Grünn (or Grün) Marx." In his show, among other spectacular feats, he performed a Harness Lift using from 25 to 30 men—"must be seen to be believed" was the way the feat was announced on his posters. Marx was, indeed, the greatest harness-lifter of his day. On one occasion—at Eastbourne, England, in 1905— he raised in this style 2000 kilos, or about 4410 pounds. This weight, minus the weight of the lifting platform and chains, would have been equivalent to that of 24 or 25 men of average size. If Marx lifted 30 men, they would either have had to be of less than average weight, or to have totalled, with the lifting platform, more than 5000 pounds. Although it was easy, in those days, to fake a Harness Lift by con-necting the lifting chains to *those supporting the lifting platform** (rather than directly from the shoulder harness to the lifting platform itself, as should be done), it is difficult to believe that Marx would resort to such trickery. In any event, Edgar Müller, the highly reputable German weightlifting statistician, gives Marx credit for a legitimate lift of the 4410 pounds stated above.

Marx was a powerfully built fellow, standing about 5 feet 11 inches and weighing at his best from 235 to 242 pounds—practically all solid bone and muscle. In addition to being the champion Harness lifter, he was also perhaps the all-time greatest exponent of the specialty of breaking horseshoes. At an exhibition in Paris in 1905, he broke with his bare hands three horseshoes (separately, of course) in the short space of 2 minutes 15 seconds. His hands were not only very strong, but also very large (each hand was about 8½ inches long by 4½ inches wide). Accordingly, he was able to use barbells and dumbbells with handles so thick that few other strong-men could even lift them off the floor, let alone to the shoulders or overhead. On many an occasion, Marx cleaned and jerked a pair of thick-handled dumbbells that he kept as "challenge" weights, the bells weighing 143 pounds and 132 pounds respectively, and each bell having a handle 2¾ inches in diameter. Marx also performed a one-hand snatch of 154 pounds, the bar again being 2¾ inches thick.

At Prof. Desbonnet's physical culture school in Lille, France, Marx readily lifted from the floor to the "hang" position, first with his right hand and then with his left, a barbell of 226 pounds that had a handle about 2⅜ inches (actually, 60 mm or 2.36 in.) in diameter. This was on the famous occasion (in 1897) when "Apollon" (Chapter 4) was present. Slyly remarking, after making his lifts, that he (Marx) was

---

* The mechanical principle involved here is the same as where, sitting in a swing, one can "lift" oneself with very little effort by pulling inwardly on the two support-ing ropes.

the only man who could thus pick up the 226-pound "unliftable" barbell, Marx waited for the giant Frenchman's reaction. It was then that Apollon almost "snatched" the bar that Marx had lifted only hip-high! Actually, Apollon pulled the bar high enough *to* snatch, but not dipping under it to get his arm straight (he declined to use such "technique"), the bell slipped from his grasp and crashed to the floor behind him. This was one of the greatest exhibitions of grip-strength on record. Although Marx could lift the bell only as high as the "hang" position, he was one of the very few lifters of that day who could do even that, and probably made the lift with less effort than did any of the other men. In other words, during the 1890s, which marked the beginning of a 20-year "Golden Age" for professional strong-men, the only man who could surpass John Marx in the lifting of thick-handled barbells and dumbbells was Apollon.

Still another difficult feat that Marx evidently could do was to break coins with his fingers. When Marx was on tour in the United States, about 1900, he is said to have presented the gymnastic instructor, Prof. Paulinetti, of Philadelphia, with a 10-cent coin that he broke in Paulinetti's presence. This was a more difficult feat, in view of the small size of a dime, than the breaking of quarters and half-dollars —feats which Marx was also said to be capable of doing. This great strong-man from Luxembourg died in London in 1912.

7. GEORGE HACKENSCHMIDT, "The Russian Lion." (See Plate 8.) This strong, quick and agile Russian strong-man and wrestler was doubtless one of the greatest athletic "supermen" of all time. His remarkable ability in weightlifting becomes truly extraordinary when it is considered that he practically discontinued this sport (at least so far as making attempts at records was concerned) at the early age of 20. At that time he concentrated his practice on Greco-Roman wrestling, in which activity he was soon to become the world's champion.

George Hackenschmidt was born on August 2, 1878, at Dorpat, a town in what was then the Estonian province of Russia. His ancestry was German, Swedish and Russian. Although his parents were of quite ordinary physique, he had a brother and a sister, both younger than he, who were above average in strength. His maternal grandfather was a powerfully-built Swede, six feet in height; and from him "Hack" feels that he acquired his liking for bodily exercises, which came about at an early age. When only nine, he was acknowledged the strongest boy in his school, and four years later he won a prize as the best gymnast of his age. At that time he weighed 122 pounds, although he was only 4 feet 7½ inches in height, being of a rather heavyset build. He could, even then, clear his own height in a running high jump, and once sprinted 197 yards in 26 seconds (equivalent to 100 yards in about 13¼ seconds). In dumbbell lifting, he could (at the same age of 13) press a weight of 36 pounds 16 times with his right hand and 21 times with his left—the latter effort being equivalent to a single press with about 60 pounds. At the age of 17 he became a member of the Reval Athletic and Cycling Club, and in the last-named sport won several important races. He likewise became a first-class swimmer. The chief gymnasium activities of the aforementioned club were weightlifting and wrestling, and in the sport of lifting Hack soon became the recognized champion. In wrestling, for which at first he had little liking, it was to be several years before he took up its practice in earnest.

By July 1897, when he was just turning 19, Hack had grown in height to 5 feet 8½ inches, in weight to 176 pounds, and in weightlifting ability to the point where he could raise in the two hands continental press a barbell of 243 pounds. About this time, having sustained a slight injury in his work as an engineer (for he was still an amateur athlete), Hack, in seeking medical treatment, was fortunate in meeting a Dr. von Krajewski, who happened to be visiting the doctor on whom Hack had called for treatment. Dr. Krajewski, besides being at the time physician to His Majesty Czar Nicholas II, was founder of the St. Petersburg Athletic and Cycling Club, and was virtually the patron-saint of athletes in Russia. After giving Hack a physical examination, Dr. Krajewski predicted for him an exceptional success as a professional strong-man and wrestler, if only he would put himself under the Doctor's supervision. To this Hack agreed, and went to live and train at Dr. Krajewski's palatial home in St. Petersburg (now Leningrad), in which the Doctor had a completely equipped gymnasium. This was in January 1898.

Between February 1898 and June 1900—on which latter date Hack became a professional athlete (Greco-Roman wrestler)—he made the following weightlifting records: Right Hand Press (a bent press preceded by a "hip toss"), 255½ pounds. This was performed in Moscow in February, 1898. On April 27, he improved on this poundage by making his best official one hand put-up of 269½ pounds (just a half-pound more than Sandow's official record). Unofficially, he raised, sometime later, a bar of 291 pounds. On April 27 also, while weighing 190 pounds, he made an official world's amateur record in the Right Hand Snatch by raising 197.3 pounds. During the same month, he did a Right Hand Jerk (shouldering the barbell with two hands) of 231½ pounds, and a left hand lift in the same manner of 205 pounds. In the Two Hands Snatch he raised 251.3 pounds (which was only 2.2 pounds under the world record held by the Frenchman, Pierre Bonnes); and in the Two

Hands Clean and Jerk 308.6 pounds. That the latter lift was not his limit is indicated by his record of 197.3 pounds in the Right Hand Snatch, which was equivalent to a Two Hands Clean of about 315 pounds, and to the fact that in the two hands jerk from the shoulders he was capable of about 350 pounds. Lying flat on his back, he pulled over his face and then pressed a barbell weighing 361½ pounds (and having 19-inch discs), which lift was destined to be the world record for over 18 years. In the Pull-Over and Press in Wrestler's Bridge he did 311½ pounds (which he pressed twice, and which was equivalent to pressing about 324 pounds once). This lift, which Hack performed in Vienna on August 2, 1898 (his twentieth birthday), at a bodyweight of 195 pounds, remained the official world record for over 50 years!

Hack became the Greco-Roman professional wrestling champion of the world at Vienna in April 1901. His prowess in this sport is described later (Chapter 7). Hackenschmidt was a superlative example of the benefits of sustained physical training, and even when in his seventies could do a standing jump over the back of a chair. "Hack" died in London on February 19, 1968, at the age of 89 years.

8. G. W. ROLANDOW. (See Plate 9). What a wonderful all-around strength-*athlete* this splendidly formed strong-man was! That this evaluation of Rolandow is no exaggeration on the writer's part may be seen from the following brief account of some of the things he could do.

Rolandow was born in Switzerland, on May 6, 1874, of German-Swiss parents. He became a naturalized American citizen about 1896 and made his home in New York City. His real name was Gottfried Wuthrich. He said that he picked his professional name, Rolandow, from a beer advertisement. Probably the fact that this name sounded somewhat like Sandow had something to do with its choice. For the name Sandow was uppermost in Rolandow's thoughts, and for several years, around the turn of the century, he persistently challenged Sandow to a public contest. At one time a friend of Rolandow's actually deposited $25,000 with a New York newspaper to go to the winner of a Sandow-Rolandow weightlifting match, but Sandow, who had more to lose than to gain by such a test, wasn't interested. If such a contest *had* come about, Rolandow would probably have won it, since for about ten years he had trained with the specific object in view of bettering each and all of Sandow's performances.

Before becoming a professional athlete (exhibitor and instructor), Rolandow was a star performer for one of the leading amateur athletic clubs in New York City. Representing this club in various track and field meets, Rolandow made some creditable records, especially considering that he was rather small for the weight events (he was 5 feet

9¾ inches tall and weighed between 175 and 180 pounds). He put the 16-pound shot 45 feet, threw the 16-pound hammer 162 feet, and did equally well in sprinting and in throwing the javelin and the discus. He also became a first-class boxer, wrestler, and bag-puncher, and a champion handball player and rope-skipper. He likewise excelled in hand-balancing and in various forms of gymnastics. The fact that he had been physically inferior and with no interest in athletics up to the age of 16 showed the extent of his later determination to excel.

In weightlifting, Rolandow accomplished the following lifts: One Hand Snatch, 180 pounds right and 170 pounds left; Two Hands Continental Jerk with barbell, 310 pounds; Bent Press from Shoulder, 298 pounds right and 265 pounds left. In a two-hand grip lift, hands to sides and using special grips, he raised 1650 pounds, a remarkable performance. In supporting a weight on his knees and shoulders in a bridge (the so-called "Tomb of Hercules"), he was capable of 3500 pounds. In tearing cards, he could tear into halves at one time 162 cards, or three decks plus six cards over.

But Rolandow's greatest ability, undoubtedly, was in *jumping* with weights, in which he was in a class by himself. Here are some of the things he could do: (1) jump over a table 36 inches high and 25 inches wide while holding in each hand a 75-pound dumbbell; (2) jump forward and backward over the shaft of a 200-pound barbell held in his hands; (3) perform a standing back somersault while holding a 60-pound dumbbell in each hand. An observer, Thomas W. McGrew, says that he saw Rolandow do a back somersault with a *barbell*, and that he never heard of anyone else so much as trying it!

Having heard that the famous prize-fighter, John L. Sullivan, once did 5000 rope-skips without a miss, Rolandow determined to do at least double that number. Making a test, he did 15,000 consecutive skips—a world record at the time. Rolandow died in New York City on December 6, 1940, at the age of 66 years.

9. LIONEL STRONGFORT. (See Plate 9). This one-time exhibiting strong-man gained his greatest fame after he had retired from the stage and had launched his mail-order course in health and body-building. From 1898 until perhaps 1935 or so, his advertisements grew in volume and scope until finally they appeared in practically every popular magazine published. His always-used, full-length front pose became familiar the world over, and his advertising literature reached out to prospective pupils from Alaska to Zanzibar. But to repeat, "Strongfort" had first been known as a strong-man, although his claim to be "The World's Strongest Man" was an example of the flamboyant style he was to use later in his mail-order advertising. This claim was unsupported by

any sort of evidence. In fact, on at least one occasion his claim was to cause him considerable embarrassment!

"Lionel Strongfort," whose real name was Max Unger, was born in Berlin on November 23, 1878. He commenced his stage performances at an early age, perhaps about 1897, which unfortunately for him was the very time when Arthur Saxon (who was the same age as Strongfort) was coming into the limelight. Conveniently ignoring the ability of Saxon (see below), who could have toyed with any of Strongfort's barbells, Strongfort claimed to hold the world record in the Bent Press with 312 pounds (and to raise that poundage at each of his two-a-day theatrical performances!). On the occasion of one of his nightly challenges to the audience, at the London Pavilion, Piccadilly Circus, early in the 1900s, the well-known lightweight professional, Albert Attila (no relation to Louis Attila), "jumped the stage," bent-pressed Strongfort's "challenge" barbell with ease, and, after much ado, collected the promised £25 award. Attila's estimate of the alleged "312-pound barbell" was that it weighed *probably* about 190 lbs. Various bits of evidence point to the probability that Strongfort, as a record test, could have bent-pressed some amount between 225 and 240 pounds. These figures are a far cry from his claim of 312 pounds.

An interesting circumstance is that while Strongfort claimed a record in the bent press—which he never held—he was relatively much better in the One Hand Snatch, although the latter fact was never publicized. Al Treloar, who was familiar with Strongfort's abilities, once informed me that Strongfort could readily snatch 175 pounds with his right hand. At that time (about 1902), Strongfort weighed only about 177 pounds himself, his one hand snatch thus being a fine lift. Perhaps it was because a much heavier poundage could be *claimed* in the Bent Press than in the One Hand Snatch that Strongfort chose the former lift for his sensational theatrical announcements.

In his "Human Bridge" act (see Plate 9), which he performed at the New York Hippodrome, Strongfort used to sustain momentarily the weight of a bridge, automobile and passengers totalling about 3200 pounds. For this feat his exceptionally strong legs stood him in good stead. Warren L. Travis (see below) said that he was willing to wager that Strongfort could have supported in this manner 4000 pounds as a record attempt. Notwithstanding this, Strongfort—as in the poundage of his Bent Press—couldn't refrain from exaggerating his "Human Bridge" feat, and claiming that the total load was "approximately 7000 pounds"(!)

Strongfort, like G. W. Rolandow, patterned many of his feats after those which had been made popular by Sandow, and which demonstrated agility as well as strength. One of these feats was to do a standing back somersault while holding in his hands two "56-pound" (35-pound?) dumbbells. Remarkably, Strongfort was exactly the same height (5 feet 7.7 inches) as Sandow, and at his heaviest bodyweight also weighed nearly the same (184 pounds). Strongfort, however, was more symmetrically proportioned than Sandow in respect to relative lengths of legs and trunk. Sandow was superior in muscular development from the hips up, especially in the shoulders (deltoids), upper arms, and abdominals. Strongfort had splendidly developed thighs. At latest report, he was still hale and hearty although approaching 90 years of age!

10. ARTHUR SAXON. (See Plates 10 and 11). Biographers usually have their favorite subjects, and one of mine has always been Arthur Saxon. Next to Eugen Sandow, he was certainly the most *interesting* professional strong-man of the last hundred years, and his remarkable and spectacular feats are still discussed whenever present-day strong-men start reminiscing. Unlike many another performer of his day, Saxon insisted on making *genuine* lifts.

Saxon's real name was Artur Hennig. He was born in Leipzig, Germany, on April 28, 1878. With the exception of a short period toward the end of his professional career, Arthur Saxon never performed his stage act alone, although he would occasionally lift alone in public when feeling in the mood for bettering some one of his records. Principally, he was the central figure in what came to be known (between 1897 and 1914) as the Arthur Saxon Trio. While this trio of strong-men was composed, from 1904 on, of Arthur and his two younger brothers, Hermann and Kurt, in the beginning, because of the immaturity of the latter, a number of older strong-men, mostly fellow-Germans, teamed up for varying lengths of time with Arthur. To recount the rather complex history of the Trio and its various members is not essential here.

Arthur, who was six years older than Kurt, and four years older than Hermann, left school at the age of 14 to become a stonemason's apprentice. At the same time, along with a few friends, he commenced the practice of weightlifting. This, at first, took place in the cellar of his parents' home in Leipzig. Making rapid progress in strength and lifting ability, Arthur at the age of 16 joined the Athletic Club "Atlas" in Leipzig, and within a few months was acknowledged to be the strongest man in the club. At 17 (in 1895) he became a professional performer, displaying his strength in German fairs and carnivals. For some reason —perhaps because Eugen Sandow had made such a great name as a strong-man through his ability to put up heavy weights with one arm— Arthur also adopted the Bent Press as his special lift, and before long became a truly phenomenal performer in it. While, as we have seen,

Sandow's best official record in the Bent Press was 269 pounds—made in 1891, when he was 24 years of age—Arthur Hennig at the age of only 18 was regularly raising 386 pounds in the Two Hands Anyhow, the first stage of which consisted of a Bent Press of 267 pounds!

Ultimately, Saxon attained poundages in the Bent Press and the Two Hands Anyhow (with barbell and ringweight) that left earlier record-holders such as Sandow, Cyr, Barré, and Holtgrewe hopelessly outclassed. Since Saxon's records in both the foregoing lifts remain unequalled after more than 60 years, a brief recounting of his successive record performances in them—particularly in the Bent Press—may at this point be appropriate.

When the Arthur Saxon Trio was giving music-hall performances in England, Arthur's first public record in the Bent Press was on April 8, 1903, when he raised 314 pounds. This was at the old South London Palace, London Road, S.E. On November 24, 1904, in a private demonstration at the Sandow School of Physical Culture in Liverpool, he raised 331 pounds, this consisting of a thick-handled barbell weighing 160 pounds, to which were tied two dumbbells weighing 90 and 81 pounds respectively. Again in London, at the previously-mentioned South London Palace, on January 4, 1905, he made his best official record by raising 335¾ pounds. This lift, according to W. A. Pullum, who witnessed it, was made on an ordinary six-foot steel bar of one-inch diameter, loaded mainly with 15-pound plates. Saxon actually arose with the weight before his arm was fully straightened, and had to stagger forward to "lock" his arm (elbow) and save the lift. On another occasion, in October 1904, when the Trio visited the oldtime Scottish strongman Donald Dinnie, who had cast aspersions on Arthur's alleged abilities, Arthur "converted" him by bent-pressing an aggregation of Dinnie's own weights that weighed 340½ pounds. Arthur's bodyweight at the time was only 191 pounds. This would have been equivalent to a lift of 356 or 357 pounds had Saxon been at his usual bodyweight of 200 pounds.

In London, at the old National Sporting Club, on January 29, 1906, Saxon attempted to bent-press 350 pounds in order to settle a wager. However, his use of a badly-balanced, globe-ended barbell with a handle only one inch in diameter, along with a shaky floor (boxing ring) and various other factors, caused him to fail to make the lift. No fewer than six times he pressed the weight (which actually scaled 353 pounds) to a straight arm; but each time the sand-filled spheres caused the bar to roll back into his fingers, and he finally had to give up. However, about this time, Saxon made his highest unofficial Bent Press, at Apollo's (William Bankier's) physical culture school in London. As in his exhibition at the National Sporting Club, the lift was attempted under anything but ideal conditions. A number of failures took place (this time because various small weights became untied from the barbell handle) before Saxon finally was able to lock his arm and stand erect with the weight. This, when placed on the scales, proved to be no less than 386 pounds! It should have answered eloquently the question that had prompted Saxon to make the lift, namely, a query by "Apollo" as to whether it was true that Saxon had ever put up 300 pounds with one arm! Saxon's bodyweight at the time of this phenomenal lift was about 203 pounds. As to Saxon's generally accepted "official" record of 371 pounds in the Bent Press, there is actually some doubt as to whether he was able to stand erect with the barbell after getting it to a straight arm. However, his 386-pound unofficial lift in London, along with the fact that on a number of occasions he lifted his two brothers, Hermann and Kurt, in a *sitzapparat*, the total weight of which was approximately 370 pounds, would indicate that he was fully capable of the 371-pound "official" lift referred to above. This controversial lift by Saxon was allegedly performed in Stuttgart, Germany, on December 12, 1905. It is interesting to note that in the accompanying reproduction (see Plate 10) of one of the Saxon Brothers' theatrical posters the record one-arm lift claimed for Arthur is 335 lbs., 12 oz. This is the amount that he lifted in London on January 4, 1905. Curiously, the artist has shown all the barbells as being the wheels and axles of railway cars rather than the globe-ended "stage" bells that the Saxons customarily used. I wonder if any "old-timer" knows whether, *after* December 1905, the Bent Press claimed for Arthur on his posters was 371 pounds?

An equally detailed commentary could be given on Saxon's various records in the Two Hands Anyhow lift. Suffice it to state here that his official record in this style—when bent-pressing a barbell with his right hand and then bringing up a kettlebell with his left hand—was 202 kilos or 445.33 pounds. This lift was performed in Leipzig on November 3, 1905. The most remarkable feature of Saxon's Two Hands Anyhow lift was the amount that he was able to raise from the shoulder with his *left* arm after he had completed the overhead lift with his right arm. On the occasion of the Saxon Trio's visit to Donald Dinnie, when Arthur bent-pressed for the old Scotchman a barbell weighing 340½ pounds, he made another lift—a Two Hands Anyhow— of 380 pounds. In the latter, the weight brought overhead with the *left* arm was no less than 150 pounds! Arthur's brother Kurt says that Arthur could clean and jerk with two arms a barbell of 275 pounds, shift it into his right hand, stoop low and grasp with his left hand one end of a barbell of 149 pounds, which he would stand on end, turn over to the shoulder, and finally jerk aloft, making a Two Hands Anyhow of 424 pounds. Imagine jerking 149 or 150 pounds with one hand while already supporting 275 pounds overhead on the other arm—what truly phenomenal ability Saxon had in this style of lifting!

Be all this as it may, Arthur Saxon could be rated as a prodigy only in feats of *combined* strength and specialized skill, such as the foregoing—in which he was unique—and in other events depending on his oversized hands and powerful grip, in which he was equalled or surpassed only by a few other strong-men of his time. However, as an all-around lifter he was excellent, in the so-called "quick" lifts as well as in sheer one and two arm pressing and curling power.

Other than in the Bent Press and the Two Hands Anyhow, Arthur Saxon's best barbell and dumbbell lifts (in the standard competitive events then in vogue) were, as follows. (The lifts followed by *est.* are closely estimated figures based on Saxon's known lifting records and capabilities):

> Right Hand Snatch (officially), 195 lbs.; ditto (unofficially), 210 lbs.; Right Hand Clean and Jerk (est.), 250 lbs.; Right Hand Swing with Dumbbell, 187 lbs.; Right Hand Military Press (est.), 130 lbs.; Two Hands Military Press (est.), 260 lbs.; Two Hands Snatch (est.), 263 lbs.; Two Hands Clean and Jerk, 336 lbs.; Two Dumbbells Clean and Jerk, 288½ lbs.; Two Hands Continental Jerk (officially), 345 lbs.; ditto (est.), 365 lbs.; Pull-over and Press on Back with Bridge, 386 lbs. A rather unusual lift, which may not have represented his limit, was when, in front of Warren L. Travis, Saxon rolled up his back and then jerked from behind his neck a barbell weighing 386 lbs.

Some of Saxon's more remarkable feats of hand and finger strength, also of supporting on his feet, are listed later in this chapter and in Chapter 5 under their respective headings.

Despite the known capabilities of Arthur Saxon in numerous different feats of strength and skill, there appears to be a widespread and persistent confusion about his status as a "strong-man." While he was billed on his theatrical posters as "The Strongest Man on Earth" (he *had* to make sensational claims in order to receive billings), it is to be doubted whether he could foresee that a lot of later writers on weightlifting would take the claim literally. Away back in 1911, when Saxon was still performing regularly, Alan Calvert, in his book *The Truth About Weight-lifting* pointed out (p. 84) that "There are four amateurs and two professionals in the city of Vienna, three amateurs in Germany and one professional in Sweden, who could take Saxon's measure in those lifts which require pure strength." The four Viennese amateurs to whom Calvert alluded were probably Josef Steinbach, Berthold Tandler, Josef Grafl, and Karl Swoboda. The two Viennese professionals were probably Michael Mayer and Karl Witzelberger. The three German amateurs were probably Alois Selos and Heinrich Rondi and possibly Hans Hagstotz, although several other names suggest themselves. The Swedish professional was doubtless Arvid Anderson. The only point in which Calvert erred was in his use of the common phrase "pure strength." Actually, there is *no* feat in weightlifting, gymnastics, or any other field of muscular effort that can be performed by "pure strength." *Skill*, and very often *speed*, are factors present in all acts of bodily strength, and these factors depend very largely on the degree of specialized training through which the performer has put himself.

After the disbanding of the Saxon Trio due to World War I, Arthur resumed work as a "solo" performer in 1920. In Duisberg, Germany, he contracted plural pneumonia and there died, on August 6, 1921, at the age of 43.

11. WARREN L. TRAVIS. (See Plate 12). Right in the middle of the "Golden Age" of professional strong-men was Warren Lincoln Travis, of Brooklyn, New York. Travis made most of his records in 1907, and for years after that was recognized by the *National Police Gazette* as "The Strongest Man in the World." He was presented by publisher Richard K. Fox with a diamond-studded belt (worth, it was said, $2500) emblematic of that title. This belt had been made up originally to be presented to the winner of a contest between Eugen Sandow and Louis Cyr. However, since Fox was unable to induce Sandow to lift publicly against Cyr, that contest never materialized.

Travis himself, possibly because of lucrative real estate deals, was able to wager as much as $10,000 against any disputant of his "title." The size of this wager was alone sufficient to discourage any otherwise eligible competitors. But there was another factor in Travis's favor: he was not, strictly, a barbell lifter, but rather a Back-and-Harness lifter; and one of his stipulations was that the winner of the contest would be he who raised, in a series of lifts, the greatest *total* poundage! With such a näive and unsound method of reckoning prevailing, no conventional barbell lifter would have had a chance. Yet Travis actually believed in this method; and that perhaps is the reason (apart from his financial stipulations) why no public contest ever took place between him and any opponent.

Actually, while Travis was very capable in his chosen forms of lifting, he was neither big enough (he stood 5 feet 8 inches and weighed at his best 185 pounds) nor strong enough to have had any chance against the various European champions at barbell lifting who were active in his day. Arthur Saxon—with whom Travis assertedly tried to get a match when the Saxon Trio was in this country in 1909—would have defeated Travis decisively unless a number of heavy "poundage" lifts had been included in the contest for Travis's benefit.

But in the Back Lift with platform, Harness Lift, Hand and Thigh Lift, and various specialties of hand and finger strength, Travis was unquestionably a marvel, especially considering his limited size and bodyweight. Travis had been an adopted child, and his real name was Roland Morgan. He was born in Brooklyn on February 21, 1876. That city he made his lifelong home. His best lifts as a professional were made at an exhibition he gave at the Brooklyn Athletic Club on November 1, 1907. His bodyweight then was 185 pounds. Here are the records he established, in front of numerous athletes and sportsmen, on that date: Back Lift, 4140 pounds; Harness Lift, 3985 pounds; Hand and Thigh Lift, 1778 pounds; Two Finger Lift, 1105 pounds. In all these lifts, iron (not people) was used. Four days later, on November 5, at the same place, he did a One Finger Lift of 667 pounds. In this style of lifting he used a tight "finger-ring," which was padded, and rested the lifting hand about halfway up on the thigh. Unofficially, Travis on several occasions exceeded his best official Back Lift, his highest record being a lift of 25 men in overcoats, who, together with Travis's lifting platform, weighed an estimated 4240 pounds. Travis's numerous feats of hand and finger strength, as well as certain feats of supporting, are listed later in this chapter and in Chapter 5.

Travis performed a great deal of "endurance" or repetition lifting, in which, for example, he would do a Back Lift, or a Hip Lift, of 1000 pounds 1000 times in as short a period of time as possible. He persisted in doing such strenuous work right up to the time of his death. In the last performance of his strong-man act at the World's Circus Side Show, Luna Park, Coney Island, on Saturday night, July 12, 1941, Travis suffered a heart attack and expired. He was 65 years of age. It was the feeling of some of his friends that if only he had taken things a bit easier in his later years, he could have lived to a ripe old age.

12. JOSEF STEINBACH. (See Plate 13.) While all eleven of the previous subjects in this series were *professional* strong-men, this celebrated weightlifter from Vienna was for several years (1904–1906) the world's amateur champion. Although he never became a professional strong-man, he did relinquish his amateur status, late in 1907, by competing for a brief period as a professional wrestler. Essentially, however, Steinbach was an example *par excellence* of the amateur "Continental" type of weightlifter of his day.

Josef Steinbach was born on March 21, 1879, at Horschaù, near Pilsen, Bohemia. This district was then a part of Austria-Hungary, but is now in Czechoslovakia. Steinbach's forebears were all farmers, of

German-Bohemian stock, and had resided in the district for generations. At the age of 15, Josef went to Vienna, to work in a tavern. He was noticed, on account of his strength, by a Viennese lifter named Bartasek, who introduced him to the weightlifting club "Sparta." This was early in 1898, when Steinbach was going on 19. Due to his natural great strength and athletic aptitude, he rapidly rose to first place among Viennese lifters. He was, in turn, a member of the Athletic Clubs "Sparta," "Hercules," and the Viennese Turnverein "Austria." In 1900, he was adjudged the champion of the Association of Austrian Athletic Clubs, in 1902 of Austria-Hungary, and in 1904 of the world (at Vienna). In the latter contest, which comprised eight different styles of lifting, Steinbach was over 100 pounds ahead of the second-place man, Josef Grafl.

At the age of 25, in 1904, Steinbach stood 5 feet 10 inches and weighed 252 pounds. He had, however, an oversized waist (43 inches), as was typical of German and Austrian heavyweights of his time, and his true *muscular* bodyweight was probably about 232 lbs. He was powerfully developed all over, as the illustration of him in Plate 13 shows.

Besides winning the world's championship in 1904, at Vienna, Steinbach won the same title *twice* during 1905—once at Berlin, and again at Duisburg (Germany). In most of these competitions, eight different lifts were used, these being usually the Right (and Left) Hand Snatch; Right (and Left) Hand Jerk, Continental style; Two Hands Snatch; Two Hands Press; and Two Hands Jerk. In the two latter lifts, the barbell was brought to the shoulders in the usual German or "Continental" style, namely by shouldering it in *two* movements. But these eight "standard" lifts were not always adhered to as a set, and in some competitions the One Hand Jerk or the Two Hands Snatch was omitted and some other lift, such as the Two Dumbbell Jerk, substituted. In all these lifts, Steinbach did very well, although he was relatively stronger in putting up weights from the shoulders overhead than in raising them "clean" to the shoulders. It would appear that the bulging waists of the oldtime, beer-drinking German and Austrian heavyweight strong-men often acted as a handicap, in requiring that the barbell in a "clean" lift to the shoulders be *swung* up almost with straight arms, rather than pulled up vertically close to the lifter's center of gravity. This factor operated to Steinbach's disadvantage in his contest at Athens in 1906 against the Greek lifter Demetrius Tofalos. The details of this contest were as follows.

In 1906, which was not an Olympic year, there was held, nevertheless, an unofficial "Olympic" contest in Athens. Evidently, as in the 1896 Olympic contest in the same city, only two lifts were used, these being as before the One Hand Clean and Jerk (using a dumb-bell) and the Two Hands Clean and Jerk (using a barbell). In the one hand event the best lift was made by Steinbach, who put up 76.5 kilos or about 168½ pounds. Evidently the ruling was very strict, for in the same year in Vienna, Steinbach set an Austrian heavyweight amateur record by cleaning and jerking with his right hand a barbell weighing 106 kilos or 233.7 pounds. The latter lift was equivalent to a One Hand Clean and Jerk with *Dumbbell* of about 205 lbs. In the Two Hands Clean and Jerk, Steinbach had to yield first place to the Grecian strong-man Tofalos, who succeeded in cleaning and jerking a barbell weighing 143.9 kilos or 316¼ pounds. Although Steinbach normally was capable of cleaning this poundage as a limit effort, perhaps the fact that in this contest the 316¼-pound barbell was one that *Tofalos himself owned* (and had practiced with) explained why Tofalos was able to take it clean to the shoulders and Steinbach was not. In any event, Steinbach had to be content with doing only 136.2 kilos or 300.27 pounds—a weight that he could *military press!* After the contest, however, he took Tofalos's barbell of 316¼ pounds to his shoulders in two movements and then easily jerked it *6 times in succession.*

Although the winner of the world's championship in 1907, at Frankfurt, was the German amateur Heinrich Rondi—a lifter of decidedly less all-around ability than Steinbach—possibly Steinbach did not compete at Frankfurt. Again, in 1908, Steinbach was considered a professional, and the world's title went to one of his former Viennese competitors, Josef Grafl (see below). It is said, though, that Steinbach, lifting independently outside the contest, registered a higher total than Grafl.

Steinbach's best lifts—some of which were amateur world records at the time he performed them—were as follows. All, so far as I know, were made in Vienna.

Lift	*Kilos*	*Pounds*	*Date*
Right Hand Snatch	85.5	188.49	Sept. 8, 1907
Left Hand Snatch	80	176.37	1907
Right Hand Clean and Jerk (barbell)	106	233.68	1906
Right Hand Swing with Dumbbell	77.5	170.85	1906
Two Hands Press (Continental)	149.4	329.37	Dec. 14, 1905
Two Hands Press with Dumbbells (Continental)	140.2	309.08	Aug. 1906
Two Hands Press, sitting in chair	120	264.55	Sept. 29, 1906
Two Hands Jerk (Continental)	175.2	386.24	1907
Two Hands Jerk with Dumbbells (Continental)	152	335.10	Sept. 19, 1905

As indicated by the above lifts, Steinbach, while a good all-around barbell and dumbbell lifter, was essentially a specialist in the Two

Hands Continental Press and the Two Hands Continental Jerk, both with a pair of dumbbells as well as with a barbell. His Two Hands Press with Barbell of 329¼ pounds, made in 1905, was then the world record. His same lift with a pair of dumbbells, of 309 pounds, he improved upon in 1907 as a "professional" (wrestler) by doing 142.5 kilos or 314.15 pounds. His relatively best press, however, was when, earlier in 1907, and while still an amateur, he pressed a pair of dumbbells weighing together 126 kilos or 277.79 pounds, while standing with his *feet together*. In the Two Hands Continental Jerk with Barbell, as a "professional" he raised 178 kilos or 392.42 pounds (late 1907). But his best jerking ability was perhaps shown when, in Munich on September 12, 1907, he put up from the shoulders a barbell of 157.5 kilos or 347.22 pounds 7 *times in succession*. This was equal to jerking about 406 pounds once. The relatively slight superiority of Steinbach's jerks over his presses indicates that his jerks were probably accomplished simply by a heave and a press-out, without dipping under the bar. Such a lift today is often referred to as a "jerk-press," and is the style generally used by big men who are strong in pressing. Indeed, Tromp van Diggelen, who knew Steinbach well and often saw him train, says that a "heave and press" *was* the way that Steinbach performed his jerks.

During the period in which Steinbach was an amateur athlete, he had no desire, or urge, to publicly compete against any contemporary professional strong-man. However, after he had become a professional wrestler, he issued a challenge to Arthur Saxon to compete against him for the Professional Weightlifting Championship of the World. This challenge was issued repeatedly, and was published, among other places, in the English physical culture journal *Health and Strength* in its issue of March 12, 1910. The challenge was covered by a guarantee of $5000 by Steinbach. But Saxon had gone to the United States, and showed no inclination to meet Steinbach, even though Steinbach was perfectly agreeable to the use of four one-hand lifts (including the Bent Press) in a seven-lift contest. If Saxon had felt reasonably sure of defeating Steinbach in such a contest, he would certainly have gone after the $5000 side stake. But since he did not, it is evident that he *knew* which man would have won.

As no other lifts—such as feats of grip-strength, etc.—have been recorded for Steinbach, his records in standardized barbell and dumbbell lifting have in the foregoing account been given in some detail. Steinbach died in Vienna on January 15, 1937, when he was approaching 58 years of age. Later in 1937, a huge granite monument was erected to his memory from funds contributed by countless Austrian and German strong-men who had admired the one-time *Weltmeister* ("World-Master").

13. JOSEF GRAFL. (See Plate 13.) Next to the better-known Austrian heavyweight strong-men, Josef Steinbach and Karl Swoboda (see no. 14, following), Josef Grafl was the strongest weightlifter ever produced by that country up to the end of World War I. Grafl was also one of the tallest first-class weightlifters on record, as he stood 6 feet 3½ inches. While he weighed at his best usually around 285 pounds, some of this was excess waistline, and in "trim" condition he would have scaled about 260 lbs.

Josef Grafl was born in 1872 at Odenburg, Hungary. He went to Vienna at the age of 15, and started training with weights in 1897, when he was 25. His brilliant record as an amateur weightlifter can be summarized as follows: In contests prior to 1908, he was always behind Josef Steinbach. On December 8, 1908, at Vienna, he won the world's heavyweight title, his nearest competitor being Berthold Tandler (5 feet 6½ inches, 273 pounds), also of Vienna.* In 1909 he again won, at Vienna, this time over the famous Viennese lifters Karl Swoboda and Berthold Tandler, and Fritz Eicheldraht, of Dortmund, Germany. In 1910 the world championship was held at Dusseldorf, Germany. Grafl again took first place, the runners-up being the German champion Heinrich Rondi, and Tandler of Vienna. In 1911 there were no fewer than *four* world's championships. One of them, at Stuttgart, Germany, was won by Grafl. Another, which was held in Berlin, saw Grafl defeated by the narrow margin of 3 pounds by the colossal Karl Swoboda —even though Swoboda was not destined to reach his peak as a lifter until the following year. In a third contest, which was held in Vienna on June 29, 1911, Swoboda again won over Grafl, but only by a pound or so! The fourth world championship of that year was held at Dresden, Germany, and was won by Tandler. Grafl did not enter that contest, and probably neither did Swoboda, since Tandler was not the equal, let alone the superior, of either of these "super-heavyweight" stars.

In 1912, when the Olympic Games were held in Stockholm, Sweden, there was no weightlifting. But in 1913, in the world championship held at Breslau, Poland, Grafl again won. This made his *fifth* world title. On that occasion the runners-up were Tandler of Vienna and Jan Krause of Russia. Along with these world championships, Grafl twice won the European heavyweight title. The first time was in Vienna in 1907, Grafl's nearest competitor then being Alois Selos, of Munich. Grafl again won the European championship in 1909, at Malmo, Sweden, against Edward Danzer of Vienna, Eicheldraht of Dortmund, and Friedrickson of Copenhagen.

---

* Tandler was a brother-in-law of Karl Swoboda, having married Swoboda's sister. The two men trained together regularly in Swoboda's outdoor "gymnasium" (see p. 88).

Grafl's best lifts were as follows: Right Hand Snatch (officially), 88.4 kilos or 194.88 lbs.; ditto (unofficially), 90 kilos or 198.41 lbs.; Left Hand Snatch, 82 kilos or 180.76 lbs.; Two Hands Snatch, 117 kilos or 257.94 lbs.; Two Hands Continental Press with Barbell, 144 kilos or 317.46 lbs.; Two Hands Continental Press with Barbell, feet together, 100 kilos or 220.46 pounds *18 times in succession!;* Two Hands Continental Press with Dumbbells, 130 kilos or 286.6 pounds; Two Hands Continental Jerk with Barbell, 176.5 kilos or 389.11 pounds; Two Hands Continental Jerk with Dumbbells, 150 kilos or 330.69 pounds. Grafl, despite his great height, was superior to Steinbach and Swoboda in snatching and cleaning, and not far behind them in sheer pressing power. He could probably have made a correct Two Hands Military Press with about 280 lbs. Evidently he was relatively better at repetition lifting than in a single effort, since his feat of pressing 220 pounds 18 times with heels together was equivalent to a single press in the same style of 338 pounds!

An interesting sidelight on Grafl is that in 1913, in the first motion picture production of the story Quo Vadis?, Grafl played the part of the giant Christian captive Ursus. Cast into the Roman arena, Ursus saw galloping toward him a gigantic wild bull with his mistress, Lygia, bound onto the back of the animal. Grasping the horns of the bull, Ursus, by a prolonged, superhuman effort, succeeded in breaking the animal's neck. This life-and-death struggle made such an impression on the cheering spectators that they demanded freedom for both Ursus and the girl.

During World War I, in the Austrian offensive at Przemysl, in 1915, Grafl was killed in action. He was 43 years old. So popular had he been in Vienna that many athletic clubs were named after him, and on January 8, 1938 a special weightlifting contest was held in that city to honor his memory.

14. KARL SWOBODA. (See Plate 13.) Whenever and wherever the subject of old-time strong-men is being discussed, the name of Karl Swoboda (pronounced schwo'buda) is usually brought up. But it is doubtful whether many of those who mention this old-timer have more than a vague idea of who he was or how much he could lift. One recent weightlifter (who was a champion some years back) expressed doubt as to whether Swoboda had really pressed 352 pounds—since Swoboda was incapable of *cleaning* that heavy a barbell to his shoulders! If the aforementioned recent champion had had any knowledge of the style of two-arm shouldering that was the *standard technique* in Austria and Germany prior to World War I, he would not have raised such a silly question. While Swoboda was, admittedly, more capable in

jerking—or even in pressing—than he was in bringing a weight "clean" to the shoulders, that was simply because of his immense size and girth. In sheer strength, he was actually or potentially one of the topmost weightlifters of modern times.

Karl Swoboda, whose parents were German, was born in Vienna on July 28, 1882. In due course he became a naturalized Austrian. His interest in weightlifting began at the age of 16. His first serious training, however, did not commence until he was in his early twenties. As a young man, Swoboda followed the trade of butcher. At the age of 26 he owned his own restaurant, and he continued at this profession. At the back of his restaurant was a "beer garden," and in close proximity to it he and his friends trained with the weights. Swoboda was also a member of the Viennese weightlifting club "Türk" (named after the former world champion, Wilhelm Türk), and between this club and his beer-garden gymnasium he did all his training. Josef Grafl was a member of the same club. Swoboda won the two world's amateur championships held in 1911 at Berlin and Vienna, respectively (for the other two contests that year, see the account of Grafl, above).

In physique, Swoboda resembled the earlier French-Canadian strong-man, Louis Cyr, but was not so well proportioned as the Canadian and had an even larger waist. In height, Swoboda stood 5 feet 10½ inches, which was two inches taller than Cyr. In 1908, at the age of 26 years, Swoboda weighed from 240 to 265 pounds. From there, he gradually increased to 330–350 pounds at the age of 30 (1912), when he made his highest lifting records. By 1914, he weighed nearly 400 pounds, but by 1922 had decreased to 285 pounds. Even in strictly muscular condition he would have weighed between 250 and 255 pounds, as he had an immense frame.

Swoboda, like Türk, Steinbach, Grafl, and other amateur weightlifters in Germany and Austria prior to the year 1912, was, as previously mentioned, an exponent of the German or "Continental" school of lifting. Under this system, heavy two-arm lifts to the shoulders were performed not in one clean movement, as is the vogue today, but by first lifting the barbell onto the buckle of a specially designed, padded belt. Then, with a second heave, the bar was taken from the waist to the shoulders. Sometimes, even more than two tempos were used, but two was considered the maximum for "good" form. Thus there was a basic difference in those days between the "Continental" two-arm lifts and those performed under the strict French ruling, which permitted only "clean" (or clear of the body) shouldering. In pressing, the Continental or unrestricted style permitted two movements in taking the barbell to the chest and unlimited back-bend in the press. In the Two Hands Snatch, the huge waists of the German and Austrian heavyweights usually made it necessary for the barbell to be *swung* in a semi-circle from the ground overhead rather than "snatched"; and it was in this style that the snatches of such ponderous lifters as Steinbach, Grafl, and particularly Swoboda were performed. Hence it is hardly to be expected that these lifts could be compared with those of the later, and sensational, French champion Charles Rigoulot (see below), who used an almost acrobatic technique in getting under his weights. In short, the relatively crude styles of lifting used by Karl Swoboda and other bulky, old-time "Continental" strong-men should be taken into due consideration in assessing the records of these early champions.

Definitely, Swoboda was a specialist in the Two Hands Continental Press and the Two Hands Continental Jerk, using in both lifts a *barbell*. Unlike Steinbach, his two-arm lifts with a pair of dumbbells were not on a par (to say nothing of being better than) his overhead barbell lifts. Below are the best lifts Swoboda made under official conditions. Most of them were performed in Vienna, and all of them as an amateur, a status which Swoboda remained throughout his athletic career. To these official lifts I have added a few estimated poundages, based on his known records in associated lifts.

Lift	*Kilos*	*Pounds*	*Date*	*Place*
Right Hand Military Press	70	154.32	1912?	Vienna
Right Hand Snatch	81.35	179.34	June 29, 1911	Vienna
Left Hand Snatch	76.3	168.21	June 29, 1911	Vienna
Right Hand Clean and Jerk (est.)	100	220.46	1911?	
Two Hands Snatch	105	231.48	1911?	Vienna
Two Hands Clean with Barbell (est.)	133.5	294.32	1911?	
Two Hands Continental to Chest in two movements (est.)	160	352.74	1911?	
Two Hands Military Press (est.)	143	315.26	1912?	
Two Hands Continental Press, barbell	160	352.74	June 9, 1912	Vienna
Two Hands Olympic Press (not cleaned) 150.7 kilos 3 *times,* equal to	162	357.2	Sept. 22, 1912	Leipzig
Two Hands Continental Press, feet together	150	330.69	1913	Vienna
Two Dumbbells Continental Press	130	286.6	1911?	Vienna
Two Dumbbells Continental Jerk	145	319.67	1911?	Vienna
Two Hands Continental Jerk with Barbell, shouldered unassisted	185.6	409.18	Nov. 4, 1911	Vienna
Two Hands Continental Jerk with Barbell, assisted to shoulders 200 kilos jerked *twice,* equal to	205.3	452.7	late 1912	Vienna

Considering the poundages in the above list that Swoboda *pressed,* together with the fact that they were performed more than 50 years ago, there can be no doubt that the giant restaurant-proprietor of Vienna was a marvel in shoulder strength. His records in military pressing indicate that he should have been able to hold straight out in front of him, on stiff arms, a barbell of about 125 pounds, or to muscle-out in the Crucifix lift about 97 pounds in the right hand and 92 pounds in the left hand. And although here there is more uncertainty, one might estimate Swoboda's ability in such "power" lifts as the two hands curl, two hands dead lift, bench press, and squat. In the curl, he should have been capable of raising correctly about 225 pounds, in the dead lift at least 680 pounds (and possibly as much as 700 pounds), in the bench press about 460 pounds, and in the squat, what with his tremendously strong legs, possibly as much as 750 pounds.

However, in all-around lifting, especially the "quick" lifts, Swoboda was relatively poor. In short, while an exceedingly strong man in some respects, he was not a balanced, all-around weightlifter, as were George Hackenschmidt, Arthur Saxon, Hermann Görner (see below), and to a lesser degree Josef Steinbach, Josef Grafl, and other contemporaries of Swoboda. So, in "athletic" ability, as in physique, Swoboda could best be likened to the earlier Canadian strong-men Louis Cyr and Horace Barré. All three of these men possessed huge frames and exceedingly powerful muscles, but by letting their waistlines grow entirely out of control they greatly limited their activity and versatility and in effect restricted their strength to a few "static" feats dependent upon sheer bulk and weight. Barbell lifters today can be thankful, at least, that two of the three standard Olympic lifts place a premium on speed as well as strength, and so promote the development of a more all-around, athletic type of physique than did the old-time "Continental" system of weightlifting, in which Karl Swoboda was the premier performer.

Since Swoboda made his records during the period 1911–1913, his various "power" lifts, whether actual or estimated, should be increased by about *15 percent* in order to be brought to the level of what he could probably lift *today* if he were in his prime. A detailed discussion of the factor of time (date) in relation to athletic performances and their merits is given below.

Swoboda's records in two-arm pressing and jerking were so highly regarded in his own country that in 1912 the Austrian government issued a special 4-Heller postage stamp honoring Swoboda and the Austrian Athletic Union.

Karl Swoboda, like his predecessors Wilhelm Türk, Josef Steinbach, and Josef Grafl, when at his height of glory was a national athletic idol. When, on April 19, 1933, he passed away after a long illness, the subsequent funeral procession in Vienna was witnessed by some 50,000 persons. It was said to be the largest and most impressive funeral given to an athlete in all history.

15. MAXICK. (See Plate 14). While all the preceding subjects in this biographical series have been either heavyweights or light-heavyweights, here is a *lightweight* strong-man whose accomplishments were so extraordinary that they warrant being included in *any* list of weightlifting records.

Maxick, whose name was "anglicized" from the German, Max Sick, was anything but a man in poor health! Paradoxically, he was to become known as "The Muscular Phenomenon." He was born in Bregenz, a town in the extreme western tip of Austria, on June 28, 1882. Although as a child he had been sickly and of poor physique, by long training in weightlifting and gymnastics he became a phenomenon of muscularity and strength. Although standing only 5 feet 3¾ inches and weighing at his best from 145 to 147 pounds, Maxick set records in weightlifting that few heavyweights of his day could equal.

Tromp van Diggelen, a Dutch strong-man and wrestler, who knew and in some cases acted as a mentor to a number of the greatest European strong-men of his time, brought Sick from Munich to London, where the two men arrived on October 26, 1909. It was shortly after this that van Diggelen and an English lightweight strong-man named Monte Saldo, who was later to be associated with Sick in business, decided that the Bavarian athlete should have a name more in conformity with English usage. Accordingly, they shortened his two names into one: Maxick. While Maxick, early in 1910, did some very fine weightlifting in London, nearly all his greatest lifts were performed either in Germany (Munich) or in South Africa (Johannesburg), where in 1913 he visited Tromp van Diggelen.

Here are Maxick's weightlifting records. All were performed as a *professional* athlete and at a bodyweight that never exceeded 147 pounds:

Right Hand Military Press, 112 pounds ("performed with considerable ease").

Right Hand Snatch, 165 pounds.

Right Hand Swing with Dumbbell, 150 pounds.

Right Hand Jerk (shouldering the barbell with two hands), 239 pounds in Munich and 240 pounds in Johannesburg.

Two Hands Military Press, 230 pounds (made at a bodyweight of 145 pounds).

Two Hands Clean and Jerk with Barbell, 272 pounds.

Two Hands Continental Jerk with Barbell, 322½ pounds in London and 340 pounds in Johannesburg.

(In the Two Hands Snatch, he should have been capable of about 215 pounds.)

Of the foregoing lifts the most extraordinary were the one and two hand military presses and the one and two hand jerks. Maxick's Two

Hands Military Press of 230 pounds, which he performed in 1909, would be equivalent today to a lift in the same strict style of about 267 pounds, or to a Two Hands Olympic Press of about 312 pounds! That is to say, in pressing power Maxick was the equal, in his day, of any of the lightweight Olympic champion pressers of the present time. In the One Hand Continental Jerk, no such comparison can be made, since this style of one-arm lifting is no longer practiced.

In bringing a barbell "clean" to the shoulders with both hands, Maxick's record of 272 pounds would be equivalent to about 320 pounds today. This, while a good lift, is a long way below the 360 pounds or more that the best lightweights clean and jerk today. It is rather in the jerk from the shoulders overhead that Maxick is seen to best advantage, and his record of 340 pounds in this movement would be equal to no less than 400 pounds today. This is truly phenomenal lifting! It would appear to surpass by at least 20 pounds the best jerking ability of any present-day lightweight lifter.

Although in Maxick's day the great heavyweight professional Arthur Saxon was astonishing the world with his ability in the Bent Press, Maxick never cared about this lift. He felt that it was more a feat of long-developed skill than of straight strength. Be this as it may, Maxick must have developed a style of one-arm pressing that was nearly equal in efficiency to the Bent Press. This is deduced from the statement made by Tromp van Diggelen that in Johannesburg in 1913 Maxick "side-pressed" the 185-pound Van Diggelen no fewer than *16 times in succession with one arm.* This repetition-lift was equivalent to a single one-arm press with over 270 pounds!

Outside of straight weightlifting, Maxick showed up equally well. Indeed, in handbalancing and gymnastics he could perform some astounding feats. While I do not have any figures on his actual records in handstand press-ups, these can be deduced from his known ability to do a Two Hands Military Press of 230 pounds while weighing only 145 pounds himself. This lift, at that bodyweight, was equal to no fewer than 34 handstand press-ups on the floor, or to 21 "tiger-bend" press-ups, or to 22 handstand press-ups on a bench, touching the chest each time (a lá Siegmund Klein; see below). And since Maxick was a skilled balancer, there can be little doubt that he was actually capable of these estimated press-ups.

According to Tromp van Diggelen, who so informed me in a personal letter about 1960, here are some of the feats that Maxick performed when he visited van Diggelen in Johannesburg in 1913:

1. In a contest at finger-pulling, in which Maxick was "unbeatable,"

Maxick could pull a 200-pound opponent clear across the table that separated the two men.

2. He pressed van Diggelen (185 pounds) overhead *16 times* with his right arm, while holding in his left hand a glass of beer full to the brim, without spilling a drop. (See comments on this, above.) Earlier that same day, he had pressed Fred Storbeck (205 pounds), who was then the heavyweight British Empire Boxing Champion, *11 times* with his right arm.

3. Holding van Diggelen aloft on one arm, Maxick *ran* up two flights of stairs with him and then ran down the two flights. Then, *standing on his hands,* he in that position ran up the two flights and down again! These stairs were in the building known in 1913 as Chudleighs', but today as the Bazaar Building.

4. At the Carlton Hotel one night, six empty champagne bottles were put before him. Each of these he filled three-quarters full with water and then, taking bottle after bottle by the neck with his left hand, he brought down the palm of his right hand on the open neck, causing the *bottom* of each bottle to smash out!

As would be expected in view of his extraordinary strength, Maxick had a superb muscular development. So completely were all his voluntary muscles under his control that he could make any desired group "dance" in time to music. He was, in fact, one of the first great exponents of the art of "muscle control," and could do things in this department that astonished even the great Eugen Sandow, who himself was an expert in the art.

For many years, Maxick made his home in Buenos Aires, Argentina, where he conducted a gymnasium and health studio. He also went periodically on exploring expeditions into the Matto Grosso of Brazil. Maxick died in Buenos Aires about 1960, I believe, at which time he would have been about 78 years of age. Of him it could almost have been said, "We shall not see his like again." At least, during the period of nearly 60 years that has passed since Maxick was in his prime, no other man of his size has equalled him in all-around strength.

16. HERMANN GÖRNER. (See Plate 15). Thanks to the unremitting efforts of the German weightlifting statistician, Edgar Müller (b. 1898), Hermann Görner is without doubt the best documented strong-man of all time. In Müller's book, *Goerner the Mighty,* which was published in England in 1951, the author and longtime friend of the remarkable German strong-man lists literally *hundreds* of record-breaking feats per-

formed by Görner, all of which are fully documented. In addition, as the result of an extensive correspondence with Müller during the years 1952–1958, I received information on many of Görner's achievements that were not included in Müller's book. Accordingly, because of limitations of space, I shall here list only the chief records made by Görner, both as an amateur and as a professional strong-man. For the rest, I refer readers to Müller's book.

Hermann Görner (pronounced ger'ner) was born in Haenichen near Leipzig, Germany, on April 13, 1891. Although he was very small at birth, he grew to average size by the time he was three years old, and from then on gradually approached the herculean stature and power transmitted to him by his ancestors. Hermann's father stood 6 ft. 2¾ in. and had a very thickset frame and enormous hands. His mother, however, was only a little over 5 feet tall. In 1920, when Hermann was in his late 20s, he stood 6 ft. ½ in. in height and weighed 220 pounds. It was at that time, shortly before he decided to become a professional athlete, that he made some of his best amateur weightlifting records. These were as follows:

Lift	Kilos	Pounds	Date
Right Hand Snatch	100	220.46	Nov. 30, 1919
Left Hand Snatch	90	198.41	Nov. 21, 1919
Right Hand Clean and Jerk	120	264.55	Nov. 9, 1919
Left Hand Clean and Jerk	100	220.46	?
Right Hand Swing, with two kettlebells (officially)	96	211.64	Oct. 12, 1919
Same (unofficially)	100	220.46	Mar. 21, 1920
Right Hand Dead Lift, with barbell	301	663.59	Oct. 29, 1920
Same (unofficially)	330	727.52	Oct. 8, 1920
Two Hands Dead Lift, with barbell	360	793.66	Oct. 29, 1920
Two Hands Clean and Jerk	177	390.22	July 11, 1920
Squat, with barbell held at *chest*	215.2	474.43	Jan. 25, 1920

(with the exception of the Two Hands Clean and Jerk, which was performed in Dresden, all the above lifts were made in Leipzig).

At the age of only 22, in 1913, Görner lifted to the shoulders in two movements, "Continental" style, a barbell weighing 200 kilos or 440.92 pounds. This lift was performed at Breslau, on July 27 of that year. Görner's squat with 474 pounds held at the chest was equivalent to a regular squat (barbell across shoulders) with about 554 pounds.

In 1921, Görner became a professional strong-man. While most weightlifters who have trained since their 'teens reach their peak of strength and lifting ability about the age of 27 or so, Görner was an exception. He kept improving in most of his feats until his middle 30s, when he reached a bodyweight of 245 pounds. While Edgar Müller says that Görner's highest muscular bodyweight was 120 kilos or 264½ pounds, my own opinion is that 245 pounds represented his maximum weight in a truly muscular condition. This can be deduced from Müller's own figures, which credit Görner at 264 pounds with a waist girth of no less than 43.3 inches! When it is considered that the muscles of Görner's sides, waist, and lower back were essentially at their peak of strength when he was 29 years old, weighed only 220 pounds, and had a waist measurement of only about 37 inches (it was at that time that he made his official Two Hands Dead Lift record of over 793 pounds), it is hardly reasonable to assume that he needed a waist 6 *inches larger* in order to be at his muscular maximum. And in this connection it must again be pointed out that a hard, firm "feel" to a strong-man's limbs or body does not necessarily mean that no excess fat is present. These are the reasons why I consider a bodyweight of from 220 to 245 pounds (and no more!) to have represented Hermann Görner's best physical condition. To credit him with a heavier bodyweight would be to *penalize* him where his feats were being appraised on the basis of his bodyweight.

The number of weightlifting *styles* in which Görner made outstanding records is too great to permit all of them to be listed here.* Since many represent feats of grip-strength—which was one of Görner's strongest points—these records are reviewed in Chapter 5. Below are listed some of the best lifts in standardized styles that this herculean German strong-man made as a professional:

Lift	Kilos	Pounds	Date
Two Hands Snatch	....	297½	Sept. 4, 1926
Two Hands Swing, with kettlebells	115.5	254.63	Mar. 26, 1931
Two Hands Military Curl, barbell	100	220.46	Sept. 1, 1932
Hold Out in Front (mil. position)	50	110.23	Aug. 14, 1932
Shouldering Barbell in 2 movements	200.6	442.25	Jan. 10, 1933

(the Two Hands Snatch was made at Kalk Bay, near Cape Town, South Africa; all the other lifts were made in Leipzig, Germany).

Görner's one and two hand dead lifts are still the world's records, whether amateur or professional. His ability in swinging either dumb-bells or kettlebells from the ground overhead (either with one hand or with both hands) is also unsurpassed. However, lifting kettlebells in *any* style seems to be turning into a lost art. Görner was also for a long time the record holder in taking a barbell to the shoulder in the One Hand Clean style, having raised 135 kilos or 297.62 pounds in this manner (at Leipzig, on Nov. 9, 1919). Only the English heavyweight,

---

* Edgar Muller, on page 44 of his book, *Goerner the Mighty*, says: "During the course of my association with Hermann, I have personally witnessed and recorded as a referee approximately 1,400 different feats of strength of all varieties."

Ronald Walker, has surpassed the latter lift, by having cleaned to the shoulder (about 1938) a barbell weighing 320 pounds.

To sum up, Görner in his day was supreme in feats of back strength and gripping strength and was for a time the record holder in various other lifts, including all styles of one and two arm curling. If it is assumed that between the years 1920 and 1924 his strength increased in proportion to his increase in body weight, he would have been about 11 percent stronger at the latter date and should have been capable of a regular squat with about 615 pounds on his shoulders. Crediting him with another 11 percent in order to allow for the time (date) of his performance would bring his squatting capability up to nearly 700 pounds. Such a poundage, while highly meritorious, is no longer the heavyweight record in the squat. In the same manner, Görner's Two Hands Dead Lift would increase to nearly 900 pounds and would still be the world record. His Two Hands Curl (in military position) would similarly increase to about 240 pounds, a topnotch performance. However, in the Two Hands Military (not Olympic) Press with Barbell, Görner's best ability of about 276 pounds would be equivalent today to only about 300 pounds. This is, or was, at least 100 pounds below the ability of Paul Anderson and possibly one or two other recent "super-heavyweight" strong-men. On the other hand, Görner would certainly surpass in grip-strength all the strong-men who could surpass *him* in pressing power. Thus, in a 5-event "Power-Lift" contest (consisting of, say, the Two Hands Curl, Bench Press, Squat, One Hand Dead Lift, and Two Hands Dead Lift), Görner should rank near the top, notwithstanding that his muscular girths were not *quite* as large as those of certain other heavyweight strong-men.

Apparently Görner remained in good health until, in 1942, an operation for varicose veins initiated a condition in his blood-stream that later reacted on his organs. He died on June 29, 1956 from what was described as colic of the gallbladder accompanied by shrinkage of the liver. He was 65 years of age. Görner had no living relatives, and so bequeathed his collection of weightlifting and biographical material to his friend Edgar Müller.

17. CHARLES RIGOULOT. (See Plate 16). This French weightlifter, by virtue of a robust inherited physique and diligent, supervised training, came to be an athletic sensation in his day and subsequently one of the immortals of the "Iron Game." In the latter sport he was somewhat of a youthful prodigy; and although he was some 12 years younger than the German professional record-holder, Hermann Görner, the two men were publicly performing during the same years but in different places. Regrettably, they never met in a contest, for what a contest it should

have been! Possibly Görner's overwhelming superiority in the Dead Lifts (with their higher poundage-possibility) was the reason why no agreement from the Rigoulot camp could be reached. But this is mere speculation. Rigoulot, while not a champion in the "slow" or power lifts, exhibited dazzling speed in the snatches, swings, and clean-and-jerk lifts. Indeed, in view of his relatively short and stocky physique, he was possibly the *quickest-moving* heavyweight strong-man on record.* Here is a brief review of his athletic career and his weightlifting records.

Charles Rigoulot (pronounced ree′ga lo′) was born at Le Vesinet, a small town near Paris, on November 3, 1903. He came of sturdy peasant stock, and as a boy was above the average in strength and athletic ability. Although he was not introduced to the sport of weightlifting until he was 18 years of age, once he took it up he made exceptionally rapid progress. This was shown by his winning, on March 5, 1923, the heavyweight championship of Paris while he was still only 19 and a lightheavyweight. In 1924, while in military service, Rigoulot was permitted to train for the Olympic Games, which were to be held that year in Paris. He practiced at a gymnasium in Joinville under the supervision of skilled trainers, and made such additional improvements in lifting ability that when, in July, he competed in the Games, he was able to take first place in the lightheavyweight championship. At that time the standard set of lifts consisted of five events, including two one-hand lifts, and in these lifts Rigoulot put up the following poundages: Right Hand Snatch 192¾, Left Hand Clean and Jerk 203¾, Two Hands Press 187¼ (!), Two Hands Snatch 226, Two Hands Clean and Jerk 297½, and Total 1107¼ lbs. It is clear that Rigoulot's best individual lift on that occasion was his One Hand Snatch; next was his Two Hands Clean and Jerk, and then his Two Hands Snatch. His One Hand Clean and Jerk was relatively only fair, while his Press was positively poor. It is interesting to note that Rigoulot at no time practiced much pressing, as he believed that it detracted from his lifting speed. Yet there is the example of the Egyptian lightweight, Ibrahim Shams—to name only one other lifter—who was faster even than Rigoulot in snatching and jerking, and yet who was able to press almost the limit that muscles of the size he possessed could be expected to lift. It is certainly debatable whether slow movements of the arms, as in pressing, could have any slowing-down effect on the muscles used either in snatching or jerking, as the latter are principally the extensor muscles of the back and legs. Possibly, if Rigoulot had striven to excel in pressing as well as in the "quick" lifts, he could have made even better records than he did make,

---

* But it was incorrect to call him "The Strongest Man in the World," as nearly all Frenchmen did. Rigoulot would have had to best his German contemporary, Hermann Görner, in an all-around contest to merit that distinction.

especially in the one and two hand jerks. In fact, by giving practically no attention to the One Hand Clean and Jerk, he fell behind in that lift to the extent that he was ultimately able to raise more weight in a One Hand Snatch!

On October 6, 1925, Rigoulot became a professional athlete by meeting in a personal contest the well-known Parisian strong-man Ernest Cadine. Rigoulot had by that time systematically "highered" his lifting poundages and had left behind him amateur world records in the Right Hand Snatch of 101 kilos or 222.66 pounds, Two Hands Snatch 126.5 kilos or 278.88 pounds, and Two Hands Clean and Jerk 161 kilos or 354.94 pounds. Also, he had gained proportionately in bodyweight, and when he met Cadine weighed 216 pounds. Cadine at the time weighed 200 pounds, but since he was only 5 ft. 6 in. in height as compared with Rigoulot's 5 ft. 7.7 in., he was very nearly as large in the general girth of his body and limbs as Rigoulot; in addition, he was the more experienced lifter of the two men. Ten lifts, including pressing, snatching, swinging, clean and jerking, and the two hands dead lift were used to decide the winner of the contest, and in these lifts Rigoulot emerged with a total of 2388¾ pounds as compared with Cadine's total of 2370 pounds. From these figures it is apparent that Rigoulot's margin of superiority was very slight. Indeed, under the least change in circumstances, the outcome could have been the reverse. And it is interesting to speculate on what would have happened after this contest if Cadine, not Rigoulot, had won. Would there have been a return contest? Would Rigoulot have gone on to make the remarkable world's professional records that he did make after winning over Cadine? In other words, would the course of weightlifting history have been appreciably altered?

It was sometime after turning professional that Rigoulot put up his best performances in lifting. During the several years immediately following his contest with Cadine, he periodically—about every six months, on the average—raised his records in snatching and two-arm jerking and in the one hand swing. Here is a list of his final best marks, together with the respective dates. All the lifts, so far as I know, were made in Paris,

Lift	Kilos	Pounds	Date
Right Hand Snatch	115	253.53	Feb. 1, 1929
Left Hand Snatch	100.5	221.56	Feb. 1, 1929
Right Hand Snatch, with Dumbbell	100.5	221.56	(Fall, 1928)
Right Hand Swing, with Dumbbell	99.5	219.36	Feb. 28, 1932
Left Hand Swing, with Dumbbell	88	194.00	Dec. 5, 1933
Two Hands Olympic Press	115	253.53	(c. 1930)
Two Hands Snatch	143	315.26	May 4, 1931
Two Dumbbells Clean and Jerk	133.5	294.31	1929?
Two Hands Clean and Jerk	182.5	402.34	Feb. 1, 1929
Two Hands Dead Lift (using overgrip)	282	621.70	Jan. 16, 1926

PLATE 9

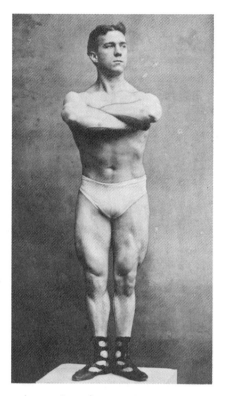

An early photograph of Lionel Strongfort (Max Unger). (30)

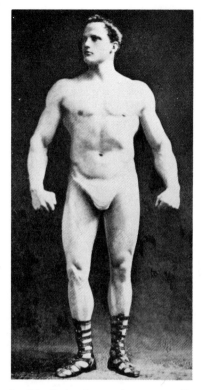

G. W. Rolandow, who repeatedly challenged Eugen Sandow to a public contest, but without result. (32)

Strongfort in his "Human Bridge" act, in which he supported momentarily a load of about 3200 lbs. (31)

Rolandow jumping back and forth over a barbell weighing 130 lbs. His best record was with 200 lbs.! (33)

PLATE 10

A theatrical poster used by the Arthur Saxon Trio in 1904–1905, when the Trio was performing in England. Shown in the three circles at the top of the poster are (left to right), Arthur, Hermann, and Kurt Saxon. (34)

PLATE 11

Hermann, Kurt, and Arthur
Saxon, c. 1905. (35)

(Right) Arthur Saxon,
"The Iron Master," showing
the position in which he
was able to "bent press"
over 370 lbs. (Drawn by
the author from a photo-
graph). (36)

Arthur and Kurt Saxon in their "Human Bridge" act at Hengler's
Circus in London, 1904–1905. (37)

PLATE 12

(Left) Warren L. Travis and two of his fancy "exhibition" weights. (38)

(Above) This old drawing shows the feat known as the "Harness Lift." In this style Travis lifted 3985 pounds (of iron) while weighing only 185 pounds himself. Brooklyn, 1907. (39)

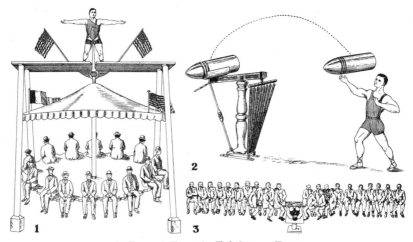

A Few of Travis's Exhibition Feats

1) supporting a revolving carousel and 14 men; 2) catching a 15-inch projectile thrown from a catapult; 3) supporting with hands and knees 26 men while lying on a revolving platform. (The artist, however, has shown the hands facing the wrong way.) (40)

PLATE 13

Wilhelm Türk, winner of the first World's Weightlifting Championship. Vienna, 1898. (41)

Josef Steinbach, Champion in 1905 and 1906. (42)

Josef Grafl, Champion in 1908, 1909, 1910, 1911, and 1913. (43)

Four Former World's Champions from Vienna

Karl Swoboda (center), Champion in 1911 at Berlin and Vienna. (44)

PLATE 14

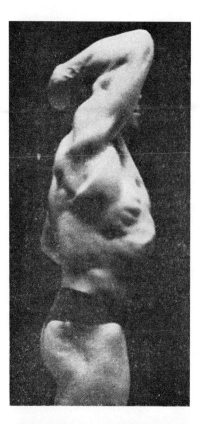

(Left) Tromp van Diggelen and his prodigy of strength, Maxick. Johannesburg, 1913. (45)

The other three views show Maxick demonstrating his remarkable ability at "muscle control." (46, 47, 48)

PLATE 15

Herman Görner performing a Two-Barbell "Sway-Press" of 275½ lbs. (142¼ right, 132¼ left). Leipzig, 1933. (49)

(Right) Görner at his best (6 ft., ½ in., 245 lbs.), being introduced by Tromp van Diggelen. Cape Town, 1926. (50)

Görner supporting on straight legs a heavy plank and 16 men, a total of over 2500 lbs. Pagel's Circus, South Africa, 1923. (51)

PLATE 16

Charles Rigoulot, while still an amateur, preparing to snatch 100 kilos (220½ lbs.) with his right hand. Paris, September 1925.

(Right) Rigoulot with his trainer, Albert Saulnier. Note the size of Rigoulot's special globe-ended barbell. (53)

Rigoulot successfully lifting the famous railway wheels of Apollon (cf. Plate 17) Paris, March 3, 1930. (54)

and in these lifts Rigoulot's bodyweight ranged from 225 to 236 pounds.

It will be noted that Rigoulot's supposed record in the Dead Lift was made only shortly after he had turned professional. His bodyweight at the time was 220 pounds, and his then-best Two Hands Clean and Jerk was only about 365 pounds. When it is considered that his ultimate record in the latter style was over 400 pounds, it can be seen that if his ability in the Dead Lift had kept apace, he would in 1929 have been capable of over 680 pounds. Even if in the Dead Lift Rigoulot had progressed only half as rapidly as in the Clean and Jerk, he should finally have been capable of at least 650 pounds.

With reference to Rigoulot's overhead barbell lifts, it should be mentioned that in them he used, not a regulation plate-loading bell, but a specially-made, shot-loading, spherical-ended bell over 8 feet in length and in which the handle was exceedingly springy. Evidently only Rigoulot had mastered the technique needed in lifting on this bar to take advantage of its springiness rather than be defeated by it. In the above list of Rigoulot's best lifts, his right hand and left hand snatches (both with barbell and dumbbell) are still the world's heavyweight professional records. Unofficially, Rigoulot did a Two Hands Clean and Jerk of 185.6 kilos or 409.18 pounds. This weight he jerked *twice* from the shoulders. On another occasion, he took to his shoulders "clean," but without jerking it, a barbell weighing 191.5 kilos or 422.18 pounds. In the Two Hands Snatch he was evidently capable of at least 150 kilos (330.69 pounds), and in the Right Hand Snatch possibly 120 kilos (264.55 pounds). These were enormous potentialities back in 1930, in a lifter whose maximum *muscular* bodyweight probably never exceeded 215 pounds.

However, Rigoulot was essentially a *specialist* in the One Hand Snatch, the Two Hands Snatch, and the Two Hands Clean and Jerk (with barbell). I have always felt that despite his superiority in these specialties, he was inferior as an *all-around* strong-man to his famous predecessor, Arthur Saxon. But such comparisons, or questions, can rarely be resolved, and we must accept each athlete for the things he does or *did* excel in.

Rigoulot retired from professional weightlifting in 1933, after sustaining a sprained hip. After that he went in for professional wrestling, from the earnings of which he was able to indulge his favorite pastime—the driving of racing cars. Rigoulot died in Paris on August 22, 1962, following the removal of one of his lungs. He was approaching the age of 60.

18. JOHN DAVIS. (See Plate 17). This well-known Negro weightlifter and strength-athlete was the first of his race to become a world amateur

weightlifting champion (Heavyweight class, Paris, 1946). Also, to date, he is the only American Negro ever to win a world weightlifting title in *any* bodyweight division. (Louis Martin, of Great Britain, a Negro heavy-middleweight, won the world title in that class in 1962, 1963, and 1965.

John Davis was born in Brooklyn, New York, on January 12 (or 19?), 1921. When only 17, he competed as a light-heavyweight in the World's Championships of 1938, at Vienna. About a year later he started making records in the three Olympic lifts, his bodyweight increasing as he progressed in strength. Sometimes he would reduce his weight so that he might continue to compete as a light-heavyweight. For example, in April 1940 he lifted in Philadelphia at a bodyweight of 197 pounds (doing 295, 280, and 365 pounds for a total of 940 pounds), yet about seven weeks later he competed in New York City at a weight of only 180 pounds (doing 250, 275, and 330 pounds for a total of 855 pounds).

Although Davis eventually became a full-fledged heavyweight, ranging from 200 to 233 pounds (at a height of 5 ft. 8½ in.), he made his best lifts relative to bodyweight when he weighed 194–196 pounds, in the latter part of 1940. At that time he pressed 310 pounds, snatched 305 (unofficially 315) pounds, and cleaned and jerked 379½ pounds. At about the same bodyweight he cleaned over 400 pounds, and jerked from the shoulders 405 pounds, but not on the same occasion in a completed lift. When making three-lift totals of over 1000 pounds, Davis always weighed over 200 pounds. On March 3, 1951, when he made his all-time best total of 1063¼ pounds, he scaled 222½ pounds, of which perhaps 210 pounds was "muscular" weight. His all-time individual best lifts were: Press 342 pounds (unofficially, 375),* Snatch 330½ pounds, and Clean and Jerk 402 pounds, a total—if made at the same time—of 1074½ pounds.

Davis was strong not only as an Olympic lifter, but also in many of the so-called "power" lifts and various feats of chinning and dipping. For example, in the Two Hands Dead Lift he did 705 pounds (bodyweight 193), and in the Squat 525 pounds eight times in succession, which was equivalent to about 570 pounds once; this also was at a bodyweight of 193 pounds. In the Two Hands Curl he did 215 pounds, and in the Bench Press 425 pounds (without specializing in either). He could pinch-lift a 75-pound, smooth barbell plate using only two fingers and a thumb. However, while he had a strong grip for feats

---

* Despite the magnitude of these Olympic Presses by Davis, it would appear that his best strictly-performed Military Press was 295 pounds twice in succession, which was equal to about 308 pounds once. This, in turn, would presuppose an ability in the Right Hand Military Press of about 154 pounds, and in the Left Hand Military Press of about 144 pounds.

such as the latter, his hands were too small for encircling and gripping really thick bars (see Chapter 4).

In chinning, Davis, at a bodyweight of 200 pounds, could at almost any time do 4 consecutive chins with his left arm, and on at least one occasion did 6 such chins. Moreover, he chinned from a "dead hang"— his arm being perfectly straight at the start of each pull-up—so there could be no argument about the validity of his "chins." At a bodyweight of 205 pounds, Davis did five consecutive one-arm chins. This was in 1941. The five chins at 205 pounds were almost exactly on a par with the six chins at 200 pounds. Both feats were equivalent to chinning once at a bodyweight of 237 pounds, or to chinning once at a bodyweight of 200 pounds while carrying 37 pounds of extra weight. These one-arm chins were equivalent also to chinning once with *both* arms at 205 pounds while carrying 190 pounds of extra weight, a total of 395 pounds. The latter figure indicates that Davis, when weighing 205 pounds, was very nearly as strong in chinning *even relative to his increased bodyweight* as when, at 177 pounds (in 1938), he had actually chinned once with both arms with 171 pounds of extra weight, a total of 348 pounds. These figures suggest also that a thoroughly skilled "chinner," who is also a thoroughly skilled Olympic weightlifter, should be able to pull up with both arms a combined load (body plus extra weight) approximately equal to his best poundage in the Two Hands Clean and Jerk with Barbell. Such comparative figures serve also to show what probably can, and what probably cannot, be done in chinning, the latter being a less well-documented form of strength than standardized weightlifting.

In view of Davis's great back and leg strength, he should have been expected to do well in standing jumping. He lived up to this expectation by doing "over 11 feet" in a standing broad jump. He also—in 1939, when weighing 200 pounds—did a standing jump over a table 30 inches high and 28½ inches wide, while holding in one hand a 15-pound dumbbell and in the other hand two five-pound dumbbells. However, the latter feat hardly compares with the jumping ability exhibited by G. W. Rolandow (see above).

By some observers, Davis is considered to have been the greatest middle-heavyweight* Olympic lifter on record. This opinion is based on the lifts that Davis made in the USA Senior Championships on May 24, 1941, at a bodyweight of 201½ pounds. These lifts were a Press of 322¼ pounds, a Snatch of 317½ pounds (though in poor form), and a Clean and Jerk of 370 pounds—a total of 1009¾ pounds. If these 1941 lifts by Davis are brought—by my time-factor procedure (which for the 3-lift total is similar to that listed for the Pole Vault in Table 27, see

---

* As a recognized bodyweight *class* in weightlifting, the middle-heavyweight (90 kilos and under) was not established until 1951.

Appendix 1)—to the poundages they would be equivalent to on July 1, 1967, they become: Press 360 pounds, Snatch 342 pounds, and Clean and Jerk 399 pounds. These three lifts make a total of 1101 pounds. It is assumed that Davis—had there been a middle-heavyweight class in 1941—could have competed in this class and made the same lifts that he made when weighing 201½ pounds. The 3-lift total of the British Negro middle-heavyweight, Louis Martin (who made his records during 1963–1965), if adjusted for time, would be over 1090 pounds. Ordinarily, for a Two Hands Clean of 400 pounds, one would expect a Two Hands Snatch of from 310 to 320 pounds. This suggests that in his snatches, Davis must have benefitted from his great pressing power. Between Davis and Martin, there would appear to be little to choose. While Davis was somewhat the stronger presser, Martin (at the time this was being written) still held the middle-heavyweight world record in the Clean and Jerk with 190.5 kilos or about 420 pounds.

All in all, John Davis has been the winner in 32 State, National, Olympic, and World weightlifting championships and Tryouts, ranging in time from 1938 to 1956. These contests, together with the dates, places, bodyweights, and poundages lifted, are listed in detail in LIFTING NEWS (Alliance, Nebraska) for February 1967. Davis was World's Amateur Heavyweight Champion in 1946, 1947, 1949, 1950 and 1951, and Olympic Champion in 1948 and 1952. His last participation in a World contest was in 1953, at Stockholm, when he took second place to the powerful Canadian heavyweight, Douglas Hepburn, whose accomplishments will now be reviewed.

19. DOUGLAS HEPBURN. (See Plate 18). This outstanding exemplar of rugged physical power was the greatest heavyweight strong-man to appear in Canada since the days of Louis Cyr and Horace Barré. Though Hepburn was once the world's Olympic weightlifting champion, he had relatively even greater ability in what are now known as the "power lifts."

Douglas Hepburn was born in Vancouver, B.C., on September 16, 1927. His father was a large man standing 6 ft. 1 in. and weighing 220 pounds. His mother was 5 ft. 4 in. and 130 pounds. "Doug" himself at the age of 17 was only of average height and weight, standing 5 ft. 8½ in. and weighing 145 pounds. It was at that age that he became interested in bodybuilding and weightlifting. Of particular interest is the fact that, solely through *training,* he was able to become a giant of muscularity and power. He frankly admits that he never was a "natural" strong-man, but instead attained his physique and strength by hard training plus an ability to progress more rapidly than the average weightlifting trainee.

Unfortunately, "Doug" had a congenital handicap in the form of a slight club foot. During an operation in his childhood to remedy this, some bones in his right ankle became fused together; and the mobility of that joint was thereby restricted. When Doug took up weightlifting, he found it difficult to "split" and dip under a weight because of his "tight" right ankle. This impairment resulted also in the girth of his right calf being several inches less than that of his left. Fortunately, this condition had no perceptible effect on his ability in pressing, curling, muscling-out, or any other form of lifting in which he did not have to flex his right ankle. Even his ability in heavy squats with a weight on the shoulders did not seem to be affected by this ankle-stiffness. However, it definitely detracted from his power and speed in lifts such as the Snatch and the Two Hands Clean and Jerk.

Hepburn reached his peak of strength and lifting power during the years 1954–1956, at which time he weighed usually between 280 and 300 pounds (at 5 ft. 9 in.). His strictly "muscular" bodyweight would probably have been about 235 pounds. Thus, both in height and "muscular" bodyweight, he was virtually a replica of his famous predecessor, Louis Cyr. Here are some of the highest *recorded* lifts made by Hepburn. However, some of them were made in 1952, before he had reached his maximum strength. Most of the lifts were made in Hepburn's home town, Vancouver.

Lift	Pounds	
Right Hand Military Press, feet apart	175	
Two Hands Press (off rack)	440	
Two Hands Press with Dumbbells	350	(175 and 175)
Press from Behind Neck	350	
Two Hands Military Curl	260	
Bench Press (correct style)	535	est. (did 580 using wide grips)
Jerk-Press (off rack)	500	
Crucifix, with dumbbells	200	(100 and 100)
Two Hands Snatch	297½	(unoff. 320)
Two Hands Clean and Press, Olympic Style	381	(unoff. 390)
Squat	760	
Two Hands Dead Lift	705	

In repetition two-arm pressing, Hepburn did 335 pounds 10 times in succession and 400 pounds 4 times in succession. This was in August, 1954. The 335 pounds 10 times was equivalent to pressing 438 pounds once, while the 400 pounds 4 times was equivalent to pressing 449 pounds (!) once. These lifts confirm Hepburn's ability to have pressed 440 pounds. The poundages recorded in the various forms of pressing listed above indicate that he was probably capable of a correct Two Hands Military Press of at least 360 pounds and possibly as much as 375 pounds.

In the Two Hands Curl, his lift of 260 pounds is the highest poundage ever recorded. On the basis of his 440-pound press from the shoulders, he *should* have been (and probably *was*) capable of a Two Dumbbell Press of about 360 pounds, a Press from Behind Neck of about 365 pounds, a Right Hand Military Press of about 185 pounds, and a correct (Military) Crucifix of about 112 pounds in each hand. These indicated abilities denote phenomenal shoulder strength. Also, due to his great curling power, Hepburn could *clean* with dumbbells about 350 pounds (175 and 175).

Hepburn's Two Hands Dead Lift of 705 pounds was a first attempt only, made without practice, and in no way indicated his limit ability in this style. In the squat, which evidently he practiced more, he eventually reached 760 pounds, which proved that his leg strength was quite on a par with his great pressing power. As to strength of hands and grip, the only information that I have on Hepburn's ability is that he was able to pick up with one hand the Louis Cyr dumbbell, which had a handle 1⅞ inches in diameter, when this dumbbell weighed 235 pounds. However, his finger strength was sufficient to enable him to bend double a Canadian dime by pressing it against an iron railing with his forefinger and thumb. The long-time champion at wrist-wrestling, "Mac" Batchelor (see Chapter 5), feels that Hepburn—when he weighed 300 pounds—could have given him possibly his hardest contest!

But just as John Davis had to give way to Hepburn, so Hepburn had to give way to the great Olympic-lift technician, Norbert Schemansky. As may be seen in the listing of heavyweight world's and Olympic champions below, Davis's highest three-lift total in international competition was 1019¼ pounds. Hepburn, in winning in 1953 at Stockholm, made a total of 1032¾ pounds. Schemansky, who won the title at Vienna in 1954, zoomed his total up to 1074¼ pounds, while the fabulous Paul Anderson (see directly below), in 1955 at Munich raised the world's-record three-lift total another 55¼ pounds to a stupendous 1129½.

20. PAUL ANDERSON. (See Plate 19). Stronger in some ways even than the mighty Canadian Douglas Hepburn was the "super-heavyweight" Olympic and power-lifter, Paul Anderson. So much publicity has been given to this strength-phenomenon that he bids fair to become a legend even during his lifetime.

Anderson was born on October 17, 1932 in Toccoa, Georgia—the small town in which he still makes his home. When in high school, he weighed from 190 to 210 pounds, and was accordingly "drafted" for the school's football team. To increase his strength and ability in football, he started training with weights, but was "advised" by his coach to leave this form of exercising alone. It was not until 1952, when he was 20, that he had the opportunity to work with the weights in earnest. This training became so fascinating to young Paul that it soon became his chief athletic activity.

In December 1952, after less than a year's training, Paul entered the State Meet in Chattanooga, Tennessee, the state in which he was then living. In winning first place in the heavyweight class in this meet, he pressed 275 pounds, snatched 225 pounds, and clean-and-jerked 300 pounds. These lifts were performed with strength to spare. After the contest, he set a new world's record in the Squat by doing 660½ pounds. Paul's bodyweight at this time was about 285 pounds.

In a little more than three years of steady training, Anderson raised his three-lift total from 800 pounds to a world's record 1175 pounds (in 1956). This total consisted of a Press of 400 pounds, a Snatch of 335 pounds, and a Clean and Jerk of 440 pounds. While the Snatch and the Clean and Jerk represented his top lifts at that time, he had on a number of previous occasions pressed more than 400 pounds—for example, at the World Championships at Munich in 1955, in which he did 409 pounds. Thus, in about three years, Anderson had increased his lifting strength about 48 percent! In the meanwhile, his bodyweight zoomed from 285 pounds to over 360 pounds, an increase of 27 percent! These figures show that *in proportion to his increased bodyweight* (and implied muscular cross-section), Anderson gained about 16½ percent in strength.

While Anderson's official amateur weightlifting records were outstanding, they did not represent his maximum power. For this we must look at some of the "unofficial" poundages he lifted in training, and at his ability in the "power" lifts as well as the three Olympic events. Some of these records were made after Anderson had turned professional, which took place in 1957. Here are some of the "Dixie Derrick's" best lifts:

Lift	*Pounds*
Two Hands Press	400—7 times in succession
Two Hands Press (off rack)	470
Two Hands Continental Jerk (shouldered in two movements?)	460 (unoff. 480)
Jerk-Press (off rack)	560
Bench Press	580 ?
Squat (partial)	1160 (prof.)
Squat, full (estimated)	900
Two Hands Dead Lift (est.)	1000 (with hands *tied* to bar)
Two Hands Snatch	336½ (unoff. 360)
Two Hands Clean and Jerk	440 (unoff. 450)
Hip Lift	4100 (prof.)
Back Lift	6000 (unoff. 6200)

Since Anderson, in accomplishing the prodigious feats listed above, weighed from 340 to 370 pounds, at a height of only 5 ft. 9 in., it is probable that he was even larger, muscularly, than either Louis Cyr, Horace Barré, Karl Swoboda, or Douglas Hepburn. From these feats it can also be deduced that Anderson, in "trim," muscular condition, would have weighed about 265 pounds. Thus he was one of the most powerfully-developed strong-men on record. Certainly his leg strength* has never even been approached by that of any other strong-man. His strength of back, chest, and shoulders also was enormous.

On the basis of the actual lifts made by Anderson listed above, his probable ability in several other events can be estimated. In a correct Two Hands *Military* Press, it would appear that he was capable of about 400 pounds. This, in turn, would indicate a Right Hand Military Press of about 200 pounds, a Left Hand Military Press of about 187 pounds, and a Crucifix with dumbbells or kettlebells of about 240 pounds (123 right hand, 117 left hand). In a *one*-leg Squat, or deep-knee bend (provided he could get into the required position!), he should have been capable of a phenomenal 270 pounds. Also, if Anderson had possessed speed and skill proportionate to his strength, he should have been capable of a Two Hands Snatch of about 450 pounds and a Two Hands Clean and Jerk of about 570 pounds!

However, despite these lifts and all the training that Anderson did, there is no mention of his having shown a degree of strength in his forearms, hands and fingers proportionate to that of his shoulders, back and legs. Even in curling, there is no record of what his limit ability was. In the same connection, it is not at all certain that he could have surpassed Douglas Hepburn in *cleaning* a pair of dumbbells. Strength of hands and grip is one of the prime characteristics of an all-around strong-man, and having possessed such strength is one of the main reasons why Cyr, Apollon, Marx, Saxon, Görner, and certain other "old-timers" attained such enduring fame.

Therefore, rather than title Anderson "the strongest man who ever lived"—as some writers have insisted on doing—it would appear more realistic to name him *possibly* the strongest man of the last hundred years *when* feats of forearm, hand, and finger strength are omitted. This is certainly no disparagement, since virtually *all* world-champion athletes today are specialists. But it would have been a more complete distinction for Paul Anderson if only he could have been the champion in *grip-strength* too!

---

* Specifically, strength of hips and thighs. It is possible that certain other strong-men, notably Louis Cyr and "Apollon," who had tremendous calf development, equalled or surpassed Anderson in the strength of these parts.

NOTE: In the listing of various weightlifting records on the following pages, limited space has made it necessary to reduce comments to a minimum. Many of the record-holders deserve special mention; but to give this attention to all would require a full-sized volume on weightlifting alone. Therefore, special comment is made only concerning performances that are outstandingly meritorious.

C. RECORDS IN THE THREE TWO-HAND OLYMPIC LIFTS

Table 1. World Records (as of August 3, 1969)

Courtesy of Oscar State, Gen. Sec'y, International Weightlifting Federation

			Kilos	*Pounds*	*Date*
Flyweight Class (114½ lbs.)					
	Press	V. Krishishin, USSR	112.5	248	8- 3-69
	Snatch	K. Miki, Japan	100	220¼	8-19-66
	Jerk	V. Krishishin, USSR	127	280	8- 3-69
	Total	V. Krishishin, USSR	332.5	732¾	8- 3-69
Bantamweight Class (123¼ lbs.)					
	Press	I. Földi, Hungary	125	275½	6-21-69
	Snatch	K. Miki, Japan	113.5	250	11-15-68
	Jerk	M. Nassari, Iran	150	330½	10-13-68
	Total	G. Chetin, USSR	367.5	809¾*	8-24-68
Featherweight Class (132¼ lbs.)					
	Press	M. Kuchev, Bulgaria	131	288¾	7-13-69
	Snatch	Y. Miyake, Japan	125	275½	10-24-67
	Jerk	I. Berger, USA	152.5	336	10-12-64
	Total	Y. Miyake, Japan	397.5	876	10-12-64
Lightweight Class (148¾ lbs.)					
	Press	E. Katsura, USSR	145.5	320¾	7-28-66
	Snatch	W. Baszanowski, Poland	135.5	298½	10-17-67
	Jerk	W. Baszanowski, Poland	170	374¾	10-17-67
	Total	W. Baszanowski, Poland	440	969¾	10-17-67
Middleweight Class (165¼ lbs.)					
	Press	V. Kurentsov, USSR	161.5	356	5-16-69
	Snatch	M. Ohuchi, Japan	145	319½	6-18-67
	Jerk	V. Kurentsov, USSR	187.5	413¼	10-16-68
	Total	V. Kurentsov, USSR	482.5	1063¼	8-31-68
Light-heavyweight Class (181¾ lbs.)					
	Press	A. Golubovich, USSR	170	374¾	7- 8-69
	Snatch	V. Belyaev, USSR	150.5	331¾	2-24-68
	Jerk	B. Selitsky, USSR	190.5	419¾	1- 2-69
	Total	A. Golubovich, USSR	490	1080	7- 8-69

* This total was equalled both by Nassiri and Földi at the Olympic Games in Mexico City (10-13-68).

Middle-heavyweight Class (198¼ lbs.)

Press	K. Kangasniemi, Finland	177.5	391¼	5-18-69
Snatch	K. Kangasniemi, Finland	160½	353¾	5-18-69
Jerk	F. Capsouras, USA	199	438¾	4-12-69
Total	K. Kangasniemi, Finland	527.5	1162½	5-18-69

Heavyweight Class (242½ lbs.)

Press	N. Mironenko, USSR	188.5	415½	7-10-69
Snatch	K. Kangasniemi, Finland	158	348¼	7-26-69
Jerk	R. Bednarski, USA	211.5	466¼	6-15-69
Total	R. Bednarski, USA	548.8	1210	6-15-69

Super-heavyweight Class (over 242½ lbs.)

Press	J. Dube, USA	209.5	461¾	8-31-68
Snatch	L. Zhabotinsky, USSR	176	388	6-25-68
Jerk	R. Bednarski, USA	220.5	486	6- 9-68
Total	L. Zhabotinsky, USSR	590	1300½	6-18-67

NOTE: The Total poundages listed in the above table (and in the table of American Records following) are those performed on *one and the same occasion* (contest). When the *separately performed* records for the Press, Snatch, and Clean and Jerk are added together, the resulting total is anywhere from 1.8 percent to 5.4 percent more than the total made at one time. In arriving at a lifter's potential, his three *best* records should be added together—or better, evaluated *separately*.

Table 2. American Records (as of June 14, 1969)

Bantamweight Class (123¼ lbs.)		*Pounds*	*Year*
Press	F. Baez, Puerto Rico	266	1968
Snatch	C. Vinci, York BC	236¾	1960
Jerk	C. Vinci, York BC	296	1956
Total	C. Vinci, York BC	760½	1960

Featherweight Class (132¼ lbs.)			
Press	I. Berger, York BC	270	1964
Snatch	I. Berger, York BC	242½	1958
Jerk	I. Berger, York BC	336¼	1964
Total	I. Berger, York BC	843	1964

Lightweight Class (148¾ lbs.)			
Press	H. Brannum, USAF	285	1967
Snatch	A. Garcy, York BC	275½	1964
Jerk	A. Garcy, York BC	352½	1964
Total	A. Garcy, York BC	909	1964

Middleweight Class (165¼ lbs.)			
Press	R. Knipp, unattached	356	1969
Snatch	P. Rawluk, USAF	306	1969
Jerk	F. Lowe, Duncan Y	395	1968
Total	R. Knipp, unattached	1000	1967

Light-heavyweight Class (181¾ lbs.)

Press	G. Cleveland, York BC	341¾	1965
Snatch	L. Riecke, NOAC	325	1964
Jerk	M. Karchut, Hammond, Ind.	406¼	1969
Total	J. Puleo, York BC	1025	1968

Middle-heavyweight Class (198¼ lbs.)

Press	P. Grippaldi, unattached	362	1968
Snatch	C. Nootens, Chicago YMCA	330	1969
Jerk	P. Grippaldi, unattached	412	1967
Total	P. Grippaldi, unattached	1050	1967

Heavyweight Class (242½ lbs.)

Press	R. Bednarski, York BC	415	1969
Snatch	R. Bednarski, York BC	347½	1969
Jerk	R. Bednarski, York BC	465	1969
Total	R. Bednarski, York BC	1210	1969

Super-heavyweight Class (over 242½ lbs.)

Press	J. Dube, Riverside AC	461¾	1968
Snatch	N. Schemansky, York BC	363¾	1964
Jerk	R. Bednarski, York BC	486½	1968
Total	R. Bednarski, York BC	1282¾	1968

NOTE: A comparison of the figures in the above table with those on the previous page reveals that American records, on the average, are about *five percent lower* than World records in the same bodyweight classes. This difference may be attributed to the much smaller *number* of weightlifters competing in the United States compared with the rest of the world. Another point is the *length of time* that American records survive. This averages no less than five years (!), as compared with only about 1.6 years for World records. This again indicates *insufficient competition.*

The following percentage ratings have been made by means of the author's method, which takes into account not only the bodyweight of the lifter, but also his height (and accordingly his muscular cross-section and body-*build*). All these factors are essential in properly evaluating lifts (or other feats) in which *speed* as well as strength come into play. Likewise, the important element of *time* (date) of performance must be taken into account, since a record that survives under steady assault for a period of 10, 20, or 30 years is manifestly a more meritorious performance than one that is broken almost as soon as it has been established. Another circumstance is that if a lifter increases his records by less than a certain average amount each year, it does not mean that he is actually improving, percentagewise. For example, in the Clean and Jerk, the bantamweight Alexei Vakhonin's lift of 314 pounds made in 1964 rates slightly higher than the one of 316 pounds which he made two years later. A number of other instances of this kind also appear in Table 3.

*Table 3. The 10 all-time leading performers in each of the
3 Olympic lifts and the total**

(Figures in parentheses are estimated muscular bodyweights) TWO HANDS PRESS [ ] Estimated from other presses

Ranking	Lifter	Nation	Bodyweight, lbs.	Height, in.	Lift Kg.	Lift Lbs.	Year	% Rating
1	Robert Bednarski	USA	245	73.0	207	456.25	1968	101.7
2	V. Krishishin	USSR	114	58 ?	112.5	248.02	1969	101.1
3	Joseph Dube	USA	316 (262)	72.0	209.9	462.75	1968	98.6
4	George Pickett	USA	300 (280)	76.5	207.4	457.25	1968	98.4
5	Emil Kliment	Austria	130	63 ?	100.7	[222]	1913	98.1
6	Victor Kurentsov	USSR	163	64.3	161.5	356.04	1969	97.8
7	Eugeni Katsura	USSR	148.8	63.5	145.5	320.77	1966	97.7
8	Paul Anderson	USA	360 (265)	69.0	208.6	460	1957	97.5
9	Imri Földi	Hungary	123	59.0	125	275.58	1969	97.2
10	Kaarlo Kangasniemi	Finland	197	68 ?	177.5	391.32	1969	97.1

TWO HANDS SNATCH

Ranking	Lifter	Nation	Bodyweight, lbs.	Height, in.	Lift Kg.	Lift Lbs.	Year	% Rating
1	Yuri Vlasov	USSR	300 (255)	72 ?	172.5	380.30	1964	102.2
2	Masachi Ohuchi	Japan	170.75	65.0	150	330.69	1967	101.9
3	Kaarlo Kangasniemi	Finland	197	68 ?	160.5	353.84	1969	101.3
4	Vladimir Belyaev	USSR	179 ?	64.9	150.5	331.79	1968	101.2
5	Yoshinobu Miyake	Japan	130	61.0	125	275.58	1967	100.7
6	Leonid Zhabotinsky	USSR	350 (275)	74.8	176	388.01	1968	100.4
7	K. Miki	Japan	122	58 ?	113.5	250.22	1968	100.0
8	Norbert Schemansky	USA	266.5 (240)	71.0	165	363.76	1964	99.9
9	(Prof.) Charles Rigoulot	France	231 (215)	67.7	143	315.26	1931	99.5
10	Waldemar Baszanowski	Poland	148	64.9	135.5	298.72	1967	99.0

TWO HANDS CLEAN AND JERK

1	Mohammed Nassiri	Iran	123.4	59.8	150	330.69	1968	101.7
2	Victor Kurentsov	USSR	163	64.3	187.5	413.36	1968	100.7
3	Robert Bednarski	USA	245	73.0	220.7	486.50	1968	100.4
4	Vladimir Belyaev	USSR	179 ?	64.9	190	418.88	1966	99.6
5	Yuri Vlasov	USSR	300 (255)	72 ?	215	473.99	1964	} 99.2
	(Prof.) Charles Rigoulot	France	236 (**215**)	67.7	182.5	402.34	1929	
6	Gyozo Veres	Hungary	181.5	64.9	190	418.88	1967	98.5
7	B. Selitsky	USSR	180 ?	66 ?	190.5	419.98	1968	98.2
8	Leonid Zhabotinsky	USSR	350 (275)	74.8	217.5	479.50	**1968**	97.7
9	Yoshinobu Miyake	Japan	130	61.0	152.5	336.20	1966	97.6
10	Frank Capsouras	USA	197 ?	70 ?	199	438.75	1968	97.3

3-LIFT TOTAL (see also Table 4)

1	Yuri Vlasov	USSR	300 (255)	72 ?	585	1289.70	1964	99.1
2	Robert Bednarski	USA	245	73.0	583.15	1282.75	1968	98.7
3	Kaarlo Kangasniemi	Finland	197	68 ?	535.	1179.47	1968	98.6
4	Victor Kurentsov	USSR	163	64.3	482.5	1063.73	1968	98.3
5	Yoshinobu Miyake	Japan	130	61.0	400	881.84	1966	97.5
6	Leonid Zhabotinsky	USSR	350 (275)	74.8	593.5	1308.44	1967	} 97.4
	Imri Földi	Hungary	123	59.0	c. 374.5	c. 825	1968	
	G. Chetin	USSR	123.4	59 ?	c. 374.5	c. 825	1968	
7	Mohammed Nassiri	Iran	148	59.8	c. 374.5	c. 825	1968	97.1
8	Waldemar Baszanowski	Poland	181.5	64.9	440	970.03	1967	96.7
9	Gyozo Veres	Hungary	148.8	64.9	496	1093.49	1967	96.2
10	Vladimir Kaplunov	USSR		62.9	432.5	953.50	1964	95.8

* As derived from the performer's *best* three lifts, performed either together or on separate dates (prior to August 3, 1969).

At various times in the past, weightlifting "ratings" have been published by authors who used naïve, unscientific methods (usually termed "formulas"), and which in consequence deprived many a worthy lifter of proper credit. It is believed that the foregoing tables—based, as they are, on *all* the factors involved in the Olympic lifts—give due percentage ratings to the various performers listed. However, it is possible that some high-ranking individuals have inadvertently been overlooked. Certainly a large number of oldtime champion Pressers have been omitted, simply because these lifters used either a strict Military Press or a Continental Press, and not a style identical to the present-day Olympic Press. The latter style, unfortunately, has not remained constant over the years, but has degenerated from what, around the turn of the century, was almost a Military (body-erect) Press into a style which, as performed by today's record-holders, permits the use of everything except an out-and-out *jerk* to get the weight from the shoulders to overhead.

In contrast to track and field athletics, the practice of which is either seasonal (scholastic) or irregular, performers of weightlifting (which is practiced mainly indoors) work *steadily throughout the year*. This is especially true among champions, near-champions, or record-holders, among whom the competition is perhaps more sustained and intense than in any other sport. While, as mentioned previously, a newly established world's record in weightlifting survives, on the average, for about 18 months, records in the three Olympic lifts continue to go up and up, even if by small increments. Accordingly, it is impossible to present a strictly "up-to-date" list of records. The purpose of the foregoing tables is to list the lifts and percentage ratings of *representative* champions and record-holders in the various bodyweight classes, rather than to "cover the field" in this sport. At the rate world competition in weightlifting is growing, such an attempt would be an endless undertaking.

As noted previously, the poundages of American records in the three Olympic lifts average about 5 *percent less* than those of World records. This lesser standard of lifting is reflected in the above percentage ratings, in which, among 42 records, only 6 have been made by lifters from the United States. These 6 records are the Presses by Bob Bednarski and Joe Dube; the Snatch by Louis Riecke; the Clean and Jerks by Bob Bednarski and Frank Capsouras; and the 3-lift Total by Bednarski. Various authors in the past, in dealing with weightlifting in the United States, have extolled the performances of John Davis, Steve Stanko, Stanley Stanczyk, Peter George, Anthony Terlazzo, Tommy Kono, Paul Anderson, Norbert Schemansky, and others. Table 4, following, gives the percentage ratings, as of mid-1969, of the 20 leading American lifters in the Olympic 3-lift total. Of these, the top 20 have an average rating of 94.3 percent. For comparison, the 10 leading performers in the World list have an average rating of 97.5 percent. This 3-percent superiority in the lifting records mainly of overseas performers is not necessarily the consequence of better training methods, but is more likely the natural outcome of these lifters having been drawn from a weight-lifting population some 100 *times as great* as that in the United States. And the champion among a vast number of competitors in any sport is almost certain to be a better performer than the champion among a comparative few.

In reference to performances in each of the separate lifts comprising the Olympic series, it should be noted that in addition to the more recent record-holders that I have listed there were many outstanding per-formers in the past. These performers have been omitted from the tables on account of their lifting *techniques* being sufficiently different from those of present-day performers to make a direct comparison impossible. Nevertheless, some mention should be made of the more notable of these old-time exponents of weightlifting. In the Two Hands Press, for example, if the three best old-time performers in either the Military or the Continental styles of pressing were rated according to their *probable* abilities in the Olympic style, these ratings would result: (1) Maxick (professional), Two Hands *Military* Press of 230 pounds at a bodyweight of 145 pounds, in 1909, 99.8 percent; (2) Emil von Mogyorossy (professional), Hungary, Two Hands *Continental* Press of 267 pounds at a bodyweight of 150 pounds, in 1910, 98.5 percent; (3) Emil Kliment, Austria, Two Hands *Continental* Press of 220½ pounds twice in succession (= 230 pounds once) at a bodyweight of 130 pounds, in 1913, 98.1 percent. Presses made in the usual Olympic style, but with the barbell being taken off a rack rather than lifted clean to the shoulders, show somewhat higher ratings. Paul Anderson, in thus raising 470 pounds, in 1957, gains a rating of 99.6 percent. A similar performance by Douglas Hepburn of 440 pounds, in 1956, rates an even 100 percent. But the most powerful pressers for their size—on account of their disproportionately short arms—are dwarfs of the type known as achondro-plastic. Throughout history, these little men have been noted for their extraordinary strength. At least two of them entered the sport of weight-lifting and set records in pressing. Americo "Firpo" Lemma, at a height of 56 inches and a bodyweight of 112 pounds, in 1938 cleaned and pressed 215 pounds. This lift rates a phenomenal 101.1 percent.* Even

---

* While, of course, no performer can be more than 100 percent efficient, the percentage ratings given in this study are influenced in some cases by factors outside the usual or normal range of conditions on which they are based. In the case of Lemma, it is the extremely advantageous leverage afforded by his *dispro-portionately short arms*. In Hepburn and Anderson it is the rating of a press *off the rack* on the same basis as if it had been *cleaned*.

Table 4.   The 20 Leading American Performers in the Olympic 3-Lift Total
(As of June 14, 1969)*

Ranking	Year	Lifter	Bodyweight Class		3-Lift Total, lbs.	% Rating
1	1968	Robert Bednarski	Super-heavy	(245)	1282¾	98.7
2	1962-4	Norbert Schemansky	Super-heavy	(240)	1211	96.3
3	1968	Joseph Dube	Super-heavy	(262)	1267	96.0
4	1951	John Davis	Heavy	(210)	1074¾	
	1967	Russell Knipp	Middle		1000	94.2
5	1968	George Pickett	Super-heavy	(280)	1261½	
	1960	Charles Vinci	Bantam		774	94.0
6	1964	Isaac Berger	Feather		843¼	
	1956	Paul Anderson	Super-heavy	(265)	1185½	93.9
7	1953	Tommy Kono	Middle		940¼	
	1966	Joseph Puleo	Middle		990	93.1
8	1965	Gary Gubner	Super-heavy	(270)	1204	92.4
9	1954	Dave Sheppard	Mid-heavy	(190)	1009½	92.2
10	1939	Anthony Terlazzo	Light		834½	92.0
11	1969	William March	Heavy	(220)	1130	91.7
12	1966	Gary Cleveland	Light-heavy		1015	91.3
13	1952	Peter George	Middle		904	
	1964	Louis Riecke	Light-heavy		1005	91.2
14	1947	Stanley Stanczyk	Middle		892½	91.1
15	1966	Anthony Garcy	Middle		947	91.0

* Performances made *prior* to 1965 are appropriately *increased* in their percentage ratings, while those made *subsequent* to 1965 are appropriately *reduced*. The totals here listed are of the performer's *best* records in each lift added together. Bodyweights in parentheses are estimated *muscular* weights.

It should be noted that in the above table (as well as in all the other lists of percentage ratings in this book) a difference of less than *one percent* is of no significance. The above rankings are made simply on the basis of the percentages resulting from the calculations, expressed to the nearest *tenth* of one percent. Thus, for example, while there is no significant difference between the respective percentage ratings of Anthony Garcy and Anthony Terlazzo, there is a definite difference between the rating of Terlazzo and those of the lifters ranked from no. 1 to no. 6.

more extraordinary was his press from the shoulders (not cleaned) of 235 pounds, which rates no less than 110.5 percent! Joe De Pietro, at a height of 58 inches and a bodyweight of 122½ pounds, in 1948 cleaned and pressed 231½ pounds for a rating of 92.8 percent. He probably could have pressed more if he had not had to shoulder the weight. Both Lemma and De Pietro had extraordinarily short arms, even for their small statures, and what they gained in pressing they lost in picking up from the floor, because of having to bend over so far. When they cleaned a weight, the lift had to be performed almost entirely by back strength. If these little lifters had possessed arms of a length proportionate to their heights, they would have pressed only about 90 percent of what they did, on account of pressing strength, at a given bodyweight, being *inversely* proportionate to the height (or to arm length).

In the Two Hands Snatch, which is a typical "quick" lift, performers having a slender build should be expected to be faster, and to lift more for their bodyweights, than heavier-built lifters who presumably have less speed. Therefore, when a lifter of heavy build makes a record in the snatch despite his build, it shows that he has *unexpectedly* great speed and consequently a high degree of lifting efficiency. The latter should be rated accordingly. Among heavyweight (and heavy-built) performers in the Snatch, three have shown a remarkable degree of speed and technique. These are the Russian, Yuri Vlasov; the French professional of the 1930s, Charles Rigoulot; and Norbert Schemansky of the United States. Among lifters of smaller size, the Japanese, with their typically short legs and easy squatting ability, seem especially suited for the Snatch (as well as the Two Hands Clean). Lifters who have great pressing power—but not correspondingly great speed in pulling a weight up—frequently end their Snatch lifts with a quick press-out, which often goes undetected by either the referee or the judges. This pressing-out—in order to finish a lift in which the weight has not been pulled high enough to dip under properly—is contrary to the spirit and ruling of a correctly-performed Snatch. It would be difficult to picture Charles Rigoulot, whose pressing ability was especially poor, performing a Snatch with a press-out at the end. The same can be said of the current heavyweight world's record holder in the Snatch, Leonid Zhabotinsky (see Plate 20), of Russia, whose Snatches are performed with admirable speed and no suggestion of a press-out. The first lifter to snatch "double bodyweight" was the Japanese featherweight, Yoshinobu Miyake. The first *lightweight* to do so was the phenomenal Polish lifter, Waldemar Baszanowski (see Plate 23). At this rate, it should be only a question of time until middleweights—and possibly even light-heavyweights—are snatching double bodyweight! Indeed, the Japanese lifter Ohuchi, in snatching 330.69 pounds at a bodyweight of 170¾ pounds, in October 1967, has closely approached "double bodyweight").

Percentagewise, at the top of the list in the Snatch is the Soviet super-heavyweight, Yuri Vlasov, with the fantastic rating of 102.2 percent. Ohuchi (just mentioned), and Belyaev, of the USSR have ratings of over 101 percent, or virtually the equal of Vlasov's.*

Coming now to a consideration of performances in the Two Hands Clean and Jerk, at the top of the list is the Iranian bantamweight, Mohammed Nassiri, with a rating of 101.7 percent. Second is Victor Kurentsov, of the USSR, with 100.7 percent; third is Robert Bednarski of the USA, with 100.4 percent; and fourth is Vladimir Belyaev of the USSR, with 99.6 percent.

Close on the heels of these three present-day record-holders is the Clean and Jerk record of the French professional lifter, Charles Rigoulot, who made most of his best lifts during the years 1929–1931. While Rigoulot's bodyweight in a strictly "muscular" condition was probably not over 215 pounds, his actual weight at the time he made his Clean and Jerk record of 402.34 pounds was 236 pounds. This bodyweight, at his height of only 5 ft. 7.7 in., gave him an exceedingly stocky physique. Yet despite this supposed deterrent to activity and agility, Rigoulot was able to move with the rapidity of a middleweight. One should bear in mind, however, that in all the "quick" lifts made by Rigoulot with a barbell, he used a specially-designed, shot-loading bell with globular rather than plate-loading ends. This barbell was over 8 feet in length, and the great distance between the globes made the handle exceedingly springy. And since, after the initial momentum imparted to the bar, the lead shot inside the globes would be momentarily suspended in space (and therefore not being "lifted"), it is quite likely that Rigoulot got an advantage out of using this barbell, even though the technique of handling it was a special one that had to be learned. What he could have lifted if he had used a regulation plate-loading barbell will never be known; but such a bell might have had the effect of lowering his rating (99.2 percent) in the Clean and Jerk to 97 or 98 percent. In any event, he was a phenomenon in the Snatch (either with one or both hands), and in the Clean and Jerk with a barbell. Unfortunately, Rigoulot's disinclination to practice the Press—on the supposition that

---

* The percentage system introduced here makes use of the figure 100 as a convenient index of a "maximum" performance. However, the main purpose of the percentage ratings is to indicate the *relative* standings of the performers listed. Certainly the figure 100 is a desirable maximum. Therefore, if an appreciable number of future weightlifting performances yield ratings of over 100 percent, the adopted "maximum" poundages upon which these ratings are based will have to be increased and the ratings thereby lowered—to the extent that virtually all ratings fall under 100 percent.

it would slow him down in his "quick" lifting—resulted in his 3-lift total being only about 977 pounds. This, even in view of his having lifted back in 1929–1931, gives him a 3-lift rating of only 91.2 percent.

All 10 of the listed performances in the Clean and Jerk, being over 97 percent, may, like those in the Snatch, be considered phenomenal. An unofficial lift by the Egyptian lightweight, Ibrahim Shams (see Plate 22), falls into the same select category. This was a Clean and Jerk of 160 kilos, or 352.74 pounds, made by Shams in 1939 at a bodyweight of only 142¼ pounds, and which has a rating of 94.7 percent. The lift was equivalent to one today, made by a lifter of Sham's size, of no less than 380 pounds! Shams's official record in this lift was 153.5 kilos or 338.41 pounds, which has a rating of 90.8 percent.

In the 3-lift total, it is rather remarkable that the top-ranking position (99.1 percent) should be held by a "super-heavyweight." For Yuri Vlasov (see Plate 20), when he made his phenomenal lifting records at the 1964 Olympic Games in Tokyo, weighed 136 kilos, or only about 3 ounces under 300 pounds! In assigning him an estimated *muscular* bodyweight of 255 pounds, I feel that I have put the figure amply high. Even if his effective, muscular bodyweight had been 10 pounds more than this, he would still have a 3-lift rating of 98.7 percent and would equal the number 2 performer on my list. Vlasov's compatriot, Leonid Zhabotinsky, who is the current super-heavyweight world's record holder in the Snatch and the total, is so much larger (6 ft. 3 in., 350 pounds) than Vlasov that his *muscular* bodyweight can hardly be estimated as less than 275 pounds. At this bodyweight, his 1967 three-lift total of about 1308 pounds brings him a percentage rating of 97.4.

Notwithstanding all this, records and record-holders change constantly; and doubtless by the time the foregoing review is published a whole new crop of lifters and records will be at hand for similar analysis and rating.

Table 5, following, lists the *heavyweight* lifting champions in World and Olympic competitions from 1896 to 1968, inclusive. In the early days of the sport, no specific set of lifts was agreed upon internationally, and the so-called "World" championships were mostly championships of what were then the two principal weightlifting countries: Austria and Germany. For a long time, no bodyweight *classes* were observed, although record *lifts* made by men of small size were given separate recognition. Since the majority of the heavyweight lifters in the two Germanic countries were men who loved to eat and drink, their physiques were of the type in which it was difficult to bend over and lift weights from the ground to the shoulders without brushing the belly on the way up. Accordingly, the lifts favored by these men were two-hand *barbell* lifts in which the bar—prior to pressing or jerking it overhead—

was brought to the shoulders not in a single clean movement, but by lifting it first onto the buckle of a strong, padded belt which was worn around the lifter's middle. From there the bar was heaved up to the shoulders. Sometimes the bar was even rested on the thighs prior to lifting it onto the belt. This was the manner in which Karl Swoboda of Vienna (70.5 in., 340 pounds) made his famous "Continental" style jerk of 409 pounds in 1912. To sum up, the lifts used in most of the early "World" championships were various selections from among the following styles: Right (and Left) Hand Snatch, Right (and Left) Hand Jerk (two hands to shoulder), Two Hands Snatch (occasionally), Two Hands Press and Two Hands Jerk (both the latter being shouldered in the "Continental" style).

Table 5. World and Olympic Champions in Weightlifting, 1896–1968
(Heavyweight Class)

Year	Contest	First-place Winner	Nation	Place	3-lift total, lbs.
1896	Olympic	Launceston Elliot (1 hand)	Gt. Brit.	Athens	
		Viggo Jensen (2 hands)	Denmark		
1898	World	Wilhelm Türk	Austria	Vienna	
1900	World	(no weightlifting)	————	Paris	
1903	World	Joseph Lancoud	Switz.	Paris	
1904	World	Josef Steinbach	Austria	Vienna	
1904	Olympic	Fred Winters	USA	St. Louis	
1905	World	Josef Steinbach	Austria	Berlin	
1905	World	Josef Steinbach	Austria	Duisburg	
1905	World	Emile Schweitzer	France	Paris	
1906	World	Heinrich Schneidereidt	Germany	Lille	
1906	"Olympic" (unoff.)	Josef Steinbach (1 hand)	Austria	Athens	
		Demetrius Tofalos (2 hands)	Greece		
1907	World	Heinrich Rondi	Germany	Frankfurt	
1908	World	Josef Grafl	Austria	Malmo	
1908	World	Josef Grafl	Austria	Vienna	
1908	Olympic	(no weightlifting)	————	London	
1909	World	Josef Grafl	Austria	Vienna	
1910	World	Josef Grafl	Austria	Dusseldorf	
1911	World	Josef Grafl	Austria	Stuttgart	
1911	World	Berthold Tandler	Austria	Dresden	
1911	World	Karl Swoboda	Austria	Berlin	
1911	World	Karl Swoboda	Austria	Vienna	
1912	Olympic	(no weightlifting)	————	Stockholm	
1913	World	Josef Grafl	Austria	Breslau	
1920	World	Karl Morke	Germany	Cologne	

Year	Contest	First-place Winner	Nation	Place	3-lift total, lbs.
1920	Olympic	Filippo Bottino	Italy	Antwerp	
1922	World	A. Tammer	Estonia	Reval	
1923	World	Franz Aigner	Austria	Vienna	
1924	Olympic	Giuseppi Tonani	Italy	Paris	
1925	World	(no contest)	————	————	
1926	World	(no contest)	————	————	
1927	World	(no contest)	————	————	
1928	Olympic	Josef Strassberger	Germany	Amsterdam	820¾
1929	(European)	Josef Strassberger	Germany	Vienna	821
1930	(European)	El Said Noseir	Egypt	Munich	826½
1931	(European)	El Said Noseir	Egypt	Luxembourg	897¼
1932	Olympic	Jaroslav Skobla	Czech.	Los Angeles	837¾
1933	(European)	A. Becvar	Czech.	Essen	(5 lifts)
1934	(European)	Vaclav Psenicka	Czech.	Genoa	848¾
1935	(European)	Josef Manger	Germany	Paris	870¾
1936	Olympic	Josef Manger	Germany	Berlin	904¾
1937	World	Josef Manger	Germany	Paris	903½
1938	World	Josef Manger	Germany	Vienna	971
1946	World	John Davis	USA	Paris	958½
1947	World	John Davis	USA	Phila.	1002¼
1948	Olympic	John Davis	USA	London	997¼
1949	World	John Davis	USA	The Hague	975¼
1950	World	John Davis	USA	Paris	1019¼
1951	World	John Davis	USA	Milan	953
1952	Olympic	John Davis	USA	Helsinki	1013¼
1953	World	Douglas Hepburn	Canada	Stockholm	1032¾
1954	World	Norbert Schemansky	USA	Vienna	1074¼
1955	World	Paul Anderson	USA	Munich	1129½
1956	Olympic	Paul Anderson	USA	Melbourne	1102¼
1957	World	Alexei Medvedev	USSR	Teheran	1102¼
1958	World	Alexei Medvedev	USSR	Stockholm	1068¾
1959	World	Yuri Vlasov	USSR	Warsaw	1101¾
1960	Olympic	Yuri Vlasov	USSR	Rome	1184½
1961	World	Yuri Vlasov	USSR	Vienna	1157
1962	World	Yuri Vlasov	USSR	Budapest	1190¼
1963	World	Yuri Vlasov	USSR	Stockholm	1228½
1964	Olympic	Leonid Zhabotinsky	USSR	Tokyo	1261½
1965	World	Leonid Zhabotinsky	USSR	Teheran	1235
1966	World	Leonid Zhabotinsky	USSR	Berlin	1250¾
1967	"Little Olympics"	S. Bathishev	USSR	Mexico City	1212½
1968	Olympic	Leonid Zhabotinsky	USSR	Mexico City	1262

In the contests held in Paris in 1903 and Lille (France) in 1906, the French or "clean" style of lifting was employed, even though the winner in the latter contest, Heinrich Schneidereidt (67.1 in., 194 pounds), was a German. It was not until the year 1928 that the presently used set of 3 two-hand lifts—Press, Snatch, and Clean and Jerk—was adopted by the International Federation of Weightlifting, with headquarters in Paris, as the official standard. For this reason, no listings are made in Table 5 of the lifting totals recorded (in *other* series of lifts) in earlier competitions.

One record-book states that the first "World" championship in weightlifting was staged at the Café Monico, Piccadilly Circus, London, on March 28, 1891. Actually, while this championship was "open" to the world, no foreigners entered it, and the competitors were all from Britain. Most of these lifters were not even heavyweights. The first official World's Championship was held in Vienna in 1898.

We turn now from the 3 two-hand Olympic lifts to what used to be called "strength lifts," but which are now known as "power" lifts. The set of power lifts which is currently recognized as the standard consists of three, all of which are performed with a barbell, using two hands. These are the Bench Press, the Squat, and the Dead Lift. For definitions of these lifts, see above. In competition in the Power lifts, as in the Olympic lifts, the winner is the one who amasses the highest *3-lift total*.

While the poundages given in Table 6 represent the official American records in the Power Lifts as of August 30, 1969, it should be noted that quite a number of *better* performances had been made before the present set of Power Lifts was officially adopted by the A.A.U. When rated percentagewise (and with reference to date, or time, of performance), few recently performed records in the Power Lifts rate over 90 percent, whereas when all known records are taken into account a number are found to have phenomenal ratings of from 95 to over 100 percent!

In the Bench Press, the best heavyweight record is the lift of 617¼ pounds made by Pat Casey (72 in.?, 324 lbs.) on June 17, 1967.* If we assume for Casey a *muscular* bodyweight of 270 pounds, his Bench Press has the phenomenal rating of 96.2 percent. Another high rating in this lift was achieved by John Molinaro (68 in., 300 lbs.) when he Bench-Pressed 560 pounds. If Molinaro's *muscular* bodyweight is assumed to be 230 pounds, his lift has a rating of 93.6 percent. Paul Anderson (69 in., 360 lbs.) in 1957 was capable of a Bench Press of at least 580 pounds. Assuming that Anderson had a *muscular* bodyweight of 265 pounds, the latter lift would have a rating of 92.1 percent. Whether Anderson was, or was not, a "professional" at the time he made this lift has no bearing

---

*Next in absolute poundage to Casey's lift is a Bench Press of 601½ pounds performed by James Williams at York, Pa. on August 30, 1969. I do not know his height and bodyweight.

D. AMERICAN RECORDS IN THE POWER LIFTS

Table 6.   (*as of August 30, 1969*)

Flyweight Class (114½ lbs.) None

Bantamweight Class (123¼ lbs.)		*Pounds*	*Year*
Bench Press	Enrique Hernandez, USAF	295	1967
Squat	Dave Moyer, Reading, Pa.	456¼	1965
Dead Lift	Michael Cross, Chattanooga, Tenn.	501½	1969
Total	Dave Moyer, Reading, Pa.	1160	1965

Featherweight Class (132¼ lbs.)			
Bench Press	Enrique Hernandez, USAF	319½	1967
Squat	Dave Moyer, Reading, Pa.	476	1965
Dead Lift	Allen Lord, College Park, Md.	543	1968
Total	Allen Lord, College Park, Md.	1215	1968

Lightweight Class (148¾ lbs.)			
Bench Press	William Thurber, Los Angeles, Calif.	352½	1967
Squat	William Thurber, Los Angeles, Calif.	462	1967
Dead Lift	Donald Blue, Lansing, Kansas	563	1967
Total	Donald Blue, Lansing, Kansas	1325	1969

Middleweight Class (165¼ lbs.)			
Bench Press	Robert Burnett, St. Louis, Mo.	376	1968
Squat	Leonard Ingro, Costa Mesa, Calif.	540	1968
Dead Lift	Robert Burnett, St. Louis, Mo.	668	1968
Total	Robert Burnett, St. Louis, Mo.	550	1968

Light-heavyweight Class (181¾ lbs.)			
Bench Press	Ronnie Ray, Dallas, Texas	450¾	1967
Squat	Thomas Overholtzer, Los Angeles, Calif.	666	1968
Dead Lift	R. Jackson, Kansas State Pen	672	1968
Total	Jack Barnes, Phoenix, Ariz.	1595	1968

Middle-heavyweight Class (198¼ lbs.)			
Bench Press	Ronnie Ray, Dallas, Texas	497	1969
Squat	Jack Barnes, Phoenix, Ariz.	714½	1969
Dead Lift	John Dzuerenko, Barnegat, N.J.	688½	1968
Total	Thomas Overholtzer, Los Angeles, Calif.	1675	1969

242-pound Class			
Bench Press	Mel Hennessy, Minneapolis, Minn.	542½	1969
Squat	John Kanter, Phoenix, Ariz.	764½	1969
Dead Lift	Gary Young, Portland, Ore.	770½	1968
Total	John Kanter, Phoenix, Ariz.	1905	1969

Heavyweight Class (over 242½ lbs.)			
Bench Press	Pat Casey, Norwalk, Calif.	617¼	1967
Squat	Robert Weaver, YMHA	807	1969
Dead Lift	Don Cundy, Winona, Minn.	784	1967
Total	Pat Casey, Norwalk, Calif.	2080	1967

Table 6a. The all-time leading performers in each of the 3 Power lifts
(see also the following text)

BENCH PRESS

Ranking	Lifter	Nation	Bodyweight, lbs.	Height, in.	Year	Lift, lbs.	Equivalent lift in 1965	% Rating
1	Melvin Hennessy	USA	217 (200)	66.0	1968	560	554.9	98.6
2	Pat Casey	USA	324 (270)	72.0	1967	617¼	613.5	96.2
3	Marvin Eder	USA	197	67.5	1953	485	501.8	94.2
4	John Molinaro	USA	300 (230)	68.0	1967	560	557.0	93.6
5 {	Charles Vinci	USA	123	59.0	1955	325	331.5	} 93.2
	Harold Poole	USA	162	66 ?	1966	425	423.7	
6	"Chuck" Ahrens	USA	280 (265)	72.0	1957 ?	565 e.	578.2	93.1
7	Ronnie Ray	USA	195 (180)	62.0	1968	497	490.9	93.0
8	Douglas Hepburn	Canada	290 (235)	69.0	1954	c. 535	552.0	92.9
9	Paul Anderson	USA	360 (265)	69.0	1957	580	593.6	92.1
10	William Seno	USA	195	68.0	1966	461¼	459.9	89.7

SQUAT

Ranking	Lifter	Nation	Bodyweight, lbs.	Height, in.	Year	Lift, lbs.	Equivalent lift in 1965	% Rating
1	Paul Anderson	USA	340 (265)	69.0	1957	1160	1187.0	102.3
2	David Moyer	USA	123 ?	60 ?	1965	456¼	456.6	86.9
3	Jack Barnes	USA	197 ?	70 ?	1969	714½	705.9	86.4
4	Thomas Overholtzer	USA	180 ?	68 ?	1968	666	659.6	85.8
5	John Molinaro	USA	300 (230)	68.0	1967	800	795.5	84.5
6	John Kanter	USA	240 ?	72 ?	1969	764½	755.3	83.1
7	Pat Casey	USA	316 (270)	72.0	1966	800	796.9	81.4
8	Kenji Onuma	Japan	150	64.0	1957	506	518.3	80.9

DEAD LIFT

1	Hermann Görner	Germany	220½	72.5	1920	793.66	891.4	101.5
2	Charles Vinci	USA	123	59.0	1955	600	617.5	99.7
3	John Terry	USA	132	61.4	1939	600	642.7	98.4
4	Robert Peoples	USA	189	69.0	1949	725¾	759.2	94.1
5	Bert Assirati	Gt. Brit.	240 (210)	66.0	1938	800	859.8	93.8
6	Harry Barlow	Gt. Brit.	112	59.0	1930	441¼	480.5	93.1
7	Charles Lo Monaco	USA	153	67.0	1938	600	644.8	92.9
8	Bruce White	Australia	148¾	67.0	1961	611½	618.8	92.0
9	Robert Burnett	USA	164 ?	66 ?	1968	668	662.4	89.1
10	John Molinaro	USA	300 (230)	68.0	1967	800	795.5	85.6

Figures in parentheses are estimated *muscular* bodyweights.
No ratings of 3-lift totals are here attempted, because of the obvious incorrectness of adding together three separate lifts in which the poundage-possibilities are so dissimilar.
When *separate* percentage ratings are averaged, the two highest-ranking Power lifters would appear to be David Moyer and Pat Casey.

on its merit. "Chuck" Ahrens (72 in., 280 lbs.), of Los Angeles, who like Anderson was at his best in 1957, evidently was capable, among other prodigious feats of arm and shoulder strength, of a Bench Press of between 560 and 570 pounds. He has been credited with a repetition lift in this style of 400 pounds *28 times in succession!* However, since this would have been equivalent to pressing no less than 734 pounds (!) once, evidently the 28 repetitions represented *several series* of presses. If we credit Ahrens with a Bench Press of 565 pounds, and estimate his strictly *muscular* bodyweight at 265 pounds, his lift has the fine rating of 93.1 percent. (For illustration of Ahrens, see Plate 25).

Douglas Hepburn (69 in., 235 pounds *muscular* bodyweight), of Vancouver, B.C., in 1954 did a Bench Press of 580 pounds using wide-spaced hand-grips. This was equivalent to at least 535 pounds in the style of pressing used in competition today. The 535 pounds has a rating of 92.9 percent, making it slightly lesser in merit than the lifts performed by Anderson and Ahrens. Next to Pat Casey's and John Molinaro's lifts, the best record (though unofficial) made recently is that by Mel Hennessy (66 in., 217 lbs.), of Minneapolis, Minn., who in 1968 Bench-Pressed 560 pounds. If we assume Hennessy's *muscular* bodyweight to be 200 pounds, his lift has the phenomenal rating of 98.6 percent, making it percentagewise the best recent Bench Press on record. Back in 1953, Marvin Eder (67.5 in., 197 lbs.), of Brooklyn, N.Y., Bench-Pressed no less than 510 pounds. Presumably this was with wide hand-grips. If the lift had been made under present-day ruling, the poundage would have been lessened to about 485. Even this figure has the high rating of 94.2 percent. In 1955, the Bantamweight Olympic champion (1956 and 1960), Charles Vinci (59 in., 123 lbs.) made a Bench Press of 235 pounds, which has a rating of 93.2 percent. Also about 1955, Robert Herrick (60 in.?, 118 lbs.) pressed 315 pounds lying flat on the floor. If we assume that he could, with practice, have made a Bench Press with the same poundage, his lift would have the phenomenal rating of 98.2 percent. In the Middleweight class, a very fine lift was made in 1966 by Harold Poole (66 in.?, 162 lbs.), of 425 pounds. This lift rates 93.2 percent, equalling the rating of Charles Vinci's Bench Press. Presumably Poole's lift was made outside official competition, since it surpasses by nearly 50 pounds the currently listed American record in the Middleweight class.

But the relatively greatest lying press—as well as standing press— was that performed by little Americo Lemma (56 in., 112 lbs.) back in 1938. Lying flat on the floor, Lemma pressed 280 pounds four times in succession! This was equivalent to pressing about 310 pounds once. If judged as a Bench Press, it would have the fantastic rating of 104.2 percent.

In absolute poundage, and irrespective of bodyweight and date, the highest Bench Presses would appear to be as follows: Pat Casey, 617; James Williams, 601½; Paul Anderson, 580; "Chuck" Ahrens, 565?; Douglas Hepburn, 535; Yuri Vlasov (USSR), 529; Jean Auger (Canada), 525; Mel Hennessey, 560; John Molinaro, 560; Reg Park (Prof., Gt. Brit.), 520?; Gene Roberson, 507; Terry Todd, 500; Robert Weaver, 497. The Bench Press of 529 pounds by Vlasov—who, prior to being supplanted by his compatriot, Zhabotinsky, was heavyweight world record holder in the Olympic 3-lift total—was done "without serious specialization" in this lift. Since Vlasov has made a standing Olympic Press of 435.4 pounds, he should with practice have been capable of a Bench Press of well over 550 pounds.

Again, without specialization, a number of heavyweight professional wrestlers have succeeded with high poundages either in the regular Bench Press or some equivalent style of supine pressing. Bruno Sammartino (70 in., 260 pounds) did a press lying flat on the floor of 545 pounds and a standing (Olympic-style) press of 410 pounds. "Hercules" Romero (about 250 pounds) has Bench-Pressed 502 pounds. "Chuck" Bruce (72 in., 330 pounds) did a Bench Press of 530 pounds, and—even more remarkable—a standing press of 420 pounds. It would be quite impossible to keep abreast of all the outstanding feats of lifting currently being performed by professional wrestlers, since weight-training is one of their main exercises for keeping in top-notch condition for wrestling.

Turning now to the second lift in the Power series—the Squat—the number of high-ranking performances would seem to be much fewer than in the Bench Press. By comparing a large number of performances in all three of the Power Lifts, it is found that the average, or typical, ratio of the Squat to the Bench Press is $\times 1.921 - 120.5$. This means that to be equal in merit to a Bench Press of 500 pounds, a Squat should be about 840 pounds. Thus, Pat Casey's heavyweight record in the Bench Press of 617 pounds is equivalent to a Squat with $617 \times 1.921 - 120.5$, or about 1065 pounds. Casey's best official lift in the Squat—while constituting the present heavyweight amateur record—is 800 pounds. Accordingly, while Casey has the fine rating in the Bench Press of 96.2 percent (see above), in the Squat the rating is only 81.4 percent. That the latter is at least a fair performance is shown by a comparison of it with the Squat of 506 pounds performed by the very strong lightweight Olympic lifter, Kenji Onuma (64 inches, 150 pounds) of Japan, which has a rating of 80.9 percent. John Molinaro has also made a Squat with 800 pounds, unofficially. This lift has the rating of 84.5 percent.

Paul Anderson (69 inches, 360 pounds), who in 1957, as a professional, performed a so-called Squat with no less than 1160 pounds, is beyond doubt the greatest performer in this specialty of whom there is record. However, due to the enormous girths of his thighs and calves (about 35 inches and 22 inches, respectively), and to the "interference" of his waistline with his thighs as he squats, Anderson can, or could, bend down only as far as his girths permitted. Anderson's 1160-pound lift, assuming his *muscular* bodyweight to have been 265 pounds, would give him a rating in the Squat of a phenomenal 102.3 percent. No other lifter or strong-man of any bodyweight has closely approached the latter rating.*

Among wrestlers, perhaps the strongest squatter was the English professional, Bert Assirati (66 in., 240 lbs.), who did a squat on *one* leg with 200 pounds on his shoulders. This was equivalent to squatting on both legs with about 645 pounds. On another occasion, Assirati squatted *continuously for a half-hour* while supporting a 235-pound barbell!

In the third of the Power Lifts—the Dead Lift—a fairly large series of high-ranking performances has been recorded. First in efficiency in this lift are the phenomenal records put up by the German heavyweight Hermann Görner back in the 1920s. At a height of 72.5 inches and a bodyweight of only 220½ pounds, Görner, while still an amateur, on October 29, 1920, in Leipzig, did a Two Hands Dead Lift with 360 kilos or 793.66 pounds. This, until 1969, was the official world's heavyweight amateur record. In performing this lift, Görner used an overhand "thumb-lock" or hooked grip, and not the more usual reversed grips employed by most dead-lifters. Fully equal in merit was Görner's Right Hand Dead Lift, on October 8, 1920, of 330 kilos or 727.52 pounds. This lift also was performed with a hooked overgrip, on a standard "Berg" barbell. Both it and the Two Hands Dead Lift just mentioned have phenomenal ratings of 101.5 percent. Unofficially, John Molinaro has made a Dead Lift with 800 pounds (= 85.6 percent).

A percentage rating not much under that of Görner's in the Two Hands Dead Lift was attained by the American Negro featherweight lifter, John Terry (61.4 in., 132 pounds), who in 1939 did a Dead Lift, using

---

*It should be noted also that in the system of percentage ratings adopted herein, a *symmetrical* (or, at least, a *typical* weightlifter's) *physique* is assumed. If a performer makes a record in some feat requiring only a powerful upper body, the performer could have relatively light legs and so *weigh less* for his upper body girths than would be expected. To be fair, such a man should be rated on the basis of what he *would* weigh if his legs were of a size (girth) in proper proportion to his arms and chest. Conversely, Paul Anderson, in his record-making Squat, should properly be rated on the basis of what his muscular bodyweight would be *if his arms and chest were in proportion* to his immense hips and thighs. This bodyweight would be about 283 pounds rather than 265; and Anderson's rating in the Squat would decrease from 102.3 percent to about 97.4 percent.

reversed grips, of 600 pounds. This lift has the tremendous rating of 98.4 percent. However, some of this high rating stems undoubtedly from Terry's being of short stature and having long arms, which made it possible for him to bend over less in picking up the barbell than if he had been taller and had arms of average length. Bert Assirati, the British professional wrestler mentioned above in connection with squatting, made an unofficial record in the Dead Lift of 800 pounds (in 1938). This lift—assuming Assirati's *muscular* bodyweight to have been about 210 pounds—has a rating of 93.8 percent.

A percentage rating in the Dead Lift even higher than that credited above to John Terry was attained by the American bantamweight former Olympic weightlifting champion Charles Vinci (59 in., 123 pounds). In 1955, Vinci dead-lifted 600 pounds. This lift has a rating of 99.7 percent. Another high-ranking Dead Lift was that made by the British lifter Harry Barlow (59.5 in.?, 112 pounds) of 441¼ pounds. This lift, which was made in December, 1930, has a rating of 93.1 percent.*

Next in rating to the Dead Lifts made by Terry, Vinci, and Barlow would appear to be those made by Charles Lo Monaco and Bob Peoples, both American amateur lifters. Lo Monaco (67 in., 153 pounds) in 1938 did a Dead Lift of 600 pounds. This lift has a rating of 92.9 percent. Peoples (69 in., 189 pounds), on March 5, 1949, at Johnson City, Tennessee, did a Dead Lift of 725½ pounds. This has a rating of 94.1 percent. Peoples, like Görner, used an overhand hooked grip, which added to the merit of his lift. Closely following the foregoing Dead Lifts in efficiency is one by Bruce White (67 in., 148½ pounds) of Australia, who in 1961 lifted 611½ pounds. This lift rates 92.0 percent.

Next in absolute poundage to the Dead Lifts made by Bert Assirati (800 pounds), John Molinaro (800 pounds), and Hermann Görner (793⅝ lbs.) are the following, all made by heavyweights (of the United States, unless otherwise noted): Bruce Randall (72.8 in., 355 pounds) raised 770 pounds in 1955. Ben Cote (70 in.?, 250 pounds?), of Canada, raised 750 pounds officially and 775 pounds unofficially, in 1961. Don Cundy (75 in., 270 pounds) raised 784 pounds on September 2, 1967. The latter lift, at the time this is being written, is the official American amateur record.** Terry Todd (74 in., 335 pounds) raised 738 pounds

---

*However, if the height of the bar in the Dead Lift were *in direct ratio to the lifter's height*—and not, as the existing rules allow, of a single, fixed height for all lifters—the percentage rating of Vinci's Dead Lift would reduce to about 85 percent, and that of Barlow's to about 80 percent, while the rating of the tall Hermann Görner's lift would *increase* to 106.7(!) percent.

**On August 30, 1969, at York, Pa., Cundy made a new American record by raising 801½ lbs. This lift rates 84.8 percent. About the same time, in Norway, Torkel Raundal (77 in., 300 lbs.) made a Dead Lift of 815 lbs.

officially and 750 pounds unofficially, in 1965. Gene Roberson (72 in.?, 268 pounds) raised 745½ pounds in 1966. Gary Young (240 lbs.), of Portland, Oregon, did 740 pounds in 1968. Several other heavyweight USA and Canadian lifters and wrestlers, as well as Rene Florent of France, have each dead-lifted 700 pounds or slightly over. It would appear that Paul Anderson, if he wanted to, could surpass 850 pounds— and possibly even 900 pounds—in the Dead Lift, provided he could retain his grip on the bar with such a weight. However, Anderson has long declined to surpass the 725½-pound lift of his friend Bob Peoples. Since Anderson has made a Bench Press of 580 pounds and a Squat of 1160 pounds, he should—to be proportionate to these two lifts—do a Dead Lift of about 1000 pounds!

Before leaving the subject of Dead Lifts, it should be mentioned that one other record—in addition to Hermann Görner's—in the *One* Hand Dead Lift has a very high rating. This is the unofficial Right Hand Dead Lift by the British lifter Laurence Chappell (70.5 in., 165 pounds) of 560 pounds, made in 1932. This lift, which was performed on a Pullum cambered bar—in the customary straddle position adopted by British lifters—has a rating of 97.4 percent. Officially, Chappell did 502 pounds in this lift, which poundage has a percentage rating of 87.3.

While the three aforementioned Power Lifts are becoming more popular, and attracting more competitors, year by year, they are still a long way from comparing, in organization and efficiency, with the Olympic lifts, the performers of which can be numbered in the hundreds of thousands. At present, the only nations in which the Power Lifts are practiced to any great extent are Great Britain (particularly Canada and Australia) and the United States. While many of the Olympic weightlifters in Russia and other continental European countries practice the various Power Lifts as supplementary exercises for promoting strength, no serious efforts have been made, as yet, among these lifters to surpass the American records in the Power Lifts. With a few exceptions in individual lifts—such as the Bench Presses by Pat Casey and Mel Hennessy—nothing approaching maximum efficiency in the three Power Lifts has as yet been attained. For example, the "poundage-possibility" in the Bench Press can be shown to be, on the average, about 1.35 times that in the Olympic (standing) Press.* In the Squat, the formula is 2.69 Olympic Press − 155.0; and in the Dead Lift, 1.894 Olympic Press + 97.1. On this basis, Table 7, following, shows what the records in the Bench Press, the Squat, and

---

*While the ratio between the Bench Press and the Olympic Press is *almost* a constant 1.35, actually—so far as current records are concerned—the ratio ranges from about 1.33 in the bantamweight class to 1.36 in the heavyweight class. The correct formula is: Bench Press, lbs. = 1.40 Olympic Press, lbs. − 18.0.

the Dead Lift *should be* (compared with the current records in the Olympic Press) and what, in round figures, they actually *are*.

Table 7. Potential and Actual Records in the 3 Power Lifts
(all figures to the nearest pound)

Class	Olympic Press (actual)	Bench Press Potent.	Actual	Squat Potent.	Actual	Dead Lift Potent.	Actual
Bantamweight	276	368	295	586	456	618	501
Featherweight	289	386	319	621	476	644	543
Lightweight	321	431	355	708	462	705	563
Middleweight	356	480	376	803	540	771	668
Light-heavyweight	375	507	451	853	666	807	672
Middle-heavyweight	391	530	497	897	714	838	688
Heavyweight	415	564	542	963	764	886	770
Super-heavyweight	462	628	617	1087	807	972	801

Comment on the above figures is almost superfluous. They show that the current records in the Bench Press (despite Pat Casey's extraordinary lift of 617 pounds and Mel Hennessy's almost equally remarkable 542 pounds) fall short of what they should be—in ratio to the records in the Olympic Press—by an average of over *13 percent*. In the Squat the deficiency is considerably greater—nearly *34 percent*—and in the Dead Lift about *21 percent*. With time and more extensive competition, the records in the three Power Lifts should steadily rise. Eventually, they should equal in efficiency the high standard presently exhibited in the Olympic Lifts. But until the approach of the latter stage, there is not much reason for exclaiming over record-increases of a pound or so, when the deficiencies are in *dozens* of pounds.

In addition to the standard 3-lift competition series of Power Lifts just dealt with, many other barbell lifts of the slow, or "power lift," type have long been practiced by weightlifters as part of their training routines. Among these lifts may be mentioned: (1) the Two Hands Curl (in military position); (2) the Pull-over at Arms' Length (lying flat on the floor); (3) the Pull-over and Press in Wrestler's Bridge; (4) the Reverse Curl (like the regular Two Hands Curl, only performed with the *backs* of the hands uppermost); (5) the Two Hands Press (standing) from Behind Neck; and (6)—less frequently practiced —the Bent Press. Then there are such once-popular "poundage" lifts as the Back Lift (with platform), the Hand and Thigh Lift, the Harness Lift, and others of that type. Finally, there are the well-practiced semi-gymnastic events of chinning and dipping while carrying extra weight. Records in the two latter events are given on pp. 249 and 257.

Here are some high-ranking performances in various of the slow-type lifts mentioned above.

1. Two Hands Curl (in "military," or erect, position). The best lift in this style in the heavyweight class would appear to be that of the former Canadian and World champion Olympic lifter, Douglas Hepburn (69 in., 300 pounds). In 1956, in Vancouver, Hepburn curled 260 pounds. This lift has a rating of 94.2 percent. But some of Hepburn's repetition curls indicate even greater ability. Mac Batchelor, the former world's Wrist-wrestling champion (see below), saw Hepburn curl 235 pounds 5 times in succession in "good" style. If four of these curls could have been said to be in "perfect" style, they would have been equivalent to a single Curl of 264 pounds. On another occasion, Hepburn curled 135 pounds no fewer than 35 times! 33 correct curls with this poundage would indicate a single curl with 265 pounds. Although Hepburn, when he made these lifts, weighed probably not over 235 pounds in strictly "muscular" condition, there can be no doubt that his actual weight, which bordered on 300 pounds, provided "ballast" and increased his stability during the Curling movements.

Next to Hepburn's record, the best heavyweight performance in the Curl would seem to be a lift of 255 pounds which was made by the professional wrestler "Chuck" Bruce (72 in., 330 pounds), about 1964. Bruno Sammartino, the off-and-on World's Heavyweight Wrestling Champion, curled 235 pounds. Bruce Randall (72.8 in., 355 pounds) curled 242 pounds (1954). As in the case of Hepburn, Randall's temporary great bodyweight undoubtedly helped him in this particular lift. John McWilliams (72 in., 225 pounds) has been credited with a Curl (military?) of 241¼ pounds (1954). Hermann Görner, in 1932 correctly curled 100 kilos or about 220½ pounds. While his actual bodyweight at the time was 270 pounds, his *muscular* weight was probably not over 245 pounds. The latter bodyweight would give his Curl a rating of 92.4 percent.

The most meritorious Curl on record would seem to be that performed by Robert Herrick (60 in.?, 118 pounds), who about 1955 did a Curl with 150 pounds. This lift has the phenomenal rating of 100.2 percent. The next-best Curl among smaller lifters is perhaps that of Charles Vinci (59 in., 123 pounds), who late in 1955 curled 155 pounds. This lift has a rating of 96.1 percent. In each of the latter two cases, it will be noted that the performer curled 32 *pounds more* than his own bodyweight. This is truly extraordinary.

2. Pull-over at Arms' Length. This lift is performed by lying flat on the floor and pulling a barbell from behind the head to overhead while keeping the arms perfectly straight (that is, with the elbows "locked" stiff). The two most outstanding records in this lift were, coincidentally, both made by men weighing 197 pounds. Reuben Martin, of England (72 in.), in 1950 did a straight-arm pull-over of 200 pounds. This lift rates a phenomenal 101.8 percent.* Of almost equal merit was a Pull-over of 210 pounds performed in 1953 by Marvin Eder (67.5 in.), of New York; it has a rating of an even 100 percent. The British professional wrestler, Bert Assirati, was, despite his heavy bodyweight (236–260 pounds), an expert at performing various feats of herculean gymnastics (see below). In the Pull-over at Arms' Length he did 200 pounds (1938). If we assume for Assirati a *muscular* bodyweight of 210 pounds, his Pull-over has the high rating of 95.0 percent. Back about 1925, the English professional, Alan P. Mead (73 in., 182 lbs.) did a repetition Pull-over of 70 pounds 70 times in succession!

3. Pull-over and Press in Wrestler's Bridge. In this lift the performer first assumes a supine position on the floor, on which he supports himself solely on his feet and the top of his head. It is customary to ease the pressure on the head by placing under it a firm pillow. In this position, using both hands, the performer reaches back and pulls a barbell over his face and onto his chest, from where he presses it to arms' length. Considerably the best performance in this lift was the one made by the famous Russian strong-man and wrestler, George Hackenschmidt, who pulled over a barbell weighing 311½ pounds and pressed it twice in succession. This was equivalent to pressing 324 pounds once. This remarkable lift, which remained unbroken for *over 50 years*, was performed by Hackenschmidt in Vienna on his 20th birthday anniversary (August 2, 1898), while he was still an amateur athlete and weighing only 195 pounds (at a height of 68.7 inches). This lift has the phenomenal rating of 104.0 percent.

Next in merit among performances in the Wrestler's Bridge press is one of 279 pounds, which was made by Frank Dennis (64.5 in., 151 pounds) in 1927. This lift has the exceedingly high rating of 97.5 percent. Louis Chiarelli (62 in., 152 lbs.) about 1945 did a Press in the Wrestler's Bridge position of 309 pounds, but first had the barbell *handed* to him. If only he had pulled the weight across his face onto his chest and *then* pressed it—thus making a complete lift—the lift would have gained the rating of 94.8 percent. Chiarelli also established

---

*About the same time, Martin did a repetition Pull-over of 150 pounds *12 times in succession*. Theoretically, this was equivalent to pulling-over 204 pounds once!

something of a record by *supporting* on straight arms in the Wrestler's Bridge position a load of 589 pounds. This consisted of a 419-pound barbell with a 170-pound man sitting on it.

The present heavyweight world record in the Press in Wrestler's Bridge would appear to be a lift of 375 pounds made in 1959 by Charles Davis (70 in.?, 215 lbs.). However, it was not stated whether Davis pulled the weight over his face or, like Chiarelli, had it handed to him (so that he received it at arms' length). If Davis performed a *complete* lift, it would have a rating of 93.7 percent. The "poundage-possibility" in this style of lifting is high, being on the average about 1.006 times that in the Olympic Press.

Back in 1906, Hans Schwartz, a German heavyweight wrestler, performed a remarkable feat of neck strength by first—while lying flat on the floor—pressing a barbell of 258 pounds to arms' length, *then* raising into the Wrestler's Bridge position!

4. Two Hands Reverse Curl. This lift is also, in some quarters, referred to as a "Backhand" Curl. The "poundage-possibility" in it, as compared with the regular (palms up) Two Hands Curl ranges from less than 60 percent to nearly 100 percent. The average ratio is about 83 percent. Many years ago, at the Los Angeles Athletic Club, I knew a fellow-lifter who could curl 160 pounds perfectly in the regular style, yet had difficulty with only 90 pounds in a Reverse Curl. Possibly this was because his wrists were stiff and he could not extend them (that is, bring the backs of the hands upward) to a strong degree. In contrast, I, who could lift in a regular Curl only 143 pounds, could do 140 pounds in a Reverse Curl, perhaps because my wrists were unusually flexible and could be bent upwards to a pronounced degree. This flexibility served to shorten the distance between the weight and the elbow joints, thereby reducing the leverage on the arm and forearm flexor muscles.

The highest lift in the Reverse Curl, in absolute poundage, would appear to be one by Dave Mayor (73.5 in., 265 lbs.), who in 1938 was said to have Reverse-curled 175 pounds three times in succession. This would have been equivalent to 190 pounds once. The latter lift—if it is assumed that Mayor's *muscular* bodyweight was 255 pounds—would have a rating of 92.4 percent. Al Berger (71.5 in., 220 lbs.) was also proficient at the Reverse Curl, and at a bodyweight of 193 pounds did 150 pounds (in 1939). When, in 1945, he had gained to a bodyweight of 220 pounds—with strength in proportion—he was probably capable of a Reverse Curl of 170 pounds. This lift would have a rating of 87 percent.

Among the various developmental lifts practiced by lifters and body-builders in Great Britain, the Reverse Curl is done in a modified form called a Rectangular Fix. In this lift the arms are flexed only to the stage where the forearms are horizontal (or parallel with the ground). In the latter position the barbell must be held steady for two seconds in order for the lift to be good. The "poundage-possibility" in the Rectangular Fix would appear to be identical with that in the Reverse Curl. The relatively best record in the Rectangular Fix among English lifters is that of Laurence Chappell (70.5 in., 164½ lbs.), who in 1931 raised 150½ pounds. This lift has the exceedingly high rating of 99.2 percent. An even more remarkable lift in this style is said to have been performed by the Canadian professional strong-man, Arthur Dandurand (68 in., 182 lbs.), about 1920. This was a lift of 177½ pounds. As there is no way now of checking on the authenticity of this claimed record, it can only be added that if Dandurand actually performed it the lift would have the extra-phenomenal rating of 105.2 percent. It is known that Dandurand possessed extraordinary grip, forearm, and general bodily strength from the fact that he made the best record in the popular Canadian event of trundling a loaded wheelbarrow (see p. 174).

5. Two Hands Press from Behind Neck (in standing position). This lift tests—even more than does the usual forms of the standing press—the power of the arm-extensor (triceps) muscles. The "poundage-possibility" in it is equal to 97.7 percent of that in the Two Hands Military Press, or to about 83 percent of that in the Two Hands Olympic Press. In the Press from Behind Neck, once the barbell has been raised from the shoulders to the height where the top of the head has to be cleared (and the weight directed forward), it is permissible to bend backward at the waist in order to complete the press.

Many weightlifters and bodybuilders use the Press from Behind Neck as a developer of general pressing power. In the following review of outstanding performers, space permits the mentioning of only a few of these men.

Anthony Terlazzo, the featherweight American and Olympic champion in 1936, several years later when weighing 148 pounds (height 64.5 in.) did a Press from Behind Neck of 225 pounds. This lift has the very high rating of 95.7 percent. If it be assumed that Maxick, the great Austrian lightweight professional lifter (see above) was in all respects as great a presser in 1909 as Terlazzo was thirty years later—and all available evidence supports this assumption—then Maxick (63.75 in., 145 pounds), in being capable of a Press from Behind Neck of 225 pounds, would have the phenomenal rating in this lift of 103 percent. Emil von Mogyorossy (65 in., 150 pounds), who was at one time

Maxick's partner in hand-to-hand balancing—and was an almost equally phenomenal Presser—should probably be credited with an almost equally high rating in the Press from Behind Neck.

Among recent heavyweight performers in the Press from Behind Neck, the most outstanding were Douglas Hepburn (see above), who would appear to have been capable of 365 pounds; "Chuck" Ahrens (72 in., 280 pounds); 380 pounds; and Paul Anderson, 390 pounds. These presses are simply prodigious. That by Ahrens has a percentage rating of 99.2; that by Hepburn 100.2; and that by Anderson 100.8.

Nearly equal in merit to these three lifts is onè by Mel Hennessey (66 in., 218 pounds), who in 1965 did a Press from Behind Neck in *military* position of 300 pounds. This lift would appear to have been equivalent to about 345 pounds if the usual style of pressing (with a backbend) had been employed. If Hennessey's *muscular* bodyweight be assumed as 200 pounds, his lift has a rating of 99.5 percent. Terry Todd (74 in., 335 pounds) in 1965 pressed 300 pounds from behind the neck 3 times in succession while *seated*. This was equivalent to a single press of about 332 pounds from behind the neck while standing. Possibly two or three other heavyweight lifters have made behind-the-neck presses of from 350 to 370 pounds. One is John Molinaro, whose press of 350 pounds while *seated* is equivalent to at least 360 pounds standing. This lift has the high rating of 96.8 percent. Another is Steve Merjanian of Los Angeles, who in the fall of 1966 pressed 350 pounds once from behind the neck, and 315 pounds 5 times. The latter equals 360 pounds once.

6. *Bent Press* (taking the barbell to the shoulder with both hands). This was once a highly-popular lift, both in Europe and America, when the big objective seemed to be how much weight could be "put up" with one hand. Eugen Sandow, by featuring the Bent Press in his world-wide theatrical performances in the years 1891–1902, served to introduce the lift to the public and to popularize it among lesser strong-men. But it was Sandow's compatriot, Arthur Saxon, who brought the technique of the Bent Press virtually to perfection, and left Sandow's record in this lift about 100 pounds behind.

The possibilities in the Bent Press are—in view of its being a one-hand overhead lift—simply enormous. The "poundage-possibility" is 1.1087 times that in the Two Hands Olympic Press. But to attain this degree of proficiency takes years of *daily* practice, plus the ability to master a feat that requires patience and balance rather than the "explosive" energy demanded in snatching, cleaning, and jerking. For this reason the exponents of the Bent Press to be cited here are, or were, mainly *professional* strong-men.

As noted above, the greatest performer in the Bent Press, either relatively or absolutely, was the German professional Arthur Saxon, who stood 69.6 inches in height and weighed normally an even 200 pounds. To avoid repetition here, the reader is referred to the details of Saxon's various records in the Bent Press given above.

If Saxon is to be credited with an "official" record in the Bent Press of 370 pounds, his rating in this lift is a phenomenal 103.5 percent. His highest "unofficial" lift, of 386 pounds, which was assertedly performed at "Apollo's" (William Bankier's) physical culture school in London, on July 23, 1906, has the fantastic rating of 107.8 percent. To show how extraordinary these two lifts were, it can be added that Saxon's 370-pound Bent Press would, in 1965, be equal to a similar lift of 433 pounds, and his 386-pound Bent Press to one of 451 pounds!

To weightlifting enthusiasts who have followed the feats of famous strong-men over the years, it may come as a surprise that, next to Arthur Saxon, the relatively greatest Bent-presser was not Edward Aston, nor Thomas Inch, nor either of Saxon's brothers, Hermann or Kurt. Rather, it was that great oldtime middleweight amateur lifter and strong-man, John Y. (Young) Smith, of Boston. Back in 1903, at a bodyweight of 168 pounds and a height of 66.5 inches, Smith bent-pressed with his right hand a *dumbbell* weighing 275½ pounds. This was equivalent to a *barbell* Bent Press of 313 pounds. Smith's rating for the latter estimated lift is a terrific 99.9 percent. Moreover, Smith, in contrast to most other bent-pressers, was practically as efficient with his left arm as with his right. His left-hand Bent Press with a dumbbell was 247 pounds, which was equivalent to a barbell Bent Press of about 281 pounds, and which rates 99.5 percent.

After Smith's Bent-presses, the most meritorious lift in this style would seem to be that of the English lifter, W. A. Pullum (65 in., 122 pounds), who on May 4, 1915, in London, Bent-pressed a barbell of 216 pounds. This lift has the very high rating of 97.3 percent. Pullum, while not a professional when he made this lift, became an instructor a week or two later; and he had had the advantage of daily practice in his own gymnasium (the Camberwell Weightlifting Club) over a period of years.

Fourth in efficiency in the Bent Press was the famous English professional (instructor), Edward Aston (67.75 in., 170 pounds). In 1913, at the Crystal Palace in London, Aston did a Right Hand Anyhow (one hand "all the way," standing the barbell on end to shoulder it) of 300½ pounds. This was equivalent to a Bent Press shouldered with two hands of about 310 pounds, and has a rating of 97.0 percent.

Next—practically equal in their percentage ratings—are the German professionals Hermann and Kurt Saxon, and the Swiss-American professional G. W. Rolandow. Lifting in 1906, in London, Hermann Saxon (67 in., 168 pounds) was credited with a Bent Press of 300 pounds. This lift rates 96.7 percent. Next is a Bent Press of 298 pounds performed about 1901 by G. W. Rolandow (69.75 in., 178 pounds) of New York City. This lift has a rating of 96.9 percent. Closely following in merit Rolandow's lift is a Bent Press of 300 pounds by Kurt Saxon (67.5 in., 172 pounds), performed—like that of his brother, Hermann—in London in 1906. This lift rates 95.8 percent. It would appear that since the time of W. A. Pullum, no exponent of the Bent Press of any body-weight has made a record that rates 90 percent or more. For example, the best heavyweight record made during recent years is that of Al Beinert, of Indianapolis, Indiana, who in June 1965 raised 360 pounds using a dumbbell. This was equivalent to about 409 pounds with a barbell. However, on account of Beinert's size (76 inches, 260 pounds), and the recentness of his lift, it rates only 87.5 percent.

Arthur Saxon, as a result of his long practice of the Bent Press, and also because he used an elaboration of it regularly in his stage perform-ances, became equally skilled in the lift known as the Two Hands Anyhow with Barbell and Ringweight. In this lift, after first bent-pressing a heavy barbell with his right hand, Saxon would reach down with his left hand and swing a lighter "ringweight" (often a kettlebell) to his shoulder and then press it aloft alongside the barbell. The Two Hands Anyhow—considering it from start to finish—is a drawn-out, gruelling lift requiring stamina and a high degree of technique. For this reason, few lifters have had the persistence and determination to master the lift. But with Arthur Saxon it, like the Bent Press, was a feat brought virtually to perfection; and the poundages he was able to put up in this style were truly colossal. At his usual bodyweight of approximately 200 pounds, Saxon raised first a barbell of 152 kilos (335.10 pounds) in the Bent Press, and then brought up a kettlebell of 50 kilos (110.23 pounds). This made a Two Hands Anyhow of 445.33 pounds. The lift was performed in Leipzig on November 3, 1905. It has the phenomenal rating of 100.9 percent. For details of other combinations of poundages that Saxon performed in this style, see pp. 79–80.

Outside of Arthur Saxon, only one strong-man seems to have attained a high degree of efficiency in the Two Hands Anyhow with Barbell and Ringweight. This was the one-time amateur 9-stone (126-pound) champion of Great Britain, W. A. Pullum, who has been cited above in connection with the Bent Press. Although Pullum was built along radically different lines from Saxon—he was relatively slender, and never weighed more than 122 pounds at his height of 65 inches—he was a great admirer

PLATE 17

John Davis lifting overhead the 365-pound railway wheels once owned by the French giant of strength, "Apollon." Elysee Montmartre, Paris, September 13, 1949. (55)

PLATE 18

Douglas Hepburn of Vancouver, B.C. This modern Hercules is here shown in lifting costume in 1952. In this photo, Hepburn weighs 272 pounds at his height of 5 ft. 9 in. (56)

PLATE 19

Paul Anderson, "The Dixie Derrick," doing repetition squats with a weight of 600 pounds in the basement of his Toccoa, Georgia, home. 1955. (57)

PLATE 20

The three heavyweight place-winners at the 1963 World Championships in Stockholm. No. 1, Yuri Vlasov, USSR; No. 2, Norbert Schemansky, USA; No. 3, Leonid Zhabotinsky, USSR. (58)

PLATE 21

Two phenomenal lifting records. Above, Gyözö Veres of Hungary making a record Clean and Jerk of 407¾ pounds in the light-heavyweight class, Stockholm 1963. Below, Norbert Schemansky making a heavyweight American and World record of 362 pounds in the Two Hands Snatch. Detroit, 1963. (60)

149

PLATE 22

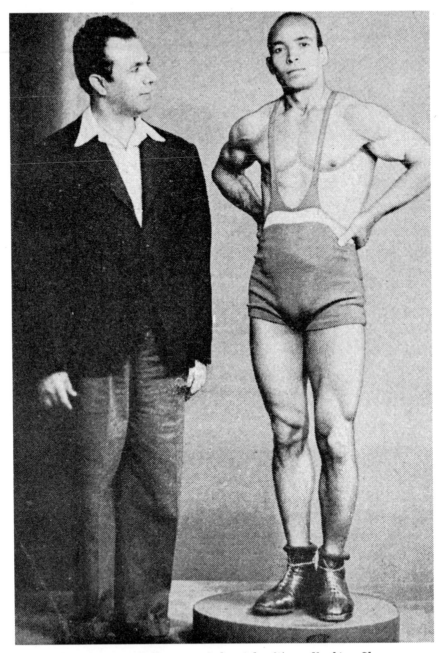

The phenomenal Egyptian lightweight lifter, Ibrahim Shams (right), who as far back as 1939 jerked 352¾ pounds while weighing only 142¼! On Shams's right is his trainer, Aziz Talaat, of Alexandria. (61)

PLATE 23

Waldemar Baszanowski, Polish lightweight, who holds the world record in the Two Hands Snatch with 298½ pounds. He is here shown making a Clean and Jerk of 363¾ pounds. Note the lifter's tremendous muscular development for a lightweight. (62)

PLATE 24

Pat Casey of Norwalk, California, holder of the heavyweight world's record in the Bench Press with 617¼ pounds. He is shown in this picture, taken in 1963, weighing 270 pounds of solid muscle. (63)

of the Saxon Trio, and practiced along the same lines followed by Arthur until he was virtually a miniature edition of him in lifting ability. Pullum, at a bodyweight of 121 pounds, on February 5, 1915, in London, made a record in the Two Hands Anyhow of 272 pounds. This weight was made up of a barbell of 210 pounds and a kettlebell of 62 pounds. This lift has the very high rating of 97.9 percent. However, Pullum, unlike Saxon, did not first Bent-press the 210-pound barbell, but jerked it from the shoulders with both hands, then "rocked" and shifted it into his right hand. The possibilities in this style of getting the heavier bell overhead with one hand are essentially the same as if the bell had been bent-pressed.

Hermann Görner in 1920 raised 430 pounds in a "two hands anyhow" lift. But the merit of this performance cannot be directly compared with the aforementioned lifts, since Görner performed his lift with four kettlebells, and in a style for which there are little or no comparative data.

It remains to make a brief mention of the best performances on record in the more familiar of the "poundage" lifts. These lifts are (1) the Back Lift, with platform; (2) the Hand and Thigh Lift; and (3) the Harness Lift.

1. Back Lift, with platform. In this style of lifting, which was popular among many old-time professional strong-men, the weight rests on top of a heavy, usually iron-bound, wooden platform, which is set across two trestles. The lifter stoops and carefully positions himself under the middle of the load, then raises the platform and load *just off* the two trestles by straightening his legs (knees). In this effort he assists with his arms by grasping and pressing strongly downwards on a sturdy stool of the proper height. But probably at least 85 percent of the lifting is done by the legs—that is, the extensor muscles of the knees and hips. The "poundage-possibility" in the Back Lift is 13.192 times that in the Two Hands Olympic Press. Here, in order of the poundages raised, are the three highest-ranking performances in the Back Lift:

6000 pounds by Paul Anderson (69 in., 364 lbs.), at Toccoa, Georgia, June 12, 1957. (A claim of 6200 pounds, at a later date, has also been made for Anderson).

4638 pounds by Jack Walsh (65.5 in., 180 lbs.), at Trenton, New Jersey, November 13, 1950. (This poundage was made up of 84 fifty-pound scale-testing blockweights on a platform weighing 438 pounds).

4140 pounds by Warren L. Travis (68 in., 185 lbs.), at Brooklyn, N.Y.,

November 1, 1907. (On another occasion, Travis lifted a platform loaded with men rather than iron, the total weight of which must have been at least 4240 pounds).

The respective percentage ratings in the Back Lift by the three above performers are, due to other factors, in inverse order of the poundages lifted. They are: Paul Anderson (assuming his *muscular* bodyweight to be 258 pounds), 97.5 percent; Jack Walsh, 97.6 percent; and Warren L. Travis, 101.6 percent. Anderson's unofficial Back Lift of 6200 pounds would have a rating of 100.8 percent, while Travis's Back Lift using live weight, if 4240 pounds, would rate 104(!) percent.

The huge French-Canadian strong-man, Louis Cyr (68.5 in., *c.* 300 pounds), was reputed to have made a Back Lift of 4300 pounds in Boston, on May 26, 1896. This was at Austin & Stone's Museum. However, the alleged 4300 pounds was not weighed, but was the combined weights of the men lifted, *as stated by themselves,* plus the weight of Cyr's platform. There is considerable doubt about the poundage of this claimed lift. Cyr's best authentic Back Lift, with weighed iron, would appear to have been somewhere between 3900 and 4000 pounds. Cyr's one-time partner, Horace Barré (69 in., 275–320 pounds), about 1896 made a record of 3890 pounds. "Nearly 4000 pounds" in the Back Lift was raised also by the Cincinnati amateur, Henry Holtgrewe (69 in., 275 pounds), in 1907; and by the French professional, George Levasseur, also in 1907. The light-heavyweight professional strong-man, F. B. Franks (68 in., 175 pounds), claimed to have made a Back Lift of 3788 pounds at New Orleans in 1924.

2. Hand and Thigh Lift. In this style of lifting, the weight is raised just off the ground, the lifter standing almost upright and raising the weight by straightening his legs (knee and hip joints). Usually the performer stands on a *platform* above the weight, and grasps with both hands a horizontal handle or bar, which is connected in the middle to a rod or chain that runs downward and is attached to the weight. The lifter retains his grip by wedging his fingers between the bar and the fronts of his thighs. Thus, since the grip is no problem, the lift is essentially a test of the power of the *extensor* muscles of the knees and hips. Here, in order of the poundages raised, are the six highest-ranking performances in the Hand and Thigh Lift:

1900 pounds by Jack Walsh (65.5 in., 180 pounds), at Trenton, New Jersey, August 1950.
1897¼ pounds by Louis Cyr of Canada (68.5 in., c. 300 pounds), at Chicago, May 7, 1896.

1805 pounds by Charles Nostramm (71 in.?, 210 pounds), at New York, c. 1900.

1778 pounds by Warren L. Travis (68 in., 185 pounds), at Brooklyn, N.Y., November 1, 1907.

1652 pounds by Paul von Boeckmann (72 in., 185 pounds), at Austin, Texas, 1893.

1640 pounds by John Y. Smith (66.5 in., 168 pounds), at Boston, Mass., 1903.

The percentage ratings in the Hand and Thigh Lift of the six performers listed above are, in order: Paul von Boeckmann, 101.8 percent; Warren L. Travis, 98.4 percent; John Y. Smith, 98.4 percent; Charles Nostramm, 97.9 percent; Louis Cyr (assuming his *muscular* bodyweight to have been 235 pounds), 94.2 percent, and Jack Walsh, 91.4 percent.

I would have guessed, offhand, that the most efficient performer in the Hand and Thigh Lift was Travis—what with his years of specialized training on this and other "power" lifts. However, Paul von Boeckmann, who lifted back in 1893, and who was of a tall and rangy build, with correspondingly smaller muscles, would appear to have been the top performer in this style of lifting. Von Boeckmann's lift of 1652 pounds in 1893 would have been equivalent to 2011 pounds in 1965! Charles Nostramm deserves special mention, since he was not a trained athlete, but did his exhibition lifting as an amateur and largely by natural strength. Travis says that Nostramm was a Swedish dock carpenter in Brooklyn, and that in the Hand and Thigh Lift he (Nostramm) could outdo all the professional strong-men of his day, with the exception of Louis Cyr, but including Travis himself. In passing, it is interesting to note that Cyr's Hand and Thigh Lift of 1897¼ pounds was equivalent to a Back Lift—the most controversial of Cyr's records—of 4215 pounds. His 1897-pound Hand and Thigh, in 1896, would be equivalent to about 2300 pounds today, while a Back Lift to be in ratio to the latter would be about 5100 pounds. For purposes of comparison and rating, it may be added that the "poundage-possibility" in the Hand and Thigh Lift is about 5.94 times that in the Two Hands Olympic Press.

3. Harness Lift. The possibilities of technical deception are so great in this style of lifting that I shall here merely discuss some of the highest recorded performances rather than list them all as "official" records. As mentioned above, whether or not a particular performance in the Harness Lift is genuine depends on the manner in which the supporting chains (from the lifter's harness to the platform being lifted) are arranged. Wherever an illegitimate hook-up of the chains is used, the maneuver is usually imperceptible to an uninitiated audience, and may be overlooked even by presumably competent judges on the stage. So far as reliable data show, the "poundage-possibility" in the Harness Lift is about 13.68 times that in a Two Hands Olympic Press. This makes the possibility about 3.7 percent greater than in the Back Lift.

The first supposedly authentic world's record in the Harness Lift was that performed by the "Alsatian" (actually, German-American) professional strong-man, Charles Sampson (67 in., 175 pounds) in London, on December 19, 1891, of 4008 pounds. Sampson became "famous" in a somewhat negative manner, by reason of having been the best-known strong-man to be defeated—on his own stage—by the celebrated Eugen Sandow. If Sampson actually raised correctly 4008 pounds in a Harness Lift at the time mentioned, the performance would have the fantastic rating of 104.4 percent. However, for several reasons —one being Sampson's claim to have broken solid *steel* chains (with links of ¼-inch thickness) on his bare upper arms—I am suspicious of the "technique" he employed in his alleged 4008-pound Harness Lift.

But far earlier than Sampson's lift was one made by the American athlete, William Buckingham Curtis, who was one of the founders of the New York Athletic Club. On December 20, 1868, in New York City, Curtis, who weighed only 165 pounds at a height of 67 inches, performed a Harness Lift of 3239 pounds. Today, this lift would be equivalent to one of nearly 4400 pounds! It has a rating of 103.9(!) percent. Presumably this was an authentic lift. It is listed in Spalding's *Official Athletic Almanac* for 1923, p. 67.

After Charles Sampson's performance in 1891, the next "record" in the Harness Lift appears to be one made by the famous Luxembourg strong-man, John Grünn Marx. Marx (70.9 in., 235 pounds) is credited with a genuine lift of 200 kilos (about 4410 pounds) at Eastbourne, England, in 1905. Due to Marx's huge size, however, his lift has a rating of "only" 95.1 percent.

The famous American professional "poundage" lifter, Warren Lincoln Travis (68 in., 185 pounds), in his exhibition at the Brooklyn Athletic Club on November 1, 1907, performed, among other highly-meritorious feats, a Harness Lift of 3985 pounds. This authentic lift, which was made up of *weighed iron*—neither men nor horses—has a rating of 96.8 percent.

Evidently the most remarkable Harness Lift on record was one made by the German amateur heavyweight lifter and strong-man, Paul Trappen (68 in., 220 pounds). At his home town of Trier, Germany, on July 5, 1914, Trappen made a lift of 2370 kilos or 5225 pounds. Earlier, on June 30, he made in practice an even higher lift: 2504 kilos or 5520 pounds. Both lifts have simply terrific ratings: the 5225-pound lift,

100.4 percent; and the 5520-pound lift, 106.2 percent! The latter lift would be equivalent today to one of over 6300 pounds.

Before concluding this review of weightlifting records, I would like to add to the standardized or "official" ones discussed above a number of lesser-known yet equally remarkable feats—mostly of an impromptu nature—performed by strong-men of the past. These feats I have entitled "Five Famous Weights and the Men Who Lifted Them."

E. FIVE FAMOUS WEIGHTS AND THE MEN WHO LIFTED THEM

1. The Apollon Railway Car Wheels

Sometime in the 1890s, the great French professional strong-man, "Apollon" (Louis Uni, see Plate 3), procured for his stage act a set of railway car wheels connected by an axle, and used the set as a ready-made barbell. This axle and wheels weighed 166 kilos (about 366 pounds). The maximum diameter of the wheels was about 26 inches, and the axle, or "barbell" handle, was 49 millimeters (1.93 in.) thick. Several differing stories have been circulated as to how Apollon used these car wheels in his act.

First, it is said that Professor Edmond Desbonnet, the oldtime French authority on weightlifting and strong-men, claimed that Apollon lifted the 366-pound car wheels *every night in his stage performance*. And by "lifted", Desbonnet meant *cleaned and jerked*. But there is probably some confusion here, between Apollon's 366-pound wheels and some that he had secured earlier—which weighed only 118 kilos or 260 pounds. A second group of followers of Apollon felt that if Apollon had lifted the 366-pound car wheels at all it was either to dead-lift them or perhaps *support* the bar across his shoulders, and that he certainly was unable to bring such a poundage "clean" to his shoulders. A third group apparently disbelieved that Apollon had ever lifted the weight in any way whatever—or possibly had ever even *seen* the car wheels!

In my article on Apollon in the April–May, 1958, issue of *Iron Man* (p. 50), I mentioned that an oldtime French circus performer, "Allo-Diavolo" (Eugen Jullien de Nozieres), claimed that Apollon had once possessed a 380-pound barbell that he kept in the gymnasium of the wrestler Paul Pons, in Paris, and that on a certain occasion—to show some of his friends what he could really do—he (Apollon) cleaned and jerked this bell with a 10-pound weight added to each end, making a total of 400 pounds! This account was given to me by "Diavolo" himself, when I talked with him in New York City in the latter part of 1953. "Diavolo" stated, further, that he had worked in the *same circuses* with Apollon for three successive seasons. However, he did not mention the years. But since "Diavolo," in 1953, was probably not over 65 years of age, and since Apollon was at his peak of strength not later than 1897, at which time Diavolo would have been about nine years of age, it is difficult to picture Diavolo "working" with Apollon in the 1890s! The point of all this is that if Apollon could have cleaned and jerked 400 pounds on any regular barbell, he could probably have lifted in the same manner the 366-pound car wheels, since the thick handle on the latter would have been the least of his difficulties. But *did* he ever clean and jerk 400 pounds? It would appear exceedingly doubtful. And whether he ever lifted the 366-pound car wheels *overhead* is something that has been both affirmed and denied.*

But there have been several other strong-men, who appeared on the scene later than Apollon, who *did* lift the 366-pound car wheels overhead, under conditions that could not be questioned. In all probability their attempts were prompted by the question of whether Apollon had ever so lifted the wheels, and indeed, whether it was possible for *anyone* to clean and jerk them.

The first man to demonstrate beyond all question that the Apollon weights *could* be cleaned and jerked was the French professional weight-lifter Charles Rigoulot. The 225-pound Rigoulot successfully raised the car wheels on March 3, 1930, at the Wagram Auditorium in Paris, before a large and enthusiastic audience. However, before doing this, Rigoulot had practiced with the weights over a period of weeks, registering innumerable failures to properly *shoulder* the awkward car wheels. And it should be noted that about this time Rigoulot was capable of raising in the Clean and Jerk over 400 pounds on a barbell having a regulation, 1.1-inch diameter handle.

Nearly twenty years were to pass before the Apollon weights were cleaned and jerked again. On September 13, 1949, John Davis of the United States, who was then the world's heavyweight amateur weight-lifting champion, lifted the car wheels in Paris at the Elysee Montmartre. However, he did not "clean" the bar in the usual manner (by taking an overgrip with both hands), as Rigoulot had done, but had to use *reversed* grips in order to retain his hold on the bar. Pulling the bar up in this manner, he loosed his right hand (supinated) grip in mid-air, catching the bar at the shoulders with both hands in a thumbless grip.

---

*If some of the more noteworthy of Apollon's other feats are to be accepted as factual, it is at least possible that he *could* have cleaned and jerked the 366-pound car wheels. I allude to Apollon's asserted One Hand Swing of five 44-pound block-weights (total: 220 pounds), which was repeated in each of his two-a-day stage performances for five successive days; to his "easy" Clean and Jerk of 341 pounds on a thick-handled barbell to "show" the Rasso Trio what he could do; and to his "near" One Hand Snatch of 226 pounds on a bar 2⅜ inches in diameter.

He succeeded in this maneuver after having failed three times to "clean" the weight in the customary style. He then readily jerked the 365-pound* car wheels overhead. But evidently the effort of raising the bar to the shoulders, even with the reversed grips he employed, was almost too much for Davis, as he suffered a momentary "black-out" after returning (dropping) the weight to the floor.

Following his exhibition of lifting the Apollon weights, Davis (see Plate 71) was roundly criticized by French weightlifting authorities because of his manner of "incorrectly" shouldering the weight. But evidently, because of the small size of his hands, it was a case of Davis's using reversed grips or not getting the weight to the shoulders at all. As his hands measured only 7.1 inches in length by less than 3.5 inches in width, it would appear that Davis performed a highly meritorious feat in raising the Apollon weights even in the style he employed. In comparing his lift with that of Rigoulot's, it should be borne in mind that Rigoulot had distinctly larger hands than Davis, and so had less difficulty in grasping the 2-inch diameter Apollon bar. Even so, he had registered many failures in his efforts to "clean" the Apollon weight. In jerking power, there was little to choose between Davis and Rigoulot. Davis put more pressing power into his jerks, while Rigoulot relied mainly on leg strength and lifting technique (speed).

But there was a *third* lifting of the Apollon car wheels, and on that occasion evidently everyone present was satisfied with the result! The date was October 17, 1954; the place, the gymnasium of Robert Cayeaux, in Lille, France; and the lifter, Norbert Schemansky of the United States lifting team. This group was returning through France from the 1954 World championships that had been held in Vienna just a week before. In those championships, Schemansky had won first place in the heavyweight division, with a new world record total of 1074¼ pounds. In an exhibition at Lille preceding his attempt on the Apollon weight, he had accomplished a sensational Two Hands Clean and Jerk with 425 pounds. So he was in top form for a try at lifting the famous Apollon car wheels. These had been brought from Professor Desbonnet's former gym in Paris to Cayeaux's gym in Lille especially for Schemansky to have a try at the formidable, improvised barbell.

Schemansky proved himself more than equal to the occasion. Employing a regular, thumbs-around overgrip, he "cleaned" the awkward, 365-pound weight with apparent ease, then jerked it from the shoulders *three times in succession.* This was equivalent to jerking 386 or 387 pounds once (on the *same* bar). Evidently Schemansky had no trouble in gripping the 2-inch diameter handle, which was made additionally

---

*Evidently the weight of the Apollon wheels varied on different occasions, as the poundage of them has been variously given as 365, 366, and 367.

difficult because of its being bent at one end, dating from the time John Davis had dropped it. However, whether the apparent ease with which Schemansky had lifted the Apollon weight proved him to be a superior lifter to Rigoulot—who had cleaned and jerked the weight *24 years earlier*—is something that can be estimated only when all the factors involved, including the date of the performance, are properly taken into account.° Just the same, Schemansky's consummate ability in handling the Apollon weight proved him to be a truly great lifter. Right after lifting it, his bodyweight was found to be 223 pounds. His height is 71 inches. For comparison, Charles Rigoulot weighed 225 pounds (probably 210 pounds muscular) at a height of 67.7 inches; and John Davis 215 pounds at a height of 68.5 inches. Douglas Hepburn declared, at the time of his winning the heavyweight amateur world championship in 1953, that if *he* ever had a chance at the Apollon car wheels, he would clean and *press* them!

2. Apollon's "Near-Snatch" of 226 Pounds

This uncompleted lift by Apollon (see above and Plate 3) constituted one of the most extraordinary impromptu demonstrations of grip-strength on record. The way it happened was as follows:

At Prof. Desbonnet's physical culture school in Roubaix, France, there was a thick-handled, unbalanced barbell weighing 102.5 kilos (about 226 pounds). The actual diameter of the handle of the bell was 60 millimeters, or about 2⅜ inches. Up until the time of which I am writing, which was about 1895, only three of the many strong-men who had tried it had been able to lift this barbell off the floor with one hand. These "grip-men" were Léon Sée (65.75 in., 155 lbs.) and E. Vandenocke (66 in., 165 lbs.) of France, and John Grünn Marx (70.9 in., 235 lbs.) of Luxembourg.

One day, Marx was present as Apollon came into the gym. Seeking to have a little fun with Apollon, Marx lifted the thick-handled barbell to a height just above his knees, first with one hand and then with the other, meanwhile slyly remarking that he was the only man who could do this. Apollon, enraged, could hardly wait until Marx had replaced the bell on the floor. Grasping it in the center with his enormous hand, he furiously snatched it to the height of his head! As he made no effort to dip under it, the bell went over his shoulder, slipped from his grasp, and landed with a crash ten feet behind him. The thickness of the bar (2⅜ inches)

°Taking these factors into account, but ignoring the *thickness* of the carwheel's axle, Schemansky's feat of cleaning the carwheels and jerking them three times in succession has a percentage rating of 88.4; while Rigoulot's single lift in the same manner (performed 24 years earlier, and at a lighter muscular bodyweight) rates 91.8 percent.

prevented its being grasped with a "hooked" grip, even if Apollon had deigned to use such an aid. This impromptu feat of Apollon's remains one of the mightiest exhibitions of gripping power ever recorded. To Marx's credit, it should be added that he knew how to get Apollon to make an all-out effort!

3. Louis Cyr's Shot-Loading Dumbbell

Less famous than Apollon's railway car wheels, but still an interesting piece of weightlifting equipment in its own right, is a shot-loading dumb-bell once used by Louis Cyr, "The Canadian Samson," and which is now in the possession of the York (Pa.) Barbell Company. Cyr used this adjustable dumbbell repeatedly, over a period of several years, in making what were then several different world records in putting up a weight from the shoulder overhead with one arm. In shouldering the dumbbell *with one hand,* Cyr used two movements: first lifting the bell onto his belt (belly), then heaving it from there to his shoulder. The lift from the shoulder overhead was not a "side press, with legs stiff,"—as one overenthusiastic biographer of Cyr has described it, but actually was performed by first *jerking* the bell partway overhead and then finishing the lift with a *push.* Cyr's records in this style of lifting were as follows:

Lift	Pounds	Date	Place
Right Hand "Jerk-Push" with Dumbbell,			
2 hands to shoulder	273¼	Jan. 18, 1892	London
Left Hand, ditto	258		
Right Hand, ditto (1 hand to shoulder)	254	May 7, 1896	Chicago

Cyr's shot-loading dumbbell, with which he made the foregoing lifts, weighed when empty 202 pounds (some accounts say 209 pounds). The bell was especially difficult to raise from the ground because of its having a thicker-than-usual handle, the diameter of the handle being about 1⅝ inches. Evidently Cyr came into the possession of this dumbbell in 1889 or earlier, since there is a record of his having put up 265 pounds with it at St. Henri, Quebec, in 1889. At that time, Cyr was 27 years of age.

Probably Cyr's most extraordinary lift with this dumbbell was when, in 1892, he was giving a performance at the Royal Aquarium in London. With the bell loaded to 240 pounds, he had just gotten it to his shoulder, when he heard—or suspected he heard—someone in the invited audience on the stage make a questioning remark. Lowering the bell to his side, he walked over to the man under suspicion and told him to either test the weight of the bell himself or shut up! Cyr then walked back to the center of the stage (during all this time he was carrying the bell at his side), swung the bell again onto his belly and up to his shoulder, and then completed the lift overhead! As the one-time British amateur weightlifting champion, Tom Pevier (who witnessed this exhibition by Cyr), remarked, "One can only imagine the strength required in the arm and hand to allow a weight of 240 pounds to be lowered quietly down in this way."

Since Cyr lifted 273¼ pounds when shouldering this dumbbell with *both* hands, but only 254 pounds when using only *one* hand, it is evident that the latter poundage must have been the limit amount—or close to the limit—that he could raise with one hand from the ground onto his middle. Such a waist-high lift would indicate that Cyr could probably have performed a *One Hand Dead Lift* on this dumbbell with about 400 lbs.

In comparison, few present-day strong-men have been able to dead-lift the Cyr dumbbell loaded even to 230 pounds. Douglas Hepburn in 1952 did a One Hand Dead Lift with this bell when it assertedly weighed 235 pounds, but this may not have been Hepburn's limit. Another Canadian lifter, Joseph Moquin (69 in., 265 pounds), is said to have taken this dumbbell *clean* to the shoulder with one hand and then pressed it "with very little effort" when the bell was empty and weighed 202 pounds. If the "clean" part of this lift was close to Moquin's limit, it would indicate that he could probably have done a One Hand Dead Lift with the bell of from 240 to 250 pounds.

Now, assuming that Cyr could have made a One Hand Dead Lift of 400 pounds (and this is only an assumption on my part) on a 1⅝-inch dumbbell handle, he would on a *2-inch* handle be expected to have been capable of about 340 pounds (see p. 209). And a 2-inch diameter handle would be a better size to use in competition, since no one except a giant of 7 feet or taller would be able, on a 2-inch bar, to use a hooked grip (or "thumb lock"). It would be very interesting if a contest were to be staged at the present time using a 2-inch diameter plain steel bar. The distance between the plates, or the innermost collars, should be sufficiently great (perhaps 6 inches) that no assistance could be gained by pressing the plates or collars with either edge of the hand. Indeed, the ruling should say that the dumbbell must be lifted with the handle *level*, and raised to at least the height of the knees and held there for at least 2 seconds. If such a "grip-lift" contest is ever held, I shall be most interested to know the results. Is there a man in the world today who can do a One Hand Dead Lift of 340 pounds on a 2-inch bar?

4. Thomas Inch's "Unliftable" Dumbbell

Thomas Inch (70 in., 210 pounds) was an English professional strong-man, born in 1881. For some years, with offices in London, he conducted a widespread business in health and muscular development by correspondence. For this, he recommended what is known today as "weight-training." Inch once held British professional records in the Right Hand Bent Press from Shoulder, with 304½ pounds, and the Two Hands Anyhow (change-over style), with 356½ pounds. The Bent Press record was performed in 1913, at Scarborough, England (on the 13th attempt!). The Two Hands Anyhow was done some years later. Inch also did a Right Hand Military Press of 112 pounds, and a "Side Press" of 201 pounds. The latter lift is essentially a Bent Press performed with straight legs, and with the lifting arm kept free of the body.

But Inch's main claim to fame was in his strength of grip, which he had developed over a period of years by special exercises and lifts. By these means he became capable of doing a One Hand Dead Lift of 402 pounds on a 1½-inch, straight bar.* However, his interest had been stimulated in grip-strength long before he made the latter lift, by the following circumstance. Quite by chance, he had come into possession of a heavy, unwieldy, cast-iron dumbbell having a short and thick handle. At first, Inch could not lift this bell off the ground with one hand; but after long, daily practice, he became able to do so. Finding, then, that no one else could lift the bell, he offered increasingly higher amounts, up finally to £200 (then nearly $1000) to anyone who could do so. For over fifty years, it would seem, no one appeared who could lift Inch's "Challenge Dumbbell," as he called it. Finally, Inch himself, passing into his 60s, became unable to lift it.

In 1956, at the annual Aberdeen (Scotland) Sports Revue, the Thomas Inch Challenge Dumbbell was brought onto the stage for all and sundry to have a go at. The bell was then owned by the Reg Park Barbell Company, Ltd. As long as Inch himself had possessed the bell, he had kept all information on its size to himself. (I know, because I once inquired of him concerning it.) But now, the dumbbell was on public view, and upon being measured its dimensions proved as follows: weight, 172 pounds; overall length, 20 inches; diameter of each sphere, 8½ inches; circumference of handle, 7¾ inches (which would make the diameter 2.47 inches); length of handle between spheres, 4 inches. The last-mentioned factor would alone suffice to stop any really large-handed lifter from picking up the bell, since anyone having a hand much wider than 4¾ inches could not get his fingers to fully encircle the handle. As Inch often mentioned that Edward Aston, and even Arthur Saxon, had failed to lift the bell, undoubtedly this was the reason—since both men, according to Inch, had "enormous" hands. Actually, Saxon's hands were

---

*But probably with a hooked grip, although such essential information is hardly ever added.

nearly 4¾ inches wide; so it can be seen why he was "unable" to lift Inch's Challenge Dumbbell. That Saxon's gripping strength was inferior to Inch's is unthinkable.

On the aforementioned occasion, at Aberdeen (October 26, 1956), not one, but *three* contestants each lifted Inch's dumbbell! The first was John Gallagher, a 165-pound weightlifter from Glasgow. Gallagher lifted the 172-pound bell with his right hand almost to knee height. The second man to succeed was a powerful heavyweight from Kintore, named Douglas Cameron. He, like Gallagher, raised the bell approximately to knee height, when it slipped from his grasp and crashed to the floor. Next, the well-known Scottish Games athlete, Henry Gray, was called out from the audience and asked to make a try. Gray, a big, rangy fellow standing 6 ft. 4 in. and weighing 252 pounds, was already somewhat of a celebrity from having lifted and carried the famous Dinnie stones (see below). Grasping the handle of the Inch dumbbell, Gray pulled it *chest high*! If only he had known how to turn the bell over, he could have "cleaned" it. But whether he could then have gotten the bell from the shoulder to arm's length overhead is a question. Gray was known also as one of the two or three men ever to toss the famous Braemar caber, which was 19 ft. in length and weighed close to 120 pounds.

During the course of bringing the aforementioned dumbbell into the limelight, it developed that there was a *second* Inch dumbbell, somewhat smaller than the "number one," and weighing 153 pounds. It also had a 2½-inch handle. This dumbbell is said to be (or to have been, in 1956) owned by a Welsh amateur lifter named Tom Fenton, who was formerly a pupil of Inch's.*

On a later occasion, at the "Mr. Universe" competition in London in 1957, the 153-pound Inch Challenge Dumbbell no. 2 was successfully lifted knee-high both by John Gallagher of Scotland, and Jacobus Jacobs (6 ft. 2 in., 230 pounds) of Capetown, South Africa. It was then announced that *this* dumbbell had previously been lifted *only* by Thomas Inch during the past 52 years. Another lifter (not at the "Mr. Universe" show) who was able to lift Inch's 153-pound bell knee-high was Hubert Thomas, of Wales.

The merits of the foregoing liftings of the Inch Dumbbells as compared with those made on *other* thick-handled barbells and dumbbells, by other strong-men, are discussed below.

5. The Dinnie Stones

Every nation, at a given time, has its athletic idol; and the idol of

---

*The statistics on the two Inch dumbbells, and on the competition held at Aberdeen, were kindly furnished to me by David Webster, of Glasgow, who was M.C. at the show.

Scotland a hundred years ago was a versatile superman named Donald Dinnie.

This remarkable all-around athlete was born on July 8, 1837, at Blanacraig, near Aboyne, Aberdeenshire. He came into his prime in the 1860s and '70s, long before Sandow, Cyr, and Apollon were heard of and before the modern "strong-man" boom was fairly started. Dinnie as a young man was a handsome fellow (see Plate 27) 6 ft. ½ in. tall and with muscles of exceptional quality and power. In his athletic prime he weighed about 218 pounds, thus being about the same height and weight as was Jim Jeffries, the onetime heavyweight boxing champion. But while there is no mention of Dinnie's ever having been a boxer, it would appear that he tried his hand at nearly every other athletic sport. The measure of Dinnie's prowess may be appreciated from the fact that during his long career as a Highland Games' athlete and as a professional wrestler he was the recipient of over 100 medals and won no fewer than 7500 cash prizes totalling over $100,000! He was also the winner in more than 200 weightlifting contests. Dinnie was ideally proportioned for a big man, combining great strength with exceptional speed, agility, and endurance. His long career before the public extended from 1853 (when he was 16) to 1900 (when he was 63!)—a record perhaps unequalled by that of any other athlete of any era.

Here is an example of how strong Dinnie was in a simple feat of lifting and carrying. This information was kindly furnished to me by David Webster of Glasgow, a famous strand-pulling expert and an authority on Donald Dinnie. Outside the hotel in Potarch, Scotland, are two large and heavy boulders which used to be used in tethering horses (while their masters went into the hotel to refresh themselves). One of the boulders weighs 340 pounds and the other 445. In the top of each weight is fastened a ring made of ½-inch round iron and just large enough to grip with one hand. Few men can lift even the smaller of these stones off the ground with one hand. The story is that Dinnie's father was able to lift the 445-pound stone onto a wall 3½ feet high and that Dinnie himself carried both stones (one in front of him and the other behind) a distance of five or six yards. On October 29, 1954, a contest was held by the Spartan Physical Culture Club in the Music Hall at Aberdeen, with a prize of £20 offered to anyone who could carry with one hand the 340-pound "Dinnie steen" a distance of 20 yards. No one succeeded in covering this distance, but the prize was given to Henry Gray, who carried it 18 yards before his grip gave out. This young and powerful athlete could not pick up the 445-pound stone with one hand, let alone carry it! I understand, however, that the latter stone *was* lifted off the ground by John Gallagher, the Scottish Dead Lift record holder and a man known to have a very strong grip.

More recently, in 1964, Dave Prowse (6 ft. 7 in., 273 lbs.), then the British heavyweight Olympic champion weightlifter, succeeded repeatedly in lifting the two Dinnie stones together—a total weight of 785 pounds. However, in order for his grips to hold, Prowse had to use lifting-straps, which ran around his wrists and attached to the handles on the stones (see Plate 28).

To refer once more to Donald Dinnie—this time to his *continuing* strength—it is said that even when 75 years of age he could still muscle-out a 56-pound weight on one hand!

F. "MR. AMERICA" TITLE-HOLDERS

If the term super-athletes is taken to include all men whose muscular development, strength, and agility is far beyond that of the average athlete, the various holders of the annual "Mr. America" title, must be given mention. This is equally true of the winners in the annual "Mr. Universe" contest—as well as lesser contests of a local or regional title— which must be bypassed here because of limitations of space.

It is still a common misconception—among persons who have not looked into the matter*—that title-holders and contestants of the "Mr. America" type are simply a group of slow-thinking, "muscle-bound" mirror athletes, whose muscles are useless in any "practical" test (the favorite of which seems to be boxing). While this summary misinterpretation of a splendid group of athletes should be dismissed as so much "sour grapes," let us take a critical look at a few of the "Mr. Americas" listed in the adjoining table.

The first "Mr. America," Bert Goodrich, used to come to my gymnasium in Los Angeles to work out. This was in 1928, when Bert was 21. He and his partner were then training for a handbalancing act in vaudeville. Goodrich in due course became one of the most capable "understanders" (supporters) in that profession. In addition to his gymnastic ability, he was equally capable in track and field. When weighing over 200 pounds, he could run the 100 in 10 seconds flat, and at a lighter bodyweight once ran it in 9.8. His best time for 220 yards was even more remarkable, 21.4 seconds, and he put the 16-pound shot 47 feet. He was so capable in boxing that he was offered an attractive contract, but took an offer in vaudeville (handbalancing) in preference to it. In 1928, when I measured him (at 190 pounds), Goodrich had a truly classical figure, with muscles that were certainly as "practical" as they were handsome.

Frank Leight, "Mr. America" of 1942, holds (or held) the world record in the sit-up, or Abdominal Raise. In 1942, he sat up (with his feet held

---

*The philosopher Herbert Spencer considered one of mankind's worst evils to be the principle of "condemnation prior to investigation."

down, of course) while holding behind his neck a barbell of 154½ pounds! He also made a remarkable record in a repetition Two Hands Press by pressing a 150-pound barbell 35 *times in succession*. As to his "practical" physical ability, Leight was for several years a police officer in New York City!

Steve Stanko, "Mr. America" of 1944, was one of the greatest amateur weightlifters ever produced in this country. He was the National heavy-weight lifting champion in 1938, 1939, and 1940. He was the first lifter in the world to total over 1000 pounds in the three Olympic lifts, ac-complishing this epochal feat in 1941 with a Press of 310½ pounds, a Snatch of 310½ pounds, and a Clean and Jerk of 381 pounds—a total of 1002 pounds. The ability to perform the three Olympic lifts with the poundages that Stanko was accustomed to handle denotes a "Super-athlete" in the fullest sense of the word. Stanko was also a "Mr. Universe" (in fact, the *first*, in 1947).

Space here forbids a mention of all the other men who have won the title "Mr. America." Steve Reeves became a motion picture actor, starring in a series of Italian-produced films, including *Hercules, The Giant of Marathon,* and others of that type. George Eiferman and Jack Delinger were all-around strength athletes, some of whose feats are mentioned later in this book. Harry Johnson became a "Mr. America" at the age of 35—a testimonial to his enduring physical fitness. Val Vasilieff has performed a correct Two Hands Curl of 220 pounds, a Press of 315 pounds, a Snatch of 270 pounds, a Clean and Jerk of 360 pounds, a Bench Press of 450 pounds, and a Two Hands Dead Lift of 600 pounds. No man can perform all the foregoing lifts—or even a Curl of 220 pounds and a Clean and Jerk of 360 pounds—without possessing tremendous strength combined with speed and agility. This combination of qualities is indispensable toward even reaching the finals in a present-day "Mr. America" contest, let alone emerging as the winner. And the "stiffness" of the competition itself becomes greater year by year!

As will be seen in Table 8, the majority of the holders of the "Mr. America" title conform fairly closely in height and weight, although there is a wide range in these measurements when the smallest and largest individuals are compared. The height ranges from 66 to 73 inches, with the typical value being 70 inches. The bodyweight, as would be expected, shows a proportionately greater variability, ranging from 168 to 223 pounds. The average weight is 200 pounds. The Weight/Height, or bodyweight per inch of height, is an index of the general muscular cross-section (relative girth, squared) of the body. It shows that the smallest-muscled "Mr. America" was Jules Bacon (1943); and the two largest-muscled were Steve Stanko (1944) and John Grimek (1941). The average Weight/Height is about 2.857. With

Table 8. "Mr. America" Title-Holders

Year	Name	Height, In.	Bodyweight, lbs.	Weight Height
1939	Bert Goodrich	70.5	195	2.766
1939	Roland Essmaker	71.0	180	2.535
1940	John Grimek	68.5	183	2.671
1941	John Grimek	68.5	221	3.226
1942	Frank Leight	71.2	209	2.935
1943	Jules Bacon	68.0	168	2.471
1944	Steve Stanko	71.5	223	3.119
1945	Clarence Ross	69.5	192	2.763
1946	Alan Stephan	71.5	205	2.867
1947	Steve Reeves	73.0	192	2.630
1948	George Eiferman	67.5	195	2.889
1949	Jack Delinger	67.0	195	2.910
1950	John Farbotnik	69.0	195	2.826
1951	Roy Hilligenn	66.0	178	2.697
1952	Jim Park	69.6	185	2.658
1953	Bill Pearl	71.0	201	2.831
1954	Dick Dubois	73.0	215	2.945
1955	Steve Klisanin	70.0	185	2.643
1956	Ray Schaefer	70.5	210	2.979
1957	Ron Lacy	68.5	185	2.701
1958	Tom Sansone	71.0	212	2.986
1959	Harry Johnson	69.0	186	2.695
1960	Lloyd Lerille	66.0	185	2.803
1961	Ray Routledge	72.0	210	2.917
1962	Joe Abbenda	72.0	200	2.778
1963	Vern Weaver	69.5	205	2.950
1964	Val Vasilieff	71.0	212	2.986
1965	Jerry Daniels	72.0	220	3.055
1966	Bob Gajda	69.0	195	2.826
1967	Dennis Tinerino	72.0	220	3.055
1968	Jim Haislop	71.0	220	3.099
1969	Boyer Coe	69.0	210	3.043
	Average (32)	70.0	200	2.857
	Range	66-73	168-223	2.47-3.23

a height of 70 inches, and a bodyweight of 200 pounds, the girths are about as follows: neck, 17.4 inches; biceps (average of right and left sides), 17.3; forearms, 13.6; wrists, 7.5; chest (normal), 47.7; waist (normal, *not* retracted), 31.9; hips, 39.8; thighs, 24.9; knees, 15.6; calves, 16.5; ankles, 9.3; shoulder breadth (bideltoid), 22.0. The outstanding distinctions of this physique are the relatively small hips, very small waist, large upper arms and chest, and proportionately even greater breadth of shoulders. Because of the neck being hardly any larger than the flexed upper arms, it is appreciably too small for the chest. Actually, the "Mr. America" physique is markedly specialized in its proportions, and is attainable only by those whose natural skeletal proportions make possible a very small yet muscular waist in combination with a huge chest and broad shoulders. Such a small Waist/Chest ratio is not necessarily ideal; otherwise the muscular yet relatively large waists of models such as Sandow, Al Treloar, Siegmund Klein, Hermann Görner, and many others would have to be labelled too large.

While the title "Mr. America," in reference to the winner of a physique contest, was not conceived and introduced until 1939, it should be noted that a number of such contests had been held in this country in earlier years. Noteworthy were those sponsored by Bernarr Macfadden, the publisher of *Physical Culture* magazine, in 1900, 1903, 1915, 1920 and 1921.

In having mentioned above Al Treloar, perhaps a few additional words about this famous professional athlete will not be out of place. In one sense, he can be considered as having been the real *first* "Mr. America" (even though such a title was not then in vogue), because of his winning of first place in the "open" physique contest sponsored by Bernarr Macfadden in New York City in December, 1903. The adjoining photograph (Plate 27) shows how Treloar looked shortly after winning the contest. His height was 70.5 inches and his weight 186 pounds. Despite being less heavily muscled than recent "Mr. Americas," he was all-around strong-man. In addition, either in college (Harvard) or afterward, he was a track athlete, oarsman, wrestler, tumbler, gymnast, and juggler—in short, a super-athlete. By reason of this athletic versatility—plus the more important ability of being able to impart his knowledge to others—Treloar in 1907 became Physical Director of the Los Angeles Athletic Club and held that position continuously until 1949, a period of 42 years! Meanwhile—due in no small measure to his own ability as an instructor—he had the satisfaction of seeing the LAAC become one of the world's greatest athletic establishments.

5.

Miscellaneous Feats of Strength and Endurance

NOTE: "Records" that come under this heading are so numerous that only the more outstanding of them can be listed here. The accounts of these performances have, in most cases, been extracted or summarized from magazines such as *Iron Man, Strength and Health, Physical Culture, Health and Strength* (London), and various old annuals and almanacs in which such "records" are listed. In some instances, the accounts have been copied direct from news dispatches; and in hardly any of these accounts has an effort been made to "track down" their reliability. Accordingly, no responsibility can be assumed here for the authenticity of the performances quoted. It would appear that the great majority of them are factual, although in some cases possibly exaggerated (or mis-described) to a certain degree. No order or systematic arrangement of the various feats has been attempted, as they are obviously too diversified for this to be done. The *order* in which the individual performances are listed does not necessarily indicate their respective merits.

A. SHOULDERING, CARRYING, SUPPORTING, AND CLIMBING (WITH EXTRA WEIGHT)

These feats are among the most "natural" and elementary ones—such as would occur to ordinary workmen and non-athletes—and require a minimum of skill. They test the overall strength of the body—especially the back and legs—and in most cases require exceptional organic power and stamina as well as immediate muscular strength. Accordingly, in the majority of these feats the performer has been a *heavyweight*.

1. Arthur Dandurand (68 in., 185 pounds), a French-Canadian professional strong-man, active in Montreal during the 1920s, was able to shoulder unassisted a Ford automobile engine weighing 455 pounds, walk with it a distance of 84 feet, and lower it onto a table. He could

Trotting while carrying over 400 lbs. (Drawing by Clyde James Newman)

also shoulder a barrel of beer weighing 500 pounds, or lift (from the ground?) a railroad rail weighing 780 pounds.

2. Ian "Mac" Batchelor (74 in., 300 lbs.) shouldered (by tilting over) a telephone power pole 40 feet long, weighing (estimated) 700 to 800 pounds, and walked with it for over 300 feet before heaving it off his shoulder. This feat was witnessed by a group of employees of the Pacific Telephone Company in 1948, in Los Angeles. On another occasion, on a movie studio lot, Batchelor carried on his back a small horse weighing 600–700 pounds, walked 20 feet with it, then carried the animal up a steel ladder 16 feet high.

3. Horace Barré (69 in., 275–320 lbs.), a French-Canadian professional strong-man, is said to have once shouldered (tilted over) an enormous barbell weighing 1270 pounds, and to have walked with it about 50 feet. This was in 1896, when Barré was training in Louis Attila's gymnasium on 28th Street in New York City. This claimed feat has never been authenticated. However, in view of Hermann Görner's 1104½-pound carrying feat in the same manner (see no. 4, following), it just might have been possible.

4. Hermann Görner (72.5 in., 220 lbs.), the famous German professional strong-man, carried strapped to his back a grand piano weighing

1444 pounds a distance of 52½ feet. Leipzig, June 3, 1921. Another carrying feat by Görner was to stack 100 bricks into a special hod, and carry the load on his shoulders up the staircase of a piano factory. Leipzig, May 10, 1912. The bricks used each measured 10¼ in. long by 5⅜ in. wide by 2 9/16 in. thick, and weighed 4 kilos or 8.82 pounds. The entire load of bricks plus the hod weighed 1124½ pounds. Carrying a weight on one shoulder only, Görner walked the length of a circus arena with a load of 1104½ pounds. The load was made up of two barrels connected by a special bar. On each barrel sat two men. This feat was performed by Görner during every show, in Pagel's Circus, Capetown, South Africa, 1935.

5. William Pagel (71.3 in., 238 pounds) was a circus proprietor and strong-man in Australia and South Africa about the turn of the century. One of his most spectacular exhibition feats was to carry a horse (said to weigh about 1000 pounds) up two vertical ladders about 12 feet high. The rungs of each ladder were about 9 inches apart, and Pagel would stand between them and mount the ladders to a height of about 9 feet (12 steps) by raising one foot on each ladder, alternately, meanwhile bracing his hands on the rungs. The horse that he carried was suspended from a harness which fit over Pagel's neck and around his waist. The strong-man would slowly climb the two ladders and then come down in the same manner. (See Plate 28). Another of Pagel's feats was to resist the pull of *two pairs* of horses pulling in opposite directions against his arms, in the manner employed earlier by Louis Cyr (see Plate 4).

6. William Carr (76 in., 336 pounds), of Blyth, England, in 1798 is said to have carried on his shoulders an anchor weighing *1120 pounds* for a distance of *half a mile*. If true, this would appear to be the greatest feat of carrying ever performed.

7. Hugo Lauffer, a railway porter in Vienna, carried two pieces of luggage, weighing together 132 pounds, from Vienna to Paris, a distance of 750 miles, in 25 days. Lauffer, it may be presumed, had a full night's rest between each day's 30-mile walk with the luggage.

8. A porter in Cairo, aged 42, was credited with carrying a piano over a mountainous goat-path several miles long. The piano, an upright grand, was said to weigh about 6 hundredweight (about 672 pounds). The porter carried it strapped to his back, with one of the straps passing around his forehead. This feat was performed sometime in the 1920s.

9. William Cahill of Portland, Oregon, when only 17 years of age, carried across his shoulders a sack of sand weighing 125 pounds for a distance of 26½ miles without resting, on September 30, 1943. The time required was 8 hours, 45 minutes.

10. Around about 1910, a contest was held to determine who could carry a barrel of salt (about 300 lbs.) the greatest distance. There were about 30 competitors. The winner was a French-Canadian named Oulette (75 in., 215 pounds), who carried a barrel a distance of 5 miles, 352 yards. He could have carried it farther, but did not have to, as all the other contestants had given up at shorter distances.

11. Elzear Bacon (74 in., 320 pounds), of Montreal, Quebec, could walk a distance of 30 feet while carrying on *one shoulder* a beam of lumber weighing 1003 pounds. This was in early 1955.

12. Julius Cochard (70.9 in., 200 pounds), an early-day French professional strong-man, won a sack-carrying contest by carrying on his shoulders a sack weighing 220 pounds while walking from Paris to Reims, a distance of about 112 miles. Cochard covered the distance in 166 hours, which included six nights of rest; even so, it was a gruelling task.

13. Giovanni Battista Belzoni, who lived from 1778 to 1823, was an Italian archeologist who for a time found it necessary to support himself by being a professional strong-man! He was of gigantic proportions, standing over 6 feet 6 inches and weighing nearly 300 pounds; and evidently he possessed great natural strength. One of his stage feats was to support on his shoulders an iron frame with steps projecting from its sides, on which stood *eleven* men. The total load was over 1700 pounds; yet with it Belzoni was said to have "walked easily around the stage." Even to have *shuffled* across the stage, keeping the legs straight, with such a load, would have been a tremendous feat.

14. Cripus Maltese (68 in., 230 pounds) was a Sicilian of great natural strength who followed the occupation of longshoreman and lived in Brooklyn, New York. On one occasion, within the space of 30 minutes, he carried 35 barrels each weighing 250 pounds up three flights of stairs. At another time he lifted 50 heavy wine barrels onto a truck. He was able to shoulder (tilt over) a 1600-pound anchor. These and other feats he performed either in his daily work or to entertain his friends. The date was about 1913.

15. James Welsch, of Tweedhopefoot, Scotland, was known as "The Scottish Giant." One of his feats was to carry, strapped to his back, a load of flour weighing 280 pounds for a distance of 24 miles, during which he rested only once.

16. "Maciste" (Bartelomeo Pagano; 70 in., 240 pounds), an Italian movie strong-man of the silent screen days, once carried a heavy field piece on his shoulders up a mountainside of the Alps during World War I.

17. "Klondike Mike" (Michael Ambrose) Mahoney (74 in., 200 pounds) carried a small (150-pound?) piano, strapped to his back, over the Chilkoot Pass, Alaska, from the 2300-foot level to the summit (3500 ft.), a distance of about ⅛ mile, with four short rests (February 1898). But a number of gold-miners are said to have each carried anywhere from 300 pounds to 400 pounds in *gold* over the same pass. They would certainly have had an incentive!

18. Jean Pocette, a French-Canadian guide, of Noranda, Quebec, carried 880 pounds on his back a distance of 100 yards, *c.* 1960. Pocette was the champion in the yearly contest known as "Tump-line" carrying. The "tump-line" is a strong leather or fabric strap which is passed across the forehead and fastened at the back of the load being carried. This procedure helps stabilize the load. Pocette could also stand *erect*, but without walking, with a 1200-pound "tump-line" load.

19. Some years ago, in Paris, a wheelbarrow contest was held annually. A course 20 meters (about 66 feet) long and up a slight grade was marked out. A heavy wheelbarrow was loaded up to 500 kilos (about 1100 pounds) to start with. After all the competitors had wheeled this load up the grade, another 50 kilos (110 pounds) was added. The winners usually managed to wheel about 800 kilos (1760 pounds). Whether this event is still being held, I do not know. Using probably a different type of wheelbarrow, Arthur Dandurand of Montreal (see no. 1, above) wheeled a load of lead ingots, weighing 4300 pounds, a distance of 23 feet. This feat was performed in contests at St. Hyacinth Park and at Sohmer Park, Montreal, 1908. Another of Dandurand's feats was to carry a barbell weighing 400 pounds at arm's length overhead on one hand, a distance of 30 steps. (See also no. 46, below).

20. Away back in 1793, Gustave Rehard, chief of a band of thugs in Lons, France, broke up a fight between two members of his gang, who were duelling with knives atop a billiard table. Rehard got beneath

the table, lifted it on his shoulders and carried it, along with the struggling highwaymen, a distance of 20 feet.

21. An old-time Birmingham (England) lightweight (?) strong-man, who took professionally the name of H. Paolias, in his stage act used to lift from the floor onto the top of his head a sofa weighing perhaps 100 pounds on top of which reclined his wife (c. 125 pounds?). This—in contrast to lifting a barbell—was a feat that the entire audience could appreciate.

22. "Milo" (Luigi Borra), a top-notch middleweight Italian strong-man, wrestler, and balancer of the 1890s, was said to have been able to cross the stage while carrying a barbell and men on his shoulders, totalling 1100 pounds (London, 1892).

23. Possibly the greatest poundage ever to be *supported* on the shoulders was that held up by Hermann Görner during his circus performances in the 1920s and 1930s. This, a load of approximately 4000 pounds, consisted of a heavy wooden bridge over which was driven an automobile and six passengers. Görner formed the support of one end of the bridge, which rested on his shoulders as he stood erect. As the car moved over the bridge, Görner supported momentarily perhaps as much as 2500 pounds. Another spectacular supporting feat performed by Görner was to support on the soles of his feet, while lying on his back, a heavy plank on which were seated as many as 24 men. His record in this feat was 4123 pounds, which he did as one of his regular circus performances in London, on October 12, 1927.

24. Arthur Saxon in his stage and circus acts made a regular feature of supporting a plank and men on the soles of his feet. His heaviest support in this manner was 3200 pounds, which he did in 1907.

25. Joseph Mongelli (65 in., 155 pounds), of Astoria, Long Island, an ice-man by profession, but also a strong-man, could perform the following feats of carrying: (1) with a 325-pound block of ice on his back, walk up three flights of stairs, or walk eight city blocks; (2) with the same block of ice perform three deep knee bends; (3) with the 325 pounds on his back, and carrying (with tongs) 120 pounds of ice in his right hand and 60 pounds in his left hand, walk one block with the entire load of 505 pounds. In supporting the 325-pound block of ice on his back, Mongelli did not grasp the ice-tongs, but kept them in place by pushing steadily on one of the handles with the side of his head!

26. Noah Young (71 in., 208 pounds) *ran* a mile in 8½ minutes while carrying a 150-pound man on his back. This was on the 1/10-mile track in the gym of the Los Angeles Athletic Club, February 23, 1915.

27. Joe Nordquest (67.5 in., 190 pounds), a weightlifter with one artificial leg, *hopped* a half-mile on his good leg on the beach at Ashtabula, Ohio, 1917.

28. Norman Perdue, a professional hand-to-hand balancer, carried his wife, sitting on his shoulders, from the ground level to the top story of the Empire State Building, New York City, a height of 102 stories or over 2000 upward steps. However, this feat, remarkable though it was, is far outclassed by the porters of Tai Shan, China, who in one locality carry human beings (paying guests!) in chairs strapped to their backs up a mountainside flight of 6700 steps! Some of these porters are said to be able to *trot* up the steps!

29. Leon Avazian of New York City ran up the stairs to the top of the Woolworth Building—a height of 55 stories or 1520 steps—in 9 minutes. (*c.* 1927?). In 1921, Howard Roome, a Yale football star, had similarly run up the 44 flights of stairs of the Equitable Building, New York City, in 8 minutes 51 2/5 seconds.

30. In earlier days, the trade in tea between West China and Tibet was carried on solely by human carriers. This procedure still continues to a certain extent, since no vehicular transportation can compete with the low cost of human labor. The carrier's outfit consists of a framework fitted to his back, along with a sturdy pole on which to rest, having a grooved T-shaped top into which the carrier sets the framework, thus making it unnecessary to put the load down. Usually a stop is made every hundred yards or so. A supply of straw sandals protects the feet and prevents slipping. The packages of tea, which average about 25 pounds each, are bound to the back frame up to a total load, in some cases, of 400 pounds. This load is carried, on the average, about 12 miles, over difficult and rarely level roads and paths. In another part of China—between the packinghouse at Yaan and the market in Kangting—tea farmers plod the 150-mile distance while carrying usually a load of about 220 pounds, but sometimes as heavy as 400 pounds. This trip is covered in from 20 to 22 days, the carriers thus averaging only about seven miles a day. While walking this distance, each man stops and rests about 120 times. As recently as 1945, each of these tea-carriers was paid only about 23 cents a day!

31. Thomas Topham, the famous English strong-man of the early 18th century, (see chapter 3), is said to have *run* (jogged) a half-mile while carrying on one shoulder a keg of nails weighing "about three hundred-weight" (336 pounds).

32. Ben Butler (178 pounds), a strongman-wrestler of Waterville, Maine, could walk (shuffle?) 40 steps while carrying on his shoulders a load of 1000 pounds (1950). On this basis, the *strongest* super-heavyweight should be able to "walk" 40 steps with about 1680 pounds on his shoulders.

33. J. C. Tolson (65.5 in., 159 pounds), a British professional strong-man and physical instructor, by training three months (sometime in the 1930s) especially for the feat, was able to carry on his shoulders a special bar with *eight men* (four on each side) hanging from it. The weight of the eight men, without the bar, was 1138 pounds. With this load on his shoulders, Tolson "walked" (shuffled?) twice around the clubroom without a rest. This was an extraordinary feat for a middle-weight.

34. The army physical instructor at Woolwich, England, in 1901, was Sergeant Hawthorne. He was regarded as one of the strongest men in the entire British forces. One of his feats was to support on one shoulder a gun (without its carriage) weighing 400 pounds, and to maintain it in that position while it was fired and against its recoil.

35. A market "carrier" in Paris, to qualify for the job, at one time was required to *run* 200 meters while carrying 200 kilos (about 440 pounds) on his head! Some of these market porters are able to carry two carcasses of beef on their shoulders at one time—a load of from 800 to 1000 pounds—and to walk with the load for a distance of several hundred feet (cf. item no. 49, following).

36. Rama Murti Naidu (67 in., 195 pounds) was a professional strong-man of Madras, India, who was known as "The Indian Hercules." He could support momentarily a 7000-pound elephant on a cushioned plank across his recumbent body (*c.* 1910). The author who reported this performance said that Naidu actually appeared to flatten out under the tremendous weight, but after the elephant had passed over, immediately stood up and bowed to the crowd of 2000 spectators, who cheered wildly.

37. The professional acrobats of Arabia have long been known for their proficiency in tumbling and pyramid-building. In the latter event they often build up to *five high*, each man standing on the shoulders of one or more below him, with the entire pyramid consisting of as many as 24 men. But sometimes the bottom man supports *all the rest* of the troupe; and it has been known for one man to support (but not carry) 14 others, a total load of perhaps 1800 to 1900 pounds. Naturally, during this feat, the bottom man must keep his legs completely straight (see also section "R" below).

38. Ole Petersen, aged 22 (74.5 in.), of Auburn, Wisconsin, was said to have carried two sacks of salt, *one under each arm*, up a steep flight of steps 8 feet high, and returned down the steps with them. Each sack weighed 330 pounds, making a total of 660 pounds.

39. Anton Riha of Bohemia *supported* 1400 pounds of miscellaneous weights in a standing position. A drawing of him shown doing this appears in Plate 28. It is doubtful if he attempted to move, even shuffle, with this load. The placing of so many of the weights below the shoulder level made the supporting of them much easier on the back. Another Austrian strong-man, B. Stein of Vienna, made a then-record on September 8, 1891 by similarly supporting 2000 pounds. The record today would appear to be that made by Hermann Görner (see no. 23, above).

40. In the latter part of 1905, a stair-climbing contest was held in the Eiffel Tower. There, 300 competitors assembled to climb the 729 steps up the long, winding staircase leading to the second platform, which is 373 feet high. All wore rubber-soled shoes, as the weather was wet. The winner, a man named Forestier, reached the top in 3 minutes, 12 seconds.

41. In the year 1798 a boy was born in North Carolina who, when he attained his full size, turned out to be the largest human being on record up to that time. His name was Miles Darden. He stood 7 feet 6 inches in height and weighed 1020 pounds. While he could not have been called a "strong-man" in the usual sense of the words— let alone a "super-athlete"—he *must* have been very strong even to have moved. When he walked, he would be carrying a load of about 850 pounds heavier than a man of ordinary size has to carry. Darden's chest measured well over 80 inches, and he had perhaps the most powerful pair of lungs of any man who ever lived. This was demonstrated whenever he engaged in a spell of hog-calling, at which time his tremendous voice could be heard for miles through the hills.

42. Oom Cornelis Joubert was a "natural" strong-man of South Africa whose feats are there becoming legendary. He died in Volksrust in 1949 at the age of 97. Once, angered by an unruly horse, he struck the animal between the eyes with his bare fist. The horse dropped dead! He was warned never to strike a man. As a young man, Joubert took part in several African wars. Although he was wounded repeatedly, he always refused anesthetics and endured in silence the removal of bullets and spearheads from his body and limbs. He claimed that his most difficult feat was performed during the Boer War (1899) when, in order to remove his sick wife from the path of advancing British troops, he carried her two miles over rough terrain atop a mattress on his back. While the combined weight of his wife and the mattress was only about 200 pounds, Joubert had to carry the load the entire two miles in a bent-over position.

43. In 1958, a stone-raising and carrying contest was held in Boise, Idaho, among the Basque residents of that state. In walking with weights, Juan Uberuaga carried two 103-pound stones equipped with handles a distance of 240 yards. In a rock-tossing contest, Martin Idoeta won by tossing a 105-pound stone a distance of 10 ft. 11 in. In shouldering a 235-pound "stone" (actually a concrete pipe 18 inches in diameter and about 3 feet long), Jose Maruri won by lifting the pipe to his shoulders 13 times in less than 4 minutes. Whether this Basque stone-lifting contest is an annual event in Boise, I do not know.

44. Olinto Ancilloti, an old-time Italian professional strong-man, devised a supporting feat of a gymnastic nature that made him a sensation with his audiences. *Hanging by his knees* from supports attached to a trapeze, he would support either a horse or an ox by means of a sling under the animal's belly to which a harness around Ancilloti's body was attached.

45. Ralph Robbins, of Detroit, Michigan, supported a 525-pound barbell at his shoulder on one hand (*c.* 1950).

46. George Lurich (69.3 in., 187 pounds), the famous old-time Russian wrestler and strong-man, in one of the features of his stage act supported 5 *men* (a total weight of over 700 pounds) on his upraised right hand. Part of the weight rested on his shoulders. With this load, he would "walk" across the stage (1902). (See also no. 19, above.)

47. The German professional strong-man, Arthur Saxon (69.6 in., 200 pounds), who had relatively enormous hands, was a wonder at

handling and supporting heavy, thick-handled barbells with one hand. One of his feats was to bent-press two men seated in a sling—the total weight of which was 314 pounds—then "toss" this weight from his right hand to his left hand overhead! New York City, 1909.

48. Although there were many capable athletes in the Revolutionary War (George Washington was himself a champion broad-jumper and a first-class wrestler), perhaps the strongest man in the entire Continental army was a gigantic Virginian named Peter Francisco (78 in. and 260 pounds at the age of 16!). While fighting with the American forces, and during an emergency, he carried a 1200-pound cannon on his shoulders "a considerable distance."

49. Aloysius Marx (68.3 in., 230 pounds), a German professional strongman who "discovered" the great Luxembourger, John Grünn, and with him formed the act known as the "Brothers Marx" was himself possessed of great natural strength. On April 17, 1890, at the P.A.T. Club in St. Louis, he "marched" with a weight of 1065 pounds on his shoulders; this consisted of a barbell of 265 pounds and three heavy men.

50. In the early 1900s, in Wainwright, Alberta, Canada, there was a railroad construction supervisor named Daniel Dempster. While his physique was nothing unusual (74 in., *c.* 180 pounds), his strength was astonishing. On one occasion, becoming impatient with a group of workmen who were taking too long to carry a 30-foot rail to the point of construction, Dempster walked up, grasped the rail at the middle, ordered the workmen to let go, and carried the rail alone to the track. The rail, which was of the common size known as 80 lb. (the weight per yard), weighed 800 pounds!

51. Jack Fasig, who in the 1920s and 1930s was known as the "Monster of Manheim" (after his home town in Pennsylvania), stood 6 feet 11 inches, weighed 362 pounds, and evidently was a phenomenon of natural strength. One of his regular chores, which he performed once or twice a month, was to walk three miles from his farm to a feed mill, where he would buy two 100-pound sacks of scratch feed for his game chickens. He would then walk back to his farm carrying a sack "under each arm." His neighbors along the way would engage him in conversation in order to see how long he would stand talking before putting down his two sacks. The record claimed by one friend of Fasig's was 27 minutes! Fasig was also credited with being able to lift overhead one of the 100-pound sacks of grain 40 times in succession with either

hand. If true, this was most extraordinary. Fasig tried his hand both at boxing and wrestling. Although he had no skill in either, his sheer strength was so overpowering that none of his opponents in either sport cared to meet him a second time.

52. In the exhibition supporting feat known as "The Tomb of Hercules" (for illustration, see Lionel Strongfort in his "Human Bridge" act, Plate 9), Hjalmar Lundin (210 lbs.), a Swedish professional strong-man and wrestler, would regularly support about 4000 pounds. For this, he would use 20 heavy roustabouts from the circus, who sat, 10 on a side, on a "see-saw" plank over 20 feet in length. At one of his performances he had both of his arms broken when the load came down on him (*c.* 1900). Lundin could also *support*, but not walk with, a weight of 1500 pounds on his shoulders.

53. The German strength-statistician, Theodor Siebert, writing in the periodical *Athletik* in 1927 (p. 844), tells of Greek fishermen who regularly carry on their backs loads ranging from 400 to 800 pounds. The diet of these men consists mainly of rye bread, grapes, raisins, and figs. In Smyrna (now Izmir), Turkey's Asiatic seaport, one porter carried on his back a load composed of a barrel of sugar weighing 400 pounds, plus two sacks of coffee weighing 200 pounds each—a total of 800 pounds—a distance of 100 "steps" from his house to the wharf. The usual load carried by the porters in Izmir is 560 pounds and frequently 840 pounds is seen. On one occasion one of the strongest porters carried three sacks of coffee weighing together 960 pounds. The Turkish porters in Constantinople (now Istanbul) used to carry regularly 600 pounds, sometimes at a *trot*, and some of the strongest porters carried 800 pounds.

54. In "sprinting" while carrying extra weight, the German strong-man Hermann Görner, in 1912 while still an amateur (he then stood 72.5 inches and weighed about 208 pounds), covered 100 meters (109.36 yards) in 18.4 seconds while carrying 220½ pounds (a 110¼-pound kettlebell in each hand). This, in some quarters, was hailed as an extraordinary feat of combined strength and activity. However, some years earlier, Gustave Fristensky (72.8 in., 200 pounds), who was known as "The Bohemian Hercules," ran the same distance while carrying 90 kilos (198.4 pounds), in only 14 seconds. No matter how these two performances are compared, it works out that Fristensky's feat was more meritorious than Görner's, since the latter strong-man carried only about 11 percent more weight than Fristensky, yet required over 30 percent more time to cover the same distance. Fristensky was a true

"super-athlete," combining strength, speed, agility and endurance. At Rotterdam in 1903, he won the Greco-Roman wrestling championship of Europe (112 wrestlers entered the competition). He also won prizes for his physique and muscular development in 1905, 1907, 1909 and 1910. He never won top honors in weightlifting, perhaps only for the reason that he favored "repetition" lifts rather than maximum single efforts. However, the training that he followed made him an *all-around* athlete rather than a specialist.

55. A fine all-around feat of strength, as well as an entertaining exhibition, is to support either a person or a barbell at arm's length overhead on one hand, then lie down full-length on the floor and return to the standing position while maintaining the weight on a straight arm. The two best performances I have listed for this lift are as follows. In 1905, in New York City, Otis Lambert (P*; 65.6 in., 161 pounds) lay down and got up while holding on one hand overhead his stage partner, Adolph Nordquest (68.3 in., 195 pounds), plus a 25-pound dumbbell— a total weight of 220 pounds. This lift has the extraordinary rating of 97.4 percent. Proportionately the next-best lift (as well as probably the world's heavyweight record) was made about 1940, when John Collins (71 in., 200 pounds?), at Muscle Beach, California, lay down and got up while supporting overhead a man weighing 265 pounds. This fine lift rates 91.3 percent. No one else, to my knowledge, has accomplished a lie-down and get-up that rated 80 percent or over.

56. Once approximately every ten years, near Interlaken, Switzerland, a festival is held called the *Unspunnenfest*. One of the athletic events on the program is the tossing, for distance, of a 184-pound boulder called the Unspunnen stone. The stone is rounded and football-like in shape, and measures about 18 inches in length by about 13 or 14 inches in diameter or thickness. The performer raises the stone with both hands first to his chest, and then if possible onto the crown of his head. From there the stone is heaved forward onto the ground. In August, 1968, some 25 contestants managed to heave the stone, the winner attaining a distance of 3.02 meters (about 9 feet, 11 inches), a new record. The Unspunnen stone bears various incised and painted dates, of which the most prominent are 1805 and 1905—the year that the festival was first held, and its centenary anniversary, respectively.

---

*Denotes professional.

B. BARREL AND SACK LIFTING AND CARRYING

A weightlifting event popular in Germany and Austria in the 1890s was the pressing and jerking, respectively, of heavy filled beer barrels. Although breweries today use stainless steel barrels, up until about 1940 wooden barrels were still in common use, and such barrels were the ones used by the old-time German and Austrian weightlifters.

1. Hans Beck (66.5 in., 242 pounds) was the German amateur heavyweight lifting champion in 1895 and 1897, and the European champion (at Rotterdam) in 1896. In his home town of Munich, on September 25, 1896, Beck shouldered and then pressed three times in succession a 71-liter (18¾-gallon) barrel of beer weighing 113 kilos or 249 pounds. These three presses in succession were equivalent to a single press of about 268 pounds. On the same occasion, Beck shouldered and *jerked* an 81-liter (21⅜-gallon) barrel weighing 125 kilos or 275½ pounds. Obviously, the press was the better of these two lifts.

2. Alois Selos (67.7 in., 275 pounds) was the German amateur heavyweight lifting champion in 1905. He shouldered and pressed a filled 71-liter barrel of beer, the same as did Hans Beck, but pressed it only once to Beck's three times.

3. In *shouldering* heavy barrels, one of the greatest performers was "The Canadian Samson" Louis Cyr, who is credited with having brought to the shoulder, *using one hand only,* a barrel filled with sand and water weighing 445 pounds. In this one-arm lift, Cyr would use his right knee to help raise the barrel through the final stage (see Plate 4).

4. In the early 1800s there was a gigantic Austrian named Franz Wintersteller (74.5 in., 362 pounds), who was known as the strongest man in the Tyrol. It is said that on one occasion, in order to discourage a visiting strong-man who wanted to wrestle him, Wintersteller said, "With pleasure, but first let us have some beer." The visitor being agreeable to this, Wintersteller rolled out an oversized barrel of 113 liters, and to the visitor's astonishment raised it to his shoulders, pulled out the plug with his teeth, and had a good drink in that position. Replacing the barrel on the ground, Wintersteller said, "Now, my friend, if you want me to wrestle with you, you must first take a drink of beer just as I have done it." Needless to say, there was no wrestling match, as the barrel that Wintersteller raised to his shoulders weighed, with its contents, over 360 pounds! It is doubtful whether any other

man—not only in the Tyrol, but in the whole world—could have duplicated Wintersteller's feat at that time.

5. Hermann Görner in 1910, when he was only 19 years of age and weighed about 198 pounds, lifted from the floor by the chimes (the edge, or rim) a beer barrel of 200 liters (52 5/6 gallons) weighing 595¾ pounds and placed it on one end upon a table.

6. John Y. Smith (66.5 in., 165 pounds), the famous old-time middle-weight strong-man of Boston, was a sailor in his younger days, at a time when sailors were required to climb up and down the rigging of a vessel, and to pull on thick hawsers and cables. From years of performing such work, Smith acquired a remarkable strength of grip, and extraordinary toughness in his hands and fingers. One of his unequalled feats was to lift a 200-pound barrel by the metal hoops (not the chimes, but the *hoops!*). He could also lift off the ground by the chimes a 52-gallon wooden barrel filled with water, weighing 585 pounds.

7. Arthur Dandurand (68 in., 185 pounds) of Montreal could shoulder a barrel weighing with its contents 500 pounds (*c*. 1910).

8. Sebastian Miller (P; 69 in., 280 pounds), the old-time German professional strong-man and wrestler, in a friendly test with Arthur Saxon, lifted with one hand, by grasping the chime *(edge or rim)*, a heavy barrel that Saxon was unable to lift similarly. This, too, was when Miller was past his prime. The weight of the barrel was not stated (*c*. 1909).

9. "Apollo" (William Bankier), the old-time "Scottish Hercules" (66 in., 176 pounds), in his music-hall act in the 1890s, had a sack of flour weighing 20 stone or 280 pounds, which he challenged members of his audience to lift. Referring to this sack, Thomas Inch, writing in *Health and Strength* (London), November 5, 1921, p. 323, says:

> "The sack was tightly pressed down, and was quite unlike an ordinary sack of flour. It did not stand very high, and the contestants had to lie down against it, then get it on their backs and walk off the stage with it. If they were fortunate enough to get the sack on to their backs, it invariably rolled off, and I remember once, when on a visit to Leeds, the audience were more amused by the antics of the contestants with the "lucky bag", as it was called, than with the leading comedian, especially when one unfortunate succeeded in rolling the sack across his neck and pressing his nose into the stage when he received the full benefit of the 280 lb. weight. The prize was £10, and I believe one of the few who ever succeeded was (Edward) Aston . . .

PLATE 25

Chuck Ahrens (6 ft., 280 lbs.) muscling-out a 75-lb. girl on one arm. "Muscle Beach," California, August 1957. (64)

PLATE 26

*John Grimek, the only competitor ever to win the title of "Mr.
America" twice in succession (1940 and 1941). He was also "Mr.
Universe" (1948) and "Mr. U.S.A." (1949). (65)*

PLATE 27

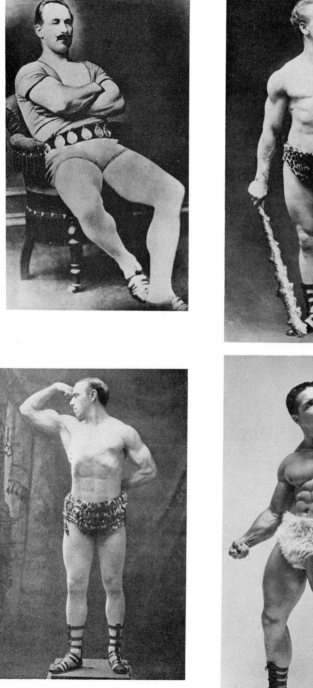

Four world-famous strong-man models of different epochs. Upper left: Donald Dinnie, the early Scottish "all-rounder" (c. 1865); upper right: Eugen Sandow, in 1902; lower left: Al Treloar, in 1903; lower right, Bill Pearl, "Mr. America" of 1953, "Mr. Universe" of 1953, "Mr. U.S.A." of 1956, and "Mr. Universe" of 1967. (66–69)

PLATE 28

Anton Riha of Bohemia, supporting 1400 lbs. (70)

William Pagel of South Africa, carrying a 1000-pound horse up and down a ladder. (71)

Dave Prowse (6 ft., 7 in., 273 lbs.) lifting together the two famous "Dinnie Stones" of Scotland. One stone weighs 340 lbs., the other 445 lbs. (72)

PLATE 29

Frank "Cannonball" Richards "stopping" a 104-lb. missile. (73)

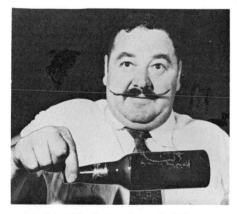

(Left) "Mac" Batchelor holding a beer bottle horizontally by a pinch-grip of finger and thumb. (74) (Right) Batchelor working up a heavy wine bottle through his hand by finger and thumb strength. (75)

PLATE 30

An iron bar, ⅝-inch square by 5 inches long, bent into a U-shape with his bare hands by "Samson" (Alexander Zass) in London, 1924. Several years later, "Young Apollon" (J. C. Tolson) is said to have performed the same feat. The bar is shown here in its actual size. (76)

PLATE 31

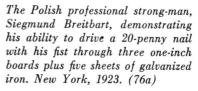

The Polish professional strong-man, Siegmund Breitbart, demonstrating his ability to drive a 20-penny nail with his fist through three one-inch boards plus five sheets of galvanized iron. New York, 1923. (76a)

PLATE 32

*John Grünn Marx, "The Luxembourg Hercules," and a repro-
duction of a horseshoe, actual size, that he broke with his bare
hands in less than a minute. Paris, 1905. (77)*

10. The Arthur Saxon Trio, when exhibiting in England just after the turn of the century, had a "challenge" sack which, like Apollo's, weighed 280 pounds. The terms under which a member of the audience had to lift this sack in order to collect the prize money were that the sack should be lifted from the floor onto the shoulders, then carried off the stage, body erect. During the several years that the Saxons performed in England, no "challenger" ever succeeded in thus lifting the sack. Hermann Saxon (67 in., 168 pounds), who was then only a youth, used to show the audience how "easy" it was to do the feat, regularly every Friday evening.

11. The Saxons had an even heavier "emergency" sack, which only Arthur (69.6 in., 200 pounds) could lift. This sack, which the Saxons had covered with slippery chalk, was filled in a way that made it an unbalanced, tricky affair. It weighed just over 300 pounds. Arthur could shoulder this unwieldy sack, then jerk-press it to arms' length overhead!

12. At the Strong-man Contest held by the Basques of Idaho, at Boise, in 1958, there was a sack-lifting event in which 100-pound bags of salt were used. This event was won by Santiago Basterrechea, who succeeded in lifting *three* 100-pound bags and supporting them, one atop the other, on his chest, leaning well back from the waist.

13. August Johnson, a 64-year-old iceman, carried a 32-pound sack of coins in one hand—without once shifting the sack to the other hand or resting it against his body—for the distance of a mile. Prior to Johnson's effort, 30 other contestants had each failed to carry the sack the entire distance. 1958.

C. REPETITION LIFTING

Although this type of weightlifting is not practiced much anymore (except for exercise and development), in earlier days it was quite popular, and in it some extraordinary records were set up. The styles of lifting usually chosen for repetition lifting have been: (1) one- and two-arm pressing, the one-arm lifts being performed usually with a solid iron dumbbell; (2) deep-knee bends (or squats on toes); (3) foot-pressing (performed with a barbell supported on the soles of the feet while lying on the back); and (4) sit-ups or abdominal raises (rising from a supine position to a sitting position on the floor, the legs out straight in front, with or without a barbell held back of the neck). Some of the more remarkable "endurance" records in these four events are listed below, along with a few records in other forms of repetition lifting. Unless otherwise noted, the performers are from the U.S.A. (P=professional.) Where the height and the bodyweight are not given, in parentheses following the performer's name, it means that these items are unknown to the writer. Following each repetition record is the estimated poundage that would be equivalent to that record if the weight were lifted only *once*. (In cases where the number of repetitions is so great as to make this estimation uncertain, it is omitted.)

1. Pressing (or pushing) or jerking a dumbbell from the shoulder overhead with one arm

(NOTE: *For the difference between a press and a push, see the definitions in Chapter 4.*)

1. Using a Bent Press, G. W. Rolandow (P; 69.75 in., 178 pounds) raised a 138-pound dumbbell from the shoulder overhead 18 times in succession. Presumably he lowered the weight each time using *both* arms. New York City, 1900. This was equivalent to bent-pressing *once* a dumbbell of about 255 pounds.

2. Louis Cyr, "The Canadian Samson," (P; 68.5 in., c. 300 pounds), did a one-arm "put up" of 132½ pounds *36 times in succession*. Chicago, May 7, 1896. (This lift, in some reports, has been given as 162½ pounds, which apparently was a misprint. Also, in some lists, it was stated to be a one-arm *push*, whereas it was actually a one-arm *jerk*).

3. Michael Mayer (P; 66.1 in., 242 pounds), of Austria, *pushed* a dumbbell of 50.2 kilos (110.67 pounds) 30 times. Vienna, Feb. 6, 1900. (= 209 pounds once).

4. Josef Grafl (75.5 in., 286 pounds), of Austria, standing *with his heels together,* pressed a dumbbell of 50 kilos (110.23 pounds) 20 times with his right hand and 17 times with his left hand (Vienna, 1913). This was equivalent to pressing *once*, with heels together, 175 pounds with the right hand and 166 pounds with the left hand.

5. "Romulus" (Cosimo Molino), of Italy (P; 63 in., 167 pounds), *pushed* a 109-pound dumbbell 22 times. London, Feb. 29, 1892. (= 180 pounds once).

6. G. Tsambaris, of the Greek-American Athletic Club, *pushed* a 104-pound dumbbell 23 times. New York City, Jan. 16, 1914. (= 175 pounds once).

7. G. W. Chadwick *pushed* a 100-pound dumbbell 30 times. New York City, Feb. 22, 1915. (= 189 pounds once).

8. William Conture (149 pounds) *jerked* a 110-pound dumbbell 27 times. Bath, Maine, Feb. 11, 1892. (= 200 pounds once!)

9. Father B.H.B. Lange (68 in., 232 pounds), of Notre Dame University, did a *military press* with either hand of 75 pounds 25 times. Austin, Texas, 1921. (= 130 pounds once with either hand).

10. William P. Caswell (64.5 in., 140 pounds), of England, *jerked* a 56-pound blockweight 100 times in 4 minutes 28 seconds. London, *c.* 1900. He also jerked the same weight 50 times in 1 minute 28 seconds.

11. George Clifford of London *jerked* a 56-pound dumbbell 120 times in 6 minutes 22 seconds. London, 1897(?).

12. Alfred (Staff-Sergeant) Moss (67.5 in., 182 pounds) *jerked* a 56-pound blockweight 100 times in 2 minutes 52 seconds. Aldershot, England, *c.* 1900. (*cf.* no. 10, above).

13. G. N. Robinson *pushed* a 51-pound dumbbell 80 times. San Francisco, Nov. 20, 1883.

14. A. A. Hylton *pushed* a 50-pound dumbbell 94 times. San Francisco, May 19, 1885.

15. Adrian P. Schmidt (P; 62.5 in., 130 pounds) *pushed* a 35-pound dumbbell 100 times. New York City, *c.* 1900.

16. G. W. W. Roche *pushed* a 25-pound dumbbell 450 times. San Francisco, Nov. 25, 1875.

17. Anthony McKinley of Ireland *pushed* a dumbbell weighing 12 lbs. 1½ oz. 16,000 times in 2 hrs. 57 min. 50 sec. Ballycastle, Ireland, Dec. 26, 1904.

18. A. Corcoran pushed a 12-pound dumbbell 14,000 times. Chicago, Oct. 4, 1873.

19. H. Pennock *pushed* a 10-pound dumbbell 8431 times in 4 hrs. 34 min. New York City, Dec. 14, 1870.

20. Ed C. Stickney *pushed* a 4-pound dumbbell 6000 times in 59 min. 53 sec. (Thus averaging almost exactly 100 pushes per minute). Lynn, Mass., June 22, 1885. (I understand that in some of the repetition lifts with light dumbbells, the performer would *keep* his upper arm in a vertical position and do all the lifting by raising and lowering his *forearm*).

21. Anthony McKinley of Ireland *pushed* a 4-pound dumbbell 10,000 times in 1 hr. 6 min. 45 sec. (Thus averaging about 150 pushes per minute!) Ballycastle, Ireland, Jan. 9, 1905.

2. Jerking a barbell overhead with one arm

1. George Lurich (P; 69.3 in., 187 pounds), a famous Russian strong-man and wrestler, jerked from the shoulder 220 pounds 6 times, 199 pounds 10 times, 179½ pounds 15 times, and 162 pounds 17 times. Germany, 1899. Each of the first three of these repetition lifts was equivalent to a single lift of about 262 pounds, and the 162 pounds 17 times to a single lift of 245 pounds. Lurich's record single one-arm jerk was one of 121 kilos or 266¾ pounds. This extraordinary lift was made at the Meteor Athletic Club in Prague, Czechoslovakia, in February 1902. It has a rating of 94.2 percent.

2. X. Jung (heavyweight) of Germany, jerked 70 kilos or 154¼ pounds 22 times. Wurzburg, Germany, Aug. 31, 1900. (= 253 pounds once).

3. K. Schuster (heavyweight), of Germany, jerked 50 kilos or 110¼ pounds 55 times in 2 min. 25 sec. Nürnberg, Germany, Sept. 21, 1900.

3. Pressing (or pushing) or jerking a pair of dumbbells overhead with both arms

1. Steve Gob (68 in., 181 pounds) pushed a 103-pound short barbell with his right hand and a 101-pound dumbbell with his left hand, together, 20 times. New York City, 1948. (= 164 pounds right hand and 161 pounds left hand, once). This is one of the greatest feats of dumbbell pressing on record, rating 101.7 percent.

2. Joe Lauriano *cleaned and pressed (pushed)* a pair of 75-pound dumbbells 16 times (i.e., 16 cleans and 16 pushes). York, Pa., 1950.

3. Frank Dorio (165 pounds) *pressed* a pair of 60-pound dumbbells

together 25 times, while sitting. Los Angeles, Calif., 1951? (= 103½ pounds in each hand once).

4. Donald Dinnie (P; 72.5 in., 218 pounds), of Scotland, "put up" (jerk-pressed ?) a pair of 56-pound dumbbells 52 times. Aboyne, Scotland, c. 1865.

5. Launceston Elliot (73.5 in., 210 pounds), of England, raised two 60-pound dumbbells *from the ground overhead* 30 times. London, c. 1900.

6. John Grimek (68.5 in., 195 pounds) pushed a pair of 50-pound dumb-bells together 45 times. York, Pa., Sept. 1948. (= 117½ pounds in each hand once). He also pressed a pair of 20-pound dumbbells together 145 times.

4. Pressing (or pushing) or jerking a barbell overhead with both arms

1. *Karl Swoboda* (70.5 in., 360 lbs.) of Vienna, *pressed* 110 kilos (242½ pounds) 12 times in *strict military style*, with heels together. Vienna, Aug. 27, 1912. (= 330 pounds once).

2. Josef Grafl (75.5 in., 286 lbs.) of Vienna, *pressed* 100 kilos (220½ pounds) 18 times (not military, but with heels together). Vienna, 1912. (= 338 pounds once).

3. Malcolm Brenner (73 in., 228 lbs.) *pushed* 250 pounds 10 times. Los Angeles, Calif., 1951. (= 327 pounds once). He also pushed 185 pounds 27 times (= 330 pounds once).

4. John Grimek (68.5 in., 195 lbs.) *pushed*—using a forward lean—225 pounds 14 times. York, Pa., 1948. (= 319 pounds once).

5. Frank Leight (71.2 in., 209 lbs.) *pushed* 150 pounds 35 times. New York City, 1942. (= 300 pounds once).

6. John Lopez (205 lbs.) *pushed* 150 pounds 37 times. He also pushed 300 pounds once. Los Angeles, Calif., Sept. 30, 1942.

7. "Romulus" (Cosimo Molino), of Italy (P; 63 in., 167 lbs.), *pushed* 168 pounds 20 times (= 267 pounds once), and 179 pounds 18 times (= 274 pounds once). London, March 12, 1892.

8. Karl Svenson (165 lbs.) *pushed* 85 kilos or 187.4 pounds 16 times. 1904. (= 276 pounds once).

9. Norman Stanway (123 lbs.), of Canada, *pushed* 125 pounds 20 times (= 198 pounds once), and 160 pounds 10 times (= 209 pounds once). Winnipeg, Manitoba, 1954.

10. About 1948, in the USSR, a contest was launched to discover who could lift a 72-pound barbell overhead with both arms the greatest number of times, consecutively. Trained weightlifters were excluded. The contest enjoyed great popularity, with over 30,000 men taking part in the Ukraine alone. In the Georgian finals at Tbilisi, one Alex Khatiashvili *jerked* the barbell overhead no fewer than 170 times! Shortly thereafter another competitor, Shalva Mdinaradze, did the lift 173 times! However, Mdinaradze must have taken rests of several seconds' duration between each repetition—or longer rests between *series* of repetitions— since he required 20 minutes to perform the 173 counts. The amount of time required by Khatiashvili was not stated.

5. Miscellaneous repetition lifts to the shoulders or overhead

1. Andre Rolet (P; 68.5 in., 176 lbs.), of France, lifted with both hands a 44-pound blockweight (having handles on each end of it) from the ground to arms' length overhead 1300 times consecutively in 2 hours. North Island, France, April 1921.

2. Gustave Fristensky, a famous European strongman-wrestler, at the age of 19 (1899), at the Athletic Club Hellas, in Brno (Czechoslovakia), won a competition in which 24 lifters were entered by performing the following repetition lifts: (1) cleaning with both arms from the "hang" position, *without lowering* the bar from there, 88 pounds 50 times, 110 pounds 40 times, 132 pounds 28 times, and 154 pounds 16 times; (2) jerking with both arms a barbell of 176 pounds 26 times, 220 pounds 18 times, and 282 pounds once. Of the latter lifts, relatively the best was the 220 pounds 18 times, which was equivalent to jerking 308 pounds once.

3. Hans Frohner, a pupil of Adrian P. Schmidt, alternately *curled* a pair of 8¼-pound dumbbells 14,000 times in 1 hr. 45 min. New York City, 1900. (Schmidt, who was a great "endurance" lifter himself, considered Frohner's performance "phenomenal").

4. Hermann Görner (72.5 in., 208 lbs.), the world-famous German

strong-man, did a Right Hand Swing with a kettlebell weighing 50 kilos (110¼ pounds), 48 times in succession. Leipzig, July 14, 1912.

5. Ewald Redam (P; 67 in., 160 lbs.), of Germany, at the age of 19, did a Two Hands Snatch of 51 kilos (112½ pounds) 42 times in succession. A few minutes later, he followed this with a Right Hand Swing (dumbbell) of 112½ pounds 26 times. Leipzig, 1904.

6. Frank Merrill (P; 70 in., 165 lbs.), a one-time National Champion on the Roman rings, performed a Lateral Raise Lying with a pair of 48-pound dumbbells 16 times in succession. Midland, Texas, Feb. 1929. This repetition lift was equivalent to raising a pair of 70-pound dumbbells once, and has the phenomenal rating of 97.1 percent. The Lateral Raise, lying, is performed by raising the dumbbells stiff-armed from the floor, with the arms out to the sides at shoulder level. Merrill (whose real name was Otto Poll) was the *second* man ever to appear* in the rôle of Tarzan in the silent movies, the first being Elmo Lincoln (71 in., 210 lbs.).

6. Knee-bending, or squatting (with and without extra weight)

1. Max Danthage (68 in., 159 lbs.) of Vienna, performed 6000 consecutive deep knee bends (on toes) without extra weight in 3 hrs. Vienna, June 4, 1899. He also performed 50 knee-bends while holding a barbell of 100 kilos (220½ pounds) on his shoulders. Sept. 12, 1896.

(I understand that many years after Danthage's record there was a contest in deep knee bending without weights between two physical culturists, one of whom was a vegetarian while the other included meat in his diet. One of the two contestants (which one I do not know) quit after performing 8000 knee-bends, while the other, equally exhausted, did only about ten more! If any reader has further information about this contest, I would be most grateful for it.)

2. Henry Fletcher performed 76 deep knee bends with 200 pounds. San Diego, Calif., c. 1945.

3. H. P. Hansen (heavyweight), of Denmark, squatted with 277 pounds 65 times in succession. Copenhagen, March 19, 1899.

4. Kimon Voyages (67 in., 190 lbs.) did 100 consecutive flat-footed squats with 200 pounds on his shoulders, and 50 squats with 300 pounds. New York City, Jan. 1949.

---

*Or at least to be widely publicized.

5. George Eiferman (67.5 in., 195 lbs.), "Mr. America" of 1948, did a *one-leg* squat (flat-footed) 150 times in succession. (*c.* 1950). This feat was equivalent to doing a squat on both legs while carrying on the shoulders a weight of about 550 pounds.

6. The professional wrestlers of India can each, on the average, per- form in their training *five series* of 300 "dunds" (body-swaying floor- dips), followed by *three series* of 1000 "batticks" (knee-bends, on toes). As most of these wrestlers are heavyweights, it can readily be seen why they acquire extraordinary development of the muscles of the chest and thighs. Another leg exercise used by some of the East Indian wrestlers is to *leap* repeatedly as high as possible from a low knee-bend position. One of these wrestlers is said to have performed 700 such leaps in succession!

7. Juan Ferrero, who once won the title *"Le plus bel athlete"* in France, did a Squat with 187 pounds 75 times, 220½ pounds 60 times, 253½ pounds 35 times, 308½ pounds 7 times, 330½ pounds 3 times, and 374¾ pounds once. Of these poundages, the most meritorious was the single effort with 374¾ lbs.

8. —— Adelhaid, a heavyweight Russian strong-man, performed 14 knee bends (on toes) while holding at arms' length overhead a barbell of 90 kilos (198.41 pounds). (= *c.* 250 pounds once).

9. William Boone (265? lbs.) performed 16 squats with 400 pounds and 3 with 515 pounds (*c.* 1945). The 16 squats with 400 pounds were equivalent to about 510 pounds once, and the 3 with 515 pounds to about 540 pounds once.

10. Karl Heim, of Germany, performed 1114 knee bends without extra weight, in 9 min. 45 sec. Ingolstadt, Germany, 1909. These knee bends were performed at the rate of about 114 per minute, or nearly 2 bends every second.

11. George Hackenschmidt (P; 68.7 in., 205 lbs.), of Russia, performed 50 consecutive "Hacke" (or "Hocke") lifts with 50 kilos (110¼ pounds). This feat was done in front of the famous German weight-trainer, Theo- dor Siebert, at Alsleben, Germany, Feb. 15, 1902. "Hack" also performed a single lift in the same style with 85 kilos (187¼ pounds). The latter was equal to a flat-footed squat with about 522 pounds on the shoulders. The "Hacke" lift is performed by knee-bending on the toes while hold- ing a barbell *with the hands together* behind the hips, thus leaving the

back muscles out of the effort and doing all the work with the legs.

12. Hermann Gassler (68.5 in., 209 lbs.), of Germany, who in 1912 held several world's records in barbell lifting, performed a "Hacke" lift with 55 kilos (121¼ pounds) 20 times in succession. These repetitions were equivalent to lifting about 162 pounds once in the same style, or to doing a regular Squat with about 470 pounds on the shoulders. That Gassler had very strong legs was demonstrated also when he performed a "Cossack dance" while carrying a man weighing 160 pounds!

13. Henry "Milo" Steinborn (P; 68.25 in., 210 lbs.), who virtually "introduced" the Squat, as a weight-training exercise, to American weightlifters in the early 1920s, once performed 33 successive squats with a barbell of 315 pounds. Los Angeles, Feb. 1926. While theoretically these squats were equal only to about 480 pounds once, actually Steinborn, several years earlier, in Germany, had squatted once with 553 pounds. On the other hand, Kimon Voyages (see no. 4, above), who could squat 50 times with 300 pounds—which was equivalent to doing 525 pounds once—actually could not squat once with more than 400 pounds. These two examples show how "endurance"—or the ability to perform a high number of repetitions—may vary among individuals having approximately the same degree of *momentary* strength.

7. Pressing a barbell on the soles of the feet ("Foot-pressing")

1. Rudolf Klar (67.5 in., 174 lbs.), of Germany, foot-pressed 150 kilos or 330½ pounds 34 times in succession, 160 kilos (352¾ pounds) 20 times, and 200 kilos (440¾ pounds) 12 times. The latter lift was equivalent to a single foot-press with about 500 pounds, or to squatting with 454 pounds.

2. Anton Endres, of Germany, foot-pressed 101 kilos (222¾ pounds) 241 times consecutively. Apr. 8, 1896.

3. Ewald Redam (P; 67 in., 168 lbs.), of Germany, foot-pressed 52 kilos (114½ pounds) 1000 times. Leipzig, 1910.

8. The sit-up, or abdominal raise

In performing a sit-up without extra weight, a considerable number of records are at hand. The following list doubtless represents only a portion of these records, and there may be intermediate figures that I have been unable to collect.

1. 3100 consecutive sit-ups were performed by Bill Ghesquire (aged 14), Detroit, Mich., 1946.

2. 3201 by Bill Wolhschlegel in 2 hrs. 16 min. Aurora, Ill., 1930.

3. 4417 by Jerry Hornig (aged 16) in 3 hrs. Fresno, Calif., *c.* 1950. During this endurance feat, Hornig lost 8 pounds.

4. 5555 by William Froehlig, 1945. (see no. 7, below).

5. 6033 by Angelo Poffo in 4 hrs. 10 min. Downers Grove, Ill., 1948.

6. 6034 by Ed Beranek in 5 hrs. 54 min. Yale Univ., 1946.

7. 6250 by William Froehlig in 3 hrs. 42 min., *c.* 1946 (see no. 4, above).

8. 6429 by Edward O. Spratt in nearly 10 hrs.! 1946.

9. 6600 by Leon Cronsohn (aged 20) in 3 hrs. 40 min. Brooklyn Central YMCA gym, May 28, 1948. Cronsohn's feet were *not* held down. (see no. 11, below).

10. 8043 by Barry Barrett (aged 19; 70 in., 175 lbs.), hands clasped behind head, knees bent partway. San Rafael, Calif., Feb. 6, 1960. This performance took 6 hrs. 9 min., and during it Barrett lost 7 pounds.

11. 10,000 (and some over) by Leon Cronsohn, at Siegmund Klein's gym, New York City, 1950. (see no. 9 above). Cronsohn also did 1506 consecutive sit-ups with 20 pounds behind his neck, *without his feet being held down.*

12. 14,000 by John Greenshields in 6 hrs. 10 min. Tampa, Florida, Oct. 24, 1964.

13. Alan P. Mead (73 in., 182 lbs.), of England, performed 70 consecutive sit-ups with 70 pounds. London, *c.* 1925.

14. Kimon Voyages (67 in., 190 lbs.) did 105 consecutive sit-ups with 70 pounds. New York City, May 1948.

15. Frank Leight (71.2 in., 209 lbs.) did 100 sit-ups with 60 pounds, also one sit-up with 154½ pounds. The latter lift constituted a heavyweight world record at the time. New York City, 1942.

16. Gene Jantzen, at a bodyweight of 195 pounds (height 69 in.), performed 5300 consecutive sit-ups without extra weight. Bartelso, Ill., c. 1950.

17. Jerry Salzman performed 201 sit-ups with a 25-pound dumbbell held behind his neck. *c.* 1940.

18. Jack Greenlees, a professional handbalancer, is said to have performed 5 successive sit-ups while holding behind his neck a 168¼-pound (!) barbell. His feet were held down by two men (1946). No information was given as to Greenlees's height and bodyweight. In any case, the 5 repetitions with 168¼ pounds were equivalent to a single sit-up with at least 195 pounds. This was a phenomenal performance, far surpassing any other record in the Abdominal Raise. Its rating, in all probability, would be in the neighborhood of 100 percent.

D. "MUSCLING OUT" (STRAIGHT-ARM HOLDING OUT AT SHOULDER-LEVEL)

While many claimed "records" have been published and quoted in this style of lifting, few of them have been performed in the correct manner. A true "muscling out" feat should be performed with the body perfectly erect and the elbows perfectly straight. When *two* weights are held out simultaneously in this manner, one in each hand, the lift is known as the "crucifix." Although in this feat it is common practice to use a dumbbell, or a pair of dumbbells, a better balance may be obtained by using kettlebells (or ringweights), since in such weights the center of gravity is *below* the performer's hand, or hands, rather than above or on a level with the hands. Where the *correct* position is assumed in the Crucifix, the "poundage-possibility" is 60 percent of that in a correct Two Hands Military (*not* Olympic) Press with barbell. Thus, if a lifter can perform a correct Two Hands Military Press with 200 pounds, he should be expected to be capable of a Crucifix with 120 pounds—that is, 60 pounds in each hand (or the equivalent in total poundage). The weight, or weights, should be held out in the straight-arm position for at least two seconds.

In contrast to these rules, a so-called "crucifix" is often performed with the body bent far back at the waist, with the wrists strongly flexed (so as to shorten the distance from the shoulders to the hands), and with the arms brought forward so as to use the pectoral (front chest) muscles as well as the deltoids. Such a lift, if viewed from the front, may, it is true, show the arms in a straight line with the level of the shoulders; but since the body is bent so far backwards the spirit of the lift is being violated, and the feat becomes one of gymnastic contortion rather than sheer shoulder strength. By extreme proficiency in this incorrect form of "muscling out," a lifter may be able to hold out momentarily as much as 20 percent more weight than he could handle in a correctly-performed Crucifix. No man, so far as I know, has ever performed a *correct* Crucifix with the equivalent of his own bodyweight, although several lifters have claimed to have done such a poundage (without giving the details as to how they did it). However, among today's record holders in pressing, such a feat would appear possible. For example, a 150-pound lifter who can Olympic press 320 pounds *should* be capable of a correct Crucifix with 160 pounds (80 pounds in each hand).

Here are a few "records" in muscling-out weights, with critical comments on each.

1. Louis Cyr (P; 68.5 in., c. 300 lbs.), "The Canadian Samson," performed a correct Crucifix lift with a 94-pound dumbbell in his right hand and an 88-pound dumbbell in his left hand, a total of 182 pounds. Chicago, May 7, 1896. He also held out momentarily with his right hand, with a slight body-bend, a dumbbell of 104 pounds. London, Jan. 19, 1892. While Cyr has been credited with holding out a barbell of 129 pounds with his right hand, such a lift—in view of his known strength otherwise—would have been impossible for him, no matter what position he assumed for it.

2. "Apollon" (P; 74.8 in., 264 lbs.), the gigantic French strong-man, held out "very correctly" on the palm of his right hand a French block-weight of 50 kilos (110¼ pounds). Paris, 1892. This lift was equivalent to muscling-out about 85 pounds with a kettlebell. Probably, as a limit test, Apollon could have performed a Crucifix with about 180 pounds (say, 95 pounds right and 85 pounds left). However, that he ever held out with one arm—as some reports have it—either 154 pounds (!) or 176 pounds (!!) is preposterous.

3. Peter Kryloff (P; 69.3 in., 203 lbs.), of Russia, has by some authors been credited with a Crucifix of 180 pounds (90 pounds in each hand), c. 1900. However, it is probable that in this lift Kryloff used an incorrect style such as was employed also by George Hackenschmidt (see no. 4, following).

4. George Hackenschmidt (P; 68.7 in., 210 lbs.), the world-famous Russian strong-man and wrestler, held out dumbbells of 90¼ pounds right hand and 89⅝ pounds left hand, simultaneously. St. Petersburg,

Feb. 15, 1902. This lift, in comparison to the performances of the French professional strong-man, Victorius, was—in Hackenschmidt's own words —"in a less strictly correct style." From the fact that "Hack's" best Two Hands Military Press was about 250 pounds, he would be expected to have been capable of a *correct* Crucifix with about 75 pounds in each hand.

5. Douglas Hepburn (69 in., 260 lbs.), of Canada, held out correctly on his right hand a dumbbell weighing 102½ pounds. He maintained himself in an erect position by holding onto a tree with his left hand. Vancouver, B.C., Apr. 29, 1951. Since Hepburn at the latter date had not attained his full strength, it would seem that when he did—in 1954–1956—he could probably have performed a Crucifix with about 112 pounds (!) in each hand.

6. Although I have never heard or read of Paul Anderson (69 in., c. 360 lbs.) having performed a Crucifix lift, it would appear—in view of his tremendous strength in pressing—that with due practice he *should* have been capable of holding out correctly no less than 240 pounds (say, 123 pounds right and 117 pounds left)!

E. BLOW RESISTING

This type of performance, while far removed from conventional weightlifting, must nevertheless be classed as a specialized form of strength-feat. It may be likened, in its requirements, to the feat of *supporting* heavy loads on the recumbent body. Although blow-resisting constitutes a "passive" (immobile) form of effort, perhaps it—and the conditioning necessary to develop it—is, in its way, as beneficial and useful as the more familiar forms of strength-demonstration. Two main variations of body-blow resisting may be recognized: (1) where the performer, lying in a recumbent (supine) position, allows weights to fall, or a person to jump, onto his naked abdomen; and (2) where the performer, in a standing position, resists heavy blows directed to his abdomen or mid-section.

Here are a few examples of the first type of resisting:

1. Joe Zimmerman (145 lbs.), while lying on the ground, allowed his brother, Dick (150 lbs.) to jump off the top of a six-foot stepladder, while holding a 50-pound dumbbell in each hand, onto his abdomen. York, Pa., Mar. 7, 1938.

2. Harold Ansorge (P; 71.9 in., 220 lbs.), as one of his regular exhibi-

tion feats, while lying on the ground, allowed his sister, Jean (125 pounds) to jump off the top of an 18-foot ladder onto his abdomen. Grand Rapids, Mich., 1944.

3. Jan Peter Müller (P; 72 in., 180 lbs.), of Denmark, author of the widely-distributed book on physical culture, *My System,* gave special attention to the development of his abdominal muscles. With reference to his strength in these muscles, he says: "I can allow an iron ball weighing half a hundredweight (56 pounds) to be dropped from a height of four feet on my naked abdomen, or a man weighing 216 pounds avoirdupois and wearing thick-soled boots to jump eight feet and land on the aforesaid part of my body, or an iron-tyred wheelbarrow with a load of 360 pounds avoirdupois to be wheeled over me."

It is interesting to evaluate each of the above feats in terms of "foot-pounds" resisted by the abdominal muscles of the recumbent performer. In no. 1, it can be calculated that the speed of Dick Zimmerman, in dropping from a height of six feet, is 19.6 ft. per sec. This, multiplied by Dick's bodyweight plus two 50-pound dumbbells—a total of 250 pounds —gives 4900 as the number of "foot-pounds" dropping onto Joe Zimmerman's abdomen.

In no. 2, the speed of Jean Ansorge is 34 feet per second, and this, multiplied by her weight of 125 pounds, gives 4250 "foot-pounds."

In no. 3, the 216-pound man dropping (at a speed of 22¾ feet per second) from a height of eight feet onto Müller's abdomen gives 4914 "foot-pounds."

However, in order to derive a more accurate estimation of the pressure resisted by the abdominal muscles in each of the above cases, the area of the surface (soles of the feet) coming into contact should be taken into account. When the estimated foot-size is thus considered in each case, it is found that Joe Zimmerman sustained on his abdomen a pressure of about 131 pounds per square inch; Ansorge, about 127 pounds per square inch; and Müller, about 126 pounds per square inch. It is difficult to estimate how much pressure Müller withstood in allowing the 56-pound iron ball to drop onto his abdomen, since the surface of the ball was *round* rather than flat. Thus the amount of surface on the ball that came into contact with Müller's abdomen at the instant of contact would depend on how much his abdominal muscles were compressed by the impact. However, a rough estimation indicates that in this feat Müller probably withstood somewhat *less* pressure than where he allowed the 216-pound man to "jump" (drop?) on him.

The foregoing three instances, in which falling objects were resisted, would seem to compare very favorably with the feat of Rama Murti Naidu, "The Indian Hercules" (see p. 177) in *supporting* momentarily a 7000-pound elephant on *a much greater surface* of his recumbent body.

Of the second type of blow-resisting, I shall give only one example, as this, I believe, is without parallel.*

Back in the 1920s there was a carnival and fair performer named Frank Richards, who, because of his specialty, became known as "Cannonball" Richards. Through many years of training, he had become able to withstand blows to his body that would have incapacitated anyone else. Richards was a large man, weighing about 240 pounds, and apparently fat, although carrying thick, powerful layers of muscles underneath. He would allow any man in the world to try to faze him with blows from his fist to Richards's torso. Jack Dempsey in 1927 (the year he fought Jack Sharkey) made a determined effort to "bother" Richards, by pounding his mid-section with some 75 to 80 punches (covering the solar plexus, the heart, and the kidneys), but with no effect whatever. Several years before this, Richards had appeared at the Los Angeles Athletic Club, and in an exhibition given on the roof of the building invited all and sundry to take punches at his body. Several of us used a four-by-four timber as a battering ram against his abdomen, but this, too, proved ineffectual.

Tiring of such "feeble" efforts to disturb him, Richards progressed to where he would allow a heavy sledgehammer to be pounded against his abdomen. Even this in time became boring, and it was then that Richards developed his cannonball act. In this he used a 12-foot-long cannon transported on truck wheels, which fired a steel ball 9 inches in diameter, weighing 104 pounds. Standing about six feet in front of the mouth of the cannon, and with a heavy, spring-supported wall of canvas about the same distance behind him, Richards would receive the full force of the fired cannonball directly in his midriff. The blow would usually knock him clear back into the canvas "net," but he always emerged unhurt. One reason for this was that Richards knew exactly how and where to position himself so that the cannonball would hit against the "best-cushioned" part of his torso. Even so, he said that the shock of receiving the cannonball was so great that he did not care to go through the performance more than twice a day (see Plate 29).

---

*However, the middleweight Russian strong-man, "Samson" (Alexander Zass), as part of his stage performance in 1924, used to catch in his *arms* a 104-pound girl who was "fired" out of a cannon 42 feet away from him. The girl's speed was said to be 45 mph (= 66 ft. per sec.), and the impact of her body some 2150 pounds (?). Doubtless, from the distance she had to travel, she was "fired" in an arc, rather than straight forward like Richards's cannonball. Coincidentally, both Richards's cannonball and Samson's girl weighed the *same.*

F.   FEATS OF GRIP-STRENGTH
(WITH BARBELLS AND DUMBBELLS)

NOTE: *In order to make valid comparisons between the various performances listed here, it is necessary (1) to convert all the lifts to the* same diameter of bar; *and (2) to convert the poundages lifted to the* same date *(year). By estimating all lifts as though they were performed* on a 2-inch diameter bar, in the year 1965, *a more accurate estimation of the relative grip-strengths of the various performers can be determined.*

This procedure is applied also to the feats of pinch-gripping listed under heading G.

While percentage-ratings, based on the performer's height, bodyweight, and date of performance can be made of all grip-feats, it should be noted that these feats are dependent mainly upon the muscular power of the hands, fingers, and forearms, and that the size and strength of these parts may vary considerably in relation to that of the body as a whole. Therefore, percentage ratings which are not based on the size of the hands and forearms, rather than the entire body, can give only approximate evaluations.

1. Hermann Görner (72.5 in., 220-265 lbs.) performed, among many others, the following feats of grip-strength:

a. Right Hand Dead Lift of 330 kilos (727½ lbs.) on a 1.1-inch barbell handle, using a hooked over-grip. Leipzig, Oct. 8, 1920. This was equivalent to lifting about 590 pounds on the same diameter of bar, *without* hooking the thumb.

b. Right Hand Dead Lift of 251.5 kilos (554½ lbs.) on a 30 mm. (1-3/16-inch) straight, non-revolving, barbell handle, using a regular (unhooked) grip.

c. Right Hand Snatch or Swing, keeping the arm straight, of 77 kilos (169¾ lbs.) on a bar 60 mm (about 2⅜ inches) in diameter. This evidently was not his limit poundage.

From these three lifts, it can be estimated that Görner was capable of a Right Hand Dead Lift on a 2-inch diameter dumbbell handle (see p. 162) of about 395 pounds. This denotes gripping strength of a truly phenomenal degree.

2. "Apollon" (P; 74.8 in., 264 lbs.) once pulled to shoulder height a 2⅜-inch bar weighing 226 pounds. This uncompleted lift (see above) was equivalent to a Right Hand Dead Lift on a 2-inch bar (see above) of about 360 pounds. Projected to the year 1965, Apollon's lift on the 2-inch bar would be equivalent to about 440 pounds, and Görner's lift to about 450 pounds!

3. John Grünn Marx (P; 70.9 in., 235 lbs.), "The Luxembourg Hercules," could regularly perform a Right Hand Snatch of 70 kilos (154¼ pounds) on a barbell handle 2¾ inches in diameter. It would appear that his limit in this lift was about 167 pounds. He could also do a One Hand Dead Lift, readily with either hand, of 226 pounds on a 2⅜-inch bar. On a 2-inch bar, it would appear that Marx could have raised about 330 pounds (in 1965 = *c.* 400 pounds).

4. Dominique Rest, an old-time heavyweight professional strong-man, about 1880 did a One Hand Snatch of 82.5 kilos (181¾ lbs.) on a bar 55 mm (2.16 inches) in diameter, finishing the lift with a Bent Press. This was a terrific feat of gripping, being equivalent to doing a One Hand Dead Lift with about 314 pounds on the same bar, or with about 338 pounds on a 2-inch bar (in 1965 = 430 pounds!).

5. Simon Bauer, an old-time German professional athlete, at a bodyweight of only 141 pounds, about 1890 did a One Hand Snatch of 70 kilos (154¼ pounds) on a bar 55 mm (2.16 inches) in diameter! This was equivalent to doing a One Hand Dead Lift with about 266 pounds on the same bar, or with about 286 pounds on a 2-inch bar (in 1965 = 342 pounds!). Thus Bauer, in proportion to his size (height and bodyweight) showed a strength of grip fully equal to that of the heavyweight grip-champion, Hermann Görner.

6. Arthur Saxon (P; 69.6 in., 200 lbs.) did a Right Hand Snatch of 93.5 kilos (about 206 pounds) on a bar 42 mm (1.65 inches) in diameter (1904). However, it was not stated whether or not Saxon used a hooked grip in making this lift. If no hooked grip were used, the lift would have been equivalent to a One Hand Dead Lift with about 415 pounds on the same thickness of bar, or with about 355 pounds on a 2-inch bar (in 1965 = 417 pounds!). Such a lift—not using a hooked grip—might just have been possible for Saxon, who had relatively enormous hands. If so, it would have been phenomenal.

7. Louis Cyr (P; 68.5 in., *c.* 300 lbs.), in his contest with August Johnson in Chicago, on April 1, 1896, is said to have lifted 525 pounds on a dumbbell having a 1½-inch diameter handle. If he did, he almost certainly used a hooked grip. This would have been equivalent to lifting about 426 pounds on the same bar *without* a hooked grip, or to lifting about 340 pounds on a 2-inch bar (in 1965 = 410 pounds). Cyr had an exceedingly strong grip, provided the bar lifted was not too thick for his length of hand (about 7¾ inches). However, in lifting on bars over,

say, 2 inches in diameter, he could not cope with larger-handed strong-men such as Görner, Apollon, Marx, and Saxon.

Another splendid example of grip-strength performed by Cyr was to snatch with each arm (keeping the arm practically straight) a barbell weighing 188½ pounds that had a handle 1⅛ inches in diameter. Chicago, May 7, 1896. Since Cyr was right-handed, and nearly seven percent stronger on that side than on his left, it can be assumed that with his right hand he could, as a limit effort, have snatched at least 200 pounds on a 1⅛-inch bar. This would have been equivalent to doing a One Hand Dead Lift on a 1⅛-inch bar with about 406 pounds, or on a 2-inch bar with about 342 pounds (in 1965 = 412 lbs.). This estimation checks very well with that made for Cyr in his contest with Johnson (see above), and confirms his prodigious strength of grip.

8. August Johnson (P; 71 in., 205 lbs.), the powerful Swedish strong-man who contested with Louis Cyr in Chicago on April 1, 1896, was said to have made in that contest a One Hand Dead Lift of 475 pounds on the same 1½-inch diameter bar on which Cyr raised 525 pounds. As in Cyr's case, Johnson undoubtedly used a hooked grip in making his lift. *Without* a hooked grip, he would have raised about 363 pounds on the 1½-inch bar. This, in turn, would have been equivalent to a lift of about 290 pounds on a 2-inch bar (in 1965 = 350 pounds).

9. Ernest Cadine (P; 66 in., 198 lbs.), the famous French professional weightlifter, is said to have performed a Right Hand Dead Lift with the Apollon car wheels and axle (see above) when these weights weighed 367 pounds. Paris, 1925. The diameter of the axle (handle) was 49 mm or 1.93 inches. Since Cadine, even if he had proportionately large hands, could not have secured a hooked grip on this bar, and would have had to lift it with a regular (unhooked) grip, if he actually did so it would have been a remarkable feat of grip-strength for a man of Cadine's size. It would have been equivalent to doing about 355 pounds on a 2-inch bar (in 1965 = 394 pounds).

10. Jean Baillargeon (P; 73 in., 212 lbs.), of Quebec Province, Canada, was one of a family which included six brothers and six sisters, all of whom were exceptionally strong. Jean's specialty was feats of finger and grip strength. At the Apollo Health Studio in Columbus, Ohio, in 1951, he picked up with his right hand a 167-pound dumbbell that had a handle 2⅜ inches in diameter, and *passed it* from one hand to the other several times. No other man who had ever come to the gym had been able to lift this dumbbell even off the floor. It would be interesting

to know how much Baillargeon could lift, in a limit effort, on a 2-inch handle.

11. Edward Aston (P; 67.75 in., 168 lbs.), who once claimed the title "Britain's Strongest Man," was an exceptionally capable all-around barbell lifter, and in addition possessed large hands and a strong grip. In Paris, in 1913, he did a Two Hands Dead Lift of 225 kilos (496 pounds) on a bar 2¼ inches in diameter, using an overgrip. This was equivalent to doing a One Hand Dead Lift on a 2-inch bar with about 278 pounds (in 1965 = 318 pounds).

12. John Y. Smith (66.5 in., 165 lbs.), the famous old-time middleweight strong-man of Boston, had exceptionally strong and tough hands and fingers. He was in his prime about 1903, when he was 31 years of age. About that time, he once picked up a 220-pound barbell in his right hand and a 200-pound dumbbell in his left hand, and with these two weights walked 75 yards (another account says 200 yards!). The bar on each bell was 1½ inches in diameter. This, and other feats of gripping performed by Smith, indicate that his strength in such feats was about 75 percent of Hermann Görner's. This means that in a Right Hand Dead Lift on a 2-inch diameter bar, Smith in 1903 should have been capable of about 286 pounds (in 1965 = 337 pounds).

13. Arthur Dandurand (P; 68 in., 182 lbs.), of Canada, was one of the greatest light-heavyweight strong-men on record. He was equally strong all over, including his grip. About 1920, when he was 42 years of age, he did a Right Hand Dead Lift of 552 pounds. In his prime, about 1905, he should have been capable of about 580 pounds. This would have been equivalent to lifting, on a straight, 2-inch bar, about 315 pounds (in 1965 = 354 pounds).

14. Bob Bainhardt (70 in., 210 lbs.) was able to do a partial Two Hands Dead Lift, raising the weight about 6 inches from off a stand, with a barbell weighing 1250 pounds! In doing this he used reversed grips, but without any wrist straps or other artificial aids. Minneapolis, 1965.

G. LIFTING WEIGHTS WITH A PINCH-GRIP

NOTE: *Under this heading are included (1) pinch-lifts made on flat, iron barbell plates; (2) the same made on wooden planks; (3) chinning on rafters by means of a pinch-grip; (4) lifting barbell plates by their hubs; and (5) various comparable feats in which the adduction (bringing together) power of the fingers is used, such as holding out billiard cues between the fingers.*

1. Arthur Saxon (P; 69.6 in., 200 lbs.), as one of the feats in his act with the Ringling Brothers' Circus in 1909–10, used to snatch with one hand a 90-pound wooden plank while grasping it with a pinch-grip. The plank, which was of rough hemlock or spruce, was 10 inches wide, 3 inches thick, and about 15 feet long; it was used by Saxon to support, on his feet, from 12 to 14 men. The snatching of this plank was equivalent to picking off the ground by a pinch-grip a flat, iron barbell plate weighing about 113 pounds (in 1965 = 131 pounds).

2. Earlier, when the Saxon Trio was performing in England and on the continent, Arthur used a larger plank in his foot-supporting feat, capable of "seating" up to 21 men. This plank, according to the German strength-statistician Edgar Müller, was 23 feet long, 10 inches wide, 4 inches thick, and weighed 224 pounds. If so, the wood must have been of a heavier variety than that used in Saxon's 15-foot plank; otherwise the 23-foot plank would have weighed only about 184 pounds. Müller says that with the 23-foot plank (which was *4 inches* thick, remember) Saxon could perform a Two Hands Clean and Jerk! This would have been a phenomenal feat even if the plank weighed only 184 pounds, and it would seem impossible that Saxon could have performed it if the plank weighed 224 pounds.

3. Warren L. Travis (P; 68 in., 190 lbs.), who in 1909–10, while the Arthur Saxon Trio was in the United States, trained with the express object of having a weightlifting contest with Arthur. Travis, while known primarily as an expert in back-lifting and dead-weight lifting, also was very capable in various specialized feats of grip-strength, even though his hands—in contrast to those of Saxon—were only of average length and width (although very thick and muscular). Here are three of the pinch-grip lifts that Travis performed:
   a. Lifted a plank (of yellow pine), weighing 210 pounds, off the floor with two hands.
   b. Similarly lifted an iron elevator counterweight, 6 inches wide by 4 inches thick by about 34 inches long, weighing 210 pounds.
   c. Snatched with two hands a plank weighing 140 pounds.

4. "Apollon" is said to have once picked up a 90-pound barbell plate, 4.7 inches (!) thick,* gripping it between his four fingers, which were

---

*Another account says 3 inches thick, increasing slightly toward the middle.

bent, and the *palm* of his hand. He then "muscled-out" the plate in front of him, and in that position carried it the length of the gymnasium! Paris, *c*. 1892.

5. Hermann Görner (P; 72.5 in., 290 lbs.), the heavyweight champion of grip-strength, once pinch-lifted 111 pounds. This weight consisted of two large iron barbell plates in the middle and two smaller plates on the outside, the four being held together by a chair-leg forced into them like a shaft. The width of the two larger plates together, where Görner pinch-gripped them, was 2⅜ inches. Leipzig, July 10, 1934. This feat was performed without any special practice having been given to pinch-gripping. Since Görner's grip-strength otherwise was about 8 percent greater than Arthur Saxon's, it is probable that his potential in pinch-lifting a barbell plate was about 130 pounds (in 1965 = 141 pounds).

6. Al Berger (71.5 in., 193 lbs.) of Philadelphia, was one of the best performers at feats of pinch-grip strength ever to be seen in this country. While, later on, he increased in bodyweight to over 220 pounds, here are some of the feats he performed, in 1941, at a weight of 193 pounds:
   a. Pinch-lifted a 75-pound plate (1-inch thick) with 33 pounds added, a total of 108 pounds.
   b. Lifted "clean" to the shoulder a 75-pound plate (1-inch thick) in each hand.
   c. Lifted "clean" to the shoulder two 35-pound plates with one hand.
   d. Similarly lifted one 75-pound plate with 10 pounds added (on a short dumbbell bar through the center of the plate).
   e. Chinned 12 times in succession with a pinch-grip on rafters (30 inches apart).
   f. Chinned similarly 6 times with 10 pounds added.
   g. Chinned similarly once with 43 pounds added.
Since Berger was able to chin once while supporting 236 pounds (193 plus 43 pounds extra) with both hands, or 118 pounds with one hand, he should have been capable of picking up with a pinch-grip a plank weighing at least that amount (118 pounds). In fact, since the "poundage-possibility" in pinch-lifting a wooden plank is 1 1/7 times that of a smooth, iron barbell plate, Berger *should* have been able to pinch-lift a plank weighing about 123 pounds.

7. Ian "Mac" Batchelor (73 in., *c*. 300 lbs.) of Los Angeles was for many years the recognized champion at "Wrist-wrestling" (see p. 287). In addition, he made a specialty of various kinds of gripping and finger

strength. For example, he could bend metal bottle-tips between his thumb and forefinger as easily as the average man could break a peanut shell. In fact, between his thumb and clenched fist, he once bent 500 beer-bottle caps in succession during a period of 20 minutes. He also filled a beer bottle with 63 tightly-bent caps in 2 minutes. Again, he was able to bend simultaneously a cap in each hand, using the thumb and index finger only and keeping the finger *straight*. He once pinch-gripped an 80-pound iron plate in each hand and carried them 30 feet. Each plate was about 16 inches in diameter and 1½ inches thick. He also pinch-lifted a "steel facing plate" at the Douglas Aircraft plant that weighed over 100 pounds. When weighing 300 pounds, "Mac" could hang by one hand from a vertical climbing rope ("no locked thumb"); he considers this probably his most meritorious gripping feat.

One of Batchelor's more outstanding feats of finger strength was to grasp a large (2 to 2½-ft. high) wine bottle at the top or neck, and then work the bottle upwards by working the fingers downwards. This is a difficult feat with a large, tapering bottle alone; but "Mac" has done it with one of the very large wine bottles mentioned above, *filled with lead shot!* Another feat performed with a bottle was to pinch-grip between his two thumbs the very lip of a beer bottle and hold the bottle parallel to the bar. In Plate 29 "Mac" is shown performing a variation of the latter feat—using his forefinger and thumb—also his feat with the large wine bottle.

8. Charles Vansittart (P; 72 in., 182 lbs.) was an old-time English music-hall entertainer known professionally as "Vansart, the Man with the Iron Grip." That this title was fully appropriate will be seen from the following recital of some of the things that he could do.

One of Vansittart's unique feats was to tear a new tennis ball in half. Sometimes he would vary this by simply gripping the ball so hard that it burst! Another of his exhibitions was to grasp a champagne bottle (filled with shot and weighing 12 pounds) by the neck with one hand and gradually work it up with the fingers alone until the base of the bottle was in his palm (cf. Mac Batchelor's feat, above). Still another feat was to grasp four clay pipes in each hand—one stem between each two fingers, and with the bowls in the palms—and by suddenly clenching both hands smash the eight bowls into fragments. This was accomplished not so much by gripping the bowls as by pressing in on them with terrific adductor-muscle strength (of the fingers).

Again, Vansittart was the greatest of all the "billiard-cue performers" of his time (which was about the turn of the century). Fastening four billiard cues together, he would allow the tip of one of them to project just far enough to be grasped between his index and middle fingers, the palm of his hand facing the floor. Then, by turning his palm halfway upward, and by pressing down hard with the index finger and using the second as a fulcrum, he would raise the bundle of cues from the upright (hanging) position until they were fully horizontal, holding them in this position for several seconds. Many other feats with the cues were in Vansittart's repertoire.

Chinning on a single rafter. (Drawing by Clyde James Newman)

In pinch-gripping, "Vansart," in his music-hall act, would pass a 56-pound blockweight repeatedly across the face of an assistant who lay supine on the stage. This weight was pinch-gripped across the *bottom*, usually by two fingers and thumb, although it is said that he *could* lift in this manner as much as 65 pounds using only his index finger and thumb. 65 pounds in the latter style would be equivalent to about an even 100 pounds using the whole hand. (in 1965 = 119 pounds).

9. Henry Sincosky (67 in., 175 lbs.) could chin on rafters about 18 inches apart, and also walk along them, using a pinch grip, for 5 or 6 feet. He would do this by chinning halfway, giving a kick and hitch with his legs and arms, and moving one hand ahead a few inches. Philadelphia, *c.* 1915. Charles McMahon, who witnessed this feat, says that he never heard of anyone else being able to do it.

10. A number of heavyweight lifters have each performed a Two Hands Snatch by grasping the *rims* of the largest plates at each end of the barbell. In this manner Weldon Bullock, about 1940, snatched 135 pounds; Steve Stanko, about 1942, snatched 145 pounds; and Hermann Görner, in Leipzig on Oct. 20, 1931, snatched 75 kilos (165¼ lbs). In Görner's case the lift was more meritorious than the poundage alone would indicate, by reason of the plates being *flat* (1 3/16 inches thick) and therefore being pinch-gripped.

11. J. C. Tolson (65.5 in., 159 lbs.), a British professional strong-man known as "Young Apollon," about 1933 could lift a block of lead weighing 65 pounds by pinch-gripping with the *index finger and thumb of one hand only* an English penny that had been soldered in an upright position to the top surface of the weight. The English penny is a bronze coin of a size almost identical to that of a United States' half-dollar (i.e., about 1.22 inches in diameter by 0.08 inch thick). Out of twenty other strong-men who tried to lift this weight, in the manner that Tolson had employed, only one succeeded. He was the British amateur weightlifting record-holder Laurance Chappell (70.5 in., 165 lbs.), who had recently established a middleweight world's record in the Right Hand Dead Lift, with 502 pounds.

12. William P. Caswell (64.5 in., 140 lbs.) was a London music-hall strong-man who specialized in feats of grip-strength. Although he was only a lightweight, he had hands of large size, and thick, calloused fingers resulting from years of specialized work requiring strength and toughness. One of his feats, possibly unequalled, was to pinch-grip with one hand, *using the thumb and forefinger only*, on a 56-pound blockweight, the stud or eye through which the ring of the weight ran, lift the weight from the ground with this meager grip, turn it over at shoulder-height, then press it overhead! Some other feats in this category performed by Caswell were these: (1) he "cleaned" to the shoulders a barbell of 190 pounds having a regulation-sized bar, using only his two middle fingers; (2) he did a Bent Press with a barbell of 160 pounds by supporting the bar in the middle with only his forefinger and thumb! (3) he juggled a 56-pound ringweight, somersaulting it and catching it by the ring with only a little finger! Like "Apollo" (William Bankier), Caswell was able to hold five billiard cues in a horizontal position by the mere squeezing-together of the first two fingers of his right hand.

13. Jim Pedley (P; 68 in., 180 lbs.), who for several years was instructor

in Eugen Sandow's school of physical culture in London, could take hold of the outside (end) nuts of a shot-loading dumbbell weighing 200 pounds—using the tips only of his thumbs and fingers—shoulder the weight and press it overhead, afterwards lowering the bell to the ground with the same meager grip.

14. John McLoughlin (68 in., 205 lbs.), of the German-American Athletic Club of New York City, could in 1954 pinch-grip two 35-pound Olympic plates face to face, and walk around the gym "several times" (over 100 yards?) while retaining his grips on the plates. McLoughlin also holds the world record in the Two Finger Lift on a barbell (see below).

15. Stanley Krsysanowski could lift a 112-pound anvil by the horn and walk with it a distance of 8 feet (*c.* 1945).

16. Otto Poll (P; 70 in., 165 lbs.), who was known in motion pictures as Frank Merrill, was the second man to play the part of Tarzan, the first man being Elmo Lincoln (71 in., 210 lbs.). Both these men performed in the silent-picture era. However, Merrill was a skilled gymnast, who before going into the movies had held the National Championship on the Roman rings for several years in succession. Despite being rather lightly-built below the waist, Merrill was a first-class *all-around* performer in the gymnasium, being proficient in bar-vaulting, standing jumping, lifting weights (in certain specialties), etc. One of his feats of grip-strength, which he used in playing the part of Tarzan on the screen, was to hang (swing) by one hand from a climbing rope (with knots on it) while carrying ("rescuing") with his other arm a girl (Natalie Kingston) weighing 122 pounds—a total one-hand grip of 287 pounds (*c.* 1922).* (See Plate 33.)

17. Walt Metzler (*c.* 170 lbs.) could do a pinch-grip chin on two 2-inch thick rafters while carrying a 75-pound barbell plate hanging from his waist. On the basis of Al Berger's feats (see no. 6, above), it would appear that Metzler should have been capable of pinch-lifting an iron barbell plate of about 112 pounds, an extraordinary feat.

18. Stan Nicholes (*c.* 175 lbs.) could perform the following remarkable feat of pinch-grip strength. Using a large plate weighing 75 pounds, he would grasp the hub of the plate with his palm facing forward, stand erect, then curl the plate to his shoulder and press it aloft. From there he

---

*On one occasion, the rope broke, and both Merrill and Miss Kingston fell from a considerable height, she landing on top, and Merrill sustaining severe injuries.

would reverse the procedure until the plate was again flat on the floor, retaining his pinch-grip on the hub throughout! Melbourne, Australia, 1963.

19. Jack Fritsch was able to pinch-lift one of the *new-design* York 45-pound barbell plates by the hub with an extra 10 pounds added. Another of his feats was to pinch-lift two 45-pound plates placed together with the smooth sides out. York, Pa., 1965.

20. Dr. Daniel Siss, a dentist, had such a strong grip in his finger-tips that he was often able to extract children's teeth, and sometimes those of adults, without using forceps. This same ability, it is said, was possessed by many of the dentists in Japan in earlier days. These men developed this strength by the daily practice of pulling out pieces of wood driven into a plank.

Franz Föttinger, holding out 28½ lbs., gripping only a needle.

21. In the early 1890s, in central Europe, an extraordinary feat of finger strength was gradually developed by an amateur specialist named Franz Föttinger, of Vienna. A remarkable circumstance was that Föttinger, when performing his lifts in 1896, was 59 years of age. But he had practiced his specialty so constantly and for so many years that his age was not a factor of great importance. His special lift was as follows: He had two wooden blocks, one attached to the other with a cord. On the bottom of the lower block some additional weights were fastened. On top of the upper block he had an ordinary needle stuck in until less than an inch of the needle's length projected above the wood. Grasping the needle with his thumb and forefinger only, Föttinger would lift the collection of weights off the floor to the height shown in the

accompanying drawing. The total weight of the two blocks and additional weights was 28½ pounds. Fottinger used to offer 100 gulden (then about $40) to anyone who would duplicate his feat, but his money was pretty safe!

22. Joseph Mongelli (65 in., 155 lbs.), a strong-man of New York City, had large hands and, in one respect at least, unique finger strength. He could take an unshelled Brazil nut, place it on a table, grasp the middle finger of his right hand with his left, bend the right finger back as far as possible, then, releasing the finger, let it snap forward and downward on the nut. Invariably, the hard-shelled Brazil nut would be smashed into fragments! He could do the same with ice-cubes, and won many a bet from persons who, understandably, doubted that such a feat was possible (c. 1940).

23. "Batta" (Charles Estienne) was a French professional strong-man renowned for his strength of fingers and grip. Yet Batta could not equal the feat of a country clergyman he once met, who could crush a grain of wheat between his finger and thumb. The parson admitted that several years' practice had been necessary before he himself was able to accomplish this feat (c. 1895).

24. "Maciste" (Bartolomeo Pagano), the old-time Italian motion picture Hercules could open an ordinary can of sardines by using his fingers only. He would press his fingers strongly into the narrow strip of tin that would ordinarily be rolled up with the can-key. Separating this strip from the rest of the can by the pressure of his finger-tips, "Maciste" would then pull the top off the can.

25. Here is another feat of grip-strength by John Y. Smith, which may be compared with those performed on a vertical climbing rope by "Mac" Batchelor (no. 7, above) and Frank Merrill (no. 16, above), respectively. Smith could hang by one hand from a vertically-fixed belaying pin while holding in the other hand a 100-pound dumbbell—a total one-hand support of about 265 pounds.

26. Roberto Heydrich, of Havana, Cuba, could pinch-lift, using only the first two fingers and thumb of one hand, a blockweight 4.7 inches wide weighing 48½ pounds, to which extra weights were added, bringing the total up to over 70 pounds. 1955.

27. Samuel Olmstead (P; 69 in., 165 lbs.), a vaudeville strong-man and (later) the proprietor of a bodybuilding gym in New York City, could

hold out at arm's length *six* billiard cues simultaneously, maintaining the cues in a horizontal position simply by gripping them (by strength of the adductor muscles) between his index and middle fingers (c. 1930). This feat was performed also by Charles Vansittart (see no. 8, above) some 30 years earlier. "Apollo" (William Bankier), "The Scottish Hercules", of about the same period as Vansittart, in his stage act similarly held out *five* cues.

28. William J. Hunt (P; 66 in., 154 lbs.), while primarily a "herculean handbalancer" (see below), equalled the records of Charles Vansittart and Samuel Olmstead (see above) by holding out horizontally from the shoulder *six* billiard cues together, gripping them between the index and second fingers only. England, June 25, 1954. Hunt was then 45 years of age.

29. Perhaps the greatest recorded example of strength of the adductor muscles of the fingers was that performed by the 18th-century English strong-man, Thomas Topham (see Chapter 3). One of Topham's exhibition feats was to place the bowl of a strong (clay ?) tobacco pipe between his first and second fingers, then break the pipe-bowl simply by pressing his fingers together sideways! London, 1741.

H. BAR, NAIL, CHAIN, AND HORSESHOE BREAKING

NOTE: *One of the favorite and most impressive feats of old-time professional strong-men was the breaking of chains (so-claimed) on the arms and the chest. On the upper arm it was done by bending the arm and expanding the biceps; and on the chest by inflating the lungs and "throwing out" the muscles of the upper back. But these alleged accomplishments lent themselves to trickery of various sorts, although an expert performer could make the feat appear realistic and genuine.*

Charles Sampson, the old-time German-American strong-man who was "defeated" by Eugen Sandow at the Royal Aquarium Theatre in London, in 1889, attempted to use his trick "chain-breaking" feats in that contest, but was properly barred from doing so by the judges. A faked photograph shows Sampson breaking on his right upper arm a chain in which the links appear to be at least ¼-inch, or possibly 5/16-inch, in thickness. Now, according to my engineering handbook, a wrought-iron chain with links ¼-inch in caliber will withstand a load, or pull, of 3200 pounds before breaking. With 5/16-inch links the breaking strength is 5000 pounds. Even a chain with links only 3/16-inch thick (which is usually the smallest size listed) will withstand a pull up to 1800 pounds. Whether it is possible to develop an expansive power in the lungs and chest muscles sufficient to break—without using any trickery, or "doctored" links—even a ⅛-inch solid link chain (which will support 800 pounds), I do not know; and as for breaking such a chain around the biceps, I simply cannot imagine it.

Among performers who "break" chains on their chests and arms, the chain used is generally of the kind that has links made of wire bent into an S or an 8 shape, which actually part, or spring open, under pressure, rather than break. This is quite a different matter from breaking a chain with welded links, as the pull required to part the S-shaped wire links is within the range of human strength. Even in using such a wire chain, it is customary to place a leather or metal belt under the chain in order to prevent bruising, pinching or cutting of the skin, although some professional exhibitors have, by long practice, so toughened their skins that they can part wire chains around the chest or biceps without such protection.

Looking at the subject of "chain-breaking" from a realistic standpoint, it can be said that if a man bound to a post or wall by chains connected to metal wrist or ankle bands, or around his waist—as was done with prisoners in former times—could break such chains by sheer pulling power, and so free himself, there would be some point in admiring such a feat of strength. But what has such a practical application of physical power got to do with parting a wire chain on the biceps or around the chest?

While the exhibition feats of bar-bending, nail- (and spike-), breaking, and horseshoe-breaking may—like that of chain-breaking—also be faked, it is equally true that many perfectly genuine performances in these specialties have been made. Some of the more outstanding of these legitimate examples follow.

1. Thomas Topham (see Chapter 3), the famous English strong-man of the eighteenth century, may well have been a genetic anomaly, or "freak," of muscular power. Otherwise it would be difficult to account for the prodigious strength he possessed in every part of his body. One of Topham's regular exhibition feats was to take a large iron kitchen poker (about a yard long and nearly an inch in diameter) and bend it nearly to a right angle by holding it in his right hand and striking it with great force upon his bared left forearm. An even more extraordinary feat was the following: Taking an iron poker of about ¾-inch diameter and placing the center of it on the back of his neck, he bent it by pulling forward on the ends of the bar. But the extraordinary part was that after he had thus bent the poker, he was able to *straighten it out* simply by reversing the direction of his pull on the ends of it! The remarkable thing about this feat was that, in an ordinary person, the

muscles that bring the elbows backward are not nearly so strong as those that bring them forward; yet Topham performed both movements with equal facility.

2. Siegmund Breitbart (P; 73 in., 225 lbs.) was a famous Polish strong-man who appeared with his elaborate stage act at the New York Hippodrome in 1923. He would bend an iron bar 7 feet long by 1¾ inches wide by ½-inch thick into the shape of a three-leaf clover; and a ⅝-inch square bar 10 inches long into a horseshoe shape. He also per-formed various spectacular supporting feats, and "broke" link (jack) chains with his hands and by expanding his chest. But his most sensa-tional and unbelievable act was to bite through steel chains with his teeth. While most dentists claimed this feat to be impossible, the story is that Breitbart, in order to prove the actuality of the feat, once stopped at the Krupp Steel Works in Essen, Germany, and before the com-pany's engineering experts bit clear through a *steel* bar 5 mm (3/16-inch) thick. Secondly, he bit into a steel bar 11 mm (7/16-inch) thick to a depth of 1½ mm (1/16-inch). The engineers then placed these steel bars between two tool-cutting machines, and found that the pressure required to indent them to the same depth that Breitbart had done was 2500 pounds! After all this, the officials of the Krupp Works signed a document attesting to the legitimacy of Breitbart's performances.

For a long time, I, and everyone with whom I discussed Breitbart's alleged chain-biting feat, believed the performance to be faked. But later on another strong-man appeared, having a similar power in his teeth and jaws, and whose metal-biting ability could not be doubted. This circumstance made Breitbart's feats equally credible. The second "metal-biter" was Joe Greenstein, whose feats will now be described.

3. Joe Greenstein (P; 64 in., 140 lbs.), of the Bronx, New York, was a sideshow and carnival strong-man known as "The Mighty Atom." He also appeared in vaudeville, both in Europe and the United States, over a period of about 20 years. He was still able to perform many of his feats when past 80 years of age. He could "break" by chest expan-sion as many as three chains placed together, of a size designated as #8 or #10 jack chain. This consisted of S-shaped links of the type that could be parted rather than broken, as described on p. 221. Green-stein could also bend an iron bar or a horseshoe with his *teeth* while one end of the bar was fixed (as in a vise). The bar that he used for this purpose was usually one of ½-inch mild cold-rolled steel, 8 or 9 inches long. This size of bar he could also bend into a U-shape with his hands. But Greenstein's most extraordinary and spectacular feat far

transcended these chain-breaking and bar-bending exhibitions. He could *bite* a nail in half! That he actually possessed the ability to do this he demonstrated on many different occasions. On one of these, about 1934, when he was 53 years of age, Greenstein walked into the well-frequented New York gymnasium operated by Siegmund Klein and before the incredulous stares of Klein and about a dozen of his pupils who were working-out in the gym at the time, proceeded to bite in two a 20-penny nail that Klein—after satisfying himself that it was a strong and sound one—supplied. Klein's description of the act was as follows: "Greenstein placed the nail in his mouth, clamping it between his molars and holding onto the head of the nail with his fingers. Then with tremendous pressure he bit into the nail, and one could hear the teeth crunching as though they were being ground. He then turned the nail a little and bit again. On the last bite he just bent the nail slightly—and presto, it was in half!" Also, ". . . all of us checked his teeth to see that there were no special mouthpieces or caps over his teeth." Greenstein was capable also of performing with a *25-cent coin* the same feat of biting and breaking. For an account of his ability in *bending* coins, see Section I. See also no. 11, p. 228.

4. Charles Vansittart (P; 72 in., 182 lbs.), an English music-hall performer, was known professionally as "Vansart, the Man with the Iron Grip." He had extraordinary strength in his arms and upper body, especially his hands and fingers. Below the waist he was relatively undeveloped. One of his feats of bar-bending was to bend into a U-shape a wrought-iron spike ⅜-inch square by 7 inches long; moreover, he bent it in the most difficult way, so that the bend came *diagonally* across the section of the spike rather than on its flat side. "Vansart" was active around the turn of the century. George Gouin, a professional contemporary strong-man was said to be capable not only of bending a spike of the same size as Vansart's, but of *restraightening* it!

5. "Samson" (Alexander Zass), a Russian middleweight (64.5 in., 156 lbs.) professional strong-man, may have been more capable at bar-bending than even Vansart. Samson was said to have been able to bend into a U-shape, with his bare hands, a bar of iron ⅜-inch square and only 5 inches long! This feat was witnessed by the famous English weightlifter, Edward Aston, in London in 1924. In bending the bar, Samson would start by pressing it downward on one thigh just above the knee. He would then bend it further, in front of his chest, with his hands alone. This feat was fully equivalent to bending a *railroad spike*,

which if 5 inches long would be either ½-inch or 9/16-inch in thickness. Truly phenomenal! (See also no. 7, following.)*

6. "Young Apollon" (J. C. Tolson), a professional strong-man of Dewsbury, England (65.5 in., 159 lbs.), could bend *four 60-penny nails together*, a world record. A 60-penny nail is 6 inches long and from .26 to .28 of an inch in diameter. Another of Tolson's feats was to bend around his bare neck a bar of mild steel, ½-inch square and 10 inches long, into a U-shape. Once, for a wager of £100, he bent into a U-shape a *steel* carriage-bolt, with a nut on one end, the bolt being ⅝-inch diameter by about 6 inches long (*c.* 1927). Tolson, it is said, finally became able to duplicate Samson's feat of bending a ⅝-inch square iron bar only 5 inches in length.

7. "Samson" (Alexander Zass), some of whose bar-bending I have described in no. 5, above, was capable also of some extraordinary feats in *driving* nails. One of these exhibitions was to *pound* a 5-inch spike through a 3-inch-thick plank, using only the palm of his bare hand. He would then *pull the spike out of the plank* by hooking a single forefinger around it. In bending a long strip of iron into a scroll, Samson would customarily use a piece 7 feet long (the same length as Breitbart used) by 1¼ inches wide by ⅜-inch thick. Thus, in cross-section, Samson's piece of iron was only a little over half as strong as Breitbart's, since, as related above, the bar used by Breitbart had a section 1¾ inches wide by ½-inch thick.

8. The usual method of driving nails with the hand is to *hold* the nail between the second and third fingers, so that the head of the nail comes about in the middle of the palm. The palm is protected by the use of a small pad, either of thick leather or some soft material rolled into a pad. The nail is then driven into, or through, a board or other material by a powerful, fast downward blow of the fist. Siegmund Breitbart (see no. 2, above) was perhaps one of the best at driving nails in this manner. Holding a 6-inch spike, Breitbart could drive it through three one-inch thick boards plus five sheets of galvanized iron, two of the sheets being alternated between the boards and three sheets lying on top of them (see Plate 31). Another remarkable feat of Breitbart's was to *tear* in two a sheet of galvanized iron about six inches square and nearly ⅛-inch thick!

---

*While in my drawing (Plate 30) I show a piece of ⅝-inch square iron 5 inches long, as per Edward Aston's description, I do not see how, in using such a short length, anyone could bend a bar of this thickness unless the iron in it were relatively soft. In none of the bar-bending feats I have listed is the *grade*, or quality, of the iron or steel specified, and this can vary greatly.

9. Arnold Dyson, in a contest held in England during March 1954, won the title of British Bar and Nail-breaking Champion. Some of Dyson's record feats were to: (1) break 5 nails, each 6 inches long, in 1 min. 35 sec.; (2) break 4 large 6-inch nails in 59 seconds; (3) break an iron bar 18 inches long by ½-inch diameter in just over 20 seconds; (4) break an iron bar 12 inches long by 7/16-inch diameter in just over 20 seconds.

10. Harold Cope, of Derbyshire, England, in 1958 broke a single 6-inch nail in 5.8 seconds, and five nails of that size, one after the other, in 59 seconds. However, Cope took 48 seconds to break an iron bar 18 inches long by ½-inch diameter, whereas Dyson (see above) did the feat in 35 seconds officially and "just over 20 seconds" unofficially.

11. While a number of professional strong-men* have claimed to be able to bend, twist and break *horseshoes* with their bare hands, the recognized "champion" in this specialty was John Grünn Marx (70.9 in., 235 lbs.), "The Luxembourg Hercules," whom I have referred to repeatedly in connection with feats of gripping strength. At an exhibition in Paris in 1905, Marx broke three shoes in succession in 2 minutes, 15 seconds. And they were not small horseshoes, either. An illustration of one of the shoes broken by Marx under official conditions shows it to be 5½ inches wide, 5½ inches long, and made of a piece of flat iron over an inch wide. Evidently Marx was able to bend and break such a horseshoe in less than a minute (see Plate 32).

I. COIN BENDING AND BREAKING

NOTE: *A widespread aura of suspicion attaches to this feat: first, because of its seeming impossibility; secondly, because so many old-time professional strong-men faked the performance by "doctoring" their coins before breaking them. A third reason, which has probably influenced the opinion of many amateur strong-men, is the statement made by a number of well-known professionals that the feat clearly is impossible. Some of these "doubting Thomases" were men who themselves possessed exceptional finger and hand strength in other areas.*

For example, Edward Aston, the one-time professional champion weightlifter of Great Britain, in his book, How to Develop a Powerful Grip, *says, p. 32 (in speaking of the possibility of breaking an English penny): ". . . I made a test that finally convinced me and that con-*

---

*In addition to these professionals, there was Maurice Saxe, a Count of Saxony in the 18th century, who possessed great all-around "natural" strength. According to the historian, Guillaume Depping, Maurice "Having on one occasion stopped at a village during fair-time, to have his horses shod, he got a number of new shoes, of which he cracked five or six as if they had been glass."

sisted of placing a penny in a vise, gripping the free end with a pair of pliers and employing the full powers of my arms to break the coin. I found that it took thirty movements backwards and forwards before there was any sign at all of its rupturing. That test proved to my satisfaction that to break a penny with the hands alone was not possible . . ."

But Aston was dubious also about anyone being able to tear three decks of playing cards with the hands—a feat that has definitely been performed repeatedly by numerous vaudeville strong-men. Then there were the dentists who, in signed affidavits, solemnly declared that to bite into an iron bar with the teeth was "impossible." What, then, about the performances of Siegmund Breitbart and Joe Greenstein? In view of the performances with coins now about to be cited, it would seem pointless to deny the possibility—not only of bending coins with the fingers, which Aston admits can be done—but also the more difficult procedure of breaking them into two pieces. For there are "super-athletes" possessing great finger strength.

1. The most famous of these old-time strong-men was "Cyclops" (P; 66 in., 250 lbs.), a Polish exhibitor around the turn of the century. His real name was Franz Bienkowski, and he was known in theatrical and wrestling circles throughout Europe as "The Coin-breaker." In front of Professor Edmond Desbonnet, the French authority on weight-lifting and strong-men, "Cyclops" broke a 10-centime piece, a bronze or copper coin practically identical in diameter to a United States silver half-dollar (1.22 inches), but considerably thinner. In front of Theodor Siebert, the contemporary German authority, he broke several 10-pfennig nickel coins and one 20-pfennig silver coin, using, according to Siebert, "solely the thumb and forefinger of one hand!"

2. Charles Sampson (P; 67 in., 175 lbs.), who was a stage-partner of "Cyclops" (see no. 1, above) back in the 1890s, also claimed to be able to bend and break coins. However, Sampson's claims in this department were under suspicion. One theory has it that he carried around in his pockets an assortment of prepared coins, and that he would substitute one for each coin that was given to him to break. It would seem, however, that the probability of his having had prepared coins of every date and denomination was so remote as to make this theory absurd Certain it is that Sampson did at times break coins under conditions that would have made any faking of the feat difficult if not impossible. For instance, a wager of $500 was once made by a sportsman in New Orleans that Sampson could not break a freshly-minted 25-cent piece. Sampson accepting, the pair went to the mint then in New Orleans,

where Sampson, before several witnesses, proceeded to break a new quarter-dollar into halves within a period of three minutes. He then assertedly broke a half-dollar coin in less time than it had taken him to break the quarter.

3. Charles Vansittart (P; 72 in., 182 lbs.), an English music hall entertainer known professionally as "Vansart, the Man with the Iron Grip", could break an English penny with his fingers. The method he employed was to hold the penny between his forefinger and thumb, then break the coin by pressing it against the ball of the other thumb. The suggestion has been made that possibly the *composition* of the coins in those days made them more *brittle* than coins which were minted later on. The English penny, which is of bronze or copper, is practically identical in diameter and thickness to the French 10-centime piece.

4. Léon Sée (65.75 in., 155 lbs.) was a French amateur strong-man renowned for his strength of fingers and grip. At the first attempt, he picked up with one hand the "unliftable" barbell that once reposed in Professor Desbonnet's Physical Culture School in Roubaix (see above). It is interesting to note that "Cyclops" (see no. 1, above) could not pick up this barbell with one hand, despite his terrific finger-strength in bending and breaking coins. Desbonnet attributed to Sée also the ability to *break* coins, but did not specify what the size of the coins was.

5. William P. Caswell (P; 64.5 in., 140 lbs.), like Vansart, was an English music-hall performer whose specialty was feats of finger and grip strength. Using the same "technique" as that employed by Vansart, Caswell could bend and break with his fingers an English penny. Another feat performed by Caswell was to place either a penny or a two-shilling piece under the middle finger of his left hand so that the edges of the coin rested on the tops of the index and third fingers. Then, using the heel of his clenched right fist as a hammer, he would come down on the left middle finger with such a powerful blow that the coin would split in two!

6. "Morrison—the American Hercules" was a professional who performed *c.* 1905. W. A. Pullum, the British authority on weightlifting, tells of seeing Morrison "tear" three half-crown silver coins into halves, one after the other, before an astonished audience. The British half-crown is 1.30 inches in diameter, or slightly larger than a United States half-dollar.

7. John Grünn Marx (P; 70.9 in., 235 lbs.) is said to have presented the gymnast Prof. Paulinetti of Philadelphia with a 10-cent piece that he broke in Paulinetti's presence (*c.* 1900). This—in view of the small size

of a dime—was a more difficult feat than the breaking of quarters and half-dollars, feats that Marx was also said to be capable of doing.

8. Count Felix von Luckner, the famous German naval officer known during World War I as "The Sea Devil," was said to be able to *break* a United States 25-cent piece in half. He could also *bend* a dime to the extent that a match could be slipped under the arch in the coin.

9. Gerald Kersh, the famous British novelist, is said to have been able to bend (and break?) coins with his fingers.

10. Richard Bullis of Los Angeles, in the 1930s was said to have been able to *bend* a 50-cent piece.

11. A considerable number of strong-men, amateur as well as professional, have been able to bend a dime by holding it between the front *teeth* then pushing upwardly on the coin with the thumb. Gregory Paradise, a 125-pound Canadian strong-man, could thus bend a 25-cent piece to a right angle (*c.* 1920). Joe Greenstein could similarly bend either a quarter or a half-dollar. It is rather surprising that neither Samson (Alexander Zass) nor Siegmund Breitbart—both of whom were exceptionally capable at nail and bar bending and had strong jaws and excellent teeth—ever claimed to be able to bend or break coins.

J. CARD TEARING

NOTE: The tearing in two of one or more decks of playing cards is a specialized feat of hand and finger strength that lends itself well to stage or exhibition work. It was featured by many an old-time vaudeville or music-hall performer. Since even the "record" performances in this feat were made usually as a regular, routine part of a strength act (rather than as a single "official" attempt), no exact dates have been recorded for these performances. Therefore, in listing them, the best that can be done is to give the known year, or an estimate of it, in which the performer was active. Again, since no significant correlation exists between the size of the performer and his proficiency in card-tearing, in the following listings the height and weight are omitted. The performers are all professionals, unless otherwise noted.

1. Eugen Sandow, the "Non-pareil" of old-time strong-men, in his stage performances tore in half three full decks of cards. 1893–1902. According to Al Treloar (see no. 4, below), Sandow would tear the three decks usually in from 16 to 18 seconds.

2. G. W. Rolandow, a contemporary of Sandow, who challenged him repeatedly to a public contest, was able to tear three decks of cards plus 6 cards over, a total of 162 cards. New York City, *c.* 1900.

3. Charles Vansittart, "The Man with the Iron Grip," could easily tear three decks of cards. London, *c.* 1900.

4. Albert Treloar, longtime physical director of the Los Angeles Athletic Club, in his vaudeville performances and at the Club "smokers," regularly tore 3 decks of cards. He did not, however, hold the three decks in the manner generally used in holding one or two decks (and then tearing them with an S-shaped twist), but held the cards on one knee with his left hand, using an "overgrip," then *sheared* the 3 decks into halves gradually by gripping them firmly with the fingers of his right hand and pressing downward with the "heel" of his right thumb. While Treloar ordinarily could tear the 3 decks in a reasonably brief time (usually about 20 seconds), at one of his "smoker" exhibitions the cards started to slip, and Noah Young, who was watching the performance, says that Treloar had such a struggle and took so long to finish the job that he (Young) was "sweating blood" in sympathy for Treloar by the time he got done! Treloar started his card-tearing act in 1894, and in 1922—28 years later—stated that he was still improving his "technique" in the feat!

5. Noah Young, who was the heavyweight amateur champion weightlifter of the United States during the years 1915–1920, and during that time represented the Los Angeles Athletic Club, had large hands, a strong grip, and could tear 3 decks of cards largely by sheer strength. In fact, he and Al Treloar could each tear 4 decks, but found that it took too long for the feat to be a good one for exhibition.

6. Mark Jones, who was one of the greatest lightweight strong-men and all-around gymnasts ever developed at the Los Angeles Athletic Club, was a contemporary and close friend of Noah Young. The contrast in the sizes of the two men was outstanding. Yet Jones also could tear 3 decks of cards. How, with his small hands, he managed to do this I do not know, as at the time I knew Jones he had "retired" from demonstrations of this sort.

7. David Willoughby, the author of this book, in addition to being the light-heavyweight amateur champion weightlifter of Southern California during the years 1922–1925 (and National Olympic Champion in 1924), practiced various specialty feats such as spike-bending and card-tearing.

He could tear 2½ decks of cards into halves, 2¼ decks into quarters, and one deck into eighths. He could also tear one deck into halves in one clean twist.

8. Herman G. Bush, of Hannibal, Missouri, made somewhat of a specialty of card-tearing. When only 16 years of age he could tear a deck into eighths. Later on, he became able to do this in less than 10 seconds. He tore *40 separate decks* into halves in succession in less than 20 minutes. Another feat was to tear a deck into halves with his left hand while gripping the other end of the deck with his *teeth*. He felt that his most difficult performance was to tear a new deck into halves without removing them from their box or container, 1948. How would he have felt to learn of the feat performed by John Valentine (no. 9, following)?

9. John Valentine, of Leeds, England, was a very capable all-around middleweight strong-man. Once, when somebody had questioned his ability to tear cards, he went out and purchased two new decks and tore them together into halves *without removing them from their containers, c.* 1950.

10. "Batta" (Charles Estienne), the famous old-time French professional, was said to have been able to tear a deck of cards into halves by holding it *between the forefinger and thumb* of each hand only. Paris, *c.* 1897.

11. Tom Pevier, the old-time amateur weightlifting champion of England, tells of having a friendly contest with John Grünn Marx, in which Marx tore through 2 decks of cards before he was able to finish one deck. London, c. 1905.

12. "Young Apollon" (J. C. Tolson), an English professional noted especially for his feats of finger and grip strength, is said to have been able to tear 3 full decks of cards into *quarters*. This must be a record. Dewsbury, England, *c.* 1933.

13. Paul von Boeckmann, the old-time strong-man and health specialist of New York City (*c.* 1900), could take a deck of cards and *tear out of one side of the deck, with his forefinger and thumb, a small piece the size of a quarter-dollar.* He did this by first "breaking" the deck in the usual way, then working his thumb around the break in a semi-circle (see Plate 33). While this feat by von Boeckmann has been considered one of the most difficult of all card-tearing variations, Herman

Bush (see no. 8, above) says that he performed it "very easily" the first time he tried it!

14. Harold Ansorge, a heavyweight professional strong-man of Grand Rapids, Michigan, could perform a feat with a deck of cards very similar to that just described in connection with Paul von Boeckmann. The only difference was that Ansorge would tear a piece about 1¼ inches *square* out of the *corner* of the deck. This feat was illustrated by Bob Ripley in one of his "Believe It or Not" cartoons in 1939.

15. Adrian P. Schmidt, the well-known old-time instructor and featherweight strong-man of New York City, was said to be able to tear a corner out of 2 decks of cards placed together, c. 1896.

16. Hermann Görner when once asked, "What can you do in tearing a pack of cards?" replied "I don't know." Upon then being handed some new cards—110 in number—Görner tore the stack in half in exactly one second!

K. DYNAMOMETER GRIPPING

In all forms of strength-testing, it is desirable to use, wherever practicable, some form of resistance that can be accurately *measured*. Hence the usefulness and reliability of barbells and dumbbells, which can be placed on a scale and *weighed*. For testing the strength of one's grip, or hand-squeeze, there is a device that registers the amount of resistance in another way. It is called a hand dynamometer. This device is available in several different styles, according to the source of manufacture. However, in each of these styles the basic principle of the device is the same. This principle is the squeezing together of the two "sides" of the dynamometer in one's hand against the resistance of a spring, or springs. The "grip-machine" that may appropriately be considered first is the one known as a Collin's dynamometer. An illustration of it is shown here.* This hand dynamometer consists of a single elliptical spring, about 5 inches long by 2⅜ inches wide, with a rack-and-pinion arrangement in the center which moves an arrow on a radial, calibrated dial and thereby records (in kilograms or pounds) the amount of pressure applied to the spring. On this instrument the "average" man (69 in., 155 lbs.) can squeeze with his right hand about 112 pounds, and with his left hand about 102 pounds.

Before listing the performances of various strength-athletes and "grip-men" on the Collin's dynamometer, it will be helpful to describe another type of gripping device known as the Regnier dynamometer.

*Collin's hand dynamometer.**

This for the reason that some performers used the Collin's dynamometer, others the Regnier, and a few *both* devices. From the latter information, it is possible to convert the performances made on a Collin's dynamometer to those made on a Regnier dynamometer, or vice versa. Thus a direct comparison of all performances can be made.

In the Regnier dynamometer, the spring is of a long and narrow shape, designed for the use of both hands simultaneously. At least two positions for using the Regnier dynamometer are recognized: first, the *position libre*, or free style, which will not be considered here; and secondly, the *position reglem*, or regular style used for determining one's strength of grip. About 53 percent more, on the average, can be registered in the *position libre* than in the *position reglem*. In the latter style the instrument is held close to the chest, one hand above the other; and the spring is compressed by a squeezing of both hands combined with an inward pushing of the arms. The Regnier dynamometer as thus used tests the strength of the grip, and to a lesser extent that of the pectoral muscles of the front chest. Experience has shown that, on the average, the amount that can be gripped on the Regnier dynamometer is equal to ⅝ (62.5 percent) of the *combined* right and left hand grips on the Collin's dynamometer. For example, if a performer gripped on the latter device 125 pounds with his right hand and 115 pounds with his left hand—making a total of 240 pounds—he would be expected to grip on the Regnier dynamometer ⅝ of 240, or 150 pounds. Conversely, the expected poundage on the Collin's dynamometer (right and left hand squeezes combined) is 8/5, or 1.60, times that on the Regnier dynamometer.

Here are some recorded performances on both types of dynamometers, one being converted to the other. The figures, which in most cases were originally recorded in kilograms, are given only to the nearest pound; and those in parentheses are the *estimated* figures. Where the left-hand

---

*On the dynamometer pictured in this illustration, the dial registers only up to 180 pounds. There are, however, other makes that register to well over 200 pounds.

grip is unknown, it is estimated as being 92 percent of the right-hand grip, this being the average ratio observed among strong-men.

Table 9. Records in gripping on hand dynamometers.

Year	Nation	Performer	Collin's dynamometer		Regnier dyna- mometer	Equivalent in 1965 to
			Right Hand	Left Hand		
1928	USA	David Willoughby	192	174	(229)	(252)
1908	Belgium	Gustave Empian	(217)	(199)	260	(302)
1925	France	Ernest Cadine	229	214	(277)	(307)
1909	Poland	Stanislaus Zbyszko	(229)	(211)	275	(319)
1895	France	"Batta" (Chas. Estienne)	(222)	(205)	267	(323)
1901	France	Leon See	(235)	(217)	282	(335)
1903	France	Pierre Bonnes	(243)	(221)	291	(343)
1902	Gt. Brit.	Jim Pedley	(248)	(228)	298	(353)
1920	Germany	Hermann Görner	(314)	(288)	(376)	(423)
1892	France	"Apollon" (Louis Uni)	(294)	(270)	(352)	(431)

In the above table, the only performers to have not set their records when they were in their physical primes are Apollon and Görner, and for these two strong-men all three poundages are estimated. Apollon made an actual record of 153 kilos (337.3 pounds) on a Regnier dynamometer in 1902, when he was 40 years of age. At his best, perhaps ten years earlier, he should have done about four percent more, or 352 pounds, as shown in the table. Görner, on December 12, 1949, when he was nearly 59 years of age, squeezed 130 kilos (286.6 pounds) with his right hand on a Collin's dynamometer. In his prime, about 1920, he should have done nearly ten percent more, or 314 pounds. This would have been equivalent to 376 pounds on a Regnier dynamometer.

The final column on the right in Table 9 shows what each performer would be expected to squeeze on a Regnier (two-hand) dynamometer if he were in his prime in the year 1965 and made his effort then. With Apollon being at his best in about 1892 and Görner about 28 years later, it would appear from the projected poundages that Apollon had a slight edge over Görner, at least in gripping on a hand dynamometer if not on a thick-handled barbell.

It is only fair to add that a person may have a strong hand-grip in other directions without necessarily being able to make a good showing on a hand dynamometer. Much depends on how well the performer is able to *apply* the strength of his grip to the size and shape of the object being gripped. Back in 1893, Dr. Dudley Allen Sargent of Harvard University, in testing the famous Eugen Sandow on a Collin's-type dynamometer, found Sandow's right-hand "squeeze" to be only 75 kilos or about 165 pounds. Similarly, about 1920, Warren L. Travis, who could lift more than 100 pounds with a pinch-grip, registered only 150 pounds on a Collin's dynamometer. In contrast, a person may have exceptional ability in squeezing on a "grip-machine" without being strong otherwise. Such possibilities and uncertainties help to make physical tests interesting. One never knows when a truly phenomenal ability may be discovered!

L. ONE-FINGER LIFTING AND FINGER PULLING

NOTE: One of the lifts that was popular among old-time German and Austrian strong-men was the raising of heavy weights just off the ground using only a single finger. Usually the finger employed was the middle one, since that is the longest, and normally the strongest, of the four. But some strong-men became such specialists at the feat that they made records using each of their four fingers separately. Originally these lifts were performed by hooking the lifting finger through a plain iron ring. Possibly the lift was "discovered" by someone who tried to lift one of the heavy stones to which horses could be hitched, and which had an iron ring fastened in its upper surface. In any event, the lift was a legitimate test of finger strength until a specially-designed, padded ring was introduced, into which the lifting finger fit so tightly that it was impossible for it to straighten out from the pull of the weight. In the following list of performances, the lifts were made on a plain iron ring— rather than a padded "finger ring." Lifts in the latter style are indicated by an asterisk.

1. Louis Cyr (P; 68.5 in., c. 300 lbs.) lifted off the ground with his middle finger a weight of 552½ pounds. Chicago, May 7, 1896.

2. Bergman Rottenfusser, while standing on two stools, lifted 552 pounds about 20 inches off the floor with his middle finger.

3. Lorenz Geer, a middleweight strong-man of Munich, lifted 557½ pounds with his middle finger.

4. George Rock lifted 569 pounds with the middle finger.

5. Hans Steyrer, of Munich, who was known as "The Bavarian Hercules," was somewhat of a specialist at one-finger lifting. In one of his per-

PLATE 33

(Above, left) Frank Merrill as "Tarzan". (78)

(Above, right) Deck of cards torn by Paul von Boeckmann. (79)

(Below, left) An old-time finger-pulling contest in the Tyrol. (80)

(Below, right) Hans Steyrer lifting 500 German pounds with one finger. Munich, c. 1878. (81)

PLATE 34

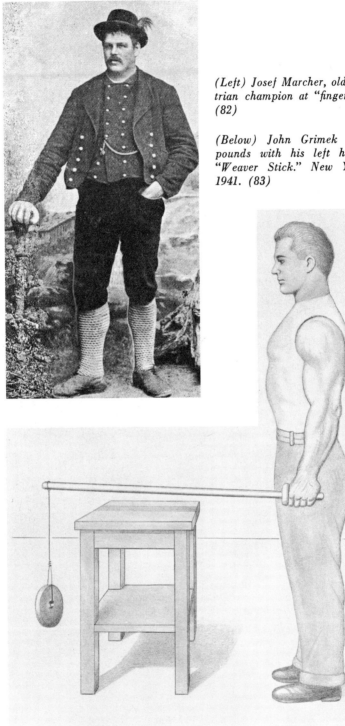

(Left) Josef Marcher, old-time Austrian champion at "finger pulling." (82)

(Below) John Grimek lifting 10 pounds with his left hand on a "Weaver Stick." New York City, 1941. (83)

PLATE 35

Siegmund Klein, famous bodybuilding instructor of New York City, illustrating the style in which he performed 19 consecutive handstand pushups on a bench at a bodyweight of 148 pounds. Klein could still approximate this record when past 40 years of age. (84, 85).

PLATE 36

(Above) Jules Keller, the "upside-down man." (86)

(Left) Joe Duncan Gleason (top) and partner doing a fine hand to head balance on the roof at the Los Angeles Athletic Club. Gleason was a former National Champion on the Roman Rings. (87)

Two poses by the phenomenal equilibrist, Gilbert Neville. On the left he is balancing on a hand-grip pedestal, and on the right on a free-to-move slackwire! (88, 89)

PLATE 37

Bob Jones, performing his famous "thumb-stand" on Indian clubs. Pine Bluff, Ark., Sept. 8, 1929. (90)

PLATE 38

Coulter and Shaffer—Equili-
bristic Feats of Strength

Introducing difficult feats in
hand-to-hand balancing

*(Above, left) Prof. P. H. Paulinetti.
(91)*

*(Below, left) Ottley Coulter and
Charles Shaffer. (92)*

*(Right, above and below) The Erik-
son Brothers. (93, 94)*

PLATE 39

(Top) "The Carmenas," a top-ranking brother-and-sister balancing act from Germany. (95)

(Bottom) Bert Goodrich (right) and his partner, Nelson, going through their hand-to-hand routine. (96)

PLATE 40

Two unusual feats performed at "Muscle Beach."

(Left) Harold Zinkin supporting about 240 pounds (Dolly Zinkin and Abbye Stockton). (96a)

(Right) John Collins supporting 260 pounds on one arm. The girl is Dee Fritz, and the topmounter, Renald, of Rudy and Renald, handbalancers. (96b)

formances at the Circus Herzog in Vienna, in 1879, he lifted a foot off the ground, using his middle finger, a block of marble weighing 582 pounds. This block, which was presented to Steyrer when he left the circus, later—gaining fame with the years—became virtually a "museum piece."

6. Michael Schart lifted 605 pounds with his middle finger. London, 1893.

7. Perhaps the greatest of all the old-time exponents of finger-lifting was Philip Brumbach, the father of the famous strong-woman Katie (Brumbach) Sandwina. Brumbach is credited with having lifted with his middle finger 642 pounds, with his fourth finger 551 pounds, and with his little finger 441 pounds. Munich, c. 1880.

8. Warren L. Travis (P; 68 in., 185 lbs.) lifted 667 pounds with his middle finger.* Brooklyn, N.Y., Nov. 1, 1907.

9. Jack Walsh (P; 65.5 in., 180 lbs.) lifted 670 pounds with his middle finger.* Trenton, N.J., Nov. 13, 1950.

10. R. S. Weeks (69 in., 220 lbs.) lifted 760 pounds with his middle finger.* Myrtle Beach, S.C., c. 1942.

11. Hermann Görner (P; 72.5 in., c. 245 lbs.), using "reverse grips" on a barbell (that is, with the palm of one hand facing forward and the palm of the other hand facing the body) lifted with his two middle fingers 140 kilos or 308½ pounds. Using the index and middle fingers of each hand in an "overgrip" (that is, with the backs of both hands facing forward) he lifted a barbell of 175 kilos or 385¾ pounds. In a similar lift but using a "reverse" grip, he raised 275 kilos or 595¼ pounds. All these lifts were well under Görner's maximum ability. Leipzig, c. 1925.

12. John McLoughlin (68 in., 205 lbs.), of the German-American Athletic Club of New York City, using "reversed" grips on a barbell, lifted with his two middle fingers 411 pounds. 1954.

13. Arthur Saxon (P; 69.6 in., 200 lbs.), the celebrated German professional strong-man, possessed extraordinarily large and thick hands, fingers and wrists. Although generally remembered for his world's record one-arm overhead lift (a Bent Press of 370 pounds performed in Stuttgart in 1905), an even more extraordinary feat he is said to have

performed was to raise overhead (Bent Press), *using his little finger only*, a weight of 135 kilos (297.6 lbs.)! This weight was supported by a strong leather loop into which Saxon hooked his little finger—naturally as far down as possible. Surely this lift must represent one of the greatest feats of finger-*supporting* strength on record. Thomas Inch tells how Saxon, for a wager, once played the part of a lamb being led to its slaughter by taking on a 336-pound bully who delighted in breaking the fingers of his opponents in pulling and twisting contests. Some of the bully's "past victims" were on hand to watch Saxon turn the tables on the finger-twister.

14. Thomas Topham, the great 18th-century English strong-man (see Chapter 3), is credited, among many other feats of finger strength, with having taken a "200 weight" (224 pounds) with his little finger and raising it "gently" over his head. While this was considerably less than Saxon's similar lift of 297 pounds, it should be noted that Saxon used a Bent Press to raise the weight overhead, whereas Topham declined to use "scientific" methods and relied wholly on his abnormal strength. What a phenomenal specimen he must have been!

1. *Finger Pulling*

This event, like finger-lifting, was popular among old-time German and Austrian strong-men. In these regions it is still a regular competitive test. However, today it is performed with a rubber-covered, oblong steel ring, into which the opponents hook their middle fingers. This is a fairer test than when—as was the rule for many years—fingers alone were hooked together, as it eliminates the possibility of a thick-fingered competitor causing his opponent's finger to be partly straightened out even before the pulling commences! Again, the object today is no longer to straighten out one's opponent's finger, but to pull his shoulders across the centerline of a table. Finally, there is less chance of trickery in the new style.

Years ago, at a gymnasium which I then conducted in Los Angeles, the giant German wrestler, Hans Steinke, was quite vexed after having lost a finger-pulling contest to a smaller and obviously less-strong wrestler. After teasing Steinke a while, this smaller wrestler divulged to Steinke that his middle finger had once been broken and had knitted so as to make the terminal joint partially bent. Thus, to have defeated his opponent, Steinke would have had to re-break the man's middle finger!

The recognized champion in finger-pulling, in the days when two opponents simply hooked their middle fingers and pulled, was Josef Marcher, of the Austrian Tyrol. Marcher was a giant of a man, standing

6 feet 3 inches and weighing 280 pounds (see Plate 34). It is easy to see why he won all his matches, since his hands and fingers were simply enormous. Consequently, when a thinner-fingered opponent hooked fingers with Marcher, the smaller man's fingers would be partly opened-out to start with.

A feat with which Marcher used to demonstrate his finger strength was to hang by his middle finger from an iron ring while holding in his left hand a weight of 120 pounds. This made a total support of about 400 pounds. One would think that this would have made a one-finger lift from the ground easy for Marcher, yet he failed to thus lift a weight of 460 pounds which had been raised with the middle finger by Franz Stöhr, the contemporary Austrian weightlifting champion. On the other hand, Marcher is said to have defeated in finger-pulling contests both Stöhr and Hans Steyrer. This, in view of Marcher's enormously thick middle finger and the advantage it gave him, is not surprising. Possibly, if either Stöhr or Steyrer had competed against Marcher and had used a padded metal ring, such as is customary today, he might have held his own against Marcher. The latter athlete was born at Kirchdorf, in the Tyrol, in November 1863, and was at his best in finger-pulling in the late 1890s.

Adrian P. Schmidt, the old-time featherweight strong-man and physical instructor of New York City, was evidently a wonder at finger-pulling, even though he weighed only 126 pounds. But he was also tricky, and would "get the jump" on his opponent by quickly shifting *his* finger from the middle phalange to the distal phalange of his opponent's finger. By such means he is said to have "defeated" such celebrated strong-men as Warren L. Travis, Joe Nordquest, and the German champion Karl Mörke. If a padded metal ring had been used in these contests, there can be little doubt that the outcomes would have been different.

The most recent Bavarian champion in this event of which I have information is Willi Lehner, a 230-pound athlete who out-pulled all his opponents in 1961. From the available information concerning Lehner's training methods, they appear to have been very similar to those used by Josef Marcher in the 1890s. In Germany and Austria the sport of finger-pulling is called *Fingerhakelm* (see Plate 33).

M. LEVERAGE LIFTING BY "WRIST" STRENGTH

The above heading applies to feats in which weights are lifted and held out by strength of the forearm muscles which *abduct* the wrist (that is, maintain the hand in line with the forearm). A typical example is where a heavy sledgehammer is grasped at the end and held horizontally, either at shoulder-level or any lower point. Another example is the familiar one of holding a chair upright while grasping one of its front legs at the bottom with one hand. But there are better ways of testing one's "wrist" strength in this manner, so that a more accurate recording of the strength required can be made. One of these ways is as follows. A round lifting stick (such as a mop handle) is used which has the following dimensions: diameter, about one inch; length, 42 inches. About 25 years ago, my friend and fellow-enthusiast, George Russell Weaver, who was then living in Brooklyn, popularized this leverage "wrist" test there and in Manhattan. The stick he used, which was of the dimensions given above, came to be known as a "Weaver stick." Weaver's description of the details of his stick is as follows:

Half an inch from one end, cut a notch. *Exactly* 36 inches from the *center* of this notch, circle the stick with a line. Get two metal right-angles at a hardware store, and screw them into the top and bottom sides of the stick so that the rear edges of the right-angles come exactly to the circled line. (The top side of the stick is the side where the notch is cut.) If one angle has one screw-hole, and the other angle has two screw-holes, the screws will not conflict. You can shave the top and bottom of the stick a little with a knife, at these places, to make a flatter base for the angle. This leaves a "handle" just 5½ inches long, which you can tape to a thickness that suits your hand and affords a good grip.

It is important that the following rules be observed. The stick must be lifted approximately parallel to the floor, and *not* with the weighted end tilted downward. Above all, the stick must be lifted straight **up** from the chair; there must be no rocking of the stick on the chair before lifting. The lifting hand and arm must remain free of the body. And the heel of the hand must remain on *top* of the stick; if the hand twists around under the stick, the lift is no good and cannot be allowed. The stick, when lifted, need not be held for any length of time; but it must be clearly lifted free of the chair (an inch is enough) and held in control (one second is enough).

This lift may also be made by turning the back on the weight and grasping the stick with the little-finger toward the weight, instead of with the thumb toward the weight. More weight can be lifted in this manner. When lifting with the back toward the weight, the body may be bent forward as the lift is made.

(For an illustration of the position to be assumed in making a Forward Lift on a Weaver stick, see Plate 34).

Many years before George Weaver thought up his leverage lifting stick, Paul von Boeckmann of New York City, who found that he was good at this sort of lifting, used to win bets by raising weights on the end (straw) of an ordinary broom. He, like Weaver, soon saw that it was essential to establish a fixed distance on the stick between the center of the weight and the front (thumb-side) of the lifting hand. By doing this, he eventually made a record by lifting 11½ pounds at a distance of 36 inches in front of his grip. This was equivalent to raising the same amount in a Forward Lift on a regulation Weaver stick. At the age of 62 (in 1933), von Boeckmann could still raise 9½ pounds in this manner!

Weaver's tests with his stick revealed a remarkable *range* in ability among the various persons who lifted on it. In this lift (in the Forward style) the "average" man would seem to be capable of about 4 pounds. Yet Warren L. Travis, the one-time world's champion in back and harness lifting, and who in addition had a very strong grip, could raise only 4¼ pounds. The best performance in the Forward Lift recorded by Weaver was a *left-hand* lift of 10 pounds by John Grimek. Later, in York, Pa., Grimek is said to have raised 11¾ pounds in this style with his *right hand.** The latter lift would appear to be the present world record. Steve Stanko and John Davis, who were then at their best, each lifted 8 pounds.

In the Backward Lift, the highest poundage recorded by Weaver was 12½ pounds. This was performed by John Protasel, of New York City. However, in order to be equal in merit to John Grimek's Forward Lift of 11 pounds, a Backward Lift should be about 15½ pounds.

It would certainly be interesting to know what such strong-men as Cyr, Barré, Apollon, Marx, Görner, and others of great hand and forearm strength could have lifted on a Weaver stick. However, any guesswork in this direction could be highly unreliable. One would suppose that thick wrists and tight wrist ligaments would be of great assistance in this lift; yet actually some strong-men who possessed these attributes did very badly on the Weaver stick, while others, who had more slender wrists and limber wrist joints, did unexpectedly well.

But it *is* possible to estimate with a fair degree of accuracy what certain athletes could probably have lifted on a Weaver stick from what they were *known* to have accomplished in holding out sledgehammers and other objects in a "leverage" manner by "wrist" strength.

Arthur Dandurand (P; 68 in., 185 lbs.), the great Canadian light-heavyweight strong-man, at the age of 50 (!) could hold out at arm's length with either hand, gripping the handle at the end, a 12-pound sledge hammer 36 inches in length. This was equivalent to not only lifting a Weaver stick off a table, but *holding it at shoulder-level with the arm straight*, with a weight of about 8¾ pounds. Considering Dandurand's

---

*However, from the description of Grimek's feat, in the November, 1943 issue of *Strength and Health*, the distance from the notch on the stick to the front of the lifter's hand was only 33¾ inches. This would reduce Grimek's lift from 11¾ to 11 lbs.

age at the time he made this demonstration, he should surely have been capable of lifting on a Weaver stick in the usual manner at least 10 pounds when he was in his prime.

An equally remarkable lift, considering the age of the performer, was made by an old-time exhibitor in Germany named Josef Siegl. In 1893, at the age of 68 (!) Siegl was able to hold out, on a stick 56 inches in length, a weight of 5 German pounds (= 5.51 English pounds). This was equivalent to holding out at least 8 pounds on a regulation Weaver stick. Siegl, however, had made a specialty of this lift for many years and for that reason was probably at 68, almost as capable in it as he had been in his prime. In any case, he won many a bet by being able to do it.

Henry Holtgrewe (69 in., 280 lbs.), "The Cincinnati Strong-man", had 15½-inch forearms and was very strong at all kinds of wrist-leverage tests. (See Plate 5). One of Holtgrewe's feats, which he performed in the presence of Ottley Coulter, when way past his prime and out of condition, was to place a common brick (6 pounds) on the straw of a broom, then lever up the broom and brick, keeping the broom horizontal, by grasping the end of the handle with the *back of his hand uppermost and his thumb toward the brick*. This tested the *supinator*—rather than the abductor—muscles of the forearm. Holtgrewe performed this feat with great ease. Coulter, after some practice, was just barely able to do it. As will be noted, this lift was different from lifting on the Weaver stick, where the forearm is more *perpendicular* to the floor.

Ernest Cadine (P; 66 in., 198 lbs.), of France, in his stage act performed a feat similar to that described for Henry Holtgrewe above. The only difference was that Cadine employed 5 billiard cues, grasping them together at their small ends and holding them in a horizontal position at arm's-length out from the shoulder. In order to properly compare Cadine's feat with that of holding out a 6-pound brick on the straw of a broom, it would be necessary to know the length and the weight of the billiard cues used by Cadine. Unfortunately, such essential information is almost always omitted from the published accounts of feats of this nature.

Murl Mitchell of Los Angeles, who in 1945 placed second in the 123-pound class in the Senior National Weightlifting Championships, used to perform this feat of "wrist" strength. Grasping in each hand a 25-pound sledgehammer at the end of its 30-inch-long handle, he would hold both hammers at arms' length in front of him at shoulder-level, then slowly lower (by bending the wrists toward the forearms) the hammers until they gently touched his eyeglasses! This feat uses the same muscles as the Backward Lift on a Weaver stick, but in a different manner. As I have no other records of its kind with which to compare it, I can only say that Mitchell's feat appears to be a terrific one!

With reference again to Paul von Boeckmann (see above), here is another feat that demonstrated his remarkable strength in "leverage" lifting. He had an iron Indian club, about 20 inches high, that weighed between 80 and 85 pounds. Grasping this club at the small end with his hands close together (in baseball bat style), von Boeckmann could readily lever it up and over his shoulder. But evidently, for anyone else it was a terrific feat. Sandow, who tried it, couldn't budge the club from the floor. Charles Atlas, at a much later date, managed to tilt it slightly. Only one man other than von Boeckmann ever succeeded in getting it to the shoulder. This was Joe Nordquest (67.5 in., 190 lbs.), who, after a tremendous effort, was able to shoulder the club in the prescribed manner.

Finally, here is a feat which, though not of the same nature as those cited above, must still have required great "leverage" strength in the wrists and grip. Jack Smith, one-time rookie with the New York Yankees, was said to be able to *break* a baseball bat with his bare hands! (How—by slugging it against a brick wall?)

N. CHINNING

NOTE: *While "weightlifting," using a barbell, a dumbbell, or any of the other pieces of apparatus designed for the purpose, is perhaps the most generally used method of testing a person's muscular strength, it should be remembered that there are other, equally valid methods, some of which are performed with weights and some merely by raising one's own bodyweight. In the latter category are such time-honored feats as "chinning" on the horizontal bar and "dipping" on the floor or on the parallel bars. These events, along with others of a similar nature, will be dealt with in the following pages.*

Before reviewing various records that have been made in one-arm and two-arm chinning, it will be well to consider some of the basic principles applying to this form of gymnastic ability, so that any particular record may be properly evaluated, or rated, and compared with others of its kind.

First, let us consider the chinning ability of the "average" young man of college age. At a height of 69 inches and a bodyweight of about 155 pounds, he can pull himself up on a horizontal bar, or "chin" himself, about 9 times in succession. This is equivalent to chinning once while carrying about 35 pounds of extra weight, a total lift of about 190 pounds. This represents a "chinning strength" of about one-half of what it might be if the "average" young man developed himself muscularly to ideal bodily proportions and built up his bodyweight to 170–175 pounds.

By the application of certain principles of bodily efficiency, as deduced from the average or typical performances of athletes in general, it is possible to "predict" with a fair degree of accuracy what a man should be able to do in one kind of effort from what he has been known actually to do in another, provided the same groups of muscles are being tested in both feats and the performer has endurance—or the ability to repeat an effort—in typical proportion to his momentary strength. Thus, we are able to say that if a man is able to chin himself 24 times with both arms (with the hands facing toward the body), he should be able to chin himself once with one arm, provided he has practiced both feats equally and is therefore able to adopt and apply the most advantageous "technique" in each. From this we can see that it is quite beyond the strength of the "average" man to chin himself with one arm, since he is able to chin only about 9 times with both arms (instead of over 20 times). However, numerous gymnasts have each chinned themselves repeatedly with only one arm; and some of the records established both in one-arm and two-arm chinning are quite extraordinary, as will shortly be related.

To "chin" once with one arm is equivalent to chinning once with both arms while carrying extra weight equal to two-thirds of the performer's own bodyweight. Thus, for a 150-pound man to do a one-arm chin, is equivalent to his doing a two-arm chin while carrying 100 pounds of extra weight. It should be noted that, whether live or dead weight be used, the extra weight should always be so attached to the performer's body that when he first starts chinning the extra weight starts being lifted also. To have the extra weight, on the contrary, leave its support only after the performer is one-half or two-thirds of the way up to the chinning bar is not a complete lift and should not be claimed as one.

A comparison of various records in both one-arm and two-arm chinning shows that, on the average, the number of two-arm chins possible is equal to 6 times the number of one-arm chins (average of right and left arms), plus 18. Thus, if a man can chin once with either arm, he should be expected to chin 24 times with both arms; twice with one arm, 30 times with both arms; 3 times with one arm, 36 times with both arms; and so on, adding 6 two-arm chins for every additional pair of one-arm chins. Thus, when a performance of 14 one-arm chins (with either arm) is reached, it is found to be equivalent to about 102 two-arm chins.

In the following review, my object is not to list at length all the better-known performances in chinning, but rather to comment on some of the more remarkable of these performances. Each will be rated, percentage-wise, on the basis of what the performer's record is equivalent to in chinning with both arms while carrying extra weight.

1. Perhaps the greatest performer in one-arm chinning was Gilbert Neville (P; 66 in., 126 lbs.), a professional equilibrist, who did much of his training in the "weight room" of the Los Angeles Athletic Club, in 1918–1919. The late Al Treloar, Physical Director of the L.A.A.C. for over 40 years, who knew Neville's powers from first-hand observation, says that Neville could put a shot-loading belt around his waist to increase his weight by as much as 56 pounds (that is, to 182 pounds), then perform five or six chins with his left arm. Six one-hand chins while carrying 56 pounds of extra weight was equal: (1) to one chin while carrying 72 pounds of extra weight, a total of 198 pounds; (2) to one two-arm chin with 204 pounds of extra weight, a total of 330 pounds; (3) to 19 consecutive one-arm chins without extra weight; and (4) to about 132 consecutive two-arm chins without extra weight! This chinning ability was truly phenomenal, and is reflected in his fantastic percentage rating of 106.0 (see Table 10). A remarkable fact about Neville was that he was tubercular, and eventually succumbed to that disease, even though for a while he developed himself into a prodigy of gymnastic strength. Two old-time champion boxers—Joe Gans (lightweight world champion, 1901–1908) and George Dixon (featherweight world champion, 1892–1900)—also were tubercular; and there have been a number of other champion athletes similarly afflicted. (For a description of some of the feats that Gilbert Neville performed in *handbalancing*, see p. 267).

2. Closely following in merit the performance of Gilbert Neville was that of Bert Assirati (66 in., 240-266 lbs.), who in 1938, at a bodyweight of 240 pounds, performed 3 successive one-arm chins. This was equivalent to one chin while weighing 261 pounds, or to one two-arm chin with 195 pounds of extra weight, a total of 435 pounds. On this basis Assirati receives a rating of 105.3 percent—as in the case of Neville, a fantastic performance. The records of Neville and Assirati indicate that, in chinning, no one type of body-build is superior, since two physiques as dissimilar as those of these two champion "chinners" could hardly be found.

3. Third in percentage rating (101.2) is Harry Rogal, a small man of the same slender build as Neville. Rogal's ability is discussed below, in connection with that of Lillian Leitzel.

4. Fourth in ability in chinning—so far as my records go—was Jasper Benincasa (67.5 in., 140 lbs.), of Brooklyn, New York, who could chin *14 times in succession with either arm*. This was equivalent to chinning once with either arm while carrying 60 pounds of extra weight, or once with *both* arms while carrying 204 pounds of extra weight (the same

as Gilbert Neville, above). An even greater ability is indicated by the fact that Benincasa chinned 3 times in succession with both arms while carrying 185 pounds of extra weight. This was equivalent to chinning once with 213 pounds' extra weight. Another indication of this gymnast's phenomenal ability is that he could perform a *one-arm planche* (front lever) while supporting himself from the ring by only his middle finger! Brooklyn, 1940.

Doubtless, at this point many readers will be asking, "What about Lillian Leitzel?" This petite, one-time star gymnast (57 in., 95 lbs.) of Ringling Brothers and Barnum & Bailey Circus is generally credited with having set a world record in one-arm chinning by doing 27 consecutive pull-ups with the right arm and 17 with the left arm. This asserted performance took place at William Hermann's Gymnasium in Philadelphia, in 1918. Moreover, it is said that when Leitzel (Lillian Alize Pelikan) did these chins it was not in an attempt to set a record, but merely as a warm-up (!) for some other gymnastic work she was going to do for a photographer. Despite all this, I have never been able to accept Leitzel's alleged one-arm chinning records for the following reasons.

First, let us ignore the fact that she was a woman and therefore not as suited to gymnastic work (especially efforts of strength rather than endurance) as a well-trained male subject. Judged purely by masculine standards, Leitzel's asserted feat of chinning 22 times with one arm (the average of her 27 chins right and 17 left) was equivalent: (1) to her doing approximately 150 (!) consecutive chins with both arms; (2) to chinning with either arm while holding a weight of 62 pounds in the other hand; and (3) to chinning with both arms once while carrying 166 pounds (or no less than 74 *percent* over her own bodyweight) in extra weight. But actually, one is not warranted in assuming that a woman athlete or gymnast, no matter how long trained, is *fully* (that is, 100 percent) as strong as an equally well-trained male athlete or gymnast. The basis of comparison here should be the *bodyweight per inch of height*. On this basis, even the strong-woman Katie Sandwina, who lived in a circus from the time she was born, was scarcely more than two-thirds (67 percent) as strong as her male contemporary Arthur Saxon, whom she fully equalled in weight per inch of height.

Lillian Leitzel's weight/height was 95 pounds divided by 57 inches, or 1.667. For comparison, Harry Rogal's (see Table 10, following) was 108/64, or 1.688. These figures are so nearly identical that from them a reliable estimate can be made. A male gymnast of Rogal's ability, weighing 1.667 pounds per inch of height (the same as Leitzel), would be expected to chin with 1.667/1.688, or 98.8 percent, of the total poundage that Rogal could raise with both arms. This, as Table 10 shows, was 108 plus 178, or 286 pounds. And .988 $\times$ 286 is 283 pounds. If we credit Leitzel with having had a full two-thirds of the strength of the best male chinner of her weight/height, she would be expected to chin (both arms) with a total of ⅔ $\times$ 283, or about 188 pounds (that is, 95 + 93). Using the ratios applying to one-arm chins and to repetitions, it then works out that Leitzel may have been capable of: (1) a single one-arm chin while carrying 18 pounds' extra weight; (2) about 54 consecutive two-arm chins; and (3) 6 one-arm chins. This estimate, I feel, gives Leitzel the maximum of due credit. Several years ago, a report came from Europe stating that a girl gymnast named Blanche Rassana had set a record by performing 6 consecutive chins with one arm. If Leitzel had performed 27 legitimate chins, it is most probable that some other girl gymnast would have performed somewhere near that number. It can only be surmised, therefore, that Leitzel must have performed her chins—if she actually did the number claimed for her— with a great amount of body momentum, similar to that which she used in performing her spectacular "giant revolutions" high up in the tent in the circus (see Part 3).

In two-arm chinning (without extra weight), the highest authentic number of repetitions performed would appear to be that of Anton Lewis of Brockton, Mass., who sometime in April 1913, did 78 consecutive chins. But there have been several men who each performed 12 one-arm chins with their stronger arm, which would be equivalent to about 80 two-arm chins. Marvin Eder (see Table 10, below) is said to have performed 80 "wide-arm" chins when weighing 190 pounds or more. One professional gymnast claims to have done 84 chins at a bodyweight of 153 pounds. And during World War I, there was a report that an American soldier (name not given) had succeeded in performing nearly 100 two-arm chins. Gilbert Neville's record in chinning, if converted from the year 1918 to its equivalent merit today, would denote an ability to perform about 180 consecutive two-arm chins!

The first man to do 12 one-arm chins would appear to have been A. Cutter of Louisville, Kentucky, who performed the feat on September 18, 1878. On the same occasion he also did 6 one-arm chins using only the *little finger* of one hand. The latter feat was an example of remarkable finger strength as well as chinning ability. I once knew a handbalancer named Johnny Daum, who was the top-mounter in an act known as "The Bel-Thazers." Daum could do 11 successive correct one-arm chins on an ordinary Roman ring, and on at least one occasion did 12 chins. These were with his right arm. With his left arm he could not chin more than once, which would indicate that his ability with his right arm was a highly specialized attainment. One who could do 12 chins with his right arm should, if he were proportionately well-developed on his left side, do at least 6 chins with his left arm.

Here, out of many listed performances in chinning over the years, are what would appear to be ten of the best, with the percentage rating of each.

Table 10. Some records in chinning.

Ranking	Name	Body-weight, lbs.	Performance	Equal to a 2-arm chin (total), lbs. Then	1965	Year & Place	% Rating
1	Gilbert Neville	126	6 one-arm chins with 56 pounds	330	373	1918 Calif.	106.0
2	Bert Assirati	240	3 one-arm chins	435	468	1938 London	105.3
3	Harry Rogal	108	3 one-arm chins with 50 pounds	286	306	1940 Wisc.	101.2
4	Jasper Benincasa	140	3 two-arm chins with 185 pounds	353	378	1940 N.Y.	99.2
5	John Davis	190	3 one-arm chins with 25 pounds	390	417	1940 N.Y.	96.0
6	Joseph Prada	120	1 one-arm chin with 56 pounds	293	329	c. 1920 ?	95.2
7	Steve Stanko	220	3 one-arm chins	398	427	1939 Pa.	93.9
8	Marvin Eder	197	6 two-arm chins with 125 pounds	379	392	1953 N.Y.	88.6
9	Jack Delinger	200	5 chins with either arm	385	394	1957 Calif.	88.5
10	Ed Kreusser	235	30 two-arm chins	400	402	1963 Calif.	86.4

Some other interesting performances in chinning are the following:

FRANCIS LEWIS (158 lbs.), of Beatrice, Nebraska, in May 1914 did 7 consecutive chins using only the middle finger of his left hand. He could also chin once with the little finger of either hand, or 50 times in succession using both arms.

OSCAR MATTHES (58.7 in., 107 lbs.), of Lawrence, Mass., was known in the 1890's as "The Miniature Sandow." He could chin 3 times with his right arm or 42 times with both arms.

ROBERT SNYDER (64.5 in., 130 lbs.), the well-known former lightweight champion lifter of Hagerstown, Md., when weighing 130 pounds could do 9 consecutive one-arm chins with his right arm. *c.* 1917.

ADRIAN P. SCHMIDT (P; 126 lbs.,) the old-time physical instructor and strong-man of New York City, was reputed to do 10 consecutive chins using only the middle finger of his right hand.

EUGEN SANDOW (P; 67.7 in., 186 lbs.), according to Al Treloar (who for a season was Sandow's assistant in his stage act), could do a one-arm chin with a single one of any of his ten fingers, including the thumbs! Treloar said that he saw Sandow do these chins on a loop of rope which was suspended backstage. When chinning with one of his thumbs, Sandow contrived to assist it with the palm of his hand, but it was a terrific feat just the same.

PAUL VON BOECKMANN (P; 72 in., 180 lbs.) of New York City, could perform 3 consecutive chins using only the middle finger of his right hand.

BOYD SHEARER (160 lbs.) of Portland, Oregon, in 1925 could do a one-arm chin while holding a 40-pound dumbbell in his other hand.

STANLEY BALLIS (c. 135 lbs.) at the age of 15 could chin 7 times with his right arm, also once while holding 30 pounds in his left hand. He could also chin once with both arms while carrying a 135-pound assistant who clung to him. Again, he could chin 6 times in succession while pinch-gripping two 4-inch-thick rafters.

EVERETT MARSHALL, the one-time heavyweight professional wrestler, could do a one-arm chin when weighing 226 pounds, also 28 chins with both arms (*c.* 1927).

MALCOLM BRENNER of Los Angeles, Calif., in 1951 performed 28 consecutive chins with both arms when weighing 235 pounds. This was essentially equal to the performance of Ed Kreusser at the same bodyweight (see Table 10).

In passing, it should be noted that performances in chinning *cannot* be rated percentage-wise in *direct ratio* to the Power Lifts or to other "strength" feats with weights. The formula I have used in rating the chinning performances listed in Table 10 is: Two-arm chin (including

extra weight carried) = 0.755 Two Hands Olympic Press + 146 lbs.*
This indicates that chinning is relatively easier for small men of light
bodyweights, and that *slender* arms make it easier to conclude the movement of pulling up to the bar (and gaining a "rest" between repetitions,
especially in "endurance" chinning). For this reason, exceptional merit
attaches to the performance of Bert Assirati (see Table 10), who had
the ability to chin 3 times with one arm despite weighing 240 pounds
or more and having very *thick* arms.

For some reason, when both arms are used together, one's chinning
strength is only about 75 percent as much as would be expected on the
basis of one arm. From the standpoint of kinesiology, points like this are
exceedingly interesting; and an attempt to find out *why* the body reacts
this way in chinning should be made by some student, or students, who
have the time and the interest to give to the problem.

O. ROPE CLIMBING

The official competitive rope climb, as recognized by the Amateur
Athletic Union, is to a height of 20 feet, using the hands alone. The
climb is made on a Manila rope, 2 inches in diameter. The rope climb
has been a standard, yearly event since 1888.

So far as I know, the record time for climbing a 20-foot rope is that
which was made by Don Perry, at Champaign, Illinois, on April 3, 1954.
His time was 2.8 seconds.

In climbing 25 feet, the record is held by Garvin S. Smith, with 4.7
seconds, at Los Angeles on April 19, 1947. Smith has climbed a 25-foot
rope in under 5 seconds in 17 consecutive gymnastic meets. His best
unofficial record is 4.2 seconds.

One rarely reads of rope climbs of more than 25 feet, but in the early
1920s Louis Weissman of New York City, made a climb of 40 feet in
16-3/5 seconds, which he claimed as a world record. He also climbed
16 feet in 3-2/5 seconds and 25 feet in 6-1/5 seconds. Manifestly, in
climbing 40 feet, the last 15 feet was much harder than the first 25.

Even better than Weissman's record was one made by Frank ("Tarzan") Merrill (70 in., 165 lbs.) of Los Angeles, who *c.* 1928 climbed 45
feet, from a sitting start, in 16 seconds flat. Considering Merrill's weight
—even though he had a gymnast's build—this was a remarkable performance.

---

*In rating chinning, the performer's height is to be ignored. This is in contrast to
pressing, where a lesser height at a given bodyweight is an advantage.

P. DIPPING, ON THE FLOOR AND ON THE PARALLEL BARS

NOTE: *Floor-dipping—or, as it is often called, "push-ups"—is perhaps one of the most familiar of all non-apparatus exercises. It consists merely of lowering and raising the body by bending and straightening the arms while supporting oneself face-down on the floor on the hands and toes and with the entire body straight. In this exercise the "average" young*

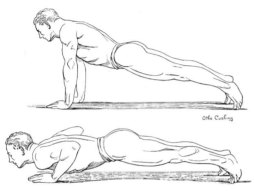

The correct manner of performing a floor-dip, as illustrated by Otho Cushing.

man (69 in., 155 lbs.) of college age can do about 16 repetitions. In the more difficult exercise of dipping on the parallel bars (and in which the entire weight of the body is supported on the hands), he can do about 7 repetitions. The latter effort is equivalent to dipping in the same manner once while carrying about 34 pounds in extra weight, which makes the average man's dipping strength about 155 plus 34, or 189 pounds. This single effort, in turn, is equivalent to performing a Bench Press with about 137 pounds. However, an ordinary man who weighed 155 pounds at the start, but who built himself up to 170 pounds and acquired maximum strength for that bodyweight, might do as much as 400 pounds in the Bench Press, or dip on the parallel bars while carrying 300 pounds' extra weight. Thus it can be said that the average college student is only from one-third to two-fifths as strong in his arm and chest "pushing" muscles as he might become if he trained regularly with weights.

In the floor dip, the average man's pushing muscles have to raise somewhere around 100 pounds (not including the weight of the arms), as compared with about 135 pounds in the parallel bar dip. Of course, in the two different forms of dipping the muscles are used in slightly different ways, and this complicates the matter of making comparisons between them.

Here are some of the many recorded performances in "repetition" floor-dips.

1.   Two-arm dips

1. Eugen Sandow (P; 67.7 in., 186 lbs.), 200 times (*c.* 1893).

2. Melvin Tampke (185 lbs.), 200 times (*c.* 1917).

3. Dr. Robert Meals (64 in., 130 lbs.), 424 times. Los Angeles (*c.* 1915).

4. Charles Somlo, 555 times in 20 minutes. Siegmund Klein's Gym, New York City, June 16, 1949. (Witnessed by Klein, Frank Leight, and others in the gym). Somlo claimed to have done over 600 dips in private.

5. Kimon Voyages (67 in., 190 lbs.), 625 times. Brooklyn, N.Y. 1942.

6. John Lopez (aged 16), 664 times. Santa Paula, Calif. March, 1953.

7. Mark Evans (over 200 lbs.), 1000 consecutive dips in 17 min. 5 sec. Hayward, Calif. 1956. Evans also performed 150 dips in 1 min. 30 sec. 1954.

8. The professional wrestlers of India can each, on the average, perform in their training five *series* of 300 "Dunds" (body-swaying floor-dips) and three *series* of 1000 "batticks" (knee-bends, on toes). As most of these wrestlers are heavyweights, it can readily be seen why they acquire such extraordinary development of the muscles of the chest and thighs.

9. Borgia Vincent did 25 floor-dips on his thumbs alone. Brooklyn, N.Y. 1946.

10. Fukashi Iwashita did 6 floor-dips while supporting 155 pounds on his back. Honolulu, Hawaii. Nov., 1954.

11. Charles Szynkiewicz performed a full dip, while supporting himself on three boxes rather than on the floor, with 200 pounds on his back. Worcester, Mass. c. 1945.

12. Dan Lurie performed 25 "extension" press-ups (arms stretched overhead and body supported on fingertips and toes). Brooklyn, N.Y. 1942.

13. Mel Crosby did 5 "forearm dips" (his feet being on the seat of a

chair) while supporting 120 pounds on his upper back. Melrose, Mass. c. 1945.

14. Louis Goelz—at the age of 75 years—could *support* himself in the full extension position with 155 pounds on his back! Denver, Colo. 1956.

2. One-arm dips

1. Ted Breitenbach (aged 18), 61 times. New Orleans, La. 1936.

2. Jim Sligh, 72 times. Long Beach, Calif. *c.* 1940.

3. Jim Daniel, 82 times. Chicago, Ill. 1944.

4. 84 times. I have no name to go with this record, but it was the best mark posted for the Naval Aviation Cadets' gymnastic program during World War II. Their other records were: regular (two-arm) floor-dips, 325 times; floor-dips on fingertips, 84 times; extension (full-length) press-ups on floor, 25 times; push-ups on low parallels (feet also resting on bars), 202 times.

5. Dudley Osborn could perform 30 consecutive one-arm dips at a body-weight of 260 pounds! Nebraska, 1964. He could also, at the same body-weight (and a height of 72 inches) do 20 consecutive straight-arm "exten-sion" floor-dips!

6. Dave Mayor (73.5 in., 265 lbs.), who was at one time the American amateur weightlifting champion, could do 30 consecutive one-arm dips "comfortably." York, Pa. 1938.

3. Parallel Bar Dips

As mentioned earlier, the "average" young man (69 in., 155 lbs.) can perform about 16 floor-dips but only 7 dips on the parallel bars (where he must push up nearly his entire bodyweight). And according to the records of the Naval Aviation Cadets' gymnastic program (see above), while the greatest number of floor-dips was 325, the greatest number of parallel bar dips was only 34. From the available data, it would appear that the record in floor-dipping (1000 times) is equivalent to somewhere between 110 and 120 parallel bar dips. While the latter number has not, so far as I know, been actually performed, it has been closely approached, and is probably within the capacity of some present-day expert in this gymnastic specialty. Below are some of the best records that *have* been performed.

'Dipping on the parallels.' (Drawing by Otho Cushing)

1. Charles Chadwick (72.25 in., 182 lbs.), the intercollegiate champion strong-man back in 1896, dipped on the parallel bars "over 70 times".

2. Even earlier, in 1879, William Blaikie, in his book *How to Get Strong and How to Stay So,* cited, without mentioning by name, a gymnast in New York City who could do over 80 parallel bar dips, even though he weighed over 180 pounds.

3. Tony Sansone (P; 72.2 in., 178 lbs.) performed 84 consecutive dips. Brooklyn, 1940.

4. Jack La Lanne (P; 67 in., 175 lbs.) performed 80 consecutive dips on bars spaced 34 inches apart. Oakland, Calif., 1945. He also did a total of 1000 (!) dips, performed in series with rests between but keeping his position on the bars throughout. The time required was 34 min. 41 sec.

5. An unnamed gymnast who weighed 160 pounds is said to have performed 90 dips.

6. Another unnamed gymnast who weighed only 120 pounds is said to have done 110 dips.

7. In pressing up on the parallel bars with extra weight attached to

the feet, the outstanding performer was Marvin Eder (67.5 in., 197 lbs.), of Brooklyn, N.Y. Sometime in 1953, Eder is said to have pressed up while carrying on his feet two men weighing together 435 pounds! If this lift was correctly performed, it has the fantastic rating of 104.9 percent.

8. Even surpassing Eder's phenomenal performance, on a smaller scale, was that of Gerald McCabe (125 lbs.), who in 1952 did a press-up on the parallel bars while carrying 260 pounds. This would be equivalent to 270 pounds in 1965, and has the exceedingly high rating of 105.5 percent. McCabe also pressed 330 pounds while lying on the floor, for a rating of 95.3 percent. This, even in 1952, was considerably better than the present-day American record in the Bench Press in the Bantamweight class.

Q. HANDSTANDING AND DIPPING (See also p. 277 ff)

NOTE: *In dipping in the handstand position, one's strength is less than in either the floor-dip or the parallel bar dip. Quite apart from the skill and energy required merely to maintain one's balance while in a handstand, the muscles involved in the pressing movement are less powerful. In the floor-dip, the chief muscles involved are the pectorals (front chest), the triceps (back arm), the front portion of the shoulder (deltoid) muscle, and the* serratus magnus *of the lower sides of the chest, which pulls the shoulder-blades forward as the body is pushed to arms' length. In addition there is, of course, the necessity of keeping the trunk and the legs straight, which puts a mild tax on the abdominal muscles and those of the groin and the front-thigh. In the parallel bar dip, the same muscles are used as in the floor-dip, with the exception of those of the abdomen and thighs; in addition, in depressing or pushing the arms downward, the* latissimus dorsi *and the* teres major *muscles of the back-armpit region are brought strongly into play. In dipping in the handstand position, the movement (so far as extending the arms is concerned) is almost identical to that made in doing a two-arm press with a barbell, bending back at the waist. Accordingly, the muscles involved are the deltoids (mainly the anterior portion, but also some of the lateral fibers), the* triceps brachii, *the* serratus magnii, *the middle portions of the* trapezii, *and the muscles of the forearm which flex the wrist (and so keep the arms at right angles to the palms of the hands). Therefore, anyone who is proficient in doing handstand dips and push-ups is bound also to be a good overhead presser when standing on his feet and using a barbell, whether or not he has ever before trained with this invaluable apparatus.*

To do a dip and push-up in the handstand position is equivalent to doing a two hand; military (not Olympic) press with a barbell weighing 79 percent of the performer's bodyweight. For handstand dips on low parallel bars, the ratio is 90 (instead of 79) percent; and for dips on the high parallel bars (where the shoulders are lowered clear down to the bars) the ratio is 96 percent. Below are a few of the many outstanding performances recorded in handstand dipping and pushing-up. Wherever the bodyweight of the performer is known, his record in the handstand push-ups is converted into an equivalent lift in the Two Hands Military (not Olympic) Press with Barbell.

1. Eddie Harrison (148 lbs.) could do 15 consecutive handstand pushups on the edge of a table, touching his chest on each lowering (*cf.* Siegmund Klein, no. 2, following). Harrison's 15 pushups were equivalent to a single Two Hands Military Press with Barbell of about 210 pounds. York, Pa., *c.* 1945.

2. Siegmund Klein (P; 64.5 in., 148 lbs.) was noted for his exceptional pressing ability, having made an American professional record in the Two Hands Military Press of 229½ pounds at a bodyweight of 152 pounds. New York City, Jan. 12, 1935. Here are some of Klein's records in handstand dipping: 19 consecutive handstand pushups on a bench, touching his chest on each lowering (see Plate 35); 13 consecutive "tiger bend" (elbow-stand) press-ups; one "hollow-back" handstand pushup while carrying (strapped on his back) a dumbbell weighing 75 pounds. All the foregoing feats were performed before witnesses in Klein's gym in New York City, the last-named feat on Jan. 19, 1945, when Klein was nearly 43 years of age. His 19 pushups on a bench were equal to 30 pushups on the floor. When Klein was 67, in 1969, he could still do 12 or 13 handstand pushups any time.

3. Joe Nordquest (67.5 in., 168 lbs.) did 28 handstand pushups on the floor. Astabula, Ohio. 1915. Later on, when Nordquest had increased in weight to 190–200 pounds, he was still adept at all types of hand-standing, including jumping off a 30-inch-high table onto the floor in a handstand. His 28 pushups at 168 pounds were equivalent to a single Two Hands Military Press with 241 pounds.

4. Ed Theriault, at a bodyweight of 132 pounds, did 18 consecutive hand-stand pushups between chairs, which were equivalent to a single Two Hands Military Press of 195 pounds. Montreal, *c.* 1950.

5. John Davis, the former heavyweight American amateur weight-

lifting champion, in 1939, at the age of 18, did 10 consecutive handstand pushups on the high parallel bars at a bodyweight of 200 pounds. These 10 pushups were equivalent to a single Two Hands Military Press of 251 pounds, which was just about what Davis could actually press at that time. He was also able to do a handstand jump from a table 36 in. high to the floor.

6. Maxick, the phenomenal old-time lightweight lifter was a wonder at handstand pushups. Just how many repetitions he could perform, I do not know; but his Two Hands Military Press record of 230 pounds at a bodyweight of 145 pounds is equivalent to 22 consecutive pushups on the high parallel bars or to 34 pushups on the floor.

7. First Sergeant Burko, of the United States Marine Corps stationed at San Diego, Calif., is said to have performed 27 consecutive handstand pushups on the floor. His bodyweight was not given.

8. Jack La Lanne (P; 67 in., 178 lbs.) did 15 consecutive hollow-back handstand pushups on pedestals. He is credited with having done 40 consecutive handstand pushups on the floor. Even though La Lanne's various feats show him to have disproportionately great "repetitional" ability, his 40 handstand pushups would be equivalent to a Two Hands Military Press of at least 270 pounds. This number of handstand pushups (on the floor) is the greatest number of which I have a record. They were performed in an exhibition given by La Lanne at the Naval Hospital, Sun Valley, Idaho, about 1942. (However, see the record of J. Salmacy, following.)

9. To do a dip and press-up in the "tiger-bend" or elbow-stand position is equivalent to doing a Two Hands Military Press with a barbell weighing the *same* as the performer.* J. Salmacy (64 in., 134 lbs.) of Iran, in 1948 at the age of 34, performed 27 consecutive tiger-bend press-ups. This phenomenal performance was equivalent to doing a Two Hands Military Press with no less than 240 pounds! Actually, Salmacy had a record in the Right Hand Military Press of 115¾ pounds, which was equivalent to a Two Hands Military Press of 232½ pounds. This indicates that he was even more capable as a handbalancer than as a weightlifter, notwithstanding that in the latter he was a feather-weight national champion. Salmacy's 27 tiger-bend press-ups would be equivalent—if only he had performed them—to 41 or 42 regular push-ups on the floor.

---

*Also, the number of tiger-bend press-ups to be expected is about two-thirds of the number that can be performed on the high parallel bars (or on a bench or horizontal ladder, touching the chest on each lowering).

10. William J. Hunt (P; 66 in., 154 lbs.) of Darwen, England, was a remarkably capable "herculean handbalancer," as the following review of some of his records will show. He was perhaps at his best about 1939, although he was still active 15 years later. In the tiger-bend press-up, he ultimately reached 16 repetitions. This feat was almost exactly equal in merit to his record of 220¼ pounds in the Two Hands Military Press, which he performed at a bodyweight of 150 pounds. Even more remarkable was his press-up from a tiger-bend while holding 75 pounds in his teeth. Other feats were these: (1) in a handstand, jump over a bar 17½ inches high and remain in a balance; (2) jump backwards in a handstand onto a table 23½ inches high; (3) drop in a handstand from the top of a 6-foot ladder onto the edge of a table supporting the ladder.

11. Gordon Campbell, another British handbalancer, could drop into a handstand from a height of 4 feet while blindfolded. Another of his feats was to cover a distance of about 100 feet while walking in a handstand position on his *fingertips*. He could also do 10 handstand pushups while on his fingertips (1951).

12. Oscar Bradley jumped over a bar 17 inches from the floor while holding a handstand. He could also do a handstand pushup 15 times in succession while balancing on his thumbs, index and middle fingers. New York City, *c.* 1948.

13. Mahmoud Namdjou (60 in., 123 lbs.), of Iran, was a former world's bantamweight weightlifting champion, as well as an expert handbalancer. He could perform 20 consecutive tiger-bend press-ups, the equivalent of a single Two Hands Military Press with about 196 pounds (1948).

14. Marvin Eder (67.5 in., 190 lbs.) performed 25 consecutive handstand pushups on a horizontal ladder. This was equivalent to doing the same on high parallel bars, and equalled a Two Hands Military Press with barbell of about 315 pounds. The latter poundage is just about what Eder was capable of pressing at the time, since a year later, at a bodyweight of 210 pounds, he pressed 350 pounds in near-military style and was able to do a Crucifix with a 100-pound dumbbell in each hand. Brooklyn, N.Y. 1952.

15. Francis Gerard (P; 67 in., 175 lbs.), of the Belgian handbalancing team of "Manuel and Francois," could do a "press-up" (jerk-up?) from an elbow-stand or tiger-bend *on one arm* 10 times in succession! He had a phenomenal development of the triceps (*c.* 1903). (See Plate 41).

16. Alex Bernard could perform 12 or more consecutive handstand "press-ups" with the arms *straight* throughout, and supporting the weight *on the thumbs only*. Hayward, Calif. 1954.

17. Tom Fitzsimmons was able to dip over 20 times consecutively while maintaining a front planche (straight-arm) handstand balance! Richmond Hill, N.Y. (*c.* 1945).

18. Jules Keller, a professional equilibrist of the 1890s, who had congenitally undeveloped legs, compensated by developing tremendously strong arms. Standing on his hands, he could "jump" over an obstacle 4 feet high! Again, he could jump downward in a handstand from a platform 9 feet high.* He could also dance a jig on his hands with great ease. (See Plate 36).

19. Joe Branco (145 lbs.) could do 24 consecutive handstand pushups on the floor. He could also do 5 handstand press-ups on a *horizontal bar* (not parallels). Again, he could walk on his hands while supporting a 145-pound training partner on his neck. Fall River, Mass. 1940.

20. Al Treloar (P; 70.5 in., 186 lbs.), former vaudeville strong-man and sculptor's model, once, while posing for an art class, held a stationary balance on two hands for 8 *minutes*. New York City, *c.* 1900.

21. "Chesty" Staccato, a circus acrobat, held a stationary balance on two hands for 6 min. 4 sec. He also *jumped*, while holding a *one-hand stand*, 64 times in succession, each jump moving him forward about 6 inches.

22. Prof. Paulinetti (Philip Henry Thurber), the famous old-time equilibrist, held a perfect one-hand stationary balance on the floor for 1 min. 30 sec. He also held a headstand for 5 minutes with his body held perpendicular to the ground throughout.

---

* Gymnastic feats performed by individuals having undeveloped (and therefore, disproportionately light) lower bodies bring up the question of how much credit such performers should be given (that is, how their performances should be evaluated). If Keller, while holding a handstand, was able to drop from a height of 9 feet, and Hunt (see No. 10, above) from only 6 feet, it can be estimated that if both men hit the floor with the same impact, Keller, by falling at the rate of 24 feet per second, as compared with Hunt's 19.6 feet per second, must have weighed only about 82 percent as much as Hunt. If it is assumed that Keller's *upper* body weighed the same as Hunt's, it works out that Keller's legs must have weighed about 30 pounds *less* than Hunt's. If Hunt weighed 30 pounds less below the waist, it is quite probable that he, too, could have dropped in a handstand from a height of 9 feet! On the other hand, Keller's phenomenal handstand "high jump" of 4 feet has not been even remotely approached by any other performer.

23. Bert Assirati (P; 66 in.), the one-time European professional wrestling champion, was in addition a record-holding weightlifter and a skilled performer on gymnastic apparatus. He could hold a one-hand stand when weighing no less than 266 pounds! London, 1938.

24. Maurice King is said to have held a one-hand stationary balance for 4 min. 30 sec.! Santa Monica, Calif.

25. John McLoughlin (68 in., 205 lbs.), of the German-American Athletic Club, New York City, could do a "handstand" using only his thumbs (1954).

26. Peter Schaaf of Chicago could do a one-hand balance on his *fist*.

27. Ray Salter of St. Mary's, Pa., could walk on his hands while balancing on a pair of crutches, his hands being 47 inches above the floor.

28. Mark Jones, a featherweight professional strong-man and equilibrist who trained at the Los Angeles Athletic Club in 1918–1920, was a fine all-around gymnast as well as a near-champion weightlifter. One of his stunts was to do a one-hand stand on the cornice of the LAAC roof, over 100 feet above the sidewalk! Another feat, very easy for him, was to roller-skate in a handstand.

29. George Lapausky of Hershey, Pa., could ice-skate for about 25 yards while standing on his hands (*c*. 1940).

30. John Lucyn, a professional handbalancer of Philadelphia, could do a one-hand stand and at the same time hold a 100-pound dumbbell in his other hand. I believe that Joe Nordquest (see no. 3, above) could also perform this feat.

31. "Milo" (Luigi Borra), the old-time Italian middleweight strong-man and wrestler, was also an expert at heavy supporting and juggling and handbalancing of all kinds. One of his feats was to do a stationary one-hand stand on an unfixed (that is, free to move) 50-pound iron ball. He could press up into a handstand (on two high pedestals) twice in succession while holding 150 pounds suspended from a chain held in his teeth by a mouthpiece. This and other pressing feats indicate that Milo could probably have done a correct Two Hands Military Press with 210 to 215 pounds, which was a fine performance for a middleweight back at the turn of the century.

32. Gilbert Neville (P; 66 in., 126 lbs.) was a prodigy of gymnastic strength (see p. 251). At his height and weight, he looked (when dressed) more like a weakling than a phenomenal athlete with muscles of steel. L. Frank Baum, famous author of the *Wizard of Oz* books, got the idea for his "Herkus" (her-cues—a race of slender men of gigantic strength) from watching Neville in his workouts at the Los Angeles Athletic Club. Among other difficult balancing feats, Neville could perform a one-hand stand *on a swinging slackwire!* (See Plate 36). I saw him do this extraordinary balance during one of his exhibitions at the LAAC in 1919. Only one other gymnast, so far as I know, performed this feat, and that was a Swedish professional named Alfred Arnessen, who exhibited about 1900. Another of Neville's feats was to take a free one-hand stand on a pedestal, lower his body until his legs were in a sitting or half-lever position (that is, straddling his supporting arm), and from there raise into a handstand 14 times (!) in succession. When using a brace on his arm, he could increase the number of raisings to 23. Another of Neville's feats that indicated phenomenal pressing strength was to perform a handstand dip and press-up while carrying an extra 112 pounds. As his stage partner, Paula Armstrong, usually weighed about 110 pounds, it may well be that Neville used her in performing this record handstand press-up. This feat was equivalent to Neville's doing a correct Two Hands Military (not Olympic) Press with a barbell of 188 pounds, or to performing 34 consecutive handstand press-ups. So great was Neville's triceps (back-arm) strength that it is just possible he could do a single slow *one-arm* press-up out of an elbow stand or "tiger bend". At least, he said that he *thought* he could do it; and as he was consistently accurate in describing the other feats that he could do, there is good reason to believe that this almost incredible feat was within his power.

33. Robert L. "Bob" Jones (67 in.,? 154 lbs.), who for some years was director of the Milo-BarBell Company, in Philadelphia, Pa., was famous for his ability to perform a handstand *on his thumbs alone* on two Indian clubs (see Plate 37). He would start this feat by balancing on five clubs with each hand (one finger on each club); then he would lift all his other fingers, letting the clubs fall, until he was left balancing on his thumbs alone. Even though the two clubs on which he did his thumb-stand were fastened down, there was still enough wobble in them to make the balance exceedingly difficult. Other feats of finger-supporting strength performed by Jones were these: (1) a floor-dip, using only his two index fingers *or* his two middle fingers; and (2) a handstand, using only the index and middle fingers of each hand. He could also do a one-arm handstand side-planche while holding in his

other hand a 55-pound dumbbell, as well as other balancing feats too numerous to recount here. Jones was an authority on gymnastic and acrobatic feats of all types, and I shall quote some of his opinions later in connection with certain of such feats.

34. James Powers of Medford, Mass., ran 71 feet on his hands, following it with a walk of 393 feet in the same position.

35. Val de Genaro won a "walking-on-hands" race of 100 feet in 21.6 seconds. York, Pa. 1940.

36. Claude Pyle (aged 14 years), of Los Angeles, Calif., walked 25 feet on his hands in 3.1 seconds. c. 1945.

37. Donald Doxtad, of Fort Banning, Ga., walked 400 yards, continuously, on his hands (1944). Another of his feats, in handstand position, was to walk up a flight of 285 steps, turn around, walk down, and then walk an additional 300 feet!

38. Siegfried Waisberger, a German professional acrobat, in order to gain publicity, walked on his hands a distance of about 175 miles, covering on the average about two miles a day. 1958.

39. Johann Huslinger walked on his hands from Vienna to Paris, a distance of 871 miles! Huslinger averaged 10 hours of walking a day for 55 days (= 550 hours at 1.58 MPH).

40. Glenn Sundby (65 in., 142 lbs.), of Santa Monica, California, is editor of *The Modern Gymnast*. In December 1949, while he was a member of the Wayne-Marlin Trio (an acrobatic-adagio act), he took time off from their engagement at the Shoreham Hotel in Washington, D.C., to show that he could walk on his hands down the 898 steps of the Washington Monument, a height of over 500 feet. Sundby (who in his act took the name Marlin) felt that while this would not be a difficult stunt for one trained to walking on his hands, it was for him, who was "just a handbalancer" and did not do much walking. But he accomplished the feat—resting upright for a moment on most of the 50 landings of the iron staircase—in 1 hr. 10 min. Sundby's performance, much to his surprise, received widespread publicity, being among other places in one of Ripley's "Believe It Or Not" cartoons. After that, a number of other handbalancers repeated the stunt. The fastest time for the walk, it would appear, was that made by a fireman from Norfolk, Virginia, who before making his attempt practiced several *months*

especially for it, doing this in the training tower in Norfolk where he was stationed. His time, presumably without rests, was about 29 minutes.

1. Hand-To-Hand Balancing

Under this heading so many fine performances come to mind that it would be impossible to describe them in the space available here. "Hand-to-hand" is a gymnastic specialty, and on it and its exponents a whole book could be written. Only the limitations of strength, suppleness, and agility of the two performers limit the number and variety of the feats they can perform. It should perhaps be mentioned that the bottom man (the one who lifts his partner) is known as the "under-stander"; while the man being lifted (who is usually the lighter in weight) is known as the "top-mounter." Here are the names of a few of the better-known hand-to-hand teams who performed during vaudeville days. In each case the under-stander is named first.

> Tony Massimo and Dave Foley
> "The Four Bards"
> "The Three Kemmys"
> Ottley Coulter and Charles Shaffer
> The Bellclaire Brothers (Benjamin and ——?)
> The Arco Brothers (Otto and Pete Nowielski)
> The Mangini Brothers (Greco and Bruno)
> The Eriksons (Karl Schneider and Hans Schumann)

More recently, there have been the teams of Bert Goodrich and George Redpath, Goodrich and Nelson, and "The Carmenas" (Adolf Kleber and his *sister*). Then, just a short time ago, there were the two German sisters, known as "The Mascotts," who performed some simply astounding feats.

Tony Massimo (68½ in., 194 lbs.), whose full name was Clevio Massimo Sabbatino, was known in his vaudeville days as "the strongest under-stander in the business." Of him Alan Calvert wrote, "This Massimo is as strong as a horse, as quick as a cat, and as supple as a contortionist." What higher praise could be given an athlete? His partner, Dave Foley, was rather heavily built for a top-mounter (64.5 in., 156 lbs.), yet Massimo handled him as though he were a rag doll. On one occasion, he held Foley in a head-to-head balance for 11 minutes! One of Massimo's stage feats was to lie face-down with his partner doing a handstand on the soles of his feet; he would then slowly "curl" and lower him (the top-mounter) with great ease. As a record effort, he leg-curled 227½ pounds in this manner. So far as "pressing" power was concerned, Massimo could swing ("cannonball") a 180-pound top-mounter to his shoulders, then press him overhead at least 15 times in succession.

Of "The Four Bards," whom I saw perform at the old Pantages

Theater in Los Angeles in 1922, I have the recollection that one of the under-standers had exceptional leg development. Possibly the fact that he was wearing yellow tights added to this impressiveness, but the outstanding size and superb shapeliness of his limbs was evident. One of the spectacular feats performed by the Four Bards was for the two under-standers—each of whom held his partner overhead in a foot-stand —to toss the top-mounters through the air so that they *exchanged places* and ended in hand-to-hand balances. In order for this exchange to be accomplished, one top-mounter had to be pitched so high that he went over the top of the other!

"The Three Kemmys" were a team from Holland. All were of superb muscular development. The usual under-stander was Pim (Billy) Block. Although he weighed 170 pounds, Block sometimes acted as top-mounter also! One of his record feats was to have pressed one of his partners, Jack Van der Berg (115 lbs.?), in a hand-to-hand balance *43 times in succession!* When Block visited Siegmund Klein's gym in New York City, about 1930, he casually took a 100-pound barbell and held it, knuckles up, straight in front of him at arms' length, body erect! This feat was equivalent to doing a correct Two Hands *Military* Press with 250 pounds. (See Plate 41.)

Ottley Coulter (65.5 in., 148 lbs.) and Charles Shaffer (62.5 in., 120 lbs.) could perform all the usual hand-to-hand feats. Coulter had previously been a circus and carnival strong-man, specializing in back and harness lifting. Yet he readily adapted himself to handbalancing, and when weighing 165 pounds could perform 16 consecutive handstand pushups on the floor (see Plate 38). The first time I saw Charles Shaffer was at the Los Angeles Athletic Club in 1925. He was practicing repetition handstand "pushups" in a *planche* position, supporting himself on his fingertips! Shaffer's pressing strength may be gauged from the fact that he could do a Two Hands Military Press with barbell of 150 pounds when weighing only 112 pounds himself. This was equivalent to about 24 consecutive handstand pushups on the floor (see Plate 38).

The Bellclaire Brothers were regarded as one of the finest teams of hand-to-hand balancers of their time. Their most spectacular feat was where the top-mounter did a "loop-the-loop" on a specially designed structure of a roller-coaster type. At the end of his "ride," he would be propelled through the air for a distance of perhaps 15 feet, to be caught in a high hand-to-hand balance by the under-stander, Benjamin Bellclaire, who stood with his back to the loop-the-loop structure.

Otto and Pete Arco (Nowielski) were small men, but very strong. Otto was a contemporary and companion of the famous heavyweight professional wrestler Zbyszko (Stanislaus Cyganiewicz), the two having been schoolmates in Poland. Like Zbyszko, Otto Arco had been a top-notch Greco-Roman wrestler in Europe, and for his size (62.9 in., 137 lbs.) was virtually unbeatable. When weighing 137 pounds, he performed a Two Hands Continental Press of 231½ pounds, a Right Hand Snatch of 155¼ pounds, and a Two Hands Jerk (from shoulders) of 305 pounds. These lifts were made in 1907–1910. Ten years later he was doing a superb hand-to-hand act in vaudeville with his brother Pete, and he had by then increased in bodyweight to 145 pounds. Otto's most spectacular feat was to hold his brother in a high hand-to-hand balance, lower him so that Pete's feet came onto his (Otto's) knees, then—as Pete leaned forward—slowly bend backwards until the top of his head "thudded" onto the floor and Pete had gone into a hand-to-hand balance. From this "wrestler's bridge" position, Otto would then slowly return to the standing position, by holding Pete, straight-armed, as far forward as possible, which required great shoulder strength. Recently, in one of the Russian circuses, there appeared a hand-to-hand team in which the understander was limber enough to bend back and down into a wrestler's bridge while retaining his partner in a hand-to-hand balance. However, he was unable to come up again in the same manner.

Of the Mangini Brothers, I have only the information that the under-stander, Greco, could hold his brother, Bruno, in a high one-hand-to-one-hand stand for the duration of a minute, meanwhile walking for a distance of 50 feet. Bruno weighed 170 pounds (c. 1940).

The Eriksons (Karl Schneider and Hans Schumann) put on one of the greatest balancing acts of their time; the act was featured in 1946 by the Ringling Brothers and Barnum & Bailey Circus. One of the outstanding feats of this team was a head-to-one-hand stand, in which the top-mounter (who stood on his head) was tossed *from one hand to the other* by the under-stander! Another—possibly unique—stunt was a teeth-to-teeth balance, each man gripping in his jaws one end of a metal rod with a mouthpiece attached (see Plate 38).

Bert Goodrich (P; 70.5 in., 195 lbs.), who was the first official "Mr. America" in 1939, was a versatile athlete and gymnast, being equally proficient in running, jumping, ice skating and other outdoor activities, and in tumbling, aerial (trapeze) work, handbalancing, and hand-to-hand. In the latter department he worked at various times with various partners, but principally with George Redpath (163 lbs.). The performances in hand-to-hand balancing that Goodrich gave with Redpath during the 1940s proved both men to be masters of the art. Especially noteworthy were their single hand-to-hands. In one variation of these, Goodrich would support Redpath on one hand while sitting in a chair and smiling! For a photograph showing Goodrich and his partner Nelson performing a "flag," see Plate 39.

The European head-and-hand balancing team known as "The Car-menas" performed with great success several years ago in England, on the Continent, and in the United States. The under-stander in this act was Adolf Kleber, who was formerly a German Olympic weight-lifting champion; while the top-mounter was his sister. Evidently this robust girl could perform all the feats that a skilled male top-mounter could perform: single hand-to-hand, hand-to-head, foot-to-head, and of course all the two-hand balances. The featured number in this brother-sister act, as shown on American television, was a head-to-head balance in which the top-mounter *revolved* while holding the balance! (See Plate 39.)

The balancing feats of "The Mascotts" (which was strictly a feminine team) are described below, in the section on female athletes.

The limited scope of this book prevents any detailed discussion of such *group* gymnastic activities as pyramid supporting, Risley work (foot-balancing and juggling),* perch acts, etc., in all of which prac-tically unlimited variations are possible. It is seldom, in such *team* activities, that individual performers stand out so far from the others as to merit the designation "super-athletes." On the other hand, in a few acts, *all* the members of the team may be "super-athletes."

Back in 1946, when I was having some correspondence with the handbalancing expert Bob Jones, who was then conducting a training school in Philadelphia, I asked him what he considered to be the most difficult feats in this field. Here is a list of seven such feats, in diminishing order of difficulty, as submitted by Jones to me in a com-munication dated May 27, 1946:

1. One-arm balance planche (in Paulinetti's style; chest *down*, not on *side*).
2. Balancing steadily on two thumbs only (not just *supporting* one's weight). (The only balance Jones would consider as harder would be a *one* handstand on a ball set in a cup, to move freely in all directions; or still harder, a balance on one *elbow* on a stationary point).
3. Two-arm balance on a flying trapeze (ropes 8 ft. or more in length), *without* bracing one's forearms against the ropes.
4. One-hand balance on a slack wire, with a "belly" in the wire of at least 2 to 3 ft.
5. Two-arm planche (in Paulinetti's style, with *back straight*).
6. One-arm "kick-up" to a handstand from a forearm balance (after first doing the one-hand stand and lowering onto the forearm).
7. Pressing up to a *one*-hand stand.

---

* See, however, the discussion on Risley in the next section.

R. OTHER FEATS OF GYMNASTICS AND ACROBATICS

NOTE: *The feats listed under this "miscellaneous" heading are mainly "flags" on vertical or stall bars, breast-ups and crucifixes (or crosses) on the stationary (Roman) rings, and similar records of gymnastic strength. However, included also are a number of difficult performances in hand-balancing, which could equally well have been listed under that heading (see Q, above). Finally, there are a few hard-to-classify feats, requiring mainly skill and long practice, such as Prof. Patti's extraordinary specialty of going up and down stairs in a* headstand.

1. John Mueller of Ridgewood, Long Island, held a flag position on stall bars steadily for 32 seconds (*c.* 1945).

2. Lawrence Frankel of Charleston, W.Va., held a flag position on stall bars with a 50-pound dumbbell tied to his waist.

3. Jack La Lanne (P; 67 in., 175 lbs.) held a perfect flag with 77¾ pounds tied to his waist. Los Angeles, 1966.

4. Reuben Martin (P; 72 in., 197 lbs.) could "chin" on a vertical bar while holding the flag position. London, 1950.

5. Bill Trumbo (72.8 in., 225 lbs.) could "chin" on a vertical bar *13 times in succession* while holding the flag position! "Muscle Beach" (Venice), Calif., 1948. (Trumbo, who was the winner of many "best chest" awards, had a chest that measured about 51 inches in strictly *muscular* condition.)

6. "Mac" Batchelor (see p. 287) tells about a small Filipino, who weighed only about 80 pounds but had relatively powerful arms and shoulders, who could grasp one of the upright pipes supporting a volley ball net, assume a flag position, release his upper hand, and slowly lower his body into a momentary *one-arm hold-out* or planche! Los Angeles, Calif.

7. Tony Terlazzo (64.5 in., 148 lbs.), former National and Olympic weightlifting champion in the lightweight class, could, on a horizontal bar, raise his body from a full hang into a front planche *10 times in succession.* York, Pa., 1945.

8. Jack Delinger (66.5 in., 195 lbs.) could do a crucifix on the rings with an additional 45 pounds attached to his feet,* 1957.

---

* The total amount of weight (bodyweight plus extra weight) possible in the *crucifix on rings* is about the same as, or a trifle more than, the total weight possible in a one-arm *chin.* Therefore, to chin with one arm is slightly more meritorious than to perform a crucifix on the rings.

9. Jim Payne (P; 64.5 in.?, 148 lbs.) held a crucifix position on the rings while carrying 60 pounds of extra weight, 1954.

10. Bert Assirati, former British Empire and European professional champion wrestler, was also a fine gymnast. He could do a crucifix on the rings when weighing 266 pounds! London, (*c.* 1938).

11. Cliff Byers (67 in.?, 150 lbs.), Roman ring performer of the Los Angeles Athletic Club, could do an inverted (upside-down) crucifix, side crucifix (that is, with a quarter-turn), raise into a crucifix from a dead hang, do 10 one-arm chins with either arm, 15 two-arm press-ups on parallel bars from *planche* starts, and various other feats of equal caliber (*c.* 1940).

12. Joseph Prada (P; 61 in.?, 120 lbs.), a Mexican ring performer, could rise, straight-armed, into a crucifix on the rings from a dead hang, with 10 pounds fastened to his waist (*c.* 1920).

13. Joe Regnier did a full mount on the Roman rings with 50 pounds attached to his feet. Chicago, 1939.

14. Orville Wertzbaugher (148 lbs.) performed a *one-arm front planche* while holding at straight arm's length overhead (that is, horizontally) in his other hand a dumbbell weighing 55 pounds. El Monte, Calif.

15. Jasper Benincasa (67.5 in., 140 lbs.), the champion chinner (see p. 251), could hold a *one-arm front planche* on a ring, grasping the ring with his *middle finger only!* Brooklyn, N.Y., 1946.

16. Ben Piers, one-time physical director of the New Orleans YMCA on Charles Street, could do a *one-arm front planche* on a ring, grasping the ring with his middle finger only, then "chin" or pull himself up to the ring in that position! Weighing 150 pounds, he could perform this extraordinary feat when past 60 years of age.

17. Prof. Paulinetti (Philip Henry Thurber) was one of the greatest equilibrists of all time. He was in his prime during the years 1887–1900, when he appeared in the leading theaters of Europe and the United States. His last theatrical tour was in 1923, after which, at the age of 59, he settled in Philadelphia and devoted most of his time to teaching handbalancing and gymnastics. At a height of 62 inches and a weight of 125 pounds, Paulinetti was nevertheless so powerfully developed in the arms, chest, and shoulders as to be capable of planches

and balances that were beyond the capabilities of other performers. His one-arm handstand planche, for example, has never been duplicated in the style that he perfected (see Plate 28), except possibly by Gilbert Neville (see p. 267). The same is true of his two-arm handstand planche. He could dress and undress while holding a headstand on a pedestal. One of his feats requiring extraordinary strength was to do a handstand on two chairs, lower to a planche, hold it, lower to a *hanging* planche between the chairs, then return to the upright handstand position. Another of Paulinetti's many outstanding feats was to press up into a one-hand stand on a thick walking cane. He would press up, tip his hat with his free hand, then lower. He used a small socket sunk into the floor, into which he would unobtrusively fit the end of the cane. As Bob Jones says, "It was a marvelous feat, but impossible without that socket."

18. Francis Gerard was—despite his weight of 175 pounds—a fine equilibrist as well as a performer of herculean handbalancing and gymnastic feats. One of his exhibition numbers, which required extreme delicacy of balance, was to assume a handstand on the tops (thick ends) of two pairs of billiard cues. The bottoms of each pair of cues would be set on the floor a couple of feet apart (in the fore-and-aft plane), so as to form an inverted "V" support. After balancing in this position for a moment, Girard would release one of the cues in his left hand, so that he would be balancing on only three cues—two in his right hand and only a single cue in his left hand! (*c.* 1903). (See Plate 41.)

19. Frank Reckless (175 lbs.) was a professional gymnast and equilibrist, whose most spectacular feat was to support a total of 520 pounds *while doing a headstand on a swinging trapeze!* While in this headstand, he would hold in his hands the ropes of a second trapeze on which his brother (165 lbs.) held a headstand. The brother, in turn, held a third trapeze on which their sister (145 lbs.) held a back planche. The weights of the three performers, plus 35 pounds for the trapeze bars and ropes, made up the 520 pounds supported by Frank on his head! (*c.* 1935).

20. A feat somewhat comparable to Frank Reckless's, was one performed in the Moscow Circus just a few years ago. In this act, a man walked up a steeply inclined tight wire while supporting on top of his head a platform on which stood two women. (This type of act always causes the audience to breathe freely again when it is over!)

21. While dealing with head balances, perhaps the most extraordinary of all was the one performed by Alexander Patti (if I remember the

name correctly), who was a featured attraction with the Ringling Brothers Circus about 1908. Patti would go up and down a flight of stairs while balancing on his head (and if I recall, he was *bald!*). While the steps on which he performed may have been specially constructed so as to "give" a little each time Patti's head bounced onto one, the effort of propelling his body up the steps was still a tremendous one. Indeed, if any other performer has ever duplicated Patti's "walk" on his head, I have not heard of him.

22. Whether or not the following feat should be included under gymnastics, I don't know; but since it is more a feat of strength and agility than of jumping power, I shall list it here. Bill Goldmark, while holding a 100-pound barbell in both hands, could jump (forward only?) over the handle of the bell. Brooklyn, N.Y. *c.* 1945.

23. With reference to no. 22, probably the greatest of all jumpers-over-barbells was the professional strong-man G. W. Rolandow, (see Plate 9), who could jump *forward and backward* over the shaft of a 200-pound barbell! Further, Rolandow could even do a *back somersault* while holding a barbell! New York City, 1900.

24. One of the most discussed performances in equilibristics (and which, if true, would provide a fitting climax to all the foregoing ones) is the alleged feat of balancing on the tip of a single finger (see Plate 42). During the last twenty years or so, several circus performers (including at least one woman) have claimed to be able to do this feat. Franz Furtner, who was billed as "Unus," was perhaps the most publicized of these performers. He appeared before the public during the years 1948–1954. Of his "one-finger balance" I shall give the opinion of an expert in this field, Bob Jones, who analyzed the feat as follows:

> He has the best "gimmick" in the business, and in my opinion carries no weight on his hand, apparently being supported by some sort of wrist or forearm socket, with a tie-rod from it to the finger tube. All is concealed by glove, cuff and sleeve coverings until *after* he finishes the trick, when he fiddles around somewhat and removes the glove to show his hand empty and the glove ditto. He *then* bends his index finger, which he does not do at any prior time during the act. . . . His finger tube is around ⅞ to one inch in diameter, very slightly tapered to within a short distance of the end, where it tapers more sharply. The extreme end is flat, perhaps half-an-inch in diameter. . . . The finger tube fits a tapered socket perhaps half-an-inch deep in the top of the globe [on which he does his "one-finger stand", D.P.W.]. By experiment, I found that a socket *½-inch in diameter and*

5/32 *deep* affords lock enough for the balance involved! Unus is a showman and in this instance an illusionist—like the magician who "saws a woman in half"—and he *can* do real balancing. But finger balancing . . . Oh, NO!

Al Treloar, the great old-time vaudeville strong-man, and physical director of the Los Angeles Athletic Club for over 40 years, wrote about this same feat (not, however, the one by Unus) in the Club's *Mercury* magazine for November 1, 1929:

> The balancer who did the "one-finger" stand, with his finger in the candlestick, had a steel grip for the palm of his hand, fitted with a small section of steel tubing, sawed longitudinally, which supported his finger. This extended into a slot in the candlestick. The performer then did a very perfect one-hand stand on the steel grip. His problem was to conceal the grip while seeming to place only his finger in the candlestick. As I remember, he got rid of it afterward by placing it in a hat which he wore.

John Venard, of "The Two Venards," was able to perform the "one-finger balance" either on a globe or on a bottle on a table while supporting both his own weight (143 lbs.) and that of his partner, Ilse (121 lbs.). When the bottle was used, he inserted his finger into the neck. While he braced his supporting finger with his thumb, the load was borne by the single finger nevertheless. Starting out in 1930 by balancing on two hands, it took John a year to balance on one hand; three more years to balance on one finger; two more years to balance on one hand with his partner wrapped around his body; and another two years to do the latter *on one finger.*

NOTE: *Sometime after having listed the foregoing feats in hand-balancing and other forms of gymnastics, I received the following additional information pertaining to these fields and to Risley work (foot-balancing and pitching). For this material I am indebted to Victor G. Josselyn, of New York City, an old-time vaudeville equilibrist (top-mounter) who was personally acquainted with many of the performers named. While no dates are given, it is evident that the performances took place sometime during the period 1900–1930.*

A Japanese equilibrist named *Ichitsky* could hop on *one* hand down a flight of steps each about 5 inches high, then hop out to the footlights, lower into a one-arm planche, and press back into a handstand (single). On one occasion, he performed 3 one-arm lowerings to a planche and then press-ups in succession! Another of his feats was to lower into a one-arm "tiger bend" (elbow stand), his elbow coming down onto a cushion about an inch thick, then with a foot-kick regain the handstand! (*cf. Francis Gerard,* and *Gilbert Neville,* above).

Leon Serratus was a fine handbalancer who worked with a partner under the name of *Leon and Mitzi,* and later *The Ralstons.* His feature act was performed with the use of 5 or 6 pedestals, each about 9 feet high, and placed about 6 inches apart. He jackknifed into a one-hand stand on the first pedestal—a very difficult feat. He would then jump straight backwards on one hand onto each of the remaining pedestals. On the next-to-last pedestal he would "fake" the loss of balance, dropping away over on one side and recovering. In jumping to the final pedestal, he would "fake" even more alarmingly, seemingly as though he could never regain his handstand. But he would, by an exhibition of squirming and twisting that denoted phenomenal handbalancing strength. Together with an older performer who was then past his prime, Leon would hold a one-hand stand while the second man would attempt to *jump* (or *kick*) into a one-hand stand on the back of Leon's neck! Evidently no two performers ever succeeded in *holding* this balance after the topmounter had *kicked* up into it.

Gilbert Neville claimed to have performed (at the Los Angeles Athletic Club) a handstand press-up while carrying 112 pounds in addition to his own 126. With even greater facility than Leon Serratus, Neville could jackknife into a one-hand stand with feet together ("the only two men I ever knew to do it"—Josselyn). Neville's understander was a woman named Paula Armstrong, who weighed only 110 pounds. Neville trained her—so quickly that they went on the stage within *two weeks!* Obviously their more difficult feats took time to perfect. One of their stunts was for Neville to dive over a piano from a small trampoline and land in a high hand-to-hand on Paula's locked arms. This was after Gilbert and Paula were married, and it was *Paula's* suggestion that she act as Gilbert's understander!

The Great Arnson. One of this performer's feats was to pull up *with one hand* onto a pedestal and then press up into a one-hand stand! This prodigious feat was performed without any "gimmick" being used.

Charley Riley was "the best at one-hand jumping on the floor that I ever saw"—Josselyn. He jumped straight forward, bending his elbow as he jumped but landing on a straight arm. "His hand slapped the floor with a loud noise as he jumped, and he could thus hop across the width of a stage with great ease." Josselyn estimated that on each of his jumps Riley would cover between 6 and 12 inches. Josselyn says that Riley was the only performer he ever saw who would *bend* his elbow (more than slightly) as he jumped.

A recent Russian equilibrist named Egorov, who performed on the Ed Sullivan show, could jump up and down a flight of stairs on one hand. Standing on his right hand, he would jump *sideways* to the right in going up the stairs. With only a slight pause at the top, he would then hop down again. In another present-day act (Yong Brothers), the under-stander stands on his hands, and the top-mounter jumps directly from the floor into a handstand on the under-stander's *feet*—a very difficult balance.

Glenn Sundby (who is now the editor of *The Modern Gymnast*, Santa Monica, Calif.) in his earlier performances could do these feats: (1) hold a perfect two-arm planche on the floor while holding a medium-sized medicine ball between his ankles; (2) jackknife into a handstand (that is, go into it while keeping both the arms and the legs straight) while gripping 3 medicine balls between his legs—an awkward balance.

In the act known as *Wills and Hassan,* the under-stander was Lou Wills and the top-mounter "Hassan." Actually, Hassan was an English tumbler who took the name after working for awhile with an Arab troupe. Hassan was relatively tall (about 5 ft. 6 in.) for a topmounter, but he weighed only 125 pounds. The outstanding feat performed by this team was where Wills assumed the usual squatting position in which the topmounter would step onto his cupped hands and be "pitched." By this means, Wills pitched Hassan upward high enough for him to land with a straight arm on Wills's straight arm, the two thus accomplishing a "pitch-up one to one." No other hand-to-hand team, according to Josselyn, ever duplicated this one-hand to one-hand pitch-up and balance as done by Wills and Hassan. Wills, by the way, weighed usually only 150–155 pounds. Another feat performed by Wills was to do a one-arm jerk with Hassan standing on his right hand. On one occasion, Wills thus put Hassan up *14 times in succession* from the shoulder! This act first appeared in New York in the early 1900s, and was continued for 12 years. At the latter time, Hassan had reached the age of 44, and the two longtime partners separated. Wills died in 1968 at the age of 89 years.

At one stage in his career, Wills worked briefly with the famous top-mounter Gilbert Neville. In the gym, Wills held Neville in a high one-to-one handstand. Neville slowly curled down until he was straddling Wills's arm, then pressed back up (all in a one-arm balance)! This fantastic feat of hand-to-hand balancing was performed (in the 1930s) when Wills was in his early 50s and Neville his early 40s. Shortly after this, Neville's tubercular condition became active, and he had to quit work and spend his final days in a sanitorium.

Two of *The Four Usseums* performed a head-to-head balance, the top man meanwhile spinning a pole around on his feet. On each end of the pole hung one of the two other partners (each a midget weighing at least 75 pounds). Thus the under-stander had to support something like 300 pounds atop his head while most of the load was in motion. Another feat was where a head-to-head balance was assumed by the two main balancers, after which one of the dwarfs performed a handstand on the soles of the top-mounter's feet, making a three-high balance!

In the act known as *The Metzetti Troupe,* one member performed a *triple* back somersault from a teeter-board cleanly onto the shoulders of another member. The man who performed the triple somersault was Richard Metzetti, who later was to be known as Richard Talmadge of the movies, and who started therein by acting as a double for Douglas Fairbanks. When in the Metzetti act, Richard weighed only 125 pounds or so. His catcher was Charlie Metzetti, who weighed about 160. The man who jumped down onto the teeter-board weighed about 200 pounds. Another unusual feat performed by the Metzettis was this: the under-stander, leaning forwards, supported the middleman in a supine position on his back, the two men being back to back and grasping each other's shoulders. The top-mounter (probably Richard) then sat on the middleman's upraised feet, and from this position was kicked or pitched into a high double back somersault. While the top-mounter was still in the air, the middleman slid off the understander's back in time to catch the descending top-mounter on his shoulders (feet to shoulders)! This sort of foot-balancing and pitching is known as "Risley" work.* The remarkable thing is that the Metzettis were able to perform such a feat without being Risley specialists.

Here is another Risley feat, performed by a regular Risley troupe known as *The Bonhairs.* From a sitting position on the pitcher's (bottom man's) feet, one man was pitched into a back somersault and caught sitting astride the catcher's (or understander's) shoulders. Next, a second man was thus pitched onto the shoulders of the man who was already sitting on the catcher's shoulders, making a three-man-high setup. Thirdly, another man was pitched up and caught with his two feet in one hand by the understander (who already had two men sitting

---

* So-named after "Professor" Risley, an European equilibrist who introduced the style in the mid-1800s.

on his shoulders). Finally, the fourth man was pitched up like the third man, only caught with his two feet in the opposite hand of the under-stander. Thus the under-stander ended up supporting two men on his shoulders and one man standing in each hand. The sitting men steadied the standing men. The total weight supported by the under-stander in this difficult position was probably over 500 pounds. The last catch often knocked the under-stander down. Sometimes, if the troupe failed twice in a row, they would let the stunt go. Once, at the Hippodrome in New York City, the troupe received tremendous applause and had to make a curtain call. For an acrobatic act, this was most unusual praise.

Another troupe of Risley performers was that known as *The Kikuta Japs*. In nearly all Risley work, the top-mounter is pitched either from a sitting to a standing position on the feet, or reversely. Hardly ever is he pitched from standing back to standing, which is very difficult. One of the Kikutas did a half-twisting back somersault, feet to feet. He informed Josselyn that he had also performed the same feat while making a full twist. This same Kikuta was also a wonder at jumping in a handstand position, and could cross the stage rapidly while making 2½-foot jumps.

The Yakopis were a famous teeter-board troupe from South America. One of their possibly unique feats was to pitch (from a teeter-board) a topmounter (who did a double back somersault) onto the shoulders of a *three-man-high column,* making a four high! This feat, which was very difficult, was regarded by most professionals as "foolhardy." The topmounter was, of course, a small man, weighing perhaps 110 or 115 pounds. In the same category was a *quadruple* somersault, in which the performer would land in a large, padded chair held on the catcher's shoulders. Ringling Brothers Circus had them discontinue this feat, on account of its dangerousness. In practice, the Yakopis troupe was able to perform a "four-high somersault down, caught by the bottom man." In this, the topmounter on the four-man-high column would do a back somersault off the shoulders of the third-high man. The latter, and the man beneath him (that is, the two middle men in the column), would then jump out of the way so that the down-coming, somersaulting top-mounter could be caught on the shoulders of the under-stander! Still another difficult feat performed by the Yakopis was a *tandem* somersault off the teeter-board onto the catcher's shoulders. In this, one of the pitched men sat on the other's shoulders. An even more difficult variation of this tandem pitch and catch (which was performed only in practice) was done with the top man *standing*, rather than sitting, on the lower pitched man's shoulders! The top-mounter of course squatted down in a tight ball and gripped the lower man's forearms.

The Three Melvins was one of several fine handbalancing acts to have originated in Reading, Pa. *The Four Bards* was another such act. The Melvins did a three-high, middleman out, half-back down. That is, the top-mounter, standing on the three-high setup, jumps upward and does a half-back somersault; the middleman jumps out of the way, and the topmounter is caught hand-to-hand by the under-stander. This feat is difficult to control; and the top-mounter is heavy to catch, as he is heading straight down. Two of the "Melvins" were brothers, whose real name was Siegfried.

One of the many pyramid-building troupes to come out of Arabia was called *The Abdullas*. The "supporter" in this troupe was a tall, rangy fellow, not very strong-looking, known as "Big Ab." He was said to have held the record by supporting 14 other men. The Arabs call the usual type of pyramid (in which the center of gravity is low) a "tuckle." A more difficult type, in which only 6 men are supported, is a 3-high. In this pyramid, 3 men stand on the supporter's shoulders, and 3 men on *their* shoulders. This is called a "top-heavy" pyramid.

In an old-time act known as *The Franklin Troupe*, the under-stander would walk up and over and down a flight of steps while carrying the middle man standing on his shoulders, and a boy (weighing under 100 pounds) who held a headstand on the middle man's upstretched right hand (cf. *The Mascotts*, Part 3).

One of the greatest tumblers was an American professional named *Eddie Prevost*. One of his stage routines was what is known as a "4-way cross." In a cross routine, the tumbler starts in one direction with one routine, finishes with either a half-twist or a one-and-a-half twist, and returns with another routine. Prevost is said to have been the only tumbler to have thus "crossed" the stage 4 times while using *difficult* routines.

A woman acrobatic dancer named *Mariam La Velle*, who was a pupil of the famous instructor Lou Wills, was able to do a walk-over-forward (walking somersault) in ballet shoes, taking off from the toe (ballet position) and landing on the toe! Wills himself said, "I don't know how she did it." Only a minimum of help could be gained from the jump leg, and the "arm lift" had to be applied to the maximum. "A difficult feat, requiring a great deal of 'know how.'"

A top-mounter named *Gene Darmon*, who weighed 125 pounds, used as an under-stander his *mother*, who weighed only 105! One of the items in their routine was for Gene to jump from the small of the back of his mother to a position where he was standing atop her head.

A difficult feat on a pair of horizontal bars is where the performer first does a "giant swing" on one bar, releases his grip, and, as he flies through the air, does a *double somersault* before catching onto the second bar. Using 3 bars, a straight back somersault has been done over the second (middle) bar to catch on the third bar. The latter feat is usually done with a half-twist, which makes it easier. The flying double somersault was performed (possibly only) by a horizontal bar artiste named *Chevet*. Lou Wills (see above) rated the latter somersault as "perhaps the most difficult feat ever done in acrobatics."

As to standing ("spot") flip-flaps, Billy Nelson, of the famous Nelson family, did 75 spotting flip-flops on a table in 60 seconds! This feat he performed on many occasions; and he would ask the spectators to take out their watches and time and count the flip-flaps.

S. EXPANDER PULLING

This exercise is also known as strand-pulling or rubber-cable stretching. In some instances the "strands" are of molded *flat* rubber, rather than round cords; again, they may be coiled steel *springs* that the performer attempts to "stretch" or open out. There is an organization, with headquarters in England, known as The International Steel Strandpulling Association. This organization keeps records, in the numerous styles of strand-pulling included under its rules, in much the same manner as weightlifting records are kept. Indeed, there are even bodyweight classes. The techniques of all these styles of strand-pulling, and the records made in them, pertain to a specialized form of gymnastics that is too extensive to be dealt with here.

Among old-time professional strong-men, I know of only two who made prominent use of "expanders" in their stage exhibitions. One was Fred Rollon, a phenomenally developed German athlete and sculptor's model, who was said to be able to stretch a collection of rubber strands further than could be accomplished by a team of horses. However, the position adopted by Rollon to accomplish this feat was not stated. He could very well have performed a Hand and Thigh Lift, or even a Harness Lift, with the elastics!

During the 1890s, in France and Belgium, the recognized champion at expander-pulling was a Belgian light-heavyweight named Joseph

Vanderzande. Like Fred Rollon, Vanderzande had an extraordinary muscular development—especially of those muscles of the arms, chest, and shoulders that are brought into action in expander-pulling. In pressing-out an expander in the back-press position, Vanderzande could perform several repetitions with 20 rubber strands that were said to have a combined resistance of 294 pounds. This is only slightly under the British amateur heavyweight record today in the pull known as the Two Arms Back Press at Attention.

Occasionally, alleged record performances are published in which it is stated merely that so-and-so stretched a certain number of cables. Even if the maximum resistance of these cables is stated—and it hardly ever is—there is no way of knowing just how much strength would be required to stretch the cables the particular distance that the performer in question stretched them. Obviously, if a 6-foot performer attempts to do, say, a back press with an expander having a chosen amount of resistance, he has to exert considerably more force than does a 5-foot (and shorter-armed) performer attempting the same feat. The reason for this is, of course, that in stretching an elastic material the pull required is not *constant* (as it is in lifting a weight), but *increases* according to the *distance* the elastic is stretched.* Some strand-pulling enthusiasts, in attempting to minimize the latter fact, may point out that certain records were made by performers who had a "long" reach. This in no way disproves what has just been remarked. Rather, it indicates that such occasional long-armed record-makers may possess compensating advantages in leverage (e.g., narrower shoulders in relation to length of arms), *as well* as greater muscular strength.

In short, because of factors of leverage that vary from individual to individual, a performance in strand-pulling cannot be a consistent measure of the force (strength $\times$ speed) expended in the performance. Thus the records in this sport cannot be accurately compared, by the usual means, with those in other sports.

In England, as I have mentioned, the Strand-Pullers' Association has rules and regulations similar to those in weightlifting. However, as the event is not practiced on a comparable scale in the United States, and since the rules and records connected with it are quite extensive, no reason exists for quoting these records here.

T.   WRIST-WRESTLING

This form of strength-demonstration, which formerly boasted only an

---

* This property of elastics serves to differentiate strand-pulling from *all other forms of athletics and gymnastics*. In the latter activities the controlling factor is *gravity, or weight*.

occasional outstanding exponent, has during recent years increased in popularity to the stage where it is now a well-organized, national sport.

As a "man-to-man" test, wrist-wrestling brings into action the entire arm, and perhaps to an equal extent certain muscles which act on the shoulder joint. In this test the opponents sit at a table across from each other, rest their elbows on top of the table, and grasp each other by the right hand. The elbows of each man are placed on the table in line and a few inches apart. The forearms are held upright and the hands are clasped in what is known as a thumbs-grip, which means that the thumbs are hooked together. (In Plate 43, the latter grip is shown in the photograph of "Mac" Batchelor and Earl Audet. The drawing by Clyde Newman, which was made years before the present thumbs-grip was officially adopted, shows the usual hand-grip.) The left (or free) hand and arm of each man must be placed in a fixed position (of which there are several different variations), and must remain there during the course of the contest so that no advantage may be gained. The opponents must remain seated with their feet on the floor. When these preliminary conditions have been complied with, the contest is ready to begin. The object of each competitor is to force his opponent's arm down sidewise and forward until the back of his hand touches the table.

For this sport, the term "wrist-wrestling" is the one most generally used. But there are other designations, such as "arm-wrestling" and (in England) "arm turning." Still another term is "Indian wrestling", but this actually refers to a different event—in which the opponents, taking a hand-shaking grip, push against each other in a *standing* position, each trying to force the other to move his feet.

Wrist-wrestling is practiced the world over, and—like many another man-to-man test—doubtless had its beginning in the days of the cavemen. Many a celebrity admits to having indulged in this test in his younger days. Abraham Lincoln, despite his lanky build, was said to be good at it. So, too, was said to be the novelist Jack London whose virile fictional character "Burning Daylight" may have been merely an extension of his own rugged constitution. Among old-time strong-men and wrestlers, many had the reputation of having been formidable wrist-wrestlers. Henry Holtgrewe, "The Cincinnati strong-man," is said never to have been defeated at it. But I should imagine that either of two contemporaries of Holtgrewe—the giant Canadians, Louis Cyr and Horace Barré—might have proved too much even for the 280-pound Cincinnatian. Eugen Sandow, it is said, was defeated in wrist-wrestling, in 1896, by a New York druggist named L. F. Fendler, who in turn was beaten by the 126-pound strong-man Adrian P. Schmidt. The latter is said also to have put down the arm of the *Police Gazette* champion

strong-man, Warren L. Travis. Joe Nordquest, about 1917, defeated a
man (unnamed) who had claimed to be the wrist-wrestling champion.
In turn, Nordquest's arm was put down by the handbalancing under-
stander, Franklin D'Amour. Maxick, the one-time champion lightweight
professional weightlifter was possibly unbeatable at his weight in wrist-
wrestling. Writing to his former mentor, Tromp van Diggelen of South
Africa, in 1936, Maxick, who was then living in Buenos Aires, Argentina,
said that he had beaten all the heavyweights there who would wrist-
wrestle with him, and that he was quite sure he could put down even
the arm of Hermann Görner in this test! Considering that in 1936 Maxick
was 54 years of age, one can only imagine what a terror he must have
been in this man-to-man test in his prime. However, that he could have
put down the arm of the giant Hermann Görner is exceedingly doubtful.
As to Görner's ability in this test, here is what his biographer, Edgar
Müller, wrote about him in his book *Goerner the Mighty*, 1951, p. 119:

> Hermann possessed amazing forearm and wrist strength, which he
> demonstrated in no uncertain manner in the sport of "Wrist Wrestling."
> On 17th December, 1934, our hero took on six famous International
> Professional Wrestlers in Leipzig's Crystal Palace. At this particular
> time Hermann and myself were judges in the Professional Greco-
> Roman Wrestling Contest. The opponents of Hermann in Wrist Wres-
> tling were all well over 6 ft. in height, the tallest of them being no
> less than 6 ft. 4½ in. All six men were beaten by Hermann in just one
> minute. This was startling tribute to his terrific wrist and forearm
> strength, as some of the men he beat possessed biceps of over 18 in.
> In this contest the six men were seated at a table on one side, whilst
> Hermann occupied the opposite side of the table. Starting with the
> first man, he rapidly downed his arm and carried on along the row
> of men until he came to the sixth. As has been already stated, he
> flattened the forearm of the sixth man before one minute had elapsed.
> At the finish of this contest Hermann called out smilingly, "Next gen-
> tleman, please," but there were no takers. This demonstration of his
> overwhelming strength left his audience gazing at him in amazement.

Others who were reputed to excel at wrist-wrestling were the huge
Polish Greco-Roman and catch-as-catch-can wrestling champion, Stanislaus Zbyszko; the Luxembourg "breaker of horseshoes," John Grünn
Marx; Arthur Dandurand, the light-heavyweight Canadian all-around
champion strong-man; Harold Ansorge, a professional strong-man of
Grand Rapids, Michigan; Al Berger of Philadelphia, who was especially
capable at all types of forearm and grip tests; and Bruno Sammartino,
the contemporary heavyweight professional wrestling champion.
I almost forgot to mention a real old-timer who should, by all signs,

have been supreme at this test. This was "Apollon," the French giant (74.8 in., 264 lbs.), who had a muscular forearm measuring over 16 inches and a grip which must have been nearly, if not actually, the equal of that of Hermann Görner's. What a contest it would have been between Apollon and Görner in wrist-wrestling, if each man had been in his prime at the same time!

During recent years, the greatest exponent of wrist-wrestling was Ian "Mac" Batchelor (P; 73 in., c. 300 lbs.) of Los Angeles, who reigned undefeated in this sport over a period of no less than 25 years (1931–1956). Batchelor, who was a bartender, had an excellent opportunity in this profession to engage in wrist-wrestling. Despite countless encounters—when some husky, after a few beers, would challenge "Mac" to have a go with him—"Mac" invariably emerged the victor.

Perhaps one of Batchelor's most formidable opponents was the former professional football player Earl Audet. The two men met in an "official" contest at the Embassy Auditorium, Los Angeles, on December 16, 1946. Batchelor won from the 280-pound Audet in two straight "falls," each taking less than 30 seconds. As a result of this contest, which was witnessed by a large audience, Batchelor was awarded the title "Wrist-Wrestling Champion of America." (See Plate 43.)

Since 1962, the town of Petaluma, California, which is located about 30 miles north of San Francisco, has been the site of an annual series of championships in wrist-wrestling. Winners in each of the three body-weight classes are named World Champions. There is even a competition for women (see Part 3). The winners in the men's heavyweight division have been as follows:

1962	Earl Hagerman	(67 in., 205 lbs.)
1963	Duane "Tiny" Benedix	(75 in., 282 lbs.)
1964	Joe Schuler	(73 in., 285 lbs.)
1965	Arnie Klein	(72 in., 225 lbs.)
1966	Mike Rowe	(73 in., 230 lbs.)
1967	Larry Finley	(77 in., 330 lbs.)
1968	Duane "Tiny" Benedix	(75 in., 280 lbs.)
1969	Duane "Tiny" Benedix	(75 in., 280 lbs.)

The 1969 championships were held on the evening of Friday, May 2, at the Petaluma Veteran's Memorial Building, before an audience of over 2000 persons. No fewer than 101 contestants were entered in the various bodyweight classes. In the heavyweight finals, Duane "Tiny" Benedix of Livermore, California, defeated Larry Finley, the champion in 1967, of Penngrove, California. In the middleweight (175–200 lbs.)

finals, Jim Pollock, of Palo Alto, defeated Rich Kennedy. In the light-weight (under 175 lbs.) finals, 16-year-old Mike Dolcini of Petaluma, defeated George Quevillon of Ceres, California, after a hard struggle.

While wrist-wrestling would appear to constitute a test of sheer man-to-man strength, actually a goodly degree of skill or acquired proficiency enters into it, as is true of any other test. This is indicated by the fact that occasionally a small but skilled competitor will defeat an opponent who is stronger than himself in every other way. The contests between Adrian P. Schmidt and his larger opponents in this test afford pertinent examples. Again, there is the instance, away back in the 18th century, of the famous Maurice Saxe, Count of Saxony, who was a very strong man and good at wrist-wrestling, but who was given his hardest tussle in this test by a woman! This was Mlle. Gauthier, an actress who was then appearing in the *Comédie Française*. This relatively slight woman nevertheless possessed great strength of arm, as "She could with her fingers roll up a piece of silver plate with as much ease as the renowned Englishman, Topham."

Evidently one of the things a contestant in wrist-wrestling should strive to do at the outset is "lock" his arm (elbow joint), so that there is the least possible angle between his upperarm and his forearm. In relatively slender-armed contestants, this "locking" is easier than in those having relatively short and thick arms. The "locking" of the arm is for the purpose of supplying *passive resistance*, thereby causing one's opponent (if inexperienced) to tire himself out trying to unbend the locked arm, before any actual "wrestling" begins. But toughening-up of the muscles and ligaments for the particular stresses occurring in wrist-wrestling is important also, and this can be done only through long practice or training. In the retired undefeated heavyweight champion, "Mac" Batche-lor, the development of the ligaments surrounding the elbow joint was so pronounced as to be noticable even to an inexperienced observer. Batchelor says that during his 25-year reign as wrist-wrestling champion he had approximately 4000 matches, none of which lasted over *two minutes*. Perhaps the late novelist Ernest Hemingway should have been informed on the latter point before he wrote *The Old Man and the Sea,* in which he had The Old Man engage with a tough opponent in a wrist-wrestling match that lasted *two days!*

(Much of the foregoing data pertaining to the organized wrist-wres-tling championships that are now an annual event in Petaluma, Cali-fornia, was supplied by my friend Bert Elliott who was himself for several years a leading contender in this sport in the middleweight class and who is presently an official referee and an authority on the subject. D.P.W.).

PLATE 41

(Top) The phenomenal Belgian gymnast and equilibrist, Francis Gerard. 1903. (97)

(Bottom) "The Three Kemmys," Dutch handbalancers, in a statuary tableaux. At the right is Billy Block, the herculean understander. c. 1930. (98)

PLATE 42

EGEIS

"Egeis," an European equilibrist, being held in a "one-finger" balance by his feminine partner. (98a)

PLATE 43

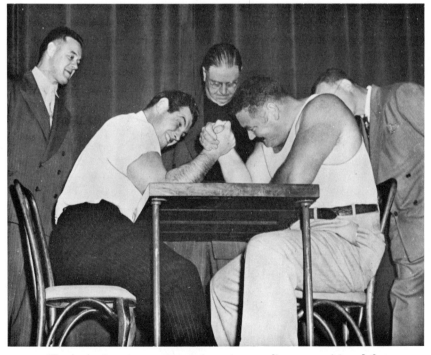

(Top) An imaginary contest in wrist-wrestling as envisioned by the old-time pen-and-ink illustrator, Clyde James Newman. (99)

(Below) A real contest in which "Mac" Batchelor (right) put down the arm of his challenger, Earl Audet, twice in succession. For this, Batchelor was awarded the title "Wrist-wrestling champion of America." Embassy Auditorium, Los Angeles, Calif. December 16, 1946. (100)

PLATE 44

Signor Lawonda, "The Iron-Jawed Man." Drawn by the author from a photograph taken in the 1890s. (101)

PLATE 45

(Top) José Meiffret, and the 275-gear (!) bicycle he designed.
(101a)

(Bottom) Meiffret setting his paced bicycle record of 127.24
MPH, near Lahr, Germany. (102)

PLATE 46

Tom Burrows, of Australia, a famous old-time club-swinging champion. (103)

PLATE 47

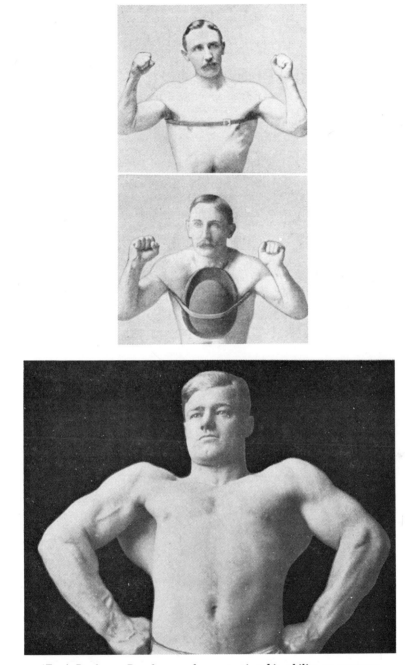

(Top) Paul von Boeckmann demonstrating his ability to contract and expand his chest. (104)

(Bottom) Joe Nordquest showing his remarkable "muscular" chest expansion. (105)

PLATE 48

"Blondin" (Jean Francois Gravelet), crossing the Niagara River on a tightrope while carrying his manager, Harry Colcord, on his back. The lines seen on all sides of the tightrope are guy wires, which were necessary to keep the rope from swaying excessively. (106)

U. STRENGTH OF NECK AND JAWS

The strength of the muscles of the neck and throat may be demonstrated in various ways, as are illustrated in the performances of circus and carnival strong-men. More often than not, these demonstrations are displays of the *resisting* strength of the neck rather than feats of actual lifting. By long and specialized practice, certain athletes have developed a degree of resistive strength in their necks that is simply astonishing.

One of the simplest feats—so far as position is concerned—is to hang by one's *chin* from a horizontal or a parallel bar. Some performers are able to do this feat even while holding extra weight in their hands. Hanging similarly by the *back* of the head and neck is easier, since the muscles of the nape of the neck are normally much stronger than those on the front-neck or throat. Some women gymnasts are able to hang by the backs of their necks, but I do not recall ever seeing one who could hang by her *chin*.

Even more difficult—and dangerous—is the feat of allowing oneself to be hanged. Martin "Farmer" Burns, the great old-time light-heavyweight wrestler, once demonstrated the extraordinary strength of his neck muscles by having himself "hanged" in an exhibition. He took the "drop" as in a genuine hanging, and complained afterward only of a sudden shutting-off of his circulation, that he had not anticipated!

More recently (1938), Lawrence Heffernan, an amateur strong-man of New South Wales, in his public exhibitions made a regular act of hanging himself. It was not stated whether Heffernan took a "drop" as he was hanged, in the manner that Farmer Burns did; but he *was* able to support himself for some time by his neck alone, and this in itself demonstrated the remarkable strength of his neck muscles. As a "conditioning" exercise for his feat of hanging, Heffernan, using a leather harness around his head and under his chin, would attach a 100-pound kettlebell to the harness, then whirl it around by the strength of his neck!

Saxon Brown, a British professional strong-man of the 1930s, once allowed himself to be hanged by the neck for a period of 7 minutes 10 seconds.

The English historian Plot (1686) cites instances in which the person, either man or woman, could not be hanged on account of the larynx or windpipe having been turned into *bone*. One man, for this reason, survived no fewer than 13 hangings! After his ultimate death it was found that his windpipe was turned into bone. A woman, named Judith de Balsham, similarly recovered after hanging for nearly 24 hours!

"Mac" Batchelor, whom I have mentioned in connection with wrist-wrestling, knew a strong-man named "Death Valley Mac," who would lie face-up on the floor, then allow Batchelor (who weighed 300 lbs.) to stand on one foot on his throat. Batchelor mentioned another man—a circus performer—who could thus support over 600 pounds! One professional strong-man even claimed that he could allow a loaded auto to run over his neck!

A feat performed by certain Japanese wrestlers also demonstrates this type of resistive neck strength. In this feat, one of the troupe lies on his back on the wrestling mat. A long, somewhat flexible wooden pole is laid across his throat and four heavy men, two on each end of the pole, are requested to bear down on the pole with all their weight. Although thus pinned to the mat, the agile Japanese wrestler is able, by means of his powerful neck muscles, to extricate himself from under the pole by performing a quick flip!

Another type of neck strength is exemplified in feats where weights are carried on top of the head, or are balanced on the chin or the forehead. As these are essentially *supporting* feats—in which little or no motion takes place, and the muscles act *statically* to maintain the balance—the amount of weight that can be borne in them is enormous. The old-time Italian strong-man and equilibrist, "Milo" (Luigi Borra), had a 17½-inch neck at a height of 65 inches and a weight of 161 pounds. One of his feats was to balance on a pole ("perch") on his chin a platform holding a man and a 400-pound field gun and carriage, a total weight of more than 600 pounds! Another of his performances was to balance a 100-pound "stage" cannon on a perch on his chin, knock away the perch, and catch the falling cannon on his neck and upper back.

Even heavier weights can be supported in the position known as the "wrestler's bridge." However, when a platform is placed on the performer's body in this position, the weight is usually arranged so as to come mostly over the *knees* rather than the head and neck. In this "wrestler's bridge" position, Robert Strikland of Yarmouth, Nova Scotia, supported a platform on which stood six men—a total load of about 1200 pounds.

Various "Iron Jaw" acts may be seen at circuses and carnivals in which the performer hangs by his teeth from a trapeze, or in the same position slides down an inclined tightwire. Such acts are tests of the strength of the neck muscles quite as much as of the teeth and jaws. In these exhibitions the performer fastens his teeth upon a special mouthpiece, which is shaped (thickened) inside the mouth so as to provide a solid surface that exactly fits the front portion of the *palate*. By this means the stress, or pull, comes upon the maxillary bone of the upper jaw rather than upon the teeth. And so long as the performer keeps his teeth gripped on the thinner and softer outside part of the mouthpiece—which is usually a strong leather strap—it is virtually impossible for the mouthpiece to pull out of his mouth from any load that he is likely to support. Some "Iron Jaw" performers *do* support substantial loads in this manner, such as the weight of two or three other persons in addition to himself.

The famous Polish professional strong-man Siegmund Breitbart (73 in., 225 lbs.), in a street exhibition aimed at attracting people to the theater in which he was appearing, performed the following feat in Washington, D.C., on the afternoon of Tuesday, November 27, 1923. He was chained to the seat of a truck, which was filled with 50 men and was drawn by a team of horses. The horses were connected to the truck solely by a harness which ended in a mouthpiece that Breitbart gripped between his teeth. "In this manner, the strange-looking vehicle made its way from Keith's Theatre to F Street, F to Fourteenth, Fourteenth to G Street, and G Street back to Keith's entrance.

A most unusual feat of pulling with the teeth was performed about 1945 by Joe Tonti of Midland, Pa. He would stand on his hands, then walk backwards while pulling a five-ton truck by means of a "bit" held in his teeth.

So far as the amount of weight pulled goes, the record would appear to be held by Andre Jean le Gall, the one-time town crier of St. Servan, France. In a contest against a number of other "iron jaw" performers, held in 1949, le Gall defended his title by starting and pulling with his teeth a train of four freight cars, the asserted total weight of which was 326 tons or 652,000 pounds! (One might well ask whether this contest was "on the level"—or downhill!

In the lifting of heavy weights off the ground with the teeth, usually the same type of mouthpiece is used as that employed by other "Iron Jaw" performers. Two main styles of teeth-lifting are recognized: (1) where the performer lifts the weight while keeping his hands behind his back; and (2) where he braces his hands on his knees. The first style is, of course, the more difficult, as a considerable strain is thrown upon the back muscles as well as those of the neck and shoulders. The records in the two styles of teeth-lifting, so far as my listings go, are as follows:

Hands behind back: 311 pounds, by Warren L. Travis (P; 68 in., 200 lbs.), Brooklyn, N.Y. March 20, 1918.

Hands on knees: 550 pounds, by Joseph Vitole (P), New York City. 1922.

Joe Lambert (P) of Boston at a bodyweight of only 133 pounds, raised in the hands-on-knees style 397 pounds (*c.* 1925).

Using a head-harness rather than a mouthpiece, and bracing his hands on his knees, Carl Pape of Chicago lifted 580 pounds (*c.* 1940).

Also using a head-strap, but lying face-up on a bench, Ed Quigley

(66 in., 200 lbs.) used 200 pounds as an *exercise* for the muscles on the front of his neck! By this and other such means, Quigley acquired a neck measurement of 19½ inches (1962).

Joe Ragusa, a heavyweight professional strong-man of the 1950s, could, in a standing position, lift 655 pounds by means of a strap that was attached to each end of a barbell and passed over the back of his neck. He made the lift *without* bracing his hands on his knees. However, the strap passed over the very *base* of Ragusa's neck, whereas the harness used by Carl Pape (see above) fitted over his *head*, thereby putting a greater leverage on the back-neck muscles. So it would be difficult to say which neck-lift—Pape's or Ragusa's—was the more meritorious. Another exhibition feat performed by Ragusa was to pull a truck, loaded with 12 tons of material, with his teeth, after the fashion of Siegmund Breitbart (see above).

The famous 18th-century English strong-man Thomas Topham (see Chapter 3) lifted with his teeth (gripping on a mouthpiece) a six-foot-long table, at the far end of which was attached a 56-pound weight, and with the two nearest legs of the table resting on top of his knees. At an even earlier date, Godfrey Witrings, a butcher of Newcastle, England, had performed a lift very similar to Topham's. But Witrings used a table 6 ft. 10 in. in length, and let the near legs rest on his body, with his hands behind him. Also, there was no extra weight attached to the table. The weight of the table was 56 pounds; and since the legs of it were located about 10 inches back from the ends of the top, it can be estimated that the pull on Witrings's teeth was about 170 pounds. Making a similar calculation for Topham, it would appear that his 6-foot table, with a 56-pound weight added to the far end of it, placed a pull on Topham's teeth of nearly 500 pounds.

Plot, the English historian (1686), who gave the account of Godfrey Witrings just quoted, mentioned two other instances of strength of the teeth and jaws. Nicholas Cooper could lift from the floor with his teeth a man weighing 300 pounds and set him upon a table. A "cord" was tied around the body of the man being lifted, and presumably to this cord, or rope, some sort of a mouthpiece was attached. This teeth-lift by Cooper, made without the aid of special apparatus, would appear to be fully as meritorious as the one performed in 1918 by Warren L. Travis (see above). Plot's other example was Thomas Wall of Wolverhampton, who could bend with his teeth a large nail or a tenterhook. It was found that Wall's incisor teeth were exceptionally *thick* (from front to back).

Signor Lawonda, who exhibited in the 1880s with P. T. Barnum's circus, was known as "The Iron-Jawed Man." One of his feats was to support, by means of a mouthpiece, a cask on which sat four men (see Plate 44). Assuming the four men to have averaged 150 pounds each, the total load supported by Lawonda's teeth and jaws was from about 700 to 1000 pounds, depending on the amount (if any) of liquid in the cask.

In 1879, at the Hippodrome in Paris, a strong-man named Joignery, as part of his performance, supported "for several minutes" the weight of a horse and rider suspended from his teeth.

Another French circus performer, an acrobat (name not given), was said to be able to *chew* in half, within several seconds, a rope about 1½ inches in diameter!

An "Iron Jaw" feat commonly used by performers in this field is to lift with the teeth a person seated in a chair. In commencing this feat, the performer has to go down on one knee in order to grasp between his jaws the lower rung of the chair. To provide a better "grip" for the teeth, this rung can be wound with adhesive tape. After seeing that the person being lifted is properly balanced on the chair, the performer stands upright, meanwhile grasping the two *front* legs of the chair. Finally, with the balance attained, and with the two *back* legs of the chair resting against his chest, the performer releases his grips on the front legs. I do not know what was the greatest amount ever lifted in this manner, but it must have been well over 200 pounds. Harold Ansorge (P; 71.9 in., 220 lbs.), of Grand Rapids, Mich., in his stage act in 1944 used to lift his sister Jean (125 lbs.) in this chair-lift with ease. The adjoining sketch shows a similar lift being performed by two of the members of the Rasso-Caccetta Trio, back in the 1890s. In 1922, John Hajnos (66.5 in., 180 lbs.), who was then known as "The Navy Hercules," used to lift a 165-pound sailor in this "iron-jaw" test.

Lifting a girl in a chair by the teeth, as performed by one of the Rasso-Caccetta Trio, c. 1892.

As to the actual "gripping" strength of the teeth and jaws, there are quite a few figures available from various dynamometer tests. In one such test, made in 1938 by Dr. Peter J. Brekus of the University of Minnesota dentistry department, 108 of the university's athletes were each requested to bite as hard as they could on an instrument that Dr. Brekus invented and which he called a gnathodynamometer. These athletes averaged about 72 inches in height and 176 pounds in weight. Their average "biting power" (or pressure exerted between the upper and lower molar teeth) was 126 pounds° Sometime later, Dr. L. M. Waugh, a New York orthodontist, took one of Dr. Brekus's gnathodynamometers with him to the far north to study the biting power of the Eskimos. This was found to be much greater than that of white Americans living under modern, artificial conditions. Many of the Eskimo men—as well as some of the women—had a biting power of over 330 pounds. Even the children showed as high as 175 pounds.

In the experiments of Regnard and Blanchard at the Sorbonne in Paris, it was found that a crocodile weighing only about 120 pounds was able to exert a biting power of no less than 1540 pounds. An average-sized dog, weighing 44 pounds, registered a bite of 363 pounds. On the basis of this dog's biting strength, a full-grown lion or tiger should be capable of biting with a force of perhaps 1200–1500 pounds. In an experiment made by the eminent French naturalist, Count Buffon, a man was found who could exert a force of 534 pounds with his jaws. In view of these figures, it is difficult to imagine a man capable of biting into a *steel* bar to the depth of 1/16 inch, with a pressure of 2500 pounds! Yet that is what the Polish professional strong-man, Siegmund Breitbart, is credited with having done. The biting ability of Joe Greenstein, "The Mighty Atom," who could chew into a wrought-iron nail, was scarcely less extraordinary (see Section H).

V. LOG CHOPPING AND SAWING

In Australia, an event used to be held which was known as an "Axeman's Carnival." Whether it is still held I do not know. In this event a series of logs, each about 4 feet long and 20 to 22 inches in diameter, is arranged in a row. The top of each log is first trimmed flat to enable the axeman to plant his feet firmly. Standing on the log in his stockinged feet, with axe poised above his head, the axeman awaits the signal "Go!" He then chops rapidly into the log until he reaches the center, turns quickly around, and completes the job by chopping to the center of the log from the other side. A good axeman will thus chop through a 20-

---

° When the biting power of the jaws is measured between the front *incisors* rather than the molar teeth, it averages only from 40 to 45 percent as great.

inch-diameter log in less than a minute!

The world record for one-man sawing, through a 32-inch-diameter log, is 1 minute 26.4 seconds, by Paul Searles of Seattle on November 5, 1953. The record for two-man sawing, through an 18-inch-diameter log, is 10.2 seconds, by Ernest Hogg and William Donnelly, at Southland, New Zealand, on December 4, 1955. This record was exactly equalled by N. Thorburn and M. Reed, at Whangarei, New Zealand, on March 3, 1956.

W.   TUG-OF-WAR

In the small central California town of Tuolumne, a tug-of-war championship has been held every year since 1901. Each team is made up of six men; and the pulling is done on a long, wooden frame fitted with cleats, or steps, on which the competitors brace their feet. The rearmost, or "anchor," man on each team is fitted with a special steel-and-leather belt weighing 70 pounds, around which, or whom, the 2-inch-diameter pulling rope is looped. The contests are grueling trials of strength and stamina, with skinned hands being a common occurrence and more serious injuries an occasional result. A time-record was set in 1960, when two teams pulled against each other for an hour and fifteen minutes before one of the teams won.* While in these contests the "action" may be painfully slow, the spectators are thrilled by the struggle and enjoy the tenseness, suspense, and uncertain outcome. For any man to be able to pull with all his strength for an hour or more certainly denotes extraordinary endurance, both mental and physical.

X.   CYCLING

Statistics on bicycle racing are varied and extensive. There are paced and unpaced records, over distances ranging from 200 meters to 100 kilometers, both indoors and outdoors; standing and flying starts; road races ranging from 25 miles to 100 miles, and over durations of 12 hours and 24 hours; annual world championships, both road and track; annual "tours" of Britain, France, and Italy; annual Grand Prix de Nations races; amateur and professional categories, etc. From the statistics pertaining to these events, only the more outstanding records can be listed here. As in nearly all instances the best records have been made by professional rather than amateur cyclists, the following figures refer to professional performances.

---

* This, however, is not the *world's* endurance record. Some years earlier, at Jubbulpere, India, in a tug-of-war between Companies E and H of the 2nd Derbyshire Regiment, the contest went on for 2 hours 41 minutes, with Company H winning.

Table 11. Outdoor world's professional bicycling records,
from unpaced standing start

Distance	Time	Performer	Nation	Place	Year	MPH
1 kilometer	1:02.6	Morettini	Italy	Milan	1961	35.73
5 kilometers	6:02.4	L. Faggin	Italy	Milan	1961	30.87
10 kilometers	12:22.8	R. Riviere	France	Milan	1958	30.12
20 kilometers	24:50.6	R. Riviere	France	Milan	1958	30.01
One hour: 29 miles, 938 yds.		R. Riviere	France	Milan	1958	29.53
100 kilometers	2:20:44.8	M.Di Benedetti	Italy	Milan	1942	26.49

With a flying start, Daniel Morelon, of France, cycled 200 meters in 10.72 seconds, at Zurich, Switzerland, November 4, 1966. This was at the rate of 18.66 meters per second, or 41.73 mph. Unofficially, Antonio Maspes of Italy cycled 200 meters in 10.6 seconds (= 42.21 mph), at Milan on August 28, 1962.

Over a distance of 500 meters with a flying start, the record is held by Morettini, of Italy, who in 1955 set a mark of 28.8 seconds (= 38.84 mph).

Evidently the best time for a short distance from a *standing* start was the ¼ mile in 27-1/5 seconds made by William Spencer, at Newark, New Jersey, on June 9, 1926. This was at the rate of 16.18 yards per second, or 33.09 mph. For a mile from a standing start the best time is that of Reginald McNamara, who covered the distance in 1 min. 45 sec., at Newark, New Jersey, on September 17, 1916. McNamara's record was at the rate of 34.28 mph.

These figures indicate that a bicyclist is relatively "slow" in getting under way, and requires about 7 seconds to cover the first 50 yards. If a race were to be staged between a bicycle rider, a sprinter (runner), a greyhound, and a Thoroughbred racehorse, the cyclist would be the last to get started, but would catch up with the human runner at about 100 yards. It would be about a half-mile before the cyclist would overtake the greyhound; while the racehorse would keep about 100 yards ahead of the bicycle rider for several miles. If the respective speeds of these four imaginary racers are plotted in yards per second in relation to distance, it is interesting to see that, after the initial "sprint" of a hundred yards or so, all four racers gradually *decelerate at approximately the same rate*. This, in turn, would seem to indicate that the physiology associated with prolonged effort in lower animals (specifically, mammals) is essentially the same as that in man.

The duration record for bicycling is said in some sources to be 125 hours, by Anandrao Halyalkar, on a track at Shivaji Park, Bombay, India. Halyalkar pedaled steadily from 1 P.M. on April 14 to 6 P.M. on April 19, 1955. Even if he had averaged only 16 mph, he would have covered 2000 miles! However, an American professional cyclist named Miller rode continuously during *six days* a distance of 2192 miles!

In motor-paced cycling records, the speed attainable may be as much as three times as great as that made in unpaced cycling.

On June 30, 1899, Charles Murphy of Brooklyn set a world record when a railroad train paced him for a mile over a level stretch of track on Long Island. His time was 60 seconds flat, or 60 miles an hour. Murphy accomplished this feat using a bicycle with a gear of 120. By arrangement with the railroad officials, a special 4-foot-wide wooden track was laid down over the ties for a distance of nearly three miles. The coach behind which Murphy cycled was lengthened at the rear by a wooden wall, or hood, several feet wide, which extended across the top, on both sides, and clear down to the rails. Murphy, cycling inside this hood, and keeping about four feet behind the rear platform of the train, was completely freed of wind pressure. The latter circumstance shows the great amount of retardation that occurs in fast racing, even in a cyclist who is crouched together so as to present the least possible surface to the wind.

In Paris in 1928, Leon Vanderstuyft of Belgium, in a motor-paced record attempt (from a standing start), lowered Murphy's mark substantially by cycling 76 miles and 504 yards (= 76.286 miles) in an hour. This, while not a maximum motor-paced speed record, is the greatest distance covered to date in one hour of non-stop cycling. It was performed on the Monthléry Motor Circuit, Paris, on September 30, 1928.

Even more extraordinary, so far as absolute speed is concerned, was the record made by Alfred Letourner, of the U.S.A. On May 17, 1941, paced by a racing car, Letourner cycled a mile on a concrete highway in 33.05 seconds (= 108.92 MPH).

In France, José Meiffret was a cyclist who had a determination to someday break the "barrier" of 200 kilometers per hour (= 124.27 mph). He may have been actuated also by Letourner's record, which equalled 175.29 Km/H. In 1951, Meiffret set a new record of 175.61 Km/H (= 109.13 MPH), but was dissatisfied with this slight advance over Letourner's mark. Ten years later, on the newly-opened Autobahn near Freiburg, Germany, Meiffret reached 186.625 Km/H (= 115.96 mph). Finally, on July 20, 1962, he attained the speed of 204.778 Km/H (= 127.24 mph). In making the latter two records, Meiffret used a bicycle of his own design, which had 172 teeth on the pedal sprocket and only 17 teeth on the rear hub. This made the gear a fantastic 275! The pedal sprocket was over 20 inches in diameter, and the rear wheel was about 15 percent greater in diameter than the front wheel. As it was impossible for Meiffret to pedal off to a start with his 275 gear ratio, he had to be *towed* until the wheels were turning fast enough for him to pedal. He was paced by a Mercedes 300 SL sports car, which was fitted at the back with a windshield that was wide and deep enough to completely free Meiffret from wind pressure. The cyclist also wore intercom headphones to keep in touch with the auto driver. Despite these preparations and precautions, Meiffret, prior to setting his records, had several near-fatal accidents, and was saved only by timely surgery. He sacrificed a great deal in order to set a record that others would be content to let stand (see Plate 45). Meiffret's present ambition (per personal communication, Jan. 27, 1968)—and, he says, his final one!—is to surpass the record set by Leon Vanderstuyft in 1928 (see above) by cycling, motor-paced, 125 Km or better in one hour.

The record for distance covered during 24 hours of continuous cycling is held by Hubert Opperman, of Australia. In 1932, cycling behind an automobile, Opperman covered 860 miles and 367 yards. This was at the rate of 35.84 MPH.

A few words concerning the *modus operandi* of bicycle racing may help the unfamiliar reader to better understand the merits of the foregoing records. To start with, the "gear" of a bicycle is derived by multiplying the number of teeth in the front (or pedaling) sprocket by the wheel (tire) diameter in inches, then dividing by the number of teeth in the rear sprocket. This is essentially the same as relating the *diameters* of the two sprockets and of the tire.

In an ordinary racer-type bicycle, having a tire diameter of 27 inches, the "gear" most often used in competition is about 86. Using this "gear" (or sprocket) ratio, every turn (revolution) of the pedaling sprocket causes the rear sprocket (and wheel) to turn 3.18 times. If the gear were 100, the ratio of turns would be 3.70 times. That is, the ratio of the revolutions of the rear wheel and sprocket to the pedaling sprocket (with a tire diameter of 27 inches) is equal to .037 times the "gear" of the bicycle. It used to be that the gear was referred to as so-and-so many *inches,* as for example a 66-*inch* gear. This is still done in some quarters. It is really the easiest way of expressing the gear, since 66 inches, for example, means that every full turn of the pedal sprocket is equivalent to the revolution of a wheel 66 inches in diameter. The diameter of the pedaling sprocket may vary greatly, according to the "gear" desired, but for unpaced racing usually ranges between 7 and 9 inches. For paced racing, the diameter of the sprocket may be as much as twice the latter figures.

An unpaced cyclist, using the normal 86 racing gear, with tires 27 inches in diameter, covers about 7.45 yards per second or 15.3 miles per hour with each turn of the pedal sprocket. A champion sprint cyclist, moving at the speed of 42 miles per hour ($=$ 20.53 yards per second), would thus have to turn the pedal sprocket 2.75 times per second.

Using a high gear, while not necessarily requiring an increase in the number of wheel-turns (or leg movements) per second, calls for increased *effort* because of the greater foot-pressure required to turn the wheels. Thus, Meiffret's 127 MPH record (in which he made 2.28 leg movements per second using a 275 gear) is more meritorious than Murphy's 60 mph (in which he made 2.83 leg movements per second using a 120 gear). Additional credit, too, must be given Meiffret in view of the fact that he was 50 years of age when he made his record. In performing the latter, it can be calculated that the rear wheel of the bicycle had to turn on the average no fewer than 10.185 times (!) for each turn of the sprocket on which Meiffret was pedaling. The one kilometer over which he cycled at 127 mph required only 17.58 seconds to cover! (See Plate 45.)

It is interesting to note that the speed made by women cycling champions in comparison with that made by men bears a similar ratio at a given distance to that made in sprint and middle-distance *running*. If a woman cyclist performs the same number of leg-movements per second as a man, she has to use a lower gear, in conformity with her lesser strength. If a man uses, for example, a bicycle of 90 gear, a woman, in order to go 90 percent as fast, has to use a gear of 81.

Professional bicycle racing in Europe is a major sporting industry. The chief cycling countries on the Continent are France, Italy, Luxembourg, Belgium, Holland, Switzerland, and Spain. The Tour de France, an event which was inaugurated in 1903, costs its promoters today about $500,000 a year. The *Union Cycliste Internationale*, with headquarters in Paris, lists 97 countries now affiliated with it. And the sport is still spreading.

Amateur cycling races are represented in the Olympic Games. The events now on the program are these: (1) 1000 meters sprint; (2) 1000 meters time-trial; (3) 2000 meters tandem; (4) 4000 meters individual pursuit; (5) 4000 meters team pursuit; (6) road race (over varying distances, depending upon where Games are held); and (7) road team time-trial. All the races are unpaced and from a standing start.

In the circus, the first man to perform the spectacular feat of looping-the-loop on a bicycle was "Allo Diavolo" (Eugen Jullien de Nozieres), a Frenchman who was featured by the Forepaugh and Sells Brothers Circus in the early 1900s. His act was described thus: "The veritable cap-sheaf of all hazardous exploits—the extreme and absolute limit of sensationalism reached at last. Beyond the tremendously terrible temerity and illimitable, inimitable intrepidity of DIAVOLO, no man may go."

But evidently the press-agents who thus extolled the merits of Diavolo conveniently ignored those of an even more intrepid performer in another field, Blondin (see p. 320).

Y. ODDITIES AND MISCELLANEOUS

NOTE: *The following listings are of odd, miscellaneous, or "unclassifiable" feats of strength, speed, agility, and endurance. No attempt has been made to follow any "order" in the listings.*

1. Rope skipping

Back in 1889, John L. Sullivan, while training for his fight with Jake Kilrain, once skipped the rope 5000 times without a miss. Hearing of this, the professional strong-man and all-around athlete, G. W. Rolandow, of New York City, determined to do at least twice that number. Making a test he did 15,000 consecutive skips, which was a world's record at the time (1900). But since then the number has more than doubled, and the current record is 32,089 times, performed by J. P. Hughes of Melbourne, Australia, in 3 hours 10 minutes on October 26, 1953. This was at the rate of about 169 skips a minute or 2.8 skips per second. In January 1955, K. Brooks of Brisbane, Australia, performed 2001 consecutive *double* turns. The speed record is held by J. Rogers of Melbourne, with 286 turns in a minute, averaging nearly 5 turns per second! As to distance covered, Tom Morris of Melbourne in August 1935 skipped for 28 successive days from Melbourne to Sydney, a distance of 590 miles. He averaged a little better than 21 miles a day; and since with each skip he covered 6½ feet, he performed nearly 17,000 skips each day. Later the same year, during October and November, Morris surpassed this record by skipping from Melbourne to Adelaide and back, a distance of 1000 miles. Evidently, championship rope-skipping is an Australian specialty!

2. Club swinging

The most celebrated of all Indian-club swingers was Tom Burrows (P; 67 in., 140 lbs.), who was born at Ballarat, Australia, on January 26, 1868 (see Plate 46). In 1891 he went to England, where he became instructor of boxing and club-swinging at the Royal Military Gymnasium at Aldershot. One of Burrow's first records, which he performed at Cairo, in 1895, was to swing a pair of clubs, each 24 inches long and weighing 2 pounds, continuously for 26 hours and 15 minutes without a moment's rest. And as Burrows grew older he steadily improved, as the following of his records show. On October 18–19, 1904, at Montreal, he swung a pair of 4-pound clubs continuously for 43 hrs. 6 min. On June 24,

1905, at Southend-on-Sea, England, he swung a similar pair of clubs for 48 hrs. 10 min. On May 28–30, 1906, at Buenos Aires, Argentina, he swung a pair of clubs for 61 hours. Finally (at the age of 45!), at Aldershot, England, on April 16–20, 1913, he swung a pair of clubs for 107 hours! During his record-making performances, Burrows usually averaged about 120 swings (complete circles) per minute, although he would occasionally go as high as 250. Thus, during his record of 107 hours he must have swung each club some 770,000 times! Naturally this work produced tremendous forearm development, and Burrows's lower-arm muscles were like cords of steel. Burrows's series of records evidently inspired competition from some of his fellow-Australians, for in March 1913 Harry Lawson swung a pair of clubs continuously for no less than 134 hours, at Bundaberg, Australia. And a little later, Martin Dobrilla swung a pair of 3-pound, 4-ounce clubs for 144 hours, at Cobar, New South Wales, Australia. The latter, so far as I know, is still the endurance record.

3. Throwing and batting a ball
(see also Chapter 9)

Throwing, like running, jumping, and lifting, is an age-old, fundamental physical movement and test. Throwing, as far as one can, a light object, such as a baseball, is a basic test for measuring speed of arm. From the distance thrown, the speed (in miles per hour or feet per second) can be calculated, and conversely, when the speed of a pitched baseball is accurately measured, the distance that it would have gone can be estimated. Also, the *weight* of the baseball must be taken into account, as this has not always been the same. The average weight in 1962 and earlier was 5.29 ounces, while in 1963 the average was reduced to 5.11 ounces. In throwing a baseball, the average Freshman college student can do about 220 feet, while the average girl student can do only about 132 feet. The fabulous Mildred "Babe" Didrickson still holds the record for women, with a throw of 296 feet that she made in Jersey City, N.J., on July 25, 1931. The record for men was held for many years by Sheldon Lejuene, of the Cincinnati Reds, who on October 12, 1910, in Cincinnati, threw a baseball 426 ft. 9½ in. This throw was surpassed by the Southern Association outfielder Don Grate, who reached 443 ft. 3½ in. at Chattanooga, Tenn., on August 23, 1953. Thus the throw for men is about 50 percent farther than that for women. However, there is some evidence that the baseball throw for distance has not kept pace with the increase over the years in various other athletic events, probably for the reason that it is not regularly practiced. When, in 1946, Bob Feller threw a baseball at the rate of 98.6 MPH (= 144.6 ft. per second), it would appear that this was equivalent to a distance of about 452 ft. Walter Johnson, one of the all-time greatest pitchers, is said to have had an even faster ball than Feller's, but there is no record of its speed ever having been actually measured. Another greater, but less publicized, speed than Feller's had been attained in 1930 (May 23), when Mark Koenig, in a test conducted at West Point, N.Y., threw a ball at the rate of 150 feet per second (= 102.27 MPH). This was equivalent to a throw for distance of about 486 feet. When the records in throwing a baseball and in putting the 16-pound shot are compared graphically, it appears that Randel Matson's world record shot put of 71 feet 5½ inches, made in 1967, is equivalent to a baseball throw of no less than 565 feet! If a baseball were "put" in the same manner as a shot, rather than thrown, the distance to be expected, on the basis of Matson's shot put (and disregarding air resistance) would be about 506 feet. The greater estimated distance of 565 feet, given above, indicates the advantage of throwing over putting, where light objects are concerned.

It is interesting to note that at least three catchers have caught baseballs that came at a speed greater than any pitcher could have delivered them. These balls were dropped from the top of the Washington Monument, in Washington, D.C., from a height of approximately 500 feet. Accordingly, when they reached the catcher, they must have been traveling at a speed of nearly 120 MPH! The catchers were: William "Pop" Schriver, a catcher with the Chicago National League Club, on August 29, 1894; Gabby Street, on August 21, 1908; and Billy Sullivan, sometime in 1910.

In *batting* a baseball for distance, a record of 354 feet 10 inches was made by C. R. Partridge, at Hanover, New Hampshire, on October 14, 1880. In contrast, the present-day record is 610 feet, by Dick Stuart of the Lincoln (Nebraska) Chiefs, 1957. In 1956, Stuart hit 66 home runs, a performance which bears out his remarkable batting power. Babe Ruth's longest home run was one of 587 feet, made in 1919 at Tampa, Florida, in a non-league game. Mickey Mantle hit a ball 565 feet in Washington in 1953.

In throwing a cricket ball for distance, the record would still appear to be the 422 feet made by R. Percival, at Durham Sands Race Course, England, on April 14, 1889. One would have to go back almost as far in search of a record for throwing a lacrosse ball, in which a distance of 497 feet 7½ inches was reached by Barney Quinn, at Ottawa, Canada, on September 10, 1892.

An even more ancient performance in throwing is the following. Alonzo de Ojeda, a young soldier and a companion of Christopher Columbus, although only a small man, was reputed to have thrown an orange to the top of a 250-foot-high tower in Seville, Spain. This indicates that the orange was thrown at a speed of about 128 feet per second, that it took about 4 seconds to reach the top of the tower, and that the vertical throw was equivalent to a horizontal throw of about 352 feet.

The best record for throwing a 2-pound hand grenade would appear to be that made by Alfred Blozis (78 in., 240 lbs.), who was National champion in the shot put in 1940–1942. While training in the army at Fort Benning, Georgia, in 1944, Blozis threw a grenade 284 feet 6½ inches.

In throwing a common brick (8¼x4x2½ inches, weight 5¾ lbs.), the record is held by James Cantrell, with 135 feet 7 inches, made on July 17, 1965 in one of the annual contests held at Stroud, Oklahoma.

In the Basque sport of jai alai (hy-lye), the ball, or *pelota,* when flung out of the player's throwing-basket, or *cesta,* has been clocked at a speed of over 150 mph.

The longest field goal made with a basketball is 92 feet. This throw—which traveled the length of the court—was made by Jerry Harkness of the Indiana Pacers (American Basketball Ass'n.) in a game against the Dallas Chaparrals. Dallas, Texas. November 13, 1967.

On throwing a boomerang, no published records exist. However, it is said that the return-type boomerang is used by Australian aborigines to kill small animals at ranges within 400 feet, and that the war-type boomerang (which does not return to the thrower) can be thrown to a distance of over 700 feet. The ordinary (return-type) boomerang, as made by Australian "blackfellows," averages about 30 inches in length (over the curve), 2½ inches in width, and weighs about 5 pounds. Due to its peculiar shape—the cross-section being rounded on one side and flat on the other—a boomerang achieves a certain "self-propulsion" in the air, and so can be thrown to a greater distance than any other object. A native may throw a boomerang with his right hand and catch it with his left, or *vice versa.* Or, *two* boomerangs may be thrown at the same time—one with each hand. The angle (*re* the ground) at which a boomerang is thrown determines the type of curve it describes in its flight. If thrown at an angle of 45 degrees, the thrower turns his *back* to the object he wishes to strike. If thrown flatwise but with a slight upward tendency, the inclined blades, as they cut the air, will cause the boomerang to mount upwards.

In throwing a football, John Levi, an old-time All-American fullback, is said to have thrown "from goal to goal," a distance of 300 feet. In 1945, Bob Waterfield threw a football at a speed of 104 feet per second (68.18 mph). This speed would appear to be on a par with Levi's record for distance. The longest field goal (place-kick) with a football was one of approximately 67 yards, (200 feet 8 inches) made by

W. P. Chadwick at Exeter, New Hampshire, on November 29, 1887. The longest field goal (drop-kick) on record was one of approximately 63 yards (189 feet 11 inches) made by Pat O'Dea, at Madison, Wisconsin, on May 7, 1898. But O'Dea is also credited with having made drop-kicks in practice of up to 98 yards, or 294 feet.

A tennis ball can be batted at a speed of more than 163 miles per hour! In 1931, Dr. J. F. Strawinsky recorded the velocities, over a distance of 60 feet, of the services of a number of top-ranking tennis players. Each player tested was given from one to six trials. Here are the fastest speeds recorded:

John Doeg	127.8 MPH
Ellsworth Vines	128.4 MPH
Lester Stoefen	131.4 MPH
William Tilden	151.2 MPH

Doeg, unfortunately, had a somewhat lame shoulder at the time of the tests. Tilden's 151.2 mph was the average of four trials, his *best* time actually being 240 feet per second or 163.6 miles per hour! No wonder that Bill's opponents often claimed that they couldn't even *see* his cannonball service! The leading woman player tested was Helen Wills, and her highest speed of service was 87 mph, or about 53 percent as fast.

In driving a golf ball for distance, on level ground, the best record is evidently that of Craig Wood, who in the British Open Championship in June 1933 hit a ball a distance of 430 yards. Next-best to this is the record of George Bayer (77 in., 240 lbs.), who in 1953 drove a ball 420 yards. The most consistent long-distance driver in golf today is generally considered to be Jack Nicklaus, who in 1963 made the present U.S.P.G.A. record of 341 yards. Craig Wood's drive of 430 yards can be computed to have had an impact velocity of about 230 feet per second or 157 mph. The latter speed is about the same as the fastest of Bill Tilden's racket-driven tennis balls. Among women golfers, a drive of 250 yards was made by the British amateur, Cecil Leitch, in 1920. This record was substantially improved by the performance of Mildred "Babe" Didrickson, who in 1933, at the age of 19, set the present women's world record of 327 yards. Glenna Collett, who was U.S.G.A. women's amateur champion from 1922 to 1930, inclusive, did 310 yards. Third-best would appear to be a drive of 272 yards by Mickey Wright of San Diego, Calif., in September, 1966.

Shuffleboard is probably the least appreciated of all outdoor sports, in its genuine tournament form. Like golf and bowling, it is non-athletic in the sense of not requiring agility, speed of foot, or unusual strength.

However, besides the physical skills involved in the spectacular caroms and angled combinations that the leading players make, the game includes a great deal of hard hitting, which taxes the endurance of a tournament player in singles competition. It is estimated that, in "clearing the board," shuffleboard discs travel at more than 60 miles per hour.

4. Bag punching, and speed of punch

An endurance record for punching a bag was made by Tom Greenhill, who at Lismore, Australia, in July 1928, punched a bag continuously for 72 hours 10 minutes, averaging 45 blows per minute. This record was substantially surpassed by Ron Reunalf, another Australian, who punched a bag for a duration of 125 hours 20 minutes. Reunalf made his record at Southport, Queensland, Australia, on December 31, 1955.

The maximum speeds of blows delivered by boxers are said in one account to have been 135 mph (= 198 feet per second) by Jack Dempsey, and 127 mph (= 186 feet per second) by Joe Louis. However, the technique by which these alleged speeds were measured is not stated, and the figures given are manifestly much too high. The determination of the speed with which a person can move his (or her) fist in delivering a punch has long been of interest to anthropologists and physical educators as one of the basic tests of neuromuscular efficiency. Hence it is rather remarkable that more attention has not been given to the recording of data on the subject, especially as relates to boxers of championship caliber.

Back in 1884, the famous English scientist, Sir Francis Galton, in his Anthropometric Laboratory in London, measured over 500 men and 270 women between the ages of 23 and 26 as to their ability in a number of physical tests, one of which was called "swiftness of blow." In the latter test, the average speed for men was found to be 18.1 feet per second (= 12.3 mph), and for women 13.4 feet per second (= 9.1 mph). The maximum speed recorded for a man was 29 feet per second (= 19.8 mph), and for a woman 20 feet per second (= 13.6 mph). When these speeds are each *squared* (a procedure that should always be applied in such tests), it is found that the force of a blow delivered by an average woman is only about 55 percent as great as that delivered by an average man; and this percentage is even less in a comparison of the highest-rating man and woman.

In 1893, when the celebrated professional strong-man, Eugen Sandow, visited the United States, he was measured from head to toe by Dr. Dudley Allen Sargent, Director of Physical Education at the Hemingway Gymnasium of Harvard University. He was also given various tests, one of which was his speed of blow. In this test, Sandow (67.7 in., 180 lbs.) was matched against Mike Donovan, a middleweight, who was boxing instructor at the New York Athletic Club and was known to be a fast, skilful performer with his fists. The test consisted of delivering a punch as fast as possible over a distance of 40 centimeters (= 15¾ inches). The time required was recorded electrically. In 16 trials, Sandow's punching speed averaged 12 feet per second, while in 10 trials Donovan's speed averaged 16½ feet per second. From these figures it develops that Donovan, in punching, was 16.5/12 or 1⅜, times as fast as Sandow. Accordingly, Donovan, if he had been only 53 percent as strong as Sandow (which he perhaps was), could have struck a blow equally as hard as Sandow's blow. These figures—and preferably the slightly higher ones of Galton, given above—indicate also that the *maximum* speed of a punch is probably about 30 feet per second (= 20.5 mph).

It is unfortunate that some of the known hardest punchers, such as Jack Dempsey and Joe Louis, and the old-timers John L. Sullivan, Bob Fitzsimmons, Joe Choynski, and Stanley Ketchel—to name only a few—were not scientifically tested as to their speeds of punching. But it is doubtful if any of them would have punched much faster than 30 feet per second.

5. *Holding the breath under water*

A number of instances of prolonged breath-holding are on record. The feat was perhaps introduced by performers who *had* to hold their breath while under water, such as the pearl divers of Japan and Korea, and professional glass-tank exhibitionists known as "mermaids," "mermen," and "human fish." In this type of performance, women do quite as well as men.

The average person can hold his (or her) breath while under water for about a minute. The women divers of Korea and southern Japan, called *ama*, who now harvest the ocean bottom for shellfish and edible seaweeds (rather than, as formerly, pearls), usually descend to depths of no more than 80 feet, and in their descent (and subsequent ascent to the surface) hold their breath for up to two minutes. A few of these women have gone down as far as 100 feet, and have held their breath for as long as 2½ minutes. However, part of this time is taken up by the *expiration* of their breath as they ascend to the surface. Prior to diving, these women take a number of deep breaths to *hyperventilate* the lungs, then—filling their lungs to about 85 percent of their full capacity—they dive.

Many years ago, in some parts of the Tonga Islands, the native Polynesian divers used to compete in underwater *walking*. Picking an appropriate lagoon for the contest, in which the water was about 9 feet deep, a "course" would be laid off between two stakes driven into the soil on the floor of the lagoon, the stakes being some 70 yards apart. Each competitor would pick up a heavy stone for ballast, take a deep breath, then endeavor to "walk" underwater from one stake to the other. If it be assumed that the average diver would thus be able to grope his way underwater at the rate of 2 miles an hour, it would take him about a minute and 12 seconds to cover the 70 yards.

The first modern record of holding the breath while remaining under water in a tank was set by James Finney in London in 1886. He managed to stay submerged for 4 minutes 29¼ seconds. In 1893, an Australian swimmer named Beaumont surpassed Finney's record slightly by staying under water 4 minutes 35½ seconds. This was in Melbourne. Also in 1893, at Boston, Professor Enoch Lowell held his breath for 4 minutes 46 1/5 seconds (note the fractional seconds!). Whether Lowell was in or out of water was not stated. The next record, slightly less than Lowell's but made by a woman, was that of Miss Elise Wallenda (Germany), who on December 14, 1898, in a stage tank at the Alhambra, London, held her breath for 4 minutes 45 2/5 seconds. While the women divers of Korea and Japan have been commented upon as having "unusually large" lung capacities, it is interesting to note that Miss Wallenda, in contrast, had a lung capacity of only 137 cubic inches. Even in the average college girl the lung capacity is about 200 cubic inches. As Miss Wallenda was only 4 feet 9 inches in height and weighed only 91 pounds, a smaller-than-usual lung capacity would be expected, but hers was even less than the expectation. In contrast to Miss Wallenda, "Miss Niobe," a mermaid who performed at the Panama Pacific International Exposition at San Francisco in 1915, had a tremendous chest and lung capacity for her size (62 in., 115 lbs). Miss Niobe on one occasion remained under water in a glass tank for 4 minutes 20 seconds. This performance, at the time, was claimed as a world's record, but evidently those who claimed it did not know of the prior records listed above.

One of the best records in holding the breath was made by a Frenchman, M. Pauliquen, who in Paris in 1912 remained under water for 6 minutes 29 4/5 seconds.

More recently, it has been discovered that much longer breath-holding periods under water can be achieved by the expedient of breathing pure oxygen from a resuscitator-type tank for up to 30 minutes prior to submerging. Using this technique, James Ray Gordon of San Diego, in 1956 broke M. Pauliquen's 44-year-old record by staying under water an even 6½ minutes. However, prior to submerging, Gordon breathed oxygen for only a minute. He said that even on this amount he could have remained under water 7 minutes if his friends, becoming worried, had not beckoned to him to come up. Using the same technique, but breathing the oxygen for a longer period, Dr. Robert Keast, an anesthesiologist of San Rafael, Calif., in 1956 stayed under water 10 minutes 58.9 seconds. In 1957, the latter record was surpassed by Al Giddings, Jr., of San Rafael, who remained submerged for 11 minutes 40.5 seconds. In 1958, Dr. Keast regained the record by staying under water 13 minutes 35 seconds; and in March 1959 Robert Foster bettered the latter record slightly by doing 13 minutes 42.5 seconds. Before submerging, Foster had pure oxygen pumped into his lungs for *30 minutes.*

More strenuous than simply holding the breath is to *swim* for as long as possible under water. About 1927, Gus Sundstrom of the New York Athletic Club swam 100 yards underwater without using his arms. The time taken was not stated. In 1933, Bill Calhoun of Christiansburg, Virginia, swam underwater for a period of 3 minutes 48-2/5 seconds. This was at Seaside Park, Virginia Beach. The distance he swam was evidently a secondary consideration. On the other hand, the world *distance* record for swimming underwater is credited to John Howard, of the Medina Athletic Club of Chicago. In April 1938, Howard swam in this manner a distance of 413 feet; but he remained underwater "only" 2 minutes 35 seconds.

In the latter part of 1967, Bob Croft, a Navy petty officer, in a supervised physiological test, "dived" to a record depth (without using breathing apparatus) of 217 feet 6 inches. He descended by following a weighted guide-rope, and by being weighted himself with lead pieces fastened to his suit. It took Croft 40 seconds to descend to the 217-foot depth (where the water pressure was 111 pounds per square inch), and 63 seconds more to haul himself back up to the surface. He came up not by running out of air, but by excessive, painful pressure on his eardrums. Croft was chosen for this test partly because of his having an extraordinary lung capacity of 476 cubic inches (see below).

Harry Houdini (Ehrich Weiss), the world-famous "escapist," by determination and practice acquired extraordinary control of his breathing. In 1926, an Egyptian fakir named Rahman Bey put himself into a "trance" and remained in an airtight coffin for 19 minutes. He challenged Houdini to do the same. Houdini's reply (after he had "conditioned" himself for the feat by a month's practice of restricted breathing) was to permit himself to be sealed in a metal coffin and lowered to the bottom of the swimming pool in the Hotel Shelton of New York City. A physician estimated that the coffin contained enough air for 15 minutes of normal breathing. Houdini astounded the waiting audience by remaining submerged for 1 hour 42 minutes! His amazing abilities otherwise, in freeing himself from seemingly inextricable positions, demanded control and endurance of the highest order.

Opera singers, as a class, have, as would be expected, powerful lungs.

The handsome tenor, Franco Corelli (74 in., *c.* 200 lbs.) is said to be able to hold his high notes "an unearthly length of time." Once, in the opera *Turandot,* Corelli "started a note at the front of the stage, held it while he walked calmly to the rear of the stage, ran up some stairs and struck a gong three times; and he was still holding the note as he walked to the front of the stage again." Whew!

6. *Chest expansion and lung capacity*

While this accomplishment is questionable as a feat of athletics or gymnastics, it is no more of an oddity than holding the breath, and statistically it is not without interest.

The extent to which a person can "expand" his (or her) chest is dependent on the power of the lungs and on the elasticity of the ribs, the connecting cartilages, and the surrounding muscles. Large and powerful muscles on the chest and upper back can, by their tonic contraction, hinder the "expansibility" of the lungs and result in a small chest-expansion measurement. Indeed, in some very heavily-muscled strongmen, there is no expansion at all! However, this is by no means always the case. In a sport such as swimming, where lung-power is of first importance, and the muscles of the chest are conditioned for endurance rather than immediate strength, one would expect a relatively large chest expansion. The same might be said in connection with long-distance running, although in this activity there is less vigorous movement of the arms than in swimming. But despite these presumed relationships, the expectation in chest expansion in a given individual is impossible to predict, and may range anywhere from zero to many inches.

The average man has a "normal" (at rest) chest girth of about 37 inches. The normal girth is taken at the largest part of the chest, with the tape measure lying horizontally (not on a slant) across the nipples and immediately under the armpits. At the same chest level, but with all the air expelled from the lungs, the girth reduces to about 35½ inches. With the lungs fully inflated, the measurement increases to about 39 inches. That is, in the average man, the *range* in chest expansion from "contracted" (or deflated) to "expanded" (or inflated) is about 3½ inches. And usually it is this total *range* which is meant when "chest expansion" is referred to.

In the days around the turn of the century, when professional strongmen were much in evidence, it was customary for such men to claim simply phenomenal chest expansions. Eugen Sandow, for example, who had a normal chest measurement of about 45 inches and an expanded measurement of about 48 inches, in his book, *Strength and How to Obtain It* (London, 1902), claimed a *normal* chest of 48 inches and an expanded chest of 62 inches!

While an expansion from normal to expanded (inflated) of 14 inches, as was claimed by Sandow, is evidently beyond the bounds of possibility, the same amount (14 inches) of expansion from *deflated* to inflated would appear to have been attained by several professional "expansionists."

One of the most famous early performers in the latter class was "Balloon-Man" Wilson, an exhibitionist who toured with Barnum's Circus for over 25 years. Wilson had a chest expansion, from deflated to inflated, that had been measured conservatively at 12.6 inches, and may have been as much as 14 inches. This expansion was measured with Wilson standing erect. If he bent forward in exhaling, he could increase the expansion to 17 or 18 inches! His fantastic power of expansion was aided by a ruptured sternum, which he is said to have sustained from breaking chains around his chest in his exhibitions. This rupture caused his chest to bulge out abnormally during inflation. Wilson's range in chest girth was about 33 inches deflated to 46 or 47 inches inflated, with a normal girth of about 40 inches.

Paul von Boeckmann (P; 72 in., 185 lbs.) was an instructor in health and bodybuilding who was well known to followers of physical culture in the early 1900s. Though in his youth he had been a strong-man and a professional cyclist, he became much better known later as an instructor, particularly as an expert on lung development and deep breathing. As the result of special attention to breathing exercises, and to daily practice on a spirometer, von Boeckmann attained extraordinary lung power and a chest expansion of 11½ inches. During this period his lung, or "vital," capacity increased from 180 cubic inches—a poor figure even to start with—to an eventual measurement of 436 inches, which at the time was surpassed only by the world record of 460 cubic inches. This was in 1893 or 1894. Von Boeckman demonstrated his chest expansion (as shown in Plate 47) by putting a belt around his chest, letting "all" the air out of his lungs, then putting a derby hat inside the belt. Next, removing the hat and fully expanding his chest, he would fill out the space just occupied by the hat. This chest-expansion feat was performed also by Martin "Farmer" Burns (P; 69.5 in., 167 lbs.), the old-time champion wrestler who trained Frank Gotch.

More recently (c. 1933), Ben Zersen of Sioux City, Iowa, claimed to have the world's record chest expansion with a range of 10¾ inches. However, a few years earlier than this Tromp van Diggelen (68 in., 185 lbs.), a professional strong-man and physical instructor of South Africa, claimed an expansion of 14 inches, this being from 36 inches contracted to 50 inches expanded. This expansion—or something near it, as it varied—van Diggelen demonstrated repeatedly to medical men as well as in a movie made by Gaumont in London. The expansion was made possible largely by reason of an exceptionally flexible rib-box, although in an expansion of this magnitude the performer makes use of *muscular* expansion also, by tensing the muscles of the chest, spreading the shoulder-blades apart, and "throwing out" the large (*latissimus dorsi*) muscles of the upper back (see Joe Nordquest, in Plate 47).

The greatest expansion of which I have record is that of R. S. Weeks (69 in., 220 lbs.), a strong-man of Myrtle Beach, South Carolina. Weeks was in his prime in the 1940s, and at that time claimed to have a chest expansion of no less than 20½ inches! While this seems incredible, the City Recorder of Myrtle Beach—a Mr. H. T. Willcox—testified to its authenticity.

Another way in which power of lungs may be exhibited is in blowing up a hot water bottle until it bursts. Three men whom I know of—and probably others who were not publicized—have performed this feat in front of a camera. The first, in 1941, was Rocky Brooks, a former strong-man and wrestler of Sydney, Australia. The second, some years later, was Mel Robson, a weightlifter of Sunderland, England. The third is Bill Pearl, "Mr. Universe" of 1967, who does the feat as part of his stage act. When the hot-water bottle explodes, there is a tremendous "pop!" And to protect the eyes it is well to cover them with a bandage while performing this feat. Just how much air pressure is required to burst one of these rubber bottles is not stated; and since the filling is done in a *series* of efforts ("blows"), the test is one that cannot be accurately measured.

The old-time heavyweight prizefighter John L. Sullivan had a "challenge" feat with which he used to demonstrate his lung power. This was to "blow" a silver dollar out of a drinking glass (tumbler) with a single blast of air. In performing this feat, Sullivan preferred a glass that was taller and somewhat narrower than an ordinary tumbler. By blowing suddenly and hard on the floor of the glass, the coin was caused to fly up and out. Sullivan often won bets from aspirants who failed to blow the dollar out of the glass. However, he more than met his match in lung power when he challenged the huge French-Canadian strong-man Louis Cyr to do the feat.

Still another test of lung power is to see how long, or for how far, the breath can be retained while walking or running. A 100-yard sprint is usually run on a single breath, but the short duration of the effort makes this no great feat. Alan Calvert mentions a man who could run a city block (*c.* 500 feet?) on a single breath. Since this man was not a sprinter, and presumably ran at a moderate speed, his performance indicated exceptional breathing power. Emil Zatopek (68.6

in., 149 lbs.), the great Czech distance runner of the 1950s, is said to have strengthened his "will" by holding his breath while walking until he blacked-out and fell unconscious!

7. Tightrope walking (Funambulism)

The feat of walking on a stretched rope dates back to the Greeks and Romans, and even beyond, to the ancient Egyptians. Among the nations of antiquity, the inhabitants of Cyzicus (now called Kapidagi) in northwest Turkey were regarded as the most capable *schoenobates,* or rope-walkers. Not only did they walk along the ropes, but they also slid headfirst down inclined ropes on their bellies, with their arms and legs extended, and leaped and turned somersaults on the ropes with as much surety as if they had been on the ground. Sometimes they used a balancing pole (which makes the work a great deal easier), and sometimes they performed without it, on a rope that was either tight or slack. In Greece, rope-walking was mentioned shortly after the time of the instituting of the feasts of Dionysus, in 1345 B.C.

During the Middle Ages, rope-walking was a popular form of public entertainment, and historians of those times related various spectacular performances which, to the onlookers, seemed impossible. The performers, in most instances, were Italians, Frenchmen, or Portuguese.

But extraordinary as these early rope-walkers were, it is doubtful if any one of them was the equal of the 19th-century phenomenon "Blondin." This French athlete, whose real name was Jean François Gravelet, was born at Saint-Omer in 1824. His pseudonym, Blondin (blon-dan), referred to his blond hair. He commenced gymnastic training at the age of 5 years, and while still in his teens became famous for his daring performances on a tightrope. In 1859 he came to the United States, and in the summer of that year astounded his audiences by crossing Niagara Falls on a 3-inch-diameter, 1100-foot-long tightrope stretched 160 feet above the water. This act he repeated several hundred times while in this country during 1859 and 1860. He varied it in the following ways: he stood on his head, trundled a wheelbarrow across, carried his manager, Harry Colcord, on his shoulders from one side to the other (*once,* which was enough for Colcord!—see Plate 48), walked across blindfolded and with his head in a sack, and, most difficult of all, crossed the rope on *stilts* that were fastened to the soles of his shoes. On one occasion, he carried a stove, a table, and a chair out to the center of the rope, cooked an omelette on the stove, and

---

* Blondin evidently performed his eating stunt more than once, for it is said that on August 25, 1859 he took his stove out on the rope, cooked his omelet and let it down on a cord to the excursion steamboat, *Maid of the Mist,* which had drawn up in the river below him. A bottle of champagne was then attached to the cord and sent up to him in return. This he drank.

sat down and ate it!* Another time, he crossed with waste-paper baskets on his feet, and so on. Twice after his performances in 1859–1860 he returned to the United States, the last time in 1888; and although he was then 64 years of age, he carried his grown son on his shoulders across a long rope which was put up on Staten Island.

After his performances at Niagara Falls, Blondin went to England, where he exhibited at the Crystal Palace in London. After that, for the next 25 years, he traveled all over the world, performing wherever there was enough space for his high tightrope act, and wherever authorities permitted him to do his death-defying stunts. His most difficult and incredible feat was performed at the Crystal Palace in 1861, where, on a rope stretched 170 feet above the floor, and with no safety net under him, he turned a *back somersault on stilts!* Blondin, who was affectionately called "The Prince of Manila," died at the age of 73, in 1897. So great was his fame that he is mentioned in encyclopedias even today, which is a rare distinction for an athlete!

After having written the above account of Blondin, I received the following aditional information. For it I am indebted to Miss Marjorie F. Williams, City Historian of Niagara Falls, New York: Blondin was not the only tightrope performer to walk across the Falls. However, he was the first (in 1859). Later there were at least a dozen others (see below) who either tried to walk a rope across, or who did. In no case, Blondin's included, was the rope actually stretched across the Falls, as the width of the river was there too great and the air currents were treacherous.** Also, in Blondin's day, each side of the Falls was private property, but after 1885 became government-owned, New York State having title to one-half the width of the river, and Canada to the other half. Nowadays it is against the law to perform any stunts along the Niagara River, and those who have requested permission to do so have been refused, as the State no longer cares to acquiesce to the attendant type of publicity.

When Blondin made his first walk across his rope, it took him 17 minutes to go the length of it. That would have been at the rate of about a foot (step?) per second. Even though guy wires were attached to the rope to steady it, a certain amount of sway occurred in the middle, depending on the amount of slack in the rope. On one occasion, some gamblers cut the guy wires that steadied Blondin's rope, hoping that this would prevent or deter him from making his crossing. However, Blondin's balancing pole, which was very long and heavy, provided him with the necessary stability, and enabled

---

** Blondin in 1859 had his first rope stretched across the Niagara River about a mile below the Falls. His second rope, in 1860, he placed still farther downstream, where spectators could watch him from Lower Arch Bridge.

him to cross safely, much to the relief and satisfaction of his backers. (See Plate 48.)

Blondin's closest rival was a rope-walker named William Hunt, who had himself billed as Signor Farini. Hunt performed all the stunts that Blondin did, performing at the same time as Blondin (the summer of 1860), on a rope farther upstream. The gorge all the way from the Falls downstream to Lewiston was about the same height above the water, 160 to 170 feet, although the river itself varied a little in width. Hunt even carried his manager across on his back; so there was little in which Blondin surpassed him. However, Blondin was a professional ropewalker and was already well known in Europe, whereas Hunt was a medical doctor and archeologist who engaged in ropewalking as a hobby. Another performer, Signor Henry Ballini, performed nearest the Falls. He called his most spectacular stunt the "Couchant Leap." In it, he jumped from his tightrope to the river below, with a "life-saver" rubber cable attached to him. This was in August 1873.

Here are the names of the other ropewalkers who performed above the Niagara River:

Calverly, Clifford	1892, 1893
Cromwell, Charles	1874
De Leon, "Professor" (failed)	1887
Dixon, Samuel John	Sept. 1890
Hardy, James E.	1896
Jenkins, Prof. I. F. (on velocipede)	1869
Leslie, Harry	1865
MacDonald, D. H.	1893
Oliver, Joseph A. (hung by teeth)	May, 24, 1921
Peer, Steve (only fatality)	1878
Spelterini, Maria (the only woman, walked across with baskets on her feet)	1876
Williams, Oscar ("The Great Houndin")	1910

Of these performers, De Leon was forced to jump into the bushes at the side, owing to the rope being too slack. Steve Peer walked many times across the ropes of other performers, but attempted to do so one night when he was drunk. He fell off the rope and was killed. Evidently the last ropewalker to perform at the Falls was Oliver, in 1921.

A world endurance record for standing and walking on a tightrope was set in Stockholm in 1955, by Allan Lundberg, with the time of 31 hours 35 minutes. Later the same year, on May 1, Lundberg and a German rope-walker, Richard Schneider, both remained on the same rope for 33 hours 6 minutes. In January 1956, in Munich, Schneider, alone, far surpassed the latter record by remaining on a tightrope for no less than 174 hours, walking a good part of the time.

8. Dancing

The duration record for individual ballroom dancing is held by Carlos Sandrini of Buenos Aires, Argentina. In September 1955, dancing with three feminine partners in alternating shifts, Sandrini waltzed, two-stepped, and otherwise disported himself for 106 hours 5 minutes 10 seconds. Outside of *ballroom* dancing, the record would appear to be held by a woman native of Luzon, Philippine Islands, who is said to have danced continuously for 172 hours! (no name or date). Since this woman wore no shoes, one might well add "some feat!"

In this connection may be mentioned also the so-called "marathon dancing" that had a vogue in the United States in the 1930s. The rules for this stipulated dancing for 40 minutes every hour, sleeping for 15 minutes, and having the remaining 5 minutes to wake up and go to the bathroom. A couple would continue under these rules until one or the other sagged to the floor and was disqualified. The record for "marathon dancing" was set in 1932 at Atlantic City by Ruthie Smith and Frank Lo Vecchio, who held out for 3480 hours—145 days!

The "Cossack dance" is the familiar one in which the performer, while in a low knee-bend, kicks each foot out in front of him alternately. In doing this he can either remain in one position or "dance" across the floor or stage. Few persons have the leg strength to perform this dance unless they have practiced either it or appropriate weightlifting exercises, although Russian dancers do it with great ease. Hermann Gassler (68.5 in., 209 lbs.), of Germany, who once (1912) held world records in the One Hand Clean and Jerk, had very strong legs and could perform the "Cossack dance" while carrying in his arms a man weighing 160 pounds! Some years later, in vaudeville, there appeared a team of hand-to-hand balancers in which, as their *pièce de résistance*, the under-stander did the Cossack dance while holding his partner in a hand-to-hand balance at his shoulders! I do not recall the names of this extraordinary duo; but I witnessed them in practice at the Los Angeles Athletic Club about 1924, shortly before they used the Cossack dance feat in their stage act.

The so-called Limbo movement, which was introduced by dancers in the West Indies a few years ago, is where the performer, while keeping on his feet and not touching any other part of his body to the ground, passes under a horizontal bar set at the lowest level of which he is capable. The record "lowness" in this feat is credited to a Cuban dancer (name not given), who in 1962 is said to have negotiated 6½ inches.

9. Feats of acrobatic contortion

Professional contortionists are individuals whose muscles and ligaments are unusually flexible, and who have simply chosen to capitalize on their condition. They are not—as some uninformed persons may suppose—to be regarded as "freaks." While some contortionists have had to put on their acts in circus sideshows, in the company of giants, dwarfs, albinos, and other oddities of nature, the most outstanding performers of "contortion" have often been featured in the center ring of the circus. In all the early civilizations, the contortionist, or "bender," was a familiar type of acrobat, and was often represented in works of painting and sculpture. Indeed, these performers were often chosen for models because of their graceful limberness and symmetry of physique. The one-time (1904–1932?) professor of physical education at the University of Pennsylvania, Dr. Robert Tait McKenzie, was also a famous sculptor of athletes. In several of his sculptures he depicted agile models in graceful contortions. In the Hindu system of *Yoga,* the pupil is taught numerous beneficial exercises in which the chief requirement is *flexibility* of the muscles and joints. And that is what "contortion" is: simply *limberness.* As one of the attributes of physical efficiency, limberness in many cases is fully as important as strength, speed, or endurance. (See Plate 49.)

A capable contortionist can do the "splits" either with his feet directed fore and aft, which is very easy, or in the more difficult position with the feet straight out to the sides. Some performers can do these things even with their feet suported on chairs, so that their hips go below the level of their feet! They can place one of their feet behind their neck while maintaining an upright position. They can, while in a standing position, bend backward into a U-shape, so that they can touch the back of their head to their calves; or they can bend forward, stiff-legged, and touch their face to their shins. An easy feat for a "bender" is to put both feet behind his head, and, keeping them there, walk on his hands. Walter Wentworth, a contortionist who appeared before the public for many years—even until he was past 70—had a stunt which he called "Packanatomicalization." This was to stow himself away in a box that measured only 23 by 29 by 16 inches. After he had fitted himself into this box, an assistant placed *six dozen* soft-drink bottles around him, then shut the lid down!

While a fore-and-aft "split" can be performed by many a person who is not a contortionist, the sidewise split is another matter, as in doing it the heads of the thigh bones have to come nearly out of their sockets. This kind of a split thus requires extreme flexibility of the hip joints. Albert Bertrand of Sanford, Maine, was able to support his training partner overhead on one hand, then, keeping this balance, gradually lower himself into a full sidewise split. However, in a vaudeville act that I saw back in the 1920s, the male member of the team known as "The Lockfords" would perform a full sidewise split while carrying his 115-pound feminine partner on his shoulders, then slowly *rise* from the "split" until he was standing erect! This man's thigh development was simply phenomenal.

10. *Somersaulting from a trapeze*

The first (and for a long time the only) man to perform a triple somersault from a trapeze into the hands of a catcher was the Mexican aerialist, Alfredo Codona. His first success in this perilous feat was achieved in 1920. In order to perform the three somersaults in time to be caught by his partner (his brother, Lalo), Alfredo had to propel his body at a speed of over 60 mph! He usually blacked out at the top of his second somersault, and had only a split second to regain consciousness as he spun out of the third turnover and shot toward the catcher's outstretched hands. An injury sustained during the course of his act made it clear to Codona that he would never be able to do a triple somersault again. But meanwhile other aerialists were practicing the feat. In 1933, in New York City, a "triple" was accomplished by a 14-year-old performer named Tom Stickney. Then a troupe named The Alisons presented it; and about the same time, so did the Netzels, the triple being performed by a 16-year-old girl! In 1938 a troupe of aerialists from Argentina toured Europe presenting a *quadruple* somersault! Does this mean that a *quintuple* will someday be possible? In any event, a triple somersault from one flying trapeze to another is still a highly meritorious feat. The latest aerialist to perform it of whom I have heard is Victor Daniel "Tito" Gaona (b. 1948), a former Olympic-class gymnast and the former diving champion of Mexico, who in 1968 was performing with the Ringling Brothers and Barnum & Bailey Circus. Tito's "catcher" is his father, Victor Gaona, Sr.

10ª. *Somersaulting from a pair of rings*

At famous "Muscle Beach" in Santa Monica, California, many fine strong-men and gymnasts have been developed and many remarkable feats performed (see Plate 49). One of the most spectacular and difficult gymnastic feats is a high-flying double somersault called a "flippus." This is performed on a pair of swinging rings, hanging about seven feet above the ground (sand) and attached to a horizontal bar about 20 feet up. The performer of a "flippus" swings from the rings and pumps to gain momentum until his feet are pointing skyward. He then lets go, performs a double somersault (forward or backward) and finishes with a half or full twist, landing on his feet. It is said that to master the "flippus" takes about five years of hard training. One of the best exponents of it (in 1957) was Barry Toward.

11. Somersaulting from the ground and from a springboard
The first successful double back somersault was achieved in 1835 by
a tumbler named Tomkinson, who "took off" from a trampoline. However,
in those days most "leaping," as it was called in the circus (and which
included somersaulting), was performed by running down an inclined
plane, jumping onto a springboard at the bottom, and with the momentum
imparted by the springboard soaring through the air and alighting on
a straw-stuffed mattress. Where a somersault was added during one of
these leaps, it was always in the direction of the leap, and was therefore a *forward* somersault.

In the early 1800s, William H. Batchelor, "onetime champion leaper
of the world," could throw a *double* somersault over the backs of 18
horses standing "neck to neck." In this leap he covered a distance of
over 40 feet.

During the years 1840–1874, the question was repeatedly asked among
circus leapers: "Will anyone ever be able to complete a *triple* somersault
from a springboard?"

About 1859, while practicing in the winter quarters of Older and
Orton's Badger Circus, George Miller was able to perform a triple
somersault on two occasions. The third time he failed, landing on his
head and breaking his neck. Earlier that year, John Aymar, who could
readily perform a double somersault over four horses, tried a triple,
landed on his forehead, and broke his neck. Prior to this, two other
leapers—the American clown Gayton in 1842, and William Hobbes in
1846—in attempting triple somersaults, were killed. Both suffered broken
necks.

In 1860, Billy Dutton, a leaper with William Lake's Circus, at Elk-
horn, Wisconsin, successfully performed a triple somersault from an
unusually high springboard. He landed properly on his feet in a "catch
blanket." He never made the attempt again, remarking that he had
lost control after the second loop and that luck might not be with
him another time. Leapers had found that, in order to attain three
successive turns in the air, they had to rise about *a third higher* than
when performing only a double somersault.

A leaper named Ab Johnson accomplished a triple unintentionally
while attempting a double (in which he "overthrew"). But he never
"overthrew" again. In 1860, Sam Reinhardt, in essaying a triple, landed
on his back and was temporarily paralyzed. In 1870, Frank Starks similarly broke his neck.

In 1874, at St. Louis, John Worland (John Comosh) successfully
performed a triple somersault on his third attempt. In 1881 he did
triples on two different occasions—once in Eau Claire, Wisconsin and

again in La Crosse. Later, when with the Adam Forepaugh Circus at New Haven, he performed a perfect triple before a large audience, which included the mayor and various news correspondents.

Moving up to 1929, Billy Pape, a remarkable tumbler, turned a forward somersault from a short, springless take-off board over "15 standing human beings." He followed this with a round-off and (50) flip-flaps in rapid succession. On another occasion he did a forward somersault off a springboard over five elephants and two camels, a distance of 41 feet 6 inches! His speed must have been around 50 mph!

Robert Stickney, a star circus rider and tumbler, was able to perform a double forward somersault on the back of a "galloping" horse! In all such performances, the tumbler must time his somersault so that he alights when the horse's back (croup) is going *down*, not up. A number of circus riders have done a *single back* somersault from the back of one horse to another.

Very few tumblers have been able to do a double back somersault on the ground (without the aid of a springboard). When such a "double back" *is* performed, it has to be at the end of a row of flip-flaps, in order for the necessary elevation to be attained. Reputedly the first man to turn a double somersault without the aid of a springboard or trampoline was Eugene Gouleau, an old-time French middleweight tumbler and weightlifter. Gouleau was at his best in 1906, when he was able to perform a Two Hands Clean and Jerk with barbell of 292 pounds while weighing only 156½ pounds himself. Presumably he did his double somersault about that time. One of the acrobats with the Doveyko Troupe of the Moscow Circus is able to perform a back somersault while wearing a pair of 6½-foot stilts! (1963–1968). Al Treloar, who had over 50 years' experience in training and observing athletes and gymnasts, said that he saw only one tumbler—an Arab professional in the old Wood's Gymnasium in New York City—do a high, perfect, unassisted double back somersault off the floor (mat). He led into the somersault by doing a round-off and two fast flip-flaps. Dick Browning, who was at his best in 1954, was perhaps the only American tumbler who could perform a double back. He was able to attain such height in his flip-flaps that he could do a single back somersault over a bar 7 feet 6 inches high!

While holding a pair of dumbbells in the hands, a considerable number of early-day professional strong-men were each able to perform a standing back somersault. Among them were Eugen Sandow (56 pounds in each hand), "Apollo" William Bankier (30 pounds in each hand), Thomas E. White (25 pounds in each hand), G. W. Rolandow (60 pounds in each hand), Lionel Strongfort (35 pounds in each hand), and Charles MacMahon (30 pounds in each hand). Rolandow, in addition, could perform the unique feat of a back somersault while holding in front of him a *barbell* (weight not stated).

12. Juggling

Probably the two most famous European jugglers of the last hundred years were Paul Spadoni of Germany and Enrico Rastelli of Italy. Spadoni was born in 1870, and reached the peak of his skill in the early 1900s. While he did a great deal of his balancing and juggling with heavy paraphernalia, he was equally capable in handling small, light objects with speed and agility. He could either balance a small automobile (!) on a perch on one shoulder, or juggle at one time six fresh eggs. In order to show that the eggs were not hard-boiled, Spadoni, after juggling them, would break them in a plate. This six-egg feat has never been duplicated. After retiring from his exhibitions, Spadoni became one of the foremost European theatrical agents and producers.

The best feats of the versatile Italian juggler, Enrico Rastelli (1896–1931), were to juggle at one time either 12 balls or 8 plates! In these feats he is said to have been without an equal. While standing on his hands and spinning a hoop on one of his legs, he could cause a ball to "climb" from his head up his back to the sole of his other foot. All his feats were performed with "inimitable ease."

Another topnotch juggler and equilibrist of the 1890s was Paul Cinquevalli. One of his feats was to spin a heavy tub high above him on the point of a pole which he balanced, then knock the pole away and catch the tub squarely on the spike of a helmet that he wore. He also performed the "iron jaw" feat of holding by his teeth the rung of a chair in which a man was sitting. He made the feat look very easy by meanwhile sitting himself in a chair at a table, apparently reading a newspaper! He would conclude this part of his act by arising, still holding the chair and man, and strolling off the stage while he juggled three or four "cannonballs."

During recent years one of the greatest jugglers has been and is Francis Brunn. The way he is able to throw and catch spinning balls unerringly on any part of his body is simply fantastic.

But there were, and are, Oriental jugglers as well; and in their specialties they appear every bit as wonderful as their European contemporaries. One of these "Oriental" specialties is the juggling of knives. In India and China may be seen jugglers who keep in motion many pointed knives, always catching them by the handles. By throwing these knives from a distance, they can "pin" their partner against a soft board, completely surrounding his body with the daggers but never injuring his skin. In India also is performed the so-called "Dance of the eggs." The dancer, usually a woman, places on her head a large wheel made of light wood. Around the edge of the wheel, at regular intervals, are strings with loose knots at their ends, into which the dancer places the eggs as she causes the wheel to revolve. Finally, all the eggs are on the strings and are revolving so rapidly that they swing out horizontally from the wheel. The same phenomenal speed and skill that was required in putting the eggs on the strings without having one smash into another is then exhibited in *removing* the eggs one by one.

In 1967, in the Moscow Circus, which that year toured the United States, there was a Cossack riding act called The Iristons. One of the riders was Nicolai Olkhovikov, a sixth-generation circus performer and former opera singer. Standing on the croup of a cantering horse, Olkhovikov balanced four filled water-glasses on a plate atop an 8-foot pole, while he sang!

13.   Swordsmanship

Before the advent of gunpowder and rifles, the sword was an indispensable weapon to soldiers and civilians alike. With millions of men becoming skilled in its use, there were understandably some terrific exploits performed with swords, sabers, and scimitars. A scimitar was a saber having a broad curved blade with the edge on the convex side, and was used chiefly by Mohammedans—especially Arabs, Persians, and Turks.

As related earlier in Chapter 1, one of the strongest swordsmen was the gigantic King of Albania, "Scanderberg" (meaning "Prince Alexander"), who lived from *c.* 1404 to 1467. He was said to have been able to wield his huge scimitar with such force that he could cleave a man in two from head to haunches with a single blow, even if the man was clad in armor! On one occasion, when he was infuriated, with a single *horizontal* stroke of his scimitar he cut into halves at the waist two prisoners who were bound together. Whether, in these acts, Scanderberg wielded his scimitar with one or both hands, was not stated.

Turning from strength to *speed*, here is a feat of swordsmanship that was performed by Staff-Sergeant Alfred Moss (67.5 in., 182 lbs.), an instructor in gymnastics in the British Army training quarters at Aldershot, *c.* 1900. Wielding a sword horizontally, he would cut a thread by which a lemon was suspended, then, while the lemon was falling, *slice it twice* before it reached the ground! One can imagine Moss's sword swishing left-right-left so rapidly that the eye could scarcely follow it. Another of Moss's feats was to rest a broom-handle across and between two full glasses of water, then with a stroke of his sword cut the broom-handle in two without either breaking the glasses or spilling the water! He could also, with a single powerful (two-handed?) stroke cut in two the carcass of a sheep.

One of the most dextrous feats of swordsmanship ever seen was where the performer (name not given) cut in half perpendicularly a clove that stood upright on the nose of a reclining assistant, without touching the nose! In this case one might question whether the swordsman's skill was any more remarkable than the confidence and nerve of his assistant!

A short time ago, in the motion picture *Mondo Cane*, one of the episodes in the film showed swordsmen in Singapore who, with a single downward stroke, could decapitate a native ox. The sword used was broad and scimitar-like, except that the cutting edge was on the *concave* (rather than convex) side. Also, the swordsman used *both* hands together in wielding the sword, which suggests that this was probably the technique employed by the medieval warriors, mentioned above, who could assertedly cut a man in two with a single stroke.

(For other feats of swordsmanship, by medieval strong-men, see Chapter 1).

14.   Holding the arms out at shoulder level

In this feat the average man does well to last 10 minutes. Women, with their arms of lesser weight, do quite as well as men. The record is credited to a baseball player (name not given) who held his arms out steadily for 200 minutes (3 hours and 20 minutes). However, this remarkable feat was of a minor order compared with that attributed to an ancient Roman boxer named Melancomas. This boxer lived during the reign of the emperor Titus (*c.* 80 A.D.), and was held by the emperor in high regard. Melancomas was of a school of boxers whose technique was not to strike a blow, but to wear out their opponents by holding them off with straight arms. According to Dion Chrysostom, a contemporary Greek historian, Melancomas held out for whole hours, his arms extended in the face of his antagonist, who sought in vain to reach him, and bruised himself in vain efforts to break through those two muscular bars, as resistant as steel. It is said that Melancomas could remain for *two consecutive days* in this fatiguing position, while others were completely exhausted. He would leave the arena without having given or received (to his head or body) a single blow, "a feat which may be regarded as the perfection of the art of self-defence." (G. Depping, *Wonders of Bodily Strength and Skill*, 1873, p. 42. See Bibliography.) According to Depping, Melancomas "regarded with pity those of his brethren who, after heavy smashing upon each others faces, left the arena mutilated and disfigured, and considered this great waste of strength an actual proof of weakness."

As related in Chapter 1 there was in London in 1716 a giant named Thomas Fisher, who must have had strength and endurance in proportion to his height (7 ft. 5 in.), since he could hold a 10-pound weight straight out from the shoulder for *12 minutes*, continuously.

15. *Ability to withstand falls and dives*

In a free fall through space to solid ground, a few persons have survived a fall of 160 feet or so at a speed of approximately 65 mph (= 95 feet per second), with a "deceleration distance" of only a foot or less. This is said to be equivalent to a pressure of about 200 atmospheres!

Gould and Pyle, in their *Anomalies and Curiosities of Medicine* (p. 703, see Bibliography) report a case in which a person fell off a cliff 192 feet high, in County Antrim, Ireland, and recovered. They mention also where a French miner fell down a shaft 100 meters (= 328 feet) deep, into some mud and about 3 inches of water. Apparently, in falling, this man cleared the wooden structures at the sides of the shaft, as he showed no cuts or bruises, and when helped out by his brother about ten minutes later was apparently none the worse for his record-making fall. Allowing for atmospheric resistance, it can be calculated that the miner's speed in falling, when he reached the bottom of the shaft, was about 113 feet per second (= 77 mph). Accordingly, his fall took about 5.8 seconds.

Where the fall has been into deep water, a greater height and speed can be survived. For example, in 1947, Frank H. Cushing, a veteran stunt man, plunged off San Francisco's Golden Gate Bridge, a height of 238 feet above the water. However, as a precautionary measure he wore a special harness, and this probably eased his shock in hitting the water.* Even more extraordinary was when, in 1941, Keith Greene, a 19-year-old soldier from Durban, South Africa, made the record high dive by jumping from the Howick Falls into the Umgeni River, a height of 365 feet. His speed when hitting the water can be estimated as being *at least* 116 feet per second or 79 mph! This alleged feat certainly strains one's credulity.

Where the human body falls through space in random postures, its speed is retarded by air resistance from zero at the start to a maximum of nearly 50 percent. This speed, in feet per second, is equal to *9.4 times the square root* of the speed that would be attained in a vacuum. The speed becomes more or less constant in a fall of 400–500 feet, when it equals from 118 to 125 mph. However, if the body should fall steadily in a head-first or a feet-first position, rather than randomly, the speed might be as much as 50 percent greater, or in the neighborhood of 180–190 mph.

---

* On July 15, 1969, a "hippie" (James C. Layton, 20, of San Francisco), who was "high" from an overdose of the drug mescaline, jumped from the middle of the Golden Gate Bridge, landed feet-first in the water 275 feet below, and came up and began swimming. He suffered only a few bruises on his feet and ankles. Layton was one of only 4 persons to have survived the jump. 364 other jumpers have died in suicide attempts since the bridge was opened in 1937—an average of nearly one death a month.

Among circus gymnasts and acrobats, it has been demonstrated that some individuals can drop 35 feet onto the hard ground, or 25 feet onto a pavement, without injuring themselves.

16. Strength of the tendons and ligaments

Tendons, which transmit the power of the muscles to the bones, are tough, dense continuations of the "envelopes" (sarcolemmas) surrounding the bundles of muscle fibers. The strength of tendons, in resisting pulls, is said to be "equal to at least half that of the bones" (Amar, 1920, p. 99). Ligaments, which surround the joints like wristbands, thus holding the bones within a safe range of movement, are likewise composed of tough, strong material.

The strength of the tendons and ligaments was strikingly illustrated in the case of a 16th-century Frenchman named John Poltrot, who in 1563 attempted to assassinate the Duke de Guise. For this act, Poltrot was sentenced to be "quartered," or dismembered, by four horses pulling in as many directions. But the condemned man's joints and ligaments were so powerful that the "quartering" could not be accomplished, even though three fresh teams of horses in succession were harnessed to his arms and legs! Finally, he was hacked to pieces by swords. This public execution was so revolting that the King of France ordered the practice of "quartering" to be henceforth discontinued.

17. Ability to resist being lifted

In the 1920s a great deal of publicity was given to a small man who traveled all over Europe, defying anyone to lift him off the ground. The man was Johnny Coulon (109 lbs.), who during the years 1908–1914 had been world bantamweight boxing champion. Heavyweight boxers and wrestlers and champion strong-men all failed to lift Coulon, so long as he declined to be lifted. Some years afterwards, in the United States, another small man, Charlie Rose, duplicated Coulon's "resistance" act. At least two different explanations have been given of this feat. One is that the person being lifted brings about a temporary paralysis of certain nerves in the lifter, by pressing with one finger on the lifter's carotid artery (on the side of the neck), and with another finger on the lifter's pulse (on the wrist of the opposite side). The second explanation is that while the person being lifted presses on the lifter's neck, with the same hand he also presses under the chin of the lifter to an extent sufficient to throw the lifter off balance, thus making it impossible for him to exert his strength. Whatever the explanation, the fact remains that some of the world's strongest men have failed to lift Coulon and Rose when these small men resisted them, and did so easily when the "resistance" was removed.

18. Horseback riding (duration)

Innumerable records have been established in horseback riding, both for speed and for endurance. However, in the latter category, it is doubtful if the performance of John Berry, a one-time stagecoach driver in the Midwest, will ever be surpassed. On June 13, 1893, an event called "The Great Cowboy Race" took place, the starting point being the prairie just outside the town of Chadron, Nebraska. The race was to be 1000 miles, and each rider was permitted to use only two horses. Nine riders started in the race. In winning, Berry's two horses struggled "over plains, hardrock roads and clay quagmires, through cold rain, heat and dust" over the 1040 miles from Chadron to Chicago. The time was 13 days, 16 hours—an average of about 76 miles a day. On the final day, the winning horse covered 150 miles, the last 80 miles taking only 9½ hours.

After writing about the foregoing feat of horsemanship—which certainly merits recording—another instance came to hand that put it in the shade. The Abbé Nicquet, a courier of the king of France during the 16th century, rode horseback from Paris to Rome, a distance of 1050 miles, over poor roads, in 6 days and 4 hours, an average of 170 miles a day! How many horses were used during the ride was not stated.

Another riding feat of merit was when, in 1831, an English huntsman named George Osbaldiston rode 200 miles in 8 hours 42 minutes, using 28 horses. Each horse was ridden a distance of 4 miles. Thus there were 50 mountings and dismountings. Not counting these, and a six-minute "refreshment" period which was taken after the 30th heat, the actual running time was 7 hours 19 minutes—an average rate of 27.33 mph. For this feat, Osbaldiston collected 1000 guineas (then about $5000) from a colonel who had wagered that no rider could cover 200 miles in less than 10 hours.

The most prolonged example of riding—although no effort was made to establish a time record—was when, in 1924, an Argentinian, Aime F. Tschiffely, rode two Criollo horses (named Mancha and Gato) from Buenos Aires to Washington, D.C., a distance of some 10,000 miles. This famous exploit, which is thoroughly described in the author's book, *Tschiffely's Ride,* was undertaken more to demonstrate the stamina and versatility of the Criollo breed of Argentine range horses than that of the rider. However, Tschiffely certainly proved himself an extraordinary horseman in covering the long distances through jungles, mountain streams, 16,000-foot altitudes, snow, rain, deserts, heat, and about every other conceivable condition of weather and terrain.

Tschiffely mentioned several other remarkable rides made by Argentinian horsemen. One of these was when, in the year 1767, a man named Merlo carried an important message from Buenos Aires to Lima—a distance of at least 3000 miles—in 40 days, averaging 75 miles a day through all sorts of conditions. Even with an occasional fresh mount, enormous distances had to be covered. Another extraordinary ride was made in 1810 by a Major Corvalan. Leaving Buenos Aires, he arrived in the town of Mendoza, located in the foothills of the Andes, in 5 days, averaging 133 miles a day! Still another Argentinian rider, a Lieutenant Samaniego, in the War of Emancipation, in 1818, while fleeing in terror rode the 240 miles from Buenos Aires to Santiago, Chile, in only 27 hours! Certainly it would be difficult to surpass any of these *Gauchos* (cowboys of the pampas) for stamina in the saddle. But perhaps the most astonishing fact is that, over long distances, no single horse and rider has ever equalled the mileage per day accomplished by a champion long-distance human runner! (See Chapter 13).

19. Tossing the caber

This is one of the events in the Scottish Highland Games, and accordingly has been practiced since ancient times. Unlike other weight events, however, in this toss the *distance* attained is not the determining consideration. Consequently, the event cannot be rated on a numerical basis, but must be judged by the individual performance under the conditions then prevailing, including the length (which is the most critical factor) and the weight of the caber.

The caber (from the Gaelic *cabar*, a pole or beam) is a long and heavy log made from a young tree from which the branches have been trimmed. It measures in length anywhere from 15 to 20 feet, and averages in diameter from 2½ to 3 inches at the small end and up to 6 inches at the large end. Before an important contest—in order to forestall any complaints that the caber is dried-out and underweight—it is soaked for awhile in a stream, so that when used it is truly "green" wood, weighing well over 50 pounds a cubic foot. Thus a caber 20 feet in length and having an average diameter of 4½ inches would weigh, after soaking, about 125 pounds. The average caber, however, scales about 100 pounds.*

In tossing the caber, the performer stands with his foot against the small end of the caber, and several men raise it until it is standing on end. The tosser then stoops down quickly, and, lifting the lower end

---

* Dave Webster of Glasgow, who is an authority on the events of the Highland Games, says that the Braemar (Scotland) Gathering Committee possesses three cabers. In the Closed Event, for Society members only, the caber used is 17 feet 3 inches in length and weighs 91 pounds. In the Open Competition, the caber is 17 feet and 114 pounds, while the famous Braemar caber measures 19 feet 3 inches and weighs 120 pounds. (In the 1969 Games a still larger caber—19 feet and about 140 lbs.—was used. It was tossed successfully by Arthur Rowe (see Part 2) and Bill Anderson.

with both hands so that the caber rests against his shoulder, runs with it, still upright, until he thinks he has gained enough momentum to toss the light end up and over the heavy end. The caber falls on its thick end, then continues so that it "somersaults." Unless this complete turn-over is accomplished, the toss is not counted a good one; and the more in a *straight* line the caber is tossed, the greater the credit for the toss. Considering the weight of the caber, it requires a high degree of strength and activity to toss it in the specified manner. If all the competitors fail to "toss" a particular caber, a common practice is to saw a piece, or more than one piece, off the heavy end until finally someone succeeds in tossing it. An alternative, where the ground is not level (and where in the Highlands isn't it?) is to toss the caber downhill instead of uphill (or in-between). "Tossing the caber" is said to have been derived from the practical feat of pitching a log so that it would fall clear across a stream and so provide a bridge. But wouldn't it be easier to simply *stand* the log on its heavy end on the near bank of the stream and then let the light end *fall* to the other bank?

The old-time champion "all-rounder," Donald Dinnie (see p. 541), was in his prime unbeatable in this event, and in the 1860s made many fine tosses with cabers up to 19 feet in length. On September 6, 1951, George Clark, another Highlander, was widely acclaimed for his feat of tossing the heavy and cumbersome Braemar caber in good style, three times in one day. He is said to have been the first to master this largest-sized Championship caber. More recently, Henry Gray, another powerful Games athlete (see above) also tossed the Braemar caber.

20. *Pitching horseshoes*

So far as consistently perfect coordination of eye and hand is concerned, it would be difficult to top the performances of championship horseshoe pitchers. In a meet at Riverside, California, on October 23, 1934, Guy Zimmerman pitched 56 consecutive ringers! In another contest, at Des Moines, Iowa, in 1946, Ted Allen of Boulder, Colorado, scored 180 ringers out of 200 throws! While on the subject of horseshoes, it can be mentioned that two blacksmiths of St. Paul, Minnesota—J. Michael McGrath and Adolph Wondersnider, respectively—shod 127 horses (4 shoes to a horse) in 17 hours, 1912. This means that each man averaged a horse every 16 minutes or a shoe every 4 minutes.

21. *Piano playing*

A duration record for playing a piano was set in July, 1893, when J. P. Theis played continuously for 27 hours. However, more recently the time has been greatly increased. In November 1952, a player in Paris continued for 72 hours. On December 6, 1952, Noel Hylton of Los

Angeles raised the record to 80 hours 2 minutes. During this period Hylton took a five-minute rest each hour (permissible under long-distance piano-playing rules), and never repeated a tune. He played an average of 22 songs an hour, for a total of about 1760 songs, all different! But Hylton's record, remarkable as it was, was put in the shade on May 1, 1955, when Heinz Arntz of Berlin played the piano for 423 hours (= 17 days, 15 hours), stopping each hour only for the allowed five-minute rest. How many different songs Arntz played in establishing his record was not stated.

22. Rifle marksmanship

Ordinary hunting and shooting, while listed as sports, do not come under the heading of *athletics*, even though some forms require great endurance.* But where the shooting requires extreme accuracy in *marksmanship*, and so demands fine coordination between eye and hand, it becomes a form of manual dexterity which, I feel, should at least be represented here by a few outstanding examples.

Back in 1906, a vaudeville performer named Adolph Topperwein acquired a great reputation as a "trick shot" marksman through his extraordinary feats with a rifle on the stage. His most outstanding exhibition—which required great endurance as well as skill—was given one day in December 1906 at the fairgrounds in San Antonio, Texas. Perhaps I should say *commenced* one day, since his total performance extended over twelve days in a row. On each of these days, for 8 hours, Topperwein shot from *11 to 14 times a minute* at targets tossed high in the air. The "targets" were wooden cubes measuring 2½ inches on a side. On the first day he shot 6500 of these cubes without missing one! On the second day, he missed one out of 6600 shots! At the completion of his 12-day demonstration, Topperwein was exhausted, but he had missed only 9 shots out of 72,500 tries, a record which stands to this day!

Another marksman—or markswoman—of extraordinary ability was the fabulous Annie Oakley (1858–1926). At the age of 17, she was the featured rifle-shot with Buffalo Bill's Wild West Circus, and in this rôle gained an international reputation. For over 17 years she toured Europe and the United States, coming back with the circus season after season. About 1887, the Emperor of Germany, who was then Crown

---

* The late Tromp van Diggelen of Cape Town, South Africa, was not only a professional strong-man, wrestler, and proprietor of a physical culture institute, but was also an experienced big-game hunter. His opinion was that of all sports, elephant hunting is the one which demands "the most endurance, determination, and sheer physical fitness." Continuing, he says: "So it may be imagined what it means to track an elephant for 20 or 30 miles over ground that is usually hilly, rocky, or very often sandy, under the glaring tropical sun." In addition, there is the actual danger of facing the huge animal at a shooting distance.

PLATE 49

(Top) A spectacular feat of limberness and balance performed at "Muscle Beach," California, by Rus Saunders and Dolores Hoff. (107)

(Bottom) The Spurgat Brothers, who were known in vaudeville as the "Submarine Contortionists" (yes, this feat is being performed under water!). (108)

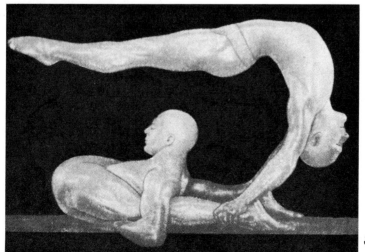

PLATE 50

The "human fly," D. D. Roland, carrying his wife around the ledge of a 22-story building. Roland performed in the 1920s and 1930s. (109)

PLATE 51

Bronze statue in the Museo delle Terme, Rome, of a Greek professional boxer resting. Attributed to the Athenian sculptor Apollonius, c. 300 B.C. (110)

PLATE 52

A woodcut of John L. Sullivan, showing the bare-knuckle champion as he appeared after his victory over Paddy Ryan on Feb. 7, 1882. (111)

PLATE 53

Robert Fitzsimmons, who fought and knocked out many of the leading heavyweights of his time, although he himself weighed only 156–172 lbs. (112)

PLATE 54

James J. Jeffries, at the age of 22, in 1897. In the author's opinion, Jeffries in his prime was the greatest heavyweight of the last 100 years. (113)

PLATE 55

Jack Johnson, who was a clever defensive boxer, but was hardly up to Jeffries, Dempsey, or Fitzsimmons as a fighter. (114)

PLATE 56

Jack Dempsey, "The Manassa Mauler," who after Jim Jeffries was probably the greatest heavyweight fighter. (115)

Prince William, had such confidence in Annie's markmanship that he permitted her to shoot the ashes off his cigarette (which he held in his lips) at a distance of 100 feet. One of Annie's favorite demonstrations was to have a five-of-hearts playing card held up at a distance of 50 feet, whereupon she would shoot in quick succession through each of the five hearts. This feat was the origin of the term "Annie Oakleys," which was applied to complimentary theater and sports events tickets perforated in a similar pattern. To demonstrate her consistent accuracy, Annie once had 5000 pennies tossed in the air in rapid succession, and out of them scored 4777 hits!

In earlier days, there were some great shots among the frontiersmen of Kentucky, who carried their carbines with them almost continuously from boyhood to old age. Audubon says that he observed one particularly skillful marksman who, shooting at night from a distance of about 40 yards, "snuffed" (but not extinguished) a candle in three out of six shots, and with the other three shots "either extinguished it or cut it immediately below the flame." Another feat witnessed by Audubon was when the famous Daniel Boone killed a squirrel at a distance of about 50 paces by shooting, not directly at the squirrel, but at the *bark of the tree* immediately under the animal. The bark, flying up, killed the animal and sent it flying through the air as though it had been in an explosion.

23. Skiing

Skiing, it would appear, is one of the most ancient sports, although at first it was used for utilitarian purposes rather than competition. A pair of crudely made skis found in a peat bog at Hoting, in east-central Sweden, has been estimated by the pollen method of dating to be between 4000 and 5000 years old. Presumably the first skis were made from the bones of large animals, and it was not until the Middle Ages that wood was substituted and the skis turned up at the front ends. World championships in skiing are now held annually under the jurisdiction of the Federation Internationale de Ski (F.I.S.). The first of these championships took place in 1925, in Czechoslovakia, and since that time have been held variously in Norway, Sweden, Finland, Germany, Poland, France, Italy, and Czechoslovakia. In 1950 the competition was held in the United States, at Lake Placid, New York, and Rumford, Maine.

Present-day ski competitions are composed of a considerable number of separate or combined events, these being mainly the following: Cross-Country (over either 15, 18, 30 of 50 kilometers); Slalom (including the Regular and the Giant Slalom, the latter being over a greater distance); Downhill Racing; Relay Racing; and Jumping. Where Downhill Racing and the Slalom are both used, the events are known as the Alpine Combined. Where the two events are Cross-Country and Jumping, they are called the Nordic Combined. All these events, with the exception of jumping (and therefore the Nordic Combined), are engaged in by women as well as men.

The most spectacular event in a ski championship is the Jump for men, in which over the years the record distance has been steadily (and enormously) increased. The first listed American record was made by Mikkel Hemmestvedt in 1887 at Red Wing, Minnesota, with a jump of 37 feet. In 1904, the record was 82 feet; and from there on the increase in distance has been continual though sometimes erratic. The American records increased almost in a straight line from 92½ feet in 1905 to 214 feet in 1919. Then there was a space of 12 years during which no records were listed. From 1931 to the present time, European records have been increasingly higher than those made by American skiers. The current world's record jump on skis is one of 145 meters (475 feet 8½ inches), made by Peter Lesser of East Germany, at Mitterndorf, Austria, on March 21, 1965. To make such a phenomenal jump requires a take-off speed of over 100 mph! It should be noted that the F.I.C. considers long jumps as official records *only for the particular hill on which the record was made*.

The 1966 World Alpine Championships were held August 5–14 at Portillo, Chile. The winners in the events that were timed were as follows: Men's Downhill, Jean-Claude Killy (France), 1:34.40; Men's Special Slalom, Carlo Senoner (Italy), 1:41.56; Men's Giant Slalom, Guy Perillat (France), 3:19.42; Women's Downhill, Erika Schinegger (Austria), 1:32.63; Women's Special Slalom, Annie Famose (France), 1:30.48; Women's Giant Slalom, Marielle Goitschel (France), 1:22.64. Wherever the women's records are lower than the men's, it should be understood that the *distances* covered by the women are shorter.

The 1966 World Nordic Championships were held February 17–27 at Holmenkollen, Norway. The winners in the events that were timed were as follows: Men's 15-kilometer Cross-Country, Gjermund Eggen (Norway), 47:56.2; Men's 30-kilometer Cross-Country, E. Maentyranta (Finland), 1:37: 26.7; Men's 50-kilometer Cross-Country, Gjermund Eggen (Norway), 3:03:14.7. From these figures it can be seen that cross-country skiing is a relatively slow means of travel, with the top speed over the shortest distance (15 kilometers, or about 9-5/16 miles) being only 11.66 MPH. This, of course, is largely due to the time lost while skiing *uphill*.

The most grueling of all ski races is the annual Vasaloppet, or cross-country race from Sälen to Mora, Sweden. The record in it is held by D. Johansson, who in 1961 covered the 54-mile distance in 4 hours 45 minutes 10 seconds (= 11.38 mph). This classic ski-race has been held each year since 1922, and in 1966 attracted 6857 contestants from 13 countries! A 50-year-old Swede, Nils Karlsson, holds the record for number of wins, having been first in the Vasaloppet 9 out of 10 times.

In skiing *downhill,* as would be expected, enormous speeds can be attained. Coming down a very steep (62-degree) slope at Portillo, Chile, on August 25, 1955, the American skier Ralph Miller is said to have reached over a short course of 50 meters a speed of 2.927 kilometers per minute (= 109.14 mph)!

Stan Baumgartner, a professional skier at Boyne Mountain resort, Michigan, could perform a flying back somersault on skis (1963).

In Norway and Sweden, and frequently in England, the word *ski* is pronounced shē.

24. Handball

The all-time greatest handball player would appear to have been the professional all-around athlete, Richard Perry "Doc" Williams of Miamisburg, Ohio. From 1900 (when he was 26) to 1948 (when he was 74!), Williams played 14,659 games of one-wall soft handball without losing a single game!

25. Other feats

NOTE: The following feats or examples, being represented in most cases by only a single performance or two, are listed without numberings. They are what may be called "unclassifiable"—perhaps even more so than some of the previous listings.

Speed of hand or fingers. This, of course, can be demonstrated in innumerable ways: striking a blow, playing a piano or a banjo, typewriting, performing feats of sleight-of-hand, etc. But a unique manner of showing how fast he could not only move his hand, but judge distance and timing to a nicety, was used by Paul von Boeckmann, the strong-man and physical instructor of New York City, c. 1900. Von Boeckmann would place 4 coins in a row on the back of his hand, toss them into the air a few inches, then catch them *separately* (the hand remaining with the back up) before they had time to fall to the floor.

In *typewriting,* the greatest number of words typed within a minute on a manual machine is 216, by Miss Stella Pajunas (c. 1957). Over the duration of an hour, Albert Tangora averaged 147 words per minute, Oct. 22, 1923.

Irvin Bauman husked 46.58 bushels of corn in 1 hour 20 minutes. Davenport, Iowa, 1940.

Earle Schmidt, of Milwaukee, Wisconsin, could hold his weight (138 lbs.) simply by pressing his hands inwardly against a 2 x 10 inch overhead wooden beam, c. 1942.

An authentic impromptu feat of strength performed in the 1890s by two British Army officers in India was as follows. A native servant fell into a deep but almost dry well, knocking himself unconscious. To get him out of the well, the lighter officer descended on the rope to the bottom. Standing in the bucket, holding onto the rope with one hand, and carrying the native in the other, he gave the signal for the other officer to draw them up (hand by hand, as there was no crank). As they reached the mouth of the well the rope snapped and the two men fell to the bottom. Unhurt, the Englishman tied the rope together, and on the second attempt both men were brought up successfully! This feat received the award of the Stanhope medal.

Joe Stecher (P; 73.5 in., 220 lbs.), the one-time world's heavyweight wrestling champion, developed the squeezing power in his legs to the point where he could burst a sack of grain by putting a "scissors" hold on it and applying pressure (see Plate 62).

A remarkable feat of endurance requiring toughness of the hands was recorded by the English historian Plot, in 1683. This was where a farmer (name not given) pulled up *four acres* of tall ("near a man's height") shrubs, known as broom, with his hands alone. To accomplish the same, other farmers were obliged to use mattocks (picks) and similar digging tools.

Talk about tough! Anthony Barker, a professional strong-man and physical instructor who ran a gymnasium in New York City about the turn of the century, would lie supine on the floor, then allow a young man assistant to jump down from a chair on a table directly onto his *face!* The young man's mother used to worry for fear that her son might sprain his ankles on Barker's handsome but cast-iron features! Another of Barker's many feats was to punch a hole with his bare fist right through the seat of a cane-bottomed chair.* Barker was a truly extraordinary strong-man, who possessed not only powerful muscles (even in his face), but also abundant, thick, strong hair and absolutely perfect teeth. Even in longevity he was a super-athlete. Born away back in 1866, he lived in good health to reach the age of 103!

Herbert Goethe, a light-heavyweight strong-man who substituted for Hermann Saxon in the Arthur Saxon Trio for one season (*c.* 1910), could support and balance a 180-pound barbell across the top of his head *without any padding or protection whatever.* In 1949, Jack Walsh (P;

---

* Barker indeed had a powerful punch; and if he had been sufficiently interested, he might have become a boxing champion. When in the Army, he had been made a boxing instructor. One time, when Bob Fitzsimmons, who was then the heavyweight champion, tried to pull an ill-chosen trick on him, Barker gave Fitz a body punch that knocked him clear across the room. Barker thinks that he could have licked Fitzsimmons in the ring, if only he had possessed a knowledge of the finer points of boxing, plus a capable manager.

65 in., 148 lbs.) of Trenton, New Jersey, is said to have similarly supported a 295-pound barbell!

Each year in Kalgoorie, a gold- and silver-mining town in Western Australia, a Shoveling Championship is held. This consists of shoveling a 2000-pound pile of ore onto a truck in the least possible time. In 1959 the contest was won by Lino Brenz-Verca, a 32-year-old Italian miner. He transferred the 2000 pounds of ore from the ground onto the truck in 62 shovelsful averaging 32 pounds each, in a total time of 2 minutes 2 seconds. Of this time, 19 seconds was a penalty for having inadvertently tossed 95 pounds of the ore *outside* of the truck while shoveling. Brenz-Verca had also won in this contest in a previous year.

Another record was set in Western Australia, in 1961, when William Hardy, a bricklayer, laid 5469 bricks consecutively during an 8-hour working period. His average time for laying a brick into place was thus only 5 seconds! A speed-record, over a period of one hour, was made in 1937 by Joseph Raglon, of East St. Louis, Illinois. With the help of assistants, Raglon laid 3472 bricks during the 60-minute period, averaging nearly a brick a second!

In Wombwell, England, there has for some years been a Hole-Digging Contest. The holes are standardized at 6 feet square by 4 feet deep, thus containing 96 cubic feet of earth. The record time for digging such a hole is 46 minutes.

In British Columbia, a yearly contest is held among lumberjacks in Pole-Climbing. The record in this event was established late in 1962 when Daniel Sailor climbed to the top of a 90-foot smooth, limbless tree in 26 seconds!

In log-rolling, or birling, the longest contest on record took place in Chequamegon Bay, Ashland, Wisconsin, in 1900. The two birlers were Allan Stewart and Joe Oliver. Stewart finally dislodged Oliver from the 24-inch-diameter log on which they were contesting, but only after a nip-and-tuck battle of 3 hours 15 minutes!

Hermann Görner performed feats that tested his strength in almost every conceivable manner. One of his more unusual exhibitions was to pick up a total of 14 bricks weighing 123½ pounds simply by *squeezing* them together sideways. At no time were either the upper arms or the bricks in contact with the body. The bricks were larger than those common in the United States (which average about 5¾ pounds), and weighed 4 kilos or 8.82 pounds each. The bricks each measured 10¼ inches long by 5⅛ inches wide by 2-9/16 inches thick.

Alan Calvert, the founder of the original Milo Bar-Bell Company and *Strength* magazine, in Philadelphia, once mentioned a strong-man who was able to hook his foot into the handle of a 50-pound blockweight and then hold his leg out straight in front of him (that is, parallel to the floor). This feat required tremendous strength in the muscles of the groin (*Psoas* and *Iliacus*) that flex the hip-joint, and to a lesser extent in the quadriceps muscles of the thigh that extend the knee.

Walking on stilts. Perhaps the most remarkable performance of this kind was when a man (name not given) from Stonington, Connecticut, on a wager, walked through the rapids of Niagara Falls on stilts! This was on March 12, 1859, just before the famous tightrope walker, Charles Blondin, walked across the falls on a rope. In this connection, Blondin's *somersault* on stilts on a tightrope 170 feet above the ground should also receive consideration!

Mountain climbing. The world's highest point, the summit of Mount Everest (29,028 feet), in the Himalayas, was reached on May 29, 1953 by the British mountaineer, Edmund Percival Hillary, and his native guide (or *sherpa*), Tenzing Norkhay. Eight previous climbing expeditions, between the years 1922 and 1953, had attained heights on Everest ranging from about 24,900 feet to 28,721 feet. Lesser peaks of the Himalayas, of over 23,000-foot elevations, were scaled between 1930 and 1960 no fewer than 54 times. But the first successful ascent of Everest, by Hillary and Tenzing, was perhaps the most spectacular of all feats of mountaineering, even though the peak was reached subsequently (1953–1965) by 10 different expeditions comprising 22 individual climbers.

The most capable mountain-climber in the world today is generally considered to be Walter Bonatti, a 37-year-old Italian alpinist. Numerous exploits in scaling sheer, vertical, ice-covered faces of mountains in the Andes, the Himalayas, and the Alps attest to Bonatti's uncanny abilities as an alpine gymnast. In February, 1965, Bonatti made one of his most difficult climbs by ascending the *north* face of the Matterhorn—a 3550-foot, icy ascent which other experienced climbers regarded as impossible. Bonatti conquered this challenging climb in "79 hours of superhuman effort." For this and other hair-raising performances Bonatti was awarded a specially-struck gold medal by President Guiseppi Saragat of Italy, attesting to Bonatti's indomitable spirit.

"Human flies." While lesser elevations are involved in the public exhibitions of the so-called "human flies" than in mountain climbing, the dangers to the performer in the latter occupation are probably even greater. Indeed, sooner or later, every "human fly" who has made his living by climbing the outer walls of tall buildings, has slipped or lost his hold and fallen, stories below, to the sidewalk. The performers of this dangerous occupation—which in many cities is now forbidden—had to develop extraordinary strength and endurance in the muscles of their fingers and hands, so as to be able to sustain their weight while

grasping whatever handholds were afforded. In Plate 50 is shown a photograph of a "human fly," D. D. Roland, who, while blindfolded, is carrying his wife on his shoulders around the ledge of a 22-story building! Roland is said to have climbed no fewer than 2500 buildings in the United States and abroad.

Karate. This form of self-defense, or unarmed combat, is said to have originated in Japan, where the name is pronounced Karl-lot-tay. The main physical attributes required in Karate are speed of movement (both in the hands and the feet) and great toughness of the skin in these parts. This toughness is developed by making a practice of striking the hands and feet against hard, resistant objects. Through long practice of this kind, many a performer of Karate becomes able to break a brick, a stack of tiles, or a 1½-inch thick hardwood board by striking it with the side of his hand. Some performers are said to be able to thus break even a 2x4 beam! The Japanese, who are the main exponents of Karate, typically are small men, weighing from 130 to 145 pounds. However, they are lean and muscular, and exceedingly quick of movement. The knuckles of their hands, particularly those of the first and second fingers, are often abnormally large, due to their being so often struck against hard objects. An All-American open championship in Karate is held each year in one of the major cities, and the various winners are identified with differently-colored *belts*, much as in the sport of Judo.

Feats of "superhuman" strength by non-athletes. Every so often, newspapers will carry the story of where a small, frail man (or even woman), while under the intense emotional strain of rescuing someone from impending death, performs a feat of strength which, under ordinary circumstances, would be impossible for any man. While some such alleged occurrences may have a certain amount of truth connected with them, probably the majority of them can be classed with other "fully documented" happenings that either did not occur or were inaccurately described. It may be significant that in practically all cases of this nature the person who is said to have performed the "superhuman" feat is an otherwise obscure individual who has never had his (or her) name in print before. I have never been an eyewitness of any act of "superhuman" strength. However, of all the countless ways in which muscular power can be demonstrated I would regard this variety as the one most open to fakery or false representation. It would seem to fall in the same category as the numerous cases of "proven" longevity, in which the individual (always from some backwoods or foreign community) is *known* to be 140, 150, or 160 years of age, even if there are no documents to show it.

6.
Boxing

The origin of boxing, or self-defense with the fists, dates back to prehistoric times. The sport attained great popularity among the Greeks and Romans, although it was practiced in a less organized fashion long before classic times. Probably one of the first representations of a boxing match is a Babylonian plaque, over 4000 years old, showing two men with raised fists facing each other. Again, on the funnel of the Hagia Triada, in Crete (dating from about 1700 B.C.), there are a number of incised figures showing boxers in various actions.

The term "pugilism" comes from the Latin word *pugil*, meaning to fight with the fists. One of the first Greek heros to popularize boxing was Theseus, whose doings are recounted in Homer's *Iliad*, and who is supposed to have lived contemporaneously with the great strong-man Herakles. But even in Theseus's time, and for centuries thereafter, boxing was no longer a simple, bare-fisted affair. Down to the beginning of the fourth century B.C., it was the custom among boxers to wind soft strips of leather around their hands and wrists, to protect their knuckles and at the same time add effectiveness to their punches. These leather strips were known as *meilichai*. Early in the fourth century they were superseded by "gloves," known as *sphairai*. These were made of hard leather, with projecting edges that could cut the flesh like brass knuckles. Still later, the Romans developed the gauntlet-like appliance known as a *cestus* (See Plate 51). This was a fist-covering made of strips of leather weighted with pieces of iron or lead, and with metal studs or spikes placed in positions over the knuckles. Naturally a blow from one of these *cesti*—which were essentially spiked *clubs*—inflicted terrible punishment; and the fighter who got in a telling blow first was usually the winner.

In boxing contests among the Greeks there was no ring and accordingly little close fighting. There were no rounds and the pace was relatively slow. A rushing, wide-open attack was—as it is today—the sign of an inexperienced fighter. Finally, there were no bodyweight classes, so that the bigger and stronger the man, usually the greater his chance of winning. With the leather thongs on the hands, gripping and wrestling were either impossible or ineffective, and a successful encounter was largely dependent upon a good defense. Blows to the body were relatively infrequent, and in those early days of boxing a fight was usually decided either by a knockout punch to the jaw or by one of the fighters acknowledging himself beaten.

Sometimes, if a fight was becoming unduly prolonged, with neither contestant showing superiority, each man, after mutual agreement, would be given a free punch at the other. In this exchange, the one whose turn came first would seem to have a great advantage, but this was not always the case. For example, in the epic encounter between the Albanian boxer Kreugas and the Italian Damoxenes, at one of the Nemean Games, Kreugas had the first turn, ". . . and his blow fell like that of a heavy hammer upon his opponent's head, which, however, withstood the onslaught" (Depping, 1873, p. 40). Damoxenes, requesting Kreugas to hold his arm above his head, then drove his leather-wrapped hand (the fingers being pointed) so deeply into Kreugas' abdomen that the blow disembowelled him and, of course, killed him on the spot. The judges, feeling that Damoxenes had deliberately killed his opponent—thus violating the spirit of the sport—banished Damoxenes and awarded the victory to the dead Kreugas, to whom also a statue was erected.* Since in this type of "free-punch" contest the fighters determined whom came first by drawing lots, from it would seem to have come the modern fight term "draw," to indicate a fight in which neither man won.

On the ancient Olympic Games program, boxing first appeared in the 23rd Games, held in 688 B.C. The victor in this first official contest was Onomastos of Smyrna. In the 27th Games, held in 672 B.C., the winner was Daippos of Crotona—the latter province being the home of the renowned sixth-century strong-man, Milo. But the most famous boxer of antiquity was Theagenes, who was born about 505 B.C. in Thasos, an island in the Aegean Sea off the coast of Thrace. Theagenes, according to the Greek writers Plutarch and Pausanias, won during the years 484–468 B.C. inclusive no fewer than 1426 consecutive victories in boxing. These bouts were engaged in with the fists covered with the soft leather strips mentioned previously. The results upon the contestants were probably much the same as if they had been wearing light boxing gloves. Later on, some of the Greek professional gladiators (see Plate 51) adopted the Roman *cestus;* but this brutal affair was not used in any of the Olympic or other amateur Games. These Grecian

---

* The Italian neo-classical sculptor, Antonio Canova (1757–1822), also made figures of both Kreugas and Damoxenes, in the postures just described. These two realistic sculptures are in the Vatican Museum, Rome.

Games continued until, with degeneracy setting in, especially in the boxing contests, the Roman emperor Theodosius abolished them in 394 A.D. With the discontinuance of the Games, boxing as a major sport went into oblivion for over 1300 years. The last winner in the Olympic Games was the Armenian boxer Varadates. Evidently his victory was held in high esteem by his countrymen, for he was later made King of Armenia.

While boxing undoubtedly was practiced in various parts of the world during the Middle Ages, it was essentially dormant during this period as an organized sport, and was not "revived" until early in the 18th century, in England. Credit for the revival is given to James Figg (1694–1734), "the father of modern pugilism." He was the first British champion—the style then being with the bare knuckles—and reigned from 1719 to 1730, when he retired undefeated.

Figg, during his lifetime, was the dominant authority on bare-knuckle boxing. His ruling was that the fighters had to continue, without rest periods, until there was a definite winner or loser. Figg's ideas were followed until 1743, when Jack Broughton, "a great fighter and student of the sport," drew up a set of rules and regulations calculated to "lessen the brutality of pugilism." So great did Broughton's fame become among British sportsmen and the public that upon his death he was buried among royalty and a few other celebrities in Westminster Abbey, London. In 1838, Broughton's rules became the basis for the London Prize Ring Rules, which governed the sport of bare-knuckle fighting until, in 1867, new rules, requiring the use of boxing gloves, 3-minute rounds with a minute's rest between, etc., were brought out under the name of the eighth Marquis of Queensberry (John Sholto Douglas). The London Prize Ring Rules continued, however, to be used until John L. Sullivan relinquished his world championship to James J. Corbett on September 7, 1892, in New Orleans, Louisiana, under the "new" Marquis of Queensberry Rules.

Whatever his merits as a boxer, John Lawrence Sullivan (see Plate 52) was the most popular pugilist of his day, and perhaps of all the pugilists from the time of James Figg on. Sullivan's defeat at the hands of Corbett came when he was 33 years of age, 20 pounds overweight, out of condition, and faced by a young, superbly conditioned athlete who was so fast and clever that Sullivan could scarcely touch him, let alone deliver one of his haymakers. In short, it was a contest in which the two fighters used totally different techniques. If the object of a fighter under the Marquis of Queensbury Rules is to win by getting his opponent to wear himself out, then Corbett was almost an ideal champion.* But if the winner is he who, in an exchange of punches, can out-weather his opponent, Sullivan in his prime (*c.* 1882, not 1892) would have been a hard man to beat.

An interesting point concerning Sullivan is that before he took up prizefighting, he trained and competed in *weightlifting*. This is especially significant in view of the use of weight-training today among practically all classes of athletes, and notwithstanding that in Sullivan's day such training was supposed to make one "slow and muscle-bound" (whatever that is). In a lifting contest against one Major Thomas F. Lynch, at Boston in 1880 (at which time Sullivan was 22 years of age), Lynch lifted a pair of 105-pound dumbbells overhead 9 times in succession, while Sullivan was unable to get the bells higher than his shoulders.

To return to the Sullivan-Corbett bout, it is the matter of *differing styles*—which prevailed then and has continued to the present day— which makes fighters (boxers vs. sluggers) so difficult to rate. Instead of more or less uniform *techniques*—such as apply in running, jumping, swimming, and other athletic events—that can be measured, in boxing (and for that matter wrestling, judo, etc.) no such exact measurement is possible. In these man-to-man encounters, unless a decisive victory —such as a knockout or a fall—is scored, the decision as to the winner rests with the referee and the judges. And, needless to say, the official decision is frequently rejected by the majority—sometimes the great majority—of the spectators and followers. Supporters of the presumably invincible John L. Sullivan simply refused to believe that their idol had been defeated by a less powerful opponent.

The factor of *subjective* opinion was perhaps never more clearly illustrated than in the "computerized" contest conducted in 1967 in an effort to determine (scientifically?) the greatest heavyweight boxing champion since the days of the great John L. Let us first review the results of this series of imaginary boxing contests, and then see how well the results tally with those of acknowledged authorities on boxing.

The "computerized" contest was conceived by Murray Woroner of Miami, Florida, and was conducted by a publicity firm in the same city. So numerous were the statistics placed on punch cards and fed into the computer that it was several months before all the results had emerged. Assertedly, each fighter was charted as to height and weight, punching power, speed, courage, defensive skill, style, native I.Q., and ability of opponents faced at peak of career. Fourteen elimination

---

* See also, in this connection, the comments on the Roman boxer Melancomas (p. 330) who won his matches by superior strength and endurance, but without giving or receiving a single blow.

contests—in each of which the computer delivered a blow-by-blow account for 15 rounds or less—preceded the final bout. The results of the 15 contests, in the order engaged in, were as follows:

	1. Jack Dempsey vs. Jim Corbett	Dempsey, by KO in 7th
	2. John L. Sullivan vs. Jim Braddock	Sullivan, by decision
	3. Joe Louis vs. Jess Willard	Louis, by KO in 15th
	4. Bob Fitzsimmons vs. Jack Sharkey	Fitzsimmons, by decision
	5. Max Baer vs. Jack Johnson	Baer, by decision
	6. Rocky Marciano vs. Gene Tunney	Marciano, by decision
	7. Jim Jeffries vs. Jersey Joe Walcott	Jeffries, by KO in 10th
	8. Cassius Clay vs. Max Schmeling	Clay, by decision
(Quarter-final)	9. Dempsey vs. Sullivan	Dempsey, by KO in 7th
(" ")	10. Louis vs. Fitzsimmons	Louis, by TKO in 10th
(" ")	11. Baer vs. Marciano	Marciano, by TKO in 14th
(" ")	12. Jeffries vs. Clay	Jeffries, by decision
(semi-final)	13. Dempsey vs. Louis	Dempsey, by decision
(" ")	14. Marciano vs. Jeffries	Marciano, by decision
(final)	15. Dempsey vs. Marciano	Marciano, by KO in 13th

Unfortunately, even electronic computers can be no more accurate than the data which are fed into them. And they can make errors, as is recognized in many "computerized" professions, where "infallible" results have occasionally to be checked by longhand methods. Quite apart from these considerations, it is safe to say that few of the above-listed boxing outcomes would be generally agreed upon. In the first place, the choice of contestants in the elimination bouts is arbitrary; and the listed outcome of the final bout still leaves undetermined the results of two of the most interesting possibilities: (1) a match between Dempsey and Jeffries, and (2) one between Louis and Marciano. Thirdly, where the outcome of a bout has to be speculative, the choice of the winner is strongly influenced by the age and experience of the person doing the speculating. Old-timers favor Sullivan, Fitzsimmons, and Jeffries, while recent fight-fans name either Dempsey or Louis. Curiously, in view of the above-listed computer results, there has never been a nation-wide poll in which Marciano was judged the greatest heavyweight. A poll, conducted in 1950, named Jack Dempsey as overwhelmingly the greatest heavyweight of the first half of the century, with 251 votes to 104 for Joe Louis, the runner-up. But it should be reflected that most of the newsmen who voted in 1950 had never seen the great old-time heavyweights who were active from 1882 to 1905. That period was truly the Golden Age of modern boxing, even though larger audiences and gate receipts were to come later on.

Prior to the above-described "computerized" contest, annual polls were published by various writers on boxing in which their choices were expressed. Nat Fleischer, Editor of *The Ring*, listed the ten all-time greatest heavyweights, in order, as: (1) Jack Johnson, (2) Jim Jeffries, (3) Bob Fitzsimmons, (4) Jack Dempsey, (5) Jim Corbett, (6) Joe Louis, (7) Sam Langford, (8) Gene Tunney, (9) Max Schmeling, and (10) Rocky Marciano. Harry Grayson, a reporter on boxing with more than 40 years' experience behind him, classed the eight leading heavyweights in this order: (1) Dempsey, (2) Johnson, (3) Jeffries, (4) Sullivan, (5) Tunney, (6) Fitzsimmons, (7) Corbett, and (8) Louis. Recently I asked Al Nelson, a lifelong student of boxing and manager of the boxing museum in Jeffries' Barn at Knott's Berry Farm, in Buena Park, California, his opinion as to the five greatest heavyweights.* Knowing all the facts and suppositions concerning each of them, Nelson named Fitzsimmons, Jeffries, Johnson, Dempsey, and Tunney.

To this somewhat diversified series of opinions, I would like to add a few observations. Clearly, among "near-heavyweights," Bob Fitzsimmons (see Plate 53) was the greatest prizefighter of the last hundred years; and only his lack of weight and strength prevented him from being the greatest heavyweight. While weighing only from 156 to 172 pounds at a height of 70.5 inches, Fitzsimmons had perhaps the hardest punch ever possessed by a boxer of his size. With it he knocked out such notables as Peter Maher (1896), Jim Corbett (1897), and Gus Ruhlin and the rugged sailor Tom Sharkey both within two weeks in 1900. Sharkey, who fought all the best heavyweights of his time, rated the greatest in this order: (1) Jeffries, (2) Fitzsimmons, (3) Joe Goddard, (4) Corbett, (5) Joe Choynski, and (6) Australian Billy Smith.

Sharkey was probably one of the few critics ever to list Joe Choynski among the leading heavyweights. Actually, Choynski weighed only about 165 pounds; but he was built along the slender lines of Bob Fitzsimmons and had, similarly, a devastating punch. Indeed, according to Jim Jeffries, Choynski hit him even harder than Fitz. In their championship fight at Coney Island, New York, in 1899, Fitz landed a haymaker on Jeffries' jaw and stepped back, waiting for the big Californian to fall. But the blow was simply shaken off by Jeff; and Fitz, having broken both his fists on Jeffries' cast-iron jaw, realized the jig was up and asked Jeff to knock him out. Choynski, in his bout with Jeffries at San Francisco in 1897, is said to have hit Jeff the hardest blow during

---

* Nelson was the principal consultant in the "computerized" contest conducted by Murray Woroner, but received little or no publicity in connection with it.

his career. Choynski's punch hit Jeff in the mouth with such force that Jeff's lips were forced back between his teeth and had to be cut back with a knife!

Jim Corbett—without doubt the greatest of all defensive boxers among the heavyweights—would appear to be under-rated in most recent polls. So long as he could keep out of reach, Corbett could probably have worn down any opponent to the point where he could step in and knock him out, just as he knocked the once-mighty John L. Sullivan out. But it is difficult for even the cleverest boxer to keep out of range indefinitely, and Corbett found this out in his championship bouts with Fitzsimmons and Jeffries. Corbett was a superb boxer and a splendidly-trained physical specimen, but he was unable to stand up under the punches from his opponents that *did* land.

Certainly, among all the heavyweights up to the year 1905, when he retired from the ring, Jim Jeffries (see Plate 54) was the greatest *all-around* performer. While he could not hit with the lightning-speed of Fitzsimmons, he had a powerful punch in each hand, and a good defense in the form of his famous "crouch." Most of all, however, he was virtually impervious to blows, either to his head, face, or body. So, about the only way he could lose a bout was on points—which he came mighty close to doing in his second match with Jim Corbett. While more recent sportswriters have extolled the abilities of Jack Dempsey and Joe Louis, contemporaries of Jim Jeffries regarded the tall (72.6 inches), 204–225 pound ex-boilermaker as a physical superman. Of him, the old master, Bob Fitzsimmons, said: "There never was another man like Jeffries. 'e's the strongest man in the world, and if 'e knew what I know, 'e would be champion till 'e's eighty years old. Nobody could ever beat 'im!"

Jack Johnson (see Plate 55), in most boxing polls, has been rated at or near the top. It would appear that the main reason for this high ranking was Johnson's "defeat" of Jim Jeffries. Before making a few comments on the latter, let us look into the respective ring records of Johnson and Jeffries. First, it is evident that Jeffries fought more "tough" opponents than did Johnson, and also disposed of more. While it is true that Johnson eventually fought a total of 90 bouts to Jeffries' 21, Johnson won only 73 percent of them (34 percent by knockouts) to Jeffries' 86 percent (52 percent by knockouts). But even these statistics omit to tell the caliber of the opponents whom Jeffries and Johnson faced. In 1905, after 6 years' experience in the ring, Johnson lost a 20-round bout to Marvin Hart, who was defeated the following year by Tommy Burns in 20 rounds. In 1908, Johnson needed 14 rounds to win from Burns, and even then did not knock him out, the bout being stopped by police. And where Jeffries, in 1897, after only a year in the ring, held the hard-hitting 165-pounder, Joe Choynski, to a 20-round draw, Johnson after two years' experience was knocked out by Choynski in three rounds, despite the fact that at that time (1901) Choynski was 33 years of age and past his prime. Again, in his fight in 1909 with the middleweight Stanley Ketchel, Johnson was knocked clear off his feet by Ketchel, although Johnson was able to come back and knock Ketchel out (in the 12th round). So far as I know, no fighter, whether middleweight or heavyweight, ever even knocked Jeffries in his prime off his feet, let alone knocked him out. In this connection, there is the story that in an exhibition bout with Jack Munroe at Butte, Montana, on December 19, 1903, Munroe—who was about the same size as Jeffries—knocked Jeffries down. The truth of the matter is that Munroe was making such a poor showing that Jeff "carried" him the first three rounds in order to give the spectators a show for their money. But Munroe took advantage of this, and managed to last through the fourth round (thereby winning $100) by running away from Jeff. Once, in chasing Munroe, Jeffries slipped and fell. The next day's newspapers said Munroe had *knocked* Jeff off his feet!

To get back to Jack Johnson, apparently his greatest achievement was his win over Jeffries after Jeff had come out of a six-year retirement. But was it an achievement for Johnson, and did he really knock Jeffries out? According to the great oldtime sportswriter, W. W. "Big Bill" Naughton, here are some of the facts connected with Jeffries' return to the ring. After his six-year-long layoff prior to training for his fight with Johnson, Jeffries was totally unlike his former self. Where he used to thrive on hard work, now it tired him out. Training was plain poison to him, and he used to say that he'd have done better if he'd gone against Johnson without a day's workout, weighing 292 pounds. The training he did do exhausted him rather than put him into condition. Despite all this, on June 15, 1910, after about 10 weeks' training, Jeff was in at least fair shape. He could run 10 miles "without too much trouble," spar or punch the bag for perhaps 15 rounds a day (without a letup), and skip rope 1500 to 2000 turns at a time (about 9 to 12 minutes steadily). Jeff had been training near San Francisco for the fight, as that is where it was scheduled to be held. Then, on June 15, the Governor kicked the fight out of California, and it was decided to hold it in Reno, Nevada. Two days before the fight, Jeff came down with a severe case of dysentery, and a day later went "haywire completely," But it was too late then to call the fight off. Jeff always said that the real reason he agreed to fighting Johnson was that he didn't have the guts to refuse to.

During the 15 rounds in the ring with Johnson, Jeff landed only two solid punches; he was oblivious of most of the fight, and Johnson was able to handle him like a baby. He was knocked down twice for the count of 9, and a third time for the count of 7, before his seconds jumped into the ring and the fight was over. Even then, Jeff wasn't "out"; and only the verdict of "technical knockout" could be rendered.

A point that seems suggestive in connection with the much-discussed possibility that Jeffries was doped before the fight is that on the day of July 3 he was a 10–7 favorite in most betting corners. Yet at 9 o'clock that night a message went over the wires to a gambling syndicate: "Cover all Jeffries bets. Johnson in." Jeff himself felt that he was a victim of trickery and that nothing short of a "shot" would explain his doped condition and physical breakdown the day of the fight. Tex Rickard, who promoted and refereed the fight, supported Jeffries's charges of having been doped. Although the motion pictures showed Jeff taking apparently a terrific beating, Jeff said, "None of it actually hurt me very much." When Jeff finally went down in the 15th round, it was probably more from sheer exhaustion (and poisoning) than from the blows administered to him by Johnson. In this review I am not attempting to detract from Johnson's merits as a fighter, but rather to express the opinion that if he and Jeffries had met when both were in their primes, Johnson would have had about as much chance of winning as Jeffries had when he staggered into the ring with Johnson in 1910. It may be added that, late in August 1904, after he had knocked out Jack Munroe in two rounds in San Francisco, and about the time he decided to retire from the ring, Jeffries invited Johnson to a *private* fight. But Johnson wanted no part of such a get-together (see *The Post*, August 3, 1935, p. 64).

One of the greatest of the old-time "near-champions" was the rugged sailor, Tom Sharkey, who fought all the leading contenders of his day. While he lost bouts with Jim Jeffries, Bob Fitzsimmons, and Gus Ruhlin, in 1898 he knocked out Ruhlin in one round. He also, in 1899, knocked out the hard-hitting Kid McCoy in 10 rounds; and in 1900 he disposed of another hard hitter, Joe Choynski, in 2 rounds.

At one time I wondered why it was that Fitzsimmons, who was knocked out on two different occasions by Jeffries, was able to knock out Sharkey (in 2 rounds), while Jeffries, in his fight with Sharkey at Coney Island in 1899, was unable to knock out Sharkey even in 25 rounds and had to be contented with a win on points. The answer to this is as follows. Ten days before the fight, Jeffries was running from the gym upstairs, when Ernest Roeber, a one-time champion wrestler and a camp aide of Jeffries, in fun tossed a medicine ball at him. Seeing, out of the corner of his eye, the ball coming at him, Jeff threw up his left hand to ward it off. When the ball hit, Jeff's arm was dislocated at the elbow. Roeber reset the arm; but a doctor who was consulted a couple of days later and who was a specialist in such cases, said, "No fighting for six months." In the second round of his fight with Sharkey, Jeffries scored a knockdown with a left hook, after which his left arm was useless the rest of the fight. (In those days, a fighter did not ask to have the fight stopped because of an injury.)

In the foregoing recounting, I have dwelt on the career of Jim Jeffries for two main reasons: first, because most present-day boxing fans seem to be unfamiliar with Jeffries's true stature as a fighter; and secondly, because certain present-day newswriters rate Jeffries below Jack Johnson.

After Jeffries, and up to the present day, it is generally conceded that the greatest of the heavyweight boxing champions was Jack Dempsey (see Plate 56). Certainly he was the most popular and most widely publicized. At his best, and with no flukes or "long counts" occurring, Dempsey could probably have beaten (besides Jess Willard) Gene Tunney, Max Baer, Joe Louis, Rocky Marciano, and all the lesser champions from then on. But whether he could have knocked out in his prime John L. (Lawrence) Sullivan in 7 rounds (as the "computerized" contest would have it)—or in any number of rounds, for that matter—is still a question.° And that Dempsey could have defeated the Jim Jeffries who twice knocked out both Fitzsimmons and Corbett, and who went 23 rounds with the durable Tom Sharkey with only one good arm, I find it impossible to believe.

Therefore, to sum up, my choice of the eight greatest Marquis of Queensberry heavyweight champions, in order, would be: (1) James Jackson "Jim" Jeffries; (2) William Harrison "Jack" Dempsey; (3) Robert Prometheus "Bob" Fitzsimmons; (4) Jack Johnson; (5) James John "Jim" Corbett; (6) James Joseph "Gene" Tunney; (7) Joseph Lewis Barrow "Joe Louis"; and (8) Rocco Marchegiano "Rocky Marciano". Probably somewhere among these eight should be the "near-champion," Tom Sharkey. Beyond this number, it would seem to be anyone's guess!

A. NAT FLEISHER'S ALL-TIME RATINGS OF PROFESSIONAL BOXERS:
(other than Heavyweight)

Light Heavyweights: (1) Kid McCoy, (2) Jack O'Brien, (3) Jack Dillon, (4) Tommy Loughran, (5) Jack Root, (6) Battling Levinsky, (7) George Carpentier, (8) Tom Gibbons, (9) Jack Delaney, (10) Paul Berlenbach.

° It should be noted that wherever Sullivan failed to knock out an opponent, it was only because the opponent (including Corbett) had no desire to mix with Sullivan. In contrast, Dempsey, being eager to exchange punches, would have found a worthy opponent in the John L. of 1882 (*not* 1892).

Middleweights: (1) Stanley Ketchel, (2) Tommy Ryan, (3) Harry Greb, (4) Mickey Walker, (5) Ray Robinson, (6) Frank Klaus, (7) Billy Papke, (8) Les Darcy, (9) Mike Gibbons, (10) Jeff Smith.
Welterweights: (1) Joe Walcott, (2) Billy Smith, (3) Jack Britton, (4) Ted Kid Lewis, (5) Dixie Kid.
Lightweights: (1) Joe Gans, (2) Benny Leonard, (3) Owen Moran, (4) Freddy Welsh, (5) Battling Nelson.
Featherweights: (1) Terry McGovern, (2) Jim Driscoll, (3) Abe Attell, (4) Johnny Dundee, (5) Johnny Kilbane.
Bantamweights: (1) George Dixon, (2) Pete Herman, (3) Kid Williams, (4) Joe Lynch, (5) Bud Taylor.
Flyweights: (1) Jimmy Wilde, (2) Pancho Villa, (3) Frankie Genaro, (4) Fidel La Barba, (5) Benny Lynch.

Here are some additional and miscellaneous items of information on boxers and boxing that the reader may find of interest (but the list could be indefinitely prolonged!)*

Jim Jeffries, while training at Lake Merritt, in Oakland, California, was timed repeatedly by Dewitt Van Court (who was then boxing instructor at the Los Angeles Athletic Club, and who started Jeffries out as a boxer) at 11 seconds for 100 yards, which Jeff ran while wearing heavy training clothes. While at Jim Corbett's training camp at Carson City, Nevada, in 1897, Jeffries found that he could outsprint Corbett any time, much to Corbett's chagrin! John L. Sullivan, after seeing Jeffries in shape, pronounced him: "The fastest big man I ever saw in the ring."

Joe Choynski, who seldom weighed over 162 pounds in fighting trim, attributed his shoulder development and great hitting power largely to his previous trade of candy-puller! While in his fight with Bob Fitzsimmons, at Boston in 1894, Choynski lost the decision, he had first nailed Fitz with a terrific righthand punch to the jaw that felled the lanky Cornishman "like a poleaxed steer."

Stanley Ketchel, the great middleweight, ascribed his hitting power to a job he once had which required him to toss bricks into an open freight car.

Bob Fitzsimmons, before becoming a boxer, had worked as a blacksmith. Prior to his winning of the heavyweight championship from Jim Corbett, in 1897, Fitzsimmons had a blacksmith shop in Newark, New Jersey. In that smithy, whenever he needed money, Fitz would make horseshoes which he was able to sell to a noted sportsman for $50 each! Of Fitzsimmons, his conqueror, Jim Jeffries, said: "The trickiest man who ever fought in the heavyweight division, and he could hit

---

* See also Chapter 5, on the speed of punches.

like hell. A guy could make just one mistake against old Fitz." John L. Sullivan described Fitzsimmons as: "A fighting machine on stilts."

While the blow with which Fitzsimmons won the championship from Corbett was popularly described as a "solar plexus" punch, actually it was a left hook to the liver.

Even before the days of Fitzsimmons and John L. Sullivan, there were bare-knuckle fighters who could knock their opponents cold with their first solid punch. One of these was the giant Englishman, Peter Corcoran, who was 6 ft. 7 in. tall. During his six years as British champion (1770–1776), Corcoran won at least ten of his victories with single punches.

Joe Walcott (61 in., 135 lbs.), who was known as "the Barbadoes demon," was said to be able to hit harder than either Fitzsimmons or Choynski. Walcott knocked out Choynski in 7 rounds, after Choynski had fought Jim Jeffries a fierce 20-round draw.*

The two tallest heavyweight boxers were Gogea Mitu of Romania (b. 1914) and Jim Cully of Ireland, who came along a few years later. Each stood 7 ft. 4 in. in height. Mitu was also the heaviest boxer on record, weighing (in 1935) 327 pounds. Cully weighed 273 pounds. But away back in the 1840s there was a fighter from Michigan named Charles Freeman who stood 6 ft. 11 in. and weighed nearly as much as Mitu, namely 323 pounds. Freeman had previously been an acrobat (!), and despite his great size could still do flip-flaps and somersaults. More recently (1955), in Johannesburg, South Africa, there was an aspiring heavyweight contender named Ewart Frederick Potgieter, who stood 7 ft. 2 in. and weighed 310 pounds. Ed Dunkhorst, a heavyweight who scaled 312 pounds, was knocked out by a "solar plexus" blow from Bob Fitzsimmons, who at the time was at his heaviest ring weight—172 pounds!

The two tallest of the heavyweight boxing champions were Primo Carnera, who stood 6 ft. 5.4 in. (not 6 ft. 5¾ in., as usually stated), and Jess Willard, who stood 6 ft. 5¼ in. (not 6 ft. 6¼ in., as usually stated). Evidently the commonly-published heights of many of the heavyweight champions were taken *with shoes on*. The following heights are quoted from the accurately-taken measurements secured by Dr. Dudley Allen Sargent, Physical Director of the Hemingway Gymnasium at Harvard University, who during the years 1880–1920 measured a great many of the leading athletes in all lines of sport: Bob Fitzsimmons 5 ft. 10½ in. (not 5 ft. 11¾ in.); Jim Jeffries 6 ft. 0.6 in. (not 6 ft. 1½ in.); and Jack Johnson 6 ft. 0.7 in. (not 6 ft. 1¼ in.). It is probable also that the actual heights of Jack Dempsey and Gene Tunney were each an inch less

---

* But it may have been that his fight with Jeffries had taken something out of Choynski. For it was said that once a fighter had been pounded by Jeffries's heavy fists, that fighter was never quite the same again!

than the published 6 ft. 1½ in., and that Jim Corbett, Jack Sharkey, and Max Schmeling each stood an even 6 ft., rather than the asserted 6 ft. 1 in. The shortest of the heavyweight title-holders was Tommy Burns (champion from 1906 to 1908), whose publicized height of 5 ft. 7 in. may have been even less.

The only boxer ever to hold the top three weight titles: heavy, light-heavy, and middle—but not during the same period—was Bob Fitzsimmons, who ranged in weight from 156 to 172 pounds. Henry Armstrong held *simultaneously* the three world titles in the featherweight, welterweight, and lightweight divisions (1937–1938).

The longest glove fight on record was between Andy Bowen and Jack Burke, who on April 6, 1893, in New Orleans, fought for 7 hrs. 19 min. (110 rounds) to a "no contest" decision when they refused to continue.

7.
Wrestling

Wrestling, like its kindred sport, boxing, is of great antiquity. Indeed, some historians consider it the oldest of all sports. A story has it that Eve must have been the first wrestler, since the Bible says "Eve wrestled with her conscience." While mythology attributes the origin of wrestling in Greece to the great Athenian hero, Theseus, there is historic evidence to show that the sport was practiced in other places thousands of years before Theseus's supposed time. There has been found, for example, in ruins at Kyafaje, near Baghdad, Iraq, a bronze statuette showing two wrestlers coming to grips. This statuette is believed to have been made by a Sumerian sculptor approximately 4800 years ago. And in Egypt, paintings on the tomb of nomarch Beni Hasan XVII (c. 1850 B.C.) show series of wrestling holds practically identical with those used in modern freestyle wrestling (see Plate 57).

With a few modifications, the Greeks adopted the Egyptian form of wrestling, and it soon became one of their most popular and widely practiced sports. Plutarch regarded wrestling as the most artistic and requiring of skill of all the forms of Greek athletics. Gymnasiums were founded in the chief Greek cities for the training of men and boys in military exercises, and to each gymnasium was given the name *palaestra*, from the Greek word meaning wrestling school. There were two principal styles of grappling. One was called "upright wrestling," in which the object was to throw one's opponent to the ground (i.e., off his feet). In this style, three falls were necessary to decide the winner. The second style of competition was called "ground wrestling." In it the contest was continued, even after a fall, until one of the wrestlers acknowledged defeat. Ground wrestling was generally practiced inside a building, but on ground which had been watered until it was muddy and slippery.

Upright wrestling was the only form permitted in the pentathlon (the Greek 5-event competition consisting of running, broad jumping, throwing the discus, throwing the javelin, *and* wrestling) and in major wrestling competitions. Ground wrestling was not recognized as a separate competition, but was merely the style used in the pankratium (a combination of boxing, wrestling, and kicking). In the gymnasium, both upright and ground wrestling were part of the regular training. To sum up the rules of Greek wrestling: (1) if any part of the body above the knees touched the ground, it was counted a fall; (2) if both wrestlers fell together, the fall did not count; (3) to win, a wrestler had to throw his opponent three times; (4) to trip one's opponent was permitted, but it was not enough merely to throw an opponent; the winner had to perform with grace and skill.

Greek mythology abounds with tales of wrestling bouts between mighty heroes and their opponents. There are the matches between Hercules and Antaeus; Hercules and Achelous; Theseus and Cercyon; Ajax and Ulysses; Dares and Entellus; to name only a few. The most famous actual wrestler and strong-man of antiquity was Milo of Crotona, about whose exploits mention is made at the beginning of the book. That Milo was a prodigy of muscular might, there can be no doubt. He won wrestling championships in Olympiads 61 (?), 62, 63, 64, 65, and 66—a period of 20 years between 536 and 516 B.C. Again, he won in seven Pythian, nine Nemean, and ten Isthmian Games. In one of Milo's matches—perhaps when he was past his prime—he and a young wrestler named Lysander had wrestled two hours without either man gaining a fall, when suddenly Lysander dropped lifeless to the ground. The judges awarded the wreath of victory not to Milo, but to Lysander, on the ground that it was not Milo, but Death, who had conquered the noble athlete from Sparta! (In one book on wrestling, it is stated that in the Greek wrestling bouts of Milo's day there was no winner until one of the contestants was "sent into eternity." This is not true. In later times, especially in the arenic contests in Rome, some contestants in the pankratium did meet their deaths as the result of brutal injuries; but never in a Greek wrestling match did one contestant try to kill the other, and the accidental death of Lysander from exhaustion was certainly an exception, if not actually the only one of its kind).*

Wrestling, besides being one of the oldest sports, was (and is) also one of the most universally practiced ones. As far back as history goes, there are references to the wrestlers of various Old-World countries: Egypt, India, China, Assyria, Persia, Mesopotamia, Ethiopia, et al. And

---

* We must here note, however, the death of the sixth-century B.C. Greek pankratiast, Arrichion of Phigaleia, who is said to have died in a contest with an unnamed opponent who was strangling him. But, so the story goes, Arrichion, kicking his right foot back in an expiring effort, dislocated the ankle of his opponent, who had locked his foot in the bend of Arrichion's knee. Suffering this injury, Arrichion's opponent signalized his defeat, *after* which Arrichion expired and was awarded the victory posthumously. The credibility of such an occurrence hinges on whether the effects of strangulation could cause death *after* the victim had still possessed enough strength to disable his strangler.

doubtless, during the same period, many of the primitive races and tribes in the then "undiscovered" New World each had their local wrestling champion. It is not within the scope of the present book to cover, even scantily, the long history of wrestling from antiquity to the present day. Rather, the chief object here shall be to refer to a few outstanding facets of the sport and to some of the most famous exponents of it.

Of considerable antiquity is the Sumo wrestling of Japan. In this form of wrestling, great size and weight are the prime requirements, and gigantic individuals have resulted from the age-old practice of marrying the sons of Sumo wrestlers with the daughters of other Sumo wrestlers. Few of these wrestlers weigh less than 300 pounds, and some range as high as 400 pounds and over. The first historical record of a Sumo wrestling match dates back to the year 24 B.C., during the sixth year of the reign of Emperor Surnin, when a courtier named Tiamanokehaya challenged any man in Japan to a contest. A wrestler named Nomi-No Skikune took up the challenge and defeated the boastful Tiamanokehaya. Today, Sumo championships are held in Tokyo twice a year, for ten days in May and ten days in January during the prolonged New Year's celebration. To get into "condition," the Sumo wrestlers not only train by having practice matches throughout the year, but also strive to gain as much weight as possible. The latter is accomplished by consuming "ten or more times as much food" as the average man, in addition to drinking great quantities of sake (rice-beer) and regular Western beer. The winner of each ten-day national Sumo contest is privileged to wear a huge white rope belt, known as the Yokozuna. This belt identifies him as the champion until he is defeated. Plate 58 shows two champion Sumo wrestlers, Tochikiyama and Nishinoumi, who each reigned back in 1926.

Sumo wrestling is carried on in a rope-marked ring, 12 to 15 feet in diameter and covered with a thin layer of fine sand. Prolonged introductions, salutations and other ceremonies are a preliminary to the match itself, which is usually over within a minute or so. A match is won by toppling an opponent off his feet, or by shoving at least one of his feet outside the ring. Sumo wrestling consists of 48 permitted holds or throws. They are classified into 12 throws, 12 lifts, 12 twists, and 12 throws over the back. An interesting point is that some of the larger wrestlers, especially the taller ones, exhibit distinct signs of *acromegaly* (a glandular disorder producing post-adolescent gigantism).

As one of Japan's time-honored sports, Sumo wrestling has had its ups and downs. Today, despite the competition from Judo and from the entire agenda of Olympic events introduced during recent generations, the sport is riding a wave of great popularity. One reason for this is that Sumo lends itself well to exhibition via television. As a result, many Europeans and Americans who had previously regarded the Japanese as being a nation of physically small people have been astonished to learn that Japan is the only nation in which a race of gigantic supermen is systematically bred. Recent champions of Sumo are said to earn—like the top-ranking American professional wrestlers—from $50,000 a year upward.

While various other nations in Asia have each had, for untold centuries, their particular forms of wrestling, perhaps the most publicized wrestlers have been those from India, where they are known as *pahlewans* ("strong-men," or "champions"). Like the Sumo wrestlers of Japan, the Hindu pahlewans may be regarded as a special *breed* of athletes. However, unlike the Japanese, the Hindus do not strive to attain great stature and weight alone, but train so as to acquire pronounced endurance as well as strength and skill. As mentioned in Chapter 5, the training of the Indian wrestlers consists largely of two or three exercises which they repeat hundreds of times. One of these exercises is called "dunds," and may be described as a form of body-swaying floor-dips, or pushups. The average wrestler performs each day about 1500 "dunds," divided into five series of 300 repetitions each (however, some individuals prefer a larger number of series and a smaller number of repetitions in each series). The second exercise is simply knee-bending repeatedly while keeping on the toes, with the heels raised. This exercise the Hindus call "batticks" (or baithaks). During a training session, these knee-bends are performed 3000 times or more, usually in series of about 1000 repetitions each. A third exercise is to *leap* repeatedly as high as possible from a low knee-bend position. This movement also is repeated hundreds of times. While such prolonged "endurance" exercises would reduce an average-sized man to skin and bones, their effect on the Indian wrestlers—nearly all of whom are heavyweights—is to produce an enormous development of the chest and the thighs. Strangely, in these wrestlers the forearms and the calves remain relatively small, while the upper arms become only moderately developed in proportion to the huge chest and thighs. Also, the entire physique in these Indian wrestlers is notably *smooth* in appearance, all parts (especially the mid-section!) being covered with a thick layer of fat. Why the Japanese Sumo wrestlers acquire from their training a massive development of the *calves* as well as the thighs, while the Indians do not, is difficult to understand. Possibly the small-calved condition is a *racial* peculiarity. Even the few Hindu women wrestlers of whom photographs have been published are seen to possess disproportionately small and shapeless lower legs.

On the question of whether the East Indian wrestlers are more capable than those of Europe and the United States, there are diverse opinions.

Some writers, both Indian and European, on the subject have cited various Hindu wrestling champions as being invincible. In contrast, I have before me a letter from an Indian wrestling enthusiast in which he opines that the Hindu system of training produces only obese, sluggish individuals, "good only for wrestling, overeating and sleeping." Again, during the 1930s, among a troupe of Hindu wrestlers which toured the United States, certain of them engaged in "shooting" matches with ordinary (not champion) American wrestlers and were held to draws or even defeated.

Part of the difficulty of comparing Hindu and occidental wrestlers stems from the fact that *differing styles* of wrestling are followed. In India the contestants wrestle in sand, or even ankle-deep mud, and employ a style comparable to the Greco-Roman, in which all holds below the waist are barred. Also, as in Japanese Sumo wrestling, a "fall" may occur if any part of a contestant's body other than the soles of his feet hits the ground. Thus a match may be over in a matter of seconds (see Gama vs. Zbyszko, below). So it may be said that while the Hindu wrestlers are skilled at wrestling in a standing position, they are at a disadvantage in the occidental free-style form of grappling in which most of the time is spent with the whole body (not just the feet) on the mat.

One of the first great modern Hindu wrestling champions was Gulam (or Ghulam) (68.5 in., 287 lbs.), who was born in the Punjab, India, in 1860 (see Plate 59). In the early 1900s, Gulam, accompanied by a small troupe of other Indian wrestlers, defeated all the European grapplers (some 50, it is said) who would face him. But much more publicized, and more recent, among the Hindu wrestlers than Gulam was Gama (67 in., 220–250 lbs.; see also Plate 59). Gama's real name was Gulam Mohammed. He was born in the Punjab in 1878, of Kashmiri wrestling stock. He became recognized as the champion of India in 1909, after defeating Rahim Sultaniwala (6 ft. 11 in., 270 lbs.). In England, in 1910, in a private get-together, Gama threw the well-known American wrestler, Dr. Benjamin Roller, twice within 7 minutes (another account says 13 times within 13 minutes!). The famous Pole, Stanislaus Zbyszko (68.9 in., 250 lbs.) was then called upon to uphold the prestige of occidental wrestling. In a match held at the Holborn Empire Theater, London, Gama threw Zbyszko to the mat in a few seconds—and there Zbyszko stayed, huddled up on his hands and knees, for 2 hours and 45 minutes! This would seem to indicate that Gama was comparatively inexperienced in ground wrestling. In disgust, Gama returned to India, where, in 1928 (*eighteen years* later!) Zbyszko challenged him to another match. This time, Gama, who was then 50, threw Zbyszko, aged 48, in *ten seconds!* (But perhaps just off his feet.) In 1918, Gama had turned over his title to his younger brother, Imam Bux, who weighed only 182 pounds but was virtually unbeatable at that weight. However, this transfer of his title was not because Gama had gotten out of condition. Even at the age of 69, it is said, Gama trained by performing 2000 dunds and 4000 baithaks daily, followed by a walk-and-run of 4 miles and a series of wrestling bouts extending without rest over three or four hours! In wrestling tradition, Gama married one of the daughters of Gulam. Although the age-old sport of wrestling still lives on in India, none of its champions, so far as I know, have visited America during recent years.

Just before and after the turn of the century, a number of professional wrestlers from Turkey toured the United States and evoked a considerable amount of interest by their great size, exotic appearance, and manifest wrestling ability. Chief among them was the celebrated Yousouf Ishmaëlo° (74 in., 265 lbs.), who created a sensation wherever he went (see Plate 60). He was the first, and the most colorful, of the "terrible Turks" to compete against American wrestlers. Shortly after Yousouf had arrived in the United States, in 1897, he was matched against the former American wrestling champion, Henry Clayton (70 in., 195 lbs.), who on the mat took the name of Evan Lewis and was known as "the Strangler." That is, he was the original "Strangler Lewis." Since Lewis had won from nearly everyone who had opposed him, including the famous "Jap" Matsada Sorakichi, he regarded the Turk, Yousouf, as just another set-up. But he was to learn differently. When Lewis and Yousouf met, the huge Turk, who appeared to be loaded with fat, turned out to be quick and graceful as a cat and possessed of incredible strength. He simply grabbed Lewis, slammed him face-down to the mat, and sat astride him applying a scissors. Lewis soon gave up. In the second fall, Lewis was thrown similarly in even less time. Ernest Roeber, the Greco-Roman wrestling champion, was Yousouf's next victim. He lasted no longer than had Lewis. About this time, the lightweight wrestling champion, George Bothner, who was the epitome of skill and had thrown many of the leading heavyweights, thought he might have a chance to win some easy money by standing up against the Turk for 15 minutes, $100 being the amount offered by William Brady, Yousouf's manager, to anyone whom the Turk could not throw within that time. But like Yousouf's other opponents, Bothner was picked up bodily, raised overhead, and dashed to the mat. So hard did Yousouf throw him that Bothner's neck was wrenched and it was several days before he could look straight ahead again!

Unfortunately for Yousouf, he insisted on carrying all his mat earnings in gold coins stored in a belt around his waist, which he wore day and

---

° *Not* Yussif Mahmout, who appeared on the wrestling scene some years later and was a smaller man.

night. In 1898, he became homesick, and quietly booked passage on the French liner, *La Bourgoyne*. The ship was wrecked off the coast of Nova Scotia in collision with a British sailing vessel, the *Cromartyshire*. While Yousouf was adjudged a good swimmer, he declined to part with his gold-filled belt and so drowned, along with 560 other passengers. So, it could never be learned whether Yousouf could have defeated all the American and European champions who appeared in action during the early years of the 20th century. Nouroulah, a Turkish wrestler who came to the United States during that time, was even bigger than Yousouf (Nouroulah being 78¾ in., 344 lbs.), but evidently was not in the same class as Yousouf in strength, speed, and wrestling ability. In addition, Yousouf had possessed a degree of pride and self-confidence that made him absolutely fearless of any opponent. What a match it would have been between him and the Hindu, Gama!

As to who, in America, was the greatest heavyweight among the many catch-as-catch-can wrestlers who were active during the years 1900–1910, let us briefly review the qualifications and records of a few of the most eligible candidates.

First, there was Martin "Farmer" Burns, who was born in Springfield, Iowa, on February 15, 1861 (see Plate 60). Burns trained and developed himself into one of the most versatile and scientific catch-as-catch-can wrestlers the sport has ever known. However, since at his best he weighed only 165–170 pounds (at a height of 69.5 in.), he was not quite big enough or strong enough to compete on even terms with the best heavyweights of his time. His position among the heavyweight wrestlers of his day could be likened to that of Bob Fitzsimmons among the heavyweight boxers: a supremely capable performer *for his size*. On April 20, 1895, Burns won the professional wrestling championship of America by throwing Evan Lewis, the Strangler. In 1897 he was defeated both by Dan McLeod (another light-heavyweight) and Tom Jenkins. In December 1899, Burns met and started training Frank Gotch (see Plate 62). It is said (and I have no way of checking on the report) that in a private match—*after* Gotch had thrown Hackenschmidt—Burns defeated Gotch. Again, it is said that Ed "Strangler" Lewis declined to meet Burns on the mat (at which time Burns was past 60 years of age!).

Another truly great old-timer was Dan McLeod, although, like Farmer Burns, he was only a light-heavyweight (67 in., 176 lbs). McLeod was not only a highly-skilled wrestler, but earlier, in 1892, had represented the United States in a track and field meet in Australia, where he won first places in the hammer throw, shot put, pole vault, broad jump, high jump, and tossing the caber! While, in 1904, Frank Gotch defeated McLeod on the mat, it should be noted that Gotch was then only 26 years of age compared with McLeod's 44 years, and that despite his great skill McLeod was then past his prime in strength and staying-power. From 1913 to 1920, McLeod was wrestling instructor at the Los Angeles Athletic Club. He died in June 1958, at the age of 98 years.

Next in line, chronologically, was Tom Jenkins (69.1 in., 200 lbs.), who was born in 1872 and from 1898 to 1903 was the recognized American champion. On February 22 of the latter year, in his home city of Cleveland, Jenkins threw Frank Gotch (71 in., 200 lbs.), his leading opponent, in two straight falls. However, on January 27, 1904, at Bellingham, Washington, Gotch retaliated by throwing Jenkins once and then being awarded the second fall on a foul. Gotch thus became American champion. About Jenkins and Gotch, more will be said shortly, in connection with a review of some of the more notable matches engaged in by the contemporary European heavyweight champion, George Hackenschmidt.

In my opinion—and the opinions of many other followers of the mat game—the Russian strong-man and wrestler, George Hackenschmidt, was not only the greatest Greco-Roman but also the greatest catch-as-catch-can wrestler of recent times[*] (see Plate 61). I can imagine someone saying: "How can that be so, if Hackenschmidt was defeated twice by Frank Gotch?" To reply to this question, let us look into some of the matches between Hackenschmidt and various opponents, and between Gotch and some of the same opponents. The factor of respective ages can be disregarded, since both Gotch and Hackenschmidt were born in the same year, 1878, Gotch on April 27 and Hackenschmidt on August 2. Moreover, both men commenced their wrestling careers at about the same time—1898—although Gotch became a professional within a year, while Hackenschmidt wrestled as an amateur until June 1900.

While it is well known that wrestlers, as a class, retain their strength and skill longer than other types of athletes, still there is an inevitable deterioration with age, and few wrestlers are in as good condition after they have passed 40 years as they were at 25 or 30. An exception was Zbyszko, who won the world title from Lewis when he was 41 (see Plate 62). Tom Jenkins was perhaps still in his prime at the age of 32, in 1904. In January of that year, as related above, Jenkins lost his American title by being thrown (once) by Gotch. Yet there was little to choose between the two men, and Gotch was having plenty of trouble keeping from being thrown.[**] On July 2, 1904, at Albert Hall in London, Jenkins wrestled Hackenschmidt, Greco-Roman style, and was thrown twice within 35 minutes. In a return match in New York City on May

[*] For a review of Hackenschmidt's records in weightlifting, see Chapter 4.
[**] In fact, so roughed-up was Gotch in every one of his eight matches with Tom Jenkins (of which Gotch won 5, and Jenkins 3) that in some quarters Gotch's death at the early age of 39, of nephritis, has been attributed to those bouts. (See, for example, the article by Dan Daniel in *Ring Wrestling* for October, 1967, p. 6.)

4, 1905 (catch-as-catch-can style), Hackenschmidt again threw Jenkins in two straight falls, the first in 31 min. 15 sec., and the second in 22 min. 4 sec. In contrast to the Gotch-Jenkins bouts, Hackenschmidt at no time was in difficulty from Jenkins, and was the aggressor throughout. According to a newspaper report the next day, "Jenkins was handled like a pigmy in the hands of a giant. Hackenschmidt broke holds as if they were the clutchings of a child".

Later in 1905, on October 2, in London, a top-ranking Turkish wrestler named Ahmed Madrali (73 in., 224 lbs.) threw Jenkins twice within less time (19 min. 48 sec. and 22 min. 46 sec., respectively) than it had taken Hackenschmidt. However, "Hack" had previously, on January 30, 1904, in London, thrown Madrali with the first hold he got on him, dashing the Turk to the mat so hard that his arm was broken and he was unable to continue. In a second match with Madrali, this time under catch-as-catch-can rules, at which style the Turk was regarded as "absolutely invincible," Hackenschmidt threw the Turk in two straight falls, the first in 1 min. 34 sec., and the second in 4 minutes. Thus "Hack" proved himself to be not only the superior of Jenkins—with whom Gotch had had great difficulties—but of a Turkish wrestler who had easily defeated Jenkins, and who Hackenschmidt described as "a most formidable opponent, one of the strongest, if not actually the strongest, man I have ever encountered".

Of other matches engaged in, both by Gotch and by Hackenschmidt, against top-ranking opponents, a long series could be presented if space allowed. The main point is, was Gotch really a better wrestler than Hackenschmidt? Their first match took place on April 3, 1908, at the Dexter Park Pavilion in Chicago. The "official" verdict of that match was that after 2 hrs. 3 min. of grappling, during which time neither wrestler had gained a fall, Hackenschmidt "quit," thereby conceding victory to Gotch. However, to attain his end, Gotch had resorted to every unfair tactic he could think of (oiling his body, rubbing the oil into Hackenschmidt's eyes, butting, gouging, scratching, and even punching the Russian in the nose). For such unsportsmanlike actions Gotch should have been disqualified immediately, and the match awarded to Hackenschmidt on a foul. But the referee, Ed Smith, a Chicago sports editor, was exceedingly pro-Gotch and equally anti-Hackenschmidt (as was also the audience). Under such conditions, how could "Hack" possibly have won?

Of the second Gotch-Hackenschmidt match, which took place in Chicago on September 4, 1911, only a few words need be said. For that match, "Hack" (68.7 in., 215 lbs.) had trained himself into superb physical condition. His training partners while in Chicago were "Americus" (Gus Schonlin), Dr. Benjamin Roller, and Jacobus Koch—all champions in wrestling, but with whom "Hack" simply toyed. However, accidents are unforeseeable, and only two weeks before his match with Gotch was to be held, an accident was sustained by Hackenschmidt which changed the whole course of his future. While training with Dr. Roller, "Hack," in coming out of a hold, somehow tore the semi-lunar cartilage in his right knee. If the reader has ever suffered such an injury (I have, on three separate occasions), he will know that all he can do is "favor" the joint, and that it cannot possibly heal itself within two weeks. So, with such an injury—and not wishing to disappoint the large audience—Hackenschmidt went into the ring with Gotch on the due date, and allowed Gotch to have his two "falls."*

Jack Curley, who sponsored the 1911 Gotch-Hackenschmidt match, and who knew full well the abilities of all the wrestlers of that period, considered Hackenschmidt the greatest, with Jenkins second and Gotch third.

About the time of Gotch's retirement from the mat, early in 1913, the two leading contenders for his crown were Henry Ordeman and Jess Westergaard. In an elimination match, Ordeman threw Westergaard. In 1914, at Minneapolis, Charles Cutler threw Ordeman in two straight falls. Then Dr. Roller threw Cutler, who in turn threw Roller. Between July 1914 and July 1915, Roller and Cutler each held the title twice. Then came the first of the great post-Gotch wrestlers, Joe Stecher (73.5 in., 210–220 lbs.), who on July 5, 1915, at Omaha, threw Cutler in two straight falls. For this victory, Stecher became recognized as the world's heavyweight wrestling champion. He also, because of his powerful leg holds (see Plate 62), became known as "the scissors king."

After winning the title from Cutler—by having thrown him twice within 27 min. 30 sec.—Stecher wrestled Ed "Strangler" Lewis (72 in., 228 lbs.) at Evansville, Indiana, and made him give up in two hours. In a return match, at Omaha, on July 5, 1916, the two men wrestled to a 5-hour draw. On April 9, 1917, again at Omaha, Stecher lost his world title (under not altogether satisfactory conditions) to Earl Caddock (71 in., 190 lbs.), who was known as "the man of a thousand holds." In 1920, after both men had served in World War I, Stecher won back the title from Caddock, in New York City, after 2 hrs. 5 min. 30 sec. of hard wrestling.

Ed "Strangler" Lewis (b. 1890), whose real name was Robert H. Friedrich, was one of the greatest wrestlers to appear during the 15-year

---

* I have not taken the facts of the two Gotch-Hackenschmidt matches merely from news accounts. In 1927, at my gymnasium in Los Angeles, I had them direct from Ivan Linow, a top-notch wrestler who was one of the training partners of Hackenschmidt.

"revival" era of the sport following World War I (see Plate 63). Lewis won the world's title from Joe Stecher on December 13, 1920, in New York City, in a see-saw battle that was largely a contest between Stecher's body-scissors and Lewis's headlock. But Lewis did not retain the title for long, since in 1921 the veteran Pole, Stanislaus Zbyszko (68.9 in., 255 lbs.), defeated him in a one-fall match. But Zbyszko was in turn defeated by Lewis, at Wichita, Kansas, on March 22, 1922. The match, in which Lewis won two falls and Zbyszko one, was described as "one of the fastest, cleanest wrestling tilts ever staged in this country in which a title was at stake." Lewis then kept the title until January 8, 1925, when, at Kansas City, Missouri, he was defeated and succeeded by Wayne "Big" Munn (78 in., 260 lbs.).* However, Munn held the championship only a brief three months, at which time he went down to defeat at the hands of Zbyszko, who thereby became world's champion a second time.

During all this, Joe Stecher had been awaiting a chance to win back his crown. The chance came on May 30, at St. Louis, when and where Stecher defeated the ageing Pole, Zbyszko, in two straight falls (Zbyszko therefore having held the title only six weeks). On the same day, at Michigan City, Indiana, Ed "Strangler" Lewis avenged his previous (January 8) defeat by Wayne Munn by tossing Munn for the second and third falls, Munn having won the first. This was a well-attended match, witnessed by nearly 21,000 persons. The total receipts were $64,162, of which Lewis received $30,000.

After Stecher had again become champion, the bout he regarded as his toughest was that with Jim Londos, in Philadelphia on June 10, 1926. Nearly two hours passed before Stecher emerged the victor, and during most of that time Londos was the aggressor. During the following two years, Stecher defended his title successfully against a number of outstanding challengers, among whom were the giant Russian, Ivan Padoubny (72.8 in., 248 lbs.), who in Paris, 21 years previously, had won the world's Greco-Roman championship; Dick Daviscourt (71 in., 230 lbs.), a rough and aggressive headlock expert; and Jim Browning (74 in., 226 lbs.), whose body scissors was said to be as powerful as Stecher's. However, on February 20, 1928, in St. Louis, Stecher, in meeting Ed

---

* Lewis, who died on August 7, 1966, at the age of 76, had a wrestling career which spanned 44 years and included 6200 matches, of which he lost only 33. During this period he earned $3 million dollars. One of his biggest purses came in his match with Gus Sonnenberg, in 1932, for which he received $25,000. On October 11, 1928, while he was still going strong, Lewis appeared in my gymnasium in Los Angeles for a news photo. Although I was a weightlifter and had never done any wrestling, I was happy to pose alongside Lewis in the photograph shown in Plate 63.

Strangler Lewis for the third time, was forced to relinquish his title to the powerful headlock champion, who had gained the first and third falls.

Shortly after Lewis had taken the championship from Stecher, the leading wrestlers, along with their respective managers, split up into several independent combines (cliques), each of which recognized only its own "champion." During 1929–1930, continuity in the succession of heavyweight champions came to an end, with Lewis, Dick Shikat, Gus Sonnenberg, Hans Steinke, Jim Londos, Ed Don George, Jim Browning, and various others either claiming the title or clamoring for a chance at it.

On August 23, 1929, Dick Shikat (72 in., 217–225 lbs.) won from Jim Londos (66 in., 185 lbs.), and thereby became one of the regional or group champions. Similarly, Gus Sonnenberg had become "champion" by defeating (unexpectedly) Ed Lewis on two different occasions during 1929. It would appear that Sonnenberg (68 in., 200 lbs.), an ex-football player, by using "flying tackles" and billy-goat butting, ushered in what was essentially a new era in professional wrestling, with just about anything and everything being permitted. Certain it is that from that time to the present day, clean, scientific wrestling has either been replaced, or relegated to second place, by phony, slapstick tactics and ludicrous costuming and posturing which—as one critic put it—"would be tolerated in no other sport." But perhaps the wrestling-minded public prefers exhibitionism to straight wrestling because of the former being more lively and unpredictable (and actually contributing a higher percentage of *injuries* than legitimate wrestling).

Of the wrestlers prominent during the decade 1930–1940, probably the best were Hans Steinke (74 in., 240 lbs.), Dick Shikat, and Ray Steele (or Pete Sauer; 73 in., 218 lbs.). Under 200 pounds, far and away the best wrestler was the "Greek Adonis," Jim Londos. During his long career on the mat, Londos had won from such outstanding heavyweights as Stecher, Caddock, Shikat, Browning, Steele, Everett Marshall, and even Strangler Lewis. But it should be added that Lewis had previously thrown Londos on no fewer than 14 different occasions, and that when Londos finally won over him—on September 30, 1934, in Chicago—Lewis was 44 years of age and past his prime. That match, incidentally, drew a crowd of over 35,000 spectators, and yielded a record-making $96,302 in gate receipts.

The number of professional wrestlers who have appeared in action in this country from 1940 onward is so great that it is beyond the scope of this volume to list more than a small fraction of them here. During the 1950s, the wrestler who came closest to being recognized as the undisputed world champion was Lou Thesz (b. 1920; 73 in., 225 lbs.), who during 15 years on the mat (up to 1953) had engaged in some 2500 matches and won over 90 percent of them. Other top-notch wrestlers of this period were Verne Gagne (72 in., 220 lbs.), Frank Sexton (75 in., 235 lbs.), Gene Stanlee (73 in., 230 lbs.), Antonino Rocca (72 in., 226 lbs.), Don Eagle (73 in., 218 lbs.), and the late Italian giant, Primo Carnera (77.4 in., 260 lbs.). Carnera—despite all the criticisms of his abilities—was the only athlete during recent generations to have been both a world's champion boxer and a leading contender in professional wrestling.

One of the greatest—probably *the* greatest—present-day wrestling champions is Bruno Sammartino (70 in., 260 lbs.) of Pittsburgh. Certainly he is among the two or three strongest men in the entire profession. That is probably because Sammartino, from the very commencement of his career, has trained steadily with weights. In various of the "power" lifts, Bruno has raised very respectable poundages. He has pressed 545 pounds while lying flat on the floor; made a standing (Olympic-style) press of 410 pounds; squatted with close to 700 pounds across his shoulders; picked up in the dead lift 705 pounds, and curled in good style 235 pounds. In all probability, if Sammartino had not chosen to concentrate on wrestling, he could have become a champion performer in the three official Power Lifts. One of the sensational feats that Sammartino performed in the wrestling ring was to lift "Haystacks" Calhoun—who stood 6 ft. 4 in. and weighed 641 pounds (!)—off his feet and crash him to the mat!

A number of other present-day or recent professional wrestlers have proven to be exceedingly strong, and have performed well in the "power" types of weightlifting. "Chuck" Bruce (b. 1942; 72 in., 330 lbs.) in 1962 had a chest girth of 62 inches, neck 23½, biceps 22½, thighs 34, and calves 21. He did a standing press of 420 pounds, bench press 530, curl 255 (a record), and squat 675. "Hercules" Romero (c. 250 lbs.) has made a dead lift with 700 pounds, a bench press (officially) with 502, and a squat with 650. "The Mongol" (69 in., 238 lbs.) took a regulation basketball and squeezed it with his arms against his chest until it broke at a seam. He then inserted his hands and pulled it apart until it was in a flat piece. The basketball had previously withstood the weight of a 225-pound wrestler standing on it without effect.

After having put down the foregoing facts and figures on wrestlers and wrestling, I found that there were numerous other items of information that could not be listed conveniently either in chronological or geographical order, but which might prove of interest to readers. Some of these items (in no order whatever!) follow:

The longest wrestling match on record was between John Shea, of Saginaw, Michigan, and Alfred Davey, of England. The match, which was in the Cornish style, was held at Ishpeming, Michigan in July, 1908, and went for 11 hours 30 minutes before one of the wrestlers (which one, I know not) finally gained a fall.

Probably the quickest fall on record occurred when Frank Gotch, in his match with Stanislaus Zbyszko on June 1, 1910, in Chicago, took the first fall in 6¼ seconds! When the bell rang, Gotch came out as though to shake hands with Zbyszko, who extended his hand to do so. But since the two men had already shaken hands before going to their respective corners (which act Zbyszko evidently had forgotten), Gotch ignored Zbyszko's hand, dived for the Pole's legs, and got a hold with which he soon had Zbyszko's shoulders on the mat.

Zbyszko, whose real name was Cyganiewicz, and who stood only 68.9 inches in height, at one time weighed 276 pounds and then had a 22-inch (!) flexed upper arm. Besides being a wrestler, Zbyszko was a linguist, having mastered Greek and Latin, and being able to read and speak "with fair fluency" English, French, German, Italian, Spanish, Portuguese, Russian, Hungarian, Turkish, and all the Balkan dialects! Zbyszko, despite his few defeats on the mat when he was long past his prime, is nearly always listed among the ten greatest heavyweight wrestlers of the present century. He died at his farm in Missouri (where he and his younger brother, Wladek, raised hogs) on September 23, 1967, at the age of 87 years.

The wrestler with the highest earnings was probably Ed "Strangler" Lewis, who during a career covering 44 years and 6200 matches, is said to have received more than $3,000,000. Another well-rewarded wrestler was Jim Londos, who in 1935, in his title match with Dan O'Mahony (which Londos lost) is reported to have received $100,000— a record sum for a single match. During 15 years of steady wrestling engagements, Londos is said to have amassed a fortune of nearly $2 million. The most money earned during a single year is probably the $180,000 which was paid to Antonino Rocca in 1958.

The tallest wrestler was perhaps the German giant Zehe—known professionally as "Gargantua"—who performed in the 1950s, stood 7 ft. 6 in. in height, and weighed about 400 pounds. The heaviest wrestler was doubtless William J. Cobb, who on the mat was known as "Happy Humphrey," and who in 1960 is said to have scaled 802 pounds. Later on, Cobb made medical history by successfully reducing his weight to a normal 230 pounds. During World War II, there was in Japan a Sumo wrestler (name not given) who stood 6 ft. 2 in., weighed a solid 535 pounds, and had a 30-inch biceps. However, if we are to believe the history books, there was in ancient Afghanistan a wrestler beside whom even the biggest Sumo wrestlers would appear dwarfed. He was an apparently invincible giant named Rustum, who, legend has it, was 9 feet in height and weighed 652 pounds!

In the wild and mountainous north countries of England, the accepted style of wrestling is what has long been known as the Cumberland and Westmoreland style. It is said to have been brought to England by the Vikings, sometime between the years 870 and 920. In this form of grappling, the first man who goes down is the loser. Consequently, as in Japanese Sumo wrestling, the bouts are usually of short duration. The world's champion in Cumberland-Westmoreland wrestling for over 30 years was George Steadman (71 in., 260 lbs.). He held his title against all comers from 1870, when he was 24, to 1900, when he was 54! At the latter age he was still undefeated; but he then retired.

Thomas Nicholson, an old-time English wrestler, was, because of his extraordinary stamina, known as "the Iron Man." On one occasion, after dancing all night at Penrith, he walked 25 miles to Ambleside and there, in a wrestling tournament, threw in succession four heavyweight opponents!

Speaking of old-time English wrestlers, how about that 18th-century phenomenon of muscular power, Thomas Topham? (see Chapter 3). For Topham, in addition to possessing fantastic all-around strength, was described also as "the champion wrestler of his day." As previously related Topham, despite having a limp (because of a leg injury sustained earlier), once took on six wrestlers, one after the other, and brought all six to the ground "in an unconscious form" within five minutes! How would Hackenschmidt, or Gotch, or any of the recent champion wrestlers, have fared against Topham, who had merely to get hold of an opponent once?

Among the earlier presidents of the United States, wrestling, in one style or another, was a favorite sport. George Washington (74 in., 215 lbs.) was a first-class wrestler, even at the age of 15. When he was 18 he defeated a wrestler who had the reputation of being the best in north Virginia. Abraham Lincoln, whose great height and rangy build (76 in., 180 lbs.) fitted him more for a runner and jumper than a wrestler, nevertheless could hold his own either in wrestling or rough-and-tumble fighting. When only 18, he defeated in a wrestling match the champion of Louisiana, Jack Armstrong, at New Orleans, after a hard struggle. He also, when President, was the first to establish wrestling in the armed forces as a means of physical training and self-defense. Other presidents who practiced wrestling were Andrew Jackson, Ulysses S. Grant, Zachary Taylor, Theodore Roosevelt, and William H. Taft. That Taft, who weighed over 300 pounds, was remarkably strong is shown by the fact that once, while remaining seated in a chair, and using only one hand, he grabbed a man and with a single sweep of his arm threw the man clear over his shoulder.

Joe Stecher developed the remarkable power of his famous "scissors" hold by squeezing 100-pound sacks of grain between his legs until the sacks burst (see Plate 62). A little later, Jim Browning developed an equally powerful scissors combined with what he called an "airplane spin." While Stecher had practiced his scissors on grain sacks, Browning used wine casks filled with water. These he would whirl around above his body, while keeping them in a firm grasp between his knees. Through this practice, Browning became able to handle his human opponents on the wrestling mat in the same way.

A perennial question among sports-followers is, "Can a wrestler beat a boxer?" It should no longer be a question, since it has already been answered several times, always in the affirmative. The first notable instance occurred when, in 1887, the fabulous John L. Sullivan went into the ring with his trainer, the Greco-Roman wrestling champion William Muldoon. Sullivan started the proceedings by tripping Muldoon. But before John L. could do anything further, Muldoon was back on his feet. Taking a waist hold on Sullivan, Muldoon slammed the prize-fighter to the mat so hard that Sullivan lay there, stunned. Time: 2 minutes! The next publicized encounter of this kind was when, sometime during the 1890s, the then heavyweight boxing contender, Bob Fitzsimmons, thought he could take the measure of the then Greco-Roman wrestling champion, Ernest Roeber. But Roeber simply grabbed Fitz's left hand, pulled him to the canvas, applied a double arm lock, and made Fitzsimmons cry "Uncle." More recently was the "match," in 1936, between the heavyweight boxing contender, Kingfish Levinsky, and the veteran wrestler, Ray Steele. The Kingfish aimed a left hook at Steele, who ducked the punch, grabbed Levinsky, and slammed him to the mat— all in 35 seconds! Even Jim Corbett, who was the cleverest of all heavyweight boxers, expressed the opinion that in such a mixed match, "nine times out of ten, the wrestler will win."

A form of wrestling that is but little known in this country is "belt wrestling." Whether it is still practiced anywhere in Europe, I do not know. But in certain countries there, about the turn of the century, it was quite popular. At one time (*c.* 1905), the acknowledged champion at belt wrestling was none other than the world-famous professional strong-man Arthur Saxon. However, in catch-as-catch-can wrestling— which evidently he did *not* practice—Saxon while in England was thrown inside 5 minutes by a quite ordinary performer.

In contrast to the field of boxing, where Floyd Patterson was the only heavyweight champion to regain the title after losing it, in professional wrestling there were *four* different champions who regained their crowns.* The first was Tom Jenkins, who had won the American title from Ernest Roeber. Jenkins lost the title to Frank Gotch on January 27, 1904, regained it from Gotch on May 19, 1905, and again lost it to Gotch on May 23, 1906. Gotch, accordingly, had won the title from Jenkins in 1904, lost it to Jenkins in 1905, and re-won it in 1906. Gotch then kept the title until he retired, early in 1913.** On July 5, 1915, Joe Stecher, by winning over Charles Cutler, became the generally accepted new world's champion. Stecher lost the title to Earl Caddock on April 9, 1917, re-won it from Caddock in 1920, lost it to Ed Lewis on December 13, 1920, regained it from Zbyszko (who had meanwhile defeated Lewis) in 1925, and finally lost it to Lewis on February 20, 1928. Thus Stecher, from 1915 to 1928, had been champion three times. Lewis, in turn, had won the world title from Stecher in 1920, lost it to Zbyszko in 1921, re-won it from Zbyszko on March 22, 1922, lost it to Wayne Munn on January 8, 1925, and re-won it from Stecher (who had meanwhile defeated Munn) in 1928. Thus Lewis, like Stecher, was crowned world champion on three different occasions. Sandwiched in between the Stecher-Lewis matches were those of Stanislaus Zbyszko, who won the title from Lewis in 1921, lost it to Lewis in 1922, regained it from Munn (who had meanwhile defeated Lewis) on April 15, 1925, and finally lost it to Stecher on May 30, 1925.

A first-class English heavyweight professional wrestler who during his prime received comparatively little publicity in the United States was Bert Assirati (66 in., 260 lbs.), of London. Starting in the early 1930s, Assirati became successively British heavyweight champion, British Empire champion, and European champion. He was, besides, a wonderfully strong weightlifter and gymnast. For example, among his various lifting records he did a strictly performed one arm military press of 160 pounds, a pull-over at arms' length lying of 200 pounds, a one-leg squat with 200 pounds, and a two hands dead lift with 800 pounds. On the rings, while weighing 240 pounds, Assirati could do either a crucifix or chin himself with one arm three times in succession. Again, even at his heaviest bodyweight of 266 pounds, he could perform a series of back somersaults (flip-flaps), and land on his feet with the lightness and grace of a ballerina! Between May 1932 and February 1933, Assirati toured the United States and engaged in a total of 65 matches, winning 63 and drawing in 2—the latter with Ray Steele and Hans Steinke respectively. And at that time, Assirati was only 20 years of age! In 21 years of wrestling, Assirati was "thrown" only once, and that was by Ivar Martensen

---

* Of the "champions" who later were put forward by various independent wrestling camps, or associations, I have not attempted to keep a record.
** After his two "wins" over the European Champion, George Hackenschmidt, in 1908 and 1911, respectively, Gotch claimed the world championship.

of Sweden (who tossed Bert out of the ring, but did *not* pin his shoulders to the mat). In two other matches against Martensen, Assirati won both times. In the United States, Assirati had wins over such outstanding grapplers as Joe Stecher, Ray Steele, Wladek Zbyszko, Jim McMillan, Dick Daviscourt, the two Dusek brothers, Gino Garibaldi, and Michel Leone. Surely, here was a wrestler who should be rated near the top in a list of the all-time greatest.

Another powerful wrestler about whom relatively little has been published was Wladyslaw Talun of Poland (b. 1913), who became known as "Iron Talun." In contrast to Bert Assirati's 5 ft. 6 in., Talun was no less than 6 ft. 5 in. in height. While he weighed around 280 pounds, he was so tall and thick-boned that he appeared to carry no excess fat whatever. Talun's wrists each measured 9 inches around, and the length of each of his hands was an extraordinary 9-7/8 inches! Stanislaus Zbyszko, who had "discovered" Talun while on a talent-hunt in Europe just before World War II, regarded the young Polish giant as a physical phenomenon. Up to the end of 1940, Talun had engaged in 247 matches without ever having his shoulders pinned to the mat. After that time, I have not kept abreast of his record.

During recent years, it has, for some reason, become the practice to call any wrestler having acromegalic features an "Angel." The first of such wrestlers to become widely publicized was Maurice Tillet of France, who became known either as "the French Angel", or simply "the Angel". When Tillet came to the United States in the late 1930s, his acromegalic status had progressed to the stage where his muscular strength was enormous; and at that time his head, face, and all his features were so gigantically enlarged that he looked like a bogeyman. At a height of only 68.7 inches, he weighed 278 pounds. Since from his various girth measurements it would appear that he should have weighed only about 250 pounds, it was found through X-ray studies that the extra weight could be attributed to the extraordinary *thickness* of his bones throughout his body, and to a correspondingly huge development of all his internal organs. "The Angel" knew how to act; and this ability, along with his startling appearance, caused wrestling fans to flock to his matches. Up to the year 1945, "the Angel" had engaged in 1300 matches in the United States, of which he lost only 5.

NOTE: I am aware that in the foregoing brief review of wrestling and wrestlers, I have left out of mention many an important name. However, out of the extensive literature available, I have tried to present such information as is least likely to appear in the usual books and magazines on the subject. The status of wrestling and its champions and contenders during recent years can be kept abreast of only by reading all the periodicals in this field as they appear.

8.

Archery

The bow, like the sling, was originally an Asiatic weapon. When the Persian king, Xerxes I, and his army invaded Greece in 484 B.C., almost all the soldiers were equipped with bows. But the Asiatic bow differed from that used in Greece; the first was shaped like a crescent, while the Greek bow was made of two crescents joined by a handle in the middle. That the bows used by heroes of the Homeric age required great strength is indicated in the story of Ulysses, whose great bow only he could bend. And as well as strength, the Homeric heroes were credited with great skill; for Ulysses not only bent his bow with ease, but sent an arrow through 12 small consecutively-placed rings without touching any one of them.

In Rome, while the bow was not looked upon as a national weapon, certain emperors practiced with it so assiduously that they acquired extraordinary skill. Domitian (51–96) was said to have had a young man stand some distance from him, with one hand raised and his fingers spread apart, and to have shot arrows through the spaces between the man's fingers without even grazing the skin. The Emperor Commodus (161–192) was equally adept. In the Roman arena, one of his exhibitions was to have a troop of ostriches run by at top speed, and to decapitate each of the birds with a single arrow. The arrows he used for this had crescent-shaped iron heads.

In ancient Britain the greatest archer was, of course, the legendary Robin Hood. This cheery outlaw was credited with being able to cover, in three shots, the distance of a mile. In a contest described by Sir Walter Scott, in his *Ivanhoe*, Scott gives Hood the name of Locksley. His competitor was one of the royal archers, named Hubert. After Hubert had placed an arrow near the center of a distant target, Hood (or Locksley) placed one even nearer the center, remarking that Hubert had not allowed for the wind. One of the spectators, Prince John, was displeased with Hubert's showing, and told him that with his next shot he had better do better, "or else!" Hubert, thus exhorted, placed an arrow in the exact center of the target. Put upon his mettle, and activated by Prince John's remark that it would be impossible for him to surpass Hubert's last shot, Robin Hood placed his next arrow right on top of Hubert's, splitting it down the middle!

In our own country, Hiawatha, according to legend, could shoot 12 arrows one after the other so swiftly that before the first fell to the ground the last had left the bowstring!*

An extensive literature recounts innumerable other early exploits with the bow; but it is to be doubted whether the *actual* performances of those archers surpass those which have been performed during recent years by modern champions.**

Some sports writers have questioned whether archery, as it is ordinarily practiced today, is any more a form of athletics than is golf, shuffleboard, or bowling. At least, in archery and golf, the strength required can be measured in the distance that the arrow is shot or the golf ball is driven. Endurance, of course, enters the picture where numerous successive efforts are made. Here are a few statistics on these aspects of archery.

The "all-time" world's record for distance attained with a bow and arrow was made in Turkey in 1798, by Sultan Selim III (1761–1808). Presumably the Sultan used the style now known as "freestyle shooting," in which the archer lies on his back, braces his feet against the bow, and draws the bowstring with both hands. The Sultan attained a distance of 972 yards 2¾ inches—about 5½ city blocks!

During recent years, the best mark in freestyle shooting was established by Don Lamore, at Lancaster, Pa., on August 22, 1959. With a bow having a pull of 250 pounds, he reached a distance of 937 yards 4½ inches.

In "flight shooting," by which is meant shooting in an erect standing position and drawing the bowstring with one hand, a record that stood for over a hundred years was made in London in 1796, by the visiting Ambassador from Turkey. In order to prove his point that Turkish bows were superior to those of England, the ambassador (name not given) removed from one of the exhibition cases in the Diplomatic Building

---

* A little figuring shows that, if we credit Hiawatha with a shooting range of 600 yards (or about 13 yards farther than Robin Hood was said to have reached), and an elevation angle of 45 degrees, the initial speed of his arrows would have had to be 240.6 feet per second (= 164 MPH), and each arrow would be in the air for 10.57 seconds. If Hiawatha shot 12 arrows during the 10.57 seconds, he would have had to place them in his bow at the rate of one arrow every .88 of a second! And if his range was *less* than 600 yards, the rate at which he shot the arrows would have had to be *greater* in the same proportion!

** These champions are recruited from a population of amateur archers which in the United States alone numbers over 2 million. A second factor in the probable superiority of modern archery champions is the high quality and uniformity of the bows and arrows they use.

a Turkish bow of the Seljuk Period (1000–1300 A.D.), and with it shot an arrow a distance of 482 yards. This bow was, and possibly still is, preserved in the Museum of the Toxophilite Society. The present-day record in flight shooting is held by Don Lamore, with a distance of 850 yards (1959).

The "endurance" record in archery is generally attributed to a 17-century Japanese champion, Wada Daihachi. In a contest held in 1676, lasting 24 hours, Daihachi is said to have shot 8133 arrows into a target placed 128 yards away. This was at the average rate (not counting rests) of 5.65 arrows per minute. The modern record—of 5583 shots during 24 hours—was made in Tokyo in 1852. This was at the average rate of about 3.88 arrows per minute. While Daihachi is said to have used a bow of 80 pounds pull, the distance (128 yards) that he shot his arrows required a pull of only about 50 pounds.

Incidentally, the pull, or "weight," required in a bow is in ratio to the *square root of the distance* the arrow can be shot. Accordingly, the distance attainable increases more rapidly than the pull of the bow—in fact, in ratio to the pull *squared*. Thus the average bow for men, having a pull of 45 pounds, can shoot up to about 95 yards; while the average bow for women, having a pull of 30 pounds, shoots only 42 or 43 yards. When, in 1950, the women's flight record of 505 yards was performed, the bow used must have had a pull of 103 or 104 pounds—over three times the pull of the average woman's bow. The men's world record in freestyle shooting, of about 937 yards (see above), was made with a bow requiring the tremendous pull of 250 pounds. The women's record in the latter style is 575 yards 2 feet (1958).

Bows of heavy "weight" have been used in hunting as well as for flight and freestyle shooting, and some spectacular exploits have been made in the killing of big game animals with arrows rather than bullets. The famous archer Howard Hill using a bow of 172 pounds' pull, killed a full-grown African rogue elephant with a single arrow!

In contrast to the use of the bow in feats of distance shooting—or in the killing of large game animals—is the following record in which extreme delicacy and phenomenal accuracy of placement were required. The feat was performed many years ago by an East Indian archer named Baquir Khan Najmai Sani. He was given three arrows, with which to shoot at a target consisting of a fragile glass bottle on which was placed a thin wafer of wax; on top of the wafer was placed a grain of rice, and on top of the rice a grain of black pepper. At a distance of ten yards, Sani with his first arrow shot the pepper off the rice; with his second arrow, the rice off the wax wafer; and with his third arrow, the wafer off the bottle—without touching the bottle!

9.

Baseball

In this chapter, the main object will be to present a few new thoughts on an old subject, rather than burden the reader with a mass of statistics on the innumerable achievements that have been catalogued in baseball. Whole volumes have already been devoted to this subject, and even in these the authors usually end up by giving only the records *per se,* and *without* giving explanations or mentioning important modifying factors.

One of the most often-quoted records connected with professional baseball was George Herman "Babe" Ruth's hitting of 60 home runs in 1927.* But this was by no means his greatest achievement. In order to arrive at the "Babe's" true ability, one should examine his all-around playing record as of the year 1920, when, at the age of 24, he was a trim-waisted athlete in his prime. When this is done, Ruth's incomparable record as a ball player is clearly seen.

My friend, George Russell Weaver of St. Petersburg, Florida, is a great enthusiast about various sports, including weightlifting, tennis, and baseball. In 1956, he made a thorough analysis of the batting records of the leading sluggers, both in the era of the "dead ball" (from 1904 to 1919) and in that of the "lively ball," which has been in use since 1920. Weaver's research, which took several months to complete, was carried on at the Helms Athletic Foundation in Los Angeles. Early in 1968, Weaver worked up a more comprehensive list of ratings, which covers the entire period from 1884 to 1967. Here, published for the first time, are the properly-determined all-around standings of *Baseball's Greatest Hitters,* as per the rating formula developed by George Weaver. The ratings resulting from Weaver's formula were selected "blindfold," above those published in *Life* and *Look* magazines, as the only acceptable ones by the famous veteran baseball expert Frederick G. Lieb. The so-called "time" factor (actually, a "change of

---

* In that same year, on a day in February at Wrigley Field Chicago, Ruth gave an impromptu exhibition of his extraordinary batting powers. For a whole hour he stood at the plate, facing one pitcher after another, and during that time batted out *125 home runs!*

PLATE 57

(Above) Egyptian wrestling as depicted on a tomb over 3800 years old. (116)

(Below) A bout between ancient Greek wrestlers, as shown on a vase painting. (117)

PLATE 58

Two Sumo wrestling champions of 1926. On the left is Tochiki-yama, and on the right Nishinoumi. The "umpire" standing between them is of average size for a Japanese, which shows how huge the two wrestlers are. (118)

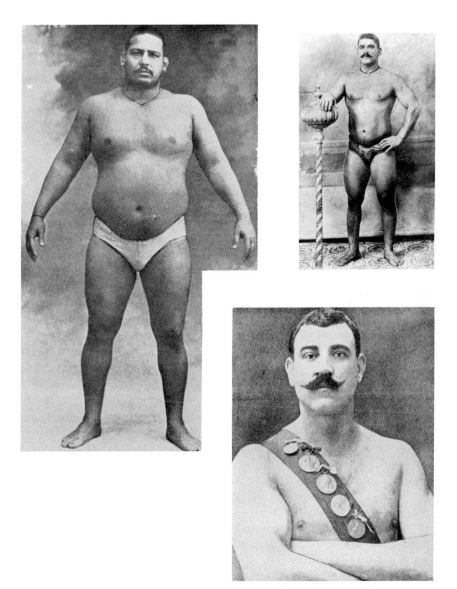

PLATE 59

On the left is the great Hindu champion wrestler, Gulam;
and on the upper right his successor (and son-in-law), Gama.
On the lower right is the great French Greco-Roman wrestler,
Paul Pons, who in the early 1900s was second only to Hackenschmidt, (119–121)

PLATE 60

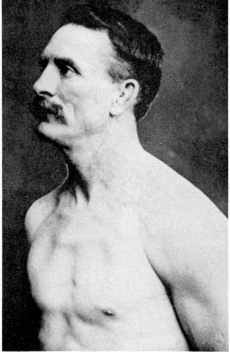

(Above) Yousouf Ishmaelo, the original "Terrible Turk," who went down with the French ship La Bour-goyne *when it sank in 1898. (122)*

(Below) Martin ("Farmer") Burns, who was one of the greatest light-heavyweight wrestlers, and who trained Frank Gotch to succeed him as American champion. (123)

PLATE 61

George Hackenschmidt, "The Russian Lion," who was a fine all-around athlete and sportsman and one of the top-ranking wrestlers of modern times. (124)

PLATE 62

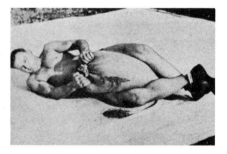

(Above) The one-time world's catch-as-catch-can wrestling champion, Frank Gotch (1878–1917). (125)

(Lower left) The great Polish wrestler, Stanislaus Zbyszko, as he appeared just before he came to the United States in 1909. (126)

(Lower right) Joe Stecher, showing how he developed his powerful leg scissors by squeezing sacks of grain until they burst. (127)

PLATE 63

Ed "Strangler" Lewis and the author, David Willoughby, in a photograph taken on October 11, 1928 in Willoughby's Gymnasium in Los Angeles, California. (128)

PLATE 64

John P. (Honus-Hans) Wagner, in
the author's opinion the greatest all-
around player of them all. (128a)

conditions markedly affecting batting" factor) is, according to Weaver, the most important of the several factors incorporated in his rating formula. This formula, the reasons for which it was evolved, and the ratings as derived from its application to the leading hitters of the period 1884–1967, are all explained in the following elucidation by George Weaver. I am greatly indebted to him for his unique discussion.

Although it is played in a few other countries, such as Cuba and Japan, baseball is primarily a sport of the United States, and is, in fact, described as "America's national game." It is actually a derivative of two English games, cricket and rounders; and although, in the past, it was often a bewildering puzzle to visiting Englishmen, its characteristics should by now be too familiar to need description.

In this discussion we are concerned with the leading players in the history of American major-league baseball, as far back as the available records allow us to go toward 1884, when overhand pitching began and the schedule reached 100 games. Since that year, there have actually been six major leagues, but only two of these have lasted over the years—the National League and the American League.

Baseball is a *balanced* game. The proportions of the diamond, devised by Alexander Cartwright in 1845, give such a balance between pitcher,

MEANING OF BASEBALL ABBREVIATIONS

G	Number of games played.
AB	Number of times at bat.
R	Number of runs scored.
H	Number of hits made by batter, or allowed by pitcher.
TB	Total bases on hits (hits plus doubles plus twice the triples, plus three times the home runs).
2B	Two-base hits (doubles).
3B	Three-base hits (triples).
HR	Home runs (homers).
BA	Batting average (number of hits divided by times at bat).
SA	Slugging average (total bases divided by times at bat).
IP	Number of innings pitched by a pitcher.
BB	Number of bases on balls (walks to first base, on four bad balls given by pitcher).
SO	Number of strikeouts by batter or pitcher (three balls missed by batter, or not swung at but called good by umpire).
ERA	Earned run average of pitcher: number of "earned" runs allowed per nine-innings.

hitter, and fielders that the basic rules of the game have not changed in over a hundred years. Thus, while records are constantly surpassed in most athletic sports, baseball averages merely fluctuate. The game does have one defect: from the statistical viewpoint, all ball parks should have the same internal shape and dimensions. In other words, the home-run distances, both horizontal and vertical, should be uniform. This decidedly is not the case. We have to accept this imperfection, and disregard it.

A. BASEBALL'S GREATEST HITTERS

The question of the game's greatest batters has long been a leading interest of the fans and a leading problem for the statistician. It is widely recognized that the standard batting averages are an unreliable index of hitting prowess, since they take no account of the *length* of the player's hits. Consider the case of the 1913 National League batting champion and the runner-up:

PLAYER	AB	H	TB	2B	3B	HR	BA
Jacob Daubert	508	178	215	17	7	2	.350
Clifford Cravath	525	179	298	34	14	19	.341

It is perfectly obvious that the real batting champion was Cravath and not Daubert. This fact is indicated by the so-called slugging average. Where the batting average measures *only* the *frequency* of hitting, the slugging average measures *both* frequency and *power*. Daubert's slugging average was .423, while Cravath's was .568.

Consider the even more outrageous case of the 1949 American League batting championship:

PLAYER	AB	H	TB	2B	3B	HR	BA
George Kell	522	179	244	38	9	3	.3429
Ted Williams	566	194	368	39	3	43	.3428

It need hardly be said that Williams's hitting was far superior to Kell's. The slugging averages show this: Kell, .467, Williams .650.

There is reason to believe, however, that the slugging average is not the best possible index. In 1954, Branch Rickey, a famous baseball executive, presented a formula developed with the help of leading baseball statisticians and research mathematicians, which indicated that extra-base power was 75 percent as important as frequency of hitting.

The results of applying this formula to the problem of baseball's greatest hitters were presented in *Life* magazine. They showed Babe Ruth, Ted Williams, and Lou Gehrig as the three greatest hitters, but unfortunately they also showed Ty Cobb in 23rd place, and such acknowledged greats as Wagner, Lajoie, and Jackson nowhere at all. Rickey himself admitted the unfairness of this, but had to accept it as unavoidable.

But why should an apparently valid formula result in such an obviously unfair rating of great hitters? The reason is simple and universally acknowledged: because the nation-wide excitement produced by Babe Ruth's new major-league record of 29 home runs in 1919 caused the baseball magnates to introduce a new and far livelier ball, which truly revolutionized the game. It was possible to hit twice as many home runs with this new rabbit-ball, and batters began to swing for the fence as they never had before. Thus, all power-hitting records made before 1920 became non-comparable with those made since then.

At least they are not comparable directly, as they stand. But I believe that the great hitters of baseball *can* be fairly compared, on the basis of their records, whether they batted against the dead ball or the lively ball, and regardless of other changes as well.

The secret of rating major-league batters is to *relate their performances to the conditions, varying from year to year, that affect batting possibilities for players in general.* And these possibilities are unfailingly reflected in the *league* batting and slugging averages.

Thus it is meaningless to record that Honus Wagner batted only .354 in 1908 while Bill Terry batted .401 in 1930, unless this is related to the fact that the *league* batting average was only .239 in 1908, whereas it was .303 in 1930. Similarly, it is pointless to record that Wagner had a slugging average of only .542 in 1908, while Hack Wilson had a slugging average of .723 in 1930, unless you relate this to the fact that the *league* extra-base average was only .067 in 1908, whereas it was .144 in 1930.

While the change to the lively ball in 1920 (which jumped the home-run record from 29 to 54) is the outstanding example of the variation in conditions affecting batting possibilities, there are a number of other such variables. The lively ball itself was made extra-lively in 1930 in the National League, with the result that Bill Terry hit .401 and Hack Wilson hit 56 homers. In 1931 the ball was made less lively: the batting champion hit .349 and the home-run champion hit 31 homers.

In 1931 the sacrifice-fly rule was changed in a way that subtracted points from the batting averages. Later it was changed again, so that some points were restored to the batters.

In Babe Ruth's day the players had to bat in semi-darkness when the late afternoon sun started to throw shadows on the field, or when a heavy overcast gave aid to the pitchers. Today there are push-button lighting systems that take care of such conditions.

On the other hand, we have had in recent years a wonderful development of pitching skill. Young pitchers have appeared, armed with fast balls, changes of pace, palm balls, knuckle balls, screwballs, and sliders. In addition, a commentator complains, managers "now platoon their pitchers." The hitter no longer has a chance to adjust to the pitcher, and the pitcher is no longer allowed to tire. A ball club, runs the complaint, now has "four or five starters, a couple of late-inning retrievers, a couple of middlemen, and a few for long relief or extra starts." In addition to this, the glove used by the fielders has been greatly increased in size in recent years; it now grabs balls that would have gone through for singles in earlier years. And the pitcher's mound was lowered from 15 to 10 inches in 1969.

All of these varying conditions can be *automatically compensated for* by the use of a formula that relates each player's performance to the *league average* for the year in question. In this way, it is possible to compare fairly the hitters of any year and either league.

Accepting Rickey's determination of extra-base hitting as having three-fourths the importance of frequency hitting, I have devised this formula for the rating of batters.

$$\left(PBA \times \frac{.303}{LBA} \right) + \frac{3}{4} \left(PEBA \times \frac{.145}{LEBA} \right) = \text{Batting Rating}$$

Here PBA is the player's batting average for the year, LBA is the league batting average for that year, PEBA is the player's extra-base average, and LEBA is the league extra-base average. Any appropriate figures can serve as the dividends: I chose .303 as the highest league batting average so far recorded, and .145 as a comparable figure for the league extra-base average.

The most practical way to apply this formula is to rate each player at his peak—his one best season. This is particularly interesting to the reader, as he is thus presented with the details of the great batter's performance during his greatest year. In this way we also avoid the vitiating influence of the illness and injuries that have adversely affected the lifetime averages of some great hitters, and the fact that others have insisted on playing for several seasons after the natural decline of athletic aging was obvious. There is also a reason (constantly overlooked) why the lifetime averages of such players as Browning, Brouthers, and Anson, which are often cited, are not valid: they include the 1887 season, when batters were allowed four strikes, and a walk (base on balls) was recorded as a hit! For this reason, also, no player's 1887 batting average should ever be cited as an example of hitting prowess. (If the walk-equals-hit rule had existed in 1923, Babe Ruth's batting average that year would have been .542, and his lifetime average would be .355 instead of .342.)

It is not claimed that the use of each player's one best year invariably gives unquestionable results. No one would deny that Joe DiMaggio was a greater hitter than Norman Cash. Joe batted over .300 ten times and Cash only once. Why Cash dropped from a league-leading .361 to only .243 the following year (while still hitting home runs at the same rate as before) is one of baseball's mysteries. The fact remains that Cash is the only man to hit as high as .360 since Ted Williams and Mickey Mantle in 1957. In fact, no other hitter but these three has gone that high in either league since 1948. This exceptional batting average, coupled with his home-run hitting, means that Cash's 1961 performance is definitely worthy of remembrance. Here follow, then, my ratings of baseball's greatest hitters, based upon each one's greatest seasonal performance. For inclusion in this table, a minimum of 400 times at bat is required.

Baseball's Greatest Hitters
(those rating over .659)

BATTER	YEAR	G	AB	R	H	TB	2B	3B	HR	RAT-ING
1. George (Babe) Ruth	1920	142	458	158	172	388	36	9	54	.896
2. Lou Gehrig	1927	155	584	149	218	447	52	18	47	.770
3. Ted Williams	1957	132	420	96	163	307	28	1	38	.754
4. Ty Cobb	1917	152	588	107	225	336	44	23	7	.753
5. John Wagner	1908	151	568	100	201	308	39	19	10	.753
6. Rogers Hornsby	1925	138	504	133	203	381	41	10	39	.732
7. Stanley Musial	1948	155	611	135	230	429	46	18	39	.728
8. James (Jimmy) Foxx	1932	154	585	151	213	438	33	9	58	.726
9. Napoleon Lajoie	1904	140	554	92	211	304	50	14	5	.713

10. Mickey Mantle	1956	150	533	132	188	376	22	5	52	.698
11. Carl Yastrzemski	1967	161	579	112	189	360	31	4	44	.697
12. Joe Jackson	1912	152	572	121	226	331	44	26	3	.694
13. James Seymour	1905	149	581	95	219	325	40	21	8	.689
14. Charles (Chuck) Klein	1933	152	606	101	223	365	44	7	28	.685
15. Ed Delahanty	1893	132	588	145	218	346	31	20	19	.681
16. Joe Medwick	1937	156	633	111	237	406	56	10	31	.680
17. Tris Speaker	1912	153	580	136	222	328	53	13	9	.679
18. John Mize	1940	155	579	111	182	368	31	13	43	.672
19. George Sisler	1920	154	631	137	257	399	49	18	19	.671
20. Willie Mays	1965	157	558	118	177	360	21	3	52	.671
21. Frank Robinson	1966	155	576	122	182	367	34	2	49	.671
22. Al Simmons	1930	138	554	152	211	392	41	16	36	.668
23. Harry Heilmann	1923	144	524	121	211	331	44	11	18	.668
24. Norman Cash	1961	159	535	119	193	354	22	8	41	.663
25. Joe DiMaggio	1941	139	541	122	193	348	43	11	30	.660

And here are the holders of the major-league records in the various departments of hitting, with each champion's rating, by the Weaver formula, for the year in which he made his record. The All-Time records are from 1884 onward; the Modern records are from 1900 onward.

Department	Player	Record	Year	Rating
Slugging Average	Babe Ruth	.847	1920	.896
Total Bases	Babe Ruth	457	1921	.831
Runs (Modern)	Babe Ruth	177	1921	.831
Home Runs (154 Games)	Babe Ruth	60	1927	.775
Batting Average (Modern)	Rogers Hornsby	.424	1924	.726
Hits	George Sisler	257	1920	.671
Batting Streak (Games)	Joe DiMaggio	56	1941	.660
Runs Batted In	Hack Wilson	190	1930	.632
Batting Average (All-Time)	Hugh Duffy	.438	1894	.623
Home Runs (162 Games)	Roger Maris	61	1961	.594
Three-Base Hits	John Owen Wilson	36	1912	.575
Two-Base Hits	Earl Webb	67	1931	.543
Runs (All-Time)	William Hamilton	196	1894	.483

Hamilton was not an extra-base hitter, but combined a high batting average with amazing base-stealing ability: he stole as many as 117 in a season, and seven in one game.

And here are the all-time leaders in Total Bases: Babe Ruth, 457 (85 singles, 44 doubles, 16 triples, and 59 home runs) in 1921; Rogers Hornsby, 450 in 1922; Lou Gehrig, 447 in 1927; Chuck Klein, 445 in 1948; Hack Wilson, 423 in 1930.

The above tables show conclusively that Babe Ruth was, without question, the greatest hitter in the history of baseball. In fact, no other batter has ever remotely approached his greatest record, which is not his 60 home runs, as commonly stated by sports writers, but his .847 slugging average in 1920, which he also practically equalled the following year. The closest approach to this record was made by Lou Gehrig, who had an average of .765 the same year that Ruth hit 60 homers.

But the hitting records alone do not reveal the true greatness of Babe Ruth as a super-athlete. For he was not only a fine outfielder and a good base-runner before he allowed himself to become fat, but in his earliest years he was a great pitcher. In 1916 he was the leading pitcher in the American League, winning 23 games and losing 12 for a .657 average, and, more importantly, leading the league in earned-run average with a low 1.75, to do which he merely had to outpitch such moundsmen as Walter Johnson, Hubert Leonard, Eddie Cicotte, Bob Shawkey, Urban Faber, Stanley Covaleski, Jim Bagby, and Ernie Shore!

Lou Gehrig's list of batting achievements is formidable. For five years he was overshadowed by Ruth, but he tied Ruth in homers in 1931, and then led the league in 1934 and 1936. In 1934 he was both batting and slugging champion, and was slugging champion again in 1936. He led the league in RBIs five times, and holds the league record of 184. He had a slugging average of over .700 three times, and he amassed more than 400 Total Bases five times, more than any other player. He hit two homers in a game 45 times, and cleared the bases with a home run 23 times, more than any other player. He was also the first player of this century to hit four home runs in one game, which he did in 1932. And finally, there is the incomparable, magnificent *balance* of his long-distance hitting in his greatest year. When Ralph Kiner hit 54 home runs, he hit only 19 doubles and 5 triples. When Roger Maris hit 61 homers, he hit only 16 doubles and 4 triples. But no batter, except Gehrig, has ever hit as many as 50 doubles, 10 triples, and 40 home runs in the same season. And when Gehrig, in 1927, hit 52 doubles, 18 triples, and 47 home runs, he performed a feat of balanced power-hitting that may never be equalled.

B. BASEBALL'S GREATEST PITCHERS

We must now consider the fascinating question of baseball's greatest pitchers, restricting ourselves in this case to the twentieth century. The original method of rating pitchers statistically was by the Won-Lost Percentage, the ratio of the number of games won to the number pitched. This method, however, ignored the influence of the other eight players on the winning or losing of a game. In a rating of pitchers by lifetime Won-Lost Percentage published a few years ago, Walter Johnson was 23rd, whereas every baseball expert would rank him among the very greatest. The admitted fact is that, when Johnson was in his prime, his club, the Washington Senators, "bore slight resemblance to a baseball team," and this great pitcher "was surrounded by mediocrity and lack of talent."

A much better method of rating pitchers is the Earned Run Average, a really complex statistical calculation which does give the pitcher credit for a good performance regardless of what the other players on his team may do. Unfortunately, some of the greatest pitchers, like Cy Young and Christy Mathewson, pitched for years before this method was devised.

In August 1956, *Esquire* magazine published an article entitled *The Twenty Greatest Pitchers of All Time,* by Max Carey, formerly one of baseball's greatest base-stealers, who had studied the game closely for 45 years. In Carey's analysis (which was actually restricted to the 20th-century pitchers) many different items connected with pitching were rated and averaged. By this method, Christy Mathewson was selected as the greatest of all pitchers; and after him, in this order, Carey listed Grover Alexander, Walter Johnson, Cy Young, Carl Hubbell, Bob Feller, Robin Roberts, Lefty Grove, Dizzy Dean, Mordecai Brown, Eddie Plank, Bob Lemon, Chief Bender, Hal Newhouser, Ted Lyons, Herb Pennock, Dazzy Vance, Eppa Rixey, Red Ruffing, and Rube Waddell.

Other great pitchers have appeared since Carey made his selection. Perhaps the best way to bring things up to date would be to list some outstanding achievements and the present (1969) record-holders in the various categories that relate to pitching, restricting ourselves to the 20th century.

MOST GAMES WON: Walter Johnson, 416. (Cy Young won 511 games, but more than half of them before 1900.)

MOST GAMES WON IN A SEASON: Jack Chesbro, 41, in 1904.

MOST CONSECUTIVE GAMES WON: Carl Hubbell, 24, at the end of 1936 and the beginning of 1937.

MOST CONSECUTIVE GAMES WON IN A SEASON: Richard (Rube) Marquard, 19, in 1912.

MOST SEASONS WINNING THIRTY GAMES: Christy Mathewson, 4 (30, 33, 32, 37).

HIGHEST WON-LOST PERCENTAGE IN A SEASON, WITH THIRTY GAMES: Lefty Grove, won 31, lost 4, percentage .866, in 1931.

MOST SHUTOUTS: Walter Johnson, 113.

MOST SHUTOUTS IN A SEASON: Grover Cleveland Alexander, 16, in 1916.

MOST OPENING-DAY SHUTOUTS: Walter Johnson, 7.

MOST CONSECUTIVE SHUTOUTS: Don Drysdale, 6, in 1968.

MOST NO-HIT GAMES: Sandy Koufax, 4.

MOST CONSECUTIVE NO-HIT GAMES: John Vander Meer, 2, in 1938.

MOST CONSECUTIVE HITLESS INNINGS: Cy Young, 23, in 1904.

MOST STRIKEOUTS: Walter Johnson, 3497.

MOST STRIKEOUTS IN A SEASON: Sandy Koufax, 382, in 1965.

MOST SEASONS WITH 300 STRIKEOUTS: Sandy Koufax, 3 (306, 382, 317).

MOST STRIKEOUTS IN A NINE-INNING GAME: Steve Carlton, 19, in 1969; Sandy Koufax, 18, in 1959; Robert Feller, 18, in 1938. (Feller actually struck out 18, 17, 16, 15, 14, 13, 12, 11, and 10 batters in various games!)

MOST CONSECUTIVE INNINGS WITHOUT A BASE ON BALLS: Christy Mathewson, 68, in 1913.

LOWEST BASE-ON-BALLS AVERAGE PER INNING FOR A SEASON: Charles (Babe) Adams, 18 walks in 263 innings, average .068, in 1920. (Christy Mathewson's average in 1913 was .069, 21 walks in 306 innings.)

MOST CONSECUTIVE SCORELESS INNINGS: Don Drysdale, 58, in 1968.

LOWEST EARNED RUN AVERAGE IN A SEASON: Hubert Leonard, 1.01, in 1914.

Probably the greatest pitching ever seen in the heat of a pennant race occurred in 1908. That year Ed Walsh won 40 games and lost 15 for a .727 average. In the last eight days of the season he appeared in six games. He pitched both games of a doubleheader and won both, allowing 3 hits in the first and 4 in the second. Then, with two days of rest, he lost a 1–0 game, allowing only 4 hits, walking only one man, and striking out 15 batters. His opponent, Addie Joss, who had pitched three one-hit games the previous year, pitched a perfect game.

Lefty Grove led the league in earned-run average nine times (four years straight). Sandy Koufax led the league five times (five straight years before he voluntarily quit pitching). Grover Cleveland Alexander led five times (three years straight). And Walter Johnson led four times.

Walter Johnson led the league in strikeouts twelve times (eight years straight). Bob Grove and Dazzy Vance both led the league seven times (and seven straight years). Rube Waddell led seven times (six years straight). Bob Feller led seven times (four years straight). Grover Cleveland Alexander led six times (four years straight). Christy Mathewson led six times (three years straight). Dizzy Dean and Warren Spahn led four times (and four straight years). Sandy Koufax led four times.

This matter of strikeouts brings up a curious and little-known record. When young Herbert Score, playing his first season in the majors, led the league with 244 strikeouts in 227 innings, he became the first pitcher in baseball history to strike out as many men as the number of innings he had pitched (requiring a minimum of 180 innings). His average was 1.07 per inning. When Sandy Koufax fanned 382 men in 336 innings in 1965, he surpassed this with 1.14 strikeouts per inning. But in the same year, Sam McDowell struck out 325 men in 273 innings, an even better average of 1.19 strikeouts per inning. At the end of the 1968 season, after eight years in the majors, Sam McDowell had struck out 1384 men in 1304 innings.

Koufax is the only pitcher in baseball history who has more strikeouts than innings pitched during an entire career. He actually fanned 2396 batters in 2325 innings, during twelve years.

Strikeouts, however, are generally accompanied by walks. The man with tremendous speed is usually somewhat lacking in control. Feller, who formerly held the strikeout record with 348 (although the latest research now credits Waddell with 349 in 1904), also held the record for walks given in a season, no fewer than 208! On the other hand, the mark of the greatest pitching is precisely the small number of walks given in comparison with the number of strikeouts. Feller struck out 348 and walked 153. Koufax fanned 382 and walked only 71. If we study the best years of the famous strikeout artists, we find that while Mungo, Feller, McDowell, Grove, and Newhouser did strike out two or three times as many men as they walked, Koufax, Marichal, Mathewson, Johnson, and Young actually struck out five or six times as many as they walked.

In his wonderful analysis of the elements of hitting and pitching greatness in the *Esquire* article cited above, Branch Rickey, on the evidence of his statisticians, concluded that while the walks and hits allowed by the pitcher are of vital importance, the number of strikeouts had an extremely low correlation with the earned-run average.

Accepting Rickey's evaluation of strikeouts, and seeking a formula that could be applied to pitchers active before 1912, when earned runs were first tabulated, I arrived at the following calculation:

$$\frac{H + BB}{IP} - \frac{1}{8}\left(\frac{SO}{IP}\right) = \text{Pitching Rating}$$

Here H is the number of hits allowed, BB is the number of walks (bases on balls) given, SO is the number of strikeouts, and IP is the number of innings pitched. Applying this formula to each player at his peak, his one best season, and requiring a minimum of 180 innings pitched, the leading modern pitchers would be rated thus:

Baseball's Greatest Pitchers

Pitcher		Year	IP	H	BB	SO	ERA	Rating
1. Walter Johnson	R	1913	346	232	38	243	1.14	.692
2. Sandy Koufax	L	1965	336	216	71	382	2.04	.712
3. Bob Gibson	R	1968	305	198	62	268	1.12	.743
4. Christy Mathewson	R	1908	391	281	42	259	....	.743
5. Luis Tiant	R	1968	258	152	73	264	1.60	.744
6. Dave McNally	L	1968	273	175	55	202	1.95	.750
7. Addie Joss	R	1908	325	232	30	130	....	.752
8. Grover Cleveland Alexander	R	1915	376	253	64	241	1.22	.763
9. Juan Marichal	R	1966	307	228	36	222	2.23	.770
10. Cy Young	R	1905	321	245	30	208	....	.776
11. Ed Walsh	R	1908	464	343	56	269	....	.787
12. Mordecai Brown	R	1908	312	214	49	123	....	.794
13. Dennis McLain	R	1968	336	241	63	280	1.96	.801
14. Hubert Leonard	L	1914	222	140	60	174	1.01	.803
15. Chief Bender	R	1910	250	182	47	155	....	.839
16. Guy (Doc) White	L	1906	220	162	38	102	....	.851
17. Joel Horlen	R	1964	211	142	55	138	1.88	.852
18. Charles (Babe) Adams	R	1919	263	213	23	92	1.98	.854
19. Dean Chance	R	1968	287	213	62	230	2.45	.858
20. Eddie Cicotte	R	1917	346	246	70	150	1.53	.859
21. Jack Chesbro	R	1904	454	337	87	240	....	.869
22. Don Drysdale	R	1964	321	242	68	237	2.19	.873

The earned-run average (ERA) has been given where available.

If we turn to the many all-star teams that have been selected by baseball experts and famous players, we find that the names most frequently repeated in the pitching staffs chosen are, in this order, Christy Mathewson, Walter Johnson, Cy Young, and Grover Cleveland Alexander; and, after that, Bob Feller and Lefty Grove. Connie Mack, a man of unequalled experience, stated that George (Rube) Waddell "could have been the greatest pitcher of all time" if he had taken base-ball seriously and made full use of his natural gifts. Max Carey, also, in his *Esquire* analysis says that, "had the southpaw possessed normal intelligence, he would have become the greatest of all." Connie Mack says that Waddell's fireball almost equalled that of Walter Johnson, and his curve was faster and deeper than that of any other pitcher. In exhibition games, when holding a slight lead in the ninth inning, Waddell is alleged to have called in the outfielders and infielders to sit on the grass while he struck out the last three men.

Christy Mathewson possessed, to a high degree, the seriousness and intelligence that Waddell lacked. He studied every batter, and, says Max Carey, "never made the same mistake twice." He mixed his speed-ball, his curve, and his fadeaway (screwball) with great skill and marvel-ous control. Carey thinks that Mathewson's greatest achievement was pitching three straight shutouts against the Athletics in the five-game World Series of 1905. In summary, says Carey, Mathewson combined all the talents of body, mind, and heart that any athlete could hope for.

C. THE GREATEST PLAYERS

Strangely enough, baseball experts seem never to have selected any all-star teams of the greatest *fielders* in the various positions. Many ex-perts have chosen all-star teams, but the players have always been selected on the basis of their all-around play, their combination of batting and fielding and baserunning talents. An examination of a number of such teams chosen prior to 1969 shows that the majority selections would be: Gehrig at first base, Eddie Collins at second, Wagner at short, Traynor at third, Ruth in left field, Tris Speaker in center, Cobb in right field, and Cochrane catching.

However, in July of 1969, the Baseball Writers Association of America voted on candidates for an all-time all-star team with the following results:

First base: Lou Gehrig.
Second base: Rogers Hornsby.
Shortstop: John (Honus) Wagner.
Third base: Harold (Pie) Traynor.
Left field: George (Babe) Ruth.
Center field: Joe DiMaggio.
Right field: Ty Cobb.
Catcher: Gordon (Mickey) Cochrane.
Right-hand pitcher: Walter Johnson.
Left-hand pitcher: Bob (Lefty) Grove.
The pitchers, presumably, were chosen for their pitching ability only.

D. THE GREATEST PLAYER OF ALL

And now for the ultimate question. Who deserves to be called the greatest baseball player of all time? Actually, only three men are ever mentioned for this honor: Babe Ruth, Ty Cobb, and Honus Wagner. The choice of Ruth is based on the fact that he was a supremely great hitter, and had, previously been a great pitcher. This, however, is not quite what is meant by the greatest all-around player. The choice, then, is between John Peter Wagner and Tyrus Raymond Cobb. The vast majority of experts today choose Cobb. John McGraw, Ed Barrow, and Branch Rickey, however, chose Wagner (see Plate 64).

Whenever anyone does mention Wagner as the greatest, the proponents of Cobb become greatly excited, and produce panegyrics of the famous outfielder that describe how he dominated every game he played in, what an incomparably fierce competitor he was, how his dazzling baserunning would upset the enemy pitchers and hustle the opposing fielders into errors, how he was equally great in bunting or slashing long hits, and so on. But these eulogies all have one peculiar characteristic: they are always concerned with Cobb's greatness on *offense*, as a superlative exponent of *attack*. Cobb's greatness here must be admitted, although my rating of the greatest hitters shows Cobb and Wagner as virtually equal (with Wagner, however, being the greatest right-hand hitter, and Cobb the fourth-best left-hand hitter). But what about *defense?* It is easy to think of outfielders who have been rated higher than Cobb, defensively: Oscar Felsch, Harry Hooper, Tris Speaker, Stanley Musial, Joe DiMaggio, Chuck Klein (with his 44 assists in one season). But what infielder was ever rated, defensively, above Wagner?

It seems to me that the answer to the problem can be found in six indisputable facts:

When they were in their prime, Ty Cobb was the greatest hitter in the American League, and Honus Wagner was the greatest hitter in the National League. Cobb was the greatest baserunner and base-stealer in the American League, and Wagner was the greatest baserunner and base-stealer in the National League. Cobb was a very good outfielder, and Wagner was the greatest infielder in the National League. In fact, as a leading baseball writer puts it, nobody has ever disputed Wagner's right to be called the greatest infielder the game has ever known.

Actually, Wagner was a third-baseman during his last year in the minors, and he was an outfielder during his first year in the majors. He did not settle down as a shortstop until his seventh year in the National League. As an outfielder he displayed the same great throwing that he displayed as an infielder. And so, when Barrow and McGraw picked him as the greatest all-around player, Grantland Rice had to say: "From that all-around stand, they could be right. Wagner could play more positions better than either Cobb or Ruth."

On the basis of hitting, running, and fielding, then, it seems obvious to me that the greatest all-around baseball player in the history of the game was John Peter (Honus) Wagner.

The only time Cobb and Wagner faced each other was in the 1909 World Series. Cobb stole two bases and batted .231. Wagner stole six bases (three in one game) and batted .333. The record of six stolen bases stood for 57 years; the record of three in a game was not tied until 1965 and again in 1967, and has not been surpassed.

John Wagner led the National League in batting eight times, more than any other player; Rogers Hornsby and Stanley Musial each made it seven times. Wagner also led the league in slugging six times. He led in two-base hits eight times, in three-base hits three times, and in stolen bases five times. He batted over .300 for 17 consecutive seasons; finally, when he was 40 years old, he fell below that figure. Even when he was 41, he was able to play in his club's full schedule of 156 games, hitting 32 doubles, 17 triples, and 6 home runs—against the dead ball of 1915. When he retired, he held the National League lifetime records for runs, hits, doubles, triples, extra-base hits, total bases, runs batted in, and stolen bases. As a right-handed batter, he had further to travel to first base than Cobb did, but he was just as famous for beating out infield grounders. At bat he simply had no weakness, and could hit a bad ball as well as a good one if a hit was needed.

On the base paths he was one of the fastest men in baseball. Almost six feet tall and carrying 200 pounds of bone and muscle, with bowlegs and long apelike arms, he was a fantastic sight as he scurried around the bases, his legs churning like mad and his body close to the ground. He was a master slider, and yet, unlike Cobb, he would rather be tagged out than injure an enemy fielder.

As a shortstop, no one could equal Wagner at covering a wide range of territory. He seemed to have the reach of an octopus. Actually, he was a keen student of batters, and thus developed remarkable anticipation. In addition, as Fred Lieb says, "he was much faster than the more graceful Lajoie." He also had hands and fingers of extraordinary size, with which he could spear or smother anything that came anywhere near him, in the air or on the ground. And finally, he possessed one of the greatest of all throwing arms, in which respect he was far ahead of Cobb. Robert Smith, in his *Baseball*, thus describes the strength and versatility of Wagner's throwing: "His throws, from any position, crouched, off balance, falling down, or moving, were straight and hard, accurate as bullets. He threw overhand, underhand, with a quick snap, or a pendulum swing, as the situation demanded."

In summation, Smith describes Wagner as having possessed the muscular control and agility of an acrobat, the keen eyes and perfect judgment of a juggler, and the hand and shoulder strength of a circus strongman. More picturesquely, it was once said that "he walks like a crab, plays like an octopus, and hits like the devil." In the sober pronouncement of Ed Barrow: "So uniformly good was Wagner as a player that it is almost impossible to determine whether his highest point of superiority was in his fielding, in his batting average, or in his base running. He was a topnotcher in all."

This should be enough. And yet there is a bonus. For Wagner was admired as widely for his personality as he was for his playing.

10.
Tennis

NOTE: *For the following concise account, I am again indebted to George Russell Weaver, who has an encyclopedic knowledge of tennis and has seen most of the great players in action.*

Starting with the beginning of the 20th century, the first two great players of lawn tennis (so-called, though sometimes played on clay, cement, asphalt, or indoors on wood) were the British Doherty brothers, Reginald and Hugh. They were a marvelous, harmonious doubles team, and were equally great in singles. Reginald was tall and thin, while Hugh was relatively short and compact in build. Reggie was the more brilliant, and could defeat Hugh when they met, but his health was uncertain, and Hugh had a better record against other players. Reggie won the Wimbledon singles title (the unofficial world's championship) four straight years, 1897 to 1900. Then Hugh won the title for five straight years, 1902 to 1906. The brothers teamed to win the Wimbledon doubles title eight times. Dr. Philip Hawk, a lifelong student of tennis, ranked Hugh Doherty as the second greatest court-coverer and the second greatest strategist of the game.

Meanwhile, the United States had produced a player who is seldom mentioned today, but who was, in my opinion, one of the greatest of champions, Malcolm Whitman. He won the American singles title three straight years, 1898 to 1900, and proved himself superior to both Hugh and Reginald Doherty in international singles matches. Qualified critics believe that he could have continued to win the American championship indefinitely, but his family persuaded him to quit the game and concentrate on a professional career. Thereupon William Larned took over, and won the American championship seven times with very sound and solid baseline driving.

Hugh Doherty remained supreme in England until 1906, and then came two great Australasian players, Norman Brookes and Anthony Wilding. Brookes was a unique player, a remarkable volleyer who used an odd, loosely-strung racket. He was noted for his tactical acumen. Wilding, on the other hand, was a model of the tall, handsome, athletic male, and played a splendid all-around game. Brookes won at Wimbledon in 1907 and again in 1914. Wilding won in four straight years, 1910 to 1913, and then was killed in World War I.

In 1912 the "California Comet," red-haired Maurice McLoughlin, swept through the American singles championship with the most dynamic game that had ever been seen up to that time on the tennis courts. With tangled-up, wretched footwork on his groundstrokes, and with an awkwardly weak backhand drive, he combined a thunderous if erratic forehand drive, and the most terrific services and overhead smashes that anybody had ever seen. Gifted with tremendous energy, his whole game was acing service, net-rushing, volley and smash.

McLoughlin pulverized both Brookes and Wilding in the 1914 Davis Cup matches, and was an overwhelming favorite to win the American singles crown afterwards. But a new genius of the courts appeared, stood in close to McLoughlin's service, took it on the rise, shot it back before the Comet could reach the net, and scored a startling victory. This was Richard Norris Williams (see Plate 66), rated by Tilden as second only to Cochet for pure instinctive genius. Williams had deliberately developed the most recklessly daring game ever seen on a tennis court: he had a very fast first service, and often tried for aces on his second service; he made his drives off the rising bounce of the ball, which shot them back very quickly but required the most difficult timing; he tried to make his drives skim over the net with practically no margin of safety; he walked about the court, making volleys and half-volleys from any and every position; he actually often aimed at the lines for the pure thrill of seeing the chalk fly.

With such a game, Williams was likely to be defeated by almost any good player when his "touch" was "off," but when it was "on" he was unbeatable, and produced the most dazzlingly brilliant tennis that was ever seen. In 1916 he defeated William Johnston in the American singles final, displaying wonderful mastery of his difficult game. Service in the war, however, caused him to lose something of the precise coordination required for consistent winning. Yet every once in a while he would produce a sample of his greatest game, as when, in 1924, he swept the new Wimbledon champion, Jean Borotra, off the court in straight sets, 6–2, 6–2, 6–2. And in 1925, in the Pennsylvania State Singles Championship, though losing to Tilden in five sets, he produced in one set the greatest tennis, unquestionably, that has ever been played. For although Williams often made far more errors than most other topflight players (because of the difficult and daring nature of his game), in this set against Tilden he actually made only one error! Tilden himself, who made only five points, and lost every game in the set, stated that he was playing at the very top of his form—*whenever he could get his racket on the ball,* which was hardly ever!

In 1925, Williams teamed up with Vincent Richards and, playing a less daring and reckless game, won the American doubles championship two years in succession.

Vincent Richards (see Plate 67) has been generally recognized as the greatest all-around volleyer in the history of tennis, and second only to Borotra as a high volleyer. Being of less than average height (5 ft. 7 in.), he volleyed well back from the net, better to protect himself against lobs. From this position, his low volleying was phenomenal. Lunging like a hawk on the wing, he would shoot back the attempted passing shots of the greatest baseline drivers. Being a wonderful half-volleyer and a decisive smasher, he was naturally one of the great doubles players. In fact, he won the American doubles championship, with Tilden, when he was only 15 years old!

In fact, Tilden and Richards won the professional doubles title 27 years after they had won the amateur title, when Tilden was in his fifties and Richards was in his forties!

Another great player of the twenties was William M. Johnston (see Plate 66). Being only 5 ft. 8 in. tall and weighing but 130 pounds, he was known as "Little Bill" Johnston, in contrast to "Big Bill" Tilden, who stood 6 ft. 1 in. and weighed 165 pounds. This relatively frail man had one of the most tremendous forehand drives in tennis history, made with the longest swing of any player. Johnston actually swung his racket completely around his head like a whip when making his forehand drive. Most opponents found its thunderous speed simply unplayable, and were blown off the court in straight sets. Johnston was also one of the most decisive of high-volleyers.

And so we come to William T. Tilden himself (see Plate 65), universally acknowledged by sports experts and tennis authorities as the greatest player of them all. Tilden attempted a very difficult thing: to master every stroke of the game and every method of play, and in groundstrokes to become equally adept at topspin and undercut. He succeeded, but went through years of defeat on the way. Hence he did not win his first American singles championship until he was 27 years of age, in 1920. He won this title seven times in all, six years in a row, and in doing so he played against the greatest competition any champion has even had. After he was 34 years of age, the two great Frenchmen, Cochet and Lacoste, were able to defeat him; yet he won his last American singles championship at 36, and then won the Wimbledon title at 37.

Tilden possessed one of the greatest services in the history of tennis; he had one of the greatest forehand drives; his forehand chop was hardly surpassed even by Wallace Johnson; his backhand groundstroke was the greatest ever seen, equally wonderful with topspin or with undercut (since he used mostly his slice in his later years, the younger sports writers were sometimes unaware that he had formerly shown the greatest of all backhand topspin drives); his drop shot (just over the net) equaled those of Ramillon and George Lott; his stamina and courage were outstanding; he was an expert volleyer and half-volleyer; Dr. Hawk ranked him as the greatest of all court-coverers, and one of the leading strategists.

After Tilden appeared to be through as a player, he turned professional and seemed to be rejuvenated! He swept Cochet off the court, and scored an overwhelming series of victories over Kozeluh, Nusslein, and Richards, the other leading professionals. He won the American professional singles championship for the last time in 1935, when 42 years of age.

During Tilden's last amateur years, three great French players appeared: Henri Cochet, René Lacoste, and Jean Borotra. From 1924 to 1932 the French singles championship was won by one or another of these Three Musketeers, and the same thing was true of Wimbledon from 1924 to 1929. Lacoste and Cochet also won the American singles crown. Of these three major championships, Borotra won four times, Lacoste six times, and Cochet seven times.

Lacoste was one of the very greatest defensive players, a tireless retriever and wonderful court-coverer, an extremely accurate baseline driver who was noted especially for his backhand. He was also a keen student of opponents and ranked highly among the great strategists. As a baseliner he was supreme during his playing years.

Exactly the opposite was Jean Borotra, the Bounding Basque, who might justly be called the Douglas Fairbanks of the tennis courts. He rushed to the net at all times, and Tilden rates him as the greatest all-around net player, surpassing Richards and McLoughlin. He is universally acknowledged as the greatest high-volleyer in the history of the game, and no player excelled him in the leaping smash.

Borotra holds the distinction of being admittedly the greatest *indoor* tennis player of all time. He used to make business trips to the United States in alternate years, and he won the American indoor singles championship in 1925, 1927, 1929, and 1931. In 1948, with Marcel Bernard, he won the American indoor doubles championship, and he was then in his fiftieth year! He truly deserves to be called a super-athlete!

The third Musketeer of France, Henri Cochet, was considered by Tilden to be one of the authentic geniuses of tennis. Cochet was the shortest great player (5 ft. 6 in.) and had the most bewildering game of any. He had copied the mid-court half-volleying game of Dick Williams, but instead of Williams's great service he had a soft service that looked easy to hit, and instead of Williams's lightning backhand drive he had a backhand that seemed defensive and weak. His forehand drive, however, though not extremely fast, was taken off the rising bounce and often sharply angled; it was used very effectively. As a low-volleyer, Tilden ranked him second only to Vincent Richards, and as a half-volleyer the greatest in tennis history.

From 1926 to 1932 Cochet won the French singles championship in every alternate year, and in the Davis Cup matches he was unbeatable on the French clay courts—until his invincibility was ended by the marvelous play of Ellsworth Vines. Cochet's game had something of the "magical" quality seen in the play of Richard Williams.

Ellsworth Vines (see Plate 67) won his first American singles title at the age of 18. After conquering Cochet on the Frenchman's own clay court, he defeated him in straight sets on grass in the final of the American singles championship. According to Tilden, he had the greatest service *and* the greatest forehand drive in the history of tennis.

Vines had also a fast backhand drive, and was a decisive volleyer. He resembled Dick Williams in one respect: he hit very flat, net-skimming drives. Thus a slight lessening of accuracy would cause many of his drives to hit the net. With full control, his service and drives, according to expert opinion, constituted the most devastatingly destructive armament ever displayed by a tennis player. When Vines demolished Austin in the Wimbledon final, when he annihilated Cochet at Forest Hills, and when he blasted Perry off the court in their second New York match as professionals, Vines produced a game of such overwhelming power and accuracy that critics said they had never seen its equal.

After Vines turned pro, Fred Perry ruled the amateur world for about four years, winning French, English, and American singles crowns. He was a wonderful all-court player, with a forehand drive that Tilden rated second only to that of Vines. Made with the Continental grip, it lacked the terrific speed produced by Vines, Johnston, Hunter, and Tilden. But Perry was a wonder at returning wide balls and hitting on the run. He was a clever strategist, had marvelous stamina, and covered the court like an antelope. On a short ball, he often followed a running drive to the net for a winning volley.

From about this time, amateur male players began to turn pro as soon as they won a couple of national championships. The first of these later great players was Donald Budge, who became the first man to win the Australian, French, English, and American singles titles in one year. He had a game of great power, with a wonderful service, a backhand drive second only to Tilden's, a terrific smash, great stamina, and the highest day-after-day standard of play (according to Tilden) of any player. Budge was at his best when he hit his forehand drive naturally, from an open stance, instead of restricting his power by turning sideways and crossing his left foot over, as in his later losing matches with Riggs. Tilden rated Budge as the third hardest hitter in tennis, after Kovacs and Vines. This Frank Kovacs, incidentally, was a puzzle. He often looked like the greatest player in the world, seeming to have everything: service, forehand and backhand drives, volley and smash, developed to a superlative degree. Yet he would lose. He was certainly never rated highly in match-temperament, and seemed unable to concentrate on the game with real seriousness. However, after turning pro, he did win the national professional doubles title three times.

After Budge joined the pros, Robert Riggs was the amateur leader for several years. A short player, with turned-out feet, he was rated by Tilden as the greatest baseliner of all, surpassing Nusslein, Kozeluh, and Lacoste. In accuracy, Tilden rated him first; in court-covering, second only to Perry; in match-temperament, second only to Frank Hunter; and as a tactician, second only to Norman Brookes. However, he had no great strokes. Power players like Vines, Budge, and Kramer at their best would beat Riggs; but when they began to falter in their later years, as Budge did, Riggs would emerge the victor through his tireless retrieving and accurate placements.

Next came Jack Kramer, who in 1947 won the Wimbledon singles, the Wimbledon doubles, the American singles, and the American doubles titles. When he turned pro, he defeated Riggs by a wide margin in a series of matches. Then Richard Gonzales won the American amateur singles crown twice, and when he turned pro Kramer defeated him by a wide margin. Then Frank Sedgman, a superlative volleyer, won the Wimbledon singles, and twice took the American singles crown. Turning pro, he also was beaten by Kramer in a series of matches. As a pro, Kramer developed the net attack to its ultimate degree of power. From 1948 to 1953 no professional appeared who could defeat him.

After Kramer quit the game, Gonzalez, matured and improved, decisively defeated Sedgman, Trabert, Rosewall, and Hoad. As an amateur, Lewis Hoad had previously won the Australian, French, English, and American singles titles in one year.

Finally, Rodney Laver won these four major singles titles in 1962. Then he, also, turned pro. In 1968, when the Wimbledon tournament was opened, for the first time, to both amateurs and professionals, Rod Laver became the first player to win the men's championship; and he successfully defended that title in 1969. Moreover, in 1969 he duplicated his 1962 feat of winning the Australian, French, Wimbledon, and American singles titles in the same year, thus becoming the first player to make this Grand Slam *twice.*"

Meanwhile, Roy Emerson of Australia, remaining an amateur, won 12 major national single titles in seven years, a male record. In 1968, Arthur Ashe won both the American Amateur Singles Championship and the new American Open Singles Championship.

In tennis, doubles and singles are two different games. George Lott has been called the world's best *doubles* player. His twist service, excellent volleying, quick-dipping drives and dink-shots, masked lob, and knowledge of doubles strategy were especially well suited to the team game. He won more major doubles championships than anyone else.

Among other players who specialized in doubles may be mentioned Jacques Brugnon, Wilmer Allison, John Van Ryn, Randolph Lycett, John Bromwich, Lester Stoefen, Perrine Rockafellow, and William Aydelotte.

Looking back over this concise survey of men's tennis, I find that five names stand out: first, Tilden; after him, for consistent greatness, Budge and Kramer; and for unequalled heights of brilliance, Vines and Williams.

Among the women players, four names are outstanding: Lenglen, Wills, Marble, and Connolly. Though often photographed in rather acrobatic poses, Suzanne Lenglen's game was actually one of extreme accuracy. For years she was unbeatable in France and England, and then turned pro. She collected 21 major national championships in singles or doubles.

Helen Wills won her first American singles title at 17, and at 18 won the Olympic singles championship. She holds the singles record with 19 major national championships. Her total of 29 major titles in singles or doubles was the record until Brough and Osborne (see chart). For a period of 6 years, Helen Wills never lost even a *set* (much less a match) to any woman player; she seldom allowed even four games in a set. For consistent power and accuracy on both forehand and backhand, her driving has never been equalled by any woman player. She also had the best feminine service of her time.

Alice Marble won 5 national singles crowns and 12 national doubles titles and then turned pro. She had a wonderful service, and was superior to Helen Wills as a volleyer and smasher.

Maureen Connolly, a shorter player, possessed the most solid baseline-driving game since Helen Wills. She won her first national singles title at 16, and in 1935 she won the Australian, French, English, and American singles crowns, the only woman to do this. While still in her teens, she won two French, three English, and three American national singles championships. She then suffered an injury that ended her career.

The tennis writers of 1955 ranked the women players thus: first,

Helen Wills; second, Alice Marble; third, Maureen Connolly; fourth, Suzanne Lenglen; fifth, Pauline Betz; sixth, Helen Jacobs; seventh, Molla Mallory.

The most successful singles player in recent years has been Margaret Smith, the Australian, who has chalked up 12 national singles victories since 1960. In 1967, Billie Moffitt (now better known as Billie Jean King) won the American singles, women's doubles, and mixed doubles titles, as well as the Wimbledon singles, women's doubles, and mixed doubles titles. In 1968 she won the first open Women's Singles Championship at Wimbledon.

A word should be said about the great *doubles* players. Elizabeth Ryan was long regarded as the greatest woman doubles player, having won 23 national championships in England and America with more than a dozen different partners. Sarah Palfrey was a superb doubles player, winning 15 national championships outdoors and 5 indoors. Hazel Hotchkiss (better known as Mrs. Hazel Wightman) won 13 national doubles titles outdoors and 15 indoors, in a career covering 35 years, from 1909 to 1943.

But the greatest of all women doubles players were Louise Brough and Margaret Osborne. Playing together, they won 17 national women's doubles titles, taking the American championship in nine successive years! Louise Brough won 25 national doubles crowns and 6 singles; Margaret Osborne won 28 doubles and 6 singles. Winning her first national championship in 1941, Margaret Osborne won her last in 1962. In these 22 years, she won 34 national championships in singles or doubles. (See chart.)

In *indoor* tennis, Nancy Chaffee won the American singles and doubles titles for three successive years, 1950 to 1952.

Mary Kendall Browne owns the distinction of having been a leading tennis player and a leading golfer at the same time. She won the American singles tennis crown for three straight years, 1912 to 1914. In 1924 she reached the final of the American national amateur golf championship, and in 1925 she won the American national women's doubles tennis championship.

Among the more recent multiple winners in singles and doubles should be mentioned Doris Hart, Shirley Fry, Althea Gibson, Darlene Hard, and Maria Bueno.

What women players have *men* most enjoyed watching, or considered outstanding for beauty or grace or charm of personality? These names have probably been most often mentioned: Alice Marble, Gertrude Moran, Kay Stammers, Eileen Bennett, Evelyn Colyer, and Lili de Alvarez.

As for the most beautiful of all *strokes*, not the greatest in attacking power, but those which, in rhythmic smoothness and linear perfection, most satisfy the eye, my own choice would be the service of John Doeg, the forehand drive of Henry Austin, the backhand drive of Jack Crawford, the volley of Vincent Richards, and the smash of John Doeg. The service and smash of Doeg, it should be added, did have tremendous speed as well as perfection of form. The same was true of the smash of Maurice Jackson. Perfect form was also combined with great power in the forehand drive of Gerald Patterson.

In regard to perfect form, it needs to be pointed out that the super-athletes of tennis, in actual match play, do not usually adopt the sideways stance that has for years been taught, in tennis manuals and clinics, as correct form for the forehand drive. When they do sometimes use a closed stance, with its restriction of body rotation, they are likely to put the ball into the net and then wonder why. The ideal footwork and body position for a powerful forehand drive are best shown in the movie-strip of Gerald Patterson in Parmly Paret's book *Mechanics of the Game* (which also has movies of the perfect volleying of Vincent Richards). Cochet's book on tennis also has a movie-strip of his forehand drive which shows the proper footwork and body position. The movie of Bruce Barnes in Dick Bradlee's book *Instant Tennis* is also good. Everyone interested in this subject should study the articles by Harwood White in *Tennis* magazine from January to March 1932, and in *American Lawn Tennis* from November 1948 to April 1949, and also June 1950. The first step in the development of super-athletes should be professional instruction based on a knowledge of anatomical and mechanical *facts* instead of on the thoughtless repetition of traditional theories that are at variance with the actualities of match play.

In recent years, owing to the influence of Jack Kramer, tennis has suffered a change that is causing much concern. The leading male players have, one and all, gone back to the 1912 net-rushing game of Maurice McLoughlin. This game was exciting when pitted against a baseline game, a mid-court game, or an all-court game. But with everyone playing it, the result is a monotonous succession of serves and volleys from which spectators can learn nothing about the real game of tennis. The great all-court game exemplified by Wilding, Johnston, Tilden, Crawford, von Cramm, Perry, Vines, and Budge, with its exciting baseline rallies, its sudden changes of pace and depth, its variety of spins, its miracles of court covering and retrieving, and its fascinating strategical maneuvers, has been replaced by "just a mad dash followed by a fine reflex action." Reflecting on the true greatness of this sport and its wonderful history, recalling the thousands of men and women who have been thrilled by the marvelous court-covering and retrieving of Tilden, Perry, Riggs, Kozeluh, Manuel Alonzo, Sidney Wood, and Bryan Grant, one realizes what a tragedy this is. But the balance of the game can be restored, so that spectators can again thrill to the spectacular retriever as well as to the spectacular volleyer and smasher, by saying goodbye to the fast grass court, and standardizing tournament play on a slower clay or composition surface. Or if grass must remain, a slower tennis ball should be manufactured and used. Since doubles (which is essentially a net game) would still remain for the big serve-and-volley boys, not to mention indoor singles play on wood, there is every reason why this needed change of playing surface, or ball, should be made, and with as little delay as possible. One of the clearest indications of Tilden's supremacy is the fact that, in addition to winning the American National Singles Championship seven times, on grass, he also won the American Clay Court Singles Championship six years in succession.

RECORD NUMBER OF WINS IN OUTDOOR NATIONAL CHAMPIONSHIPS FROM 1897 TO 1969

Championship	Men		Women	
Australian Singles	Roy Emerson	6	Margaret Smith	7
	Jack Crawford	4	Nancye Wynne	6
French Singles	Max Decugis	8	Suzanne Lenglen	6
	Henri Cochet	5	Mlle. Masson	5
English Singles	Hugh Doherty	5	Helen Wills	8
	Rodney Laver	4	Dorothy Douglass	7
	Anthony Wilding	4		
	Reginald Doherty	4		
American Singles	William Tilden	7	Molla Mallory*	8
	William Larned	7	Helen Wills	7
	Rodney Laver	3		
	Frederick Perry	3		
	Malcolm Whitman	3		
All Four Singles	Roy Emerson	12	Helen Wills	19
	Rodney Laver	11	Margaret Smith	16
English Doubles (Straight or Mixed)	Hugh Doherty	8	Elizabeth Ryan	19
	Reginald Doherty	8	Louise Brough	9
	Randolph Lycett	6	Suzanne Lenglen	9
American Doubles (Straight or Mixed)	William Tilden	9	Margaret Osborne	22
	George Lott	8	Louise Brough	16
All Four Doubles	George Lott	11	Margaret Osborne	28
	William Tilden	10	Louise Brough	25
	Hugh Doherty	10		
	Reginald Doherty	10		
All Eight Championships	William Tilden	20	Margaret Osborne	34
	Roy Emerson	16	Louise Brough	31

*Molla Mallory's 8 American titles include the Patriotic Championship that was substituted for the regular National Championship in 1917 because of the war.

10a. BADMINTON

The origin of badminton is said to have been in India, hundreds of years ago. The game may be described as a miniaturized form of tennis, played with a shuttlecock instead of a ball, confined to volleying, and demanding the utmost of agility and quickness. From India the game was brought to England in the 1860s. Its present name comes from that of the residence of the Duke of Beaufort in Gloucestershire, at which venue in England it was first played. Up until 1893, when the first Badminton Association was formed, the rules of the game were somewhat variable and unstandardized, but from that time on the game increased in uniformity and popularity. About that time, also, it came to be played in the United States. By 1930, badminton was well on the way to becoming an international game, with national championships being held in Australia, Denmark, India, Malaya, Norway, Sweden, Mexico, the Netherlands, and the United States. Today badminton is a well-organized sport, with world and national competitions held yearly. Our space here will be given mainly to a review of the respective championships of a man who was possibly the greatest badminton player among men, and a woman who was certainly the greatest among women.

David G. Freeman, formerly of Pasadena, California, reigned supreme in amateur badminton from 1939 to 1942, and from 1947 to 1953 (from 1943 to 1946 the American championships were discontinued because of the war). During this period Freeman dominated amateur badminton as thoroughly as Bill Tilden had dominated tennis some two decades earlier. Freeman was U.S. Men's Singles Champion in 1939, 1940, 1941, 1942, 1947, 1948, and 1953; and English Men's Singles Champion in 1949. He was also U.S. Men's Doubles Champion for five years with three different partners (Chester Goss, Webster Kimball, and Wynn Rogers).

As an example of Freeman's fantastic ability, it is said that in the middle of a rally he could drive the shuttlecock at any chosen spot and make a "bullseye." Both in accuracy of placement and in ability to retrieve, Freeman is considered to have been the greatest male badminton player produced in America, and to rank at or near the top among the greatest seen anywhere, even to the present day. Freeman was a very "colorful" player (to one spectator his game suggested the antics of a Comanche Indian war-dancer!) and only those who have watched him in action can realize how fantastically phenomenal his retrieving was. (See Plate 68.)

The outstanding player among the professionals was Jack Purcell, the Canadian. His game was based on continual attack, the exact opposite of Freeman's original game. (Dave started as a defensive player, a retriever pure and simple, and later rounded out his game with the necessary attacking strokes.) Purcell combined devastating power with consistent accuracy, and was considered the greatest all-around player in the game. When Freeman became the leading amateur, a match was finally arranged between them, and Freeman won in two straight games. In a return match, Dave won again, but this time had to go three games.

Among women exponents of the game, Judith Devlin (since 1961, Judith Devlin Hashman) stands supreme. Her record is even more remarkable than that of David Freeman. Indeed, it is probable that in no other women's sport has there been a champion who reigned so long and outstandingly.

Judith was born in 1935 at Winnepeg, Canada, and started playing badminton when she was seven years old. She had the benefit of expert coaching from her father, J. Frank Devlin, a six-time winner of the English Men's Singles Championship. Beginning in 1949, Judith won the United States Junior Girls' Singles Championship six times in a row. She also won the Junior Girls' Doubles Championship five straight years (with three different partners) and the Junior Mixed Doubles title three times.

She won her first American Women's Doubles Championship in 1953, and won the Women's Singles Crown the following year. In 1967 she won the American Women's Singles, Women's Doubles, and Mixed Doubles crowns. In these 15 years, she piled up a total of 56 national championships in the United States, England, and Canada.

Championships	United States	All-England	Canadian
Women's Singles	12	10	3
Women's Doubles	12	7	3
Mixed Doubles	8	0	1

The All-England title is considered the world's championship. In addition to the above, Judith has won the championships of Germany, Sweden, Ireland, Scotland, Jamaica, and the Netherlands. It would appear safe to say that this record of championships has never been approached by any other athlete, man or woman. Thus her record stamps her as the outstanding woman athlete of modern times in any one sport. Every year some member of the feminine sex is elected by sportswriters as the Woman Athlete of the Year, and the winner has often been a star in golf (which is hardly in the same class as badminton in respect to the *athletic* ability required); yet not once, from 1954 to 1967, has Judith Devlin Hashman been accorded this well-merited honor.

In the doubles game, Judith's sister, Susan Devlin Peard, was a player of championship caliber, having been Judith's partner in no fewer than 20 of her doubles championships.

Another outstanding woman player was Ethel Marshall, who won the American Women's Singles Championship for seven years consecutively, from 1947 to 1953.

David Freeman, incidentally, owns the distinction of having been a two-sport champion. In his teens, before he decided to concentrate on badminton, he won the American National Junior Singles Championship in tennis.

The distance record for driving a badminton "bird" or shuttlecock is held by Frank Rugani. On February 29, 1964, in San Jose, California, Rugani drove a shuttlecock 79 feet 8½ inches.

11.
Ice Skating (speed)

Ice skating, in a primitive form (using skates made of bone) is believed to have originated in Scandinavia before the beginning of the Christian era, and is mentioned in Scandinavian literature of the second century. Today it is a widespread sport, and the records in it, like those for bicycle racing, are varied and numerous. There are world and national records, outdoors and indoors, for both men and women, over distances ranging from 50 yards to 10,000 meters (about 6¼ miles). Beyond this, a few individuals have established records from 25 miles up to 100 miles. One skater—William Donovan of New York City—in March 1885 skated 1093 miles and 660 yards in 12 days, averaging over 90 miles a day! This was for a wager of $1000. The following world's records were all performed by amateurs, on *curved* tracks.* The standard racing distances in international competition are all in meters.

Table 12. World records in ice skating (outdoor, except at 75 yards)

Distance	Time	Performer	Nation	Place	Year	MPH
50 yards	0:04.4	Fred J. Robson	USA	Toronto	1916	23.24
60 yards	0:06.0	Fred J. Robson	USA	Pittsburgh	1916	20.45
75 yards	0:07.8	Fred J. Robson	USA	Pittsburgh	1916	19.70
100 yards	0:09.4	Charles Jewtraw	USA	Lake Placid	1923	21.73
220 yards	0:17.8	R. McDermott	USA	St. Paul	1961	25.28
440 yards	0:34.6	Tom Gray	USA	St. Paul	1965	26.01
880 yards	1:13.3	Andy Karanek	USA	St. Paul	1961	24.56
¾ mile	1:55.8	Clas Thunberg	Finland	Lake Placid	1926	23.31
1 mile	2:38.2	Clas Thunberg	Finland	Lake Placid	1926	22.76

*On a straightaway track, the professional skater Norval Baptie is credited with covering 440 yards in 28-1/5 seconds, 880 yards in 1 minute 2/5 second, and 1 mile in 2 minutes 8 seconds. These records were made at Lake Minnetonka, Minnesota, on December 28–29, 1898. The 440-yard record was at the speed of 31.91 mph! By many observers, Baptie was considered the greatest speed ice skater on record.

2 miles	5:33.8	E. Schroeder	USA	Minneapolis	1934	21.56
3 miles	8:19.6	Ross Robinson	USA	Lake Placid	1930	21.61
5 miles	14:16.9	R. Wurster	USA	St. Paul	1965	21.00
500 meters	0:39.5	Evgeni Grishin	USSR	Alma Ata, Russia	1963	28.31
1000 meters	1:22.8	Evgeni Grishin	USSR	Alma Ata, Russia	1955	27.01
1500 meters	2:03.9	Kees Verkerk	Holland	Inzell, Ger.	1967	27.08
3000 meters	4:26.8	Rudi Liebrecht	Holland	Oslo, Norway	1965	25.33
5000 meters	7:26.6	Kees Verkerk	Holland	Inzell, Ger.	1967	25.04
10,000 meters	15:23.6	Johnny Hoeglin	Sweden	Grenoble, Fr.	1968	24.22

One of the items of information that the foregoing table clearly shows is the inconsistency of the records at certain distances. To be in line with the records for 50 yards and 220 yards, the record for 60 yards should be *5.2 seconds;* for 75 yards, *6.4 seconds;* and for 100 yards, *8.3 seconds.* (Here is an opportunity for some present-day sprint skater to make three new records.) The table shows also that the world records over the standardized competitive distances in *meters* are considerably better than the less-strongly-contested distances in *yards.* To gain some idea of ultimate possibilities in speed, we can compare the record in the above table for 440 yards (26.01 mph) made by Tom Gray on a curved track with that for the same distance (31.91 mph) made by Norval Baptie on a straight track. It will thus be seen that Baptie's time for the quarter-mile is 31.91/26.01, or 1.227, times as fast as Gray's time. If we apply the latter multiplier to the fastest time made over a metric distance (namely, 28.31 mph for 500 meters), it would appear that on a straightaway track the 500 meters might be covered in 1.227 × 28.31, or 34.7 mph!

Among long-distance records in ice skating may be mentioned the following, made by J. F. Donohue at Stamford, Connecticut, on January 26, 1893: 25 miles, 1:31.29.0; 50 miles, 3:15.59.4; 80 miles, 5:41.55.0; and 100 miles, 7:11.38.2. In Holland, a race is held annually over a 120-mile course through 11 cities. The best time to date over this course is 7 hours 35 minutes (= 16.45 mph), made in 1954.

A popular offshoot of ice skating is barrel-jumping. A world's championship in this event is now held each year at Grossinger, New York. The "barrels" used are cylindrical, and average about 20 inches in diameter by 3 feet in length. The distance jumped is considered to be the length between the outside edges of the two end barrels. The present record in this event was made on January 9, 1965, by Kenneth Le Bel of Great Neck, New York. He cleared 17 barrels, a distance of 28 feet 8 inches. In 1967, Jacques St. Pierre came close to equalling Le

Bel's record by jumping over 16 barrels for a distance of 28 feet 3¼ inches. In making such barrel-jumps, the skaters have to attain a speed of 24–25 mph and cover a distance on the ice of 34–35 feet.

In 1910, a world record for *high*-jumping on ice skates was claimed by John Quinn, with a leap of 4 feet 3 inches. However, 13 years earlier, on December 27, 1897, the famous all-around professional athlete, R. P. Williams (who was then still an amateur) unofficially cleared a 4 foot 6 inch fence while on skates. Whether these jumps were performed using a hurdling or a scissors technique was not stated.

(See also the comparison of ice skating with roller skating, on the following pages.)

12.
Roller Skating (speed)

The sport of skating on wheels is said to have originated in Holland in the early 1800s, when someone there attached wooden discs to shoes as a warm-weather substitute for the Hollanders' favorite winter sport of ice skating on the canals. Like ice skating, roller skating can be performed either indoors or outdoors. As a competitive amateur sport it is divided into speed or racing, hockey, and artistic. Under "artistic" are the subdivisions of Singles, Pairs, Fours, and Dance; while each of these events is divided into Senior, Intermediate, Novice, and Junior categories, for both sexes. The only statistics to be considered here are the world records in speed skating. These records, at the present time, are all held by skaters from Italy and Great Britain, where evidently more attention is given to racing than is the case in the United States. Here, the emphasis has been on artistic skating. In a survey made in 1962, it was stated that in North America alone over 20,000,000 persons enjoy the sport and diversion of roller skating.

If the following records are plotted on double logarithmic graph paper—comparing the speed in miles per hour with the distance in yards (or meters converted into yards)—it will be found that between 440 yards and 25,000 meters (or 27,340 yards), a straight-line correlation results.[*] Such a correlation is a rare occurence in athletics, since there is nearly always more of a falling-off in speed with distance, due to progressive fatigue, in other events, such as running, than there is in skating.

The "predictions" in miles per hour made from an equation which expresses the relationship of time and distance in roller skating are given in the last column of Table 13. A comparison of the predicted mph with the actual mph shows that the best performances were those made by L. Faggioli of Italy, in 1957, over the distances of 1 mile, 3 miles, 1500 meters, and 5000 meters—all of which presumably were covered in the same race. The very best of these records is at 5000 meters (= 5468 yards, or about 3.1 miles), in which the expected speed is

---

[*]The predicted figures result from the formula: log mph = 1.54696 − .051262 log distance (in yards).

Table 13.   World records in roller skating

Distance	Time	Performer	Nation	Year	Miles per hour Actual	Miles per hour formula
440 yards	0:34.9	G. Cantarella	Italy	1963	25.79	25.79
880 yards	1:13.5	G. Cantarella	Italy	1963	24.49	24.89
1 mile	2:22.5	L. Faggioli	Italy	1957	25.26	24.02
3 miles	7:28.4	L. Faggioli	Italy	1957	24.08	22.71
5 miles	14:15.1	L. Faggioli	Italy	1957	21.05	22.12
500 meters	0:43.7	G. Cantarella	Italy	1963	25.59	25.51
1000 meters	1:30.0	L. Faggioli	Italy	1957	24.85	24.61
1500 meters	2:12.4	L. Faggioli	Italy	1957	25.35	24.11
5000 meters	7:44.9	L. Faggioli	Italy	1957	24.06	22.67
10,000 meters	16:54.5	G. Venanzi	Italy	1947	22.05	21.87
15,000 meters	26:16.7	G. Venanzi	Italy	1947	21.41	21.42
20,000 meters	33:30.0	V. Pelizzari	Italy	1956	22.25	21.11
25,000 meters	44:40.1	V. Pelizzari	Italy	1956	20.87	20.87
30,000 meters	54:10.8	L. Woodley	Gt. Brit.	1960	20.64	**20.67**
50,000 meters	1:41:0.1	L. Goodchild	Gt. Brit.	1960	18.45	20.14
100,000 meters	3:23:42.0	L. Goodchild	Gt. Brit.	1960	18.30	19.44

22.665 mph, whereas Faggioli actually did 24.06 mph—or over 6 percent better. Such a difference indicates phenomenal ability.

A similar straight-line correlation results when the records in *ice* skating are plotted on graph paper. In fact, the whole series of records in both forms of skating show a remarkably similar trend. The record speeds in ice skating are, on the average, better than those in roller skating at the shorter distances, indicating that the ice skater is able to "get under way" quicker than the roller skater. The maximum superiority of the ice skater would appear to be at about 420 yards, where he is about 40 yards ahead of the roller skater. From there on, the roller skater gradually (so gradually that it takes him over 60 miles to do it!) overtakes the ice skater, until at 100,000 meters (= 62.137 miles) the two racers are theoretically neck-and-neck. The speed attained by champion roller skaters is a revelation to the average sports-follower, who in nearly every case assumes ice skating to be considerably faster.

Away back on October 22, 1893, Frank Delmont roller-skated 50 miles in 2 hours 47 minutes 45 seconds, at Buenos Aires, Argentina (= 17.88 mph). The theoretical expectation in speed today for this distance would be 19.66 mph, or 50 miles in 2 hours 32 minutes 37 seconds. The greatest recorded distance in 24 hours of roller skating is 281 miles 1006 yards, by Robert Wheeler, at Denver, Colorado, February 1917.

13.
Rowing and Sculling

Competitive rowing, using eight-man crews, has long been a classic annual event between Harvard and Yale Universities. The first race, which took place in 1852, was over a distance of 2 miles, in which Harvard won by about two lengths. From 1855 to 1875 inclusive, the distance rowed was 3 miles, and during that period Harvard won 11 times to Yale's 3 times, there being 7 years in which no races were held. From 1876 to 1966 inclusive, rowing honors between the two collegiate crews have been about evenly divided. During all this time, with only three exceptions, the races have been over a distance of 4 miles. Since 1952, the racing has taken place on Onondaga Lake, Syracuse, New York. The best time over a four-mile course was made by the University of California crew in 1939, on the Hudson River near Poughkeepsie, New York. The time was 18 minutes 12.6 seconds—an average speed of 13.18 mph. However, the speed attained in tidal or flowing (river) water is always subject to question. The highest recorded speed recorded by an eight-man rowing crew in lake water is 13.50 mph over a 2000-meter (just under 1¼ miles) course. This record (of 5 minutes 30.7 seconds) was made by the University of British Columbia crew on Lake Ontario, in August, 1962.

For comparison, in England there have been the epic annual races between Oxford and Cambridge Universities, which began away back in 1829. From the latter year to 1965 inclusive, there have been 111 races between the two universities, with Cambridge winning 61 and Oxford 50. The standard course for this race has for a long time been on the Thames River from Putney to Mortgate, a distance (upstream) of 4¼ miles. So important is this annual clash between English varsity crews that crowds numbering over a hundred thousand line the banks of the river. The best time over this course is 17 minutes 50 seconds, in a race in 1948 in which Cambridge won over Oxford by 5 lengths. The speed of the winning crew averaged 14.30 mph, which strongly suggests that the *tide* was moving in the same direction as the oarsmen.

The fastest time made by an eight-man rowing crew in England over what is known as the Henley Course (= 1 mile, 550 yards) is 6 minutes 16 seconds, made in 1965 by the Ratzeburger Club of Germany. This record, which has come down from 6:43 in 1961, 6:40 in 1962, 6:38 in 1963, and 6:25 in 1965, indicates a plausible speed of 12.59 mph.

The best single sculls record over the standard distance of 4¼ miles would appear to be 19 minutes 46 seconds, made by R. Hadfield in New Zealand on January 5, 1922. This is at the rate of 12.90 mph. In 1966, in the world championships at Bled, Yugoslavia, the 2000-meter single sculls race was won by Don Spero, of the New York Athletic Club, in the rather slow time of 7 minutes 5.92 seconds (= 10.52 MPH). Over the "dash" distance of 440 yards, there is a record of 57 seconds flat, made by Edward Healy, of Newark, New Jersey, in 1891. This equals 15.789 MPH—a truly remarkable speed for a single sculler.

It has long been recognized that a 4-mile crew rowing race constitutes one of the most grueling tests known in athletics. Such a race means sustained effort at high speed over an average period of close to 20 minutes, with no chance for even a moment's respite. With an 8-man crew, the number of strokes made in the starting spurt is 38 or 40 per minute, settling down to 32 or so over most of the distance, and increasing to 38 or 40 for a brief dash at the finish. Some championship crews have gone to 42 strokes, but could maintain that pace for only a brief period. C. S. Titus of New York, who was single sculls champion in 1902 and 1906, set a record in the latter year by reaching 48 strokes per minute. In the Royal Henley Regatta at London in July, 1936, a new world's record for stroking was set by the Japanese Olympic crew with a fantastic 56.

Experience has shown that the best oarsmen for speed as well as endurance are not powerfully-muscled heavyweights, but rather men of middle to lightheavyweight size. Edward Hanlan of Canada, who in 1882 became recognized as the single sculls champion, and was renowned for his perfection of rowing technique, stood 68.7 inches in height and weighed 166 pounds. The average height of Harvard oarsmen (senior class) over a period of years in the 1930s was found to be 71¼ inches, and the average weight 169 pounds. The heaviest crew on record was said to be the Bowdoin (Maine) College crew of 1891, which averaged 181 pounds; however, the men were lacking in speed.

Turning from racing speed to prolonged rowing endurance, a number of spectacular long-distance feats are on record. On May 12, 1877, C. A. Barnard of Chicago rowed, in a single scull, 50 miles in 8 hours 55 minutes. And away back on August 13, 1832, John Williams, in a single scull, rowed 91 miles in 11 hours 29 minutes 3 seconds. Of these two performances, that by Williams would appear to be decidedly the better, since he rowed 91 miles at 7.924 mph, while Barnard rowed "only" 50 miles at 5.607 mph.

A far more prolonged test of rowing endurance was that performed by two Norwegians, George Harbo and Frank Samuelsen. Leaving the harbor of New York City on June 6, 1896, these two rugged seamen* *rowed* across the Atlantic! Their boat, the *Fox*, was only a little over 18 feet long by 5 feet wide, and carried no mast nor sails. After a voyage that lasted 55 days and covered 3250 miles, they landed safely at the port of St. Mary's, Scilly Isles (off southwest England), having accomplished the extraordinary feat of crossing the Atlantic without benefit of sails.

Sixty years later, a single individual "rowed" across the Atlantic, although in this case sails as well as oars were used, and the voyage was from east to west. On October 20, 1956, Hannes Lindemann, a German doctor, embarked from the port of Las Palmas in the Canary Islands, and after a voyage of 72 days in a vessel only 17 feet long arrived in the harbor of Phillipsburg on the island of St. Martin, in the West Indies, a distance of over 2000 miles. During the entire trip, not once did Lindemann stand up in his small boat, and so constant were the perils from the sea and the weather that he was rarely able to sleep for longer than a half-hour at a time. He was one of the few men on record to cross the Atlantic in so small a craft, by himself, and with no outside assistance.

Another, and more recent, instance of a two-man team rowing across the Atlantic was when, in 1966, two British paratroopers stationed in the United States decided to row home to England. After weeks of preparation, and obtaining leave from the Army (without pay), Captain John Ridgway and Sergeant Chay Blyth took off from the inlet at Orleans on Cape Cod, in a 20-foot dory, the *English Rose III*. They left at 5:30 P.M. on June 4, 1966, and arrived on the west coast of Ireland on September 3, after an exhausting but lucky voyage taking some 91 days. David Johnstone and John Hoare, two other British oarsmen who had taken off two weeks earlier from Virginia Beach, Va., in a 15-foot rowboat, *The Puffin*, were never heard from again.

An interesting—but very much shorter—feat of rowing was when, on August 10, 1950, Peter Ross of England paddled his kayak across the English Channel (21 miles, at the narrowest point) from France to Dover in 4 hours 7 minutes. More remarkable still was when, in 1952, Georges Adam—a Frenchman 71 years of age—rowed from France to England and then back again to France within a period of 24 hours!

---

*Actually, the two men were clam-diggers, who worked in the clam beds along the north shore of New Jersey.

14.
Walking, or Pedestrianism

Of all physical activities, walking is the one most universally engaged in. From childhood to old age, and despite all the conveyances that man has invented to eliminate the need for walking, that need still exists. Most Americans walk entirely too little, and it is gratifying to note that a revival of the neglected art of pedestrianism is now taking place in this country. Since *some* bodily exercise is essential for the maintenance of even a fair state of health, walking offers one of the most convenient and natural means of meeting that need.

The records that have been made in competitive walking are numerous and diversified. While over short distances a surprising degree of speed can be attained, when cross-country walking is engaged in speed becomes secondary to prolonged *endurance*.

It should be interesting to compare the miles per hour in the right-hand column of the following table with the pace of the average person. The usual length of a pace, or forward step, in a man of average size has long been assumed as 30 inches. In Roman times, a "pace" was taken as the length of *two* ordinary steps, and equalled five Roman feet or 58.2 inches. Thus a single Roman step was 29.1 inches. As the average-sized Roman soldier measured only 168 cm (= 66.14 in.) in height, it is seen that the ratio of his step to his height was 29.1/66.14, or 44 percent. If we apply this ratio to the height of the average U.S. man of today, which is 69 inches, we find that a single pace equals 30.36 inches. However, as leg length increases faster than does total height, it works out that today's 69-inch man has, on the average, a stride about 44⅔ percent of his height, or 30.8 inches. As a single step in ordinary walking takes about ½ a second, there will be 120 steps per minute, and the rate of walking, in our 69-inch-tall man, will be 3½ MPH, or a mile in 17 min. 8 sec.

In comparison, a champion heel-and-toe speed walker, as seen in Table 14, is able to cover a quarter-mile at the extraordinary clip of

Distance, miles	Time	Performer	Nation	Place	Year	MPH
¼	1:22.5	F. H. Creamer	New Zealand	Auckland, N.Z.	1897	10.91
½	2:59.0	G. H. Goulding	Canada	Winnipeg, Man.	1909	10.06*
1	6:18.3	Ronald L. Zinn	USA	New York, N.Y.	1962	9.52
2	13:02.4	S. F. Vickers	Gt. Brit.	London, Eng.	1960	9.22
3	20:49.8	G. H. Goulding	Canada	Brooklyn, N.Y.	1912	8.64
4	28:06.2	G. H. Goulding	Canada	Brooklyn, N.Y.	1912	8.54
5	35:48.4	Ugo Frigerio	Italy	New York, N.Y.	1925	8.38
6	43:09.8	Ugo Frigerio	Italy	New York, N.Y.	1925	8.34
7	48:23.0	K. J. Matthews	Gt. Brit.	Coldfield, Eng.	1964	8.68
8	58:15.8	Ronald O. Laird	USA	Walnut, Calif.	1964	8.24
9	1:05:45.6	Ronald O. Laird	USA	Walnut, Calif.	1964	8.21
10	1:13:17.6	Ronald O. Laird	USA	Walnut, Calif.	1964	8.19
20	2:38:27.0	R. Hardy	Gt. Brit.	Sheffield, Eng.	1956	7.57
30	4:00:46.8	G. Klimov	USSR	Moscow, Russia	1964	7.47
52	8:11:14.0	H. V. L. Ross	Gt. Brit.	Brighton, Eng.	1909	6.35
100	18:04:10.2	T. E. Hammond	Gt. Brit.	London, Eng.	1908	5.53
131	23:57:10.0	T. E. Hammond	Gt. Brit.	London, Eng	1908	5.47

* On July 6, 1952, at Randall's Island, Henry Laskau of New York, was credited with walking a half-mile in 2 min. 48.2 sec. (= 10.70 mph). While this mark was regarded by some officials as "a physical impossibility," it appears to have been accepted by the A.A.U. If the record is correct, it surpasses all other marks over short distances. Compared with Goulding's 1909 record, Laskau's mark is over 6 percent faster.

nearly 11 MPH!* If it be assumed that such a walker uses a step 46 inches in length, it follows that he must take about 250 steps per minute, as compared with the 120 steps of the ordinary pedestrian. Thus, through training, the fastest walker is able to cover the ground about 3 *times as fast* as an ordinary walker. He accomplishes this by lengthening his stride by about 50 percent, and the frequency, or rapidity, of his steps by over 100 percent.

When the records in walking, over various distances, are plotted on a graph, it is surprising to note the almost uniform ratio that exists between them and the records in running over the same distances (above one mile). Roughly expressed, the possibilities of speed in middle-distance running average about 60 percent greater than those in walking. In the latter activity, fatigue increases with distance at a slightly greater rate than it does in running, where a more relaxed effort is possible. As a result, the records in walking over short distances are relatively better, and over long distances relatively poorer, than those over the same distances in running.

In addition to the records over distances in miles, as given in Table 14, in Europe the customary measurement is in meters (or kilometers). Over distances of 7, 8 and 9 kilometers the records are held by Ugo Frigerio, of Italy, with times of 31:16.6, 35:35.6, and 40:10.8, respectively. These marks were made in a race in New York City on March 28, 1925. They are all about on a par with Frigerio's records at 5 and 6 miles (see Table 14) made on the same date. At 10 kilometers (= 6.214 miles), Frigerio made a record on the aforementioned date of 44:38.0. This time was materially lowered in 1958 (May 7) to 42:18.3 by the Russian walker, Grigory Panichkin, at Stalinabad. Two days later, Panichkin set a record at 20 kilometers (= 12.427 miles) of 1:27:38.6. Panichkin's 10-kilometer walk was at the rate of 8.81 mph, and his 20-kilometer walk 8.50 mph. Both walks were phenomenal performances. On September 15, 1959, V. Golubrichiy, of the USSR, beat Panichkin's 20-kilometer record by covering the distance in 1:26:31.2 (= 8.62 mph).

In view of Panichkin's and Golubrichiy's fairly recent records at 10 and 20 kilometers, and Laskau's claimed record at ½ mile, it would seem that all the other marks listed in Table 14—from ¼ mile to 20 miles, at least—are subject to substantial improvement.

The greatest distance so far covered in a single hour of race walking

---

*However, over the "sprinting" distance of 100 yards, a record of only 12-3/5 seconds was established by Dr. Harry Klink, at the age of 68! This equals 16.23 mph, or appreciably faster than Jim Ryun's *running* speed over one mile! While the walking record for ¼ mile is only 54 percent as fast as the record for the ¼-mile run, Dr. Klink's walking record for 100 yards is over 72 percent as fast as the present world record (9.1 sec.) in the 100 yard dash.

is 8 miles, 474 yards, by the English walker A. G. Pope, in 1932.° This record (of 8.2693 mph) is accordingly a bit better than that listed in Table 14 for 8 miles (= 8.2384 mph), which was made by Ronald Laird in 1964. Better, however, than either of these records, when the *date* of performance is taken into consideration, is the mark of 8 miles, 438 yards in an hour set by the great English walker, G. E. Larner, on September 30, 1905. This was at the rate of 8.2489 mph.

Listed below are some miscellaneous performances in long-distance walking, along with some records over standard distances as achieved by *professional* race-walkers. The records of the latter should be compared with the *amateur* world records listed in Table 14. No particular order of listing has been attempted, except that, in general, a chronological sequence is observed.

1. One of the first widely-publicized performances in prolonged walking was that undertaken by Captain Barclay Allardyce, of Ury, Scotland. Away back in 1809, Captain Barclay, as he was called, wagered £1000 that he could walk 1000 miles within 1000 hours. The terms of the wager were that, regardless of the weather, Barclay would walk a mile every hour for 1000 consecutive hours. This he managed to accomplish, obtaining his rests during the periods following each mile's walk. Starting his race-track walk on June 1, he completed the 1000 miles on July 12, 41 days later. By assiduously placing bets on himself, the Scotsman managed to win something like $100,000 as a result of his epoch-making walk. Barclay had begun his great walking career in 1801 by walking 90 miles over a measured mile on a turnpike road in 21 hours, 22 minutes, 4 seconds. He was trained by a Mr. Smith, a Yorkshire farmer, who made Barclay live on raw meat and "hard" food, and do all sorts of rough work. One task was to send Barclay to market with a heavy load of cheese and butter on his shoulder, and allow him only 1½ hours to go 10 miles with this weight.

2. A famous early-day American walker was John Chapman ("Johnny Appleseed"). Chapman, who was born about 1775 and died in 1847, wandered for some 40 years over the states of Ohio, Indiana and Illinois helping to establish nurseries and orchards.

3. One of the first professional "pedestrians" in the United States was Edward Payson Weston (1839–1929), who in 1861 walked from his home in Boston to Washington, D.C., to attend the first inauguration of President Lincoln. His career as a professional cross-country walker began

---

°Unofficially, in 1959, the Russian walker, Gregory Panichkin, covered within an hour 8 miles, 1294 yards (= 8.7352 mph).

in 1867 when he walked from Portland, Maine, to Chicago—a distance of 1326 miles—in just under 26 days. In doing this, he won a wager of $10,000. During this walk Weston established his best record for a single day: 82 miles. On a later walk he covered 107 miles without a rest, in 22 hrs. 30 min. In 1879 he walked 550 miles in approximately 142 hours. For this he was awarded the Astley Belt as the world's champion walker. In 1883 he walked 5000 miles in 100 days. In 1909, at the age of 70, he walked from New York to San Francisco, a distance of 3895 miles, in 105 days, averaging about 37 miles a day. The following year he walked back to New York from Los Angeles (3483 miles) in only 77 days. In 1914, when he was 75, he walked from New York to Minneapolis, a distance of 1546 miles, in 61 days. One of his most noteworthy feats was to walk 1977½ miles over the turnpike roads of Great Britain, in 1000 consecutive hours, thus cutting in half the time required to cover a given distance as established in 1809 by Captain Barclay. Weston was originally a newspaperman, and in many of the towns he stopped in on his cross-country walks he delivered lectures on temperance. At the age of 88, still walking, he was struck by a taxicab and crippled. Except for this accident, he might have lived even longer than the 90 years he reached.

4. A contemporary of Weston was Dan O'Leary, who was originally a Chicago book salesman (what ideal training for a walker!). In 1875, at the age of 33, O'Leary walked 116 miles in 23 hours, 12 minutes, averaging exactly 5 mph. This was a little faster than when Weston had walked 107 miles (in 22½ hrs.). In 1902, when he was 60, O'Leary covered the 187 miles between Boston and Albany in 45 hours flat. Two years later, he walked from New York City to Toronto, Canada, a distance of 535 miles, in exactly 9 days. How much time was taken off for resting during these two performances was not stated, but in the 187-mile walk it could not have been much. In 1921, on his 79th birthday, O'Leary walked 100 miles continuously in 23 hours, 54 minutes! Whether this was within a single day was not stated.

5. A worthy successor to O'Leary was James H. Hocking of Teaneck, New Jersey. In 1920, at the age of 64, Hocking lowered O'Leary's record from New York to Toronto by covering the distance in 8 days, 3 hours. Another of the marks set by O'Leary which Hocking surpassed (in 1922) was the 187 miles between Boston and Albany, which distance Hocking covered in 42 hours, 15 minutes. In 1921, Hocking set a new record over the steep, 90-mile Mohawk Trail from Albany, New York, to Greenfield, Mass., by covering the distance in 20 hours, 30 minutes. Like Weston and O'Leary, Hocking made many walking records over various dis-

tances. No useful end would be served by quoting them all here, even if all the statistics could be located. In 1917, at the age of 61, Hocking walked from New York City to Philadelphia (97 miles) in 19 hours, 16 minutes, averaging just over 5 mph. This record, which was made between the hours of 3 A.M. and 10:35 P.M., is one of the greatest distances ever covered within a single day. Feeling energetic after reaching Philadelphia, Hocking went on towards Baltimore the next day, and covered the 205 miles to it from Philadelphia in 43 hours, 16 minutes, averaging about 4.73 mph. Hocking lowered many of the records made previously by Weston, O'Leary, John Ennis, and others. In 1924, at the age of 68, he beat Weston's New York to San Francisco record (3895 miles in 105 days) by covering the 3754 miles between Coney Island, New York, to Seal Rock Inn, San Francisco, in only 75 days, thus averaging about 50 miles a day. Hocking was born on October 15, 1856. In 1954, at the age of 98, he was still hiking! During his 75 years as a long-distance walker, he covered over 270,000 miles, *averaging* over this long period 10 miles a day!

6. In a coast-to-coast walk which ended on May 6, 1929, Abraham L. Monteverde, aged 60, of Mays Landing, New Jersey, walked from New York City to San Francisco (3415 miles) in 79 days, 10 hours, 10 minutes. While this performance has in some quarters been hailed as the official record, what about Jim Hocking's time of only 75 days, listed above? And away back in the 1890s, John Ennis had walked "from the Coney Island surf to the San Francisco surf," in 80 days, 5 hours.

7. William Gale, an English walker, covered 2280 miles in 38 days, averaging 60 miles a day. His walk ended at Bradford, England, on May 14, 1879.

8. Peter Crossland, at Manchester, England, walked 120 miles and 1560 yards without stopping. September 11–12, 1876.

9. C. A. Harriman, at Truckee, California, walked 121 miles and 385 yards without stopping. April 6–7, 1883.

10. The greatest distance covered to date in 24 hours of walking is 133 miles, 21 yards, by the English road walker, Huw D. Neilson, at Walton-on-Thames, October 14–15, 1960. This is a little better than the record made by T. E. Hammond in 1908 for 131 miles (see Table 14). Neilson walked at the rate of 5.54 MPH.

11. In 1940, seven men, consisting of three Poles, one Lithuanian, one

Latvian, one Yugoslav, and one American, escaped from a Siberian prison camp and headed south, the direction they thought would be the least-guarded. After covering about 4000 miles, which took them eight months, six survivors arrived in British India, after suffering incredible hardships. The expedition of escapees was organized and led by Slavomir Rawicz, a Polish cavalry officer, who tells of the experience in his book, *The Long Walk* (London. Constable: 1956).

12. Colonel Russell Farnum of New Hampshire, during the years 1812–13, walked from St. Louis, Missouri, to St. Petersburg (now Leningrad), Russia! The distance was at least 9000 miles. Farnum carried a 20-pound pack and a gun, and followed a course along the Missouri River to the Columbia River, thence up the Pacific Coast to Alaska. Continuing, he crossed on ice across the Bering Strait to Siberia, and from there all the way across Asia and European Russia to St. Petersburg. At the Russian capital he was acclaimed by Czar Alexander I, who called him "The lone conqueror of two continents."

13. John Snyder of Dunkirk, Ohio, in 1887 walked 25,000 miles in 500 days and was "apparently no more tired than when he began."

14. According to Gould and Pyle, *Anomalies and Curiosities of Medicine* (1937, p. 460): "A most marvelous feat of endurance is recorded in England in the first part of this (19th) century. It is said that on a wager Sir Andrew Leith Hay and Lord Kennedy walked two days and a night under pouring rain, over the Grampian range of mountains, wading all one day in a bog. The distance traversed was from a village called Banchory on the river Dee to Inverness. The feat was accomplished without any previous preparation, both men starting shortly after the time of the wager."

15. The *professional* record for walking 100 miles was held—in 1915, at any rate—by George N. Brown, who covered the distance in 14 hrs. 34 min. 26 sec. This was at the average rate of 6.86 mph. This record is no less than *24 percent faster* than the amateur world record (5.53 mph) listed in Table 14. Also, Brown's time, or mph, was slightly better than that of a *runner*, Sidney Hatch, who about the same time dog-trotted from Milwaukee to Chicago, a distance of 95.7 miles, in 14 hrs. 50 min. 30 sec. When it is considered that Hatch, during his run, stopped three times for a total of 16 minutes, it makes his actual running time for the 95.7 miles (at a rate of 6.57 MPH) almost identical to Brown's *walking* time for 100 miles!

16. A European professional walker named Anton Hanislan once (no date is given) won a prize of $2000 for pushing a special perambulator for 22 months over a distance of 15,000 miles, averaging about 22 miles a day. The remarkable feature of this feat is that in the perambulator, during the entire trip, was Hanislan's wife and his small daughter!

17. Somewhat comparable with the last-mentioned performance was that of a man (name not given) who, in the 1890s, pushed a wheelbarrow (empty or loaded?) from San Francisco to New York City in 118 days, averaging about 33 miles a day.

18. In 1865, a hunter named Thomas Keesik, who was famed for his great endurance afoot, pursued a wolf all the way from Fort Pelly to near Touchwood Hills, Manitoba, a distance of about 100 miles, until both fell exhausted. Keesik tripped and fell on top of the wolf, and, recovering first, killed it with his hunting knife.

19. In 1941, a "walking contest" was staged between Finland and Sweden, in which it was sought to determine how many competitors could walk 15 kilometers in 2 hrs. 20 min. This was approximately 9⅓ miles at the rate of 4 mph. Finland won the contest by qualifying 1.4 million walkers to Sweden's 1.1 million.

20. Bruce Neal, who for many years was a game warden in Montana, was known as "Rocky Mountain Iron Man." He was an indefatigable walker, and did practically all his walking barefooted. The soles of his feet became thickened and hardened almost like an animal's hoofs. Once, in 1915, when he was 29, Neal, on a wager, covered 68 miles between sunrise and sunset while carrying on the return trip (34 miles) a load of approximately 140 pounds. He alternated between fast walking (he used a stride of over 40 inches) and dog-trotting. On another trip he covered 71 miles over rough terrain in about 11 hours. In 1954, at the age of 68, Neal covered 80 miles within 36 hours, in the dead of winter, through blizzards and deep snow. On this trip, he condescended to wear boots and socks!

21. In the mid-summer of 1966, Jean Pierre Marquant, a 28-year-old explorer of Nice, France, walked 102 miles through Death Valley, in temperatures that ranged from 90 to 122 degrees Fahrenheit. The hike took about a week. At the end of each day, he was met by two aides in a truck, who supplied him with food and drink. In order to keep from becoming dehydrated, Marquant had to drink about 3 *gallons* of water and fruit juices daily. He was, it is said, the first person ever to have walked across Death Valley in mid-summer.

22. In the valley of Guatimapé, Mexico, in 1925, a native farmer (name not given), using a two-mule team, plowed a *straight* furrow 20 miles long! He used a primitive wooden plow and completed the job in less than two days. So straight was the furrow (its greatest deviation was only a foot, for a short distance) that engineers used it as a base for surveys in the region.

23. Dick Barstow, a professional dancer, claimed to have the world's strongest toes. In Boston, in 1927, he walked 4½ miles on the tips of his toes, over concrete pavements. Whether he did this in his bare feet was not stated.

24. During the summer of 1969, Edwin H. Paget made 41 separate ascents of Pike's Peak, Colorado (14,110 ft.). This surpassed Paget's previous record of 38 ascents made in 1968.

15.
Running

Running, like walking, is one of man's age-old, natural activities. For developing or improving one's "wind" and endurance, it is one of the best and most available exercises. Its performance requires no special equipment, only time and space. If one does not wish to run outdoors, one may run on a gymnasium track, or for that matter in one spot, doing "stationary running." This has similar effects to skipping rope. However, there is nothing quite equal to running under natural conditions outdoors, over uneven ground and occasionally uphill and down. The amount of such training being done by today's leading distance runners transcends most efforts of a similar nature performed in the past. That is one reason why the running records of today are better than those of any previous period. Another reason is because of our "population explosion," which has resulted in a larger number of students attending college and engaging in intercollegiate competition. Out of a larger college population, a greater number of exceptional performers—both potential and actual—are bound to appear.

Although men have been engaging in foot-racing since prehistoric times, only during comparatively recent years have stopwatches and electrical timing devices made it possible to record running time accurately. Table 15, following, lists the world's amateur records as of January 1, 1968, from 100 yards to the marathon. Below 100 yards the times are based on those shown on Figure 1, which charts the running times made over short distances by the Negro athletes Bob Hayes and Jim Hines, respectively, two of the fastest sprinters of recent years. A careful examination of this graph shows that a time of just under 2 seconds is required to cover the first 10 yards or "getting underway" distance. For Bob Hayes, I have estimated this time as 1.84 seconds.* The first 5 yards of this would appear to take at least 1.2 seconds and in Hayes's case about 1.3 seconds. Hayes's actual marks of 3 seconds

---

*If it is assumed that Hayes's run between 10 yards and 110 yards represents a 100-yard sprint "with a flying start," his time over this distance would be about 8.08 seconds.

flat for 25 yards, and 9.1 seconds for 100 yards (as clocked in his record-making race at St. Louis on June 21, 1963) indicate an average running speed between these distances of 75/6.1, or 12.295 yards per second (yps). If this average speed were maintained throughout, it would mean that at 60 yards Hayes's time would be about 5.85 seconds. As he reached 60 yards actually in about 6 seconds flat, it would show that between 25 and 60 yards Hayes moved at the lesser rate of 35/3.0, or 11.667 yps. From 60 yards to 75 yards—which latter distance he reached in 7.1 seconds—Hayes attained his top speed—15 yards in evidently only 1.1 seconds. This was at the rate of 13.636 yps or 27.893 mph! In other words, between 30 yards and 60 yards, Hayes *decelerated* slightly, then sped up from 60 yards on. A similar deceleration is shown in the running times attained by Jim Hines, who in three different indoor races during the winter of 1966 tied the world record for 60 yards of 5.9 seconds. Probably he was capable of the aforementioned 5.85 seconds. In May 1967, in a race at Modesto, California, Hines equalled the world record for 100 meters of 10 seconds flat. In the same race, he was clocked over 100 yards by one coach in 9 seconds flat, and by another in 8.9 seconds. If Hines was capable of 60 yards in 5.85 seconds, and 100 meters ($=$ 109.36 yards) in 10 seconds flat, and if he ran at a constant speed between 60 and 109.36 yards (which would be all that could be expected), he would have hit the 100-yard mark in 9.22 seconds. Hayes, in Tokyo in 1964, was electrically clocked over 100 meters in 9.87 seconds. The latter time is exactly equivalent to Hayes's actual record of 100 yards in 9.1 seconds. It would certainly seem that the fastest speed possible between 100 yards and 100 meters—at least at the present stage of sprinting efficiency—is about 12.6 yps, requiring 0.74 sec.

To digress a moment, it is thus exceedingly improbable that Charles Paddock, whose best time for 100 yards was 9.5 seconds, could have run 110 yards in 10.2 seconds, as he was credited with doing in Pasadena on June 18, 1921. Paddock's records of 100 yards in 9.5 seconds and 220 yards in 20.8 seconds indicate 110 yards in not less (under the most liberal estimate) than 10.36 seconds. Some of Paddock's contemporaries have insisted that he could have covered the distance from 100 to 110 yards in only 0.7 second, but I have never been able to agree with this. It is significant that Paddock's 100-meter record was 10.4 seconds, corresponding to his 9.5 seconds for 100 yards. The 100-meter record was made at Redlands, California on April 25, 1921. While every champion should be given all credit due him, to over-credit any previous record-holder means to under-credit the existing one.

Back in 1941, Harold Davis (70 in., 160 lbs.) was considered to have the fastest finish of any sprinter up to that time. In at least one of his races, Davis would appear to have reached a speed of 12.254 yps. This

Table 15. Amateur world records in running (English distances).

Distance	Time	Performer	Nation	Place	Year	MPH
20 yards	(2.6)	Bob Hayes	USA	St. Louis, Mo.	1963	15.73
30 yards	(3.86)	Bob Hayes	USA	St. Louis, Mo.	1963	15.90
40 yards	(4.2)	Jim Hines	USA	Houston, Texas	1966	19.48
50 yards	5.2	Bob Hayes	USA	St. Louis, Mo.	1963	19.67
60 yards	5.9	Jim Hines (3 times)	USA	Houston, Texas	1966	20.80
70 yards	(6.65)	Jim Hines	USA	Houston, Texas	1966	21.53
80 yards	(7.42)	Jim Hines	USA	Houston, Texas	1966	22.05
90 yards	(8.25)	Jim Hines	USA	Houston, Texas	1966	22.31
100 yards	9.1	Bob Hayes (4 times)	USA	St. Louis, Mo.	1963	22.48
110 yards	(10.01)	(Estimated on basis of 100 meters in 9.95 seconds)				22.48*
220 yards (turn)	20.0	Tommie Smith	USA	Sacramento, Cal.	1966	22.50
440 yards	44.8	Tommie Smith	USA	San Jose, Calif.	1967	20.09
880 yards	1:44.9	Jim Ryun	USA	Terre Haute, Ind.	1966	17.16
1 mile	3:51.1	Jim Ryun	USA	Bakersfield, Calif.	1967	15.58
2 miles	8:19.6	Ron Clarke	Australia	London, Eng.	1968	14.42
3 miles	12:50.4	Ron Clarke	Australia	Stockholm, Sweden	1966	14.02
6 miles	26:47.0	Ron Clarke	Australia	Oslo, Norway	1965	13.44
10 miles	47:12.8	Ron Clarke	Australia	Melbourne, Aus.	1965	12.71

Distance	Time	Performer	Country	Location	Year	mph
c. 12 5/6 miles	1 hour	Gaston Roelants	Belgium	Leuven, Belgium	1966	12.84
15 miles	1:12:48.2	Ron Hill	Gt. Brit.	Bolton, England	1965	12.36
Marathon	2:08:33.6	Derek Clayton	Australia	Antwerp, Belgium	1969	12.25

Ditto, Metric distances

Distance	Time	Performer	Country	Location	Year	mph
100 meters	10.0†	Armin Hary (plus 6 others)	W. Germany	Zurich, Switz.	1960	22.37
200 meters (turn)	20.0–	Tommie Smith	USA	Sacramento, Calif.	1966	22.50?
400 meters	44.5	Tommie Smith	USA	San Jose, Calif.	1967	20.11
800 meters	1:44.3	Peter Snell	New Zealand	Christchurch, NZ	1962	17.16
1,000 meters	2:16.2	Jurgen May	E. Germany	Erfurt, Germany	1965	16.42
1,500 meters	3:33.1	Jim Ryun	USA	Los Angeles, Calif.	1967	15.75
2,000 meters	4:56.2	Michel Jazy	France	Saint-Maur, Fr.	1966	15.10
3,000 meters	7:39.6	Kipchoge Keno	Kenya	Halsingborg, Swed.	1965	14.60
5,000 meters	13:16.6	Ron Clarke	Australia	Stockholm, Sweden	1966	14.04
10,000 meters	27:39.4	Ron Clarke	Australia	Oslo, Norway	1965	13.48
20,000 meters	59:28.6	William Baillie	New Zealand	Auckland, N.Z.	1963	12.54
25,000 meters	1:15:22.6	Ron Hill	Gt. Brit.	Bolton, England	1965	12.37
30,000 meters	1:34:01.8	James Alder	Gt. Brit.	Walton-on-Thames, Eng.	1964	11.89

*From the customary crouching (or still) start, the maximum sprinting speed (here 23.01 mph) is reached at 150 yards. From a mile or so up to 25 miles, running speed averages about 59 *percent faster* than walking speed (see Table 14).

†On June 20, 1968, at Sacramento, Calif., Jim Hines, Ronnie Smith, and Charles Greene each made the new record of 9.9 seconds.

was in the 1941 AAU 100-meter final at Philadelphia, which was won
by Barney Ewell in 10.3 seconds. In that race, Davis, who had made a
very poor start, was 3 meters behind Ewell at the halfway mark, yet
was only inches behind Ewell at the finish. If we credit Davis with
covering the 100 meters in 10.33 seconds, and with being at the 47-meter
mark (3 meters behind Ewell) in a probable 5.6 seconds, he would
have had to cover the remaining 53 meters (= 57.96 yards) in 4.73
seconds.* If this was also Davis's speed between 100 yards and 100
meters (= 109.36 yards), he would have covered the 9.36 yards in 0.77
second. This is yet another reason for concluding that Charles Paddock,
20 years earlier, could not have run from 100 yards to 110 yards in only
0.70 second, to say nothing of the 0.60 second in which he was clocked
in the same race.

While on the subject of ultimate sprinting speed, it is opportune to
mention the records of the old-time professional all-around athlete,
Richard Perry Williams (1874–1966) of Miamisburg, Ohio. The following sprinting records were assertedly performed by Williams during
1904–1906: 20 yards, 2-1/5 sec.; 50 yards, 5 sec.; 60 yards, 6 sec.; 100
yards, 9 sec.; 100 meters, 9-4/5 sec.; 135 yards, 12-1/5 sec.; 220 yards,
20-2/5 sec. There has been a great deal of questioning of the authenticity
of these figures, especially the 100 yards in 9 seconds flat. This feat was
assertedly accomplished by Williams on June 2, 1906, at Winthrop,
Massachusetts, "on a truly measured track and against 5 absolutely
perfect watches." The AAU has steadily declined to give any consideration to Williams's records simply because he was a professional. However, in the present study we are not concerned with a performer's
status—whether amateur or professional—but rather with the potentials
of human athletic capability, and whether or not a claimed record has
actually been performed.

We know that 100 yards in 9 seconds is possible today, but was it
possible back in 1906? The best amateur sprinter in the 1890s was Bernie
Wefers (72 in., 175 lbs.), who in 1895 ran the 100 in 9-4/5 seconds and
the 220 in 21-3/5. In 1896, he lowered his 220 record to 21-1/5 sec.
Unofficially, Wefers is said to have run the 100 in 9-2/5. Following
Wefers was another American sprinter, Arthur Duffey (67 in., 138 lbs.),
who on May 31, 1902, in New York, was the first to run 100 yards offi-

---

*We have seen, then, that in 1941 Hal Davis evidently was capable of a top
speed of 12.254 yps. An almost equal speed, under similar conditions, was attained
by Lloyd LaBeach of Panama, in a race against Mel Patton of Los Angeles, in
Fresno, on May 15, 1948. This race was won by Patton in 9.3 seconds. Since LaBeach
made up at the finish 2 feet of the 3 feet that he had lost at the start, it can be
computed that he reached a top speed of 12.222 yps. Expressed in another way, if
LaBeach had started even with Patton, he would have finished the 100 yards in
the then-extraordinary time of 9.245 seconds.

PLATE 65

William Tilden, tennis's greatest champion. (129)

PLATE 66

William Johnson (left) and Richard Williams. Probably in 1916, at the start of the National Championship Final. (130)

PLATE 67

Ellsworth Vines, one of the top four in any rating of tennis champions. (131)

Vincent Richards, National Doubles Champion at 15! Master of the low volley (shown). (132)

PLATE 68

(Above) Judith Devlin Hashman, of Baltimore, Md., winner of over thirty U. S. national badminton championships. (133)

(Below) Dr. David G. Freeman, of San Diego, Calif., winner of six consecutive U. S. national badminton championships during 1939–1948 (both Singles and Doubles), and the Men's Singles in 1953. (134)

John Higgins, an old-time English professional jumper of phenomenal ability. (135)

PLATE 69

PLATE 70

A Watusi champion high jumper clearing a height said to be 8 ft., 5 in. (From a foot-high take-off stone.) (136)

PLATE 71

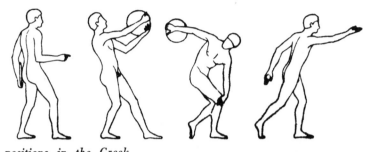

Successive positions in the Greek
or classic style of discus-throwing.
Since the discus was thrown underhand, in a sagittal rather than horizontal arc, the throw could be
likened to a toss, or pitch. (137a).

An accurate plaster copy of the statue of the Discobolus by Myron
(c. 450 B.C.) in the Glyptothek Museum, Munich. Note the relatively large diameter of the discus. (137)

451

PLATE 72

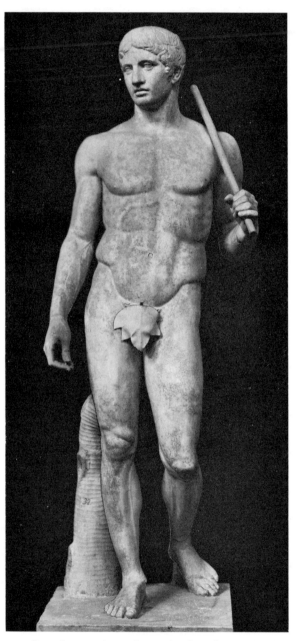

Doryphorus (spear-bearer), by the great Greek sculptor Polycletus (481–416 B.C.). This marble copy of the original bronze statue is in the National Museum, Naples. (138)

cially in 9-3/5 seconds. If tenth-second stopwatches had then been in use, Duffey could well have been credited with 9.5 sec. Another sprinter, Archie Hahn of Michigan, also in 1902 did 9-3/5 seconds. Duffey later became a professional, and then claimed to have run 50 yards in 5 seconds flat (the same as Williams claimed), 75 yards in 7-2/5, and 120 yards in 11-2/5. The latter two timings correspond with 100 yards in 9-3/5 sec. Now the question is: could Williams, in 1906, have sprinted 100 yards at such a speed that he would have won from Wefers, Hahn, and Duffey (assuming each of these sprinters to have been at his best) by anywhere from 5 to 7½ yards?

If the records claimed for Williams are compared with the general trend of sprinting speed as shown in Figure 1, it is evident that over certain distances, especially at the beginning of his races, the timing must have been incorrect. If we accept that Williams just *might* have been able to negotiate the first 50 yards in 5 seconds flat (since the amateur record is 5.1 seconds), and if—as is claimed—he ran the first 20 yards in only 2-1/5 seconds (!), he should have reached 25 yards in about 2.65 seconds. As has been noted, it took Bob Hayes 3 seconds flat to reach 25 yards and 5.2 seconds to reach 50 yards. Evidently his time for 20 yards was 2.6 seconds, or only .05 second faster than it took Williams to reach 25 yards. Thus, during the first 25 yards, Williams would have run 3.0/2.65, or 13.2 percent faster than Hayes, whereas from 25 yards to 50 yards he would have run 2.2/2.4, or about 8.3 percent *slower* than Hayes! It can only be concluded that when Williams was clocked at 20 yards (in 2-1/5 seconds), the timing was sadly inaccurate. In 1892, Edwin Bloss set the amateur record for the latter distance with 2-4/5 seconds (indoors), and this was still listed as a "noteworthy performance" as late as 1929, possibly later.

To continue, it is more reasonable—in view of present-day records—to accept that Williams ran 60 yards in 6 seconds than 50 yards in 5 seconds. Now, if Hayes ran 60 yards in the same time as Williams (i.e., 6 seconds flat), 100 meters in 9.87 seconds, and 100 yards in 9.1 seconds, then if Williams did 60 yards in 6 seconds and 100 meters in 9-4/5 seconds, his time for 100 yards (using the same intermediate ratio as in Hayes's case) would be 9.04 seconds. This is near enough to Williams's claimed 9 seconds flat, under ideal timing conditions, to give him the benefit of any doubt. Finally, if rated according to the normal trend of the 100-yard sprint record with date of performance, it would seem that Williams's time in 1906 of 9 seconds flat was equivalent to a time in 1965 of only 8.55 seconds. Since no present-day sprinter has remotely approached the latter figure,* it would appear that Richard

---

*Possibly the next-best "all-time" 100-yard record was that run by a comparatively unknown amateur sprinter, George Anderson, at Fresno, on May 11, 1935.

Perry Williams was indeed the fastest sprinter of all time. This is borne out also by his time for 220 yards of 20-2/5 seconds. This, in 1965, would be equivalent to 18.5 seconds. Moreover, in view of Williams's outstanding performances in numerous other events both in track and field, gymnastics, and weightlifting, it may safely be accepted that he was one of the greatest all-around athletes on record.

Running speed is essentially the product of the length of one's stride multiplied by the number of strides per second. Bob Hayes, at 72 inches and 185 pounds, had a sprinting stride that averaged close to 8 ft. Accordingly, in covering 100 yards in 9.1 seconds, he would have had to average about 4.7 strides (with each leg) per second. Ralph Metcalfe (71 in., 182 lbs.) was another great Negro sprinter, of about the same build as Hayes. In 1933, Metcalfe was capable of 100 yards in 9.4 seconds, which at that time was equal to the world record. Metcalfe's frequent competitor, Eddie Tolan (66.9 in., 145 lbs.) was, in 1929, the first sprinter to do the 100 in 9.5. Metcalfe had a very long stride of 8 feet 6 inches, which indicated only about 4.2 strides per second. Tolan, at the other extreme, had a stride of only 6 feet, which means that he had to average an extraordinary 6 strides per second. The great Jesse Owens (70 in., 156 lbs.) in 1936 made a then world record at 100 meters of 10.2 seconds. Owens had a stride of 7 feet 3 inches, which corresponded to an average of about 5 strides per second.

For comparison with the foregoing figures, a novice sprinter of, say, 69 inches in height, running 100 yards in 12 seconds flat, would have a stride of about 7 feet 5 inches, and would accordingly average only about 3.4 strides per second. Therefore, to become a record holder, he would have to increase the rapidity of his leg movements by about 50 percent. These figures furnish in some respects a better comparison of relative speed than do the respective running times over 100 yards (12 seconds and 9.1 seconds) of a novice as compared with a champion sprinter. Women sprinters are capable of just about as many strides per second as men; however, their strides average only about 91 percent of the length of men's strides, and their sprinting time is consequently that much slower than men's. At a given stature (standing height), a Negro's stride, in either sex, averages about 3 inches more than a white's. The longer legs, relative to stature, of Negroes provide one explanation of why they make superior sprinters. In particular, the greater length in Negroes of the lower leg in relation to the length of the thigh may be the reason.

In that race, seven out of the eight timers caught Anderson in 9.2 seconds, and the eighth timer in a probably inaccurate 9.5 seconds. Even if the latter timing were accepted, the average of all eight timings was only 9.24 seconds. That, in 1935, would be equivalent, in 1965, to 8.96 seconds. With reference to 220 yards, see (Hal Davis). p. 455.

Occasionally one will read where a sprint performance of merit is disallowed as a record because of a too-strong tail wind. How much tail wind is allowed, and how much does an excessive wind increase a sprinter's speed? The International Amateur Athletic Federation has defined the maximum allowable tail wind as 2 meters per second or 7.2 kilometers (= 4.47386 miles) per hour. But it should be noted that tail winds of lesser speed than this, which are allowable, still help a sprinter to make better time. Conversely, even in still air with no head wind, a sprinter is retarded by the wind resistance to his moving body. Finally, the sprinter's speed is affected to a small and variable degree by his *body build*—a broad body meeting with more wind resistance than a slender body of the same height. As a result of all this, many a fine sprint performance—possibly a world record—has been unfavorably influenced by the prevailing speed of the wind.

The degree to which a sprint record is affected, whether favorably or unfavorably, is in ratio to the velocity of the wind *squared*. A few examples here follow of great sprinters whose recorded speeds in certain races might have established new world records at the time, had it not been for the influence of the prevailing wind. The figures given at the end of each listing are the times as "corrected" for the wind.

Melvin Patton (1949) 100 yards in 9.1 with a 6.5 MPH tail wind = 9.25 sec.
Ralph Metcalfe (1934) 220 yards in 19.8 with a "strong" (8 MPH?)
                                        tail wind = 20.3 sec.
Harold Davis (1941) 220 yards in 20.5 with a "stiff" (8 MPH?)
    ....   head wind = 20.0 sec.?
Melvin Patton (1949) 220 yards in 20.6 with a 7.3 MPH head wind = 20.2 sec.

If there had been no headwind in Harold Davis's race, and had he covered 220 yards in 20 seconds flat, that performance in 1941 would be equivalent in 1965 to the phenomenal time of 19.4 seconds.

More about sprinters cannot be recorded in the space available here, other than to say that dozens of them, both white and Negro, were, or are, truly in "super-athlete" class. There is even a mark of 100 yards in 17.3 seconds that deserves mention. Why? Because the performer, Larry Lewis of San Francisco, made the run on his 102nd birthday! (June 25, 1969).

Turning our attention now to a distance of 440 yards, or a quarter-mile, the following very interesting opinion may be noted. In his scholarly work, *Greek Athletes and Athletics* (p. 73), H. A. Harris says that it is highly probable that the best ancient Greek runners of the *diaulos*—a distance of about 400 yards—were "fully equal to our best performers in the quarter-mile or 400 meters." If by this Professor Harris means equal *times* over different *distances*, it would seem that he is right. In that case the probable running speed of the ancient Greek runners bore to the speed of present-day runners the ratio that 400 yards bears to 400 meters. This ratio is 100.00/109.36, or .9144. If we apply it to the present-day record for 400 meters of 44.5 seconds, it means that the Greek champion could cover that distance in 44.5/.9144, or 48⅗ seconds. If we make the reasonable assumption that the Greek champion was 66 inches in height, he would have had a stride of about 84 inches and would have taken about 3.6 strides per second. A present-day 400-meter champion, running the distance in 44.5 seconds and standing 72 inches in height, would have a stride of about 94 inches and would take 3.5 strides per second. Today's 400-meter runner, if of the same height (66 inches) as the ancient Greek, would be expected to cover the distance in 46 seconds flat. Thus he would appear to be nearly 6 percent faster than his early Greek counterpart. This difference seems reasonable in view of the consideration that while today there are perhaps 50 runners to one in ancient Greece, the best athletes of those days were the culmination of *hundreds of years* of almost constant competition.

In the mile run, which appears to be a much-publicized distance (witness the former hubbub over the "4-minute barrier"), various performers at the distance have each been named as "the world's greatest runner." There have, for instance, been Paavo Nurmi (1923), Glenn Cunningham (1934), Gunder Hägg (1945), Roger Bannister and John Landy (1954), Herb Elliott (1958), and the present record holder Jim Ryun (1967). Each of these mile record holders has quite rightly been regarded, at the time, as a phenomenal performer. But note the qualification— *at the time*—and permit a short digression to be made.

The date at which an athletic performance has been established is of vital importance in the proper evaluating of any record. Yet it is a factor which, up until now, has been taken into account only by a few discerning observers who apparently were ahead of their time. Expressed in brief, the merit of a record may be assessed properly and fairly *only by comparing it with the average record of all the performers competing in the event in question at a given date*. If, for example, the average record among present-day college freshmen in the 16-pound shot put is 35 feet, and that of the world record holder, Randel Matson, is 71 ft. 5½ in., Matson's mark is 71.46/35, or 2.04 times the average. Is Matson's record actually more meritorious than that of Ralph Rose, who back in 1909 did 51 feet? The available evidence shows that in that year the *average* shot put of a freshman was not more than 25 feet, and probably somewhat less than that. Even as much as 25 feet would make Rose's relative standing 51/25, or 2.04, the equal of

Matson's. Another method of evaluation—and one that appears to provide properly for the factor of comparative performances at a given date— is to chart the world's records over the years in relation to the *population* (as of the United States) during those years. The records then appear in their true perspective.

To return to the mile running record, when it is so plotted on a graph in relation to population increase it would appear that the greatest miler was not Nurmi, nor Bannister, nor even Jim Ryun, but a pioneer English professional named Walter Goodall George (71 in., 136 lbs.).* Away back on August 23, 1885, in a mile race at Lillie Bridge Grounds, England, George won in the then-phenomenal time of 4 minutes 12¾ seconds (fifth-second stopwatches at that time having not yet come into use). This record stood for *30 years*. Even when the American amateur, Norman Taber, lowered it, on July 16, 1915, he did so by the perhaps negligible fraction of .15 second, his time being 4:12.6. As will be seen in the Appendix (Fig. 8), W. G. George's mile record stands out above all others like the proverbial lighthouse in a fog. It may be remarked also that while Roger Bannister's mile in 3:58.8 is some 25 places down from Ryun's 3:51.1 in the usual "all-time best" list, when considered according to date (1954) it is almost equal in merit to Ryun's record performed in 1967.

Passing now to the considerably longer marathon run, it may be noted that this race, like that of a mile, seems to have enjoyed more than a passing amount of interest. Perhaps this is because of its historic connection with the run from Marathon to Athens in 490 B.C. supposedly by the Greek runner Pheidippides (see listing no. 1, below). Actually to run the marathon (26 miles, 385 yards) in 2:08:33.6, as noted in Table 15, is no more extraordinary a performance than are those listed for other distances, since all are current world records. To establish a world record at any distance requires extraordinary adaptability and determination; it is simply that at differing distances the required force or effort is expended over differing periods of time. Short sprints demand intense energy and speed, while long-distance running is more a matter of lung power, circulatory efficiency, patience, and leather-tough feet. Thus many an older runner—who could make no showing whatever in a sprint—has been able to turn in a favorable performance, or at least to finish, in a race over the marathon distance. The famous Boston Marathon competitor, Clarence H. DeMar, ran in this event no fewer than 29 times, the last time when he was 61 years of age. Perhaps

---

*So far as *population increase* alone is concerned. But other factors also must be taken into account in judging the merit of an athletic performance. The procedure involved is described in the Appendix.

equally remarkable is that apparently a small number of *women* are able to negotiate this long run. For instance, in the Boston Marathon of 1966, Roberta Gibb, aged 22, of Winchester, Massachusetts, covered the distance in 3:21:30. In 1967, she ran the full distance again, in 3:27:17. In both races she finished about midway in the field.

As in the case of records in walking—perhaps even more so—only a few of the more outstanding performances in long-distance and odd-distance running can be listed here. No particular order is observed in the following examples.

1. Perhaps the most famous run in history is that attributed to the Greek runner Pheidippides, who is popularly supposed to have brought to Athens the news of the Greek victory over the Persians at Marathon in 490 B.C. It is now believed that this message was delivered not by Pheidippides, but by a fully-armed Greek soldier from Marathon whose name has not been preserved. The distance from Marathon to Athens, over the route that the Greek soldier presumably took, is slightly less than 25 miles (approximately 40,000 meters). This was the original distance for the marathon run. Pheidippides distinguished himself the day *before* the Greek victory at Marathon (when the Persians were approaching or had landed there) by taking a message from Athens to Sparta, a distance of about 158 miles. This, according to Herodotus, he covered in two days and two nights, which would have given him plenty of time to rest between spurts. He then ran back over the same route, carrying the news that the Spartan army would soon follow. Another Greek runner, Euchidas of Boetia, on another occasion, ran from Plataea to Delphi and back, about 95 miles, in one day, and at the finish fell dead (as the soldier from Marathon is said to have done). Another performance of high merit was set up by a courier from Crete, named Philonides. While in the service of Alexander the Great, Philonides ran from Sicyon to Elis, a distance of 160 miles, in 9 hours (*sic*), and returned over the same route in 15 hours. The time of 15 hours is credible (since the road used was fairly level), but the alleged 9 hours is manifestly in error. The Roman author Pliny mentions a runner who covered 235 kilometers (= *c*. 146 miles) without once stopping. This, if true, was a phenomenal performance. Pliny also mentions a child who ran almost half this distance.

2. The Incas, in the days of their glory, had an empire that extended north-south from what is now Colombia to Chile, and east-west from the Amazon valley to the Pacific Ocean. By means of their celebrated courier service, the Incas could transmit messages swiftly from one place to another over this vast area. The Inca emperor, whose capital

was at Cuzco, could have fresh fish brought to him from the ocean within two days, even though he was 350 miles from it. The couriers were called chasquis, and were stationed 1½ leagues ($=$ 5¼ miles) apart over a highway that was 2000 miles long. During a 24-hour period, in which some 53 chasquis each would run 5¼ miles in about 29 minutes, a message could be transmitted 80 leagues (280 miles). This was at an average speed of about 11¾ mph. The altitude was over 14,000 feet.

3. An American Indian runner who gained much publicity a century ago was Louis Bennett (1828–1896), nicknamed "Deerfoot." In 1861 he went to England, and there defeated the best English runners. In April 1863, in London, "Deerfoot" ran 11 miles in 56 minutes 52 seconds ($=$ 11.606 mph), and 12 miles in one hour 2 minutes 2½ seconds ($=$ 11.605 mph). Note that the rates are nearly identical. While these achievements by "Deerfoot" stood as world records for many years, it is interesting to note that the present (1966) record for one hour's running, 12.837 mph (see Table 15), is 10.6 percent faster. This may be taken as the amount that human distance-running speed has increased during the last century.

4. One of the greatest—perhaps the greatest of all—modern long-distance runners was a Norwegian sailor named Mensen Ernst. In 1834, he was astonishing all Europe by his extraordinary exploits. One of these was to run from Paris to Moscow, a distance of about 1550 miles, in 14 days, 18 hours. Although he ran over poor roads, in all kinds of weather, and swam 13 broad rivers on the way, he still averaged over 100 miles a day! In 1836, as a courier for the East India Company, he was dispatched from Calcutta to Constantinople, across the hot, desert, mountainous countries of India, Tibet, Afganistan, Persia, Mesopotamia, Syria, and Turkey—a stated distance of 5625 miles. This arduous journey was accomplished in 59 days—a speed half again as fast as that of the most rapid caravan. Ernst's actual records thus put in the shade any comparable feats of running, whether legendary or real, accomplished in antiquity.

5. Arthur Newton, a South African (white) farmer, was another great long-distance runner. To cure a weak heart, Newton ran more than 20 miles a day, on the average, over a period of 14 years (1922–1935)! During this time, he established 14 amateur running records ranging from 29 to 100 miles. In 1931, at the age of 48, Newton set a world 24-hour running record by covering 152 miles 540 yards. On November 21, 1953, in Surrey, England, the latter record was surpassed by another South African runner, Wally Hayward (66 in., 168 lbs.), aged 45, who

in 24 hours covered 159 miles 562 yards. This record was made by jogging 637 laps around a quarter-mile track.

6. In a go-as-you-please (walking and running) race over a period of 142 hours, George Littlewood of Sheffield, England, covered 623 miles, 1888. This far surpassed the feat of a Tarahumare Indian, who in 1937 received considerable publicity by covering 570 miles in 166 hours.

7. Samuel A. Johnson, aged 44, a "semi-professional" runner and news-boy of New York, wearing Indian moccasins, ran from Albany to New York City, a distance of 160 miles, in 28 hours 20 minutes. Of this time, 20 minutes was taken off for several stops to eat. While some of the time Johnson speeded up to 10 mph, his average rate over the whole distance was 160/28, or 5.714 mph, September 4–5, 1921.

8. The famous cross-country footrace sponsored by the sports promoter Charles C. ("Cash and Carry") Pyle came to be appropriately known as "The Bunion Derby." The race started in Los Angeles on March 4, 1928, with 199 contestants, including such famous runners as Hans Kolehmainen (the Finnish marathon champion) and Arthur Newton (the Rhodesian record holder). After the first 1000 miles the field had dwindled to 93, due largely to blistered feet and swollen knees and ankles. Two months after the start of the race, 71 runners had reached Chicago. On May 26, 55 runners had made it to New York City. The winner of the race was Andy Payne, a 19-year-old Indian from Clare-more, Oklahoma. He had covered the 3422.3 miles in 573 hours 4 minutes 34 seconds—an average of just under 6 mph. The 573 hours over a period of 83 days meant a running period each day of about 7 hours ($=$ 42 miles per day). For winning this grueling test, during which he lost 20 pounds, Payne collected $25,000. The next nine runners received prizes ranging from $10,000 down to $1000. The remaining 45 runners received nothing except verbal praise for their pluck and endurance. For comparison with this cross-country race, it is interesting to note that the pedestrian Jim Hocking covered a distance 332 miles longer (from San Francisco to New York City), at the age of 68, in only 75 days, by *walking*. He thus averaged 50 miles per day to Andy Payne's 42 miles (see p. 436).

9. In an east-west cross-country run, from New York City to Los Angeles (3610 miles), a record of 525 hours 57 minutes 20 seconds was set by John Salvo of Passaic, New Jersey, from March 31 to June 16, 1929 ($=$ 77 days). This is the same number of days that Edward Weston took to *walk* from east to west between the two cities, in 1910, although his

distance was somewhat less: 3483 miles (see above). Evidently Weston walked for about 9 hours each day, at a rate of about 5 mph, while Salvo averaged an actual speed of 6.86 mph, which would indicate about 7 hours' "running" each day.

10. Each year (?) a "marathon" hike is held over a trail from the foot of Mt. Whitney (California) to the summit and return—a round-trip distance of 21 miles. The men's record for this hike is (or was in 1961) held by Calvin Hansen of Colorado Springs, with a time of 4 hours 9 minutes 22 seconds (= 5.05 mph). The women's record, as of the same year, is held by Jerri Lee, of Ridgecrest, California, with a time of 7 hours 56 minutes 57 seconds (= 2.64 mph). On the basis of the men's and the women's respective records in the marathon run, the women's record in the Mt. Whitney hike would be expected to be just over 6½ hours.

11. The present-day record for a non-stop run is claimed by Jared Beads, 41, of Westport, Maryland, who in 1969 jogged 121 miles, 440 yards in 22 hours, 27 minutes (= 5.4 mph).

Here are a few additional "records" in unstandardized feats of running and hopping.

100 yards run in baseball uniform, 9.9 seconds. Jesse Owens, 1936.

Running backward: 50 yards, 6 seconds; 75 yards, 8.5 seconds; 100 yards, 13.5 seconds. All by Bill Robinson (1878–1949), the famous Negro tap dancer.

Hopping (presumably on both feet together): 50 yards, 7 1/5 seconds; 80 yards, 10 4/5 seconds; 100 yards, 13 3/5 seconds. All by S. D. See, Brooklyn, New York, October 15, 1888.

Baseball, circling bases (120 yards): 12 seconds flat. R. P. Williams, Springfield, Ohio, 1900.

Sack race (both feet in sack): 100 yards, 14 1/5 seconds. John A. Finn, Brooklyn, New York, May 1, 1929.

Every so often the question is raised as to whether a human runner can outrun a racehorse. The answer is yes, provided the distance is so great that the horse becomes exhausted from carrying its rider. This generally has to be a hundred miles or farther. In a short race or sprint, the fastest human sprinter has no chance against a thoroughbred or a Quarter horse. Even against a harness horse, while the man will of course get away quicker, the horse, sulky and all, soon catches up with him. If a human sprint champion, a greyhound champion, and a thoroughbred champion (with jockey) were to have a race, two seconds after the start the greyhound would have covered 32 yards, the horse 25 yards, and the man only 12 yards. At about 142 yards, taking 8 seconds, the horse would overtake the greyhound. After 30 seconds, the horse would have covered 605 yards, the greyhound 542 yards, and the man only 312 yards. In short, once under way, a champion thorough-bred is almost *twice* as fast as the best human sprinter. In fact, if a thoroughbred were riderless, over a course of 220 yards the horse would be able to move 2.058 times as fast as a man.

The fastest human sprinter, as we have seen, reaches a top speed, between 60 and 75 yards, of about 27.9 mph. A greyhound, between 50 and 110 yards, reaches 40.9 mph; and a thoroughbred racehorse (with jockey), between 90 and 110 yards, 47.6 mph. Riderless, between the same distances, a thoroughbred would be expected to reach 50.9 mph. The fastest starter among mammals is not the greyhound, but the cheetah, or hunting leopard. This built-for-speed animal, which can reach a top speed of 70 mph, needs only two seconds to reach 45 mph! No man-made vehicle can match this acceleration.

A word about relay racing records. The four-man time established in such a run is essentially the sum of the times of the first sprinter starting from scratch, and the next three sprinters on the team each running from a flying start. Evidently some time is lost during the passing of the baton. Thus the current 440-yard relay world record of 38.6 seconds* might be the result of the first sprinter doing his 110 yards in 10.1 seconds, and the next three sprinters averaging 9.5 seconds each. The 880-yard record of 1:22.1 (82.1 seconds) would be something like 21.0 + 20.4 + 20.4 + 20.3. The mile record of 3:02.8 (182.8 seconds): 47.5 + 45.1 + 45.1 + 45.1. The two-mile record of 7:16.0 (436.0 seconds): 111.5 + 108.2 + 108.1 + 108.1. The four-mile record of 16:09.0 (969.0 seconds): 247 + 241 + 241 + 240. It is not being said that the latter figures were the actual contributing times of each sprinter, but simply that the times were necessarily something close to these. The point is that relay races—while one of the most thrilling track events to watch—are basically composed of the joint efforts of four top-notch runners over the standard distances of 110, 220, 440 and 880 yards, and 1 mile, respectively. Potential running speed over each of these distances is best evaluated on the basis of *individual*, rather than team (relay) world records.

Hurdle races, like relay races, are essentially an offshoot of simple sprinting. According to G.H.G. Dyson, in his excellent treatise, *The Mechanics of Athletics* (1964, p. 115): " . . . the best method of clearing a hurdle or water jump is that which returns the athlete quickly to the track with a rhythm and effort akin to a running action. Hurdling

---

*This record was made by a four-man relay team from the University of Southern California, consisting of Fred Kuller, Lennox Miller, O. J. Simpson, and Earl McCullouch, at Provo, Utah, June 17, 1967.

and water jump techniques are therefore modifications of running form.'"

Basically, hurdling (and steeplechasing) is a combination of sprinting and jumping. Accordingly, it is an excellent test of speed, rhythm, and agility. Over each of the following distances, there are 10 hurdles, spaced from 10 to 38¼ yards apart according to the length of the race. Here are the current world records in hurdling: (See also Fig. 9, Appendix).

120 yards, 13.2 seconds.	Martin Lauer (W. Ger.), Zurich, Switz. July 7, 1959
	Lee Calhoun (USA), Berne, Switzerland Aug. 21, 1960
	Willie Davenport (USA), Baton Rouge, La. Apr. 9, 1966
	Earl McCullouch (USA), Minneapolis, Minn. July 16, 1967
220 yards (straight), 21.9 sec.	Don Styron (USA), Baton Rouge, La. Apr. 2, 1960
200 meters (turn), 22.5 sec.	Martin Lauer (W. Ger.), Zurich, Switz. July 7, 1959
	Glenn Davis (USA), Berne, Switz. Aug. 20, 1960
400 meters, 48.1 seconds.	Dave Hemery (Gt. Brit.), Mexico City Oct. 15, 1968
440 yards, 49.3 seconds.	Gert Potgieter (So. Afr.), Bloemfontein, So. Africa, Apr. 16, 1960

The ratio of the speed in hurdling to that in simple sprinting is, for 120 yards, 1.226; for 220 yards (turn), 1.125; and for 440 yards, 1.100. Thus it is seen that the longer the hurdle race, the more the speed approximates that of a sprint over the same distance. The standard height of the hurdles for 120 yards is 3 ft. 6 in.; for 220 yards, 2 ft. 6 in.; and for 440 yards, 3 ft.

16.
Jumping

Jumping, especially in a form requiring a quick doubling-up of the body and limbs (as in tumbling, for example), is one of the best general tests of *agility*. Such jumping is also one of the best single exercises for keeping the waist trim and for teaching the main muscle-groups of the body to work together in a coordinated effort. While in track meets only the usual three forms of jumping (i.e., the running long jump, the running high jump, and the triple jump) are used in official competition, there are a great many other forms and applications of jumping. Back in the 16th century, a whole book on the subject, entitled *Three Dialogues on the Acrobatics of Jumping*, was written by an Italian teacher of gymnastics named Saint Archange Tuccaro. In this book are mentioned no fewer than 53 varieties of jumping, including tumbling and springboard somersaulting.

In the ancient Olympic Games, jumping was not practiced as a separate event, but only as one of the five events in the pentathlon. The latter competition was introduced in the Games in 708 B.C. Evidently the only form of jumping used in official competition in these games was the broad jump. This was performed in two styles, running and standing. In both styles, *halteres* or jumping-weights were held in the hands. The same weights, which were made either of stone or metal, were used also in the gymnasium, in much the same manner as light dumbbells are used today. For this reason, some writers believe that jumping was considered the most *representative* event in the pentathlon. The *halteres* would seem to have come into existence at least by the beginning of the sixth century B.C. They were often indicated on the statues of pentathletes (performers in the pentathlon); and by the form of the *halteres* represented it has been possible to estimate with fair accuracy the *date* of a given statue.

Much controversy has taken place over the lengths of the running broad jumps assertedly made by Greek pentathletes. The most famous of these athletes was Phayllus, who twice won the pentathlon in the Pythian Games at Delphi. Phayllus has been credited with a broad jump of 55 "feet." But evidently the Greeks had no single standard for the length of a foot. The stadium at Olympia was 600 Grecian feet (= 192¼ meters, or 630.74 English feet) in length, and a foot there accordingly was 12.615 inches.* In contrast, at Delphi, where the stadium was 1000 "feet" (= 177.55 meters, or 582.51 English feet) in length, a foot was only 6.99 inches long. Applying this to the jump made by Phayllus, the "55 feet" would come down, in English measure, to 32 feet. As the advantage secured by using weights appears to be about an even 25 percent,** this would further reduce the jump by Phayllus—if performed under modern conditions—to a plausible 25 ft. 7¼ in. Using similar reckoning, the "52-foot" jump by Chionis, who won at Olympia in 664 B.C., becomes 30.29 feet with weights or 24.23 feet without.

As to the jumping-weights, or *halteres*, used by the ancient Greeks, they weighed from 4 to 5 pounds each. Some were as light as 2 pounds, and others as heavy as 6 pounds. The "take-off" for a running broad jump consisted of only a short, springy run similar to that used by a modern high-jumper. As the performer took off, he would swing his halteres vigorously forward and upward to the level of his shoulders. There he would keep them until just befort alighting, when he would throw them strongly backwards. Thus the halteres were used to increase the *momentum* of the performer and add to the length of his jump.

One of the first records in the running broad jump made in the United States was one of 23 feet, said to have been made by George Washington about 1750, when he was 18. If this is so, it would appear that Washington's record stood for *over a hundred years*. In fact, it was not until 1886 that the all-around champion of those days, Malcolm W. Ford, made a jump of 23 ft. 3 inches. Whereas Washington stood 73.5 inches in height and weighed about 200 pounds, Ford was only 67.4 in. and 153 pounds.

Around the turn of the century the most outstanding broad-jumper was Peter O'Connor of Ireland, who in 1901, at Portlaoighise, Ireland, did 25 ft. 0½ in. O'Connor's record stood for *20 years*, until on July 23, 1921, an American Negro jumper, Edwin Gourdin, surpassed it with a leap of 25 ft. 3 in. Four years later, on June 13, 1925, another Negro jumper, William DeHart Hubbard, raised the record to 25 ft. 10⅞ in. This was followed, on July 7, 1928, by a jump of 25 ft. 11⅛ in. by Edward Hamm,

---

*As the "600-foot" length of the stadium at Olympia is said to have been paced off by Hercules himself, it follows that Hercules's foot length must have been 12.615 inches. This would appear to have been *sandal* length rather than barefoot length. It would indicate that Hercules must have stood just over 6 feet in height.

**This ratio is derived from the fact that the modern broad-jump record, using weights (in this case, 5-pound dumbbells) is 29 ft. 7 in., by John Howard of Manchester, England, May 8, 1854. At the same date, the broad-jump record *without* weights was 23 ft. 8 in. (29.5833/23.6667 = 1.25.)

a white American from Georgia. The record then passed to Silvio Cator, a Negro from Haiti, who on September 9, 1928, reached 26 ft. 0½ in. Next it went to Japan's great jumper, Chuhei Nambu, who on October 27, 1931 did 26 ft. 2¼ in. The first broad-jumper to surpass 8 meters (= 26 ft. 2.92 in.) was the famed Negro track athlete Jesse Owens, who on May 25, 1935, at Ann Arbor, Michigan, jumped 26 ft. 8¼ in. (= 8.13 meters). This historic performance remained the record for *26 years*. On July 16, 1961, Ralph Boston, another American Negro, surpassed it with a jump of 27 ft. 2 in., at Moscow.

Far and away the greatest running long jump on record is that which was made at the 1968 Olympic Games in Mexico City by another Negro athlete, Bob Beamon. My graph (Figure 11) charting the long jump was made before the Olympic Games were held; and so meritorious is Beamon's performance—a leap of 29 ft. 2½ in.—that it goes clear off the graph!* Next in distance is the jump of 27 ft. 4¾ in. made by Ralph Boston, at Modesto, California, on May 29, 1965. Third-best jump was when the Russian athlete, Igor Ter-Ovanesyan, equalled Boston's 27 ft. 4¾ in. at Mexico City in 1967.

The way the running long jump is performed today puts a premium on *sprinting speed*. This has been the case at least since the time Jesse Owens (a 9.4-second sprinter) made his record jump in 1935. When the date of performance is taken into consideration—as it always should be— it would appear that Owen's 1935 jump of 26 ft. 8¼ in. is, next to Bob Beamon's 1968 record, the most meritorious performance of its kind to date. The respective merits of other long jumps by other performers are listed in Appendix 2.

A number of interesting relationships are found by comparing the running long jump with the standing broad jump, the vertical (Sargent) jump, sprinting speed, etc. Some of these relationships are discussed later. If the present record-holder, Bob Beamon, had "taken off" at the theoretically best trajectory angle of 45 degrees, he would have jumped about 31 feet rather than the 29 ft. 2½ in. he accomplished with a trajectory of about 34½ degrees. This is based on Beamon's best speed for 100 yards of 9.5 seconds. His take-off angle would denote a height at the top of his trajectory of about 40–42 inches. This refers to the actual height that Beamon raised his center of gravity. His feet, as shown in photographs, reached a height of somewhere between 66 and 72 inches.

A broad jumper does not attain or apply his *fastest* sprinting speed in his take-off, but slows down preparatory to changing his direction of travel from horizontal to the angle of his jump trajectory. It can be computed that when Beamon jumped 29 ft. 2½ in. and reached a height

---

*See the comparisons of other track and field events with this jump listed in Table 31.

(of his center of gravity) in his jump of about 41 in., his take-off speed must have been only about 9¼ yards per second, or about 88 percent of his best 100-yard sprinting speed. A detailed analysis of these and other factors involved in the running long jump are given in *The Mechanics of Athletics,* by G.H.G. Dyson, pp. 138–148. According to Dyson, the maximum height so far attained in *high* jumping (with a running take-off) is about 4 feet. This would appear to be confirmed by the estimates made in my Table 16.

In jumping, just as in all other athletic and gymnastic events, the result attained is dependent upon a combination of strength, speed, and, in most events, agility. If a broad jumper is not a fast sprinter, he must, in order to make a respectable jump, compensate by having great springing power in his legs (and also his lower back). It is said that the phenomenal Russian ballet dancer, Vaclav Nijinsky, was once (*c.* 1915?) tested to determine how far he could broad jump. With presumably only a short, springy take-off, he made only one try. It was over 26 feet! In sheer jumping power, Nijinsky probably surpassed any amateur track athlete on record. If only he had acquired the *technique* of the running broad jump, there can be no question that he would have exceeded 30 feet. This is just another instance of where a world record holder according to the rule book is not necessarily the *potential* world's greatest. And one of the objectives in the present book is to determine as far as possible the *potentialities* of human strength, speed, and endurance.

Closely related to the running broad jump is the triple jump, or running hop, step, and jump. Both events require a similar type of running take-off. Although the name "hop, step, and jump" was changed only during recent years to "triple jump," the former term was more descriptive, since actually the second and third "jumps" are not just a repetition of the first. The take-off "hop" is made off one foot, and the landing made on the same foot; on the second "step," the landing is made on the opposite foot; while the third jump is essentially a typical broad jump without a sprinting start. Thus, in the so-called "triple jump" a more diversified technique is required than in a simple running broad jump.

The first outstanding performers in the triple jump were developed in Ireland and Scotland in the late 1880s and early 1890s. In 1873, Ireland's John Daly did a double-hop and a jump of 45 ft. 4 in. In 1887, John Purcell raised the record to 49 ft. 7 in.; and a year later (1888), Daniel Shanahan did 50 ft. 0½ in.* According to the sports statistician

---

*From the meager comparative statistics at hand, it would appear that the possibility in distance with two hops and a jump is about 1.3 percent greater than in a hop, step, and jump. In a 50-foot performance, this would amount to about 7¾ in.

R. L. Quercetani, the first record-holder to use the present "triple jump" (i.e., hop, step, and jump) form was Edwin Bloss (USA), who in Chicago on September 16, 1893, made a mark of 48 ft. 6 in. In 1911, Dan Aherne of Ireland made the next noteworthy record by doing 50 ft. 11 in. Aherne's mark stood for 13 years, when in 1924, at the Olympic Games in Paris, it was beaten by a scant ¼-inch by Nick Winter of Australia. On October 27, 1931, at Tokyo, Mikio Oda of Japan set a new world record of 51 ft. 1½ in. From that date until the present time, the standard in the triple jump has advanced, through over 20 intermediate record holders, to its present level of 57 ft. 0¾ in. This fine performance was made by Viktor Saneyev of the USSR, at Mexico City on October 17, 1968.

The average figures of five world record holders in the *constituents* of the "triple jump" are as follows: hop, 20 ft. 3¼ in.; step, 14 ft. 9⅞ in.; jump, 18 ft. 4⅞ in.; total, 53 ft. 6 in. Of the total, the hop averages 37.9 percent, the step 27.7 percent, and the jump 34.4 percent. In these five instances the most consistent element is the hop, which ranges only from 19 ft. 8¼ in. to 21 ft. The most variable element is the step, which ranges from 13 ft. 1½ in. to 16 ft. 5¾ in. Of intermediate variability is the jump, which ranges from 16 ft. 2 in. to 19 ft. 8½ in.

The distance attainable in the triple jump bears a rather close ratio to that in the running broad jump, assuming of course that equal skill is acquired or applied in each event. This ratio, on the average, is approximately 2.06. Thus, for a running broad jump of 25 feet, a triple jump of equal merit would be 2.06 x 25, or about 51 ft. 6 in. To be equivalent in merit to the present world record in the running broad jump of 29 ft. 2½ in., the record in the triple jump should be about 60 ft. 4 in rather than the actual record of 57 ft. 0¾ in.

Let us now look into some of the best performances in what is today a less familiar event: the *standing* broad jump. One of the greatest amateur exponents of standing jumping, both broad and high, was Ray C. Ewry (73 in., 162 lbs.), of the New York Athletic Club. The remarkable circumstance in connection with Ewry's athletic attainments is that, as a boy, he was paralyzed and unable to walk. By dogged determination and progressive daily exercise, he overcame the doctor's dictum, and in due course emerged an extraordinary athlete. During Ewry's day, the standing jumps were regular AAU events, and in three successive Olympic Games—1900, 1904, and 1908—Ewry won first place in the standing broad jump 3 times, in the standing high jump 3 times, and in the standing hop, step, and jump twice (the latter event not being on the program in 1908). Ewry's best records were as follows: standing broad jump, 11 ft. 6 in. (New York City, August 4,

1906); standing high jump, 5 ft. 5 in. (Paris, July, 1900); standing hop, step, and jump, 34 ft. 8½ in. (Paris, July, 1900); (indoors) three successive standing jumps, 35 ft. 8¾ in. (New York City, September 7, 1903); standing jump backwards, 9 ft. 3 in.

Frequently, in early-day standing broad jumps, weights were held and swung to give added momentum and distance, just as they were used by the ancient Greek athletes in their running broad jumps. So, in listing records in the standing broad jump, it is essential to state whether or not weights were used. While it is generally assumed that Ray Ewry's official standing broad jump without weights of 11 ft. 4⅞ in. (made at the Olympic Games in St. Louis, on August 29, 1904) is the best mark on record in this event, actually there are a number of better marks. Ewry himself, according to Thomas S. Andrews's Sports Record Book, once did 11 ft. 6 in., as noted above. Here are four additional records, without weights, in the standing broad jump:

11 ft. 6 in., by Steve Gooding (USA, 198 lbs.), at "Muscle Beach", Calif., October, 1957.
11 ft. 7 in., by C. Taliclitiras (Greece), at the Olympic Games at Stockholm, July, 1912.
12 ft. 1½ in., by John Darby, Dudley, England. Date?
(Professional) 12 ft. 6½ in., by W. Barker, Wigan, England. Date?

The last-named jumper is credited also with a standing broad jump *with* weights of 14 ft. 10½ in.

Regarded by some observers as "the greatest jumper of all time" was John Higgins (see Plate 69), an English professional who stood only 63¾ inches in height and weighed 142 lbs. He was active shortly after the turn of the century. Here are some of the jumps that Higgins is said to have accomplished: running high jump with weights, 6 ft. 8¾ in.; standing broad jump with weights, 14 ft. 11½ in.; two consecutive standing broad jumps with weights, 28 ft. 10½ in.; three ditto, 42 ft. 2 in.; standing hop and one jump, with weights, 25 ft. 9 in.; standing two hops and a jump, with weights, 38 ft.; two consecutive running jumps with weights, 36 ft. 3 in.; two consecutive jumps backward with weights, 22 ft. 2 in. One of Higgins's exhibition feats was to jump over the backs of 45 chairs in succession, the chairs being 10 feet apart. He was also able to jump lengthwise over a full-sized English billiard table, or over the backs of three horses standing side by side. In his various jumps, Higgins used dumbbells that ranged in weight from 4 pounds to 17 pounds each. He regarded jumping *with weights* as the best possible means of developing all-around jumping ability.

On the basis of W. Barker's and certain other jumps both with and without weights, it would appear that Higgins's standing broad jump with weights of 14 ft. 11½ in. was equivalent to a similar jump without weights of at least 12 ft. 7¼ in. This is over a *foot* farther than the best amateur standing broad jump on record.

Another great English professional jumper was Robert H. Baker of Leeds, who in 1900 retired as undisputed world champion. In August 1898, Baker made a running high jump, without weights, of 6 ft. 8¾ in. Evidently the use of weights does not help much in jumping for height, since Baker jumped only ¾-inch higher (i.e., 6 ft. 9 in.) by using them. In three successive standing broad jumps with weights, Baker was superior even to John Higgins, accomplishing 43 feet to Higgins's 42 ft. 2 in. I regret that I have no photograph of Baker to show, for it is said that the muscular development of his legs was simply extraordinary.

A third phenomenal professional jumper was the famous old-time all-around athlete, Richard P. Williams. Indeed, in some respects, Williams would appear to have been superior both to Higgins and to Baker. In 1900, when Williams was 26 years of age, he was measured and tested by Dr. Dudley Allen Sargent, Director of the Hemingway Gymnasium of Harvard University. Dr. Sargent recorded Williams's height as 69.1 inches and his weight as 141 pounds. This, however, was before Williams started training with weights (as the result of seeing the celebrated strong-man Eugen Sandow in his stage performance). After several years of weight-training, Williams became markedly stronger (and probably quite a bit heavier), and it was between the years 1904 and 1908 that he reached his peak both of strength, speed, and jumping ability.

The jumping records credited to Williams are as follows: standing broad jump with weights, 15 ft. 4 in.; standing jump backwards with weights, 13 ft. 3 in. In contrast to these phenomenal standing jumps, Williams's record in the running broad jump is given as only 24 ft. 6 in. His standing broad jump without weights is listed in one place as 12 feet, and in another as 11 ft. 1 in. On the basis of Barker's jumps (see above), it would be expected that Williams could do a standing broad jump without weights of no less than 12 ft. 11 in.! When Dr. Sargent tested him, he found that Williams, at a bodyweight of 141 pounds, could do a standing vertical jump of 34.9 inches. That is, Williams was capable of jumping vertically and hitting with the crown of his head a disc suspended 8 ft. 8 in. above the floor. The latter jump would be equivalent to a standing broad jump without weights of about 11 ft. 6 in. Other events that indicated Williams's jumping power vertically were his "hitch and kick" (i.e., a standing jump off one foot, and kick) of 9 ft. 6 in., and his running high kick of 10 ft. 3 in. Each of these performances is the best of its kind on record, and serves to substantiate Williams's extraordinary standing vertical jump of 34.9 inches.

It is evident that Williams's best mark in the running broad jump of 24 ft. 6 in. is away under the caliber of his standing jumps. Even if Williams could standing broad jump (without weights) only 11 ft. 6 in., with his 100-yard sprinting ability of 9 seconds flat he should have been capable, with training, of a running broad jump of about 26 ft. 7 in.° Conversely, Jesse Owens, with a running broad jump record of 26 ft. 8¼ in. and an ability to sprint 100 yards in 9.4 seconds (actually, 9.37 seconds?), should have been capable of a *standing* broad jump of about 12 ft. 6 in.! For comparison with the latter figure, the average male college freshman (69 in., 155 lbs.) can do a standing broad jump of about 7 ft. 10½ in. The average woman freshman (64 in., 124 lbs.) can do 6 ft. 6¾ in. This would appear to indicate that the average college girl is 124 x 78.75/155 x 94.5, or about ⅔ (66.7 percent), as strong in jumping as the average male freshman.

An interesting and useful feature of the standing broad jump is that it provides a simple yet excellent test of the strength of the muscles of the legs and lower back. In fact, it is directly related to lifting ability in the two power lifts known as the Squat and the Two Hands Dead Lift, respectively.°° Here are a few diversified instances which show this correlation:

Performer	Bodyweight, lbs.	Broad Jump	Squat, lbs.	Dead Lift, lbs.
Average College Woman	124	6 ft. 6¾ in.	125	151
Average College Freshman	155	7 ft. 10½ in.	181	286
(Prof.) Oscar Matthes	108	10 ft. 7 in.	240	340
Bob Mitchell	148	10 ft. 5 in.	320?	460?
David Willoughby	185	9 ft. 6 in.	356	491
John Grimek	195	10 ft. 6 in.	440	600
Steve Gooding	198	11 ft. 6 in.	450?	c650
(Prof.) Hermann Görner	282	10 ft. 4 in.	565	793.66 (= former Amat. W.R.)

°While 24 ft. 6 in. is the figure usually given as Williams's record in the broad jump, in at least one list it is given as 26 ft. 0½ in.

°°The predicted poundage in the Dead Lift, which in each case closely corresponds with the above actual poundages, is: Dead Lift, lbs. = (Broad Jump, ft./5.943)² x Bodyweight, lbs. The formula for the Squat is more complex, since it involves the weight of the upper body as well as that of the barbell.

Let us turn now to the running high jump. While evidently this event was not used by the ancients—at least in official competition—nevertheless, during modern times it has had a long and interesting history. Many a man, be he warrior or ordinary citizen, has gained distinction through his ability to high-jump. It is said that in the 10th century a knight named Tzimisces was made Emperor of The Holy Roman Empire because he was able, while wearing 25 pounds of chain mail, to leap over the backs of five horses standing side by side. Abraham Lincoln was as capable a jumper as he was a rail-splitter. He could do a running high jump either over a bar placed at 6 feet above the ground, or over the back of a horse. Incidentally, the lowest point on the back of a 16-hand horse is about 5 ft. 1 inch, while the width of the back, in an ordinary saddle horse, is about 20 or 21 inches.

Some extraordinary running and standing high jumps are credited to early-day performers in England. For example, John Darby of Dudley, who is said to have performed a standing broad jump, without weights, of 12 ft. 1½ in., is credited also with a standing high jump, *ankles tied together*, of 6 feet! How this jump was done was not described; but it was added that Darby also made a jump of 6 ft. 5½ in. by taking two *hops* prior to jumping.

In various far-off countries, high-jumping has been a popular athletic event for centuries. However, in those countries, the *technique* of the jump, and the conditions under which it is performed, are so different from the running high jump as defined by the International Athletic Federation that no direct comparison of the differing styles is possible. For instance, on the island of Nias, which lies some 80-odd miles off the west coast of Sumatra, the native men practice leaping over a six-foot stone "jumping pillar."* This is a tapering, built-up column of flat stones, about 3½ feet square at the base and perhaps 20 inches square at the top. In jumping over this stone pillar, the jumper takes off from a rounded boulder that rises about 2 feet above the cobblestone street. The take-off consists of a running start of from 12 to 15 yards.

The most famous native high-jumpers are doubtless those of the Watusi tribe of central Africa. These tall, slender, long-limbed natives average well over 6 feet in height. Their interest in high-jumping comes from this athletic event having been used originally in the training of warriors. Plate 70 shows a Watusi champion jumper clearing what is said to be 2.5 meters (= 8 ft. 2½ in.). The take-off for this jump was

---

*It is said that every village on Nias Island has its jumping-pillar, and that it always stands on a paved (cobblestone) street in front of the chief's house. The pillars in the various villages range in height from 1.8 to 2 meters (about 5 ft. 11 in. to 6 ft. 7 in.).

made from a termite hill a foot or so in height. Whether the jump was thus equivalent to one of 7 feet or over with a level take-off has not been determined. In Plate 70, the man on the left is Adolf Friedrich, Duke of Mecklenburg, who describes the jumping episode in his book, *In the Heart of Africa*. In the *National Geographic* magazine for March 1952, p. 362, there is a good photograph of another Watusi jumper clearing 7 ft. 6 in. (from a foot-high take-off mound). An American athletic coach who went through the Watusi country recently was of the opinion that some of these natives could, under official conditions, probably surpass the existing world record in the high jump if they used the occidental technique. However, unless and until the Watusi jumpers perform under the *same* conditions as Europeans and Americans, it is inaccurate and unfair to credit these African natives with being better jumpers than our present Olympic and National high-jump champions.

While today a height of 7 feet in the running high jump is becoming commonplace, back about the turn of the century 6 feet was almost equally as good, considering the simpler techniques that were then employed. One of the first great high-jumpers to represent the AAU was Michael Sweeney, who came from Ireland to America in the early 1890s. On September 21, 1895, at Manhattan Field, New York, Sweeney, who was only 5 ft. 8¼ in. in height, cleared 6 ft. 5⅝ in., or 9⅜ inches over his own height. The style he used (and in some quarters is said to have originated) was a scissors combined with a backward layout. This technique became known as the "Eastern cut-off."

Sweeney's world record stood for 17 years, until in 1912 George Horine, at Stanford University, did 6 ft. 6⅛ in. Later the same year, on May 18, he raised this to 6 ft. 7 in. Yet, among professional jumpers, Robert Baker of Leeds, England—as mentioned previously—made a running high jump (without weights) of 6 ft. 8¼ in. back in 1898. Among the former and present holders of the high-jump record among amateurs, the three outstanding performers would appear to be Edward Beeson of California, who in 1924 cleared 6 ft. 9½ in., the American Negro jumper John Thomas, who in 1960 did 7 ft. 3¾ in., and the present world record holder, Valeri Brumel of Russia, who on July 21, 1963 did 7 ft. 5¾ in. So far as mastery of *technique* in the running high jump is concerned, it is evident that Brumel stands supreme. He uses the style known as the "Modified Straddle," in which the jumper's center of gravity is raised a minimum distance above the bar and may even pass *under* the bar. The first great exponent of the straddle style of high jumping was Les Steers of Oregon, who in 1941 cleared 6 ft. 11 in. In view of Steer's bodyweight having been 190 lbs. (height 73.5 in.), this was a highly meritorious feat.

In mentioning the jumper's center of gravity (CG), an interesting point is raised. Who is the greatest high-jumper: the one who clears the bar at the greatest height, or the one who raises his CG the greatest height? The two achievements are not necessarily the same, since in clearing a bar the jumper's CG is raised by a variable amount, depending on what *technique* he uses to go over the bar. In a simple, old-fashioned "scissors" high jump, the CG may have to be raised nearly a foot above the bar in order for the bar to be cleared. In the "Eastern" style reputedly introduced by Michael Sweeney in 1895, the scissors is combined with a "lay-out" as the jumper's body goes over the bar in an almost horizontal position. In this style the CG is raised perhaps 7 inches. In the "Western Roll," the differential is only about 6 inches; while in the presently popular "Modified Straddle" the jumper's CG can be anywhere from several inches above the bar to actually below it. It depends on how skillful the jumper is in literally winding his body and limbs over the bar.*

In a typical white male jumper, the CG is located at a level that averages about 57 percent of the jumper's height, or about 2 inches below the navel. Thus in a 6-footer the CG is about 41 inches above the soles of the feet. In women, the CG is only about 54 percent of the height, or about 2 inches *lower* than in a man of the same height. In male Negroes the CG averages over 58 percent of the height, or about an inch higher than in a white man of the same height. In female Negroes the CG is likewise about an inch higher (*c.* 55.5 percent) than in a white woman of the same height. The relatively higher CG in Negroes is one reason why they excel in the running high jump.

It must be evident that the *taller* a jumper is, the less credit he should be given for clearing a given height. If his legs were sufficiently long, he could simply step over the bar without lifting his body (CG) at all. Thus it is clear that the high-jumpers listed in the above table represent the approximate limit to which the performer's center of gravity can be raised in a running jump, since in each case the jumper's own height is taken into consideration. Probably there are a few other individuals who have demonstrated equal ability to spring upward into the air, but who used other styles of jumping.** It can

---

*A number of books have been published in which the various *techniques* of jumping are described. One of the best of these dissertations is *The Mechanics of Athletics,* by Geoffrey Dyson.

**Since the above was written, a new and unorthodox style of high jumping has been introduced by Dick Fosbury, of Oregon State University. In Fosbury's unique style, he approaches the bar nearly straight on, takes off on his right foot, then turns his back to the bar and arches over, face up. He ends by landing upside down on his upper back. Using this spectacular technique, Fosbury was the hit of the 1968 Olympic Games. His best jump, one of 7 ft. 4¼ in., constituted a new American and Olympic record.

be estimated that John Thomas, despite his world's third-best high jump of 7 ft. 3¾ in., because of his great height (77¼ in.) and his use of a Modified Straddle style, probably did not raise his CG more than 43 inches. The best woman high-jumper, Iolanda Balas (73 in.) of Rumania, in 1961 cleared 6 ft. 3¼ in., and in the process raised her CG about 42 inches.

Here are some figures showing the estimated heights to which the CG was raised in various famous performers of the running high jump:

Table 16.   Some Outstanding Records in the Running High Jump[*]

Year	Performer	Nation	High Jump, inches	Style of Jump	Performer's Height, in.	Height CG was raised, in.
1887	William Page	USA	76.0	Modified scissors	66.5	48.5
1962	Valeri Brumel	USSR	89.75	Modified straddle	72.9	48.25
1895?	James Ryan	USA	78.5	"Straight at bar"	72.0 ?	48.0 ?
1924	Clinton Larson	USA	81.5	Backward layout	69.5	47.9
1965	Chih-Chin Ni	China	88.6	Modified straddle?	72.5	47.3
1895	Michael Sweeney	USA	77.1	Eastern cut-off	68.25	46.0
1934	Walter Marty	USA	81.1	Western roll	73.0	45.9
1925	Harold Osborn	USA	80.9	Western roll	71.5	45.7
1956	Charles Dumas	USA	84.6	Straddle	73.5	44.7

[*] (See also Fig. 11 in Appendix).

Let us now briefly consider some of the best records in the *standing* high jump. All the jumps hereafter mentioned were made in the *scissors* (the jumper standing with his *side* to the bar) style, unless otherwise noted. Where comparison is made between contemporaneously performed standing high jumps and standing broad jumps, the average or typical ratio is found to be about 0.475. That is, for a standing broad jump of 10 feet, one would expect a standing high jump of 4.75 feet. For the existing amateur world record in the standing broad jump, 11 ft. 7 in., the "expectation" in the standing high jump would be .475 x 11.583, or 5 ft. 6 in. Actually, the best amateur record listed is 5 ft. 9¼ in., by Johan Evandt (Norway), at Oslo on March 4, 1962. The famed amateur standing jumper, Ray Ewry (USA) made a record of 5 ft. 5 in. at the Olympic Games in Paris, in 1900. Ewry's record in the standing broad jump, as mentioned previously, was 11 ft. 6 in.

However, among old-time professional jumpers, the records both in the standing broad jump and the standing high jump are appreciably better than those which were made by contemporary amateur jumpers. William Barker of Wigan, England, made an actual standing broad jump of 12 ft. 6½ in., and John Higgins, also of England, an estimated jump of 12 ft. 7¼ in. (see above). Applying the .475 ratio to the latter broad jump, one would expect a *standing* high jump of 5 ft. 11⅞ in. It would certainly appear that some of the great professional jumpers of the past were capable of a *standing* high jump (scissors style) of an even 6 feet!

Another type of high jumping, which is perhaps even less familiar to the average present-day sports follower, is that in which the jumper, from a standstill takeoff, simply jumps vertically as high as he can. Back about the turn of the century, Dr. Sargent used this vertical jump a great deal in testing the students who trained in the Hemingway Gymnasium of Harvard University. In consequence, the exercise is commonly called the Sargent Jump.* In this jump the average college Freshman (69 in., 155 lbs.) can raise himself 18 inches, while the average college woman (64 in., 124 lbs.) can do 15 inches. Thus, in the vertical jump, just as in the standing broad jump, the average college girl is just 2/3 as strong as the average Freshman. If she were equal in height and weight to the man, her jumping strength would be about 77 percent as great as the man's. Also, in the vertical jump, Negroes are said to average about 2 inches higher than whites.

It may at this point be remarked that the heights or distances attainable in *all* styles of jumping—boh standing and running—are closely interrelated. Hence the possibilities in the standing vertical jump may be deduced or estimated from the known records in other styles. A standing broad jump of 10 feet, for example, is equivalent to a vertical or Sargent jump of 27.9 inches. Conversely, Richard P. William's vertical jump of 34.9 inches (see pp. above) was equal in merit to a standing broad jump of 11 ft. 6 in. Similarly it may be computed that the estimated record of 12 ft. 7¼ in. in the standing broad jump attributable to John Higgins, the old-time English professional jumper, is equivalent to a vertical jump of 40.1 inches. Whether anyone has ever attained the latter height is unknown to the present writer.

As would be expected, some of the leading ballet dancers have been capable of extraordinary vertical jumps, but almost invariably such jumps have been made from a preliminary springing take-off. In October 1948, a photograph was published which showed the dancer Alexandre Kalioujny, leaping straight up to a height that appeared to be no less than 42 inches above the stage floor! In all probability this jump had been made from a springing take-off. The phenomenal "Russian" (actually

---

*Dr. Sargent wrote a paper in which he called the vertical jump "The Physical Test of a Man." This appeared in the *American Physical Education Review,* vol. 26, pp. 188–194, April 1921.

Polish) dancer, Vaclav Nijinsky (65 in., 135 lbs.), was said by his director, Diaghileff, to have had an "elevation" of almost three feet. However, on the basis of Nijinsky's known jumping abilities otherwise, it would seem that he must have been capable of a vertical jump of at least 38 inches and possibly even 40 inches.* The present-day Russian ballet star Rudolf Nureyev (66 in., 160 lbs.) has been credited with being able to raise himself "four feet" into the air. This height corresponds with the greatest heights that champion field athletes have been able to attain (that is, raise their centers of gravity) in the running high jump. Four feet, or 48 inches, with a springing take-off from one foot, corresponds to a standing vertical jump off both feet of about 36 inches. That is, in a running high jump, scissors style, the amount of height gained over a *standing* jump in the same style would appear to average about 12 or 12½ inches.

Evidently the latter amount should be deducted also from the leaps of African natives, such as the warriors of the Masai, who perform a great number of "bouncing" jumps prior to going on a lion hunt. In the October, 1954 issue of the *National Geographic* magazine (p. 490), one of a number of jumping Masai tribesmen appears to be jumping straight up to a height of about three feet. However, it is to be doubted if he could attain such an elevation from a still (not bouncing) takeoff. As will be seen in Table 16, the "springiest" Negro high-jumper, Charles Dumas, raised his CG less than 45 inches, which would mean that he could do a vertical jump of probably less than 33 inches.

Most so-called "natural" athletes are great jumpers. Jim Thorpe (72.5 in., 180 lbs.), the famous decathlon and all-around athlete, had a personal record in the running high jump of 6 ft. 5 in. Back in 1912, this was within 2 inches of the world record. The great old-time heavyweight boxing champion Jim Jeffries (72.6 in., 210 lbs.) said that at the age of 24 (1899) he could run 100 yards *barefooted* in under 11 seconds and could do a *standing* high jump "to the height of my shoulders." This would have been about five feet, and would have been equivalent to a running high jump, scissors style, of about 6 ft. 2 in. George Hackenschmidt, perhaps the greatest of all heavyweight wrestling champions, at the same body-weight as Jeffries but with a height of only 68.7 inches, could do a running, scissors high jump of 5 ft. 10 in. On one occasion, to demonstrate his leaping ability and general physical fitness, "Hack," with his feet together, jumped *101 times in succession* (!) over a table 32 inches high and 27½ inches wide. The 101 jumps took nearly a half-hour. Bob Mitchell

---

*Nijinsky, as is well known, is credited with having been the only dancer to achieve 12 *entrechats* while in the air. However, a 19th-century American ballet dancer (Negro?) named George Washington Smith is said to have been capable of performing "entrechats dix" (i.e., five crossings of the feet while in the air). The only woman to have been credited with 10 *entrechats* was the old-time Danish ballerina, Adeline Genée.

(65 in., 148 lbs.), who was the American lightweight amateur weight-lifting champion during the 1930s, could without training do a standing broad jump of 10 ft. 5 in., a running high jump of 6 ft. 1 in., and a standing high jump of 5 ft. 4 in. Many of the old-time American weightlifters were also all-around athletes and first-class jumpers.

In the 15th century, that universal genius, Leonardo da Vinci, evidently numbered athletics among his countless abilities. One of his feats, with which he used to astonish his visitors, was to jump upside-down up to the ceiling and kick the bells of a glass chandelier!

A number of the athletic stars in motion pictures have been capable jumpers. Apparently Burt Lancaster, who took the part of Jim Thorpe in the movie of that title, was one of these. In the silent movies, two first-class jumpers were Douglas Fairbanks, Sr. (67 in., 146 lbs.) and George Walsh. In one of his pictures, Fairbanks, with a springing take-off of only one step, jumped with both feet onto a platform 5 feet above the floor. Walsh (71 in., 180 lbs.) was said to have been a better jumper even than Fairbanks, and was a versatile all-around athlete with an ideal physique. Apparently there was nothing that he could not do! How I would enjoy seeing again some of the old William Fox movies in which Walsh was the hero!

In the gymnasium the best jumpers are of course the tumblers, some of whom have demonstrated prodigious jumping powers (such as the Arab tumbler who, at the end of several flip-flaps, did a perfect *double* back somersault!). Other great leapers were the old-time circus springboard jumpers, who would take off down an incline, running, then do a somersault, or a double somersault, over a row of horses, camels, or sometimes even elephants!

Probably one of the greatest 'natural' jumpers was Charlie Siegrist, a famous circus tumbler and all-around athlete. Siegrist could perform a *double* back somersault from the back of one cantering, bareback horse to that of another horse, following. This feat at the time was unique. Whether it has since been duplicated by some other performer, I do not know. Another of Siegrist's feats, which I saw him do sometime in the late 1910s or early 1920s, was to jump right over the head of an attendant standing in the ring. So great was Siegrist's leaping power that it was almost as though he had *hurdled* over the man! And in addition to being a jumper and a tumbler, Siegrist was an outstanding aerialist, comedy rider, clown, and wire walker.

17.
Swimming

In swimming, we come to an event in which gravity is largely eliminated by reason of the performer's body being supported in water. Consequently, the physical requirements in this sport differ somewhat from those involved in athletic events performed on the ground. With the weight of the body being, in swimming, a lesser factor than in land events, women are enabled to make a relatively better showing in swimming than in any other sport. The reason for this is that, compared with men, their buoyancy in the water is aided by their slightly lesser specific gravity.

So numerous are the various styles and distances recognized even in the standardized swimming events that no attempt will be made here to discourse on them at length. Rather, we shall endeavor simply to point out the "fatigue" element in swimming as compared with running over the same distances, and to list various performances of high merit made by professional swimmers, whose achievements unfortunately are ignored in most lists of amateur records. Neither have we made any attempt to keep strictly "up to date" on swimming records, which anyway is a practical impossibility. Most of the records in the following list are as of January 1, 1967; a few are more recent. In any case, the latest and highest record in *any* athletic event, swimming included, is not necessarily the best or most meritorious record. The element of date of performance must also be taken into account. This may be seen by referring to Figure 12.

In a comparison of the four usually employed styles of swimming listed in Table 17, it is seen that the freestyle is the fastest means of moving through the water, and the breast stroke the slowest. Taking the average "sprinting" speed in the freestyle swim as 4 miles per hour, the average in the butterfly would be about 3 2/3 mph, in the backstroke about 3½ mph, and in the breaststroke only about 3 1/7 mph. In the individual medley, the two records cited in the table are only about 2½ percent, or about 7 seconds, slower than if the separate world record times in the four different swimming styles were added together.

With reference to Table 17, if the various times (in seconds) in freestyle

Table 17. World Records in Swimming (Men's). See also next page.

Style	Distance	Time	Performer	Nation	Place	Year	MPH
Freestyle	50 yards	0:23.4	Duke Kahanamoku	USA	San Francisco	1913	4.37
	80 yards	0:42.2	Duke Kahanamoku	USA	Honolulu	1916	3.88
	100 yards	0:46.8	Steve Clark	USA	New Haven, Conn.	1961	4.37
	100 meters	0:52.6	Ken Walsh	USA	Winnipeg, Man.	1967	4.25
	110 yards	0:53.5	Robert McGregor	Scotland	Blackpool, Eng.	1966	4.20
	200 meters	1:55.7	Don Schollander	USA	Oak Park, Ill.	1967	3.87
	220 yards	1:57.0	Don Schollander	USA	Vancouver, B.C.	1966	3.85
	400 meters	4:04.0	H. Fassnacht	W. Ger.	Louisville, Ky.	1969	3.66
	440 yards	4:12.2	Greg Charlton	USA	Vancouver, B.C.	1966	3.57
	800 meters	8:42.0	Francis Luyce	France	Dinard, France	1967	3.43
	880 yards	8:55.5	Murray Rose	Australia	Vancouver, B.C.	1964	3.43
	1500 meters	16:04.5	Mike Burton	USA	Louisville, Ky.	1969	3.48
Breast stroke	100 meters	1:06.9	G. Prokopenko	USSR	Moscow, USSR	1964	3.34
	110 yards	1:08.2	Ian O'Brien	Australia	Kingston, Jam.	1966	3.30
	200 meters	2:27.8	Ian O'Brien	Australia	Tokyo, Japan	1964	3.03
	220 yards	2:28.0	Ian O'Brien	Australia	Kingston, Jam.	1966	3.04
Butterfly stroke	100 meters	0:56.3	Mark Spitz	USA	Santa Clara, Calif.	1967	3.97
	110 yards	0:58.1	Daniel Sherry	Canada	Blackpool, Eng.	1966	3.87
	200 meters	2:06.0	John Ferris	USA	Tokyo, Japan	1967	3.55
	220 yards	2:08.4	Kevin Berry	Australia	Sydney, Australia	1963	3.50
Back Stroke	100 meters	0:59.1	Charles Hickcox	USA	Tokyo, Japan	1967	3.78
	110 yards	1:01.5	John Monckton	Australia	Melbourne, Aus.	1958	3.66
	200 meters	2:09.4	Charles Hickcox	USA	Tokyo, Japan	1967	3.46
	220 yards	2:12.0	Peter Reynolds	Australia	Kingston, Jam.	1966	3.41
Individual medley	400 meters	4:45.4	Dick Roth	USA	Tokyo, Japan	1964	3.13
	440 yards	4:50.8	Peter Reynolds	Australia	Kingston, Jam.	1966	3.09

swimming are plotted on a graph in relation to the distances swum, it becomes evident that, from 200 yards on, the two outstanding performances are Don Schollander's 200 meters in 1:55.7 and Mike Burton's 1500 meters in 16:04.5. If Schollander's time for 200 meters and Burton's time for 1500 meters are connected on the graph by a straight line (and there is every reason to believe that a straight line is valid), it develops that the following improvements in time for the intervening distances should be expected: (Time, sec. = .59704 Distance, yards — 14.88).

Distance	Present record	Expected record	Difference, seconds
220 yards	1:57.0	1:56.5	− 0.5
400 meters	4:04.0	4:06.3	− 1.9
440 yards	4:12.2	4:07.8	− 4.4
800 meters	8:42.0	8:27.5	− 14.5
880 yards	8:55.5	8:30.5	− 25.0
1500 meters	16:04.5	16:04.5	± 00.0

It is evident also that Duke Kahanamoku's time of 0:42.2 for 80 yards can be reduced to 36 seconds or less. As the above list shows, the record for 220 yards is only a 5/10 second slower than would be expected. However, the shortcomings increase with distance, so that the present record for 880 yards woulds appear to be about 25 *seconds slower* than it should be. Here is an opportunity for some topnotch freestyle swimmer to prove that the world records for 400 meters, 440 yards, 800 meters, and 880 yards can indeed be better than they are (and *without* lowering Mike Burton's remarkable time for 1500 meters).

If compared with the records over the same distances made in walking, freestyle swimming is found to be, on the average, only about 35 percent as rapid a means of locomotion. However, the fatigue element, as judged on the basis of reduced speed with distance, proceeds about *46 percent faster* in race walking (up to a mile) than in freestyle swimming. Thus, while over a distance of 150 yards the record in walking is about 3 times as fast as that in swimming, when the distance of a mile is reached the ratio has diminished to 2.73. In short, since in swimming the body is largely *supported*, less energy is required to progress, and fatigue consequently mounts more slowly.

The latter statement is borne out by the swimming records established by women. Whereas in running (sprinting) the women's time for 50 yards is about 91 percent as fast as the men's, for 440 yards it is less than 87 percent as fast. In freestyle swimming (up at least to a distance of

1500 meters), the records for women average a remarkably consistent 91.49 percent of those for men, with no lessening whatever in speed as longer distances are involved. Indeed, if anything, there is a very slight *improvement* in the ratio of women's swimming speed to men's as longer distances are covered. It is generally accepted that the *skill* of women in all styles of swimming is quite equal to that of men, and that their lesser speed is due simply to their lesser ratio of strength to size. However, their *endurance* in the water is fully equal to that of men.

As to who is, or was, the greatest sprint swimmer, it is the man whom sports experts and sports followers alike have long regarded as such: Johnny Weissmuller. A glance at Figure 13 bears out this assertion. While the plotting of the records on this graph shows an erratic distribution up to about the year 1915—due to the early records being far below their potential—from 1915 on there is a reasonably good correspondence of the curve with that of population increase. In relation to the curve, Weissmuller's record of 51 seconds flat, made in 1927, is the outstanding performance.[*] It is 1.2 seconds faster than would be expected in the year 1927; and it stood for 9 years (another record, for the event) before being equalled. Steve Clark's present world record of 46.8 seconds, made in 1961, is a fine performance, but it is doubtful whether it will stand as long as Weissmuller's mark stood.

The greatest woman speed swimmer is generally considered to have been Helene Madison of Seattle, who in 1932 (aged 18, height 70.5 in.) held no fewer than 15 of the 16 women's world records, ranging from 100 yards to a mile.

Many extraordinary performances in *long-distance* swimming have been achieved over the years, mainly by professional swimmers. Some of the more outstanding of these performances will now be listed. No particular order in the listing is observed.

1. As the most famous swimming endurance test has been that of crossing the English Channel, let us look first at some of the records that have been made in this swim. The route usually taken by swimmers of the Channel is from Cape Griz Nez, France, to Dover, England. The distance is about 20 miles. The first person said to have made this difficult swim was Jean-Marie Saletti, a French soldier, who in the year of 1815 dived off a British prison ship at Dover and gained his freedom by swimming to Boulogne. The next crossing was made on May 29, 1875, by a American named Captain Paul Boynton. However,

---

[*]However, it would appear that .7 or .8 of a second may be cut off the time for 100 yards by performing in a 25-yard (rather than 100-yard) tank. All of Duke Kahanamoku's records were made in a 100-yard pool, where he was unable to benefit from a turn and kick-off.

Boynton wore a life-saving suit that buoyed him up so that he paddled, rather than swam, across the Channel. His time for the crossing was 23 hours 30 minutes.

The first generally recognized authentic swimming of the Channel was made by Captain Matthew Webb of Dawley, Shropshire, England. On August 24–25, 1875, Webb, at the age of 27, swam from Dover to Calais in 21 hours 45 minutes. The crawl stroke then being unknown, Webb used a breaststroke and a sidestroke, doing from 25 to 27 strokes a minute at the start, and 12 to the minute at the finish. As in this pioneering attempt Webb had no knowledge of the Channel's various currents, he actually swam a zigzag course of about 38 miles in order to cross the 20-mile Dover Strait. After this feat, Webb gave swimming exhibitions, and became something of a "stunt" performer in the water. Once, in the Lambeth Baths, England, he won a wager by swimming 14 hours a day for 6 days, during which time he covered 74 miles. On the afternoon of July 24, 1883, in an attempt to replenish his fading fame and fortune, Webb essayed the suicidal feat of swimming through the Whirlpool Rapids (some ¾ of a mile) below Niagara Falls. In this attempt he died; while some accounts say by drowning, others say from the terrific pressure of the waves of water that pounded him.

Although since Captain Webb's time more than a thousand attempts have been made to swim the English Channel, of these only about a hundred have been successful. After Webb's crossing, it was not until 36 years later, on September 5–6, 1911, that a second successful swim was made. This was by another Englishman, Thomas Burgess, who took 22 hours 35 minutes to make the crossing.

The record time for swimming the Channel from France to England is 9 hours 35 minutes, by Barry Watson of England in 1964. In the opposite direction, the record is 10 hours 23 minutes, by Helge Jensen of Canada in 1960. The first swimmer to cross the Channel in both directions was Edward Temme of England. In 1927 he swam from France to England in 14 hours 29 minutes, and in 1934 from England to France in 15 hours 54 minutes.

The first woman to negotiate the Channel was the famous American swimmer Gertrude Ederle who on August 6, 1926 made the crossing from Cape Griz Nez to Dover in 14 hours 31 minutes. This time was 2 hours and 2 minutes faster than the best previous record, made in 1923. The first woman to swim the Channel in both directions was Florence Chadwick (USA). On September 11, 1951, she swam from England to France in 16 hours 22 minutes, and was the only woman up to that time to do so. In 1964, Greta Andersen (USA) lowered Miss Chadwick's England-France time by swimming the distance in 13 hours 40 minutes. Miss Andersen had already, in 1958, swum in the opposite direction (France to England) in 11 hours 1 minute. On July 17, 1967, the latter mark was surpassed by Elaine Gray (England), with a time of only 10 hours 24 minutes.* It would appear that, on the average, the swim from England to France takes about an hour longer than that from France to England.

Away back in 1905, the famous woman swimmer and diver Annette Kellermann tried the Channel swim, but when only 6½ miles out from Dover (after swimming 6 hours 5 minutes) had to give up on account of seasickness. The swimmer who made the greatest number of unsuccessful attempts to swim the Channel was the Englishman Jabez Wolffe, who failed 21 times! Later, Wolffe advised and helped train Gertrude Ederle for her successful crossing in 1926.

Another famous woman swimmer who failed to conquer the English Channel was Mlle. Walburga von Icacescu, of Poland. Yet, some years earlier, in July 1900, she had swum the Danube from Vienna to Stein—a distance of 48 miles—in only 8 hours 3 minutes. This, however, was downstream, and she must have been literally swept along by the current. One of Annette Kellermann's swims also was in the Danube. On June 12, 1906, she swam 23 miles in 8 hours 11 minutes, ending at Vienna. Another of her swims was from Dover to Ramsgate, England, a distance (as swum) of about 20 miles, in 4 hours 28 minutes. This swim was made in July 1905. In it, evidently Miss Kellermann made good time, since a year later it took the English Channel aspirant, Jabez Wolffe, 6 hours 35 minutes to cover the same route.

2. A long-distance swimmer who in some quarters was regarded as the world's greatest, was Pedro Candiotti, of Argentina. He tried on some 15 occasions to swim the Paraná River from Rosario to Buenos Aires, a distance of 205 miles. Although he never succeeded in covering the entire distance, he made some highly creditable showings. In February 1935 he made his longest completed swim, in the Paraná River from Santa Fe to Zarate (Argentina), a distance of 281 miles. It took him 84 hours.

3. A swim over an even greater distance (288 miles) was made in 1939 by Clarence Giles (USA). He swam continuously in the Yellowstone River in Montana, between the towns of Glendive and Billings. He covered the 288 miles in 77 hours 31 minutes. Again, John Sigmund of St. Louis swam non-stop down the Mississippi River from St. Louis to Caruthersville, a distance of 292 miles. His time was 89 hours 42 minutes.

---

*This would appear to bear out the idea that *the longer the distance,* the better a woman swimmer compares with a man. Miss Gray's time of 10:24 is 92.15 percent as fast as the men's record of 9:35 over the same route, whereas at distances of under a mile the ratio is 91.49 percent.

4. The present record for distance covered is held by Fred Newton of Clinton, Oklahoma. In 1931, he swam down the Mississippi River all the way from Minneapolis to New Orleans. He covered the 2300 miles in 742 hours (= 30 days, 2 hours!), averaging 3.1 mph. During his swim, he gained 10 pounds!

5. The women's record for continuous swimming (in a tank) is held by Mrs. Myrtle Huddleston of New York City. In 1931, she "swam" without rest for 87 hours 27 minutes. Another accomplishment of Mrs. Huddleston was, in 1927, to swim the Catalina (California) Channel, a distance (zig-zagging) of 36 miles. Her time was 20 hours 42 minutes. Twenty-five years later, on September 21, 1952, Florence Chadwick swam the same Channel (actually, the San Pedro Channel) in 13 hours 47 minutes 32 seconds, going straight across from Catalina to Palos Verdes, a distance of only 21 miles. This success was attained after she had failed in an earlier attempt. Interestingly, Miss Chadwick covered her 21 miles at the rate of 1.523 mph, while Mrs. Huddleston swam her 36 miles at 1.739 mph. In a comparison such as this, how is one to decide which swimmer deserves the most credit?

6. George Young of Canada won the 1927 swim from Catalina Island to the California mainland in the time of 15 hours 48 minutes.

7. Tom Parks (66 in., 180 lbs.), a professional swimmer, swam from Catalina Island to the Palos Verdes mainland, on September 23, 1954, in 13 hours 25 minutes 31 seconds. He thus bettered Florence Chadwick's 1952 swim over the same course by 22 minutes 1 second. Actually, Parks was within a mile of the Palos Verdes shore in only 11½ hours, but was then carried by the tide 2 or 3 miles off course.

8. Captain Alfred Brown swam through the Panama Canal for a distance of 48 miles, at the opening in August 1914. He also swam from the Battery, New York, to Sandy Hook, in 13 hours 38 minutes. August 28, 1913.

9. L. B. Goodwin of St. Louis swam 10 miles in only 2 hours 30 minutes 49 seconds, on September 5, 1910. Presumably this swim was downstream.

10. Miss Eileen Lee of London swam 23 miles in 7 hours 1 minute, in June 1916, and 36¼ miles in 10 hours 17 minutes, on August 18, 1916.

11. Miss Mary Margaret Revell of Detroit in 1963 made several long-

distance swims in difficult waters. She was the first woman to swim the Mackinac Straits (Lake Michigan to Lake Huron), covering the 16 miles in just over 7 hours. She was also the first woman to swim the Messina Straits in Sicily, making the round trip of 13 miles in about 5½ hours. She has also swum the Straits of Bosporus, the Dardanelles, and the Black Sea.

12. On September 26, 1954, Jack Lalanne, a professional physical culturist of Oakland, California, swam the Golden Gate—a distance of about a mile—while *underwater*. He covered the distance in 45 minutes, using a frogman's suit, mask and goggles, a double oxygen tank, and a pair of oversized flippers.

In addition to the above-listed and other performances in "straight" long-distance swimming, numerous "handicap" swims of equal merit are on record. Two outstanding performers in the latter department were N. B. Coykendall and Henry Elionsky. The following statistics on the last-named two swimmers were kindly furnished by my friend and fellow sports-enthusiast, Ottley R. Coulter, of Lemont Furnace, Pa.

A. "HANDICAP" SWIMS
N. B. Coykendall

In June 1918, swam from Milford, Pa., to Delaware Water Gap, Pa., in the Delaware River, a distance of 39 miles, in 6 hours 22 minutes, the river being at flood tide after a heavy rain.

In September 1919, pulled 27 persons in a two-ton motorboat a distance of a mile, with his hands and feet shackled in regulation handcuffs. Silver Lake, Fairmont, Minn.

In July 1924, swam a mile while bound around with so much rope as to be "helpless." Also about this time he swam 150 feet while in an upside-down ("standing on his head") position. The time was 1 minute 45 seconds.

Henry Elionsky

Elionsky was a giant of a man, standing about 6 feet and with an enormous chest. It is evident that in order to have accomplished feats of swimming such as the following, he had tremendous lung power. In August 1914, Elionsky swam down the Hudson River, and from one shore to the other across it, continuously for a distance estimated to be over 60 miles. Again, he swam from the Battery, in lower New York City, to Swinburne Island and returned to the Battery, a distance of over 25 miles, with his hands and feet shackled. The time was 11 hours 30 minutes.

In November 1915, swam from the Brooklyn Bridge to Bay Ridge, with his hands and feet shackled and towing seven men in a sea dory. The distance was 7 miles, and the time 3 hours 40 minutes.

Swam from the Battery to Fort Wadsworth in the Narrows with a 200-pound man tied on his back. The distance was 10 miles, and the time 4 hours 50 minutes.

Swam Hell Gate bound in a straitjacket and with 15 feet of iron chain tied to his feet. The distance was 5 miles, and the time 2 hours 40 minutes.

In November 1915, swam Hell Gate with his hands and feet shackled and two men bound onto his back.

Swam from Bay Ridge to the Battery while tied in a chair. Time, 3 hours 20 minutes.

In October 1913, swam from the Battery to within a quarter-mile of Coney Island. The distance was 14 miles, and the time 5 hours 30 minutes.

At Palm Beach, Florida, hauled a sea dory containing nine men and carried two more on his back, with his hands and feet shackled, through five miles of heavy sea in 2 hours 50 minutes.

18.
Man Versus Wild Animals

One way in which a man may be credited with colossal physical strength is by accepting that he was able to kill a savage wild animal with his bare hands. Such a feat is one that the average man can fully appreciate, since he knows what a battle even a house cat can put up in defending itself. To increase a 7-pound domestic cat to the size of a 400-pound male African lion means to multiply its strength by 15! Yet stories have been handed down about men killing lions with their bare hands.

A perennially popular story of a man vs. lion combat is the legend of Hercules killing the monstrous lion of Nemea in its lair. The supernaturally endowed animal was able to resist the hero's arrows, his sword, and even his massive club, which he broke to smithereens on the lion's head, to have it produce only a slight ringing in the monster's ears! The only way Hercules was able to dispatch the huge cat was by getting a chancery hold on its neck and choking it to death. Afterward, and throughout his career, he used the lion's invulnerable hide as a protective cloak. In the titanic struggle, it is said that the lion bit off one of Hercules's fingers, yet strangely—although this was the first of the hero's famous twelve Labors—all statues show Hercules with a full set of ten fingers.

Another mythological figure who is said to have strangled a lion was Phylius, a friend of Hercules. Phylius, like Hercules, performed this feat as one of a number of imposed tasks. Another of these tasks was to wrestle and subdue a wild bull.

Samson—who by some classicists is regarded as the Hebrew counterpart of Hercules—is said in the Bible to have "rent" (torn apart the jaws of) a young lion that roared at him, "and he had nothing in his hands."

Polydamas (see Chapter 1), an actual Greek strong-man and pankratist of 400 B.C., is credited with the feat of strangling a full-grown lion.

In order to thus overcome a lion, or a tiger—or, for that matter, even one of the smaller great cats, such as a leopard or a cougar—it would seem that the only way to keep from being torn to shreds would be to first knock out the cat before strangling it. Whether a full-grown African lion could be rendered unconscious by a well-placed blow to its jaw is a question; but a giant orangutan was once thus knocked out by the late animal-trapper Frank Buck—and an adult male orang has a jaw almost as massive as that of a lion. A remarkable story, given out as true, is that a tiger-tamer of Calcutta, named the Sohong Swami, was accustomed to beating his captured "cats" into submission with his bare fists. Once, it is said, he knocked out a freshly caught jungle tiger in this manner, but only after being severely scratched and torn by the infuriated animal. But were the tigers that were delivered to the Swami for training full-grown specimens? Usually, animals caught for this purpose are immature ones, in which it may still be possible to inculcate new habits and responses.

Experienced wrestlers claim that a lion (or a tiger) might conceivably be strangled by applying to its head a hold similar to a "front face lock," in which the leverage on the neck is tremendous. It would be interesting to know if the Greek strong-man Polydamas (6 ft. 8 in., 300 lbs.?), first used a knockout punch on the lion that he is said to have strangled. Oh, if only someone could invent a "time-viewing" machine, with which we could *see* some of the events said to have occurred in the past!

Several instances are on record in which a man has battled with a leopard. The first of these fights of which I have heard was the one that was engaged in by Carl Akeley, a famous animal sculptor and taxidermist (it was he, in fact, who revolutionized the art of presenting realistic scenes of animal life in museum dioramas). It was on his first expedition to Africa, in 1896, that Akeley, who was then 32, had his fight with a leopard. But the leopard was a small one—a female weighing only 80 pounds—and had first been weakened by a shot from Akeley. With one of Akeley's hands gripping its neck and the other hand forced down its throat, the leopard finally relaxed. Even then, it was not dead, but had to be killed with a knife.

Frank Merrill (Otto Poll), the second of the silent-screen actors to play the part of Tarzan, had a real scuffle with a leopard in one of his jungle scenes. The animal had bitten Merrill on his leg, inflicting a severe wound, whereupon Merrill got a grip on the cat's throat and held it until the animal let go of his leg. Merrill was of the opinion that a strong man could strangle a leopard, provided the man got behind the animal and kept out of the way of its claws. He believed, however, that a lion was beyond the power of any man to overcome without at least a knife or a club.

The only instance of a staged "fight" between a man and a lion of which I know was the one in which the pioneer theatrical strong-man, Eugen Sandow, "fought" a lion in a caged arena in San Francisco in 1893. But it is significant that Sandow emerged from the combat unscathed. The lion had been muzzled and its paws mittened. Even so, if it had felt like it, the lion could have crushed Sandow's skull with a single blow. It would certainly appear that, in addition to being detoothed and de-clawed, the big cat had been given a *sedative* prior to its meeting with Sandow.

In *Outdoor Life* for March 1945 there is an account by F. Fawcett of where a big, powerful gold miner, back in the 'nineties, killed a female cougar bare-handed. The fight took place in a cave where the cougar had its lair. The man had come across two small kittens in the cave, and had taken one of them outside. As he was returning for the other kitten, the mother cougar entered the cave through another opening, and immediately sprang at the man. After a long and terrific struggle, in which the man was close to being exhausted, he managed to bite into the cougar's throat and through one of her jugular veins. This is the only apparently authentic instance I have come across in which one of the big cats was killed solely with a man's own natural weapons.

A third instance in this field is more recent. The author, Jean-Pierre Hallet, who was in the Belgian Congo in 1957, tells in his book, *Congo Kitabu,* of a fight he then had with a male leopard weighing 120 pounds. Hallet, who was a big, powerful man weighing 250 pounds, was handicapped by having lost his right hand in an earlier accident. Thus his right forearm terminated in a stump at the wrist, and it was partly with this arm that he held, from behind, the leopard's head and shoulders tightly against his chest so that the infuriated cat could not reach him with its foreclaws. Meanwile, he held the animal's hind quarters securely between his own legs. Hallet admits that he could not have killed the leopard by strangling, and that its tenacity of life and its recuperative powers were astonishing. Only when one of his frightened native bearers —all of whom had dashed off—managed to toss a knife where Hallet was able to reach it was the giant white man able to stab the leopard to death.

An old-time Italian strong-man named Peter Coutaliano traveled extensively in giving exhibitions of his strength. In the early 1900s he is said to have put on a show in Montevideo, Uruguay, in which he wrestled with a bull and killed a tiger. How the latter feat was accomplished was not explained. Could he have first knocked the tiger out (à la Sohong Swami) and then strangled it? It seems far more likely that he must have had to use some sort of weapon—a knife, a club, or a spear.

PLATE 73

George Frenn, 1967 National Champion and World Record holder in the 56-pound weight throw. 1967 National Champion and National record holder in Power Lifting (242-pound class). (139)

PLATE 74

Character and determination are expressed in the rugged features of Jim Thorpe. (140)

Jim Thorpe, the "one-man track team," at Stockholm, 1912. (140a)

PLATE 75

Richard Perry ("R.P.") Williams, one of the greatest professional all-around athletes of modern times. In this photograph, Williams is over 50 years of age. (141)

PLATE 76

Mildred ("Babe") Diarickson as she appeared shortly after the start of her fabulous athletic career. Note the boyish figure, with trim hips and well-muscled arms and legs. (142)

PLATE 77

Lillian Leitzel, one of the most remarkable woman professional gymnasts, in a photo montage taken in the 1920s. (143)

PLATE 78

Luicita Leers, woman gymnast of extraordinary ability, who appeared with the Ringling Brothers and Barnum & Bailey Circus during 1929–1933. (144)

PLATE 79

The Mascotts, a German team of equilibrists, whose remarkable feats were shown on TV in the United States. (145, 146, 147)

PLATE 80

A modern girl tumbler performing the ancient Greek exercise known as the bibasis. (148a)

Annette Kellermann, "The Perfect Woman," as she appeared in her vaudeville swimming and diving act. (148)

Speaking of bulls, it is a familiar sight at rodeos to see a cowpuncher leap off his horse and down a steer in a matter of seconds. But a steer is not a bull, and to wrestle one of the latter animals to the ground takes a long struggle by a powerful athlete. One of the lightest strong-men to successfully perform this feat was Emil Bregulla, who weighed only 178 pounds. During the early 1900s, Bregulla gave exhibitions throughout Europe in which he would throw—and sometimes break the neck of—small bulls weighing 1600 pounds or so. Bregulla got his start in this odd profession by working as a butcher's apprentice. In time he learned the best way of grasping a bull's horns and applying leverage. He became known to his audiences as the second "Ursus."

The original "Ursus" (the bear) was a giant Christian slave in the classic story, *Quo Vadis* ("Whither Goest Thou?"), by the Polish novelist Henryk Sienkiewicz (1846–1916). In an early (1913) silent-screen pro-duction of *Quo Vadis*, the part of Ursus was played by the giant Austrian strong-man, Josef Grafl (6 ft. 3½ in., 285 lbs.). Grafl's part in *Quo Vadis* is described (p. 87) in my review of his accomplishments in weightlifting, in which for several years he was the world's amateur champion.

Henryk Sienkiewicz's description in Chapter 64 of *Quo Vadis* of the original "Ursus" battling the bull is one of the most thrilling descriptions of a strength struggle in all literature. It is certainly worth repeating here:

Ursus is depicted by the author as a giant with arms like Hercules, legs like tree trunks, and a chest as big as two shields together; his strength is almost superhuman. Condemned to die by Nero, he is thrust alone and naked into the arena, before the tens of thousands of spec-tators. Resigned to death as a Christian, he kneels on the sand and prays. The crowd, eager for a new thrill, is disappointed and displeased at this display of meekness. But then, to the sound of brazen trumpets, a door in the wall opens and into the arena comes raging an enormous German aurochs, or wild bull, upon whose head lies bound the living body of the girl Lygia. Instantly the meek and resigned Ursus is trans-formed; he springs up as if touched by fire and, with the bull rushing directly at him, seizes the animal by the horns. In the stands the spec-tators hardly dare to breathe; such a spectacle had not been seen since the founding of Rome. Ursus, with his head almost hidden between his shoulders, his arm muscles nearly bursting the skin, his back bent like a bow, his feet sinking into the sand up to his ankles, stops the gigantic bull in its tracks. For what seems like a century the giant man and the giant animal are locked immovable in a titanic struggle that seems like a sculpture of Herculean repose. There is not a sound in the arena save the flaming of lamps and the crackling of torches. The mighty strugglers appear planted in the earth as if never to move again. Then suddenly to the ears of the spectators comes a dull roar like a groan. Slowly, in the iron hands of the giant, the huge head of the bull begins to turn. The face and neck and arms of Ursus grow purple; his back bends more and more. Duller and hoarser grows the groaning roar of the bull, and with it is mingled now an eerie whistle that is the breath of the giant. Farther and farther turns the head of the bull, and from its mouth creeps foam and flesh. Then a crack like the breaking of bones, and the aurochs rolls on the ground, its neck twisted in death. Ursus, his body flooded with sweat, removes the ropes from the horns of the animal and frees his mistress. The amphitheater goes wild, the very walls trembling from the roar of the thousands as they call for mercy for Lygia, mercy for Ursus . . .

To return to the question of whether an unarmed man, however strong, could overcome a lion, or a tiger, it is conceivable that he could do so *if* the animal were first rendered unconscious and was unable to defend itself. But not otherwise. For if anything will fight to its last breath it is a cat, and while the man was attempting to strangle it, even if its front legs were held immovable, its hind feet and claws would rake and tear the man's flesh to shreds.* It should be remembered that no matter how strong a man's muscles may be, they are still only flesh covered with skin, and that in a combat with a wild animal the man's strength would be no better than the power of his bodily integument to resist the onslaught of knife-like teeth and claws. This point was brought out in a fight that once occurred between a grizzly bear and a cougar. Obviously the bear was much the stronger of the two animals, and killed the cougar. But meanwhile the threshing cat had disembowelled the bear, so that it, too, died. So, to sum up, if we are to recognize the possibility of a man of "Herculean" strength, let us confine his feats within reasonable limits and admire his extraordinary muscular development as that of a super-strong athlete's, rather than of a bullet-resisting character belonging to a comic-strip.

---

*In this connection, it is said by natives of equatorial West Africa that gorillas kill leopards not by strangling them, as might be supposed, but by an open-handed blow on the side of the head. The big apes are said also to fight among themselves by "swinging their arms round like shovels."

Part 2.
ORGANIZED FIELD ATHLETICS

Organized Field Athletics

A. THE POLE VAULT

Although today the only standard vault with a pole used in field events is a vertical vault over a bar, in earlier days a horizontal vault, for distance, also was recognized. This was called the Pole Long Jump. In it, the famous Irish-American all-around athlete, Martin Sheridan, made a mark of 28 feet, at New York City, October 25, 1907. This record was improved (indoors) to 28 ft. 2 in. by Platt Adams, New York, on October 31, 1910. As recently as May 4, 1963, this horizontal vault had been increased only to 28 ft. 8 in. The latter record was made by Jeff Chase, at San Jose, California. At the same date, Chase was regularly clearing 15 feet in the usual vault for height. It does not necessarily follow that the ratio of the horizontal vault to the vertical is as 28 ft. 8 in. is to 15 ft., or 1.911, since possibly the vault for distance is limited to approximately twice the length of the pole employed. The latter, in turn, is obviously limited by the speed and power the performer is able to attain in his running takeoff.

While there is no mention of a pole vault being used by the ancient Greeks as a competitive athletic event, doubtless such a means was employed by them in warfare in order to clear moats or high walls. Even earlier, in the Tailteann Games of Ireland, which date back at least to 1829 B.C., there was an event known as a "pole-jump." Whether this jump was for height or for distance is not stated.

According to H. Archie Richardson, in his *Archie's Little Black Book* (1962, p. 41), the first track and field meet held in the United States in which the pole vault was used took place at West Roxbury, Massauchetts, in the summer of 1853. This meet was staged by the Boston Caledonian Club, an organization whose purpose was to carry on in America the athletic events used in the Scottish Highland Games.

Referring now to Figure 13 in the Appendix, it is seen that vaulters did not begin to reach their potential until about 1910—some six years after they had switched from the use of solid, hardwood poles to the lighter, more elastic bamboo ones. From 1910 on, a more or less steady gain in height was achieved, culminating in the epoch-making vault of

15 ft. 7¾ in. by Cornelius Warmerdam, at Modesto, California, on May 23, 1942. A year later, indoors, he did 15 ft. 8½ in.—a mark that was destined to remain unbroken for 14 years.

Not until metal poles were adopted, in 1957, was Warmerdam's record (outdoor) surpassed. In April of the latter year, at Palo Alto, California, Bob Gutowski cleared 15 ft. 8¼ in. Two years later—also with the use of a metal pole—Don Bragg raised Warmerdam's indoor world record to 15 ft. 9⅝ in. and Gutowski's outdoor world record to 15 ft. 9¼ in. However, Gutowski had previously set an American (but not world) record of 15 ft. 9¾ in.

In 1961, vaulting poles made of fiberglass came into general use, replacing those of metal. With the highly elastic fiberglass pole, a new vaulting technique was introduced, and the performer was literally catapulted upward as the springy bar straightened itself. As an illustration of the change brought about by the use of the fiberglass pole, it may be noted that one of its leading exponents, John Pennel (USA), between 1963 and 1966 raised his record from 16 ft. 3 in. to the then world record of 17 ft. 6¼ in., a gain of nearly 8 percent. On June 23, 1967, Paul Wilson (USA), vaulted 17 ft. 7¾ in. at Bakersfield, California. Very close to this mark was a vault of 17 ft. 7⅜ in. made by Herve D'Encausse (France), at St. Maur, France, on June 5, 1968. Next in line is the former world record of 17 ft. 7 in. set by Bob Seagren (USA) at San Diego, California, on June 9, 1967. The present record, made in June 1969 by John Pennel, is 17 ft. 10¼ in.

To refer again to Fig. 13, it is seen that Warmerdam, *in a comparison with his contemporaries* (which, along with population, is the only valid way in which to evaluate *any* athletic performance), still is one of the outstanding individual performers. His outdoor record of 15 ft. 7¾ in., made in 1942, was 10 inches higher than would have been expected in that year, and was 10 years ahead of its time. Nevertheless, today's performers with the fiberglass pole are approaching a degree of technical excellence comparable with that which Warmerdam achieved with a bamboo pole; and probably before these comments are in print a vault of 18 feet or better will have been accomplished (for ratings, see Appendix).

Away back in 1652, an English athlete trainer named William Stokes published a book entitled *The Vaulting Master*. In this book he described his methods of teaching jumping (?), and called attention to a famous contemporary "leaper" named Simpson, "who exhibited his powers at the fair of St. Bartholomew" (*with* a vaulting pole, or without?). Another author in the same field, named Strutt, says that the most extraordinary jumper (?) of whom he had any record was an 18-year-old youth, six feet tall, named Ireland, who came from the county of York.

To quote Strutt: "He [Ireland] leapt over nine horses ranged side by side, and over the man who was mounted upon the middle one. A cord, which was extended above him at the height of fourteen feet above the ground, he cleared with a single effort. With a furious bound he crushed with his foot a bladder suspended sixteen feet above the ground, and on another occasion cleared a wagon, covered with an awning, with a single leap."

The foregoing references are taken from the book, *Wonders of Bodily Strength and Skill* (1873, pp. 146–147), by Guillaume Depping. The way in which Depping quotes Stokes and Strutt, respectively, makes it appear that all the "leaps" referred to were simple, unassisted *jumps*. Yet it is evident that the jumper named Ireland must have performed a *pole vault* in order to have cleared a height of 14 feet, or to have kicked with his foot an object suspended 16 feet above the ground. As to Ireland's leaps over the nine horses and the covered wagon, respectively, these leaps could have been performed either by jumping off a springboard or, possibly, by vaulting with a pole, but certainly not by a simple running jump. Thus we have what may well have been a 14-foot pole vaulter, performing several hundred years ago!

The pole vault, especially the way it is performed today, is a highly specialized event combining both athletics and gymnastics. The ideal physique for a vaulter would appear to be a height of 6 feet and a bodyweight of 165 pounds—a combination, by the way, that was present in Cornelius Warmerdam. Thus the body-build of the typical pole vaulter is a relatively slender one. In a listing of 30 top-ranking vaulters, the height ranges from 66 to 76.5 inches, and the weight from 133 to 195 pounds. The former height and weight is that of Gerhard Jeitner (Germany), while the latter weight is that of Don Bragg (USA), who stood 75 inches tall.[*]

It is said that it takes ten years to make a great pole vaulter. From this it might be inferred that the pole vault is the most difficult and specialized of all track and field events. This is to be doubted. As indicated by the records of various top-ranking performers in the decathlon, the pole vault is hardly more difficult (*i.e.*, variable) than either the discus throw or the javelin throw, and possibly less difficult than the shot put, although in the latter event size (bodyweight) is an important factor. Other highly specialized field events are the hammer throw and the 56-pound weight throw. All the latter events are discussed under the corresponding headings, which follow.

---

[*]It is interesting to note that both the smallest and the largest men in the series of 30 vaulters previously referred to are of about the same general build; and if Jeitner and Bragg could each be converted to a height of 6 feet (72 inches), each would weigh 173 pounds.

For detailed information on the mechanics, technique, and training procedures that apply to the pole vault, the following publications are of particular value.

Doherty, J. K. 1955. *Modern Track and Field*. Englewood Cliffs, N.J.: Prentice-Hall. "The Pole Vault": pp. 345–383.

Mortensen, J. P. and Cooper, J. M. 1959. *Track and Field for Coach and Athlete*. Chapter 12: "Pole Vault." London: Prentice-Hall International, Inc.

Ganslen, R. V. 1963. *Mechanics of the Pole Vault* (5th ed.) St. Louis: John Swift & Co.

Hildreth, P. 1963. *How to Train for Track and Field*. New York: Arc Books, Inc. Putting the Shot: pp. 130–138.

Dyson, G. H. G. 1964. *The Mechanics of Athletics* (3rd ed.); Chapter 9, pole vaulting. University of London Press, Ltd.

Quercetani, R. L. 1964. *A World History of Track and Field Athletics*; Chapter 11, "The Pole Vault." London: Oxford University Press.**

B. THE SHOT PUT

"Putting the stone" is a field event of ancient origin, and from it developed today's sport of putting a 16-pound metal ball. In all probability the ancient Greeks must have practiced the feat, using stones of various weights, although the event was not standardized or used in the periodic Games, as were the discus throw and the javelin throw. At the Tailteann Games held in ancient Ireland, there was a stone-throwing contest, along with running, jumping, throwing the javelin, and vaulting with a pole. The Tailteann Games were held in August of each year at Taliti, County Meath, Ireland. The contests date back at least to the year 1829 B.C. and possibly even earlier. Thus it may be said that the field event of putting the shot (stone) is about 3800 years old.*

Although there are today a number of scholarly treatises in which the mechanics of the shot put are described, I have yet to see one in which is stated the basic fact that the distance a shot may be put (with a given amount of force) varies as the *square root of the weight of the shot*. This may be seen by reference to Table 18, below, and to Figure 15, Appendix. Indeed, the principle applies to the putting or throwing of *all* objects (discus, javelin, baseball, etc.), and is particularly accurate where the effect of wind resistance is not an important factor.

---

*Quercetani's pertains especially to successive records and record-holders.

**Another source puts the *founding* of the Tailteann Games at about 3000 B.C. The founder is said to have been one Luguid the Strong, who inaugurated the games as a memorial to his foster mother, Queen Tailte. This would make the games nearly 5000 years old.

Table 18. Shot-putting distance in relation to shot weight

Shot Weight, lbs.	Distance Put, ft. & in.	Performer	Nation	Place	Date	Predicted Distance ft. & in.
8	67- 7	Ralph Rose	USA	Travers I., N.Y.	9-14-07	69-1
12	57- 3	Ralph Rose	USA	Travers I., N.Y.	8-29-08	56-5
16	51- 0	Ralph Rose	USA	San Francisco	8-21-09	48-10
18	46- 2¾	Patrick McDonald	USA	New York, N.Y.	5-30-14	46-1
21	42- 5	Patrick McDonald	USA	New York, N.Y.	10-20-12	42-8
24	39- 3¾	Patrick McDonald	USA	New York, N.Y.	3- 6-13	39-11
27.55 (12.5 kg.)	36-11⅝	K. von Halt	Germany	Munich, Germany	5-12-12	37-3
28	39- 0½	John Flanagan	USA	New York, N.Y.	2- 4-05	36-11
33.07 (15 kg.)	34-10½	K. von Halt	Germany	Frankfurt, Ger.	6-29-21	34-1
36.74 (16.66 kg.)	31- 4	X. Geier	Germany	Munich, Germany	5-25-19	32-3
42	28-11¼	Patrick Ryan	USA	New York, N.Y.	91- 1-13	30-2
56	25- 0	Patrick Ryan	USA	New York, N.Y.	2- 6-13	26-2

The distances "predicted" in the last column above are from the formula: distance, ft. = 195.3/√weight of shot. In this evaluation, the factor of *time* (see Fig. 14) is disregarded. However, all the listed performances made by American shot-putters were established during the period 1905–1914, and during that period would not have been expected to vary more than a foot or so with a shot of a given weight. Apparently, after 1921 or so, the practice of shot-putting with weights of over 16 pounds was discontinued, at least so far as establishing records was concerned.

If the aforementioned formula were modified so as to apply to present-day shot-putting, and were based on the 16-pound shot record of 71 ft. 5½ in. made by Randel Matson (April 22, 1967), the factor or dividend 195.3 would have to be increased to 285.8. This indicates that since 1910 records in the shot put have improved over 46 percent! (If they had improved to an equal extent in, say, the 100-yard dash, the record for the latter would now be about 7 seconds!). To match Matson's current world record with 16 pounds, a 56-pound shot would have to be put 38 ft. 2 in., a 12-pound shot 82 ft. 6 in., and an 8-pound shot 101 feet!

The principle of using the square root of the weight of the shot makes it possible also to *directly compare* the shot-put records made by women with those made by men. The standard weight of the shot used by women is 4 kilograms or 8.8185 lbs. The square root of the latter figure is 2.9696. The square root of a 16-pound shot is 4.0000. Therefore, the distance that should be expected with a 16-pound shot as compared with a 4-kilo shot is 2.9696/4.0000, or .7424. Thus the former women's shot-put record of 61 feet (made by Tamara Press, USSR, in 1965), if performed with a 16-pound shot, would be 61 × .7424, or about 45 ft. 3½ in. This makes the shot-putting strength, or force, of Tamara Press, as compared with that of the men's record holder Randel Matson, 45.286/71.458, or about 64 percent. This is close to what would be expected, since the strength of a woman athlete who weighs the same *per inch of height* as a man is, on the average, as .667 is to 1.000. The lesser ratio shown by Miss Press is due mainly to her having weighed *less* per inch of height than did Matson.

The foregoing reference to bodyweight leads to the inevitable conclusion that bodily size (height and weight) are factors of such direct importance in shot putting that they should in every performance be taken into account. The situation is exactly the same as in weightlifting, where competitors are at least segregated into various bodyweight classes (and should be considered as to height also). Where this is not done, there is no way of determining the *technical efficiency* of the performer, and this is just what needs to be ascertained if improvement in technique and training methods are to be gained. There is no use exclaiming over the performance of a 300-pound shot-putter who does 60 feet, if a 180-pounder can do 59 feet. It is the latter man's performance which should be analyzed, and possibly profited by in the case of other performers. Not only that, but the 180-pound man's record should be given a higher rating than that made by the 300-pounder, even though the latter performer put the shot a foot farther in actual measurement. Perhaps he should have done *10 feet* farther.

If the record-holders in the shot put over the last hundred years are charted on a graph, taking into account their respective bodyweights, heights, and dates of performance, it is at once seen who the most *efficient* performers are, or were. The six who have accomplished the most, in respect to the physical equipment with which each was endowed, are, listed chronologically: Donald Dinnie (Scotland), Charles MacLean (Scotland), Richard Williams (USA), Charles Fonville (USA), William Nieder (USA), Arthur Rowe (England), and Randel Matson (USA). Dinnie and Williams were professional athletes. Let us now look into the performances of each of these "super shot-putters", plus a few others of almost equal caliber.

Donald Dinnie was the first great hero of the Scottish Highland Games. He was born in 1837, and competed (professionally) from age 16 to 63. During that unprecedented 47-year arduous competition, he won no fewer than 7500 cash prizes totalling over $100,000! He was a champion wrestler and weightlifter, and a topnotch runner, jumper, and weight-thrower. Also, he was one of the greatest exponents of the Scottish feat of tossing the caber (see above). Standing 72.5 inches and weighing in his prime 218 pounds, Dinnie was a model of the heavy-weight all-around athlete. He had an official record of putting the shot of 45 ft. 7 in., a mark he set in 1867. With a 21-pound stone, he made a put of an even 40 feet. This was equivalent to 45 ft. 10 in. with a 16-pound shot; and it confirmed Dinnie's ability with the latter poundage. On one occasion, Dinnie put a stone of 22 pounds a distance of 42 ft. 3 in., but as the ground was "somewhat downhill" (how much, or how little?), this remarkable put was not given credit. To indicate the greatness of Dinnie's shot-putting ability, it can be said that his 45 ft. 7 in.—performed in 1867—would be equivalent to a put of nearly 64 feet today! That is to say, Dinnie, although eminently an all-around athlete rather than a specialist, was hardly inferior, relatively, in the shot put than was Britain's greatest shot-put exponent of recent years, Arthur Rowe (see below).

Toward the end of Dinnie's athletic career, and shortly thereafter, there were a number of other first-class shot-putters and hammer-throwers in the annual Scottish Highland Games. Foremost among these were Alex Cameron (73 in., 220 lbs.), who in 1900, among other feats, put the 22-pound stone 38 ft. 9 in.; James Morrison (72 in., 231 lbs.), who also in 1900 put the 22-pound stone 37 ft. 1 in.; and Charles MacLean (70 in., 168 lbs.), who in 1899 put a stone weighing 15 lbs. 14 oz. a distance of 45 feet. With a full-weight 16-pound shot, this would have been equivalent to 44 ft. 10 in. This performance, made back in 1899 by a man who weighed only 168 pounds at a height of 70 inches, was almost as remarkable as that accomplished by Donald Dinnie. The reason why MacLean and Dinnie made such excellent records in the shot put, despite the early days in which each man competed, is because this was one of the favored events in the Highland Games, and was practiced at every opportunity.

Richard ("R.P.") Williams was in many respects the greatest all-around professional athlete this country ever produced. A summary of his many records, in gymnastics and other sports as well as in track and field, is given below. Considering that Williams, who was only 69.1 inches in height—and probably at no time while in training weighed over 160 pounds—made a shot put (with 16 pounds) of 47 ft. 9 in. just after the turn of the century, one can only marvel at the magnitude of the performance, which rates a phenomenal 101.2 percent.

Charles Fonville (74 in., 194 lbs.) was the first, and to date the only, Negro to hold a world record in the shot put. When only 21 years of age, he attained a distance of 58 ft. 0⅜ in. This was at Lawrence, Kansas, on April 17, 1948. It is said that Fonville put more speed into his shot-putting than had any performer before him. Also, he had virtually perfect coordination. So great was his speed that he was able to release the shot at the theoretically optimum angle of 45 degrees.* Unfortunately, an aggravated back injury kept Fonville from maintaining or improving upon the power with which he had made his 58-foot put.

William Nieder (75 in., 242 lbs.) in 1960 made a world record shot put of 65 ft. 10 in. This performance has a percentage rating of 97.0, as compared with that of Arthur Rowe (97.1 percent), following.

Arthur Rowe (73.75 in., 220.5 lbs.), along with the almost legendary Donald Dinnie, was one of the two greatest shot-putters produced in Great Britain to date. His best effort was recorded on August 7, 1961, at Mansfield, England, where he attained a distance of 64 ft. 2 in. It would appear that Rowe's efficiency in 1961 was sufficient to make him, percentagewise, the third greatest of all shot-putters. Rowe, who is now a professional athlete who competes regularly in the Scottish

---

*Practice has shown that for most shot-putters the ideal release angle lies between 41 and 42 degrees (see Dyson, 1964, p. 177).

Highland Games, trains with barbells and has accomplished the following lifts: Press, 334½ lbs., Snatch, 285 lbs., Clean and Jerk, 375 lbs., Press Behind Neck, 310 lbs., Bench Press, 420 lbs., Squat, 615 lbs. He is also the current (1969) champion in tossing the caber, and has tossed a 56-pound weight over a bar 16 feet high.

The most recent—and, so far as sheer distance is concerned, the greatest—of the six most outstanding exponents of the shot put is Randel Matson (78.5 in., 258 lbs.). Matson holds the current world record with a distance of 71 ft. 5½ in. This put was made at College Station, Texas, on April 22, 1967, during Matson's last appearance as a student at Texas A & M College. During that same month, he made three puts of 70 feet or more—a distance that no other shot-putter has attained even once. Matson's great height, and the corresponding elevation from which his puts are released, enables him to gain several inches in distance over his less-tall competitors by this advantage alone. In addition, he is both strong (he can do a Bench Press with 430 pounds and a Squat with 505 pounds) and quick-moving. The fact that his more recent performances are relatively better than those he made when he weighed less (e.g., 212 pounds in 1963 and 232 pounds in 1964) indicates that, while gaining in weight and strength, he lost none of his speed. Matson is also a topnotch performer in the discus throw, having produced in it the former American record of 213 ft. 9½ in. This mark was established on April 8, 1967, at College Station, Texas.*

Next to the aforementioned six shot-putters, the more efficient, in order, would appear to be: Charles MacLean (70 in., 168 lbs.), who in Scotland in 1899 did the equivalent of 45 ft.; Dallas Long (75.9 in., 250 lbs.), who in 1964 did 67 ft. 10 in.; Clarence "Bud" Houser (72 in., 180 lbs.), who in 1925 did 50 ft. 1 in.; Parry O'Brien (75 in., 235 lbs.), who in 1960 did 63 ft. 5 in.; and Jim Fuchs (74.5 in., 220 lbs.), who in 1949 did 58 ft. 4-27/64 in. (how accurate can one get?). O'Brien is said to have won no fewer than 116 consecutive shot-putting contests from 1952 to 1956. He was the top performer in this field for some years, until Bill Nieder came into the picture in 1960. Matson's closest recent rival, Neal Steinhauer (77 in., 270 lbs.), while holding the present

---

*Theoretically, Matson's mark of 213 ft. 9½ in. in the discus is equivalent to a shot put of 64 ft. 10¾ in. Conversely, his shot-put record of 71 ft. 5½ in. is equivalent to a discus throw of 235 ft. 5 in. Another great dual performer in these events was Parry O'Brien, who in 1960, in addition to putting the shot 63 ft. 5 in., threw the discus 193 ft. 2 in. Comparatively, Matson was, or is, about 91 percent as efficient in the discus as in the shot, while O'Brien was similarly about 95 percent as efficient. However, even when the respective dates of performance (O'Brien 1960, Matson 1967) are taken into account, it works out that Matson is 8.8 percent stronger than O'Brien was in the shot put, and 7.7 percent stronger in the discus throw.

indoor shot record with 67 ft. 10 in. (January 28, 1967), has a lower percentage rating than any of the foregoing performers because of his greater bodyweight.

Since in high-school competition the weight of the shot used is 12 pounds instead of the 16 pounds used elsewhere, it is interesting to make a comparison between high-school records and collegiate or world records. Here is a list of six outstanding performers with the 16-pound shot, whose earlier (high-school) records with the 12-pound shot also were available. A longer list could be compiled, but these six examples should suffice to show in a general way how high-school and collegiate records in the shotput compare.

Preformer	Distance, 12 lbs., ft. & in.	Year	Distance, 16 lbs., ft. & in.	Year	Diff., years	Diff., distance
Clarence Houser	56– 3	1922	50– 1	1924	2	−6– 2
John Kuck	55–11	1923	52– 0¼	1928	5	−3–10¾
Al Blozis	59– 0½	1938	56– 6⅛	1941	3	−2– 6⅜
Darrow Hooper	59–10⅛	1948	57– 0⅝	1952	4	−2– 9½
Dallas Long	69– 3	1958	67–10	1964	6	−1– 5
Randel Matson	66–10½	1963	71– 5½	1967	4	+4– 7

An averaging of these six sets of figures shows: (1) that the collegiate marks were set four years after the high-school marks; (2) that the average distance attained with the 12-pound shot was about 61 ft. 2¼ in., and with the 16-pound shot 59 ft. 1⅝ in., a difference of 2 ft. 0⅝ in.; (3) that the *longer* the time between the high-school record and the collegiate record, the *smaller* the difference between the two records. The latter would be expected. However, it is evident that Matson's record in the 12-pound shot is disproportionately low. Excluding Matson's marks, the average of the five other performances with the 12-pound shot is practically an even 60 feet, and with the 16-pound shot 56 ft. 8 in., a difference of 3 ft. 4 in. The distance to be *expected* with a 16-pound shot as compared with one of 12 pounds is 0.866. Therefore, *at the time* the five high-school shot-putters averaged 60 feet with a 12-pound shot, they should have averaged .866 × 60, or about 52 feet with a 16-pound shot. Since, as just seen, they actually averaged 56 ft. 8 in. (= .9444 × 60 feet), the extra 4 ft. 8 in. can be attributed to the *four years' later effort,* and to the improvement in size, strength, and shot-putting technique occurring during those four years. Hence we may conclude that a high-school athlete who becomes able to put the 12-pound shot 70 feet during his senior year, should, in his senior year in *college* be able, on the average, to put the 16-pound shot .9444 × 70, or just over 66 feet. In order to surpass Matson's 71 ft. 5½ in., the performer would have to be capable of a put of 75 ft. 8 in. or better while in high-school!

Theoretically, the velocity with which a shot leaves the putter's hand is equal to the square root of the distance attained, multiplied by the acceleration due to gravity. The generally accepted figure for the latter factor is 32.174. Expressed in a formula: Speed of shot, ft. per sec. = $\sqrt{32.174}$ × distance, ft. This may be simplified to: Speed, fps = 5.672 × $\sqrt{\text{distance}}$, ft.

Thus, theoretically, when Randel Matson made his record of 71 ft. 5½ in., the shot left his hand at a speed of 47.949 ft. per sec. (= 32.7 mph). In comparison, the average freshman college student, who puts the shot about 28 feet, gives the shot a release (or initial) speed of 30 ft. per sec. (= 20.5 mph). In short, the distance attainable in the shot put varies as the *speed of release squared*. At the stage where the shot hits the ground, its initial speed has been reduced by as much as 20 percent, depending on the release speed, angle of release, height of release, and possibly other factors. The wind resistance is customarily ignored, as its slowing effect on the shot under normal air conditions reduces the distance by only an inch or two.

The shot put is essentially an event requiring an explosive release of energy or force (strength × speed squared). As such, the performances in it may be directly compared with those in other field events in which the requirements are similar, such as the discus, the hammer, the javelin, and the 56-pound (and 35-pound) weight throws, respectively. The latter events are discussed, in that order, on the following pages. It may be noted also that the physical requirements in all the aforementioned field events are similar to those in the "quick" lifts in weight-lifting, where strength is intensified by the application of a momentary output of great speed.

For detailed information on the mechanics, technique, and training procedures applying to the shot put, the following publications are of particular value. That by Quercetani pertains especially to successive records and record-holders.

Doherty, J. K. 1955. *Modern Track and Field*. Englewood Cliffs, N.J.: Prentice-Hall. "The Shot Put": pp. 236–264.

Mortensen, J. P. and Cooper, J. M. 1959. *Track and Field for Coach and Athlete*. Chapter 13: "Shot Put." London: Prentice-Hall International, Inc.

Hildreth, P. 1963. *How to Train for Track and Field*. New York: Arc Books, Inc. "Putting the Shot." pp. 130–138.

Dyson, G. H. G. 1964. *The Mechanics of Athletics* (3rd ed.); Chapter

10, "Throwing." (pp. 174–177, 196–199). University of London Press, Ltd.

Quercetani, R. L. 1964. *A World History of Track and Field Athletics*; Chapter 14, "The Shot Put." London: Oxford University Press.

C. THE DISCUS THROW

Just as in putting the shot, hurling the discus is a field event in which height and weight (and in the discus, long arms) are an advantage, provided that speed is not sacrificed. Also, for a record or near-record performance, a good sense of balance and quick reflexes are essential. Finally, large hands and strong fingers help additionally.

In the ancient Greek athletic festivals, the discuses used varied greatly in size and weight. Pausanias says that boys used a lighter discus (Greek: *diskos*) than men. At first the discus was a circular plate of stone 10 to 12 inches in diameter. Later—about the end of the sixth century B.C.—it was made of cast metal, generally bronze. Some 15 examples unearthed at Olympia and other ancient sites show a range in weight of from 1.245 kg (= 2.744 lbs.) to 5.707 kg (= 12.58 lbs.). The average weight is 2.58 kg (= 5 lbs. 11 oz.); the average diameter about 8.4 in.; and the average thickness (between the center and the edge) 0.3 in. With a discus that may have ranged somewhere between the aforementioned weight extremes, a throw of 100 feet was considered "exceptionally good."

In the Greek Olympic Games the discus throw was a popular event, and frequently the victor or champion was immortalized in sculpture. One of the most famous Greek statues is the Discobolus, or discus-thrower, by the Athenian sculptor Myron (*c.* 490–420 ? B.C.).* Since Myron's Discobolus introduced a new era in Greek athletic art, and since our knowledge of the style of discus-throwing used by the ancients is based mainly upon this sculptured figure, a few words here about the statue may not be out of place.

Of the Discobolus, there have been recovered 12 full-size replicas and several statuettes. The most accurate copy is the marble statue in the Terme Museum, Rome. This statue preserves the original pose, whereas most other representations have the head wrongly facing forward. Plate 71 is almost an exact replica of the original statue in the Terme Museum, and is clearer in some respects because of the angle from which it was photographed and because no *support* behind the figure is shown.

According to the classicist E. N. Gardiner, seven different positions for throwing the discus are depicted in various monuments. Gardiner shows that while the swing of the arm and hand holding the discus

---

*Myron's Discobolus, however, is not believed to be a representation of any particular victor, but rather "a study in athletic sculpture" (Hyde, 1921, p. 184).

was always in the same plane (namely, in a *vertical* and not a horizontal arc), and the throw was invariably made from the position shown in Myron's statue, certain associated movements varied. The important points are that in the Greek style of discus throwing only one footstep was taken, and the body was *not* rotated as in the modern "free style," in which most performers use 1¾ turns (within a circle 8 ft. 2½ in. in diameter).

The Greek broad-jumper, Phayllus, is said also, in an inscription, to have hurled the discus 105 feet.* If the discus used by him was of the average weight of 5 lbs. 11 oz., his throw of 105 feet was equivalent to one of about 119 feet with a standard modern discus weighing 2 kg (4 lbs. 6.5 oz.). This for the same reason given in connection with shot-putting and with javelin-throwing: that the distance thrown varies *inversely as the square root of the weight of the missile.* And since the modern "free" style of throwing the discus results in a distance from one-sixth to nearly one-quarter greater than in the classic style (see Fig. 16, Appendix), Phayllus's 105-foot throw would have been equivalent to a throw today, with a 2-kilo discus, of from 138 to 147 feet. This is only about two-thirds of the distance attained by today's leading performers.

Figure 16, Appendix, shows the progress in the discus throw from the first modern Olympic Games of 1896 to those of 1964. Evidently the classic, or Hellenic, style was used only once in these games—in 1896—when the best mark at Athens, made by Robert Garrett of the United States, was only 95 ft. 7¾ in. In August 1913, E. Nicklander of Finland, using the Greek style, and presumably with a discus of the standard weight of 2 kilos, attained a distance of 136 f. 4⅝ in. In the same month and year, Armas Taipale, also of Finland, in the Olympic or "free" style, set a record of 158 ft. 4-7/16 in. This was 158.4/136.4, or 16.1 percent greater, than Nicklander's mark made in the restricted or Hellenic style.

One of the best discus throws, relative to the date of performance, was Fortune Gordien's mark of 197 ft. 2 in., made in Pasadena, California, on August 14, 1954. At that time the listed world record (which Gordien had made in 1953) was 194 ft. 6 in. However, Gordien's August 14, 1954, performance was disallowed on account of the discus he used being an *ounce lighter* than the standard weight of 4 lbs. 6.5 oz. If, using the principle stated above, the square root of 4.41 lbs. (the weight of a standard discus) is compared with the square root of 4.34375 lbs. (the weight of Gordien's discus, assuming that it was exactly an ounce lighter than the standard), it works out that Gordien's throw with the

---

*In some translations the distance is given as "five feet *less* (rather than *more*) than a hundred." However, I am here giving Phayllus credit for the longer distance.

ounce-too-light discus was equivalent to a throw of 195 ft. 8 in. with a discus of regulation weight. Thus, in effect, Gordien had surpassed his own world record by no less than 14 inches, yet received no credit for his effort because no provision is made in the rules for *calculated* performances.

Yet the rules permit a minimum weight in the discus of 4 lbs. 6 oz., that is, a *half*-ounce under the standard. This difference amounts to a little over three-quarters of one percent (actually, 0.00776). Thus, if Gordien had used a discus of the minimum *allowable* weight, instead of one weighing a half-ounce less than that, his throw, by calculation, would have been about 196 ft. 5 in. rather than the 197 ft. 2 in., and would have been passed by the judges. In any case, Gordien was deprived of a new world record by unknowingly using a discus that varied so little below the standard that an equivalent distance with a discus of acceptable weight could have been computed within an inch or so.

Another interesting instance occurred when, several years ago, Jay Silvester threw the discus 210 ft. 2½ in. In that case the factor involved was not the weight of the discus but the circumstance that the field where Silvester made his throw fell off 27 inches in the 210 ft. 2½ in. Hence the question of what distance he would have attained had the field been perfectly level becomes a simple problem of trigonometry. Assuming a uniform slope to the field, the answer works out as 210 ft. 2¾ in.! Here again was an officially unrecognized world record. At the time of writing, Silvester holds the world's best mark with 224 ft. 5 in. This phenomenal performance was made on September 18, 1968.

The most outstanding discus-throwers of recent years in addition to Silvester have been Ludvik Danek (Czechoslovakia), with the former world record of 216 ft. 9 in.,* made in Long Beach, Calif., on June 7, 1966; Randel Matson (USA), with the former American record of 213 ft. 9½ in., made in 1967; Alfred Oerter (USA), with a record of 205 ft. 5½ in., made in 1963; Rink Babka (USA), 207 ft. 5½ in., 1966; Bob Humphreys (USA), 203 ft. 5 in., 1962; and Vladimir Trusenyov (USSR), 202 ft. 2½ in., 1962. At least 20 other discus-throwers have each done over 190 feet.

Fig. 16, Appendix, shows how the leading discus throwers have stood with respect to the era in which they competed. On this basis it would appear that one of the greatest discus throwers was Armas Taipale of Finland, whose record of 160 ft. 5 in., made in 1914, was not surpassed for 18 years. Three other great throwers, all of whom competed in the 1930s, were Eric Krenz (USA), who in 1930 did 167 ft. 5⅜ in.; Harald Andersson (Sweden), who in 1935 did 173 ft.

---

*This is *relatively* better than a throw of 218 ft. 2 in. made by Danek in 1969.

11½ in.; and Willi Schröder (Germany), who also in 1935 did 174 ft. 2½ in. Not shown in Figure 16 (since it was so close to Krenz's record) was a throw of 169 ft. 8⅞ in. by Paul Jessup (USA), made in 1930. Jessup stood no less than 6 ft. 6 in. in height, and presumably weighed well over 200 pounds.

But the distance that a thrower attains, even when evaluated with respect to date of performance, is not the sole measure of an athlete's prowess in the discus throw any more than in the shot put, javelin, hammer, or any other throwing event in which height and weight are contributing factors. How the latter factors should be applied in properly rating performers in the discus throw is explained in the Appendix.*

The discus throw for women was not introduced into the modern Olympic Games until 1928, at Amsterdam. There, first place was won by Helen Konopacka of Poland, with a throw of 129 ft. 11¾ in. From that time, the record has advanced in a somewhat erratic manner to the present-day mark of 205 ft. 8½ in. The latter performance was made in East Berlin in June 1969, by Liesel Westermann (67.7 in., 176 lbs.), the extraordinary German women's champion in the discus throw.

In comparing the records of male and female athletes, it should be borne in mind that the discus used by women weighs only 1 kilogram (2 lbs. 3¼ oz.), whereas that for men weighs 2 kilograms (4 lbs. 6½ oz.). Accordingly—since the distance thrown varies inversely as the square root of the weight of the discus—if women used a 2-kilogram discus, the distance expected would be the square root of 2 (or 1.414) divided into the distance reached with a 1-kilogram discus. Thus the 205 ft. 8½ in. record of Liesel Westermann—if she had used a 2-kilo discus—would shrink to 145 ft. 5¾ in.

From 1928 to 1968 the women's records in the discus have increased, remarkably, *over 50 percent* faster than the men's records during the same period.**

With *technique* in both the shot put and the discus throw thus brought to a uniformly high level by members of the fair sex, it would appear that future increases in women's records will have to come—just as they have come in the case of men's—from the participation in these events of individuals *even bigger and stronger than they are now*, and

---

*This has reference particularly to the throw made by Armas Taipale of Finland, in 1914. When the size (77 in., 225 lbs.) of Taipale is taken into account, his otherwise remarkable performance loses much of its impressiveness.

**In a way, this is not really remarkable. Probably it is because the status of women's records in the discus in 1928 was on a par with that which had existed in the men's records in 1900. In both cases a rapid initial improvement was to be *expected* because of the relative *poorness* of the first performances.

with no diminution in speed and technique. Such individuals should appear as a statistical consequence of the accelerating population increase, and the uncovering thereby of more and more phenomenal athletic talent on the "fringe" of the population.

So closely correlated "ballistically" are the shot put and the discus throw that the distance in one event may be closely predicted from that in the other. This correlation holds true both for contemporary performances and, remarkably, for those which are compared in *time*. The conversion formulas are given in the Appendix.

As the discus throw is one of the few athletic events to have been represented in antique sculptures, there is an extensive bibliography on it, from the standpoints both of athletics and of art. The following brief list of pertinent publications could be greatly extended.

Hyde, W. W. 1921. *Olympic Victor Monuments and Greek Athletic Art*. Washington: Carnegie Inst. Wash. Pub. No. 268. Pp. 218–222: DISKOBOLOI.

Gardiner, E. N. 1910. *Greek Athletic Sports and Festivals*. London.

Gardiner, E. N. 1930. *Athletics of the Ancient World*. Oxford: Clarendon Press.

Doherty, J. K. 1955. *Modern Track and Field*. Englewood Cliffs, N.J.: Prentice-Hall. "The Discus Throw," pp. 265–284.

Mortensen, J. P. and Cooper, J. M. 1959. *Track and Field for Coach and Athlete*. Chapter 14: "Discus Throw," London: Prentice-Hall International, Inc.

Hildreth, P. 1963. *How to Train for Track and Field*. New York: Arc Books, Inc. "Throwing the Discus," pp. 138–143.

Dyson, G. H. G. 1964. *The Mechanics of Athletics* (3rd ed.); Chapter 10, "Throwing," (pp. 181–184, 193–196). University of London Press, Ltd.

Quercetani, R. L. 1964. *A World History of Track and Field Athletics*. Chapter 15, "The Discus Throw," London: Oxford University Press.

Harris, H. A. 1966. *Greek Athletes and Athletics*. Bloomington: Indiana Univ. Press. "Throwing the Discus," pp. 85–92.

D. THE HAMMER THROW

This field event originated, hundreds of years ago, from the throwing of a sledgehammer. At one time the exercise was practiced even by royalty, as is indicated by a drawing showing King Henry VIII throwing a regular sledge. Later, in the Scottish Highland Games, the event was standardized. It was then performed with two sizes of "hammers" having long, rigid wooden handles set at the ends into round iron balls. The "light hammer" weighed 16½ pounds, and the "heavy hammer" 24¾ pounds, or 50 percent heavier. Accordingly, the distance to be expected with the light hammer is $\sqrt{24.75/16.50}$, or 1.225 times the distance with the heavy hammer.

The best Scottish records up to the year 1900 were those made by G. H. Johnstone of Dunoon, who in 1893 threw the light hammer 113 ft 2 in., and in 1896 threw the heavy hammer 84 ft. 3 in. As Johnstone's record with the 16½-pound hammer is not 1.225 times the distance with the 24¾-pound hammer, but is about 1.35 times the distance, it is apparent that more speed was attainable with the lighter hammer than would be expected (which could have occurred if the lighter hammer had a *longer* handle). The 1.35 ratio is present also in the *average* of the performances of the five leading Scottish exponents with both sizes of hammers up to the year 1900.[*]

The great oldtime Scottish "all-rounder," Donald Dinnie, made the following records (and, it is added, "on level ground"): At Coupar Angus, with a hammer weighing 16 pounds, 132 ft. 8 in. (However, in this hammer the handle was "so long that a trench had to be dug in front to allow for the swing.") At Springburn, Glasgow, Dinnie threw a 17¼-pound hammer 110 ft.; and at Crieff, a 20-pound hammer 104 ft. 6 in. All these performances by Dinnie were relatively superior to those quoted above, even though Dinnie made them in the 1860s and 1870s (and with inferior hammers). No wonder that Dinnie was called by his followers "champion of champions."

The above Scottish performances in hammer throwing are quoted as a matter of historic interest. They are hardly to be compared with the records made later by the school of Irish-American performers in the United States. It was the latter group who adopted the style of hammer presently in use. In this style, the hammer is actually an iron ball with a "handle" of spring steel wire approximately 3½ feet long; the whole affair weighs 16 pounds. The throw is made from a circle 7 feet in diameter. (It was not until 1908 that these rules were adopted by the International Amateur Athletic Federation.)

Figure 17, Appendix, shows the trend of the 16-pound hammer throw from 1888, when a distance of 127 ft. 9 in. was attained by W. J. M. Barry (USA), to 1965, when Gyula Zsivótsky (74.75 in., 210 lbs.) of Hungary established the then current world record of 241 ft. 11 in. While there is an actual increase in distance between these two records of nearly 90 percent, the *expected* difference between the two years (1888 and 1965) is only 62 percent. This reduces Zsivótsky's superiority

---

[*]This does not necessarily mean that the theoretical ratio of 1.225 is invalid, but rather that the Scottish 16½-pound hammer was for some reason *disproportionately* easier to throw than the 24¾-pound hammer. In contrast, Pat Ryan's records (both made in 1913) are 189 ft. 3 in. with the 16-pound hammer and 213 ft. 9¾ in. with the 12-pound hammer. Here the ratio should be $\sqrt{16/12}$, or 1.1547, whereas it actually is *less*, namely 1.1273.

(i.e., rating in merit) over Barry to only 17 percent, even if Barry were of the same height and bodyweight as Zsivótsky, which I do not know.

While the present world champion in the hammer throw, so far as absolute distance is concerned, is Romuald Klim, the credit for top *efficiency* in this event must be given to a Japanese performer, Takeo Sugawara. In 1963, this relatively small (68.5 in., 170 lbs.) hammer expert made a phenomenal throw of 222 ft. 2½ in. This performance gains the fantastic rating of 103.3 percent (1033 points)! Next in technical merit is the throw of Norburu Okamoto (Japan), with 98.7 percent; and third, Gyula Zsivótsky's throw, which has a rating of 98.3 percent. On the basis of Sugawara's performance, it would appear that a throw of 250 feet could be made by a performer weighing under 220 pounds, provided he were at least 76 inches tall and possessed Sugawara's speed and technique. It may be that various hammer throwers other than those mentioned here have high percentage ratings, but I have been able to list only those of which I knew the height and bodyweight.

Hammer throwing, as in the other field events, requires a long period of dedicated training before the performer approaches his potential ability. However, once championship form has been acquired, the performer may stay in or near his best condition for years on end. Matt McGrath (71.75 in., 248 lbs.) started weight-throwing when he came from Ireland to the United States, in 1899 (when he was 21), reached his peak in 1911–1913 (aged 33–35), and was still good enough to win National championships in the 56-pound weight throw in 1925 and the 16-pound hammer throw in 1926, the latter when he was 48. Patrick Ryan and Patrick MacDonald were other long-active weight throwers. Ryan won the National 16-pound hammer throw every year from 1913 to 1921, inclusive—except in 1918, when it was won by McGrath. MacDonald was National champion in the 56-pound weight throw first in 1911, then 1919–1921 and 1926–1929, the latter at the age of 48! He excelled also in the shot put.

The hammer throw and the 56-pound weight throw are field events which may be directly compared with any or all of the various present-day events in weightlifting with barbells.

For detailed information on the mechanics, technique, and training procedures applying to the hammer throw, see the references given on page 513 for the shot put. The chapters on the hammer throw are as follows:

Doherty: (NOT included).

Mortensen and Cooper: (NOT included).

Hildreth: pp. 149–155.

Dyson: Chapter 10, pp. 187–193.
Quercetani: Chapter 16.

E. THE JAVELIN THROW

As the javelin was one of the two throwing events (the other being the discus) included in the ancient Greek pentathlon, it, like the discus, is of considerable interest historically. Although no full-scale Greek statue depicting a javelin thrower in action has been preserved, there are in existence two small bronze statuettes in the Metropolitan Museum of Art, New York City, besides numerous two-dimensional representations on vases and other objects, from which the Greek technique of throwing the javelin may be deduced.

The great master of the Argive (Argos) school of sculpture in the fifth century B.C. was Polycletus (Gr. Polykleitos). By most scholars he is ranked among the top three sculptors of the Golden Age, the other two being Phidias and Myron. As it is said that during this period every third man in Greece was a sculptor, the distinction attained by Polycletus, Phidias, and Myron should indicate their extraordinary abilities. The most famous work attributed to Polycletus (481–416 B.C.) is his statue called the Doryphorus (spear-bearer), which depicts an Olympic athlete* standing at ease with a javelin resting across his left shoulder (see Plate 72). While the original bronze casting of the Doryphorus has been lost, there are some 7 marble statues, 17 torsos, and 36 heads extant that have been copied from the original and which show clearly what the latter was like. The Doryphorus is of particular interest from the standpoint of anthropometry, since in the statue Polycletus is said to have embodied his conception of the ideal athlete. Polycletus also introduced the striding stance of the feet, which was a decided step forward (no pun intended!) from earlier representations in which the feet were shown stiffly (and uninterestingly) together.

Actually, the practice of javelin-throwing began long before the event was included in the Greek athletic festivals. The Tailteann Games in Ireland, for example, which may have dated back as far as 3000 B.C., featured javelin-throwing as one of its five field events. Clearly the throwing of the javelin as a peacetime athletic contest was directly

---

*While some authorities regard the Doryphorus as representing a javelin thrower, others consider it as showing a pentathlete (5-event performer). That the latter is the more likely interpretation is indicated by the somewhat heavy build of the figure, which implies that the athlete participated in wrestling as well as in track and field. Today's best javelin throwers average in weight only 186 pounds at a height of 72.4 inches. At the latter height, the Doryphorus would weigh 220 pounds.

associated with the use of the spear in war. In the latter application, distance and accuracy were vital objectives, and the training followed by the Greek warrior sought to develop both abilities. Hence the Greeks had throwing for accuracy (as at a target, and sometimes from horseback) as well as for distance. To increase the distance that a thrower might attain, a device called an *amentum* (leather thong) was used. This also imparted to the javelin a whirling motion, which steadied its flight and increased the accuracy of its placement. (For an interesting analysis of the experimental throwing of a javelin both with and without a thong, see H. A. Harris, pp. 93–95.)

As to the distance that was attained by the Greeks in the javelin throw, even less is known than in the case of the discus throw and the running broad jump. Harris (p. 95) says that in the whole of ancient literature only one passage, and that an indirect one, refers to the distance of a javelin throw. This passage is by Statius, who says that the length of a chariot course was "three times a bow shot and four times a javelin throw."

Following up the latter statement, one finds that the probable minimum length of a Greek chariot course was about 400 yards, and that accordingly the length of a Greek javelin throw must have been at least 100 yards, or 300 feet. If, considering the remote date of performance, this distance seems excessive, it should be remembered that the Greek javelin throw was made with the use of a leather thong, which acted in effect as though the javelin were being thrown with a longer arm.* Also, the length of the Greek javelin was typically 8 feet, about 6 inches shorter than the modern one; and its weight, which generally did *not* include a metal head, was from 4 to 8 ounces lighter than that of a modern javelin. In application to a distance of 300 feet with a present-day javelin weighing .8 kg (= 28.218 oz.), a javelin 4 ounces lighter would presuppose an increase in distance to about 324 feet, and a javelin 8 ounces lighter to about 354 feet. To make the comparison in a reverse manner, if the champion javelin thrower of ancient Greece were competing today, using a modern-sized javelin and no thong, he would attain a distance presumably of from 244 feet to 267 feet. The latter distance, interestingly, is just about what would be expected from the Greek's lesser stature and shorter arm length. (The average height of Greek men during the 5th century B.C. was just over 65 inches, whereas today in the United States it is approximately 69 inches. More exactly, modern man, on the average, in the United States, is nearly 6 percent taller than was the average Greek male of the

---

*Harris (1964, p. 94) says that in his experiments the use of an 18-inch-long thong, *not* twisted around the shaft of the javelin, resulted in an average increase in distance of 4 percent. This would amount to 10–12 feet.

Golden Age. If this ratio is applicable to athletes also, the average-sized Greek javelin thrower must have been about 67.7 inches in height, as compared with today's average of 72.4 inches).

Figure 18, Appendix, shows the consecutive best marks in the javelin throw from 1908 to 1968. In the 1930s, much publicity was given to the fine javelin-throwing records of the two Finnish athletes, Matti Järvinen and Yrjö Nikkanen; yet very little was published concerning an American javelin thrower, E. L. McKenzie, who substantially surpassed the records of both these top-ranking Finns. In 1936, McKenzie (72 in., 195 lbs.), while "competing in obscure industrial meets in Beverly Hills," reached a distance of 264 feet. Whatever he did after 1936, I do not know. Evidently he never competed in a sanctioned AAU field meet; but if he actually threw the javelin 264 feet in 1936—and it would appear that he did—he was far in advance of his time in this event. I have two pages of photographs that appeared in *Look* magazine sometime in 1936, showing McKenzie performing his record-making throw of 264 feet; unfortunately, the exact date of the magazine's issue was clipped from the pages. As is seen in Figure 18, it was 20 years before McKenzie's phenomenal javelin throw was surpassed. Although World War II was then going on, it is unusual for a world record in a frequently practiced athletic event to last during any period for more than a few years.

However, in all weight-throwing events—even the lightweight javelin—the height and bodyweight of the performer are factors which influence the length of his throw. Accordingly, in rating a throwing performance as to *efficiency*, the *size* of the performer must be taken into account. When height and weight, as well as date of performance, are properly considered, it develops that the most efficient javelin throwers were neither McKenzie nor Jarvinen nor Nikkanen, but rather the small (68.9 in., 165 lbs.) Finnish thrower, Jorma Kinnunen, and the even shorter (67.5 in., 168 lbs.) American thrower, Albert Cantello. The percentage ratings of Cantello and other top-ranking javelin throwers are listed in the Appendix. At the time this is being written, Kinnunen holds the world record with a phenomenal throw of 304 ft. 1½ in.

Javelin performers, whose throwing implement is relatively light, in consequence need not be so heavily built as shot putters, weight throwers, or weightlifters. The chief quality required in events using light apparatus is *speed* rather than strength. In build, the average height of 10 top-ranking javelin throwers was found to be 72.44 inches, and the average bodyweight 186 lbs. This means that the body build of javelin throwers is a trifle less heavy than that of typical all-around athletes, who at 72.44 inches would average about 192 lbs. Of 20 championship-class women javelin throwers, the average height is

67.7 inches and the average weight 152 pounds. To be of the same relative height and weight as the men javelin champions, the women should average 67.2 inches and 148.8 lbs. For both sexes, the height and weight required for the javelin throw are markedly less than for either the shot put or the discus throw.

The present-day women's world record in the javelin throw is 204 ft. 8½ in., by Yelena Gorchakova (65.75 in., 152 lbs.) of the USSR. This throw was made in the 1964 Olympic Games at Tokyo, on October 16 of that year. The javelin used was, of course, one of the .6 kg ones standard for women. With a javelin of the weight standardized for men—namely .8 kg—Miss Gorchakova's throw, theoretically, would be reduced to 177 ft. 3¼ in. To carry the comparison further, one should take into account the height and weight of the current men's world record holder, Jorma Kinnunen (Finland). As mentioned above, Kinnunen stands 68.9 inches and weighs 165 pounds., and holds the record with 304 ft. 1½ in. If Kinnunen were reduced to the height and weight of Miss Gorchakova, he would be expected to throw only about 274 ft. 6 in. Thus, Miss Gorchakova's throw, in relation to the latter distance, is 177.3/274.5, or 64.59 percent. Indeed, if Miss Gorchakova were making a record today, rather than in 1964, one would expect a distance of about 209 ft. This would make the percentage of comparison 66.55 rather than 64.59, and would substantiate the theoretical ratio of ⅔, or 66.67 per cent (the strength, or force, of a woman compared with a man *of the same height and weight*).

For detailed information on the mechanics, technique, and training procedures applying to the javelin throw, see the references given on page 391 for the shot put. The chapters on the javelin throw are as follows:

Doherty: pp. 285–311.
Mortensen and Cooper: pp. 222–235.
Hildreth: pp. 143–149.
Dyson: Chapter 10, pp. 184–185, 199–204.
Quercetani: Chapter 17.

As references on the history of the javelin throw, see also the following:

Gardiner, E. N. 1910. *Greek Athletic Sports and Festivals*. London.

Gardiner, E. N. 1930. *Athletics of the Ancient World*. Oxford: Clarendon Press.

Hyde, W. W. 1921. *Olympic Victor Monuments and Greek Athletic Art*. Carnegie Inst. Wash. Pub. No. 268. Pp. 222–228: AKONTISTAI (javelin throwing).

Alexander, C. 1925. *Greek Athletics*. New York: Metropolitan Museum of Art. "Javelin Throw," pp. 16–18. (This excellently illustrated booklet deals also with the various other athletic events practiced by the Greeks).

F. THE 56-POUND AND 35-POUND WEIGHT THROWS

Of these two throws, that with the 56-pound weight was for many years a standardized field event, while the throw with 35 pounds was not performed regularly until 1922, when it was made an annual *indoor* field event. Neither the 56-pound nor the 35-pound weight throw is practiced much, if at all, outside the United States and Great Britain; accordingly, neither event is included in the IAAF lists nor as a competition event in the Olympic Games. During the long period from 1878 to 1959 inclusive, the 56-pound weight throw appeared every year in AAU competitions. Since 1960 it evidently has no longer been a regular event, although every so often some weight-thrower will attempt a record in it (e.g., George Frenn, in 1967). Under the usual rules, both the 56-pound and the 35-pound weights are thrown from within a 7-foot circle, the thrower making a number of turns to gain momentum before releasing the weight.

The weight of 56 pounds was derived from the British half-hundred-weight. In Ireland, where weight-throwing has been a popular field event for centuries, there are (or used to be) various ways of throwing the 56-pound weight: with one hand using a run; the same without a run; with two hands using a run; the same without a run; and vertically, for height. The last-named event, which is still practiced occasionally, is discussed later on.

Figure 19, Appendix, shows graphically the trend of the best marks in the 56-pound weight throw from 1880 to 1967. It is evident that the most capable earlier performers in this highly technical field event have been, in order, Matthew McGrath (1911), John Flanagan (1907), Patrick McDonald (1911), and James Mitchel (1894). Each of these men practiced many years before attaining his potential. And each man was sufficiently big and heavy to counteract the strong centrifugal pull of the 56-pound weight as it was being whirled around. Finally, each man, despite his size, with practice became remarkably quick on his feet, so as to be able to apply to the whirling weight the maximum of *speed*.

The most recent performer to distinguish himself in the 56-pound weight throw is George Frenn of Southern California, who in 1967 established the present world record with a throw of 48 ft. 0¾ in. Frenn was also, in 1967, National Champion in the 242-pound class in Power Lifting. In that year and class he held American records in the Squat with 732 pounds, the Dead Lift with 713¾ pounds, and the 3-lift total with 1904 pounds. In the Bench Press he did 465 pounds, as compared with Mel Hennessy's record in the 242-pound class of 542 pounds. Frenn is also a creditable performer in the 16-pound hammer throw, having in

1967 made a mark of 220 ft. 11 in. Frenn (b. 1941, San Fernando, California, stands 71.5 inches in height and weighs 242 pounds in solid, muscular condition (see Plate 73).

With reference to height and weight, it is clear that these factors are of prime importance in weight throwing, just as they are in weightlifting, putting the shot, and even in the discus throw. Matt McGrath, who was an outstanding performer in the 56-pound weight throw, weighed 248 pounds at a height of 71¾ inches. Pat McDonald, another great oldtime performer, stood about an even 72 inches and weighed 250 pounds. George Frenn, the present-day record holder, is practically of the same height and weight as were McGrath and McDonald, although he is smaller waisted and of greater muscularity. Proper credit for the distance attained in throwing the 56-pound weight should, as in the shot put and in regular weightlifting, take into account the performer's height and weight. As the latter factors have always been ignored in the weight throw, it is understandable why the record holders in this event are almost always men weighing in the neighborhood of 250 pounds. While a still greater bodyweight would give still greater stability to the performer, this advantage would be offset if there were, as a consequence, a disproportionate loss in *speed*.

In the 35-pound weight throw, the current record is held also by George Frenn, with a distance of 72 ft. 9½ in. This, in comparison with his record of 48 ft. 0¾ in. with 56 pounds, yields a ratio of 72.79/48.06, or 1.513. The next-best record with 35 pounds is Harold Connolly's 71 ft. 2½ in., made in 1960. I have no figure for Connolly's record with 56 pounds. In 1954, Robert Backus did 63 ft. 5 in. with 35 pounds and 42 ft. 5¼ in. with 56 pounds. These figures yield a ratio of 1.471. It would thus appear that the possibility in distance with 35 pounds is approximately 1½ times that with 56 pounds. On the basis of the square roots of 56 and 35, respectively, the ratio should be only 1.265. This indicates that in the 35-pound weight throw some factor exists that enables *relatively* longer throws to be made than with 56 pounds. In this respect the weight throws differ from the shot puts, since in the latter the expectation in distance is directly (although inversely) in ratio to the *square roots* of the weights of the shots.

Here are a few figures concerning the 56-pound weight throw for *height*. The present record in this event is held by Jim Hannefield, who on March 2, 1968, at Long Beach, California, attained a height of 17 ft. 6½ in. Hannefield is said to weigh in the neighborhood of 300 pounds. Second in the same contest was George Frenn, with 17 ft. 2 in. Back in 1914, Pat Donovan, at San Francisco, set the previous record of 16 ft. 11¼ in. Prior to that, the best mark had been Matt McGrath's 16 ft. 6¾ in., made in 1910. McGrath's record for distance with the

56-pound weight was 40 ft. 6⅝ in. (1911). While McGrath's two records, along with Frenn's, are insufficient as a basis for determining an average ratio of height to distance, it would appear that the throw for height is somewhere between 35 percent and 41 percent of the throw for distance. In ordinary throwing, as of a baseball, the height to be expected is, theoretically, just half of the horizontal distance thrown. The lesser ratio obtaining in the 56-pound weight throw for height would appear to be due to the difference in *technique* from the horizontal throw, as in the latter the momentum is increased by the *whirling* motions of the performer. In contrast, in the throw for height, only a simple upward flinging motion is possible. Perhaps if present-day performers with the 56-pound weight would improve their technique in throwing for height, their records in this event would correspond more closely than they do now with the .407 height/distance ratio attained in 1910 by Matt McGrath.

Hannefield's and Frenn's marks for height were made by throwing the 56-pound weight upwards against a large, circular board mounted on a vertically adjustable (high-jump type) crossbar. This arrangement enables a greater height to be recorded than where—as was the fashion in some early-day contests—the weight was thrown *over* a bar or a stretched tape.

The 56-pound and 35-pound weight throws require for their successful performance the same combination of strength and speed as is required in the shot put, the hammer throw, the discus throw, and in "quick" weightlifting events, such as the Snatch and the Clean and Jerk. Thus it is readily possible to establish a series of correlation ratios for these diverse weight-using events (see Appendix).

G. THE DECATHLON

When all is said and done, it must be granted that the most desirable type of athletic ability is neither strength alone, speed alone, stamina alone, nor agility alone, but a harmonious *combination* of all four qualities. In this sense, the "best" athlete is the "all-around" athlete. And in Olympic Games competition, since 1912, the Decathlon has been accepted as the standard test of all-around athletic ability. More correctly, it might be regarded as the criterion of all-around *track and field* ability. Actually a performer might be exceedingly versatile in the four basic physical qualities mentioned above, and still not excel in the particular ten events comprising the Decathlon. Such a performer might excel in various other events, as for example weightlifting, wrestling, tumbling, standing jumping (high and broad), throwing a baseball, playing handball, feats of herculean gymnastics, fencing, and bicycling.

Surely such an athlete would be fully as worthy of the title "all-around" as would a champion performer in the Decathlon.

While it has become customary to title each successive outstanding Decathlon champion as the "greatest athlete in the world," such a title is on a par with calling the current sprint champion "the fastest man in the world." No athlete can be physically supreme in all departments any more than any individual scientist or philosopher can be supreme in the realm of thought. Thus the object here shall be not to over-emphasize the virtues of the Decathlon athlete, but to give equal praise to "all-around" athletes in general.

The first track and field events of which there is a record would appear to be those performed at the Tailteann Games in Ireland, which took place annually from at least 1829 B.C. (and probably earlier) up to 554 A.D. These events were five in number, and consisted of running, jumping, throwing the javelin, weight throwing, and pole vaulting (for distance rather than height). Whether or not an all-around championship was held using these five events is not known to the present writer. The ancient Greeks made use of a five-event track and field competition, which became known as a Pentathlon. This combination contest they introduced into the Olympic Games program in 708 B.C.

The Greek Pentathlon consisted of the following events, probably in the order named: (1) jumping (for distance, using weights); (2) running (usually a sprint of approximately 200 yards, or the length of the stadium); (3) throwing the discus; (4) throwing the javelin; and (5) wrestling (Greco-Roman style). The Greeks held versatility in high regard, and the winner of a Pentathlon received many honors. Just how the final victor in this contest was determined is a matter of conjecture. Rarely did a competitor win all five of the events, and credit seems to have been awarded on the basis of the points gained in each event.

When the first modern Decathlon competition took place at the Olympic Games in 1912, the actual (though later disqualified) winner was the renowned American Indian athlete, Jim Thorpe (1888–1953). Actually, Thorpe was one-quarter Irish as well as five-eighths Sac and Fox Indian, and he had also a little (one-eighth) French blood. By many, Thorpe (see Plate 74) has been regarded as the greatest athlete of all time. While he was outstandingly superior to his competitors in the Decathlon at the time he competed (1912), certainly he could never be judged the greatest all-around athlete on the basis of his showing at Stockholm. Here are the marks that Thorpe set there on July 13–15, 1912: 100 meter dash, 11.2 sec.; long jump, 22 ft. 2⅜ in.; shot put, 42 ft. 5½ in.; high jump, 6 ft. 1⅝ in.; 400-meter run, 52.2 sec.; 110-meter hurdles, 15.6 sec.; discus throw, 121 ft. 3⅞ in.; pole vault

Table 19. Some leading performers in the Decathlon. Author's point-ratings are corrected for date.

Rank	Performer	Nation	Decathlon Event 1 100 m	2 LJ	3 SP	4 HJ	5 400 m	6 110 m H	7 DT	8 PV	9 JT	10 1500 m	Rating, points Author's abridged method	IAAF	Year
1	Rafer Johnson	USA	10.6	24-9¼	52.0⅜	5-10	48.6	14.5	170-6½	13-0¼	233-2¾	5:09.9	8530	8683	1960
2	C. K. Yang	China	10.7	23-6⅝	43-4½	6-3⅝	47.7	14.0	134.6	15-10½	235-4¼	5:02.4	8476	9121	1963
3	Phil Mulkey	USA	10.7	24-9¾	50-3⅛	6-6¼	51.0	14.6	154-3⅝	14-4¾	221-6½	4:43.8	8361	8709	1961
4	Yuriy Kutyenko	USSR	10.7	23-0	49-4⅛	5-10⅞	50.3	15.2	154-9½	14-1¼	237-2	4:34.3	8359	8361	1961
5	Vasily Kuznetsov	USSR	10.7	24-1⅜	48-2	6-2½	49.2	14.7	163-10	13-9⅜	213-5⅜	5:04.6	8325	8357	1959
6	Robert Mathias	USA	10.9	23-5⅜	50-2⅜	6-2¾	50.2	14.7	157-11⅝	13-1½	194-3⅜	4:50.8	8302	7887	1952
7	Russ Hodge	USA	10.3	25-2¾	54-7¼	6-1½	49.3	15.2	147-6½	13-10¼	197-7½	4:43.4	8197	?	1966
8	William Toomey	USA	10.3	25-6	45-8¾	6-4⅞	47.3	14.8	147-5½	13-0	198-11	4:30.0	8192	8222	1966
9	David Edstrom	USA	10.8	23-5⅞	49-11⅝	6-1¼	49.5	14.2	151-1¾	11-5¾	218-2⅞	4:36.2	8190	8176	1960
10	Glenn Morris	USA	11.1	22-10¾	46-3¼	6-1	49.4	14.9	141-1⅝	11-6	178-10⅝	4:33.2	8138	7310	1936
11	M. Storozhenko	USSR	10.9	23-11	51-5¾	6-6¼	53.0	14.5	157-7½	13-5⅜	212-8¾	4:50.6	8050	?	1965
12	Paul Herman	USA	11.2	24-4⅛	44-0	6-2½	49.3	14.8	143-6	14-4⅜	201-3	4:35.0	7981	8061	1963
	Average (12)		10.74	24.39	48.78	6.21	49.56	14.67	150.69	13.50	211.84	4:46.2	8259	....	1959
	Maximum (best)		10.3	25.50	54.60	6.53	47.30	14.0	170.54	15.88	237.17	4:30.0	8530	....	....
	Minimum		11.2	22.90	43.37	5.83	53.00	15.2	134.50	11.48	178.88	5:09.9	8050	....	....
	Max./Min.		1.077	1.114	1.259	1.119	1.120	1.100	1.268	1.406	1.326	1.148	1.060	....	....

10 ft. 7⅞ in.; javelin throw, 149 ft. 11¼ in.; and 1500-meter run, 4 min. 40.1 sec. In the pole vault, Thorpe voluntarily dropped out at the height he was credited with, as he was afraid his weight might break the wooden pole. And in the discus throw it was evident that he used little or no "technique" and was far below his potential. In the high jump, Thorpe showed at his best, and in this event he had an unofficial record of 6 ft. 5 in. Again, in the high hurdles, Jim had a fine personal best of 15 seconds flat.

However, even if allowances were made for all these top performances and potentialities, it is doubtful whether Thorpe could ever equal the Decathlon records of the top performers listed in Table 19. Thorpe's 1912 total performance, as rated by the author's abridged method, totals 6583 points. Correcting for date of performance brings the total to 7602 points. If it is allowed that Thorpe had a potential (while performing all ten events) of 140 feet in the discus, 12 feet in the pole vault, and 15 seconds in the 110-meter hurdles, his point-rating, corrected for time, would still amount only to 8022, or just below the 12th-place performer in Table 19. To properly evaluate Thorpe's athletic greatness, one must consider not only his ability in the Decathlon, but in such other fields as football, baseball, basketball, boxing, wrestling, tennis, hockey, lacrosse, shooting, skating, archery, swimming, canoeing, golf, bowling, and virtually every other department in which natural athletic talent is an asset. So great was Thorpe's fame that in Pennsylvania a town, Jim Thorpe, was named after him. There he lies now, in the heart of the Indian country he liked best.

Bob Mathias, who won the Olympic Decathlon in both 1948 and 1952, was at the time hailed as a second Jim Thorpe. There can be no question that in the Decathlon, at least, Mathias was superior to Thorpe. In this connection, a common error in comparing the respective performances of athletes who competed in *different epochs* should here be noted. Several writers have attempted to prove the superiority of Jim Thorpe in the Decathlon over later champions such as Bob Mathias and Rafer Johnson. This they have seemingly succeeded in doing by relating Thorpe's Decathlon marks to the respective world records in each event as of 1912, and comparing the percentage results with those derived for Mathias in 1952 and Johnson in 1960. At first glance, this would appear to be a logical and fair method of comparison. However, it ignores an important factor, which is *the size of the population* from which the world records have been drawn. If only a hundred athletes compete in a certain event, or series of events, the champion among them will not surpass the average of the competitors to nearly the degree that he would if the number competing had been a *thousand* rather than a *hundred*. Conversely, if a world record has come out of a population of only a hundred competitors, the performance of the average competitor will be closer to that record than if the record had been drawn from a group of a thousand competitors. It is certainly safe to say that in 1960, or even 1952, the number of athletes competing in the Decathlon, or in track and field separately, was at least ten times as great as it was in 1912.° That is why Thorpe's Decathlon records were almost bound to be closer to the world records existing in 1912 than Mathias's were to those existing in 1952, or Johnson's to those existing in 1960. Thorpe, beyond doubt, was a phenomenal *all-around* athlete; but in the Decathlon, to date, it is equally certain that the three greatest performers were, respectively, Rafer Johnson (USA) in 1960 with 8530 points (by the author's method of rating), C. K. Yang (China) in 1963 with 8476 points, and Phil Mulkey (USA) in 1961 with 8361 points. Each of these point awards has been corrected for date of performance, as have all the other awards listed in Table 19.

Potentially, at least, the greatest of all Decathlon performers may have been the professional athlete (gymnastics instructor and track coach) Richard Perry Williams (see Plate 75) of Springfield, Ohio. Certainly he was outstanding in all the track and field events that he practiced, or attempted, and in some of them, such as sprinting and jumping, he was rarely if ever equalled. Williams was born on April 21, 1874, in Cornwall, England. He began his coaching career in 1899, at Tufts College, Massachusetts, thus becoming a professional at the age of 25. A year later he was measured and tested by the famous anthropometrist, Dr. Dudley Allen Sargent, at Harvard University. Sargent recorded Williams's height as 69.1 inches and his weight as 141 pounds. In 1902, however, after seeing the celebrated vaudeville strong-man, Eugen Sandow, perform in Boston, Williams became personally acquainted with Sandow and from him gained the desire to become as strong as possible. As a result of several years' systematic weight training, Williams built his weight up to about 160 pounds, and at that weight was able to improve on most of his previous records, especially those requiring strength.

Here is a summary of the many and varied athletic and gymnastic records set by Williams during, mainly, the years 1898–1910: 100-yard

---

°This is a most generous underestimate. According to sports statisticians who have kept a record in the matter, in the first modern Olympic Games, in 1896, the national champions who competed were drawn from a total field of fewer than 50,000 athletes. In contrast, in 1964, the field numbered more than 100,000,000 or 2000 times the number who competed in 1896. If we figure the years 1912 (when Thorpe competed) and 1952 (when Mathias competed), it works out that nearly 1500 times as many athletes comprised the field from which Mathias emerged the Decathlon champion as had been present in 1912 when Thorpe was top man. Such population figures as these greatly modify performance ratings made on the single basis of individual records compared with contemporary world records.

dash (on three separate occasions) 9 seconds flat; 100 meters, 9 4/5 sec.; 400 meters, 46 3/5 sec.; mile run 4 min. 25 sec. (equal to 1500 meters in 3 min. 56 sec.); running broad jump, 26 ft. 0½ in.; standing broad jump, with weights, 15 ft. 4 in.; standing jump backwards, with weights, 13 ft. 3 in.; Sargent (vertical) jump, 34.9 in.; running high kick, 10 ft. 3 in.; hitch and kick (i.e., a standing jump off one foot, and kick), 9 ft. 6 in.; shot put (16 lbs.), 47 ft. 9 in.; shot put (12 lbs.), 57 ft. 3 in.; discus throw, 142 ft. 9 in.; baseball throw, 415 ft. 3 in.; circling bases (baseball), 12 seconds flat; chinning the bar, 48 times; dipping on parallel bars, 55 times; high jump on ice skates, 4 ft. 6 in. One of Williams's most outstanding abilities was as a handball player. During the 48-year period between 1895 and 1943 (when he was 69!), Williams engaged in 14,657 games of one-wall handball without losing a single game! Jim Thorpe called Williams "the fastest sprinter who ever lived," and Williams surpassed Thorpe in no fewer than 19 different track and field events.

While I have not seen any published figures on what Williams could do in the hurdles, the pole vault, and the javelin throw, a figure of 8930.5 points has been given as his total score in the Decathlon, in 1912. This rating by the latest IAAF method corresponds with a rating by my own (abridged) method of 8457 points. This score would make Williams's standing in the Decathlon approximately equal in merit to his phenomenal record of 9 seconds flat in the 100-yard dash (in 1906, 1908, and 1910). Williams died in 1966, at the age of 92 years.

Concerning *all-around* athletic ability, it should be noted that many an athlete had such ability—in potential form, at least—even though he may never have practiced any of the specific events included in the Decathlon. Basically, the attributes of the "natural" athlete consist of a balanced combination of strength, speed, endurance, agility, and neuromuscular coordination. The present-day Decathlon is simply an arbitrary selection of ten track and field events in which these qualities are required. Moreover, the four field events—shot put, discus throw, pole vault, and javelin—included in the Decathlon are all highly specialized feats requiring years of practice if a championship level of performance is to be attained. In contrast, the running and jumping events—especially where the latter are not modified by the use of fancy "techniques"—express more reliably the basic physical qualities of the "natural" athlete.

Although a considerable number of essentially "all-around" athletes have already been cited in connection with various specific sports (*e.g.*, weightlifting, wrestling, acrobatics, etc.), the following list is here appended in order to bring them together in one place. These athletes, for the most part, may be termed "Decathlon strong-men." In most

PLATE 81

Katie Sandwina, as she appeared in her circus act in 1911. (149, 150)

PLATE 82

"Vulcana," an English music-hall strong-woman who, though weighing only 125 pounds herself, could raise 145 pounds over her head with one arm. (151)

PLATE 83

"Minerva," the Police Gazette's champion strong-woman of the
'90s. (152)

PLATE 84

The Flying De Pauls. In this scene the "under-stander," Nancy De Paul, is supporting the five other girls of the troupe. (153)

PLATE 85

"Christane," a European woman professional wrestler, hurling
her wrestler-husband to the mat with a flying mare. (154)

PLATE 86

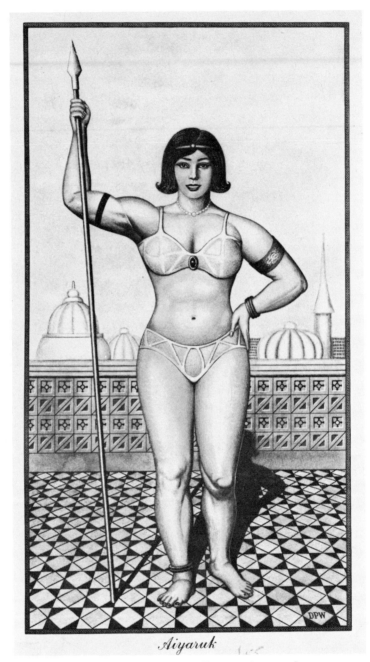

Aiyaruk

Aiyaruk, a 13th-century Tartar princess who was an invincible wrestler. (155)

PLATE 87

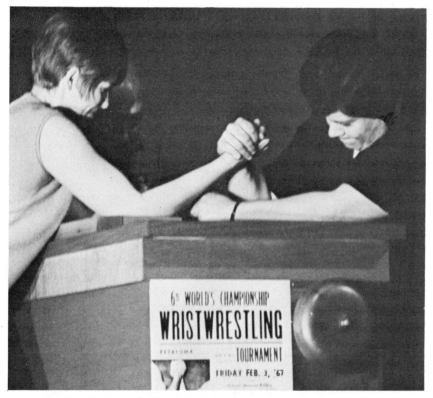

Mickie Novis of Oakland (right) putting down the arm of Mary Doughty of Petaluma, the runner-up in the woman's world wrist-wrestling championship of 1967. (156)

PLATE **88**

Margitta Helmbolt-Gummel of East Germany, world-record holder in the woman's shot put, with a distance of 65 ft., 11¼ in., made in East Berlin on September 11, 1969. (157)

respects their particular abilities are fully as indicative of general athletic prowess as are those of the formally recognized track and field Decathlon performer.

1. Some "Decathlon" Strong-men

1. ROBERT J. ROBERTS (P., 65 in., 145 lbs.) was Physical Director of the YMCA in Boston during the years 1875–1887. Here are some of the performances he made in 1875, at the age of 26: One Hand Side Press with dumbbell, 120 pounds with either arm; Abdominal Raise, 100 lbs.; Chinning, 3 times with either arm and 35 times with both arms; Standing High Jump, from either side, 4 ft. 6 in.; Running High Jump (scissors style), 5 ft. 4 in.; Shot Put (16 lbs.), 35 feet right and left; Walking, one mile in less than 8 minutes and 6 miles in an hour; Running, 100 yards in 11 seconds and 5 miles in 30 minutes. He had also learned to box and wrestle, and was a good swimmer and oarsman.

2. WILLIAM MILLER (P., 69.75 in., 196 lbs.) was born in England in 1846, but lived most of his life in Australia and the United States. In 1874 he was employed as an instructor at the Olympic Club in San Francisco, and there defeated some of the best boxers and wrestlers of the day. Shortly thereafter, in touring the United States as a professional wrestler, in 72 matches he won 55, drew 11, and lost only 6. In weightlifting, he could put up simultaneously two 115-pound dumbbells with a jerk, or push a 100-pound dumbbell with his right hand 19 times in succession. He was also proficient in gymnastics, swordsmanship, and long-distance walking.

3. CAPTAIN JAMES C. DALY (73.5 in., 205 lbs.) was born in Ireland in 1852 and performed in the United States in the 1870s. In throwing the 56-pound weight (in the Irish style, from a standing position), he did 27 ft. 2 in. In the 16-pound shot put he reached 46 ft. 8 in.; in the running high jump, 5 ft. 10 in.; in the running broad jump, 20 ft. 0¾ in.; and in the hop, step and jump, 44 ft. 8 in. As to his weightlifting ability, one of his feats was to raise 3000 pounds in the Back Lift. He was also a top-ranking wrestler.

4. DONALD DINNIE (P., 72.5 in., 218 lbs.) was the greatest all-around strong-man athlete ever produced in Scotland. He was born in 1837 and competed professionally from the age of 16 to the age of 63(!), a perhaps unique record of sustained athletic ability. During his long career as a Highland Games athlete and as a touring professional wrestler he was the recipient of over 100 medals and won no fewer than 7500 cash prizes totalling over $100,000! He was also the winner

in more than 200 weightlifting contests. In putting the shot, Dinnie was the leading performer of his day. His best official put was 45 ft. 7 in., and his best unofficial put 49 ft. 6 in. (with a 16-pound *stone*). As the latter put was made away back in 1868, it would be equivalent to over 64 feet today! Dinnie was likewise the champion at tossing the caber. In the hammer throw (using a stiff, wooden-handled hammer, as was the style in his time), one of Dinnie's best efforts was at Braemar in 1873, when he threw a 22-pound hammer a distance of 84 ft. 9 in. This was equivalent to throwing a 16-pound hammer (of the same type) 107 feet.

Here are some of the other performances that Dinnie made when he was in his prime:

  a. "Put up" (jerk-pressed?) a pair of 56-pound dumbbells 52 times in succession. This was equivalent to a single two dumbbells *press* of about 230 pounds.
  b. *Carried* together the two "Dinnie stones"—one weighing 445 pounds and the other 340 pounds—a distance of 5 yards.
  c. Put a 22-pound stone 42 ft. 3 in.; an 18-pound stone 44 ft. 8 in.; and a 14-pound stone 52 ft.
  d. Did a running high jump (scissors style) of 5 ft. 11 in.
  e. Did a running broad jump of 20 ft. 1 in.
  f. Did a hop, step and jump of 44 ft.
  g. Sprinted 100 yards in 10 2/5 seconds.

If the foregoing feats by Dinnie were converted to their respective equivalents as of today, they would *confirm* the reasons for the high esteem in which his contemporaries held him. So invincible was Dinnie in his heyday that even poets went into rhapsodies over his performances. The following is a typical ditty:

> He's springy, elastic and light when he's running,
>   Comes up to the mark in time and to spare;
> His opponents can't match him or beat him in cunning,
>   They say, "we were beat because Dinnie was there!"

5. COLONEL FREDERICK G. BURNABY (76 in., *c.* 240 lbs.) was described as being a modern Richard Coeur-de-Lion. He was born in 1842 in Bedford, England, and was killed in action in 1885 at the battle of Abou Klea, in Egypt. His relatively short life was filled with activity and adventure. While he was not a trained specialist in weightlifting nor in any other form of athletics, he excelled in anything requiring natural strength, speed, or endurance. He was an expert fencer, a skillful boxer, a horseman and an oarsman, and was very quick and agile considering his size. He "put up" with his right hand, mainly by sheer strength, a dumbbell

weighing 170 pounds. Once, in winning a wager, he ran, rowed, rode (horseback), hopped, and walked five successive quarters of a mile (that is, 1¼ miles) in less than 13 minutes. On another occasion when, as a joke, two small ponies had been driven up a flight of stairs into Burnaby's room, he couldn't induce the animals to walk *down* the stairs. Whereupon, he tucked one pony under each arm and *carried* them down the stairs himself!

6. CLARENCE WEBER (P., 72 in., 202 lbs.), around about 1910, claimed to be the champion all-around athlete of Australia. In weightlifting he established Australian professional records by doing a Two Hands Clean and Jerk of 273¾ pounds, a Right Hand Clean and Bent Press of 219½ pounds, and a Right Hand Snatch of 172½ pounds. He also did a Crucifix of 118¾ pounds (60½ right, 58¼ left), and a Wrestler's Bridge Press of 224 pounds. Weber had extraordinary leg strength, and could perform a Squat on one leg while carrying 200 pounds extra weight. From 1911 to 1914, he was the best wrestler in Australia. Previously, in 1900, he had won the amateur cycling championship of Victoria (25 miles in 1 hr. 11 min.), and also won at 5 miles. He ran 100 yards in 10-2/5 seconds, and 440 yards in 1 minute 2-1/5 seconds. In the running high jump he did 5 ft. 4 in., running broad jump 20 ft. 1½ in., and shot put 40 ft. 1½ in. He did equally well on all the gymnastic apparatus. Weber had a classical physique, and was one of the most sought-after sculptor's models of his time. Facially, he was exceedingly handsome.

7. WILLIAM BUCKINGHAM CURTIS (68 in., 168 lbs.) was born in Salisbury, Vermont, on January 17, 1837. He was one of the founders both of the American Amateur Athletic Union and the New York Athletic Club. He became known to his followers as "The father of American track and field athletics." He was also, in person, a most versatile all-around athlete, as the following list of his records shows: Running, 100 yards in 10 seconds and 440 yards in 51½ seconds; walking, one mile in 8 min. 51 sec.; 120-yard hurdles, 19 sec.; ice skating, one mile in 3 min. 18 sec.; swimming, 100 yards in 1 min. 40 sec.; single sculling, 1 mile in 6 min. 49 sec.; 2 miles, 13 min. 57 sec.; 3 miles, 23 min. 13 sec.; running high jump, 5 ft. 1 in.; running broad jump, 19 ft. 4 in.; 16-pound hammer throw (using a stiff, wooden-handled hammer), 90 ft.; 56-pound weight throw, 24 ft. Curtis was also a first-class performer in weightlifting, for his size. In New York City, on December 20, 1968, he made the first American record in the Harness Lift, by raising 3239 pounds. He also did a Two Hands Clean and Jerk with a pair of 100-pound dumbbells. This lift was performed in Chicago, on September

10, 1859. Curtis's use of "weight-training" was doubtless one of the reasons for his outstanding athletic ability. Today, a hundred years later, other track and field athletes are learning the advantages of using a similar schedule of training!

8. GENE JANTZEN (69 in., 195 lbs.) of Bartelso, Illinois, was a remarkable physical specimen, strong-man, and all-around athlete, with special ability at feats of endurance. Here are some of the things he accomplished while with the U.S. Air Force at Lincoln, Nebraska, about 1949: 500 consecutive sit-ups in 14 min., 5200 consecutive sit-ups in 3 hrs. 50 min.; 1000 chins (not consecutive) in 1 hr. 25 min.; 100-mile run in 23 hours; 21-mile swim in 11 hrs. 30 min.; 5-mile run in 26 min.; 10-mile run in 57 min.; swimming underwater, 100 yards; Two Hands Dead Lift with barbell, 540 pounds; Abdominal Raise, 130 pounds. In addition to having this extraordinary athletic versatility, Jantzen is a poet, an author, and a prize woodcarver.

9. BERT GOODRICH (70.5 in., 195–220 lbs.) of Los Angeles was the first holder of the "Mr. America" title (in 1939). Before becoming a professional hand-to-hand balancer, he had competed in school track and field events in Arizona, running the 100 yards in 9.8 seconds, the 220 in 21.4 seconds, and putting the 16-pound shot 47 feet. These were all first-class performances in 1927. Later on, when weighing well over 200 pounds, Goodrich could still run the 100 in 10 seconds flat.

10. WALDEMAR BASZANOWSKI (64.9 in., 148 lbs.) is one of the greatest Olympic weightlifters ever produced in Poland. In 1966, as a lightweight, he made a world's record Two Hands Snatch of 297½ pounds (double bodyweight). He also made a high-ranking 3-lift total of 953½ pounds (see Table 3). In addition to his extraordinary ability in the Olympic lifts, Baszanowski (at the end of 1961) was capable of the following: running high jump, 5 ft. 6 in.; standing high jump (scissors style), 4 ft. 7¾ in.; standing broad jump, 10 ft. 2 in.; 100-meter run, 11.7 sec. (= 100 yards in 10.6 sec.). These contrasting capabilities indicate a combination of strength, speed, and agility that stamps Baszanowski as being a true "super-athlete" (see Plate 23).

11. GUSTAVE FRISTENSKY (72.8 in., 220 lbs.) was known in his prime as "The Bohemian Hercules." He had one of the finest physiques ever seen anywhere, and was awarded prizes repeatedly during the years 1905–1910 for his classical figure and outstanding muscular development. Like Donald Dinnie, Hermann Görner (in 1920), Jim Jeffries, Siegmund Breitbart, and a number of other first-class heavyweight

athletes, Fristensky fell within the range of height (72–73 inches) and weight (215–225 pounds) that makes possible the maximum degree of *combined* strength and activity. Fristensky was outstanding in *repetition* weightlifting and in Greco-Roman wrestling. In the latter, he won the championship of Europe at Rotterdam in 1903 (in which competition 112 wrestlers had entered). As an example of his combined strength and speed, he once ran 100 meters in 14 seconds while carrying 90 kilos or 198.4 pounds. Perhaps, if Fristensky had had more incentive, he would have attained even greater athletic fame than he did. However, he married the daughter of a rich brewery owner in Pilsen, fell heir to the business, and thereafter did not have to worry about income!

12. G. W. ROLANDOW (P., 69.75 in., 178 lbs.) of New York City, *c.* 1900, was one of the greatest strength-athletes ever produced in this country. For his size, he combined to a remarkable degree the qualities of strength, speed, and agility. Before becoming a professional strong-man, Rolandow was a star performer for one of the largest amateur athletic clubs in New York City. There, he set the following track and field marks: 16-pound shot put, 45 ft.; 16-pound hammer throw, 162 ft. He did equally well in sprinting and in throwing the javelin and the discus. He also became a first-class boxer, wrestler, and bag-puncher; and a champion handball player and rope-skipper. He likewise excelled in handbalancing and in various forms of gymnastics. For Rolandow's records in weightlifting, see Chapter 4 where also are described his remarkable feats of *jumping* with weights. See also Plate 9.

13. AL TRELOAR (P., 70.5 in., 186 lbs.) should be included in any list of strong-man athletes. He first attained fame by winning first prize in Bernarr Macfadden's contest in New York City in 1903–1904 to find the "world's most perfectly-formed man." But before that, in 1893–1894, Treloar had worked as Eugen Sandow's assistant, and from Sandow he learned many feats of lifting and gymnastics. Treloar had also majored in physical education at Harvard University, and while there became an outstanding gymnast, wrestler, and oarsman, besides establishing a record in Dr. Sargent's strength test. Treloar started his gymnastic training at the age of 12, when he was allowed to practice at the winter training quarters in Illinois of a circus named Schep's. For three years, young Treloar specialized in tumbling, horizontal bar work, fancy horseback riding, and various forms of acrobatics. He retained this ability throughout most of his long life, and at the age of 50 was still able to perform a standing back somersault. But in addition to being an ideal all-around athlete and gymnast himself, Treloar, while Physical Director of the Los Angeles Athletic Club during the period

1907–1949 (42 years!), turned out dozens of champion performers in gymnastics, tumbling, wrestling, and weightlifting. It was in front of Treloar, in 1922, that I "tried out" for a place on the club's weightlifting team. I was accepted, and later became AAU champion of Southern California (and in 1924 of the United States). So possibly it was because of the interest in weightlifting kindled in me by Al Treloar that the present book was written.

14. BOB MITCHELL (65.5 in., 148 lbs.) was one of the greatest all-around "natural" athletes ever produced in this country. After only a year of training in weightlifting, he made a national record in the Two Hands Snatch of 215 pounds. Without special training, he was capable also of the following marks in track and field: 100-yard dash in 10 seconds or less; running high jump, 6 ft. 1 in.; standing high jump, 5 ft. 4 in. (!!); running broad jump, 22 ft. 10 in.; standing broad jump, 10 ft. 5 in. He was an equally capable gymnast and acrobat, and could dance or run up and down stairs on his hands, etc. Note in particular Mitchell's ability in the *standing* high jump. It is doubtful whether there is an athlete in the world today who can jump, scissors style, from a standing position to within 1½ inches of his own height. Mitchell made his records in the 1940s.

15. For an athlete of "super-heavyweight" proportions, BERT ASSIRATI (Prof., 66 in., 230–266 lbs.) presented a remarkable combination of strength, speed, and endurance. Back in 1938, he was a weightlifting record holder, the British Empire and World professional wrestling champion, and a gymnast who could do a one hand stand, a back somersault, a crucifix on the rings, or a one-arm chin, when weighing as much as 266 pounds! In addition to these abilities—which are commented on in detail elsewhere in this volume—Assirati was a long-distance cyclist, a champion strand-puller, and doubtless a top-performer in any other field of effort into which he entered!

16. REUBEN MARTIN (P., 72 in., 197 lbs.) of London was (about 1950) a weightlifting record holder, and a skilled handbalancer, gymnast and acrobat. His strength was shown in his Pull-over at Arms' Length of 200 pounds, and his 14 consecutive tiger-bend press-ups; while his speed was evident in his 100-yard dash in 10.3 seconds, and his 100-yard freestyle swim in one minute flat. As related elsewhere, Martin was able to "chin" a vertical bar while holding the "flag" position. In the Two Hands Clean and Jerk, he accomplished 310 pounds. For endurance, he could do 250 Indian "dunds" in succession, or 600 consecutive knee bends.

17. For a "super-athlete" of small size, it would be difficult to point out a better example than the Iranian bantamweight weightlifter MAHMOUD NAMDJOU (60 in., 123 lbs.). At the age of 16, in 1934, he was already a champion all-around athlete and gymnast. In the 1948 Olympic Games weightlifting, at London, he totalled 633½ pounds to take fifth place in the Bantamweight class. In Holland in 1949 he won the world's title with 688½ pounds. In 1950 at Paris, he retained his title with 683 pounds, and in Milan in 1951 increased his total to 699½ pounds. Namdjou could perform 20 consecutive tiger-bend press-ups, which were equivalent to doing a single Two Hands Military Press with about 196 pounds. The latter ability was confirmed by Namdjou's Olympic Press of 220 pounds. The training program in which Namdjou was an expert is known in Iran as the Zourkhaneh. It includes swordsmanship and archery, personal combat, horsemanship, "push-ups," club swinging (the heaviest clubs weighing 44 pounds), tumbling, and wrestling. In addition to being skilled in all these activities, Namdjou was an able mountaineer, skier, swimmer, oarsman (sculling), and jockey!

In addition to the 17 foregoing "super-athletes," there were, and are, a great many more whose recorded performances may not have been so extensive, yet who manifestly possessed the requisite combination of strength, speed, agility and endurance to warrant their being called by this term. Among the latter come to mind the following names: (weightlifters and "strong-men") Eugen Sandow, William Bankier, George Hackenschmidt, George Lurich, Paul von Boeckmann, Michael Dorizas, the three Saxon brothers,* Edward Aston, Adolph Nordquest, Alfred Moss, Otis Lambert, Henry Steinborn, Charles Rigoulot, Andre Rolet, Ronald Walker, Rudolf Ismayr, and a host of more recent American lifters including John Grimek, Steve Stanko, John Davis, Louis Abele, Stanley Stanczyk, Jack La Lanne, Tommy Kono, and many of today's stars. Among wrestlers there were Martin "Farmer" Burns (who possessed extraordinary abilities in various specialized tests), Dan McLeod (who was a champion all-around athlete), Jim Londos, and of course George Hackenschmidt, who was not only a world champion wrestler and weightlifting record holder, but also a local (Russian) champion cyclist and swimmer.

In some quarters, the physique of a Decathlon champion is regarded as being the ideal male physique. In a tabulation of 20 high-ranking

---

*While Arthur Saxon was not generally regarded as having speed and agility as well as strength, it may be pointed out that he could perform a One Hand Snatch with 10 pounds over his bodyweight! This, back in 1905, was extraordinary. As to endurance, Saxon when in England would cycle in good time from his home in Manchester to London, a distance of nearly 200 miles, without thinking anything of it.

Decathlon performers, the average height is 72.5 inches and the average bodyweight 183 pounds. However, the Decathlon is not necessarily an ideal "all-around" athletic test, since it is composed essentially of 4 running events (legs and lower back), 2 jumping events (legs, lower back, and abdominals), 1 gymnastic event (mainly arms and chest), and only 3 "weight" events, one of which (the javelin throw) requires more speed than strength. In short, the conventional Decathlon is lacking in strength (power) elements, since it omits such muscle-demanding events as weightlifting, wrestling, and heavy weight throwing. In contrast, the 17 "Decathlon" strong-men just listed represent a predominance of strength events. In consequence, these athletes have an average bodyweight of 186 pounds at an average height of only 69.3 inches. At 72.5 inches (the average height of conventional Decathlon performers), the proportionate bodyweight would be no less than 213 pounds. When the average body-build represented by a great number of differing athletic and gymnastic events is used as a basis, it works out that at a height of 72 inches (6 feet) the typical or "ideal" male athlete weighs 189 pounds.

Part 3.
WOMEN ATHLETES
AND GYMNASTS
AND THEIR RECORDS

NOTE: *Almost as readily as in the case of men, a full-sized book could be written on the athletic and gymnastic records made by women. As space in* The Super-Athletes *does not permit of such extensive coverage, the various women's sports here to be considered will be dealt with more concisely and in simple alphabetical order. Just as was done with men, many sports and recreational activities for women are here omitted. The reason for this, as before, is that various so-called "sports" are not really forms of athletics. Again, also, I have almost completely disregarded performances in various team games in which the ability of the individual player cannot be exactly measured. Some of the women's performances to be listed here have already been mentioned in earlier pages, to which references are made. As in the case of male athletes, the photographs shown here of women are mainly of lesser-known but highly capable performers, rather than of today's champions, whose pictures appear constantly in the usual books and magazines on athletics.*

Women's Sports

(*Listed alphabetically*)

ACROBATICS (see Gymnastics).

AERIAL OR TRAPEZE WORK (see Gymnastics).

ARCHERY. In "flight shooting," by which is meant shooting in the usual standing position, the women's distance record is 505 yards (as of 1950). In women's "freestyle shooting," in which the archer lies on her back, with the bow strapped to her feet, and draws the bowstring with both hands, the record is 575 yards 2 feet (as of 1958). The latter distance would require a pull ("weight" of bow) of about 110 pounds. For comparison, the average woman's bow has a pull of only about 30 pounds. I regret that I do not have the names of the holders of these two women's records. Compared with the men's records—approximately 850 yards in flight shooting and 937 yards in freestyle shooting—the women's record in flight shooting would appear to be about 3 percent inferior to that in freestyle shooting. For consistent accuracy in target shooting, the greatest performer among women (in America, at any rate) was Mrs. M. C. Howell. She won her first USA championship in 1883, and thereafter in 1885, 1886, 1890, 1891, 1892, 1893, 1895, 1896, 1898, 1899, 1900, 1902, 1903, 1904, 1905, and 1907—17 times a champion during a period of 25 years inclusive.

BADMINTON. The outstanding woman badminton player was Judith Devlin (since 1961 Judith Devlin Hashman). During the period 1953–1967, this remarkable woman athlete won the following numbers of championships: U.S. Women's Singles 12, All-England Singles (equivalent to World's championship) 10, Canadian Singles 3, U.S. Women's Doubles 12, All-England Doubles 7, Canadian Doubles 3; U.S. Mixed Doubles 8, Canadian Mixed Doubles 1. Thus, over a period of 16 years' competition, Miss Devlin won a total of 56 national championships. This record stamps her as the most capable woman athlete of modern times in any single sport. Miss Devlin was also selected as an

All-American lacrosse player on the woman's teams of 1954, 1955, 1957, and 1958.

BASEBALL (throw, for distance). In this event, the fabulous Mildred "Babe" Didrickson (see Plate 76) still holds the record for women, with a throw of 296 feet made in Jersey City, N.J. on July 25, 1931. This throw indicates that the ball had an initial velocity of about 117 feet per second or nearly 80 mph. In comparison, the average girl college student can throw a baseball only about 132 feet (= 78 feet per second, or about 53 mph). Thus, the "Babe" was able to put 50 percent more force into her throw than the average college girl, even though she weighed no more, and possibly less.

BASKETBALL (throw, for distance). The best record I have come across in this event is a throw of 101 ft. 6¾ in. by Nan Gindelle, Chicago, 1933.

BICYCLE RACING. The speed attainable by women cycling champions, between the distances of 5 and 20 kilometers (= *c*. 3 to 12 miles) averages about 85.7 percent of that attained by men champions. At a distance of one kilometer the women's/men's ratio is only 80.4 percent, and at 100 kilometers about 84.5 percent. Thus the speed of women in cycling, as compared with men, is appreciably less than in sprint running, where the ratio averages 90–91 percent. The explanation of this difference would seem to be that while in cycling a woman can move her legs as fast as in sprinting, in cycling a lower *gear ratio* is used by women (necessarily, because of their lesser strength) than by men, with the wheels of the bicycle accordingly turning a lesser number of times per second. Today, bicycle racing, both for men and for women, seems to be dominated by performers from France, Italy, and England. Yet there have been some outstanding performers in the United States. Back in 1900, beginning on October 6, Miss Margaret Gast (aged 20) cycled 2600 miles in alternating 12-hour periods, covering the distance in 12 days 7 hours 55 minutes. The cycling took place over the triangular-shaped record course of the Century Road Club at Valley Stream, Long Island, N.Y. Miss Gast's performance was 1100 miles farther than any other woman had cycled under the same conditions, and 600 miles farther than any man had done.

BOXING. Whether there is a recognized women's boxing champion at the present time, I do not know. Certainly this form of athletic competition among women is not generally encouraged. Back at the turn of the century there was an Irish girl named Polly Fairclough, who was then recognized as the champion woman boxer of the world. Polly appeared for a while with a traveling British circus, and offered $50 to any man in the audience who could stay with her for three rounds. As one account reads, "Many a hulking miner, longshoreman, or locally celebrated bruiser stepped into the ring, thinking to teach this pretty girl a lesson and collect some easy money. Hundreds of disillusioned fellows emerged with split lips and shiners, after taking the beating of their lives." It is said that month after month Polly trounced all comers, and that on one occasion she fought 110 victorious rounds against more than 50 men. What Polly's height and weight was is not stated, but evidently she was highly skilled in the use of her fists!

Walter Umminger, in his interesting book *Supermen, Heroes and Gods* (1963) says that in earlier days the women of various Polynesian islands used to stage friendly but fierce "boxing" bouts among their own sex. In these bouts evidently nothing was barred that would contribute to victory. The contestants would pull each other's hair, punch and kick to the stomach, and yank and pull on each other until one went down. This sounds more like the old Greek *pancratium* than like boxing!

CANOEING (see Rowing).

CRICKET (ball throw, for distance). The only women's record I have seen listed for this event is a throw of 218 ft. 2½ in. by Margaret Wilkinson (Great Britain), at Uxbridge, England, on June 26, 1948. A cricket ball is slightly less in diameter than a baseball, but weighs a trifle more. These two factors, if they cancel each other out, would indicate that the women's cricket ball throw *should* be about the same distance as Mildred Didrickson's baseball throw of 296 feet. Ignoring the lesser wind resistance encountered by a cricket ball, and considering only its greater weight, the record throw for women still figures as being at least 287 feet. Can any present-day woman player equal this estimated possibility?

DISCUS THROW (see Track and Field).

FEATS OF STRENGTH (see Weightlifting).

GOLF (hitting a ball for distance). Here, as in throwing a baseball, the women's record is held by Mildred "Babe" Didrickson. In 1933, at the age of 19 (long before she took up golf professionally), the "Babe" drove a golf ball 327 yards. Next to this phenomenal record would appear to be a drive of 272 yards made by Mickey Wright of San Diego, in September 1966. The British amateur, Cecil Leitch, in 1920 made a drive of 250 yards.

GYMNASTICS. Under this heading will be considered the available records in various gymnastic exercises (such as chinning and dipping), as well as the more difficult feats performed by professional women gymnasts, aerialists, and equilibrists.

In chinning, the "average" man, weighing 155 pounds, can chin the bar 9 times in succession, which is equivalent to chinning once if weighing about 190 pounds. The "average" young woman, who weighs 124 pounds, is only a trifle over half as strong in her arm and upper body muscles as the average man. This means that in order to chin even once she would have to reduce her weight to not over 100 pounds while retaining the arm and chest strength she has at a weight of 124 pounds. This example should indicate the basic difference in the relative strength of the upper body in women as compared with men. Women do much better athletically in feats involving the strength of the hips and thighs, as in running and jumping.

A record of 27 consecutive *one*-arm chins with the right hand and 17 with the left hand is commonly given as the women's chinning record, performed by the famous circus gymnast Lillian Leitzel (57 in., 95 lbs.) in 1918 (see Plate 77). In Chapter 5, I gave in detail my reasons for disbelieving these alleged performances, and for concluding that *six* correct one-arm chins probably represents the highest number yet performed by a woman gymnast. Six chins with either arm is equivalent to about 54 consecutive chins using both arms together.

In a like manner it can be estimated that the probable maximum number of consecutive handstand press-ups (on the floor) attainable by a woman gymnast is somewhere around 15 (the men's record is 40). I have read where a former Olympic women's diving champion is said to have performed 35 handstand press-ups, but the writer was probably confusing them with push-ups on the *floor*. The highest girl's record I have read of in regular floor-dipping is 40 consecutive dips by Judy Osborn (97 lbs.), aged 19, in 1964 (Nebraska). These 40 dips, in Miss Osborn's case, were equivalent to a single Bench Press with about 120 pounds. Lois Bosher (aged 25) of Sarasota, Florida, at a bodyweight of 128 pounds, did a Bench Press of 180 pounds. This, it would appear, was equivalent to about 50 consecutive floor-dips, or to about 17 consecutive dips on the parallel bars. All these dipping performances by young women are far surpassed by the records made by male gymnasts (see Chapter 5).

To return to Lillian Leitzel, it may be added that her real name was

Lillian Alize Pelikan. She was born in Breslau, Poland, on January 2, 1892. She performed, during the 1920s, with the Ringling Brothers and Barnum and Bailey Circus, where her gymnastic performance was featured in the center ring. Her most spectacular act was her "giant revolutions," or one-arm swings, which she worked up gradually to a record of 249 in succession. More correctly, this feat could be described as a "back-dislocation" on the rings, only performed with one arm instead of the usual two. But perhaps Leitzel's most difficult feat was that of climbing ("rolling") up a rope to the rings at the top of the tent. Miss Leitzel died as a result of a fall from a pair of rings during a performance at Copenhagen, on March 15, 1931.

Another outstanding woman professional gymnast was Luicita Leers (about 64 in., 125 lbs.?), who appeared with the Ringling Brothers and Barnum and Bailey Circus during the years 1929–1933. It is said that Miss Leers could perform all the feats done by Lillian Leitzel, but that the circus officials would not permit her to do so publicly while Miss Leitzel was being billed as their top star. Certain it is that Miss Leers could go through, with considerable ease, all the usual ring routines performed by male gymnasts: front and back planches, breast-ups, etc. Whether she could do any really difficult feats, such as a cross on the rings, I do not know. Miss Leers was born in Weisbaden, Germany, about 1907. To gain an idea of the superb development of her arms and upper body, see Plate 78.

Back in the 1920s, the Mexican aerialist Alfredo Codona received much publicity as being the only circus performer ever to do a *triple* somersault from a flying trapeze into the hands of a catcher. Yet only a decade later, the same feat was being regularly performed by a 16-year-old *girl*, who was a member of the aerial troupe known as The Netzels. Surely this girl should receive credit equal to that previously bestowed on Codona, yet nowhere have I seen her name mentioned.

As this is being written, there is an aerial troupe from Covina, California, called The Cavarettas, which is performing at the Circus Circus casino-entertainment center in Las Vegas, Nevada. This troupe consists of one young man, Jimmy (aged 19), and his four sisters: Terry (15), Marleen and Maureen (17, twins), and Kandy (22). Terry performs two difficult feats: a *triple* forward somersault into the hands of her brother, Jimmy; and a "double cutaway half," or double forward somersault with a half twist. The aerial rigging used by The Cavarettas at the Circus Circus is 55 feet up, and even though they use a safety net it does not prevent them from suffering bruises and friction burns whenever they land imperfectly in the net.

A number of outstanding handbalancing acts involving women performers have appeared in European and American circuses during recent years. Some of them have been shown on television. One of these acts was a brother-sister team known as The Carmenas (see Plate 39). In this team the under-stander was Adolf Kleber, a former Olympic weightlifting champion, while the top-mounter was his sister. Although rather heavily built, the girl could perform all the usual feats included in the routines of a skilled male topmounter. Some of these were: single hand-to-hand, hand-to-head, foot-to-head, as well as all the two-hand balances. The featured number in the Carmenas' act was a head-to-head balance in which the under-stander, using his hands, caused the top-mounter to *revolve* on his head while she held her headstand!

Another team—two German sisters—was known as *The Mascotts*. For women, performing in an essentially masculine field, they put on a truly remarkable act. Three of their many feats are shown in Plate 79. Perhaps one of the most difficult of their feats was a head-to-head balance without the use of a head ring (that is, they balanced directly head-to-head), in which the under-stander climbed a flight of steps, crossed over, and came down again while retaining the top-mounter in a balance.* As the top photograph in Plate 79 shows, not only were these two sisters expert equilibrists, but *contortionists* as well.

With reference to the "one-finger balance" performed by Franz Furtner ("Unus") and other male equilibrists, there was also at least one woman who was able to accomplish this "gimmicky" feat. This was "Princess" Elena Omar of Spain, who exhibited in 1963 and is possibly still appearing before the public.

Some years ago, a woman acrobatic dancer named Mariam La Velle could perform the difficult feat of a walking somersault while wearing ballet slippers and *remaining on tiptoe!*

One of the most impressive feats I ever saw a girl gymnast perform was a *slow* (very slow) chin and breast-up on a pair of rings. The girl (name not known) was in a vaudeville ring act in the 1920s. Her arms were models of beautiful (not over-defined) muscularity.

Here are a few additional women's performances that may be recorded under the general heading of gymnastics:

Faye Wilson (aged 19) of Aurora, Illinois, performed 1000 successive sit-ups in 46 minutes (feet *not* held down, arms swung forward on each situp). August 1930.

Kim Oetjen (aged 13), of Miami, Florida, surpassed Miss Wilson's record by doing 1448 successive situps in 1 hour 30 minutes. The style employed was not stated. June 1967.

---

*However, I have been informed by an expert in this field that *some* sort of grommet (if only the twisted hair of one of the performers) would be necessary in order to ascend and descend a flight of steps—to say nothing of turning around at the top, which is a particularly tricky maneuver.

Marion Wood (115 lbs.), a professional acrobatic dancer, could support three average-sized men together on her body while arched in a back-bend ("crab") position. Los Angeles, Calif., 1930.

Tania Warchuk, an amateur gymnast and acrobat, could do a back-bend while standing on a chair, touch the *floor* with her hands, then return to the erect position. Toronto, Canada, 1941.

HURDLING (see Track and Field).

ICE SKATING. In this sport, so many different variations are recognized that only the speed records can be mentioned here. In skating over sprint distances, women take longer to get under way than men, and attain their best relative speed only after a distance of 500 meters or so has been covered. Over 500 meters the world record for women is 44.9 seconds, made by Lydia Skoblikova of Russia in 1962. This was at the rate of 24.91 mph. Over the same (500-meter) distance, the men's record is 39.5 seconds, made by Evgeni Grishin of Russia in 1963. This equals 28.31 mph. Thus the women's skating speed is only 88 percent of the men's. Averaging the three best performers of each sex in the 1968 Olympic Winter Games, the ratio is 89.25 percent. However, in skating, women are able to *maintain* nearly their maximum speed up to at least 3000 meters or 2 miles, whereas in running their speed and endurance diminish at a more rapid rate. Thus, as would be expected, efficiency (economy of effort) is appreciably greater on skates (either ice or roller) than on one's unaided feet, as in running.

JAVELIN THROW (see Track and Field).

JUMPING. Here we have one of the best and most natural tests of combined strength, speed and agility. Indeed, jumping is a basic athletic feat worthy of thorough analysis and study. Many different styles of jumping have been developed, ranging from simple standing jumps to running high and long jumps that require long-practiced technique.

The style of jumping that requires the least practice or specialized skill is probably the standing broad (or long) jump. In this simple event the average Freshman college man (69 in., 155 lbs.) can do 7 ft. 10½ in. For comparison, the average college woman (64 in., 124 lbs.) can do 6 ft. 6¾ in. By multiplying the bodyweight in pounds by the distance jumped in inches, a simple gauge of jumping strength may be derived. From this, it follows that the relative jumping power of the college girl is 124×78.75 divided by 155×94.5, or 66 percent of that of the man. This 66 percent, in turn, is made up of perhaps 60 percent lower back strength and 72 percent strength of the extensor muscles of the hips and thighs. Briefly, then, it may be said that the average young woman, in jumping, is about two-thirds (⅔) as strong as the average young man. In actual distance, the girl's jump is 78.75/94.5, or .8333 (5/6) of the man's.

Going now from college Freshmen's records to amateur world records, we find that the amateur record in the standing broad jump for men is evidently 11 ft. 7 in. If the standing jump were used in official competition, the record could be stated with greater certainty. In any case, the 11 ft. 7 in. was performed by a Greek athlete, C. Taliclitiras, at the Olympic Games in Stockholm in 1912. If the women's amateur record should bear the aforementioned ratio of 5 to 6 to the mark set by Taliclitiras, the women's record should be about 9 ft. 7¾ in. Actually, the best women's mark on record would appear to be that made by Oddrun Lange-Hokland, of Norway, who on March 6, 1966, at Stavanger did 9 ft. 5½ in. Here, then, is an opportunity for some girl athlete to set a new world's record in the standing broad jump: simply do 9 ft. 5¾ in. or over! However, since the men's *professional* record in the standing broad jump would appear to be about 12.6 feet, a women's record of no less than 10 ft. 6 in. would seem possible.

In the standing vertical (or Sargent) jump, the average college Freshman does about 18 inches, and the average college girl 15 inches. Hence, as in the standing broad jump, the girl has a jumping strength two-thirds of that of the man, and is able to attain a distance (here vertically rather than horizontally) equal to five-sixths of that attained by the man. In these two examples the height of the vertical jump is about 19 percent of the length of the standing broad jump. However, as the distance in the broad jump increases, that in the vertical jump increases proportionately *faster*, so that to match a broad jump of 11 feet the expected height in the vertical jump would be about 32½ inches, or nearly 25 percent of the distance in the broad jump. While no world records in the vertical jump appear available, it would appear that the men's record *should* be somewhere between 35 and 40 inches, and the women's record somewhere between 28 inches and 31 inches. It would be most interesting and instructive if records were to be attempted in both the standing broad jump and the standing vertical jump by men and women track stars who excelled in the usual running jumps. Perhaps some acrobats, especially tumblers or trampoline performers, would do even better in the standing jumps.

In the running high jump, the current men's record is held by Valeri Brumel of Russia, who in 1962 did 7 ft. 5¾ in. The women's record is 6 ft. 3¾ in., by Iolanda Balas of Rumania (1961). A comparison of these two jumps yields a ratio of 75.25/89.75, or .8385. To have shown the 5:6 (.8333) ratio present in the standing broad jump, Miss Balas's high jump would have been 6 ft. 2.8 in. Thus her actual leap indicates that she possessed a degree of efficiency on a par with that of Brumel, even though she used an ordinary lay-back scissors style in contrast to Brumel's modified straddle. However, for sheer feminine high-jumping power, the palm evidently must go to Mrs. Michele Mary Brown (then Mason) of Sydney, Australia, who in 1964 made a leap of 6 ft. 0¼ in. This was 5 inches more than her own height of 5 ft. 7¼ in. Iolanda Balas's jump of 6 ft. 3¼ in. was only 2¼ inches more than her own height of 6 ft. 1 in. Valeri Brumel's jump of 7 ft. 5¾ in. was 16⅞ inches (!) more than his own height of 6 ft. 0⅞ in.

In the *standing* high jump (scissors style) for men, the best amateur record would appear to be 5 ft. 5¾ in., and the best professional record (potentially) about an even 6 feet. Assuming the women's records to be five-sixths (.8333) of these heights yields an amateur standing high jump of 4 ft. 6¾ in. and a professional possibility of 5 feet. Yet the highest listed jump is one of only 4 ft. 4 in., by Gerta Gottlieb of Austria (1934). Here is another event in which some present-day girl jumper ought to be able to set a new world record!

Now we may consider the running long jump. Ignoring very recent records—and using those that have, for both sexes, stood several years and are therefore reasonably comparable—there is the men's record of 29 ft. 2½ in. by Bob Beamon of the USA (1968) and the women's record of 22 ft. 10 in. by Tatyana Shchelkanova of Russia (1966). Interestingly, in this form of jumping, the same as in most other forms, the women's potential record is, on the average, 5/6 (.8333) of the men's. Thus, in view of the men's record being Bob Beamon's phenomenal 29 ft. 2½ in., the women's record *should* be 24 ft. 3 in.

The expectation in distance in the running long jump is closely correlated with jumping strength (*standing* jumps) and sprinting *speed*. In fact, a prediction formula may be used based on the time taken to sprint 100 yards, multiplied by the *square root* of the distance covered in the *standing* broad jump. For men, assuming a time of 9 seconds flat for 100 yards and a standing broad jump of 12.6 feet, the expected distance in the running long jump is 27 ft. 10 in.* Conversely, the present women's record of 22 ft. 10 in. is equivalent to a time in the 100-yard dash of 10 seconds flat and a standing broad jump of 10 ft. 5½ in.

Two more women's records in jumping may be mentioned. One of these is a triple standing jump and the other a triple running jump (hop, step, and jump). In the three standing jumps the record is

---

*Thus, Bob Beamon's long jump of 29 ft. 2½ in., made at the 1968 Olympic Games in Mexico City, is equivalent to a standing broad jump of about 13.2 feet and a 100-yard dash in about 8.6 seconds.

credited to Iolanda Balas of Rumania, who in 1963 covered 25 ft. 11 in. In the triple running jump the record is given as 40 ft. 1 in., by Mary Rand (Gt. Brit.) in 1959. Both these women's jumps are far below what they should be (on the basis of their equalling 5/6 of the men's records). The three standing jumps should be increased to at least 29 ft. 9 in., and the triple running jump to no less than 47 feet! Evidently neither Miss Balas (present holder of the women's world record in the running high jump) nor Mary Rand (former holder of the women's world record in the running long jump) was experienced enough in triple jumping to apply the *technique* used by long-practiced male triple jumpers. Here again is a chance for two new women's world records in jumping.

A jumping exercise that was practiced by women gymnasts and acrobats in ancient Greece was known as the *bibasis*. It consisted of leaping upward and kicking the back of the head, the body meanwhile arching backwards to make this possible. Pollux, a Roman poet, told in verse how, at one of the Spartan athletic festivals, a girl dancer made a record by doing the *bibasis* 1000 times in succession! So remarkable was this performance considered that a record of it was engraved, many years later, on the girl's tombstone. Certainly the feat denoted phenomenal endurance. In Plate 80 is shown a modern girl tumbler performing the *bibasis*.

While the following was not a jump, it required an even greater degree of flexibility in the back and hips than the *bibasis*. Some years ago, Mitzi Mayfair, an acrobatic dancer, could kick one foot backwards so far (or high) that the heel of her foot would come clear over her shoulder and touch her chest!

POLE VAULT (see Track and Field).

ROLLER SKATING. In this sport, just as in ice skating, many different categories of competition are recognized. In both fields there are Figure Champions, Dance Champions, Pair Champions, and Speed Champions. Most of these categories are further divided into World, North American, European, British, et al. Although there are more skating rinks (over 6000 at the latest count) in the United States than in any other country, and probably a proportionately greater number of competitors, the competitions do not include records of speed skating such as are tabulated for European skaters. Accordingly, the world records as listed (up to 1963, at least) are held by overseas competitors, indeed, exclusively those from Italy and Great Britain. The speed attainable in ice skating and in roller skating is nearly the same (see Tables 12 and 13).

Up to distances of 20,000 meters (approximately 12 miles), the women's records in roller skating, as in ice skating, lag behind the men's, though in roller skating at a *diminishing* rate. From, and including, 25,000 meters (about 15 miles) up to at least 20 miles (about 32 kilometers), a surprising change takes place, and the women's records become better than the men's! So far as I know, this occurrence is unique among athletic performances. Here are the respective records in speed roller skating over various distances, the men's records being listed in the top rows.

TABLE 20. WOMEN'S VS. MEN'S RECORDS IN
SPEED ROLLER SKATING

Distance	Performer	Nation	Time	Year
¼ mile	G. Cantarella	Italy	0:34.9	1963
"	A. Vianello	Italy	0:40.6	1955
½ mile	G. Cantarella	Italy	1:13.5	1963
"	A. Vianello	Italy	1:23.4	1955
1 mile	L. Faggioli	Italy	2:22.5	1957
"	B. Woodley	Gt. Brit.	2:46.2	1960
3 miles	L. Faggioli	Italy	7:28.4	1957
"	C. Barnett	Gt. Brit.	8:43.4	1962
5 miles	L. Faggioli	Italy	14:15.1	1957
"	C. Barnett	Gt. Brit.	14:27.7	1962
10 miles	L. Woodley	Gt. Brit.	28:52.6	1960
"	C. Barnett	Gt. Brit.	28:43.8	1962
15 miles	V. Pelizzari	Italy	43:09.7	1956
"	C. Barnett	Gt. Brit.	42:54.9	1962
20 miles	V. Pelizzari	Italy	57:49.3	1956
"	C. Barnett	Gt. Brit.	57:35.5	1962

Remarkable also is the fact that from 3 miles to 15 miles Miss Barnett actually *increased* her average speed! At 3 miles it was 20.63 mph, at 5 miles 20.75, at 10 miles 20.88, and at 15 miles 20.97! From there it diminished to 20.84 mph at 20 miles. Imagine *increasing* one's speed after having already skated for over a half-hour!

ROWING. The only records I find listed for women in rowing are two that were performed by Mrs. Lottie Schoemmell. One course was in salt water, from Long Beach, California, to Santa Catalina Island, a distance of 30 miles. This Mrs. Schoemmell rowed in 11 hours 29 minutes, on June 12, 1927. Her second record-making performance was to row in fresh water from Fort Ticonderoga to Lake George, New York —a distance of 32 miles—in 7 hours 48 minutes, on August 19, 1927.

However, *canoeing*, not rowing, is a regular competitive event in the Olympic Games, both for women as well as men. Some of the events are performed in regular canoes, and others in the top-covered type known as a kayak. For men, there are Kayak Singles and Kayak Pairs, over a distance of 1000 meters. For women, the same Single and Paired races are over a distance of 500 meters. The current Olympic record for men (over 1000 meters) is 3 min. 53 sec., by Erik Hansen of Denmark, 1960; while that for women (over 500 meters) is 2 min. 12.9 sec., by Ludmila Khvedosiuk of Russia, 1964. There are also annual World and National canoe and kayak championships in many categories, ranging over distances from 500 meters to 10,000 meters, and from Singles to Fours. The best Singles time for men over 500 meters in a kayak would appear to be 2 min. 4.6 sec., by John Glair (USA), 1966; and for women 2 min. 15.9 sec., by Marcia Smoke (USA), 1966. On the basis of these two marks the men's record kayak speed is 8.98 mph, and the women's 8.23 mph.

RUNNING. Despite the statement made in some quarters that women are not "built" for running and jumping, they do very well indeed in these events when they properly train for them and have reasonably good qualifications otherwise. It is said that a woman's legs are short in comparison with her trunk length (sitting height), but this is true generally only because the average woman is *shorter in stature* (64 inches) than the average man (69 inches). *At a given stature,* a woman's legs, on the average, are a fraction of an inch *longer* than a man's. Add to this the fact that most women sprint champions today are Negroes (in whom the arms and legs are relatively longer than in Whites), and it is seen that the statement that women do not make good runners because of their having relatively short legs is groundless. The main reason why women runners and jumpers do not do as well as men in these events is simply because they have *smaller muscles and less strength in proportion to their weight,* and are therefore less able to propel their body with speed and force than are men.

In running beyond sprinting distances, women's endurance and efficiency diminish at an accelerating rate, and from a distance of a half-mile onward their records become markedly slower than men's. This is shown in the following table of comparisons, in which the men's records are listed in the top rows.

Of the following performances in running by women, decidedly the best (so far as comparison with men's records is concerned) is the

Table 21. Women's vs. men's records in running (prior to 1968)

Distance	Performer	Nation	Time	Year	MPH	MPH Ratio, Women to Men
50 yards	Bob Hayes	USA	0:5.2	1963	19.67	92.9
"	Wyomia Tyus	USA	0:5.6	1966	18.27	
100 meters	Armin Hary	Germany	0:10.0	1960	22.37	90.1
"	Wyomia Tyus	USA	0:11.1	1965	20.15	
200 meters	Tommie Smith	USA	0:20.0	1966	22.50	88.1
"	I. Kirszenstein	Poland	0:22.7	1965	19.82	
400 meters	Tommie Smith	USA	0:44.5	1967	20.11	86.9
"	Sin Kim Dan	North Korea	0:51.2	1964	17.48	
800 meters	Peter Snell	New Zealand	1:44.3	1962	17.16	88.4
"	Sin Kim Dan	North Korea	1:58.0	1964	15.17	
1500 meters	Jim Ryun	USA	3:33.1	1967	15.75	82.3
"	M. Chamberlain-Stephen	New Zealand	4:19.0	1962	12.96	
1 mile	Jim Ryun	USA	3:51.1	1967	15.58	82.4
"	Doris Brown	USA	4:40.4	1967	12.84	
2 miles	Michael Jazy	France	8:22.6	1965	14.33	80.2
"	Roberta Picco	Canada	10:26.8	1966	11.49	
3 miles	Ron Clarke	Australia	12:50.4	1966	14.02	70.2
"	Ann O'Brien	Ireland	18:17.0	1967	9.85	
6 miles	Ron Clarke	Australia	26:47.0	1965	13.44	72.8
"	Ann O'Brien	Ireland	36:48.0	1967	9.78	
Marathon	Abebe Bikila	Ethiopia	2:12:11.2	1964	11.91	66.2
"	Mildred Sampson	New Zealand	3:19:33.0	1964	7.89	

800-meter record by Sin Kim Dan, of North Korea, with a ratio of 88.4. To be of equal merit, Sin's 400-meter record should be lowered to 50.8 seconds. Referring again to the table above, it may be noted that the record for 3 miles, by Ann O'Brien of Ireland, is not in keeping with her record for 6 miles. The ratio at 3 miles should be about 78.4 rather than 70.2, and this would mean to reduce the time from 18:17.0 to 16:22.7.

SHOT PUT (see Track and Field).

SWIMMING. As would be expected, women do relatively better in swimming—where the body is partially supported by the water—than on dry land, where one must fight gravity. In the following brief discussion, only freestyle swimming is considered. The fact that three other styles (backstroke, breaststroke, and butterfly) are regularly used in competition, both in individual, medley, and relay events, by both sexes, makes swimming records a subject so extensive as to require a book by a specialist on the subject.

Over the past 50 or 60 years, many outstanding women swimmers have each appeared, had their period of glory, and then made way for some new star, almost always a younger person. Here are the names, dates, and records of Olympic Games women's champions in the 100 meters freestyle:

Performer	Nation	Year	Time, sec.
Fanny Durack	Australia	1912	82.2
Ethelda Bleibtrey	USA	1920	73.6
M. Wehselau	USA	1924	72.4
Ethel Lackie	USA	1924	
Albina Osipowich	USA	1928	71.0
Helene Madison	USA	1932	66.8
H. Mastenbroek	Neths.	1936	65.9
Greta Andersen	Denmark	1948	66.3
Katalin Szöke	Hungary	1952	66.8
Dawn Fraser	Australia	1956	62.0
Dawn Fraser	Australia	1960	61.2
Dawn Fraser	Australia	1964	58.9

When the foregoing records are charted against year of performance and population, it is seen that the best records are those by Helene

Madison in 1932 and Hendrika Mastenbroek in 1936. Indeed, in many a sports poll, Miss Madison has been adjudged the all-time greatest woman sprint swimmer. At one time she held practically all the world records from 100 yards to a mile. However, this could be said also of Fanny Durack of Australia, who back in 1912–1915 was also regarded as a phenomenon. And how about Dawn Fraser of Australia, who is the only woman to have won three consecutive Olympic Games contests in the 100 meters? This brings up the old question: is it more important to set a record, or to simply *win* against one's competitors?

Swimming is the one sport in which women's endurance over long distances does not suffer in a comparison with men's. In a sense, a woman's smaller chest and lesser breathing capacity is fully compensated for by her greater buoyancy in the water and her more streamlined bodily configuration. Up to a distance of 1500 meters, at least, women's swimming records average an essentially *constant* 91.49 percent of men's. That is, their records over the greater distances are fully as meritorious and efficient as those at lesser distances.

In long-distance swimming, as for example across the English Channel, some women have done quite as well as men. Gertrude Ederle of the United States received a great deal of publicity over the years for having been the first woman to swim the English Channel.

In his book, *Athletic Records—the Whys and Wherefores* (1966), the author, George P. Meade, presents a particularly interesting and informative chapter on swimming (pp. 81–94). Meade shows, among other charted statistics, that from 1912 to 1965 records in men's freestyle swimming have improved progressively *in relation to the distances of the swims*. That is, the longer the distance, the greater the lowering of the swimming time. Meade shows also that women's swimming records are improving at a decidedly faster rate than are men's. According to his diagram (Meade, Fig. 5–2, p. 91), women's records in the 1500-meter swim—if they keep improving at the same rate as from 1920 to 1960—should, sometime between the years 1980 and 2000, equal the men's!

Among women platform and springboard divers, it is generally agreed that the greatest was Mrs. Patricia "Pat" McCormick, who was the only diver of either sex to win *four* Olympic championships. In the 1952 and the 1956 Games, "Pat" won both the platform and the springboard titles. In Plate 80 is shown a photograph of the early-day professional swimmer and diver, Annette Kellermann of Australia, who was as famous for her shapely figure as for her prowess in the water. Miss Kellermann, by her performances in vaudeville, did a great deal toward popularizing swimming and diving for women. She also introduced the one-piece bathing suit (full-length tights), thereby freeing her sex from the heavy, cumbersome outfits they had been obliged to wear prior to the 1920s.

TENNIS. On this subject, I shall turn my pen over again to George Russell Weaver;

> In a sports poll conducted in 1954, the greatest women tennis players were rated in this order: 1. Helen Wills; 2. Alice Marble; 3. Maureen Connolly; 4. Suzanne Lenglen. Althea Gibson, who won both the American and the English singles titles in 1957 and 1958, would, I presume, be rated below Lenglen.
>
> Mary K. Browne had the distinction of being both a leading tennis player and a leading golfer *at the same time!* She was American amateur singles tennis champion in 1912, 1913, and 1914. She was American amateur doubles tennis champion in 1925. She was English (Wimbledon) amateur doubles champion in 1926. And in 1924 she was finalist and runner-up in the American women's amateur golf championship!
>
> Among women's doubles players, Elizabeth Ryan had the reputation of being the greatest. I think she was an American, but she apparently lived in England. She won the American doubles title in 1926. And she won the English (Wimbledon) women's doubles championship in 1914, 1919 (there was no competition from 1915 to 1918), 1920, 1921, 1922, 1923, 1925, 1926, 1927, 1930, 1933, and 1934 (a period covering twenty years!); and she won the English (Wimbledon) mixed doubles championship in 1919, 1921, 1923, 1927, 1928, 1930, and 1932. She also won the American mixed doubles title in 1926. Thus she won 21 national doubles championships; and she won these with 12 different partners.
>
> During Helen Wills's best years no woman player won even a game (much less a match) from her. This invincibility lasted for 6 years.

In addition to the discussion by George Weaver, it may be noted that the latest No. 1 ranking player, Billie Jean King of Berkeley, California, was voted in the Associated Press's poll of 1967 the top woman athlete. During that year, Mrs. King won both the Wimbledon and the United States championships, as well as several in Australia and elsewhere. She was the seventh tennis player to be chosen the top woman athlete since the AP poll was inaugurated in 1931. The other tennis-playing nominees were: Maria Bueno (Brazil) in 1959, Althea Gibson in 1957 and 1958, Maureen Connolly in 1951, 1952, and 1953, Alice Marble in 1939 and 1940, Helen Wills Moody in 1935, and Helen Jacobs in 1933. Mrs. King was one of the first tennis champions to use the new steel racket designed by the former French men's champion,

René Lacoste. It is evident that the introduction of this metal racket may have an effect on the sport of tennis comparable to what the "lively ball" in 1920 had on baseball. If *all* the players use the new racket, which is said to possess various advantages over wooden, gut-strung rackets, competition may continue to take place on an essentially equal basis. But if some players prefer not to switch, they may find themselves falling behind the times in their game.

TRACK AND FIELD. In this category, the events of running and jumping are dealt with elsewhere under those respective headings. The usual women's field events are the Shot Put, the Discus Throw, and the Javelin Throw. Before considering these events, a word may be said about the Pole Vault.

Performances by women in the pole vault have been so few and far between that the subject may be reviewed in short order. The best mark of the several on record is the 8 ft. 6 in. vault by Diane Bragg (USA) in 1952. As Miss Bragg was the sister of Don Bragg, who later on made a world record of 15 ft. 9¼ in., it is probable that she had the benefit of her brother's coaching. Even so, her 8 ft. 6 in. vault was only about 54 percent of the men's record. Can any girl vaulter today equal or surpass the latter ratio, by doing a vault of at least 9 feet or over? At least today she would have the advantage of a fiberglas pole!

In the women's 4-kilo shot put, the record increased from a paltry 24 ft. 9¼ in. in 1919 to a substantial 65 ft. 11¼ in. in 1969. This increase is *90 percent greater* than that which took place in the men's shot-put record during the same 50-year period. Part of the women's increase is probably attributable to increase in the *size* of the performer. The record of 65 ft. 11¼ in. was made by Margitta Helmboldt-Gummel, (E. Ger.) on September 11, 1969, in East Berlin. Margitta is a veritable Amazon of 69.3 inches and 178 pounds. Her first world record, a put of 64 ft. 4 in., was made in the 1968 Olympic Games at Mexico City.

Margitta's record of nearly 66 feet with a shot weighing 4 kilos ($=$ 8.8185 lbs.) is equivalent to a put with a 16-pound shot of about 48 ft. 10 in. In comparison with the men's record by Randel Matson (78.5 in., 258 lbs.) of 71 ft. 5½ in., Margitta's record has a phenomenal rating of 101.3 percent (or 1013 points), while Matson's rating is a high 99.0 (or 990 points). (See Tables 28 and 29 in the Appendix.)

Percentagewise, the second-highest rating in the women's shot put is held, not by the previous record holder, Tamara Press, but by the record holder before *her*, the well-publicized Galina Zybina (66 in., 183 lbs.), who did 57 ft. 5 in. in 1964. Miss Press's percentage rating, on account of her large size (70.75 in., 217 lbs.), is only 90.8, while Miss

Zybina's is a significantly higher 94.1. Indeed, Tamara Press's rating is surpassed by that of her sister, Irina, who in 1965, at a height of 66 inches and a body-weight of only 150 pounds, made a put of 52 ft. 8¾ in. This gives her a rating of 93.6 percent. Miss Zybina held the women's world record from 1952, when she made a put of 49 ft. 10 in., to 1956, inclusive, by which time she had increased it to 54 ft. 11¾ in.

In third place, ranking between Galina Zybina and Irina Press, is Nadezda Chizhova (68.1 in., 196 lbs.), who did 61 ft. 3 in. in 1968. This gives her a rating of 93.8 percent.

The highest rating attained thus far in the shot put by an American woman would appear to be that of Cynthia Wyatt (66 in., 155 lbs.), who while attending college in Honolulu made a put of 48 ft. 6 in. in 1962. This put has a percentage rating of 86.5 (865 points). It is evident that if the world record in the women's shot put is to be seriously threatened by a performer from the United States, the performer will have to have the bodily size, strength, speed and technique of one of her European competitors. An absolute minimum size requirement would appear to be a height of 68–70 inches and a bodyweight of about 190 pounds. Is there no such woman athlete in the entire United States today?

In the women's discus throw, as in the shot put, a tremendous increase in distance has taken place over the years. The event was not included in the modern Olympic Games until 1928. At that time the winner was Helen Konopacka of Poland, who made a throw of 129 ft. 11¾ in. The current record is held by Liesel Westermann (67.7 in., 176 lbs.) of West Germany, with a toss of 205 ft. 8½ in., made in mid-1968. Thus the increase in the women's discus throw from 1928 to 1968 has been over 58 percent! During the same period, the men's record increased about 35 percent. Hence, as was stated previously, the women's record in the discus throw has increased, from 1928 to 1965, over 50 percent faster than the men's. But as was also pointed out, such a superiority of increase is not likely to be maintained.

Today there are at least a dozen women discus throwers who have records of 187 feet or over. The best throw, both absolutely and in relation to the size of the performer, is that of Fraulein Westermann, mentioned above. Her throw has the extraordinary rating of 98.3 percent. The next most meritorious throw appears to be that of Nina Dumbadze (USSR), who at a height of 70.5 inches and a bodyweight of 189 pounds attained a distance of 187 ft. 1¾ in. in 1952. This throw has a rating of 94.0 percent. The third-best throw, percentagewise, is that of Christine Spielberg (73.6 in., 183 lbs.), of East Germany, whose throw of 202 ft. 3 in., made in 1968, has a rating of 92.6 percent. Fourth is Yevgenia Kuznyetsova (69 in., 178 lbs.), of Russia, whose throw of 187 ft. 7½ in., made in 1964, has a rating of 92.3 percent. Fifth is Anita Henschel-Otto, (69¼ in., 187 lbs.), of Hungary, who in 1965 made a throw of 189 ft. 10 in. (= 92.2 percent).

Closely following is a rating of 91.8 percent attained by Jolán Konsek-Kleiber, (70 in., 179 lbs.), of East Germany, with a throw of 193 ft. 7⅝ in. made in 1966. The dozen or more women discus throwers who have records of 187 feet or more today are all from Europe: Russia, Germany, and Hungary. Surely, in the whole United States, there must be women athletes who have the necessary physical qualifications to equal such discus throws, even with a moderate amount of specialized training. Will they kindly step forth?

As in the shot put for women, in the discus throw a lighter implement is used than for men. The discus for women weighs only one kilo (2.2046 lbs.), or half the weight of that used by men. Hence, as the distance thrown varies *inversely as the square root of the weight of the discus*, it follows that if the weight is doubled, the distance decreases in the ratio of $\frac{1}{\sqrt{2}}$, or to .7071 of the distance attained with a discus one-half as heavy. Thus the women's record of 205 ft. 8½ in. with a 1-kilo discus is equivalent (theoretically, at least) to 145 ft. 5½ in. with a 2-kilo (men's standard) discus. Further, if the men's record of 224 ft. 5 in. with a 2-kilo discus were performed not by Jay Silvester (74.5 in., 230 lbs.), but by a man of the same height and weight (67.7 in., 176 lbs.) as Liesel Westermann, the holder of the women's record, the distance would decrease to 196 ft. 9 in. Miss Westermann's estimated 145 ft. 5½ in. (if a 2-kilo discus were used) compared with the 196 ft. 9 in. yields a ratio of 73.9 percent. In order to raise her rating of 98.3 percent to that of Jay Silvester's lofty 100.2 percent, Miss Westermann would have to increase her record only from 205 ft. 8½ in. to 210 ft. 5 in. These figures indicate that—in the discus throw, at any rate—the *technique* of women recordholders is almost on a par with that of men.

In the javelin throw, as in the shot put and the discus throw, the implement used by women performers is of a lighter weight than that used by men. However, the women's javelin is 75 percent as heavy as the men's, whereas the shot used by them is only about 55 percent as heavy, and the discus just *half* the weight of the men's discus. These varying ratios are reflected in the respective distances attained by women performers with the three types of throwing implements as compared with men. The men's javelin weighs 0.8 kilogram, or 1 lb., 12.218 oz., while the women's javelin weighs 0.6 kilogram, or 1 lb., 5.163 oz. This 3:4 ratio means that the women's javelin should be thrown $\sqrt{4/3}$, or 1.1547 as far as the men's. Conversely, a 0.8-kilo javelin should be thrown .866 as far as one weighing 0.6 kg. Thus the current women's record of 204 ft. 8½ in., made by Yelena Gorchakova (65.75 in., 152 lbs.), in the 1964 Olympic Games at Tokyo, would be equivalent to a throw with a 0.8-kilo (men's weight) javelin of 177 ft. 3¼ in. (See also Part 2, Section E.)

If it should be desired to have women's records in the shot put, discus throw, and javelin throw compare in distance as closely as possible with the records in these respective events made by men, the women's shot should weigh about 6 lbs. 7 oz. (2.91 kg.), discus 1 lb. 14 oz. (.839 kg.), and javelin less than *half* of what it weighs now, or about 10¼ oz. (.289 kg). Reduction to these implement weights would show much more directly how women's ability in the "weight" events compares with men's. Certainly the weight of the women's javelin should be reduced.

Next in distance to the javelin throw of 204 ft. 8½ in. by Yelena Gorchakova are these women's records: 201 ft. 4½ in. by Elvira Ozolina (68.75 in., 148 lbs.) of Russia, in 1964; 199 ft. 1 in. by Mihaila Penes (74 in., 209 lbs.) of Rumania, in 1964; 198 ft. 8 in. by Barbara Friedrich (68.1 in., 145 lbs.) of the USA in 1967; 198 ft. 0⅜ in. by Angela Nemeth (69.3 in., 143 lbs.) of Hungary, in 1968; 196 ft. 3 in. by RaNae Bair (71 in., 135 lbs.) of the United States, in 1967; and 195 ft. 8 in. by Danuta Jaworska (64.5 in., 139 lbs.) of Poland. Percentagewise, the above-mentioned women javelin throwers have these ratings: Danuta Jaworska, 97.3; Yelena Gorchakova, 96.8; Re Nae Bair, 95.1; Barbara Friedrich, 95.0; Elvira Ozolina, 94.6; Angela Nemeth, 94.3; and Mihaila Penes, 79.7.

As the event of Hurdling was not discussed under Running, a few words about it may be appropriate here. It is difficult to compare the efficiency of women hurdlers with that of men, since the distances at which they compete, and the number of hurdles that they must clear, are both different. Men compete at 120 yards (over ten 3 ft. 6 in. hurdles, 10 yards apart), 220 yards (over ten 2 ft. 6 in. hurdles, 20 yards apart), and 440 yards (over ten 3 ft. hurdles, 40 yards apart). In contrast, there is only one distance for women that is competed at regularly (e.g., as in the Olympic Games), and that is 80 meters (= c. 87.5 yds). In this event there are eight 2 ft. 6 in. hurdles, spaced 10 yards apart. The current women's world record for the 80-meter hurdles is 10.3 seconds, and is held jointly by Irina Press (Russia) and Pamela Kilborn (Australia), both of whom made their marks in late 1965. However, since 1964 there has been, particularly in Europe, a considerable amount of hurdle racing by women over the shorter distances: 50 yards, 50 meters, 60 yards, 60 meters, and 70 yards, as well as the standard distance of 80 meters. There have also been recent world records for women made at 100 meters and 200 meters. The latter may therefore be directly compared with the men's record time (22.5 sec.) over the same distance. The women's record, 27.4 seconds, was made by Patricia Van Wolvelaere (USA) on July 1, 1966. A comparison of these two marks 22.5/27.4, yields a ratio of 82.1. In sprinting over the same distance the ratio is 20.0/22.7, or 88.1. Another way to view it is that the man takes only 2.5 seconds longer to go over ten hurdles than if he were simply sprinting 200 meters, whereas the woman requires 4.7 seconds, or nearly twice as long, to clear the hurdles. This comparison does not necessarily indicate that women's *efficiency* in hurdling is less than men's, but more probably that their *endurance* is less. A better comparison, if it could be made, would be for a men's champion hurdler to establish a time for the *80-meter low hurdles.*

It remains only, under women's track and field, to discuss the Pentathlon. Table 22, following, lists the four best performers (as of 1965) in this five-event competition. The Pentathlon, like the men's Decathlon, is performed on two consecutive days. On the first day the events are the 80-meter low (2 ft. 6 in.) hurdles, the shot put (4 kg.), and the high jump, while on the second day come the long jump and the 200-meter dash. The figures in Table 22 show that in the Pentathlon the outstanding competitor to date has been Irina Press of Russia. She has held the World and Olympic records in this contest during 1959, 1960, 1961 and 1964. The latter year was the first time the women's Pentathlon was included in the Olympic Games program. Miss Press's best performance, as listed in Table 22, was made at the 1964 Olympic Games at Tokyo on October 16–17. However, although Miss Press amassed the highest total points, she did so mainly because of her overwhelming superiority in the shot put. Quite probably the fact that her elder sister, Tamara Press, was at the time the women's world champion in the shot put enabled Irina to profit by her sister's coaching. Also, Irina Press may have been more sturdily built (66 in., 150 lbs.) than the other competitors listed, certainly more so than Mary Rand (68.1 in., 134 lbs.), who had the build for the events in which she excelled, namely the long and the high jumps and the 220-meter dash.

The points for the Pentathlon competitors as rated by my method, as in Table 22, result from the same principles being applied as in rating men in the Decathlon. It seems highly illogical that the four women listed in Table 22 should—as by the IAAF scoring system—show an average rating of 5030 points in *five* events, whereas the two leading performers in the men's Decathlon (see Table 19) show, by the same IAAF system, an average rating of only 8902 points in *ten* events. As will be seen in Table 22, my method gives the two leading women Pentathlon performers an average rating of 4275 points. This is consistent with the average rating of 8503 points computed for the two highest-ranking performers in the men's Decathlon. As of July 1, 1969, the highest rating was still that of Irina Press.

Table 22. Some leading performers in the women's Pentathlon
(Author's point-ratings are corrected for *date.*)

Rank	Performer	Nation	Pentathlon Event					Rating, points		Year
			80mH	SP	HJ	LJ	200m	Author	IAAF	
1	Irina Press	USSR	10.7	56-3½	5-4¼	20-5⅝	24.7	4348	5246	1964
2	Mary Rand	Gt. Brit.	10.9	36-4¼	5-7¾	21-5⅞	24.2	4202	5035	1964
3	Galina Bystrova	USSR	10.7	47-5¾	5-3	20-0½	25.5	4159	4956	1964
4	Inge Exner	E. Ger.	10.8	37-10¾	5-3⅜	20-7¼	24.5	4087	4886	1965

WALKING. Few records in race walking by women appear to be available. At one-half mile, the best mark on record for women would appear to be 3:44.0, performed by Mai Johansson-Bengtsson of Sweden, in Stockholm, 1944. The men's record over the same distance is 2:59.0, by G. H. Goulding of Canada, in 1909. A more recent (1952) record claimed for Henry Laskau, of New York, reduces this time to 2:48.2. Laskau's time was thus 10.70 mph, Goulding's 10.06 mph, and Miss Johansson-Bengtsson's about 8.04 mph. So, over the distance of a half-mile, it would appear that a woman's speed in walking is not more than 80 percent of a man's. Assuming the man's length of stride (step) to be 46 inches and the woman's 42 inches, it follows that the man takes from 231 to 245 strides per minute and the woman 197 per minute.

A somewhat more favorable comparison for women walkers occurs over a distance of a mile. There the men's record is 6:18.3, by Ronald Zinn (USA) in 1962. The women's record for a mile is 7:27.2, by Mai Johansson-Bengtsson (Sweden), in 1944. Zinn's rate of speed was 9.52 mph, and Miss Johansson-Bengtsson's 8.05 mph. A comparison of these two rates shows that the woman walked about 84.6 percent as fast as the man. Over the one-mile distance, assuming the same lengths of stride as above, the man would take about 218 strides per minute, and the woman 202. These respective rates yield a ratio of 92.7 percent, which would appear to be about as fast as a woman speed walker can move her legs in comparison with a man.

WEIGHTLIFTING (and miscellaneous feats of strength). Weightlifting, either of the three Olympic lifts or the three Power lifts, has not as yet been standardized for women so that they may compete in these events in appropriate bodyweight classes. Table 23, following, has been prepared in order to propose a standard of bodyweight classes for women (in all lifts), along with corresponding poundages in the Two Hands Clean and Jerk of a merit comparable with men's records in the same bodyweight divisions as named. The average rating for the current men's world records is 98.18 percent.

In Table 23, the bodyweights proposed for women equal 76 percent of the corresponding class weights for men. The poundages in the Clean and Jerk are based on the premise applied throughout this study, namely that a woman's strength (force) *at a given height and bodyweight* is equal to ⅔ that of a man's. In this assumption, it is of course necessary to assume also that the *training* of both sexes in the event in question has been equal.

Table 23. Proposed standards for women (as compared with men) in the Two Hands Clean and Jerk with barbell

MEN				WOMEN		Proposed Standard (98.18) in THC & J
Bodyweight Kg.	Current Record, Lbs.	THC & J, lbs.	Classification (Bodyweight)	Proposed Bodywt. Kg.	Lbs.	
56	123¼	330½	Bantamweight	42.5	93¾	111.6
60	132¼	336	Featherweight	45.6	100½	136.1
67.5	148¾	374¾	Lightweight	51.3	113	188.7
75	165¼	413¼	Middleweight	57	125¾	218.3
82.5	181¾	419¾	Light-heavyweight	62.7	138¼	238.4
90	198¼	438¾	Middle-heavyweight	68.4	150¾	253.8
110	242½	479½	Heavyweight	83.6	184¼	283.3
over 110	over 242½		Super-Heavyweight	over 83.6	over 184¼	301.3

The reason for listing in the above table only the Clean and Jerk and not the Press and the Snatch is not only to avoid confusion but to stress the point that in a woman's competition the *one lift* (Clean and Jerk) should be sufficient. Further, an examination of the poundages recorded in major Olympic-lift competitions for men during recent years shows that among nearly 80 percent of the competitors (in all classes) the first ten contestants would have retained their respective positions had they contested in the *Clean and Jerk only* rather than on all three lifts. This circumstance, which can readily be verified, should be sufficient to suggest, at least, that the *Clean and Jerk alone* is all that is needed to determine the best performers in Olympic weightlifting. The Snatch, in a sense, is a mere duplication of the upward pull required in "cleaning" a barbell to the shoulders, the only difference being that the Snatch is a lighter weight pulled to a greater height. The Press, as it has been performed to an increasing extent during recent years, is no longer a standing press, but virtually a Bench Press performed while standing. Moreover, if any start of the barbell from the shoulders with a knee-jerk, however slight, should be used (as is often attempted), there is nothing to distinguish the so-called Press from a Jerk. Finally, if only the Clean and Jerk were used in all Olympic lifting, and the Snatch and the Press eliminated, the saving in time, loading of the barbell, and waiting around on the part of the lifter, to say nothing of the reduction of spectator boredom during it all, would be incalculable. I therefore here commend this proposal to the attention of the *Federation Internationale Halterophile* (International Federation of Weightlifting).

Another reason for concentrating on the Two Hands Clean and Jerk is that it is a perfect complement to the several standardized field events in which weights are used: the shot put, hammer throw, discus throw, and javelin throw, respectively. In each of these field events, as in the Clean and Jerk with barbell, the essential requirement is explosive force (generated by strength times speed). That is why shot-putters, hammer-throwers, and even throwers of the lightweight javelin, are able to better their throwing or putting distances by practicing the barbell Clean and Jerk with poundages that permit of comfortable repetitions and which may be increased as practice continues.

To return, after this extended digression, to women performers in the Two Hands Clean and Jerk, it may be said that not one on record, so far as I know, has even closely approached the perfectly rational poundages proposed as current (98.18 percent of maximum) records in Table 23. For this condition there are numerous reasons: lack of competition, insufficient numbers of competitors, unfired enthusiasm, and the still current disinclination of women (in this country, at least) to indulge in heavy exercise or sport. The latter reason, plus some of the former, accounts also for the relatively poor showing of United States women athletes in the shot put and discus throw. Only when larger numbers of well-trained, physically larger women in this country "go in" heart and soul for these field weight events, as well as truly competitive barbell lifting, will the records in these athletic activities rise to their potential levels. For this reason, the poundages in the Two Hands Clean and Jerk listed for women in Table 23 must be, for the present, regarded only as *possibilities* (but not necessarily maximums).

The only two women so far to attain even commendable records in the Clean and Jerk are Ivy Russell (65 in., 134 lbs.) of England, and Cynthia Wyatt (66 in., 155 lbs.) of the United States. In 1930, Miss Russell did a Clean and Jerk of 193 pounds. This lift has a rating of 89.7 percent, and would be equal to a lift today of about 213 pounds. About 1925, when weighing only 125 pounds, Miss Russell had done 176 pounds, which has a rating of 87.0 percent. Mrs. Wyatt, in 1962, did a Jerk of 230 pounds. This, if it were actually cleaned (and not simply jerked from the shoulders) would give Mrs. Wyatt a rating of 89.5 percent (or 895 points on the 1000 scale). This is slightly above the rating of 86.5 percent that Mrs. Wyatt attained in the 4-kilo shot put, in which she reached 48 ft. 6 in.

In connection with old-time strong-women, one occasionally reads where the Austrian professional, Katie Sandwina (71.1 in., 209.5 lbs.), jerked 130 kilos (286.6 lbs.) overhead. In some places it is even asserted that she *cleaned* this weight. In the *Guinness Book of World Records* (1967, p. 382) there is the weird statement that Sandwina did 282 pounds in a "Continental clean and jerk," *c.* 1926. First, there is no such lift as a "Continental clean." The term is self-contradictory. In earlier days, particularly among German and Austrian weightlifters (many of whom had difficulty in taking a barbell "clean" to their shoulders, on account of their big bellies), it was customary to lift the barbell first onto the buckle of a heavy belt, and from there toss it to the shoulders, the shouldering thus being performed in *two* serial movements. This preliminary lift to the shoulders, when followed by a Press or a Jerk, was termed, as the case might be, either a "Continental Press" or a "Continental Jerk." Katie Sandwina *always* shouldered her barbells in the latter two-movement style. In this manner, about 1910 or 1911 (not 1926, when she was 42 years of age), in Germany, probably Munich, which was her family's home, she shouldered and jerked 120 kilos (264.55 lbs.). With one arm, taking the weight to the shoulder with both hands, she jerked 80 kilos (176.36 lbs.). These were good lifts for a woman, even of Sandwina's size, back about 1910. The Two Hands Continental Jerk, which was considerably the better of the two lifts, would be equivalent to a *Clean* and Jerk today of about 295 pounds, and would gain the high rating of 95.7 percent.

Sandwina, whose family name was Brumbach, had parents who were both professional strength-athletes. She had also four brothers and no fewer than eleven sisters. One of her sisters, Babette Brumbach, claimed to be able to jerk more weight than Katie, namely about 285 pounds. But as Babette was of a shorter and heavier build than Katie, her percentage rating in the Jerk would probably be no higher. Katie Sandwina, and some of the feats she performed during her engagement (she was one of the star performers) with Barnum and Bailey's Circus in 1910–11, are shown in Plate 81. Beyond question, Sandwina was a remarkable "strong-woman" at the feats she chose to practice. But whether she was potentially any stronger than Tamara Press, the former Russian women's champion in the shot put and the discus throw, or than the new world's record holder in the shot, Margitta Helmboldt-Gummel of East Germany, is a question.

To repeat, present-day performances by women in barbell lifting of all kinds are far below what they should and could be. One way of providing an incentive in this sport would be to make the Two Hands Clean and Jerk a regular Olympic Games event for women. A listing of appropriate bodyweight classes in this connection is given in Table 23.

Here are some other recorded performances by women, both in barbell lifting and miscellaneous "feats of strength." There is no connection between the sequence of the listing and the merit of the performance. Most of the performances are considerably below what they might have been, even though they are, to date, the best on record.

1. Ivy Russell (65 in., 134 lbs.), of England, was trained in weight-lifting by the former 9-stone men's champion, W. A. Pullum, of London. Miss Russell's best feat was the Two Hands Dead Lift, in which she made a record of 410¼ pounds. She could also do a Bent Press with 120 pounds, a One Hand Dumbbell Swing of 92 pounds (which, in proportion to her Dead Lift, should have been about 50 *percent* higher!), a Two Hands Clean and Jerk of 193 pounds, and a Squat with 180 pounds 14 times in succession ($= c.$ 225 pounds once). c. 1930.

2. Grena Trumbo (65 in., 130 lbs.) did a full Squat with 266 pounds. Sunland, Calif. 1958.

3. Joan Rhodes (67 in., 140 lbs.), a professional strength entertainer, did a Two Hands Dead Lift with 350 pounds. London, England. 1963.

4. Petra Rivers (68 in., 138 lbs.) of Melbourne, Australia, at the age of only 14 years is said to have done a full Squat with 300 pounds! Miss Rivers is also a prospective champion in the javelin throw, having at the latest report reached over 180 feet.

5. Jean Ansorge (65 in., 128 lbs.) of Grand Rapids, Michigan, is a sister of Harold Ansorge, a former professional strong-man. Miss Ansorge's

most remarkable feat of strength was to tear a deck of playing cards into *eighths!* She could also do a One Hand Clean and Jerk with 100 pounds, a Two Hands Clean and Jerk with 155 pounds, and a Squat with 210 pounds 10 times in succession ($=$ *c.* 240 pounds once).

6. "Vulcana" (b. Kate Roberts, 1883) was an English professional strong-woman (see Plate 82). Her best feat in lifting was the Bent Press, in which she put up 145 pounds while weighing only 125 pounds herself (at a height of 64 inches). London, *c.* 1910.

7. "Miss Ella" (66.5 in., 151 lbs.) of the Schiavoni Troupe was an Italian gymnast and strong-woman. Among other feats in her performance she would carry four men around the stage on her shoulders, hold two men (totalling 260 lbs.) above her head, and do a Bent Press with 120 pounds, *c.* 1915.

8. Louise Armaindo (62 in., 122 lbs.), a Canadian professional athlete (walker, runner, and cyclist), is said to have "pressed" (bent pressed ?) a 105-pound dumbbell 5 times in succession with her right arm and 3 times with her left. Montreal, 1903.

9. Mme. Cloutier (height and weight ?), a Canadian professional strong-woman, in a contest with Flossie La Blanche, is said to have performed a Back Lift with 2500 pounds. Montreal, 1909.

10. Louise Stiernon, an old-time French professional gymnast, could, among other feats on the rings, do a back planche using one arm (flexed) only.

11. "Minerva" (Mrs. Josephine Blatt, nee Schauer) of Hoboken, New Jersey, was a huge (72 in., 230 lbs.) professional strong-woman who exhibited in the 'nineties. One of her claimed barbell lifts was a Two Hands Press of 185 pounds. This lift today would be equal to no less than 246 pounds, and would have a rating of 86.3 percent. "Minerva", in her prime, was recognized by *The Police Gazette* as being the strongest woman in the world, which she may well have been. One of the records claimed for her was a Harness Lift with 23 men, weighing with the platform and chains 3564 pounds. Evidently this lift was performed by lifting (inwardly) on the supporting chains rather than directly (straight up) on the platform. Probably, in view of Minerva's massive leg development (see Plate 83), she may have been capable of a legitimate Harness Lift of 2800 or even 2900 pounds.

12. Nancy de Paul of Sydney, Australia, was the under-stander in an acrobatic troupe known as The de Pauls (see Plate 84). Her perform-ance consisted mostly of supporting feats in which she would bear the weight of anywhere from three to five of the other girls of the same family, the five weighing together 590 pounds. In this manner Nancy de Paul is said to have supported (but not walked with) up to 800 pounds (1958).

13. "Roeder" was the name of a German professional athlete who toured the United States in 1913. Her forte, like that of Nancy de Paul's, was as a bearer or under-stander. Miss Roeder was 66 inches in height and weighed 146 pounds. As a finish to her act she would carry *six* persons off the stage on her shoulders. It is said that she could thus shuffle along for 50 feet while carrying as much as 900 pounds. The latter amount certainly is questionable, since it is almost as much weight as a *man* of the same height and bodyweight could handle.

14. Tania Warchuk (64 in., 134 lbs.) of Toronto although an amateur athlete, was a skilled acrobat, dancer, handbalancer, contortionist, judo artiste, bag puncher, and strong-woman! One of her outstanding exhibi-tion feats was to support in the so-called "Tomb of Hercules" position (for a description of which see Chapter 5, Section A) a load of 1100 pounds (*c*. 1941).

15. Perhaps equal to the supporting and carrying powers of professional strong-women is that of the women stevedores of Yamagata, Japan. One of these women can on the average carry on her back three 140-pound bales (420 pounds), and the strongest women five bales (700 pounds). During a day's work, some of these Japanese women make as many as a *hundred* trips carrying each time a full load.

16. In Portland, Maine, in 1841, there was a 19-year-old girl (name not given) who could "take up a barrel of pork" (weighing well over 400 pounds) "and carry it some distance." Some girl!

17. Among the Cherokee Indians, Lieutenant Henry Timberlake in his memoirs (London, 1765) tells of knowing an old woman, whose youngest son was about 50, who used to carry on her back daily for a couple of miles a load of wood weighing "two hundredweights."

18. A Tibetan girl of 18 "travelled one day 15 or 18 miles with a burden of 70 or 75 pounds weight. We could hardly do it without any weight

at all." Per C. R. Markham, *Narrative of the Mission of George Bogle to Tibet* (1876, p. 17).

19. The traveler, W. Bosman, speaking of the women of the coast of Guinea, says that "with a burthen of one hundred pounds on their head they run a sort of continuous trot, which is so swift that we Hollanders cannot keep up with them without difficulty, though not loaded with an ounce of weight." (London, 1814).

WRESTLING. Seemingly the sport of wrestling, among women, has never attained a high level of popularity in the United States. A magazine, devoted exclusively to the subject, and attractively gotten out, lasted just three issues. In England and on the Continent (see Plate 85) the situation would appear to be somewhat better, although not much. Meanwhile, in various oriental countries, and among certain native tribes in Africa, wrestling among women continues on as an age-old institution. In India, particularly, wrestling has for centuries been the chief sport, and is practiced by women as well as men. The greatest performers come mostly from the province of Punjab, where there are long-established *families* of wrestlers, and the sons of famous champions are married to the daughters of other famous champions. In this manner the fame and prowess of both sides is carried on, generation after generation. The style of wrestling common among the East Indians appears to have been patterned after that known among the ancient Greeks as ground wrestling, and which was used in the concluding stages of the "anything goes" combat known as the *pancratium*. Most Indian wrestling, like that of the Greeks, takes place outdoors (or in any case under an open sky, as in a courtyard) on soft ground, rather than indoors on a mat. Whether the women wrestlers train the same as the men, I do not know; but from the appearance of these oriental Amazons it could well be that their huge chests and massive thighs are the result of countless daily repetitions of *dunds* (swinging floor-dips) and *baithaks* (knee-bends).

One famous Indian wrestler named Nadir had a daughter (b. 1919) named Hamida Banu. This girl, who from childhood on was trained in the sport by her father, at the age of 19 became a professional wrestler. Over a period of several years she engaged in some 300 bouts, of which only three were with women! Although only 5 ft. 3 in. tall, Hamida was a true heavyweight, scaling 215 pounds, and evidently she had to look beyond her own sex for suitable opponents. A photograph of Hamida taken about 1940 shows the girl wearing 19 medals.

In the book *A Pictorial History of Wrestling* by Graeme Kent (1968), there is shown (p. 68) an Indian woman wrestler (name not given), rolling her male opponent onto his back for a fall. It seems as though the man was a suitor (the woman's third unsuccessful one), who was required to throw the girl if he hoped to win her in marriage, but who failed.

In this connection comes to mind the story of the mighty 13th-century Tartar princess, Aiyaruk (meaning "shining moon"), who along with being of royal lineage was an invincible wrestler! Aiyaruk was the daughter of King Kaidu, of Great Turkey (now Russian Turkestan). Kaidu had a magnificent palace in the city of Samarkand. During Princess Aiyaruk's career as a wrestler, she pinned to the mat more than a *hundred* husky suitors! Each of these men, for his failure, had to forfeit to the princess a hundred horses. According to the famous Venetian traveler, Marco Polo, " . . . the damsel by the year 1280 had thus acquired more than 10,000 horses." In the latter year there came a prince from the neighboring kingdom of Pamir, who was the champion wrestler of that country. So confident was he that he could defeat and so win the beautiful Princess Aiyaruk that he brought with him not the required hundred horses but a *thousand!* However, after a long struggle on the mat, the princess, who was a veritable giantess in size and strength, gradually wore down her determined opponent, flattened him to the ground, and added his thousand horses to her collection!

It could well be that this gigantic Tartar girl, who was said to be stronger than any man in her country, was the strongest woman as well as the mightiest female wrestler who ever lived. Making a few reasonable assumptions, the bodily size that Princess Aiyaruk would have had to possess can be estimated (because nowhere is it stated). First, although the Tartar men of her time averaged in height probably not over 66 inches, there must have been a few good-sized suitors who stood perhaps several inches more than this and weighed at least 180 pounds. Some of the challengers doubtless came from other countries (Russia ?, Turkey?, India ?), and may have been even larger. Thus, on the basis previously shown—that in order to be as strong as a man, a woman would have to weigh half-again as much—the Tartar princess would have had to weigh *at least* 275 pounds. And since she was described as being "almost a giantess," her height must have been at least 74 inches. These dimensions I have used as the basis for a drawing of Princess Aiyaruk (Plate 86). For those interested, her vital statistics would have been about 49-35-53!

After contemplating Princess Aiyaruk, it is difficult to picture any woman weighing less than, say, 200 pounds as being truly a contemporary world champion wrestler. Yet in the United States and Continental

Europe during recent years, various women professionals, some of whom have weighed no more than 130 pounds, have each claimed this distinction. It should be noted that 130 pounds in a woman is equivalent to not more than 170 pounds in a man. At the latter bodyweight a man would have to have the technique of a Farmer Burns to be a champion even in scientific wrestling, and would be far too small to withstand the battering of a real (250–280-pound) heavyweight using today's combination of wrestling and mayhem. Very probably in women's wrestling, just as in the weight events in women's track and field, the proportion of strong and active heavyweight participants has been, and continues to be, too small to yield performers of true world-championship caliber.

Currently, in women's professional wrestling in the United States, the generally recognized champion is Penny Banner (68 in., 150 lbs.). For several years previously, the top-ranking candidate was "The Fabulous Moolah" (Lillian Ellison), who was preceded by a long line of title-holders, probably the most capable of whom was Mildred Burke (63 in., 130 lbs.). Miss Burke held the American title for no less than 14 years (1939–1953), when she was dethroned by June Byers (67 in., 150 lbs.). During the last several years, the leading contenders for the title, in addition to the present holder, Penny Banner, have been mainly Judy Grable (66 in., 130 lbs.) and Rita Cortez (65 in., 140 lbs.). But the "ratings" of these and other women wrestlers fluctuate so much that it is impossible to say—without consulting the latest issue of some wrestling magazine—who are the currently recognized top-ranking contenders, as well as the champion. What is needed in women's wrestling, it would appear, are a few contenders of the size and strength of the woman champion in the following sport.

WRIST WRESTLING. A championship in this event, for men, has been held annually since 1962, in Petaluma, California. A women's championship, at the same place, has been held annually since 1966. During all 4 years the women's winner has been Mickie Novis of Oakland. In 1967 she put down the arm of runner-up Mary Doughty of Petaluma; in 1968, that of Louise Jones of San Francisco; and in 1969, that of Linda Iverson, of Boyes Hot Springs, California. In none of these women's competitions were the bodyweights listed; however, it would appear that Miss Novis, the champion, must weigh somewhere in the neighborhood of 180 pounds at a height of perhaps 66 inches (see Plate 87).

Wrist wrestling, peculiarly, is a feat, presumably of arm strength, in which certain women, even if they be of slender build, may excel. As related in Chapter 5, an 18th-century actress, Mlle. Gauthier, gave

Table 24. Women's vs. men's athletic records (as of September 14, 1969)

Event	Men's Record	Women's Record	Ratio, Women to Men
Roller skating, 10 miles	28 min. 52.6 sec.	28 min. 43.8 sec.	100.5
Sprinting, 50 yards	5.2 sec.	5.6 sec.	92.9
60 Yard Hurdles	6.8 sec.	7.4 sec.	91.9
Canoeing (Single Kayak), 500 meters	2 min. 4.6 sec.	2 min. 15.9 sec.	91.7
Sprinting, 100 meters	9.9 sec.	11.0 sec.	90.0
Swimming (Freestyle), 100 meters	52.6 sec.	58.9 sec.	89.3
Running, 800 meters	1 min. 44.3 sec.	1 min. 58 sec.	88.4
Ice skating, 440 yards	39.5 sec.	44.9 sec.	88.0
Roller skating, 440 yards	34.9 sec.	40.6 sec.	86.0
Swimming (Freestyle), 1500 meters	16 min. 4.5 sec.	18 min. 23.7 sec.	85.6
Bicycle racing, 5 kilometers	6 min. 2.4 sec.	7 min. 3.3 sec.	85.6
Walking, one mile	6 min. 18.3 sec.	7 min. 27.2 sec.	84.6
Running high jump	7 ft. 5¾ in.	6 ft. 3¾ in.	83.8
Running, one mile	3 min. 51.1 sec.	4 min. 37.0 sec.	83.4
200 meter Hurdles	22.5 sec.	27.1 sec.	83.0
Standing broad jump	11 ft. 7 in.	9 ft. 5½ in.	81.7
Running long jump	29 ft. 2½ in.	22 ft. 10 in.	78.2
Golf, drive for distance	430 yards	327 yards	76.0
Archery, Flight Shooting for distance	719 yards	505 yards	70.2
Running, Marathon	2 hrs. 8 min. 33.6 sec.	3 hrs. 7 min. 26.2 sec.	68.6
Shot Put, women's record as with 16 pounds	71 ft. 5½ in.	48 ft. 10 in.	68.3
Baseball, throw for distance	443 ft. 3½ in.	296 ft.	66.8
Discus Throw, women's record as with 2 kg. discus	224 ft. 5 in.	145 ft. 5½ in.	64.8
Weightlifting, Two Hands Clean & Jerk at bodyweight of 150 lbs.	375 lbs.	230 lbs.	61.3
Javelin Throw, women's record as with .8 kg. javelin	304 ft. 1½ in.	177 ft. 3¾ in.	58.3
Weightlifting, Squat at bodyweight of 130 pounds	470 lbs.	266 lbs.	56.6
Pole vault	17 ft. 10¾ in.	8 ft. 6 in.	47.6

Maurice Saxe, a nobleman who was noted for his great strength of arm and hand, his hardest tussle in wrist-wrestling! Virginia Hansen of Toutle, Washington, who had been trained in wrist wrestling by her father, could, it is said, put down the arm of any man she had ever been matched against. Her explanation for her success was that, "We just practiced wrist wrestling by the hour at home."

In reference to Table 24, a few comments may be made. Obviously the most questionable listings are the first, on roller skating, and the last, on the pole vault. I have taken the roller skating records for 10 miles from the *1966 Almanack of Sport* (London), p. 394, where the men's time of 28:52.6 is credited to L. Woodley of Great Britain, 1960. The women's better time of 28:43.8 is credited to Miss C. Barnett, also of Great Britain, 1962. The two years' difference in time between the two records is hardly enough to account for the superiority of the women's record. And not only does Miss Barnett surpass the men's time for 10 miles, but also for 15 miles, 20 miles, and 30,000 meters (= 18⅝ miles)! Evidently at long-distance roller skating, Miss Barnett was a phenomenon. So far as I know, she is the only woman to hold a world record that surpasses the men's record in the same sport.

As to the women's poor showing in the pole vault, this may be attributed to lack of interest and competition, along with the circumstance that women are not adapted muscularly to excel in a gymnastic event that demands *strength* rather than limberness and balance. And the stage of the pole vault where the performer must simultaneously "chin" with his (or her) arms while shooting his (or her) feet skyward must certainly be classed as a *gymnastic* (rather than athletic) movement.

In some comparisons such as are made in Table 24, other authors have attempted to show that women's athletic records have improved faster than men's. This is true, so far; but it is mainly because women have entered the field of world competition only comparatively recently. With their initial efforts in various competitive sports—track and field, for example—being inordinately poor, their records were bound to soar in merit as more and better-adapted competitors steadily entered the field. But to extrapolate this progress and make predictions on the basis of it would seem a risky procedure. Yet articles on the subject continue to appear, in which all kinds of conclusions, most of them unwarranted, are aired. The only safe course here is not to generalize prematurely, but to wait and see. In order for women to surpass men in absolute *strength*, as well as speed and agility, they would have to become *masculine* in bodily size, configuration, physiology, and even in temperament. Pity the human race if such a change should ever take place!

Appendix

A. A NEW TIME-POPULATION SYSTEM FOR RATING OR SCORING ATHLETIC RECORDS

Who's the greatest athlete? Who's the best sprinter, the best high jumper, the best shot putter? These are easier questions to ask than to answer, and there can be little doubt that every follower of sports would welcome a series of satisfactory answers. If the existing world's records in the various track and field events were the *only* records that had ever been made, there would be no problem, and each record holder could be accepted as the best performer in his particular event. However, there have been numerous world record holders ever since the first organized competitions in track and field were held nearly a hundred years ago. The problem is how to rate those champions so that each man receives full and proper credit. This cannot be done by a simple, direct comparison of records, but requires also that the date at which the record was made be taken into account and used to modify the actual record.

The reason why the *date* of performance is important is because with the passage of time there is an increase in *population*, and the larger the population the greater the *probability* of an extraordinary record. In short, athletic records, like those of height and weight or any other expressions of human diversity that can be measured, *range in magnitude in ratio to the size of the population from which the record is drawn.* Accordingly, in a large population of competitors (no matter what the events), the best performances should be *expected* to be of high caliber, and vice versa.

A second factor that should be taken into account in the "weight" events is the *size* of the performer. This means not only his bodyweight, but also his *height*. Since greater height and weight assist a performer in such events as weightlifting,* the shot put, the hammer throw, the 56-pound weight throw, and even the lightweight javelin throw, it is manifest that the factors of height and bodyweight must be incorporated into any system of rating that purports to give fair and proper credit to performances made in the weight events. Otherwise the outcome of a competition might frequently be a foregone conclusion, in which case it could hardly be judged a competition.

To make a long story short, I refer the reader now to the following series of graphs (Figures 1–21). With the exceptions of Figures 1, 3, 4, and 16, these graphs illustrate the trends of various athletic records over the years 1880–1970. Figure 1 charts the population of the United States (total), while the other graphs each show the progress in some particular athletic event *as fitted to the U.S. population*. Above each of the curves showing the trend of the actual best performances is another curve showing the assumed 100-percent (or 1000-point) performance in that event for any given year. The position of any particular record *in relation to both the lower and the upper curves* shows in a general way the merit (point or percentage rating) of that record. This holds true, however, only of the running, jumping, hurdling, vaulting, and swimming events. In the weight events—shot put, discus, hammer, javelin, and 56-pound weight throw—the merit of any particular plotted performance is dependent also upon the size (height and weight) of the performer. The reason for this is that bodily *size* is a major contributing factor in the field weight events just as it is in weightlifting. This is shown by the fact that performers in the weight events average larger both in height and weight than performers in other events, such as running and jumping, where size is of no great importance and if excessive may even be a handicap. Here are the average or typical heights and bodyweights of performers in the several weight events as assumed in the present study as a basis for comparisons and ratings.**

Event	MEN		WOMEN	
	Height, in.	Bodyweight, lbs.	Height, in.	Bodyweight, lbs.
Javelin throw	72.44	186	67.70	152
Discus throw	74.30	220	69.30	175
Hammer throw	73.20	222.5	———	———
Shot put	75.00	232.5	68.20	176
56-pound weight	75.00	232.5	———	———

---

*In the Olympic lifts, for example, while ability in the Press, at a given bodyweight, is in *inverse* ratio to the height, in the Snatch and the Clean and Jerk the reverse is the case, as in these lifts a more slender physique makes for greater *speed*.
**These heights and weights show, in a general way, that the *heavier* the object thrown, the heavier the *body build* of the performers making the throws.

In introducing here my system for rating athletic records, it is not my purpose to burden the general reader with a mass of mathematical details. However, some readers will want to know at least the principles upon which the percentage (or point) ratings are based. These principles are few in number and readily explainable. First in importance is, of course, the record itself. Second is the date the record was made. A third factor, which enters only into the performances of the "weight" events (shot put, hammer throw, 56-pound weight throw, discus, and javelin, as well as all weightlifting events) is the *bodily size* (height and weight) of the performer.

The reader is referred now to Table 25. Under the heading "rating in percent," the respective ratings were derived in the following manner. The 96-percent ratings approximate very closely to the World records that were current in 1965, after the figures were "smoothed" so as to be proportionate throughout to the 91.5-percent ratings. The latter correspond closely with the values derived by averaging the *top 50 performances in each event* recorded during 1965. The latter year, it should be stressed, is the one here adopted as the basis for all determinations of *time*. The 50-percent ratings are the assumed *average* performances of Freshman college students in 1965 (the height and weight of whom average 69 inches and 155 pounds, respectively). The 100-percent (or 1000-point) ratings are simply the figures resulting from an extrapolation of those under the 50, 91.5, and 96-percent ratings. My reason for "adjusting" the 96-percent (or 1965 World) records from the figures obtained for the 91.5-percent ratings is that an *average of 50* records of anything must be accepted as a more reliable basis for comparison than is a *single* record (i.e., a World record) of the same kind, or in the same event. Many of the figures listed under the 50-percent ratings are purely theoretical, as few if any average-sized Freshman college students compete in them, as for example in the hammer throw and the 56-pound weight throw. Where two differing figures are listed under the ratings for the weight events, the smaller figure is the assumed performance of a Freshman college student of *average* size (69 in., 155 lbs.), while the larger figure is the performance in the same event of a man of the same assumed average size as the *champion* performers in that event. For instance, in the shot put the 50-percent distance for a man of 69 inches and 155 pounds is 27 feet, while for a man of 75 inches and 232.5 pounds it is 30.822 ft.

Opposite each event is a "formula" from which the percentage rating for that particular event is derived. Each formula results from the difference between the 50-percent and the 100-percent ratings listed for that event. Here is how the formula is applied in rating a performance in the 100-yard dash:

Suppose that the time recorded was 9.3 seconds, and that the performance (for simplicity's sake) was made in 1965. Referring to the formula opposite the 100 yard dash, it is noted that the percentage rating is equal to 240.32 minus 15.86 times the time in seconds. Thus the rating is 240.32 — (9.3 × 15.86), or 92.82 percent. This can be expressed also as 928 points, the figures for the second decimal place being negligible. Now, let us suppose that another sprinter has covered the 100 yards in a tenth of a second slower time—that is, in 9.4 seconds— but did it in 1955; how does his rating compare with that of the first sprinter? First, referring to Table 27, it is seen opposite the year 1955 that the Time Factor for the 100-yard dash is 1.0131. In the running and hurdling events, the Time Factor is to be *divided into the time* (in seconds); while in the weight events, the jumps, and the pole vault the factor is to be used as a *multiplier of the distance* (in feet). Thus, for the 100-yard performance in question, we *divide* 9.4 by 1.0131. This gives 9.28 seconds (as the equivalent time in 1965). It is immediately seen, therefore, that the 9.4-second performance in 1955 is better, though only slightly, than the 9.3-second performance in 1965. Its exact rating is 240.32 — (9.28 × 15.86), or 93.13 percent (= 931 points).

In connection with the weight or throwing events, it should be noted that both in Table 25 and Table 26 the formulas specify not the distance itself, but the *square root* of the distance. This type of formula is necessary for the same reason that the expectation in distance in any throwing event varies inversely as the square root of the weight of the object thrown.

In Table 25, the formulas for rating the *weight* events apply only to the assumed *average* heights and bodyweights listed on p. 586. For every other combination of height and bodyweight in each event a specific 100-percent distance is listed, and this distance must be used to properly rate each and every performance in the weight events. The procedure, and the inclusion of numerous separate tables, is too involved to be expounded here. Just as for other track and field events, those in which weights are handled must first be "date-corrected" as per Table 27. In a shot put, for example, made in 1950, the actual distance recorded would be *multiplied* by the factor 1.0744 listed under Shot Put for that year.

Referring again to Table 25, the two columns on the right, labelled S.D. and C.V. respectively, express the *variability* of each event. The S.D. (Standard Deviation) is a conventional measure used in statistics to express the *average* degree to which each individual record in the series deviates from the mean value of the whole. The C.V. (Coefficient of Variation) is a similar measure, but one in which the *ratio* of the

Standard Deviation to the mean is expressed as a *percentage*. Thus the C.V. is particularly useful in expressing the *degree of variability* of any series of measurements (such as athletic records). In Table 25, the rightmost column, in which is listed the C.V., gives the *relative variability* of each event.

In the running events, it is seen that the greater the distance, the larger the C.V. (and accordingly, the more variable the time). Thus, while in a 100-yard dash the competitors may be separated, perhaps, by only a 2/5 of a second (or 4 percent of the time taken to cover the distance), in a Marathon run the corresponding separation would be about 6⅔ percent, or about 10 *minutes*. In Table 25, it may be noted also that the variability of the four hurdling events is in each case about the same as that of the 800-meter run. Going down the column of C.V.s, it is seen that they average about 16 percent for the three jumping events, and rise to over 34 in the pole vault. This indicates that the degree of variation in the pole vault between the performance of a novice and that of an expert is very great.

All the throwing (or weight) events, too, have a high C.V., which means, as in the pole vault, that the *range* of possibility in them is very much greater than in the running events, or even the jumps. This greater variability is shown also in the various graphs, where Figures 2, 14, 15, 17, 18, 19 and 20 show less "parallelism," generally, between the record curve and the 100-percent curve than do Figures 5, 6, 7, 8, 9, 10 and 11. In this connection it should be mentioned that the coefficients of variation in relation to *time*, as listed at the bottom of Table 27, are not for all events the same as those listed in Tables 25 and 26 for *contemporary* (or 1965) performances. In Table 25, for example, the C.V.s for the high jump and the long jump are, as would be expected, very similar, both being between 15 and 16 percent. Yet in Table 27 the C.V. listed for the long jump is only 10.26. This figure derives from the curve plotted in Figure 11, which shows that between 1930 and 1965, for example, the distance in the long jump increased less than 6 percent, while that in the high jump advanced almost 9 percent.

All the foregoing explanation may be confusing, and possibly boring, to the reader who is interested only in athletics and not also in mathematics and statistics. Yet, athletic records, no less than other kinds, can be expressed only in numbers, and it is essential that someone should try to correlate the various records in a rational manner that yields fair ratings for all performers, giving due consideration to the factors I have outlined. As no one heretofore has come forth with a system of rating that properly takes into account all the factors involved, and which correlates the performances of women athletes with those of men, the system here being introduced is respectfully submitted for application and constructive criticism to all others interested.*

The most difficult principle to "put across" in connection with the present system of rating is the date factor. To most persons, the best record is the highest record, regardless of when it was made. Yet it is not necessarily correct to say, for example, that a record of 9.6 seconds in the 100-yard dash, made in 1900, is inferior to one of 9.1 seconds made in 1965. The 1900 record, judged by the system here employed, is equal to one of 9.0875 seconds made in 1965. Thus it is a small fraction *better*. The reason for this is indicated in Figure 5. The earlier records are *necessarily* lower (or slower) absolutely than the more recent ones, for the reason that they have come out of a *smaller population of competitors*, in which the inherent variability of the event (in this case, 100-yard dash) would not be *expected* to reach a higher level. A comparable situation is in human height, or stature, which follows approximately what is known as the "normal curve" of distribution. While a giant (or a dwarf) might occur within a random population of only a few hundred persons, such an occurrence (unless in a circus or carnival!) would be exceedingly unlikely. Under normal conditions an 8-foot giant (or a 3½-foot dwarf) would be expected to occur only within a population of *several hundred million* persons. The same is true of athletic records, of all kinds. Therefore, a performance may be fairly rated as to merit only by comparing it with the *average or typical performance current at that time*. The latter, as may be seen from the numerous graphs included in Figures 1–2, varies *in ratio to the population generally*.** (The *rate* of variation, however, is usually different in one event than in another).

To sum up, and perhaps repeat, it may be said that the time factor is not a selective factor per se, but rather because it represents a change in a given population and so introduces biological variation due to modified range. That is, the larger the population of anything, the greater the range, or diversity.

Tables 26 and 29, for women, correspond with Tables 25 and 28 for men. In the former two tables are listed the formulas and ratings pertaining to women's standard field events and the outstanding performances in them. It would take an undue amount of space here to

---

*In making these comments, I am fully aware of the scoring tables originated and issued by the I.A.A.F. and by Fernando Amado of Lisbon, Portugal, respectively. The authors and compilers of these tables deserve immense credit. Yet the two systems disagree; and only that of Amado takes into account the factor of *time*. And even Amado's system makes no provision for height and bodyweight in the "weight" (field) events.

**That is, the *entire population of the nation*, and not merely the population of competing athletes in any particular event, is the decisive factor affecting *probability of performance*.

comment on all the individual performances listed in Table 28 for men and Table 29 for women. In the present system, any performance having a rating of over 900 points is good, over 930 fine, over 960 extraordinary, and over 990 phenomenal. While 1000 points was "aimed" at originally as the highest possible performance, a few altogether extraordinary feats were found later to go beyond this figure. This makes no difference in the *relative* standings, since all ratings are merely particular points on an arbitrary scale.

Far and away the men's fastest sprinter was the phenomenal professional athlete and coach, R. P. Williams. He was an equally capable jumper, although his best jumps were made from a standing rather than running start. Probably, if he had applied to the running long jump and running high jump even a fair amount of technique, he would have made phenomenal records in those events also. Even in the shot put, Williams, relative to his size (69.1 in., 160 lbs.), was the greatest performer on record. What a pity that detailed motion pictures were not taken of his performances!

Among women's track and field records, the three greatest would appear to be those by Iolanda Balas (Rumania) in the high jump, Margitta Hemboldt-Gummel (East Germany) in the shot put, and Irina Press (USSR) in the pentathlon. Perhaps many readers will be aghast and indignant because some of their favorites (even world record holders) are not included in these lists. However, the listings are unaffected by any partiality on my part, and result solely from an application of the principles previously expounded. I myself was greatly disappointed when I had to place Cornelius Warmerdam at the bottom of my listings of performances in the pole vault, since prior to figuring his point rating I had thought he was at or near the top. But that was probably from having attached undue importance to the *length of time* his record had stood. After Warmerdam's time, a great many more vaulters competed, and within this larger population a record would not be *expected* to endure as long as Warmerdam's did.

Virtually every man and woman mentioned in this book is, I feel, either a "super-athlete" or a performer verging thereupon, whether or not he (or she) is listed in Table 28 or Table 29. The latter tables, after all, list only track and field performances, and take no account of un-ratable feats in numerous other departments (boxing, wrestling, swimming, diving, rope-walking, bicycling, skating, gymnastics, acrobatics, etc).

Finally, it may be pointed out that a rating, say, of 961 points does not necessarily mean that the record is inferior to another that has been listed at 962 points. To be at all indicative of a difference, compared performances should be separated by at least 10 points (or 1 percent);

or better, by 20 points. However, when one record is 40 or more points ahead of another (as in the case of Bob Beamon's long jump compared with that of Jesse Owens), there can be no question of the superiority of the higher-rated performance.

———————

The rapidity with which track and field records have improved during recent years is a phenomenon known to every follower of athletics. It immediately raises the question, "when will the limit be reached?" Some writers on the subject have even asserted that there *must* be a "physiological limit." This, at first thought, seems reasonable. But whenever an attempt has been made to set such a limit, it has been only a matter of time—often a very short time—before the predicted "limit" was surpassed. The first widely publicized prediction of track and field "ultimates" was that made by Brutus Hamilton, of the University of California, in 1934. However, Hamilton based his "ultimates" on the assumption that the then-current record in the shot put of 57 ft. ½ in. (by Jack Torrance) was *already* an ultimate. He then predicted the limits in the other track and field events by making them proportionate to a shot put of 57 ft. ½ in. The fault there, of course, was the *assumption* that in the latter event a limit had actually been reached. So long as athletic records keep pace in general with population increase (and the results of the present study indicate that this is so), there will be no "ultimates" in them *until the population (and the number of competing athletes therein) ceases to increase.*

Today, if we followed Brutus Hamilton's principle, we could well base all the track and field "ultimates" on Bob Beamon's phenomenal long jump of 29 ft. 2½ in. made at the 1968 Olympic Games. On that basis the 100-yard dash would lower to 8.6 seconds, the mile run to 3 minutes 30.7 seconds, the high jump to 7 feet 10 inches, the pole vault to about 19 feet, and so on (see Table 31). Yet none of these improved records would be "ultimates," or "physiological limits." They would be merely performances that were equal, proportionately, to Beamon's long jump *at the time it was made.* And the latter, if the scales on Figure 10 were extended, is a performance that one would expect to see equalled in the early 1980s. So, to repeat, the only even approximate answer that can at present be given to the question, "when will the limit be reached?" is, "when the limit in *population* has been reached."

To sum up, despite all the studies that are being made, the scientific analysis of athletic records would still appear to be in its infancy. It has been said that the greatest need in athletics today is, ". . . a quantitative approach to the training of the athlete . . . the determination of the physical and physiological requirements of the event. These can best be developed from data on the current world class athletes."[*] They can, I feel, be determined even better by studying the physical, physiological, and temperamental characteristics of those athletes whose performances indicate the greatest *efficiency* in their events. This efficiency is denoted in the percentage (or point) ratings yielded by the present system of performance rating. *Sports research institutes* should be established to carry on these studies under optimum conditions.

A few comments may be added here concerning Tables 28 and 29. As mentioned before, no attempt has been made in these listings to include *all* high-ranking performances; and in some of the events even world record holders have had to be omitted. Few of the listed ratings go below 950 points. Actually, if the ratings in running include listings as low as 950, those in the "weight" events should go much lower, since the relative variability in the latter events, and even in the pole vault and the jumping events, is much greater than in even the longest of the running events (Marathon). That is why, particularly in the track and field ratings for women (Table 29), performances in the "weight" events are listed that rate considerably below 950 points.

After noting the phenomenal recent records established by Bob Beamon (USA) in the men's long jump, and by Margitta Helmboldt-Gummel (East Germany) in the women's shot put, Tables 31 and 32 were added as a matter of interest. The various estimated records listed in these tables have been set ahead chronologically so as to apply to July 1, 1970 (rather than to some prior date). In the men's table it will be seen that the best performances, next to Bob Beamon's long jump, are in the javelin throw, which is practically equal in merit, and the discus throw, which is only slightly less meritorious. In the women's performances, next to Margitta Helmboldt-Gummel's shot put, the best ratings are in the high jump, the 100 meter hurdles, and the long jump. The marathon run, too, is of exceedingly high merit.

In conclusion, it should be remembered that statistics applying to athletic performances are of a *continually changing*, rather than static, nature. Accordingly, it is the author's prerogative to revise or improve any of the formulas or ratings presented, or referred to, in *The SUPER-ATHLETES* as additional and more extensive data become available. Even though much commendable work has already been done in this field, the subject is still greatly in need of thorough mathematical analysis. It is hoped that the new approaches presented in this volume will stimulate a more widespread interest in, and study of, the basic structural, physiological, and temperamental qualities that lead to better athletic performances.

---

[*]John A. Faulkner: New Perspectives in Training for Maximum Performance. Jour. Amer. Med. Asso., vol. 205, no. 11, p. 745, September 9, 1968.

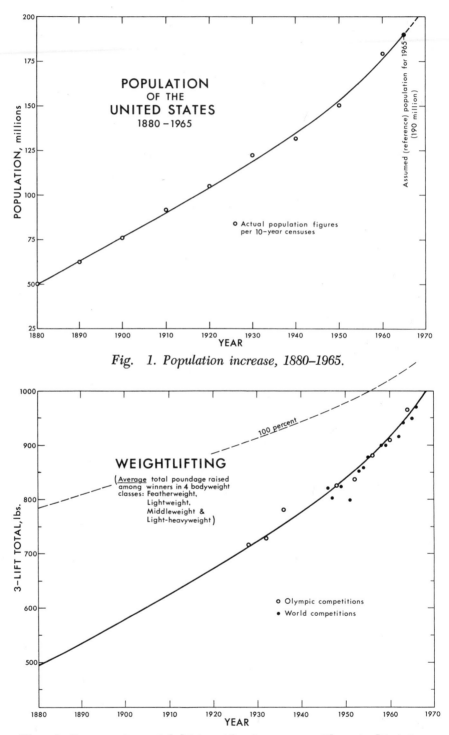

Fig. 1. Population increase, 1880–1965.

Fig. 2. Progress in weightlifting (the 3 two-arm Olympic lifts) from 1928 to 1966.

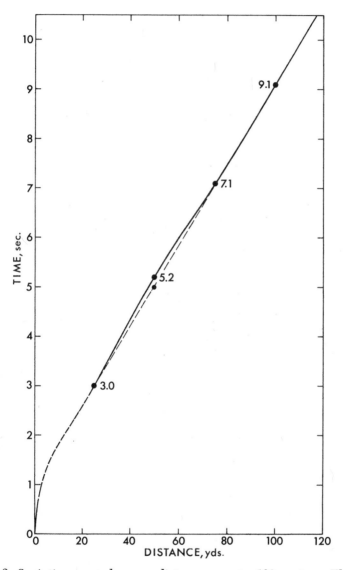

Fig. 3. *Sprinting records over distances up to 100 meters. The four points plotted on the curve (at 25, 50, 75, and 100 yards respectively) are the actual times recorded for Bob Hayes in his record-making 100-yard race (9.1 seconds). For details see Chapter 15.*

Fig. 4. Man, horse and greyhound racing.

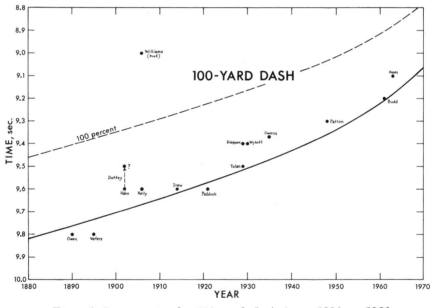

Fig. 5. Progress in the 100-yard dash from 1890 to 1963.

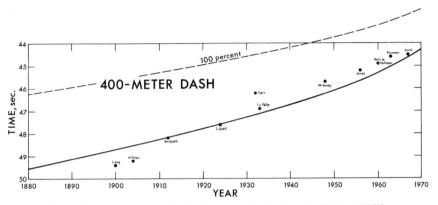

Fig.   6. Progress in the 400-meter dash from 1900 to 1967.

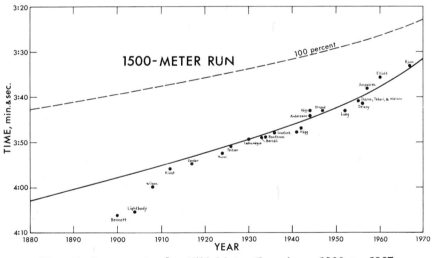

Fig.   7. Progress in the 1500-Meter Run from 1900 to 1967.

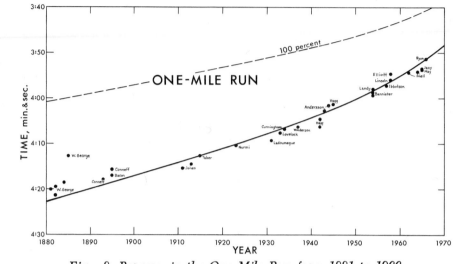

Fig. 8. Progress in the One Mile Run from 1881 to 1966.

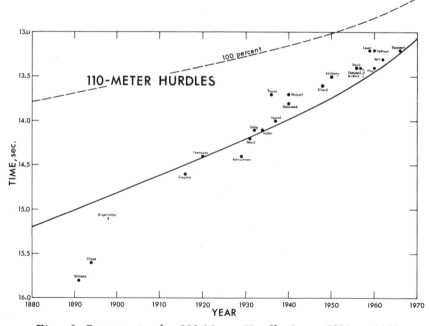

Fig. 9. Progress in the 110-Meter Hurdle from 1891 to 1966.

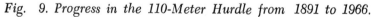

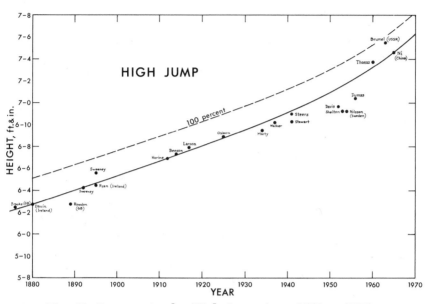

Fig. 10. *Progress in the High Jump from 1876 to 1965.*

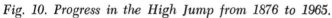

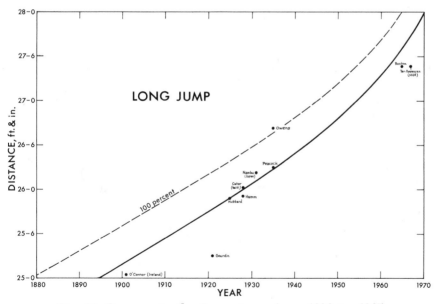

Fig. 11. *Progress in the Long Jump from 1896 to 1967.*

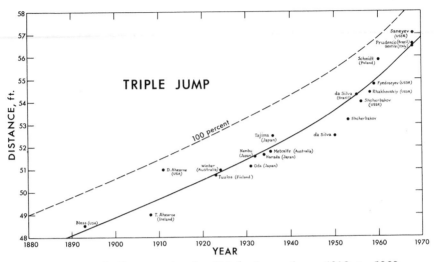

Fig. 12. Progress in the Triple Jump from 1893 to 1968.

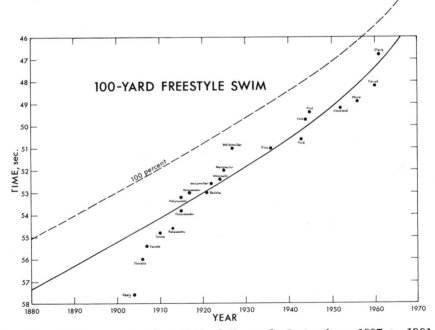

Fig. 13. Progress in the 100-Yard Freestyle Swim from 1897 to 1961.

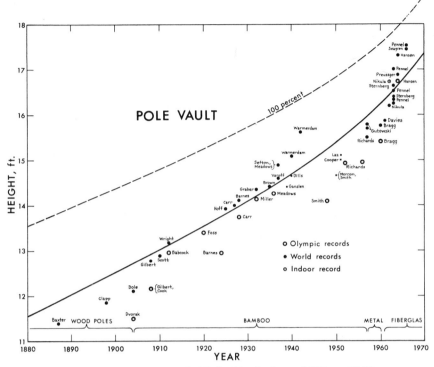

Fig. 14. Progress in the Pole Vault from 1887 to 1966.

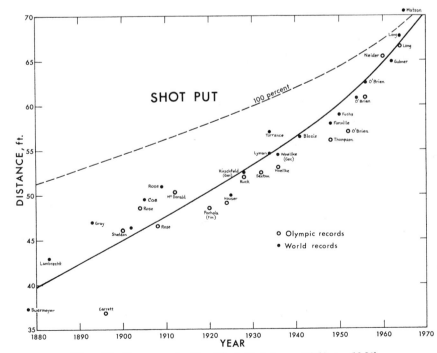

Fig. 15. Progress in the Shot Put from 1878 to 1965.

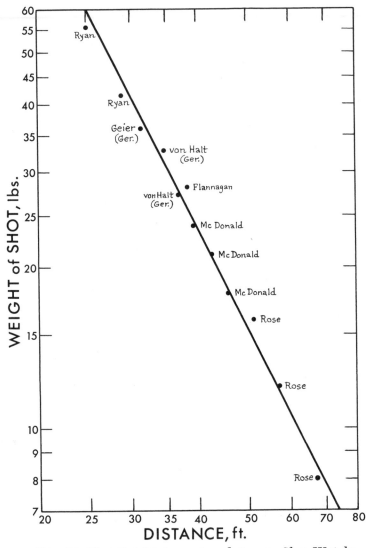

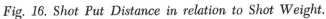

Fig. 16. Shot Put Distance in relation to Shot Weight.

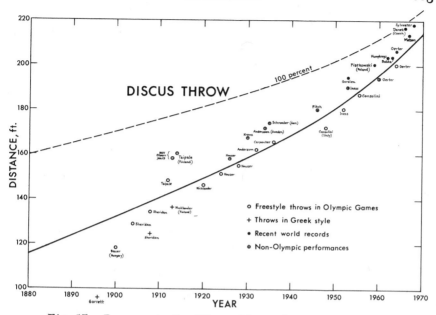

Fig. 17. Progress in the Discus Throw from 1896 to 1968.

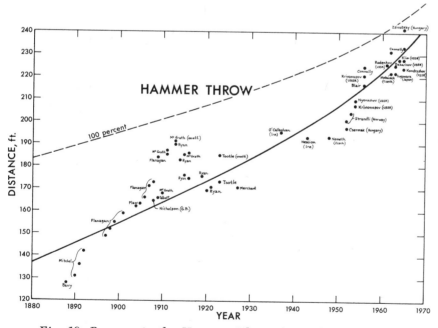

Fig. 18. Progress in the Hammer Throw from 1888 to 1965.

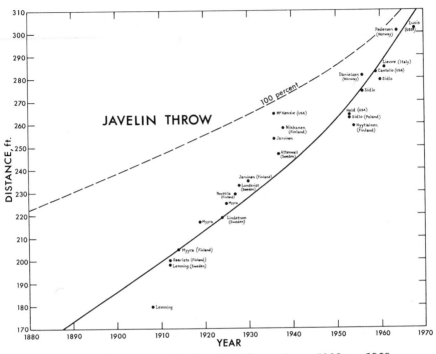

Fig. 19. Progress in the Javelin Throw from 1908 to 1968.

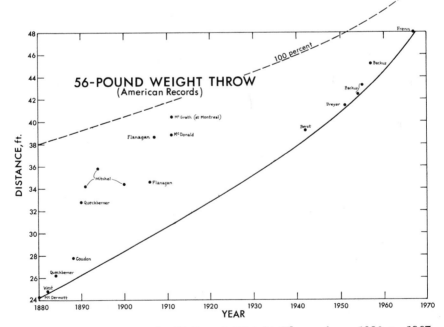

Fig. 20. Progress in the 56-Pound Weight Throw from 1880 to 1967.

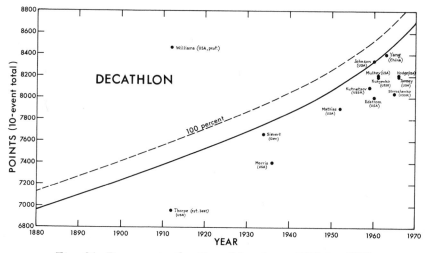

Fig. 21. Progress in the Decathlon from 1912 to 1966.

B. RATINGS OF VARIOUS RECORDS IN TRACK AND FIELD

Table 25. Relative variability of Track and Field events

(All ratings as of 1965)

MEN

Event	Rating in Percent				Formula for Percentage Rating	Time, seconds	S.D.	C.V.
	50	91.5	96	100			(yards)	
	(all times are in seconds)							
100 yard dash	12.00	9.38	9.10	8.85	240.32–15.86	Time, seconds	0.714	5.95
100 meter dash	13.06	10.20	9.89	9.61	239.50–14.51	"	0.781	5.98
200 meter dash	26.88	20.63	19.95	19.35	228.48– 6.64	"	1.707	6.35
220 yard dash	27.09	20.78	20.10	19.49	228.25– 6.58	"	1.722	6.36
400 meter dash	61.45	46.02	44.35	42.86	215.30– 2.69	"	4.21	6.85
440 yard dash	62.06	46.46	44.77	43.26	215.08– 2.66	"	4.26	6.86
800 meter run	149.10	107.72	104.31	100.42	203.13–1.027	"	10.77	7.20
880 yard run	150.05	109.40	104.90	101.10	203.20–1.021	"	10.80	7.22
1500 meter run	313.24	223.02	213.24	204.54	194.09–0.460	"	24.00	7.66
1 mile run	340.00	241.21	230.56	221.00	192.81–0.420	"	25.91	7.73
Marathon	13140	8260	7731	7261	161.75–0.008505	"	1298	9.88

					Time, seconds	(inches) / (feet)	
120 yard hurdles 18.57	13.70	13.17	12.70		208.21– 8.52	1.330	7.16
110 meter hurdles 18.62	13.73	13.20	12.73		208.07– 8.49 "	1.335	7.17
400 meter hurdles 69.59	50.90	48.87	47.07		204.50– 2.22 "	4.967	7.17
440 yard hurdles 70.08	51.22	49.17	47.35		204.17– 2.20 "	5.007	7.18
						(inches)	
High jump, ft. 4.500	7.047	7.322	7.568		16.296 Jump, ft.–23.33	8.342	15.45
Pole vault, ft. 7.175	16.197	17.175	18.045		4.600 Vault, ft.+17.00	29.557	34.33
Long jump, ft. 16.500	26.052	27.088	28.009		4.344 Jump, ft.–21.67	31.295	15.81
Triple jump, ft. 33.833	53.719	55.875	57.792		2.087 Jump, ft.–20.60	65.148	16.05
						(feet)	
Shot put, ft. 30.822 27.000 80.420	61.528	65.488	69.113		18.105 $\sqrt{\text{Distance, ft.}}$ –50.51	8.453	27.42
Discus throw, ft. 89.729 80.747	192.321	205.807	218.150		9.4386 $\sqrt{\text{Distance, ft.}}$ –39.40	28.349	31.59
Hammer throw, ft. 91.667 16.731	216.059	232.657	247.971		8.1003 $\sqrt{\text{Distance, ft.}}$ –27.56	34.504	37.55
56-lb. throw, ft. 19.000 101.410	44.683	48.130	51.291		17.839 $\sqrt{\text{Distance, ft.}}$ –27.76	7.133	37.54
Javelin throw, ft. 115.000	269.600	290.193	308.305		7.306 $\sqrt{\text{Distance, ft.}}$ –28.46	42.671	37.11

Table 26. *Relative variability of Track and Field events*

WOMEN

(All ratings as of 1965)

Event	Rating in Percent				Formula for Percentage Rating		S.D.	C.V.
	50	91.5	96	100		Time, seconds	(yards)	
	(all times are in seconds)							
100 yard dash	13.96	10.53	10.17	9.84	219.26—12.12	Time, seconds	1.046	7.49
100 meter dash	15.27	11.51	11.10	10.74	218.54—11.04	"	1.150	7.53
200 meter dash	31.94	23.60	22.70	21.90	209.05— 4.98	"	2.546	7.96
220 yard dash	32.18	23.78	22.87	22.06	208.98— 4.94	"	2.568	7.97
400 meter dash	74.50	53.60	51.33	49.31	197.63— 1.98	"	6.20	8.33
440 yard dash	75.28	54.11	51.81	49.77	197.55— 1.96	"	6.28	8.34
800 meter run	180.10	125.15	119.20	113.89	185.99—0.755	"	16.31	9.05
880 yard run	181.41	126.01	120.00	114.66	185.88—0.749	"	16.94	9.34
1500 meter run	404.02	272.37	258.45	245.79	177.67—0.316	"	40.16	9.94
1 mile run	440.80	296.20	280.40	266.59	176.51—0.287	"	44.25	10.04
Marathon	20522	12808	11973	11229	160.41—0.00538	"	2358	11.54

					Time, seconds	″	″
80 meter hurdles	15.13	10.82	10.35	9.93	195.57– 9.62	1.280	8.46
100 meter hurdles	19.67	13.92	13.30	12.75	192.03– 7.22	1.757	8.93
						(inches)	
High jump, ft.	3.750	5.852	6.081	6.283	19.740 Jump, ft.–24.03	7.716	17.15
Pole vault, ft.	4.500	12.169	13.000	13.740	5.412 Vault, ft.+25.64	28.138	52.11
Long jump, ft.	13.200	21.335	22.218	23.017	5.100 Jump, ft.–17.31	29.854	18.85
Triple jump, ft.	23.667	38.476	40.083	41.510	2.802 Jump, ft.–16.31	54.345	19.14
	22.775					(feet)	
Shot put, ft.	27.000	55.603	59.321	62.728	$18.355\sqrt{\text{Distance, ft.}}-45.37$	8.800	32.59
	61.667						
Discus throw, ft.	80.029	182.599	196.252	208.747	$9.087\sqrt{\text{Distance, ft.}}-31.29$	31.704	39.60
	58.144						
Javelin throw, ft.	75.417	189.427	204.708	218.897	$8.182\sqrt{\text{Distance, ft.}}-21.05$	35.621	47.21

Table 27. Time factors for various track and field events

(To avoid complications, the Time Factors for *women's* events are assumed to be the same as for men's)

Year	100 Yard Dash (and 100 Meters)	220 Yard Dash (and 200 Meters)	440 Yard Run	Hurdles, 110 m. & 400 m.	880 Yard Run	1 Mile Run	Marathon Run	Long Jump	High Jump & Triple Jump	Pole Vault	Shot Put, Hammer Throw, 56 lb. wt. Throw	Discus Throw	Javelin Throw
1970	0.9920	0.9915	0.9908	0.9904	0.9904	0.9899	0.9868	0.9873	0.9825	0.9739	0.9727	0.9717	0.9700
69	0.9937	0.9933	0.9927	0.9924	0.9924	0.9920	0.9897	0.9901	0.9862	0.9794	0.9784	0.9776	0.9762
68	0.9953	0.9950	0.9946	0.9944	0.9944	0.9941	0.9925	0.9928	0.9898	0.9847	0.9839	0.9833	0.9823
67	0.9969	0.9967	0.9964	0.9963	0.9963	0.9951	0.9951	0.9953	0.9933	0.9899	0.9893	0.9889	0.9883
66	0.9985	0.9984	0.9982	0.9982	0.9982	0.9981	0.9976	0.9977	0.9967	0.9950	0.9947	0.9945	0.9942
1965	1.0000	1.0000	1.0000	1.0000	1.0000	1.0000	1.0000	1.0000	1.0000	1.0000	1.0000	1.0000	1.0000
64	1.0015	1.0016	1.0017	1.0018	1.0018	1.0018	1.0023	1.0022	1.0033	1.0050	1.0053	1.0055	1.0058
63	1.0029	1.0031	1.0033	1.0036	1.0036	1.0036	1.0046	1.0044	1.0065	1.0100	1.0105	1.0109	1.0115
62	1.0043	1.0046	1.0049	1.0053	1.0053	1.0054	1.0069	1.0065	1.0096	1.0149	1.0157	1.0163	1.0172
61	1.0057	1.0061	1.0065	1.0070	1.0070	1.0072	1.0091	1.0086	1.0127	1.0199	1.0209	1.0217	1.0229
1960	1.0070	1.0075	1.0080	1.0086	1.0086	1.0089	1.0113	1.0107	1.0157	1.0248	1.0260	1.0270	1.0285
59	1.0083	1.0089	1.0095	1.0102	1.0102	1.0106	1.0135	1.0127	1.0186	1.0297	1.0311	1.0323	1.0341
58	1.0096	1.0102	1.0109	1.0117	1.0117	1.0122	1.0156	1.0147	1.0214	1.0345	1.0361	1.0375	1.0396
57	1.0108	1.0115	1.0123	1.0132	1.0132	1.0138	1.0176	1.0166	1.0241	1.0393	1.0411	1.0426	1.0449
56	1.0120	1.0128	1.0137	1.0146	1.0146	1.0154	1.0196	1.0185	1.0268	1.0440	1.0460	1.0477	1.0501
55	1.0131	1.0140	1.0151	1.0160	1.0160	1.0169	1.0216	1.0204	1.0295	1.0486	1.0508	1.0527	1.0552
54	1.0142	1.0152	1.0164	1.0173	1.0173	1.0184	1.0235	1.0222	1.0322	1.0532	1.0556	1.0576	1.0602
53	1.0153	1.0163	1.0177	1.0186	1.0186	1.0198	1.0253	1.0240	1.0348	1.0578	1.0604	1.0624	1.0652
52	1.0163	1.0174	1.0189	1.0198	1.0199	1.0212	1.0270	1.0257	1.0374	1.0623	1.0651	1.0673	1.0701
51	1.0173	1.0185	1.0201	1.0210	1.0211	1.0225	1.0286	1.0274	1.0398	1.0668	1.0698	1.0721	1.0750

1950	1.0183	1.0196	1.0212	1.0222	1.0223	1.0238	1.0302	1.0291	1.0421	1.0712	1.0744	1.0769	1.0798
49	1.0193	1.0207	1.0223	1.0234	1.0235	1.0250	1.0318	1.0308	1.0443	1.0754	1.0789	1.0816	1.0846
48	1.0203	1.0217	1.0234	1.0245	1.0246	1.0262	1.0333	1.0324	1.0464	1.0795	1.0832	1.0862	1.0893
47	1.0212	1.0227	1.0245	1.0256	1.0257	1.0273	1.0348	1.0340	1.0485	1.0835	1.0874	1.0907	1.0939
46	1.0221	1.0237	1.0255	1.0266	1.0267	1.0284	1.0363	1.0356	1.0506	1.0875	1.0916	1.0951	1.0984
1945	1.0230	1.0246	1.0265	1.0276	1.0277	1.0295	1.0378	1.0371	1.0526	1.0915	1.0958	1.0994	1.1028
40	1.0272	1.0290	1.0312	1.0326	1.0327	1.0348	1.0444	1.0442	1.0635	1.1106	1.1157	1.1200	1.1243
35	1.0312	1.0332	1.0357	1.0374	1.0375	1.0399	1.0509	1.0511	1.0741	1.1290	1.1346	1.1396	1.1451
30	1.0351	1.0373	1.0401	1.0420	1.0421	1.0448	1.0572	1.0577	1.0844	1.1467	1.1532	1.1589	1.1655
25	1.0389	1.0413	1.0444	1.0463	1.0465	1.0496	1.0633	1.0641	1.0942	1.1642	1.1715	1.1779	1.1858
20	1.0426	1.0452	1.0486	1.0506	1.0509	1.0543	1.0692	1.0703	1.1038	1.1818	1.1899	1.1970	1.2062
15	1.0462	1.0490	1.0527	1.0549	1.0552	1.0589	1.0751	1.0765	1.1132	1.1996	1.2085	1.2163	1.2269
10	1.0497	1.0527	1.0567	1.0591	1.0594	1.0634	1.0809	1.0827	1.1226	1.2177	1.2274	1.2359	1.2480
5	1.0531	1.0563	1.0606	1.0633	1.0636	1.0678	1.0866	1.0888	1.1320	1.2262	1.2468	1.2560	1.2696
1900	1.0564	1.0599	1.0645	1.0674	1.0677	1.0722	1.0923	1.0949	1.1414	1.2450	1.2665	1.2764	1.2916
1895	1.0596	1.0634	1.0683	1.0714	1.0717	1.0766	1.0979	1.1009	1.1508	1.2740	1.2864	1.2970	1.3139
90	1.0628	1.0669	1.0721	1.0753	1.0757	1.0809	1.1034	1.1069	1.1602	1.2933	1.3067	1.3181	1.3366
85	1.0659	1.0703	1.0758	1.0792	1.0796	1.0852	1.1089	1.1129	1.1696	1.3129	1.3273	1.3395	1.3596
80	1.0689	1.0736	1.0794	1.0830	1.0834	1.0895	1.1144	1.1188	1.1789	1.3327	1.3482	1.3613	1.3830
C.V.	5.95	6.36	6.86	717	7.20	7.73	9.88	10.26	15.45	28.72	30.06	31.19	33.06

NOTE: The Time Factor for the Decathlon is assumed as being the *average* of the Time Factors in the 10 track and field events of which it is composed. This makes it 1.2043 in the year 1880, or practically two-thirds (%) of the variability in the Shot Put. Thus the C.V. in the Decathlon is about 17.63.

In the women's Pentathlon, by the same method of averaging, the Time Factor for the year 1880 is 1.1866, and the C.V. about 16.11.

Table 28. Ratings of Top-Ranking Performers in Track and Field Events (Men)

(P)=Professional. Note: Height and bodyweight are listed only in those events in which they are important contributing factors.

Event	Performer	Nation	Height, in.	Body-weight, lbs.	Year	Performance Actual	Performance Corrected as of 1965	Rating, points
100 Yard Dash	(P) R. P. Williams	USA			1906	9.0 sec.	8.552 sec.	1047
" " "	William Curtis	USA			1968	10.0 "	8.743 "	1017
" " "	George Anderson	USA			1935	(P?) 9.2 "	(8.922 ")	(988)
" " "	Arthur Duffey	USA			1902	(P?) 9.5 "	(9.004)	975
" " "	Jesse Owens	USA			1935	(9.35) "	9.067 "	965
" " "	Robert Hayes	USA			1963	9.1 "	9.074 "	964
" " "	George Simpson	USA			1929	9.4 "	9.075 "	964
220 Yard Dash	(P) R. P. Williams	USA			1906	20.4 sec.	19.326 sec.	1011
" " "	Harold Davis	USA			1941	(20.0) "	(19.453) "	1002
" " "	Ralph Metcalfe	USA			1934	(20.3) "	(19.631) "	991
" " "	Roland Locke	USA			1926	20.5 "	19.702 "	986
" " "	Melvin Patton	USA			1949	(20.2) "	19.790 "	980
" " "	John Carlos	USA			1968	19.7 (200 m)	19.799 "	980
400 Meter Dash	Lee Evans	USA			1968	43.8 sec.	44.038 sec.	968
" " "	Larry James	USA			1968	43.9 "	44.138 "	965
440 Yard Dash	Ben Eastman	USA			1932	46.4	44.687 sec.	962
" "	Adolph Plummer	USA			1963	44.9 "	44.752 "	960
800 Meter Run	Rudolf Harbig	Germany			1939	1:46.6	1:43.20	971
880 Yard Run	Peter Snell	New Zealand			1962	1:45.1	1:44.54	965
1500 Meter Run	Herbert Elliott	Australia			1958	3:36.0	3:33.42	959
" "	Jim Ryun	USA			1967	3:33.1	3:33.92	957

Event	Name	Country	Year	Record	Converted	Points
1 Mile Run	Herbert Elliott	Australia	1958	3:54.5	3:51.67	955
" "	Jim Ryun	USA	1966	3:51.3	3:51.74	955
" "	Walter George	Australia	1885	4:12.75	3:52.90	950
Marathon	Clarence De Mar	USA	1922	2:18:10.0	2:09:39.2	956
"	Derek Clayton	Gt. Brit.	1969	2:08:33.6	2:09:57.8	954
"	Frank Zuna	USA	1921	2:18:57.6	2:10:06.7	953
110 Meter Hurdles	Martin Lauer	Australia	1959	13.2 sec.	13.067 sec.	971
" "	Lee Calhoun	USA	1960	13.2 "	13.087 "	970
" "	Richard Attlesey	Germany	1950	13.5 "	13.207 "	959
" "	Forrest Towns	USA	1936	13.7 "	13.218 "	959
" "	Fred Wolcott	USA	1940	13.7 "	13.268 "	954
400 Meter Hurdles	David Hemery	USA	1968	48.1 sec.	48.371 sec.	971
" "	Gerhardus Potgieter	Gt. Brit.	1960	49.0 "	48.582 "	967
" "	Glenn Davis	So. Africa	1968	49.2 "	48.631 "	965
" "	Glenn Hardin	USA	1934	50.6 "	48.733 "	963
" "	Salvatore Morale	USA	1962	49.2 "	48.941 "	959
" "	Edward Southern	Italy	1956	49.7 "	48.985 "	958
High Jump	(P) Robert Baker	USA	1898	6 ft. 8¼ in.	7.6458 ft.	1013
" "	(P) John Higgins	Gt. Brit.	(1902)	(6 ft. 8 in.)	7.5840 "	1002
" "	Valeri Brumel	Gt. Brit.	1962	7 ft. 5½ in.	7.5535 "	998
" "	Clinton Larson	USSR	1924	6 ft. 9½ in.	7.4444 "	980
" "	John Thomas	USA	1960	7 ft. 3¾ in.	7.3989 "	972
" "	Michael Sweeney	USA	1895	6 ft. 5⅝ in.	7.3963 "	972
Pole Vault	John Pennel	USA	1966	17 ft. 7 in.	17.4954 ft.	975 (17 ft. 10¾ in.)
" "	Robert Seagren	USA	1968	17 ft. 9 in.	17.4784 "	974 (in 1969=975)
" "	Paul Wilson	USA	1967	17 ft. 7¾ in.	17.4676 "	974

Table 28. Ratings of Top-Ranking Performers in Track and Field Events (Men)—Cont'd.

(P) = Professional. Note: Height and bodyweight are listed only in those events in which they are important contributing factors.

Event	Performer	Nation	Height, in.	Body-weight, lbs.	Year	Performance: Actual	Performance: Corrected as of 1965	Rating, points
" "	Claus Schiprowski	W. Ger.			1968	17 ft. 8½ in.	17.4375 "	972
" "	Wolfgang Nordwig	E. Ger.			1968	17 ft. 8½ in.	17.4375 "	972
" "	Fred Hansen	USA			1964	17 ft. 4 in.	17.4200 "	971
" "	Herve D' Encausse	France			1968	17 ft. 7⅜ in.	17.3455 "	968
" "	Cornelius Warmerdam	USA			1942	15 ft. 8½ in.	17.3263 "	967
Long Jump	Robert Beamon	USA			1968	29 ft. 2½ in.	29.0067 ft.	1041
" "	Jesse Owens	USA			1935	26 ft. 8¼ in.	28.0512 "	1002
" "	Chuhei Nambu	Japan			1931	26 ft. 2¼ in.	27.6645 "	985
" "	Eulace Peacock	USA			1935	26 ft. 3 in.	27.5914 "	982
" "	Silvio Cator	Haiti			1928	26 ft. 0¼ in.	27.5874 "	982
" "	De Hart Hubbard	USA			1925	25 ft. 10⅞ in.	27.5668 "	981
Triple Jump	Daniel Ahearne	USA			1911	50 ft. 11 in.	57.0623 ft.	985
" "	Josef Schmidt	Poland			1960	55 ft. 10½ in.	56.7522 "	978
" "	Viktor Saneyev	USSR			1968	57 ft. 0¾ in.	56.4805 "	973
" "	Naoto Tajima	Japan			1936	52 ft. 6 in.	56.2800 "	969
" "	Nelson Prudencio	Brazil			1968	56 ft. 8 in.	56.0887 "	965
Shot Put	(P) R. P. Williams	USA	69.1	160	1905	47 ft. 9 in.	59.924 ft.	1012
" "	Randel Matson	USA	78.5	258	1967	71 ft. 5½ in.	70.450 "	990
" "	Arthur Rowe	Gt. Brit.	73.75	220.5	1961	64 ft. 2 in.	65.595 "	971
" "	William Nieder	USA	75.0	242	1960	65 ft. 10 in.	67.544 "	970
" "	Charles Fonville	USA	73.5	195	1948	58 ft. 0⅜ in.	63.032 "	964
" "	(P) Donald Dinnie	Scotland	72.5	218	1867	45 ft. 7 in.	63.858 "	959
" "	(P) Charles MacLean	Scotland	70.0	168	1899	(44 ft. 10 in.)	57.307 "	949
Discus Throw	Jay Silvester	USA	74.5	230	1968	224 ft. 5 in.	220.428 ft.	1002

Event	Name	Country			Year		Metric	Points
"	Edmund Piatkowski	Poland	71.75	198	1959	198 ft. 4½ in.	205.348 "	999
"	Fortune Gordien	USA	72.75	220	1953	194 ft. 6 in.	206.975 "	978
"	Willi Schröder	Germany	72.5	192	1935	174 ft. 2½ in.	198.927 "	972 (unoff. 180-5½" = 1000)
"	Ludvik Danek	Czech.	76.0	231	1966	216 ft. 9 in.	215.181 "	969
Javelin Throw	Jorma Kinnunen	Finland	68.9	165	1969	304 ft. 1½ in.	297.425 ft.	1040
"	Albert Cantello	USA	67.5	168	1959	282 ft. 3½ in.	293.632 "	1032
"	Yrjö Nikkanen	Finland	70.5	170	1938	258 ft. 2½ in.	293.111 "	1004
"	Janis Lusis	USSR	71.0	185	1968	301 ft. 9½ in.	296.949 "	984
"	Egil Danielsen	Norway	71.75	185	1956	281 ft. 2½ in.	295.535 "	975
"	E. L. McKenzie	USA	72.0	195	1936	264 ft. 0 in.	301.352 "	975
"	Terje Pedersen	Norway	75.25	181	1966	300 ft. 11 in.	298.197 "	963
Hammer Throw	Takeo Sugawara	Japan	68.5	170	1963	222 ft. 2½ in.	225.795 ft.	1033
"	Gyula Zsivotsky	Hungary	74.75	210	1965	241 ft. 11 in.	241.526 "	983
"	Noburu Okamoto	Japan	69.8	186	1961	218 ft. 1½ in.	223.543 "	987
"	Stanislav Nyenashev	USSR	67.0	c. 200	1954	210 ft. 1½ in.	200.149 "	983
56 lb. Weight Throw	John Flanagan	USA	71 ?	210 ?	1907	38 ft. 8 in.	48.164 ft.	(1000)
"	Matt McGrath	USA	71.75	248	1911	40 ft. 6⅝ in.	49.761 "	985
"	George Frenn	USA	71.5	242	1967	48 ft. 0¾ in.	47.728 "	961
"	Robert Backus	USA	76.0	200	1957	44 ft. 8½ in.	46.494 "	951
"	Patrick McDonald	USA	72.0	250	1911	38 ft. 9⅞ in.	47.658 "	950
Decathlon	Rafer Johnson	USA			1960			981
" (=.115)	C. K. Yang	China			1963			975
" x points	Hans Sievert	Germany			1934			970
" listed	Phil Mulkey	USA			1961			962
" in Table	Yuriy Kutyenko	USSR			1961			961
" 19)	Vasily Kuznetsov	USSR			1959			957

Table 29. *Ratings of Top-Ranking Performers in Track and Field Events (Women)*

Event	Performer	Nation	Height, in.	Body-weight, lbs.	Year	Performance		Rating, points
						Actual	Corrected as of 1965	
100 Yard Dash	Marjorie Nelson	Australia			1953	10.3 sec.	10.145 sec.	963
" "	Helen Stephens	USA			1937	10.5 "	10.198 "	957
" "	Marlene Willard	Australia			1958	10.3 "	10.202 "	956
100 Meter Dash	Wyomia Tyus	USA			1968	11.0 sec.	11.052 sec.	965
" "	Diane Matheson	Canada			1956	11.2 "	11.067 "	964
" "	Wilma Rudolph	USA			1961	11.2 "	11.136 "	956
" "	Barbara Ferrell	USA			1967	11.1 "	11.135 "	956
" "	Irina Szewinska	Poland			1968	11.1 "	11.152 "	954
220 Yard Dash (turn)	Irina Szewinska	Poland			1968	22.6 sec.	22.757 sec.	200 m. x 1.0058 — 964
" " " "	Margaret Burvill	Australia			1964	22.9 "	22.861 "	960
" " " "	Wilma Rudolph	USA			1960	(23.1) "	22.900 "	958
" " " "	Nancy Boyle	Australia			1968	22.8 "	22.959 "	200 m. x 1.0058 — 956
" " " "	Betty Cuthbert	Australia			1960	23.2 "	23.027 "	952
400 Meter Dash	Sin Kim Dan	N. Korea			1964	51.2 sec.	51.133 sec.	964
440 Yard Dash	Betty Cuthbert	Australia			1964	(52.4) sec.	52.301 sec.	400 m. x 1.0075 — 947
" "	Judy Pollock	Australia			1965	52.4 "	52.400 "	945
800 Meter Run	Sin Kim Dan	N. Korea			1964	1:58.0	1:57.83	970
880 Yard Run	Dixie Willis	Australia			1962	2:02.0	2:01.35	950
" "	Vera Nikolic	Yugo.			1968	2:01.3	2:01.42	800 m. x 1.0076 — 949

Event	Name	Country	Year	Performance	Performance	Points
1500 Meter Run	P. Pigni	Italy	1969	4:12.4	4:14.50	972
" "	Marise Stephen	New Zealand	1962	4:19.0	4:17.63	963
1 Mile Run	Anne Smith	Gt. Brit.	1967	4:37.0	4:38.14	967
" "	Marise Stephen	New Zealand	1962	4:41.4	4:39.89	962
" "	Doris Brown	USA	1967	4:40.4	4:41.50	957
Marathon	Anni Pede-Erdkamp	W. Ger.	1967	3:07:26.2	3:10:07.8	990
"	Mildred Sampson	New Zealand	1964	3:19:33.0	3:19:05.0	962
"	Roberta Gibb	USA	1966	3:21:30.0	3:23:06.5	947
80 Meter Hurdles	Vyera Korsakova	USSR	1968	10.2 sec.	10.257 sec.	969
"	Irina Press	USSR	1965	10.3 "	10.300 "	965
"	Pamela Kilborn	Australia	1965	10.3 "	10.300 "	965
"	Maureen Caird	Australia	1968	10.3 "	10.358 "	959
100 Meter Hurdles	Valentina Bolshova	USSR	1966	13.0 sec.	13.023 sec.	980
"	K. Balzer	E. Ger.	1969	12.9 "	12.995 "	972
"	Niliya Kulkova	USSR	1963	13.3 "	13.252 "	963
"	Mary Rand	Gt. Brit.	1963	13.3 "	13.252 "	963
High Jump	Iolanda Balas	Rumania	1961	6 ft. 3¾ in.	6.3504 ft.	1013
"	Micheline Brown	Australia	1964	6 ft. 0¾ in.	6.0407 "	952
"	R. Schmidt	E. Ger.	1969	6 ft. 1¼ in.	6.0162 "	947
Pole Vault	Diane Bragg	USA	1952	8 ft. 6 in.	9.0296 ft.	745
Long Jump	Tatyana Shchelkanova	USSR	1966	22 ft. 10 in.	22.7805 ft.	989
"	Mary Rand	Gt. Brit.	1964	22 ft. 2¼ in.	22.2363 "	961
"	Vera Viscopoleanu	Rumania	1968	22 ft. 4½ in.	22.2139 "	959

Table 29. Ratings of Top-Ranking Performers in Track and Field Events (WOMEN)

Event	Performer	Nation	Height, in.	Body-weight, lbs.	Year	Performance: Actual	Performance: Corrected as of 1965	Rating, points
Pentathlon	Irina Press	USSR			1964			1000
"	Mary Rand	Gt. Brit.			1964			966
"	Galina Bystrova	USSR			1964			957
Shot Put	Margitta H. Gummel	E. Germany	69.3	178	1969	65 ft. 11¼ in.	64.448 ft.	1013
" "	Galina Zybina	USSR	66.0	183	1964	57 ft. 5 in.	58.013 "	941
" "	Nadezda Chizhova	USSR	68.1	196	1968	61 ft. 3 in.	60.537 "	938
" "	Irina Press	USSR	66.0	150	1965	52 ft. 8⅝ in.	53.048 "	936
" "	Maritta Lange	E. Ger.	71.7	183	1968	61 ft. 7½ in.	60.528 "	936
" "	Judit Bognar	Hungary	68.5	174	1968	58 ft. 8¼ in.	57.663 "	935
" "	Tamara Press	USSR	70.75	217	1965	61 ft. 0 in.	60.822 "	908
Discus Throw	Liesel Westermann	W. Germany	68.0	170	1968	205 ft. 2 in.	201.940 ft.	983
" "	Nina Dumbadze	USSR	70.5	189	1952	187 ft. 1⅝ in.	199.732 "	940
" "	Christine Spielberg	E. Germany	72.5	185	1968	202 ft. 3 in.	198.073 "	926
" "	Yevgenia Kuznyetsova	USSR	69.0	178	1964	187 ft. 7½ in.	188.534 "	923
" "	Anita Henschel-Otto	E. Germany	69.25	187	1966	193 ft. 7⅝ in.	191.893 "	922
" "	Jolán Konsek-Kleiber	Hungary	70.0	179	1965	189 ft. 10 in.	189.589 "	918
" "	Karen Illgen	E. Germany	71.25	196	1968	201 ft. 10¾ in.	197.650 "	914
Javelin Throw	Alevtina Shastitko	USSR	67.0	136	1962	181 ft. 2¼ in.	183.209 ft.	973
" "	Danuta Jaworska	Poland	64.6	139	1968	195 ft. 8 in.	192.106 "	973
" "	Yelena Gorchakova	USSR	65.75	152	1964	204 ft. 8¾ in.	206.362 "	968
" "	ReNae Bair	USA	71.0	139	1967	196 ft. 3 in.	193.954 "	951
" "	Barbara Friedrich	USA	68.1	145	1967	198 ft. 8 in.	196.435 "	950
" "	Elvira Ozolina	USSR	68.75	148	1964	201 ft. 4½ in.	201.795 "	946
" "	Angela Nemeth	Hungary	69.3	143	1968	198 ft. 0⅜ in.	194.219 "	943

C. NEW WORLD AND OLYMPIC RECORDS MADE AT THE 1968 OLYMPIC GAMES

Table 30. New World and Olympic track and field records made at the 1968 Olympic Games, Mexico City (final records only)

MEN

Date	Event	Performer	Nation	Record	Status of Record Olympic	World
10/13	Shot Put	Randel Matson	USA	67 ft. 10¼ in.	*	
10/14	100 Meter Dash	Jim Hines	USA	9.9 sec.	*	=
10/15	800 Meter Run	Ralph Doubell	Australia	1 min. 44.3 sec.	*	=
10/15	400 Meter Hurdles	David Hemery	Gt. Brit.	48.1 sec.	*	*
10/15	Discus Throw	Alfred Oerter	USA	212 ft. 6½ in.	*	
10/16	200 Meter Dash	Tommie Smith	USA	19.8 sec.	*	*
10/16	Pole Vault	Robert Seagren	USA	17 ft. 8½ in.	*	*
	(equalled also by Claus Schiprowski of West Germany and Wolfgang Nordwig of East Germany)					
10/16	Javelin Throw	Janis Lusis	USSR	295 ft. 7¼ in.	=	
10/17	110 Meter Hurdles	William Davenport	USA	13.3 sec.	*	* Erv Hall in semifinals
10/17	Triple Jump	Viktor Saneyev	USSR	57 ft. 0¾ in.	*	*
10/17	Hammer Throw	Gyula Zsivotsky	Hungary	240 ft. 8 in.	*	
10/18	Long Jump	Bob Beamon	USA	29 ft. 2½ in.	*	*
10/18	400 Meter Dash	Lee Evans	USA	43.8 sec.	*	*
10/20	400 Meter Relay	Charles Greene, Mel Pender, Ron Smith, Jim Hines	USA	38.2 sec.	*	*
10/20	1600 Meter Relay	Vince Matthews, Ron Freeman, Larry James, Lee Evans	USA	2 min. 56.1 sec.	*	*
10/20	High Jump	Richard Fosbury	USA	7 ft. 4¼ in.	*	

WOMEN

Date	Event	Performer	Nation	Record	Status of Record Olympic	World
10/14	Long Jump	Victorica Viscopoleanu	Rumania	22 ft. 4½ in.	*	*
10/15	100 Meter Dash	Wyomia Tyus	USA	11.0 sec.	*	*
10/16	400 Meter Dash	Colette Besson	France	52 sec.	=	=
10/18	80 Meter Hurdles	Maureen Caird	Australia	10.3 sec.	*	*
10/18	200 Meter Dash	Irina Szewinska	Poland	22.5 sec.	*	*
10/18	Discus Throw	Lia Manoliu	Rumania	191 ft. 2½ in.	*	
10/19	800 Meter Run	Madeline Manning	USA	2 min. 0.9 sec.	*	*
10/19	400 Meter Relay	Barbara Ferrell, Margaret Bailes, Mildrette Netter, Wyomia Tyus	USA	42.8 sec.	*	*
10/20	Shot Put	Margitta Hemboldt-Gummel	East Ger.	64 ft. 4 in.	*	*

Table 31. *Performances in Men's Track and Field events necessary (as of July 1, 1970) to equal in merit the Long Jump by Bob Beamon (USA) of 29 ft. 2½ in. made in Mexico City on Oct. 18, 1968**

Event	Present Record (as of Sept. 14, 1969)	Performance necessary to equal in rating Beamon's long jump	Height and bodyweight assumed for rating (weight events only)**	Deficiency in Present Record, %
100 yards	9.1 sec.	8.59 sec.	————	5.6
100 meters	9.9 sec.	9.32 sec.	————	5.9
200 meters, st.	19.5 sec.	18.56 sec.	————	4.8
220 yards, st.	19.5 sec.	18.70 sec.	————	4.1
400 meters	43.8 sec.	40.9 sec.	————	6.6
440 yards	44.8 sec.	41.3 sec.	————	7.8
800 meters	1:443.	1:35.5	————	8.4
880 yards	1:44.9	1:36.1	————	8.4
1000 meters	2:16.2	2:04.4	————	8.7
1500 meters	3:33.1	3:13.6	————	9.1
1 mile	3:51.1	3:29.0	————	9.6
2000 meters	4:56.2	4:21.5	————	11.7
3000 meters	7:39.6	6:45.0	————	11.9
2 miles	8:19.6	7:17.2	————	12.5
3 miles	12:50.4	11:18.0	————	12.0

Event					
5000 meters	13:16.6	11:44.2			10.8
6 miles	26:47.0	23:53.8			11.6
10,000 meters	27:39.4	24:49.3			10.3
3000 meter Steeplechase	8:22.2	7:11.3			14.1
Marathon	2:08:33.6	1:51:02.3			13.6
120 yard HH	13.2 sec.	12.09 sec.			8.4
110 meter HH	13.2 sec.	12.12 sec.			8.2
400 meter IH	48.1 sec.	44.8 sec.			6.9
440 yard IH	49.3 sec.	45.0 sec.			8.7
High Jump	7 ft. 5¾ in. (2.28 m)	7 ft. 11½ in. (2.43 m)			6.2
Pole Vault	17 ft. 10¾ in. (5.44 m)	19 ft. 5½ in. (4.94 m)			9.2
Long Jump	29 ft. 2½ in. (8.90 m)	29 ft. 4 in. (8.94 m)			0.0
Triple Jump	57 ft. 0¾ in. (17.39 m)	60 ft. 6 in. (18.44 m)			6.2
Shot Put	71 ft. 5½ in. (21.78 m)	75 ft. 10¾ in. (23.13 m)	78.5 in.,	258 lbs.	5.8
Discus Throw	224 ft. 5 in. (68.40 m)	233 ft. 4½ in. (71.13 m)	74.5 in.,	230 lbs.	3.8
Hammer Throw	244 ft. 6 in. (74.52 m)	264 ft. 6¾ in. (80.64 m)	73.25 in.,	247 lbs.	7.6
Javelin Throw	304 ft. 1½ in. (92.70 m)	307 ft. 0¾ in. (93.58 m)	68.9 in.,	165 lbs.	0.9
56-lb. Wt. Throw	48 ft. 0¾ in. (14.65 m)	52 ft. 4 in. (15.95 m)	71.5 in.,	242 lbs.	8.2

* If Beamon had made his record long jump on July 1, 1970 instead of October 18, 1968, the performance would have a rating of 1038.7 points instead of 1041.5.

** The heights and bodyweights assumed are those of the respective current record holders.

*Table 32. Performances in Women's Track and Field events necessary (as of July 1, 1970) to equal in merit the Shot Put by Margitta Helmboldt-Gummel (E. Germany) of 65 ft. 11¾ in. made in East Berlin on September 11, 1969**

Event	Present Record (as of Sept. 14, 1969)	Performance necessary to equal in rating Frau Gummel's shot put	Height and bodyweight assumed for rating (weight events only)**	Deficiency in Present Record, %
100 yards	10.3 sec.	9.65 sec.	——	6.3
100 meters	11.0 sec.	10.53 sec.	——	4.3
200 meters, T.	22.5 sec.	21.46 sec.	——	4.6
220 yards, T.	22.9 sec.	21.61 sec.	——	5.6
400 meters	51.2 sec.	48.2 sec.	——	5.9
440 yards	52.4 sec.	48.7 sec.	——	7.1
800 meters	1:58.0	1:51.1	——	5.8
880 yards	2:02.0	1:51.9	——	8.3
1000 meters	2:44.7	2:29.1	——	9.5
1500 meters	4:12.4	3:58.3	——	6.0
1 mile	4:37.0	4:19.4	——	6.3
2000 meters	6:09.6	5:33.0	——	9.9
3000 meters	9:48.0	8:53.6	——	9.3

Event				
2 miles	10:26.8	9:38.5		7.7
3 miles	18:17.0	15:10.8		17.0
5000 meters	16:45.0	15:39.6		6.5
6 miles	35:32.0	32:04.5		9.7
10,000 meters	38:06.4	35:17.0		7.4
Marathon	3:07:26.2	3:03:07.0		3.6
80 meter H	10.2 sec.	9.71 sec.		4.8
100 meter H	12.9 sec.	12.45 sec.		3.0
200 meter H	27.1 sec.	25.64 sec.		5.4
High Jump	6 ft. 3¾ in. (1.91 m)	6 ft. 5⅝ in. (1.97 m)		3.0
Long Jump	22 ft. 10 in. (6.96 m)	23 ft. 6½ in. (7.18 m)		3.1
Triple Jump	40 ft. 1 in. (12.22 m)	42 ft. 8½ in. (13.02 m)		6.2
Shot Put	65 ft. 11¼ in. (20.10 m)	66 ft. 3 in. (20.19 m)	69.3 in., 178 lbs.	0.0
Discus Throw	205 ft. 8⅝ in. (62.70 m)	215 ft. 10¼ in. (65.80 m)	67.7 in., 176 lbs.	4.7
Javelin Throw	204 ft. 8½ in. (62.40 m)	224 ft. 10 in. (68.05 m)	65.75 in., 152 lbs.	8.3

* If Frau Gummel had made her record shot put on July 1, 1970 instead of September 11, 1969, the performance would have a rating of 1008.2 points instead of 1013.

** The heights and bodyweights assumed are those of the respective current record holders.

Selected Bibliography

(with some annotations)

WEIGHTLIFTING AND FEATS OF STRENGTH

Aston, E. 1911. *Modern Weightlifting* . . . London. (Includes records of various strong-men, written by Tom Pevier).

Calvert, A. 1911. *The Truth About Weightlifting*. Philadelphia. (Includes numerous records up to 1910).

———— 1924. *Super-Strength*. Philadelphia. (A general review of strong-men and weight-training).

Desbonnet, E. 1910. *La Force Physique*. Paris. (Brief histories and records of leading French amateur and professional strong-men up to 1908).

———— 1911. *Les Rois de la Force*. Paris. (Biographies of several hundred strong-men of all nationalities, up to 1910).

Desaguliers, J. T. 1763. *A Course of Experimental Philosophy*. London. (A scientific account by Dr. Desaguliers, an English physicist, of the phenomenal strength of Thomas Topham, of London).

Dirscherl, J. 1926. *Schwerathletik von 1891–1926*. Berlin. (Records of European champion weightlifters).

Donaldson, C. 1902. *Men of Muscle*. Glasgow. (Biographies of Donald Dinnie and other Scottish athletes).

Guyot-Daubes. 1885. *Les Hommes-Phénomènes*. Paris. (Lists numerous feats of strength, running, swimming, etc.).

Hackenschmidt, George. 1908. *The Way to Live*. London. (An autobiography, including weightlifting records by Hackenschmidt and various contemporaries).

Inch, T. 1921–22. Strong-Men I Have Known. *Health & Strength* (London), Nov. 5, 1921 to Feb. 18, 1922, inclusive.

Maxick (Sick, Max). 1911. *Great Strength by Muscle Control*. London. (Includes Maxick's weightlifting records).

Müller, E. 1951. *Goerner the Mighty*. Leeds, England. (Lists numerous records made by Hermann Görner and other weightlifting record holders).

Murray, J., and Karpovich, P. V. 1965. *Weight Training in Athletics.* Englewood Cliffs, N.J. (A good general treatise, with numerous further references).

Pullum, W. A. 1921. *Weightlifting Made Easy and Interesting.* London. (Includes an autobiography of this remarkable featherweight strongman).

Siebert, T. 1907. *Kraftsport.* Halle, Germany. (Includes biographies and lifting records of old-time German and Austrian champions).

Willoughby, D. P. 1956–63. The Kings of Strength, Alliance, Nebraska: *Iron Man* magazine, May 1956 to April 1963, bimonthly. (An uncompleted series).

(Anonymous). 1923. *Spalding's Official Athletic Almanac.* New York: Amer. Sports Pub. Co. (This edition was one of the last to include a list of old-time records with dumbbells and barbells. It includes also various other feats and events not listed in later editions).

Periodicals

Iron Man (Editor: Peary Rader). Alliance, Nebraska. (The leading American periodical dealing with weightlifting and weight-training. Bi-monthly).

Strength & Health (Editor: Bob Hoffman). York, Pa. (An illustrated monthly on weightlifting and weight-training).

OLYMPIC GAMES

Alexander, C. 1925. *Greek Athletics.* New York: Met. Mus. Art. (32 pp., well illustrated).

Bland, E. A. 1948. *Olympic Story.* London: Rockliff.

Bloch, R. 1968. The Origins of the Olympic Games. *Scientific American,* August 1968, pp. 79–84. (Illustrates the discus throw and the long jump *with weights*).

Gardiner, E. N. 1925. *Olympia: Its History and Remains.* London: Oxford Univ. Press.

———— 1930. *Athletics of the Ancient World.* London: Oxford Univ. Press.

Grenier, H., and Gidley, L. 1932. *Olympic Games, Old and New.* Los Angeles: Am. Printers.

Grombach, J. V. 1956. *Olympic Cavalcade of Sports.* New York: Ballantine Books.

Harlan, H. 1931. *History of the Olympic Games.* Los Angeles: Sports Research Bureau.

Harris, H. A. 1964. *Greek Athletes and Athletics.* London: Hutchinson & Co.

Hyde, W. W. 1921. *Olympic Victor Monuments.* Carnegie Inst. Washington.

Mc Whirter, N. and R. 1967. *Guinness Book of Olympic Records.* New York: Bantam Books.

Osborne, C. (Ed). 1968. *The Olympic Games.* Chicago: Time-Life Books.

Ryan, A. J. 1968. A Medical History of the Olympic Games. *Jour. Amer. Med. Assoc.,* vol. 205, no. 11, pp. 715–720, September 9, 1968.

Schöbel, H. 1966. *The Ancient Olympic Games.* London: Studio Vista.

Stuff, H. S., and Moriarty, L. 1932. *The Story of the Olympic Games.* Los Angeles: Times-Mirror.

MODERN TRACK AND FIELD

(Anonymous). 1965--66. International Amateur Athletic Federation official handbook. London: I.A.A.F.

Amado, F. 1962. *Systéme Rationnel Pour Classer les Performances Athlétiques.* (2 vols). Lisbon: Federacas Portuguese de Athletismo. (The famous "Portuguese" rating tables).

Craig, A. B., Jr. 1968. Limits of the Human Organism: an analysis of world records and Olympic performance. *Jour. Amer. Med. Asso.,* vol. 205, no. 11, pp. 734–740, September 9, 1968.

Doherty, J. K. 1955. *Modern Track and Field.* Englewood Cliffs, N.J.: Prentice-Hall. (Gives ages, heights, weights, and records in men's track and field).

Dyson, G. H. G. 1964. *The Mechanics of Athletics.* 3rd ed. London: Univ. London Press. (An excellent dissertation on techniques, including a bibliography of 37 titles).

Ganslen, R. V. 1963. *The Mechanics of the Pole Vault.* 5th ed. St. Louis: John Swift & Co.

Henry, F. 1955. Prediction of World's Records in Running 65 yards to 26 miles. *Res. Quart. Amer. Phys. Educ. Asso.,* vol. 26, pp. 147–158, May 1955.

Lietzke, M. H. 1952. Running Records. *Scientific American,* August 1952, pp. 52–54. (An interesting and informative graphic analysis).

Hamilton, B. 1935. A Table of the Ultimate of Human Effort. *The Amateur Athletic,* Feb. 1935, p. 3.

Hill, A. V. 1949. The dimensions of animals and their muscular dynamics. *Royal Inst. Great Britain,* pp. 1–24. November 4, 1949.

Loesch, M. 1922. *International Athletic Annual.* Geneva: Argus Athlétique. (Lists many early-day athletic records that are difficult to locate elsewhere).

Meade, G. P. 1966. *Athletic Records: The Whys and Wherefores.* New York: Vantage Press.

Menke, F. G. 1969. *Encyclopedia of Sports.* New York: A. S. Barnes & Co. 4th Rev. ed. (An invaluable compilation of histories and records in all sports).

Mortensen, J. P., and Cooper, J. M. 1959. *Track and Field for Coach and Athlete.* London: Prentice-Hall. (Analyzes and pictures all the main track and field events).

Quercetani, R. L. 1964. *A World History of Track and Field Athletics, 1864–1964.* London: Oxford Univ. Press. (An indispensable source of statistical information).

——— (Ed). 1966. *World Sports International Athletic Annual.* The Blackburn (England) Times.

Richardson, A. 1962. *Archie's Little Black Book.* Los Angeles: Rich-Burn Pub. Co. (Gives *successive* records of various champion track and field athletes).

Seaton, D. C., et al. 1965. *Physical Education Handbook.* Englewood Cliffs, N.J.: Prentice-Hall, Inc. (Covers many sports for both sexes).

Slocum, D. B., and James, S. L. 1968. Biomechanics of Running. *Jour. Amer. Med. Asso.,* vol. 205, no. 11, pp. 721–728, September 9, 1968. (A comprehensive, illustrated analysis of the kinesiology of running).

Willoughby, D. P. 1931. How Much Faster Can Sprinters Travel? Ann Arbor, Mich.: *Jour. Health & Phys. Educ.,* vol. 2, no. 9, pp. 34–36, 46–47. Nov. 1931.

——— 1950. How Fast Can a Horse Run? Colorado Springs: *The Western Horseman,* vol. 15, no. 2, pp. 12–13, February 1950. (Charts the respective running speeds of man, racehorse, and greyhound).

GENERAL AND MISCELLANEOUS

Councilman, J. 1968. *The Science of Swimming.* Englewood Cliffs, N.J.: Prentice-Hall. (Perhaps the best single book on training for speed swimming).

Depping, G. 1873. *Wonders of Bodily Strength and Skill.* London. (Interesting and informative accounts of early-day boxing, wrestling, track and field, archery, gymnastics, acrobatics, skating, swimming and diving, and even boomerang-throwing!)

Draeger, D. F., and Smith, R. W. 1969. *Asian Fighting Arts.* Tokyo and Palo Alto: Kodansha International, Ltd. (Indian wrestling).

Edgren, R. 1926. The Big Fellow (Jim Jeffries). *Liberty,* for the seven weekly issues from July 31 to September 11, 1926, inclusive.

Fleischer, N. 1936. *From Milo to Londos.* The story of wrestling through the ages. New York: C. J. O'Brien, Inc.

Gould, G. M., and Pyle, W. L. 1937. *Anomalies and Curiosities of Medicine*. New York: Sydenham. (First edition, 1896). Includes about twenty pages on Athletics, etc.

Hackenschmidt, G. 1911. *Complete Science of Wrestling*. London: Health & Strength.

Harvey, C. (Ed). 1966. *Almanack of Sport*. London: Sampson Low. (An encyclopedia of sports from the British point of view. Includes some 2000 illustrations).

Jones, R. 1945. *The Bob Jones Books*. No. 2: Hand Balancing, by Jones and Paulinetti. Philadelphia: Published by Bob Jones. (A comprehensive instruction-book on handstanding, hand-to-hand, and other forms of balancing).

Kent, G. 1968. *A Pictorial History of Wrestling*. Feltham, England: Spring Books.

Litsky, F., and Tyno, S. 1967. *The New York Times Official Sports Record Book*. New York: Bantam Books. (A review of practically all sports records made during 1967).

May, E. C. 1932. *The Circus from Rome to Ringling*. New York: Duffield and Green. (Includes accounts of old-time circus leapers and somersaulters).

McWhirter, N. and R. 1967. *Guinness Book of World Records*. New York: Bantam Books.

Meany, Tom. 1953. *Baseball's Greatest Players*. New York: Grosset & Dunlap.

Muzumdar, S. 1942. *Strong Men Over the Years*. Lucknow, India: Oudh Printing Works. (Indian wrestlers).

Naughton, W. W. 1921. *Two-Fisted Jeff* (Jim Jeffries).

Reichler, J. 1958. *Joe Reichler's Book of Great Baseball Records*. New York: Dell Pub. Co.

Umminger, W. 1963. (Translated from the German, by James Clark). *Supermen, Heroes and Gods*. The story of sport through the ages. New York: McGraw-Hill.

WOMEN'S ATHLETICS

Amado, F. 1962. *Systéme Rationnel Pour Classer les Performances Athlétiques*. (Vol. II includes tables for rating women's track and field performances).

Mengoni, L. 1966. The A.T.F.S. (Association of Track and Field Statisticians) Handbook on women's track and field. (Lists progressive performances by women in all track and field events).

Miller, K. D. 1964. *Track and Field for Girls*. New York: The Ronald Press Co.

Pallett, G. 1955. *Women's Athletics*. Dulwich, England: Normal Press.

Pozzoli, P. 1969. *Women's Track and Field Yearbook*. Claremont, Calif.: Women's Track and Field World. (An indispensable reference work on women's track and field records).

Pugh, D. I., and Watts, D. C. V. 1962. *Athletics for Women*. London: Stanley Paul & Co., Ltd.

Quercetani, R. L. 1966. *World Sports International Athletics Annual*. The Blackburn (England) Times. (Includes world and national T and F records by women).

Seaton, D. C., et al. 1965. *Physical Education Handbook*. Englewood Cliffs, N.J.: Prentice-Hall, Inc. (Covers many sports for both sexes).

(Anonymous). 1955. *Scoring Table for Women's Track and Field Events*. London: International Amateur Athletic Federation.

Sources of Illustrations

APC = Author's personal collection of photographs, drawings, and clippings.

Frontispiece: APC.

Plate 1: 1, 2, Louvre; 3, 4, APC; 5, *Les Rois de la Force* (Paris).

Plate 2: 6, G. Depping; 7, 8, 9, 10, *Health & Strength* (London).

Plate 3: 11, 12, 13, *Les Rois de la Force* (Paris).

Plate 4: 14, 16, APC; 15, *The Police Gazette* (New York).

Plate 5: 17, 18, 19, APC; 20, Ottley Coulter (Lemont Furnace, Pa.).

Plate 6: 21, 22, N. Sarony (N.Y.); 23, *The Police Gazette* (N.Y.); 24, Warwick Brookes (Manchester, Eng.).

Plate 7: 25, APC.

Plate 8: 26, 27, Tromp van Diggelen (Cape Town); 28, 29, APC.

Plate 9: 30, 31, 32, 33, APC.

Plate 10: 34, 35, Hermann Saxon (Leipzig).

Plate 11: 36, APC; 37, Hermann Saxon (Leipzig).

Plate 12: 38, 39, 40, APC.

Plate 13: 41, 42, 43, 44, APC.

Plate 14: 45, 46, 47, 48, Tromp van Diggelen (Cape Town).

Plate 15: 49, Edgar Müller (Braunschweig, Ger.); 50, 51, Tromp van Diggelen (Cape Town).

Plate 16: 52, 53, 54, APC.

Plate 17: 55, APC.

Plate 18: 56, Douglas Hepburn (Vancouver, B.C.).

Plate 19: 57, APC.

Plate 20: 58, *Lifting News* (Alliance, Neb.).

Plate 21: 59, 60, *Lifting News* (Alliance, Neb.) and Frost.

Plate 22: 61, APC.

Plate 23: 62, Stanislaw Zakozewski (Warsaw, Poland).

Plate 24: 63, Leo Stern (San Diego, Calif.).

Plate 25: 64, Bruce Conners (Los Angeles, Calif.).

Plate 26: 65, Rosenkranz.

Plate 27: 66, David Webster (Glasgow); 67, Swiss Studios (Melbourne); 68, APC; 69, Pearl and Stern (San Diego, Calif.).

Plate 28: 70, APC; 71, Tromp van Diggelen (Cape Town); 72, David Webster (Glasgow).

Plate 29: 73, APC; 74, 75, "Mac" Batchelor (Los Angeles, Calif.).

Plate 30: 76, APC.

Plate 31: 76a, Iron Man (Alliance, Neb.).

Plate 32: 77, *Les Rois de la Force* (Paris).

Plate 33: 78, 79, APC; 80, 81, *Les Rois de la Force* (Paris).

Plate 34: 82, *Les Rois de la Force* (Paris); 83, APC.

Plate 35: 84, 85, Siegmund Klein (New York).

Plate 36: 86, *Strand Magazine* (London); 87, 88, 89, Al Treloar (Los Angeles, Calif.).

Plate 37: 90, Logue (Pine Bluffs, Ark.).

Plate 38: 91, Bob Jones (Philadelphia); 92, Ottley Coulter (Lemont Furnace, Pa.); 93, 94, APC.

Plate 39: 95, *Skill* magazine (Blackpool, Eng.); 96, APC.

Plate 40: 96a, 96b, Joe Mahalic (Los Angeles, Calif.).

Plate 41: 97, APC; 98, Siegmund Klein (New York).

Plate 42: 98a, Skill magazine (Blackpool, Eng.).

Plate 43: 99, APC; 100, "Mac" Batchelor (Los Angeles, Calif.).

Plate 44: 101, APC.

Plate 45: 101a, 102, José Meiffret (Perthes, France).

Plate 46: 103, *Health & Strength* (London).

Plate 47: 104, 105, APC.

Plate 48: 106, Marjorie F. Williams (Niagara Falls, N.Y.).

Plate 49: 107, Art Allwine (Los Angeles, Calif.); 108, APC.

Plate 50: 109, APC.

Plate 51: 110, Museo delle Terme (Rome).

Plate 52: 111, APC.

Plate 53: 112, Al Nelson (Bellflower, Calif.).

Plate 54: 113, Al Nelson (Bellflower, Calif.).

Plate 55: 114, Al Nelson (Bellflower, Calif.).

Plate 56: 115, Al Nelson (Bellflower, Calif.).

Plate 57: 116, 117, Munich Museum.

Plate 58: 118, *Asia* magazine (New York).

Plate 59: 119, 120, 121, APC.

Plate 60: 122, *The Police Gazette* (New York); 123, APC.

Plate 61: 124, APC.

Plate 62: 125, 126, 127, APC.

Plate 63: 128, APC.

Plate 64: 128a, Pittsburgh Baseball Club.

Plate 65: 129, Acme (New York).

Plate 66: 130, Paul Thompson (New York).

Plate 67: 131, 132, Paul Thompson (New York).

Plate 68: 133, 134, American Badminton Association (Pasadena, Calif.).
Plate 69: 135, APC.
Plate 70: 136, APC.
Plate 71: 137, Glyptothek Museum (Munich).
Plate 72: 138, National Museum, Naples.
Plate 73: 139, George Frenn (North Hollywood, Calif.).
Plate 74: 140, 140a, APC.
Plate 75: 141, Carl W. Williams (Springfield, Ohio).
Plate 76: 142, APC.
Plate 77: 143, APC.
Plate 78: 144, Siegmund Klein (New York).
Plate 79: 145, 146, 147, *Skill* magazine (Blackpool, Eng.).
Plate 80: 148, APC.
Plate 81: 149, 150, APC.
Plate 82: 151, APC.
Plate 83: 152, APC.
Plate 84: 153, *Iron Man* (Alliance, Neb.).
Plate 85: 154, *Skill* magazine (Blackpool, Eng.).
Plate 86: 155, APC.
Plate 87: 156, Wayne Drumheller (Petaluma, Calif.).
Plate 88: 157, Pete Pozzoli (Enfield Lock, Eng.).

Name Index

* Name in Footnote

633

Subject Index

Addenda

(These entries are not included in the indexes)

A. WEIGHTLIFTING—OLYMPIC LIFTS (AS OF MAY, 1970)

Press

MEN

	Name and Nation	Kilos	Lbs.
(114) Flyweight class	V. Krishishin (USSR)	113.5	250
(123) Bantamweight Class	R. Belenkov (USSR)	122.5	270
(132) Featherweight Class	I. Földi (Hungary)	131.5	289¾
(148) Lightweight Class	N. Dehnavi (Iran)	146	321¾
(181) Light-heavyweight Class	H. Bettenberg (Sweden)	174.5	384½
(198) Middle-heavyweight Class	S. Poltoratskii (USSR)	182	401¼
(242) Heavyweight Class	V. Yakubovskii (USSR)	195	429¾
(over 242) Super-hvy. Class	S. Reding (Belgium)	218.5	481½

Snatch

(132) Featherweight Class	Y. Miyake (Japan)	125.5	276½
(148) Lightweight Class	W. Baszanowski (Poland)	136	299¾
(181) Light-heavyweight Class	M. Ohuchi (Japan)	152.5	336
(198) Middle-heavyweight Class	K. Kangasniemi (Finland)	161	354¾
(242) Heavyweight Class	K. Utsar (USSR)	165	363¾

Jerk

(114) Flyweight Class	V. Krishishin (USSR)	128.5	283¼
(132) Featherweight Class	Y. Miyake (Japan)	153	337¼
(148) Lightweight Class	W. Baszanowski (Poland)	170.5	375¾
(181) Light-heavyweight Class	G. Ivanchenko (USSR)	191.5	422
(198) Middle-heavyweight Class	V. Kolotov (USSSR)	200.5	442
(242) Heavyweight Class	Y. Talts (USSR)	212.5	468¼
(over 242) Super-hvy. Class	V. Alekseev (USSR)	223.5	491½

Total

(114) Flyweight Class	V. Krishishin (USSR) Smetanin (USSR)	337.5	744
(123) Bantamweight Class	I. Földi (Hungary)	370	815½
(148) Lightweight Class	W. Baszanowski (Poland)	445	981
(181) Light-heavyweight Class	G. Ivanchenko (USSR)	500	1102¼
(198) Middle-heavyweight Class	K. Kangasniemi (Finland)	530	1168¼
(242) Heavyweight Class	J. Talts (USSR)	550	1212½
(over 242) Super-hvy. Class	V. Alekseev (USSR)	607.5	1339¼

B. WEIGHTLIFTING—POWER LIFTS
(AMERICAN RECORDS AS OF FEBRUARY, 1970)*

Bench Press

	Name and Place	Lbs.
(165) Middleweight Class	Joseph Leonardis, Boston	390½
(over 242) Super-hvy. Class	James Williams	628

Squat

(123) Bantamweight Class	Dave Moyer, Reading, Pa.	464½
(148) Lightweight Class	Thomas LaFontaine, Detroit	488
(165) Middleweight Class	J. B. Adams	550
(198) Middle-heavyweight Class	Jack Barnes, Phoenix, Ariz.	720
(242) Heavyweight Class	George Frenn, N. Hollywood, Calif.	765

Dead Lift

(over 242) Super-hvy. Class	Don Cundy, Winona, Minn.	801½

Sit-ups
15,011 consecutive sit-ups, by John Greenshields, Tampa, Florida, on June 6, 1966. Time, "less than 6 hours."

Chinning the Bar
106 consecutive pull-ups with both arms, by William D. Reed, University of Pennsylvania, June 23, 1969.

C. BASEBALL

In 1969, Steve Carlton, pitcher, struck out 19 men in a nine-inning game, breaking the record of 18 made by Bob Feller in 1938 and tied later by Sandy Koufax (twice) and by Don Wilson.

In 1970, Tom Seaver equalled Carlton's record of 19 strikeouts in nine innings. In the same game, Seaver set a new record with 10 successive strikeouts, breaking the record of 9 straight which had stood for 86 years! At the moment of publication, it seems certain that Tom Seaver's 1970 record will place him among the "greatest modern pitchers" as listed on page 405. On July 25, 1970, having pitched 189 innings, his rating was .819, which if maintained would place him fifteenth.

D. TENNIS

In 1970, Margaret Smith (Mrs. Margaret Court) won the Australian

---

* Late in 1969, John Citrone of England did a bench press of 490 pounds at a body-weight of 175 pounds.

women's singles championship for the ninth time (see table of listings on page 417). She also won the French singles championship and the English (Wimbledon) singles championship, thus equalling Helen Wills's record of 19 wins in the four major singles championships.

E. WORLD SPEED SKATING RECORDS

MEN

Distance	Time	Name and Nation	Place	Date
500 meters	39.2	Erhard Keller (W. Ger.)	Inzell, West Ger.	Jan. 28, 1968
	39.2	Anatolyi Lepeshkin (USSR)	Alma Ata, USSR	Jan. 26, 1969
	39.2	Keichi Suzuki (Japan)	Inzell, West Ger.	Mar. 1, 1969
	38.8	Anatolyi Lepeshkin (USSR)	Medeo, USSR	Feb. 7, 1969
1000 meters	1:19.5	I. Eriksen (Norway)	Inzell, West Ger.	Mar. 1, 1969
1500 meters	2:02.2	Cees Verkerk (Neth.)	Davos, Switz.	Feb. 9, 1969
3000 meters	4:17.4	Dag Fornaess (Norway)	Cortina, Italy	Jan. 29, 1969
5000 meters	7:13.2	Cees Verkerk (Neth.)	Inzell, West Ger.	Mar. 1, 1969
10,000 meters	15:03.6	Cees Verkerk (Neth.)	Inzell, West Ger.	Jan. 28, 1969

WOMEN

Distance	Time	Name and Nation	Place	Date
500 meters	44.4	V. Krasnova (USSR)	Yerevan, USSR	Feb. 22, 1969
1000 meters	1:30.0	E. van de Brom (Neth.)	Davos, Switz.	Feb. 9, 1969
1500 meters	2:18.5	Johanna Schut (Neth.)	Inzell, West Ger.	Feb. 22, 1969
3000 meters	4:50.3	Johanna Schut (Neth.)	Inzell, West Ger.	Feb. 23, 1969
5000 meters	9:01.6	Rimma Zhukova (USSR)	Medeo, USSR	Jan. 24, 1953

F. AMATEUR WORLD RECORDS IN TRACK WALKING

MEN

5 miles	34:21.2	Kenneth Matthews (Gt. Brit.)	London, England	Sept. 28, 1960
10 miles	1:09:40.6	Kenneth Matthews (Gt. Brit.)	Walton-on-Thames, Eng.	June 6, 1964
20 miles	2:31:33.0	Anatoliy Vedyakov (USSR)	Moscow, USSR	Aug. 23, 1958
30 miles	4:00:06.2	Christoph Höhne (E. Germany)	East Berlin, Ger.	Oct. 18, 1969

Road Walking—Men

San Francisco to New York 66 days Flt. Sgt. P. Maloney and Stf. Sgt. M. Evans
Ending on June 17, 1960

Road Walking—Women

San Francisco to New York 86 days Dr. Barbara Moore (aged 56)
Ending on July 6, 1960

G. SWIMMING—MEN

(World records)

Freestyle

Distance	Name and Nation	Time	Place	Date
100 meters	Michael Wenden (Australia)	52.2	Mexico City, Mexico	Oct. 19, 1968
200 meters	Don Schollander (USA)	1:54.3	Long Beach, Calif.	Aug. 30, 1968
200 meters	Mark Spitz (USA)	1:54.3	Santa Clara, Calif.	July 12, 1969
800 meters	Mike Burton (USA)	8:28.8	Louisville, Kentucky	Aug. 17, 1969

Butterfly

Distance	Name and Nation	Time	Place	Date
100 meters	Mark Spitz (USA)	55.6	Long Beach, Calif.	Aug. 30, 1968
200 meters	Mark Spitz (USA)	2:05.7	West Berlin, Germany	Oct. 8, 1968

Backstroke

Distance	Name and Nation	Time	Place	Date
100 meters	Roland Matthes (E. Ger.)	57.8	Werzberg, E. Ger.	Aug. 23, 1969
200 meters	Roland Matthes (E. Ger.)	2:06.4	East Berlin, Germany	Aug. 29, 1969

Breaststroke

Distance	Name and Nation	Time	Place	Date
100 meters	Nikolai Pankin (USSR)	1:05.8	Magdeburg, E. Germany	Apr. 20, 1969
200 meters	Nikolai Pankin (USSR)	2:25.4	Madgeburg, E. Germany	Apr. 19, 1969

Individual Medley

Distance	Name and Nation	Time	Place	Date
200 meters	Gary Hall (USA)	2:09.6	Louisville, Kentucky	Aug. 17, 1969
400 meters	Gary Hall (USA)	4:33.9	Louisville, Kentucky	Aug. 15, 1969

H. SWIMMING—WOMEN

(World records)

Freestyle

100 meters	Dawn Fraser (Australia)	N. Sydney, Australia	58.9	Feb. 29, 1964
200 meters	Debbie Meyer (USA)	Los Angeles, Calif.	2:06.7	Aug. 24, 1968
400 meters	Debbie Meyer (USA)	Los Angeles, Calif.	4:24.5	Aug. 25, 1968
800 meters	Karen Moras (Australia)	Edinburgh, Scotland	9:02.5	July 18, 1970
1500 meters	Debbie Meyer (USA)	Louisville, Kentucky	17:19.9	Aug. 17, 1969

Butterfly

100 meters	Ada Kok (Netherlands)	Budapest, Hungary	1:04.5	Aug. 14, 1965
200 meters	Ada Kok (Netherlands)	Blackpool, England	2:21.0	Aug. 25, 1967

Backstroke

100 meters	Karen Muir (South Africa)	Utrecht, Netherlands	1:05.6	July 6, 1969
200 meters	Susie Atwood (USA)	Louisville, Kentucky	2:21.5	Aug. 14, 1969

Breaststroke

100 meters	Catie Ball (USA)	Los Angeles, California	1:14.2	Aug. 25, 1968
200 meters	Catie Ball (USA)	Los Angeles, California	2:38.5	Aug. 26, 1968

Individual Medley

200 meters	Claudia Kolb (USA)	Los Angeles, California	2:23.5	Aug. 25, 1968
400 meters	Claudia Kolb (USA)	Los Angeles, California	5:04.7	Aug. 24, 1968

I. TRACK AND FIELD—MEN

Running

Event	Name and Nation	Time	Place	Date
100 yards	William McGee (USA)	9.1	Houston, Texas	May 16, 1970
440 yards	Curtis Mills (USA)	44.7	Knoxville, Tenn.	June 21, 1969
10 miles	Ron Clarke (Australia)	46:44.0	Leicester, England	Nov. 9, 1968
20,000 meters	Gaston Roelants (Belgium)	58:06.2	Louvain, Belgium	Oct. 28, 1966
30,000 meters	James Hogan (USA)	1:32:25.4	Walton-on-Thames, Eng.	Nov. 12, 1966

Hurdles

Event	Name and Nation	Time	Place	Date
120 yards	Irving Hall (USA)	13.2	Knoxville, Tenn.	June 19,1969

Field Events

Event	Name and Nation	Time	Place	Date
Hammer Throw	Anatolyi Bondarchuk (USSR)	247 ft. 7 in. (74.48)	Rovzo, USSR	Oct. 13, 1969
Decathlon	William Toomey (USA)	8417 points*	Los Angeles, Calif.	Dec. 10-11, 1969

* 1st day: 100 m. 10.3 sec.; Long Jump 25 ft. 5½ in.; Shot Put 47 ft. 2¼ in.; High Jump 6 ft. 4 in.; 400 m. 47.1 sec.
2nd day: 110 m. Hurdles 14.8 sec.; Discus 152 ft. 6 in.; Pole Vault 14 ft. 0¼ in.; Javelin 215 ft. 8 in.; 1500 m. 4:39.4

J. TRACK AND FIELD—WOMEN

Running

Event				
100 yards	10.0	Chi Cheng (Taiwan, China)	Portland, Oregon	June 14, 1970
100 meters	11.0	Wyomia Tyus (USA)	Mexico City, Mexico	Oct. 15, 1968
	11.0	Chi Cheng (Taiwan, China)	Vienna, Austria	July 18, 1970
220 yards (turn)	22.6	Chi Cheng (Taiwan, China)	Los Angeles, California	July 3, 1970
	4:15.0	Maria Gommers (Holland)	Sittard,	Oct. 25, 1967
1500 meters	4:12.4	Paola Pigni (Italy)	Milan, Italy	July 2, 1969
	4:10.7	Jaroslava Jehlickova (Czecho.)	Athens, Greece	Sept. 20, 1969
1 mile	4:36.8	Maria Gommers (Holland)	Leicester, England	June 14, 1969

Hurdles

Event				
100 meters (2 ft. 9 in.)	12.8	Pamela Kilborn (Australia)	Melbourne, Australia	Dec. 17, 1969
200 meters	26.2	Chi Cheng (Taiwan, China)	Walnut, California	May 25, 1969
	25.8	Pamela Kilborn (Australia)	Melbourne, Australia	Dec. 17, 1969

Field Events

Event				
Shot Put	67 ft. 0¾ in. (20.43)	Nadezhda Chizova (USSR)	Athens, Greece	Sept. 16, 1969
Discus	209 ft. 10 in. (63.96)	Liesel Westermann (W. Ger.)	Hamburg, Germany	Sept. 27, 1969